Distances a[...] s

The mileage chart shows distance[...] AA-recommended routes. Using m[...] normally the fastest route, though [...]

The journey times, shown in hours and minutes, are average off-peak driving times along AA-recommended routes. These times should be used as a guide only and do not allow for unforeseen traffic delays, rest breaks or fuel stops.

For example, the 378 miles (608 km) journey between Glasgow and Norwich should take approximately 7 hours 28 minutes.

Journey times

The upper-right triangle of the chart gives journey times; the lower-left triangle gives distances in miles. Place-name labels run diagonally across the chart in the following order:

Aberdeen, Aberystwyth, Barnstaple, Birmingham, Brighton, Bristol, Cambridge, Cardiff, Carlisle, Carmarthen, Dorchester, Dover, Edinburgh, Exeter, Fort William, Glasgow, Gloucester, Guildford, Hereford, Holyhead, Hull, Inverness, Kendal, Leeds, Lincoln, Liverpool, Maidstone, Manchester, Middlesbrough, Newcastle, Northampton, Norwich, Nottingham, Oxford, Penzance, Perth, Peterborough, Plymouth, Portsmouth, Preston, Salisbury, Sheffield, Shrewsbury, Southampton, Stoke-on-Trent, Stranraer, Taunton, Wick, York, LONDON

Distances in miles (one mile equals 1.6093 km)

Atlas contents

Scale 1:200,000 or 3.16 miles to 1 inch

30th edition June 2015

© AA Media Limited 2015

Original edition printed 1986.

Cartography:
All cartography in this atlas edited, designed and produced by the Mapping Services Department of AA Publishing (A05308).

This atlas contains Ordnance Survey data © Crown copyright and database right 2015 and Royal Mail data © Royal Mail copyright and database right 2015.

 This atlas is based upon Crown Copyright and is reproduced with the permission of Land & Property Services under delegated authority from the Controller of Her Majesty's Stationery Office, © Crown copyright and database right 2015, PMLPA No.100497.

 © Ordnance Survey Ireland/ Government of Ireland. Copyright Permit No. MP000115.

Publisher's Notes:
Published by AA Publishing (a trading name of AA Media Limited, whose registered office is Fanum House, Basing View, Basingstoke, Hampshire RG21 4EA, UK. Registered number 06112600).

All rights reserved. No part of this publication may be reproduced, stored in a retrieval system, or transmitted in any form or by any means – electronic, mechanical, photocopying, recording or otherwise – unless the permission of the publisher has been given beforehand.

ISBN: 978 0 7495 7686 8 (leather)
ISBN: 978 0 7495 7685 1 (standard)

A CIP catalogue record for this book is available from The British Library.

Disclaimer:
The contents of this atlas are believed to be correct at the time of the latest revision, it will not contain any subsequent amended, new or temporary information including diversions and traffic control or enforcement systems. The publishers cannot be held responsible or liable for any loss or damage occasioned to any person acting or refraining from action as a result of any use or reliance on material in this atlas, nor for any errors, omissions or changes in such material. This does not affect your statutory rights.

The publishers would welcome information to correct any errors or omissions and to keep this atlas up to date. Please write to the Atlas Editor, AA Publishing, The Automobile Association, Fanum House, Basing View, Basingstoke, Hampshire RG21 4EA, UK. E-mail: roadatlasfeedback@theaa.com

Acknowledgements:
AA Publishing would like to thank the following for their assistance in producing this atlas:
RoadPilot mobile Information on fixed speed camera locations provided by and © 2015 RoadPilot Ltd. Crematoria data provided by the Cremation Society of Great Britain. Cadw, English Heritage, Forestry Commission, Historic Scotland, Johnsons, National Trust and National Trust for Scotland, RSPB, The Wildlife Trust, Scottish Natural Heritage, Natural England, The Countryside Council for Wales (road maps).

Road signs are © Crown Copyright 2015. Reproduced under the terms of the Open Government Licence.

Transport for London (Central London Map), Nexus (Newcastle district map).

Printer:
Printed in China by Leo Paper Products.

Route planner

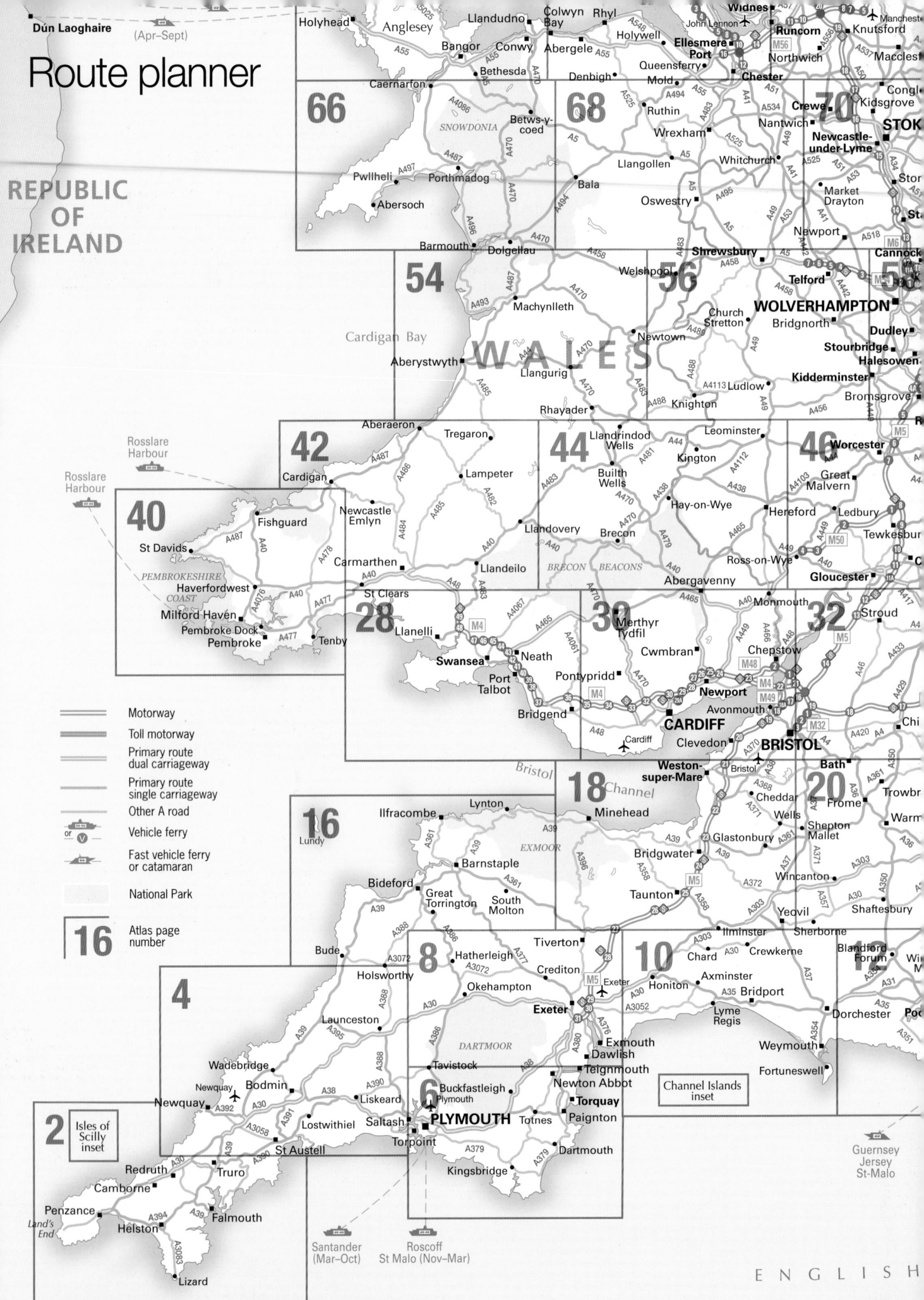

Dún Laoghaire (Apr–Sept)

REPUBLIC
OF
IRELAND

Rosslare Harbour

Rosslare Harbour

ANGLESEY
Holyhead
Bangor
Conwy
Bethesda
Caernarfon
SNOWDONIA
Pwllheli
Abersoch
Porthmadog
Barmouth
Dolgellau
Betws-y-coed
Llandudno
Colwyn Bay
Abergele
A55
Rhyl
Holywell
Queensferry
Denbigh
Mold
Ruthin
Wrexham
Llangollen
Bala
Oswestry
Whitchurch
Newport

66   **68**   **70**

John Lennon
Widnes
Runcorn
Ellesmere Port
Northwich
Chester
Crewe
Nantwich
Newcastle-under-Lyme
Knutsford
Macclesfield
Kidsgrove
STOKE
Market Drayton
Cannock

Machynlleth
Newtown
Welshpool
Shrewsbury
Church Stretton
Bridgnorth
WOLVERHAMPTON
Dudley
Stourbridge
Halesowen
Kidderminster
Bromsgrove

54   **56**   **59**

WALES
Cardigan Bay
Aberystwyth
Llangurig
Rhayader
Llandrindod Wells
Kington
Leominster
Ludlow
Knighton
Worcester
Great Malvern
Hereford
Ledbury
Tewkesbury

42   **44**   **46**

Aberaeron
Tregaron
Lampeter
Builth Wells
Hay-on-Wye
Ross-on-Wye
Gloucester
Cardigan
Newcastle Emlyn
Llandovery
Brecon
BRECON BEACONS
Abergavenny
Monmouth
Stroud
Chepstow

40   **28**   **30**   **32**

PEMBROKESHIRE COAST
St Davids
Fishguard
Haverfordwest
Milford Haven
Pembroke Dock
Pembroke
Carmarthen
Llandeilo
St Clears
Tenby
Llanelli
Neath
Swansea
Port Talbot
Pontypridd
Bridgend
Merthyr Tydfil
Cwmbran
Newport
Avonmouth
CARDIFF
Cardiff
Clevedon
Bristol
BRISTOL
Weston-super-Mare
Bath
Cheddar
Wells
Shepton Mallet
Frome
Trowbridge

Bristol Channel
ENGLISH Channel

16   **18**   **20**

Ilfracombe
Lynton
Minehead
Lundy
Barnstaple
EXMOOR
Bideford
Great Torrington
South Molton
Bridgwater
Taunton
Glastonbury
Wincanton
Yeovil
Shaftesbury
Sherborne

4   **8**   **10**

Bude
Holsworthy
Hatherleigh
Crediton
Tiverton
Chard
Crewkerne
Blandford Forum
Launceston
Okehampton
Exeter
Honiton
Axminster
Bridport
Lyme Regis
Dorchester
Wadebridge
Newquay
Bodmin
DARTMOOR
Tavistock
Exmouth
Dawlish
Teignmouth
Newton Abbot
Weymouth
Fortuneswell
Liskeard
Buckfastleigh
Torquay
Paignton

2   **6**

Isles of Scilly inset
Newquay
Lostwithiel
St Austell
Saltash
Torpoint
PLYMOUTH
Totnes
Dartmouth
Redruth
Truro
Camborne
Penzance
Land's End
Helston
Falmouth
Lizard
Kingsbridge

Channel Islands inset

Santander (Mar–Oct)
Roscoff St Malo (Nov–Mar)

Guernsey Jersey St-Malo

ENGLISH

Legend

- ═══ Motorway
- ═══ Toll motorway
- ─── Primary route dual carriageway
- ─── Primary route single carriageway
- ─── Other A road
- Vehicle ferry *or* V
- Fast vehicle ferry or catamaran
- National Park
- **16** Atlas page number

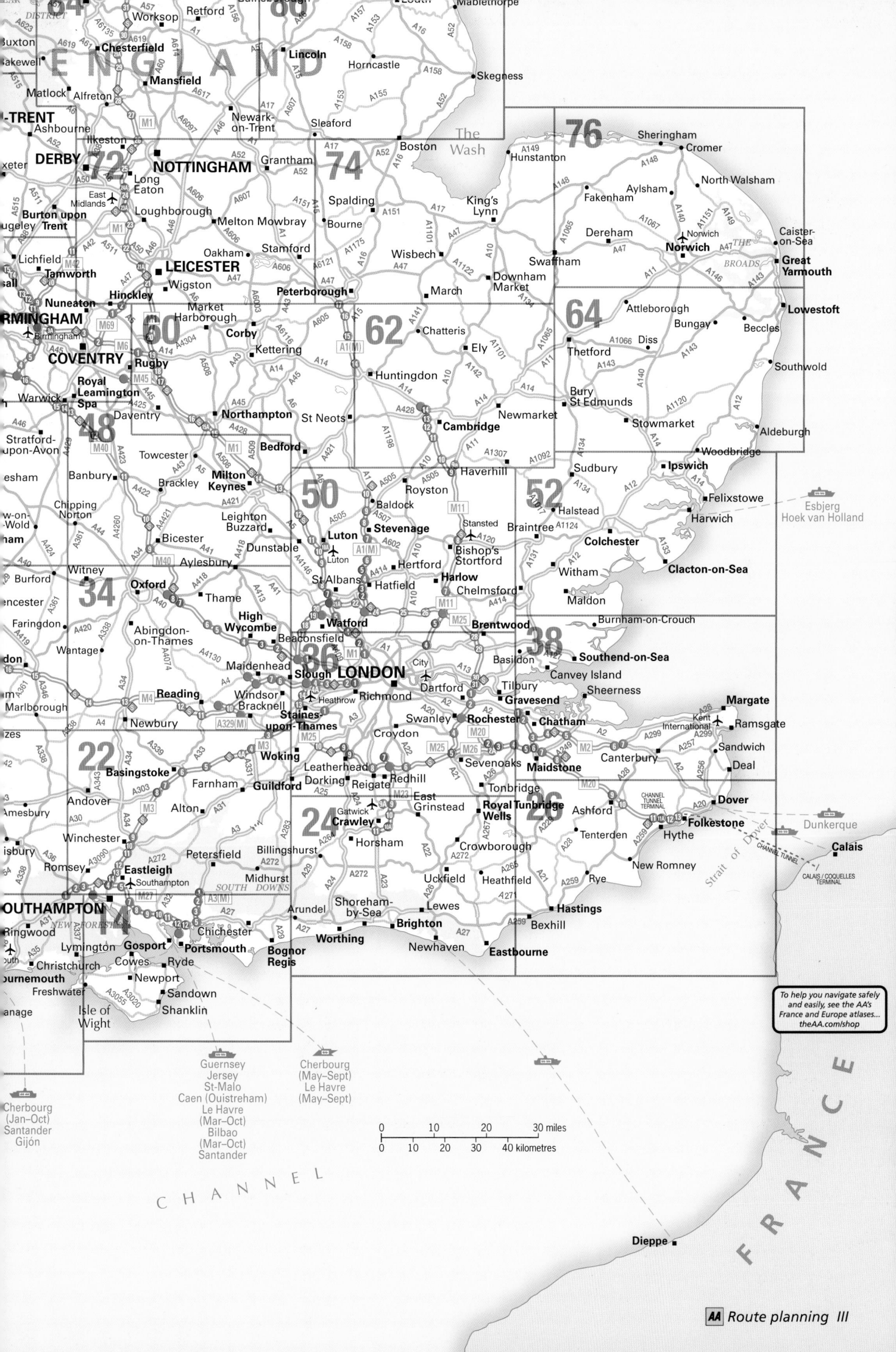

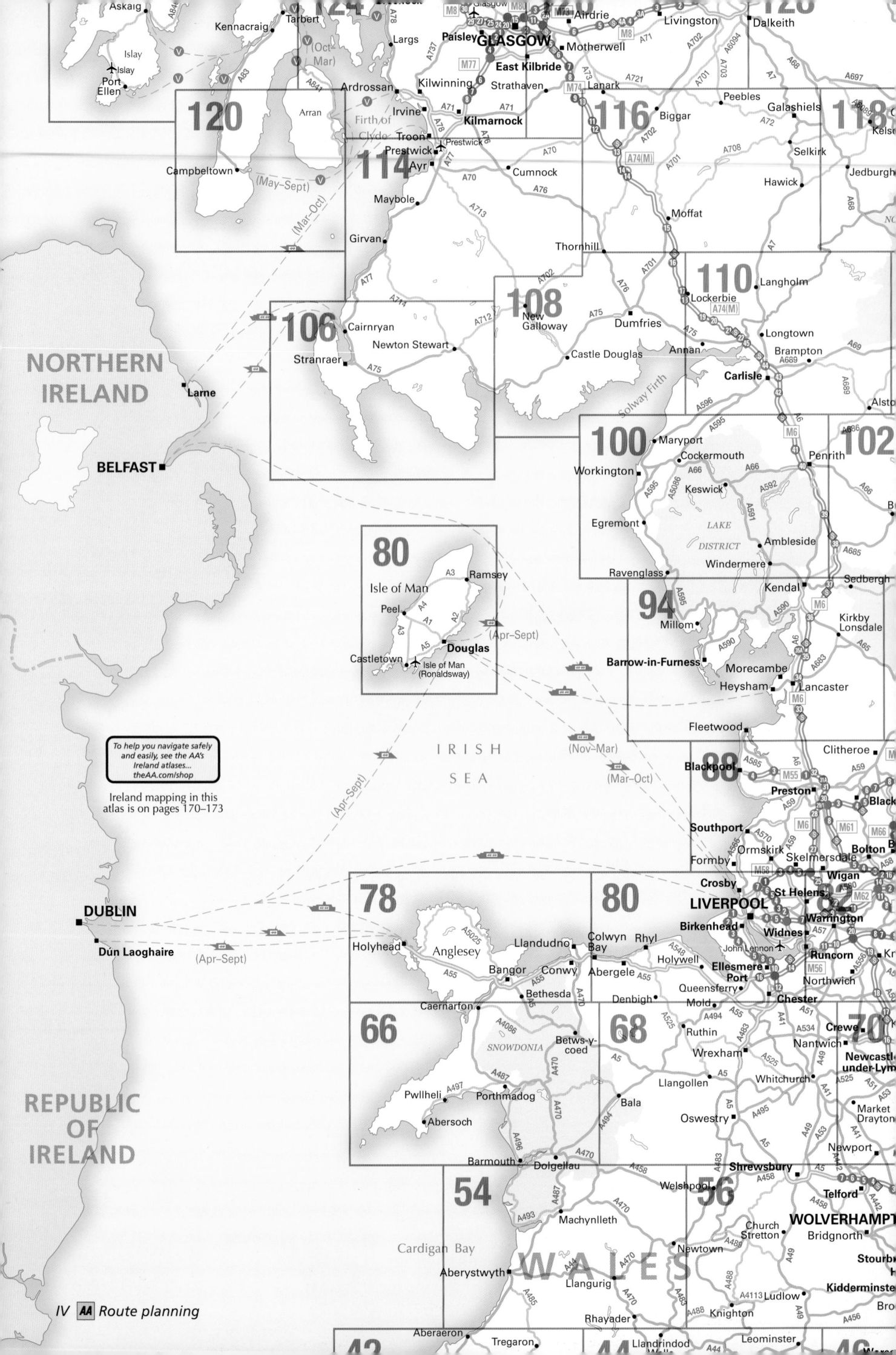

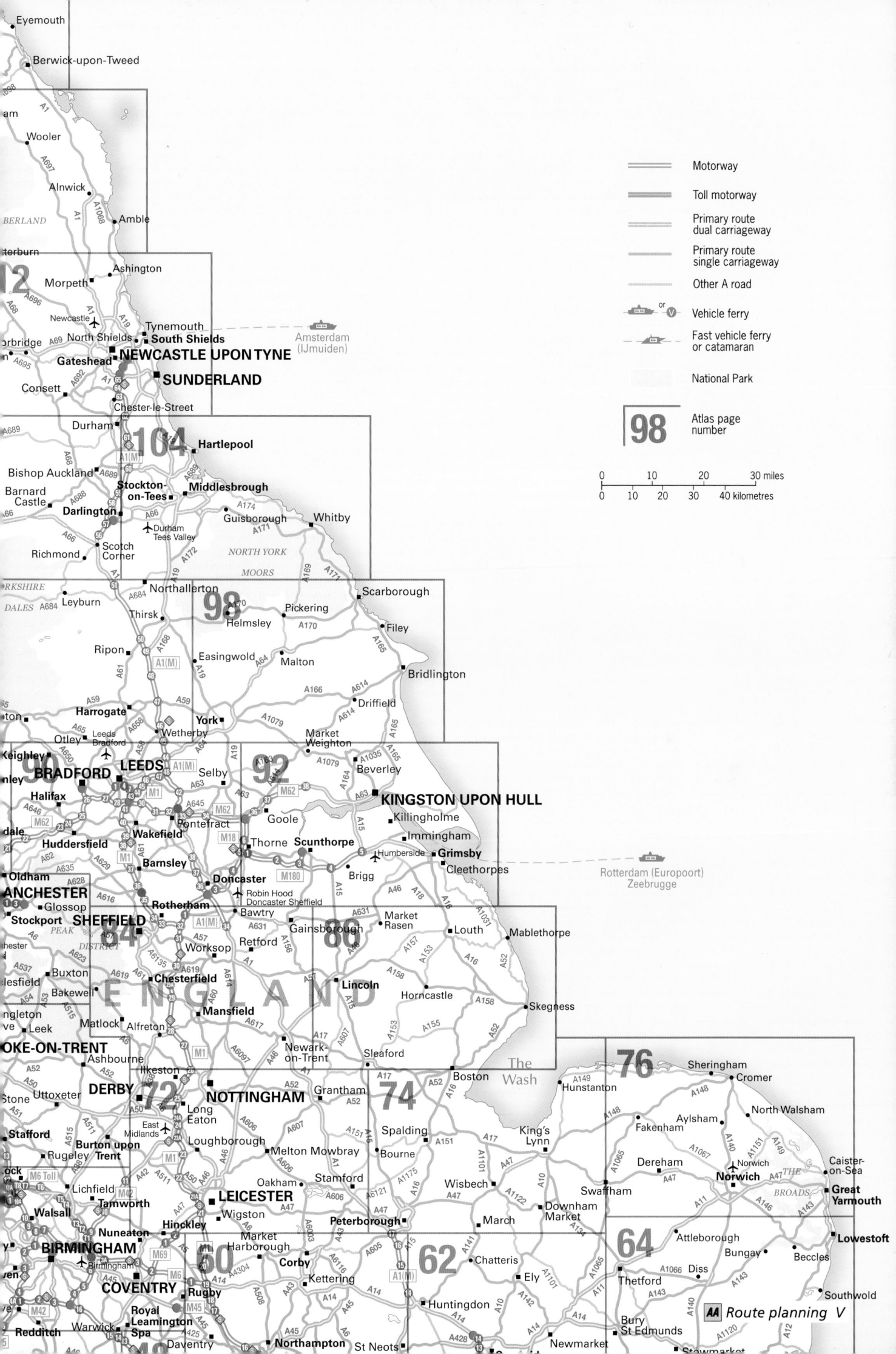

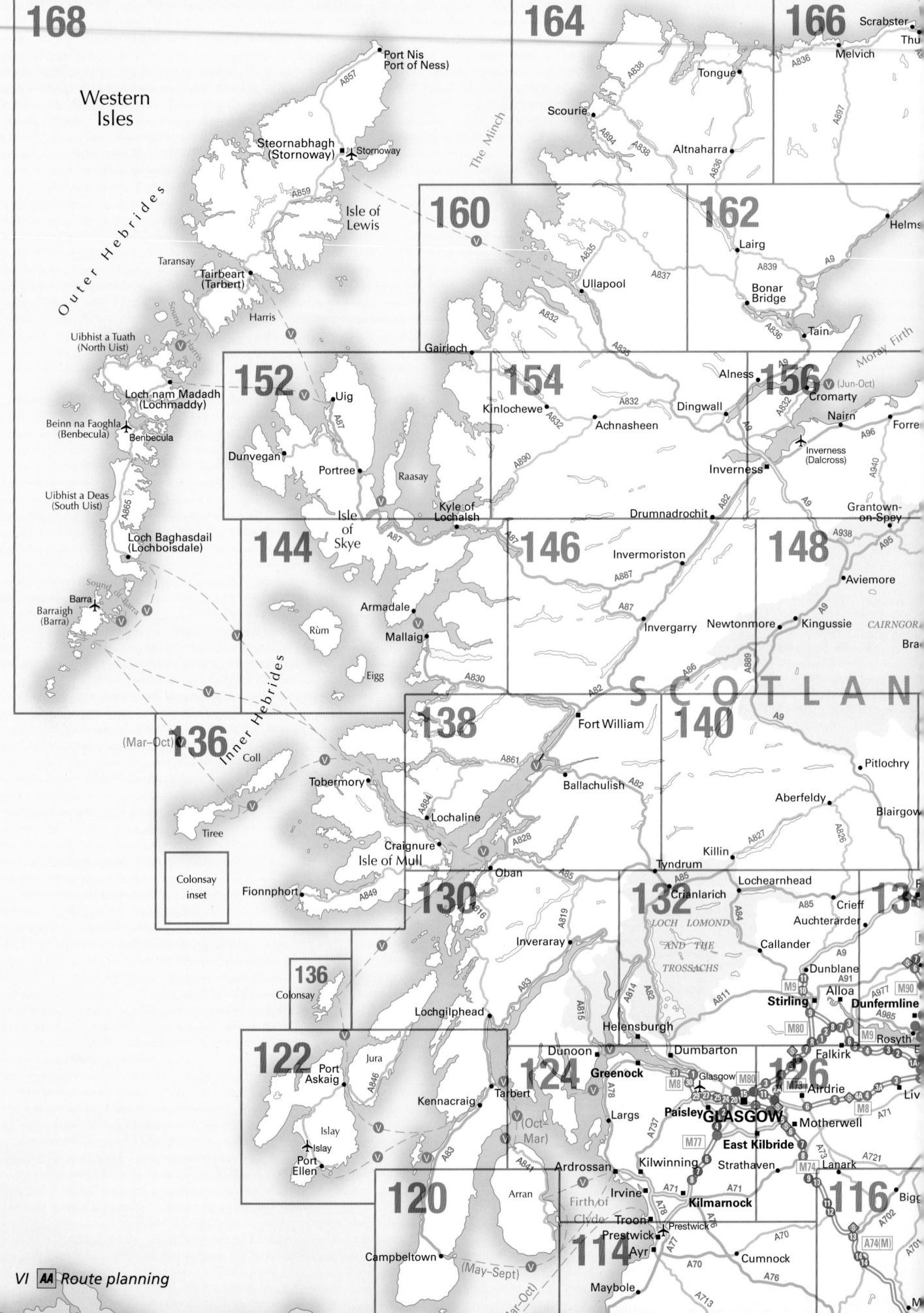

168

Western
Isles

Port Nis
Port of Ness)

A857

Steornabhagh
(Stornoway)   ✈ Stornoway

Isle of
Lewis

A859

Outer Hebrides

Taransay

Tairbeart
(Tarbert)

Harris

Uibhist a Tuath
(North Uist)

Loch nam Madadh
(Lochmaddy)

Beinn na Faoghla
(Benbecula)
Benbecula

Uibhist a Deas
(South Uist)

A865

Loch Baghasdail
(Lochboisdale)

Sound of Barra

Barra
Barraigh
(Barra)

164

A838

Tongue

Scourie

A894

Altnaharra

A836

A838

The Minch

166   Scrabster
Thu

Melvich

A836

A897

160

Ⓥ

Gairloch

A832

A835

162

Lairg

A839

Bonar
Bridge

A836

Tain

A837

A9

Helms

Moray Firth

152   Ⓥ

Uig

A87

Dunvegan

Portree

Raasay

Isle
of
Skye

Kyle of
Lochalsh

154

Kinlochewe   A832

Achnasheen

A890

A832

Alness

Dingwall

156   Ⓥ (Jun–Oct)
Cromarty

Nairn

Inverness
(Dalcross)   ✈

Inverness

A832

A9

Forre

A96

A940

Grantown-
on-Spey

A938

144

A87

Armadale

Mallaig

Rùm

Eigg

A830

146

Invermoriston

A887

A87

Invergarry

A82

A86

148

Aviemore

Newtonmore   Kingussie   *CAIRNGOR*

Bra

A9

A889

A9

136   Ⓥ (Mar–Oct)

Coll

Inner Hebrides

Tobermory

A884

Lochaline

Tiree

Craignure

Isle of Mull

A849

Colonsay
inset

Fionnphort

138

A861

Ballachulish   A82

A828

Oban

A816

A85

130

Inveraray

A83

Fort William

S C O T L A N

140

A9

Pitlochry

Aberfeldy

A827   Blairgow

A826

Killin

Tyndrum

A85

Lochearnhead

132

Crianlarich

*LOCH LOMOND
AND THE
TROSSACHS*

A84

A82

A811

A814

Callander

A85   Crief

Auchterarder

134

A9

Dunblane

A91   Alloa

Stirling

M9

M80

M9

A977   M90

Dunfermline

A985

Rosyth

Falkirk

M80

136

Colonsay

Ⓥ

122

Port
Askaig

Jura

A846

Islay

A83

Ⓥ

Islay
Port
Ellen

Lochgilphead

A815

Kennacraig   Tarbert

Ⓥ

Ⓥ (Oct
– Mar)

Helensburgh

Dunoon

124

A78

Greenock

Largs

Dumbarton

Glasgow   M80

M8

M8

126

Airdrie

Liv

A8

M8

Paisley   **GLASGOW**   Motherwell

M77   **East Kilbride**   A73

A737   Kilwinning   Strathaven   M74   Lanark

Ardrossan   **Kilmarnock**   A71   A721

120

Arran

*Firth of
Clyde*

Irvine   A71

114   Troon   A77

Prestwick   ✈ Prestwick

Ayr   A70   Cumnock

Campbeltown   (May–Sept)   Maybole   A76

116   Bigg

A74(M)

A70

A713

Stromness
Kirkwall
Lerwick
Kirkwall
Orkney
Islands

Shetland Islands
are on page 169

St Margaret's
Hope

Gills

John o' Groats
A836

Wick John o' Groats
A882
Wick
A99

158

Cullen
Banff
Fraserburgh
A98
A98
A90
A941
A96
Keith
A95
Turriff
Aberlour
Huntly
A952
Peterhead
A90
A947

Lerwick

Oldmeldrum
Ellon
A90

150

intoul
Inverurie
Aberdeen
A96
Aberdeen

A93
Ballater
Banchory
A90
Stonehaven

42

A90
Brechin
Montrose
Forfar
A92
A94
A90
A92
upar Angus
Arbroath
Carnoustie
Dundee
Newport-on-Tay
A92
St Andrews
A91
A91
Cupar
A915
A917

Glenrothes

Kirkcaldy

Firth of Forth

NORTH
SEA

Dunbar
A1
EDINBURGH

128

Dalkeith
Eyemouth
A6094
A703
A7
A68
Berwick-upon-Tweed

Peebles
A697
Galashiels
A898
Coldstream
A1

118

A72
Kelso
A708
Selkirk
Wooler
Jedburgh
A697
Hawick
A68
Alnwick
A1
A1068
NORTHUMBERLAND
Amble

FERRY INFORMATION

Hebrides and west coast Scotland
calmac.co.uk	0800 066 5000
skyeferry.co.uk	
western-ferries.co.uk	01369 704 452

Orkney and Shetland
northlinkferries.co.uk	0845 6000 449
pentlandferries.co.uk	0800 688 8998
orkneyferries.co.uk	01856 872 044
shetland.gov.uk/ferries	01595 743 970

Isle of Man (see also pages XII-XIII)
steam-packet.com	08722 992 992

Ireland (see also pages XII-XIII)
irishferries.com	08717 300 400
poferries.com	08716 642 020
stenaline.co.uk	08447 70 70 70

North Sea (Scandinavia and Benelux)
dfdsseaways.co.uk	08715 229 955
poferries.com	08716 642 020
stenaline.co.uk	08447 70 70 70

Isle of Wight
wightlink.co.uk	0333 999 7333
redfunnel.co.uk	0844 844 9988

Channel Islands (see also pages X-XI)
condorferries.co.uk	0845 609 1024

France and Belgium (see also pages X-XI)
brittany-ferries.co.uk	0871 244 0744
condorferries.co.uk	0845 609 1024
eurotunnel.com	08443 35 35 35
dfdsseaways.co.uk	08715 229 955
poferries.com	08716 642 020
myferrylink.com	0844 2482 100

Northern Spain
brittany-ferries.co.uk	0871 244 0744
ldlines.co.uk	0844 576 8836

EMERGENCY DIVERSION ROUTES

In an emergency it may be necessary to close a section of motorway or other main road to traffic, so a temporary sign may advise drivers to follow a diversion route. To help drivers navigate the route, black symbols on yellow patches may be permanently displayed on existing direction signs, including motorway signs. Symbols may also be used on separate signs with yellow backgrounds.

For further information see *www.highways.gov.uk*, *trafficscotland.org* and *traffic-wales.com*

Motorway

Toll motorway

Primary route
dual carriageway

Primary route
single carriageway

Other A road

Vehicle ferry

Fast vehicle ferry
or catamaran

National Park

114 Atlas page
number

0   10   20   30 miles
0   10   20   30   40 kilometres

Traffic signs

Signs giving orders

Signs with red circles are mostly prohibitive. Plates below signs qualify their message.

Entry to 20mph zone

End of 20mph zone

Maximum speed

National speed limit applies

School crossing patrol

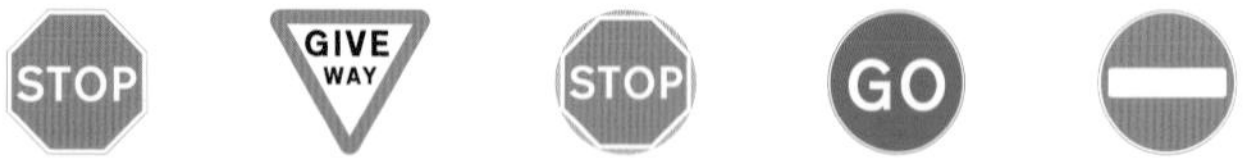

Stop and give way

Give way to traffic on major road

Manually operated temporary STOP and GO signs

No entry for vehicular traffic

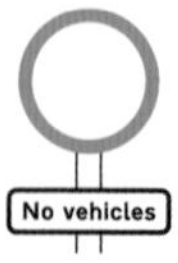

No vehicles except bicycles being pushed

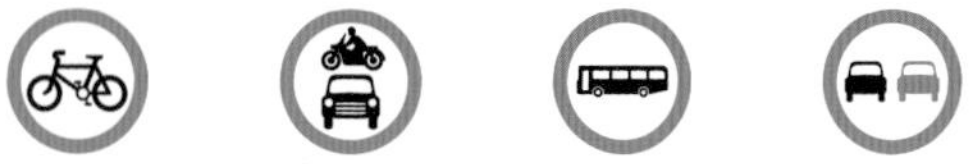

No cycling

No motor vehicles

No buses (over 8 passenger seats)

No overtaking

No towed caravans

No vehicles carrying explosives

No vehicle or combination of vehicles over length shown

No vehicles over height shown

No vehicles over width shown

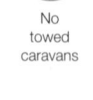

Give priority to vehicles from opposite direction

No right turn

No left turn

No U-turns

No goods vehicles over maximum gross weight shown (in tonnes) except for loading and unloading

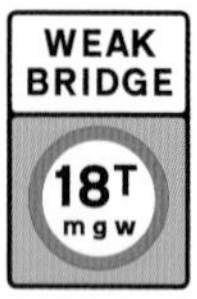

No vehicles over maximum gross weight shown (in tonnes)

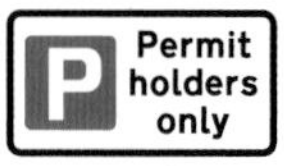

Parking restricted to permit holders

No stopping during period indicated except for buses

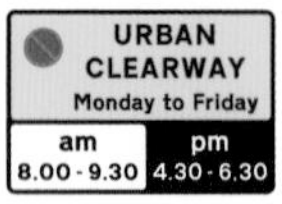

No stopping during times shown except for as long as necessary to set down or pick up passengers

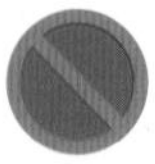

No waiting

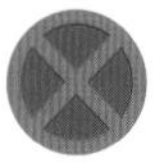

No stopping (Clearway)

Signs with blue circles but no red border mostly give positive instruction.

Ahead only

Turn left ahead (right if symbol reversed)

Turn left (right if symbol reversed)

Keep left (right if symbol reversed)

Vehicles may pass either side to reach same destination

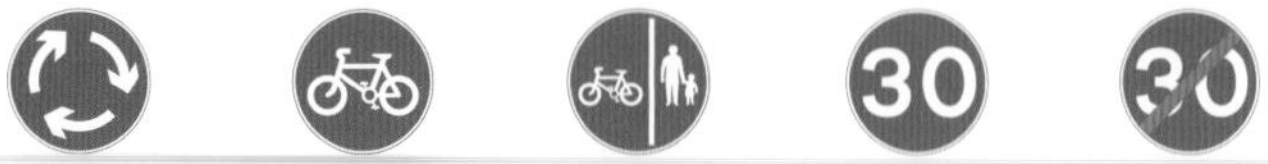

Mini-roundabout (roundabout circulation – give way to vehicles from the immediate right)

Route to be used by pedal cycles only

Segregated pedal cycle and pedestrian route

Minimum speed

End of minimum speed

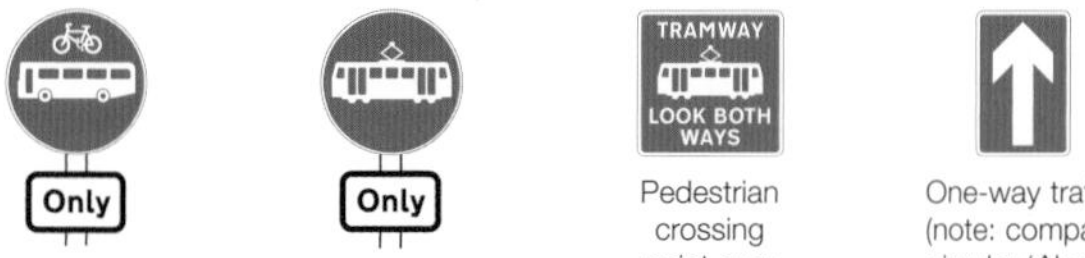

Buses and cycles only

Trams only

Pedestrian crossing point over tramway

One-way traffic (note: compare circular 'Ahead only' sign)

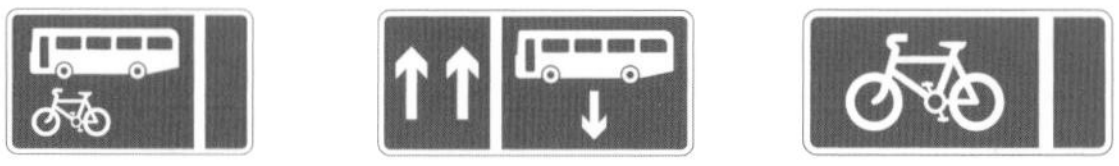

With-flow bus and cycle lane

Contraflow bus lane

With-flow pedal cycle lane

Warning signs

Mostly triangular

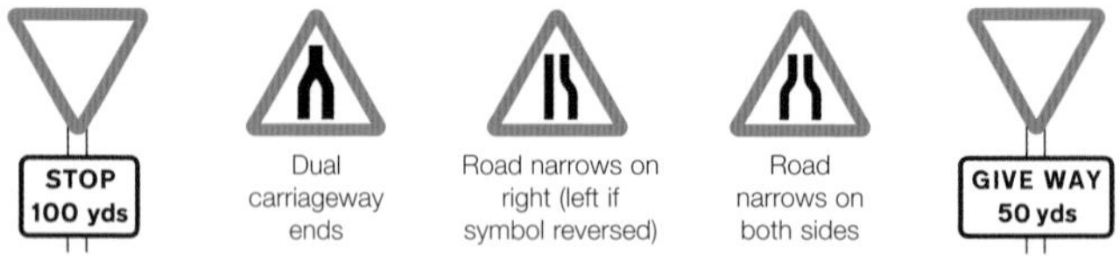

Distance to 'STOP' line ahead

Dual carriageway ends

Road narrows on right (left if symbol reversed)

Road narrows on both sides

Distance to 'Give Way' line ahead

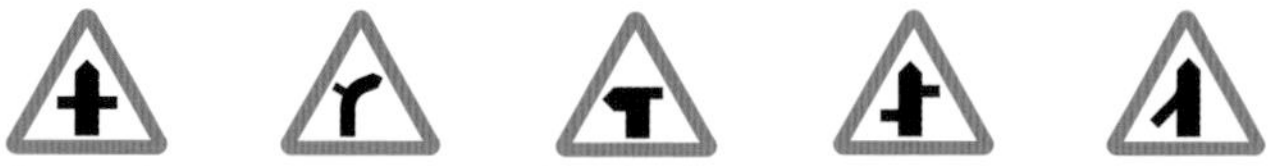

Crossroads

Junction on bend ahead

T-junction with priority over vehicles from the right

Staggered junction

Traffic merging from left ahead

The priority through route is indicated by the broader line.

Double bend first to left (symbol may be reversed)

Bend to right (or left if symbol reversed)

Roundabout

Uneven road

Plate below some signs

Two-way traffic crosses one-way road

Two-way traffic straight ahead

Opening or swing bridge ahead

Low-flying aircraft or sudden aircraft noise

Falling or fallen rocks

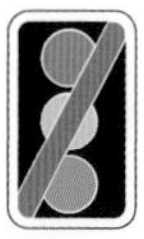

Traffic signals not in use

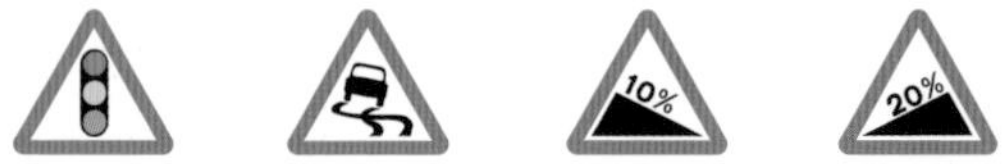

Traffic signals

Slippery road

Steep hill downwards

Steep hill upwards

Gradients may be shown as a ratio i.e. 20% = 1:5

Tunnel ahead

Trams crossing ahead

Level crossing with barrier or gate ahead

Level crossing without barrier or gate ahead

Level crossing without barrier

School crossing patrol ahead (some signs have amber lights which flash when crossings are in use)

Frail (or blind or disabled if shown) pedestrians likely to cross road ahead

Pedestrians in road ahead

Zebra crossing

Overhead electric cable; plate indicates maximum height of vehicles which can pass safely

Available width of headroom indicated

Sharp deviation of route to left (or right if chevrons reversed)

Light signals ahead at level crossing, airfield or bridge

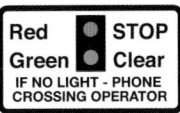
Miniature warning lights at level crossings

Cattle

Wild animals

Wild horses or ponies

Accompanied horses or ponies

Cycle route ahead

Risk of ice

Traffic queues likely ahead

Distance over which road humps extend

Other danger; plate indicates nature of danger

Soft verges

Side winds

Hump bridge

Worded warning sign

Quayside or river bank

Risk of grounding

Direction signs

Mostly rectangular

Signs on motorways – blue backgrounds

At a junction leading directly into a motorway (junction number may be shown on a black background)

On approaches to junctions (junction number on black background)

M1
The NORTH
Sheffield   32
Leeds   59

Route confirmatory sign after junction

Downward pointing arrows mean 'Get in lane'
The left-hand lane leads to a different destination from the other lanes.

The panel with the inclined arrow indicates the destinations which can be reached by leaving the motorway at the next junction

Signs on primary routes - green backgrounds

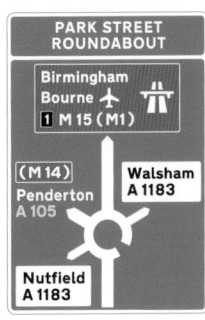
On approaches to junctions

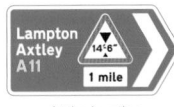
At the junction

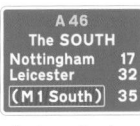
Route confirmatory sign after junction

On approaches to junctions

On approach to a junction in Wales (bilingual)

Blue panels indicate that the motorway starts at the junction ahead.
Motorways shown in brackets can also be reached along the route indicated.
White panels indicate local or non-primary routes leading from the junction ahead.
Brown panels show the route to tourist attractions.
The name of the junction may be shown at the top of the sign.
The aircraft symbol indicates the route to an airport.
A symbol may be included to warn of a hazard or restriction along that route.

Signs on non-primary and local routes - black borders

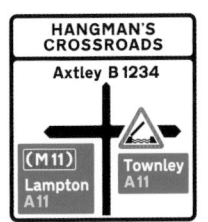
On approaches to junctions

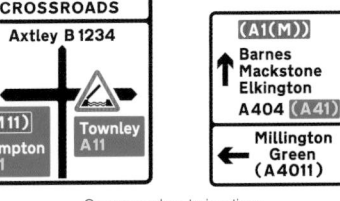

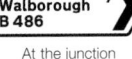
At the junction

Direction to toilets with access for the disabled

Green panels indicate that the primary route starts at the junction ahead.
Route numbers on a blue background show the direction to a motorway.
Route numbers on a green background show the direction to a primary route.

Emergency diversion routes

In an emergency it may be necessary to close a section of motorway or other main road to traffic, so a temporary sign may advise drivers to follow a diversion route. To help drivers navigate the route, black symbols on yellow patches may be permanently displayed on existing direction signs, including motorway signs. Symbols may also be used on separate signs with yellow backgrounds.

For further information see highways.gov.uk, trafficscotland.org and traffic-wales.com

Note: The signs shown in this road atlas are those most commonly in use and are not all drawn to the same scale. In Scotland and Wales bilingual versions of some signs are used, showing both English and Gaelic or Welsh spellings. Some older designs of signs may still be seen on the roads. A comprehensive explanation of the signing system illustrating the vast majority of road signs can be found in the AA's handbook *Know Your Road Signs*. Where there is a reference to a rule number, this refers to *The Highway Code*, which is detailed in the AA's guide. Both of these publications are on sale at theaa.com/shop and booksellers.

Channel hopping

For business or pleasure, hopping on a ferry across to France, Belgium or the Channel Islands has never been easier.

The vehicle ferry routes shown on this map give you all the options, together with detailed port plans to help you navigate to and from the ferry terminals. Simply choose your preferred route, not forgetting the fast sailings; then check the colour-coded table for ferry operators, crossing times and contact details.

Bon voyage!

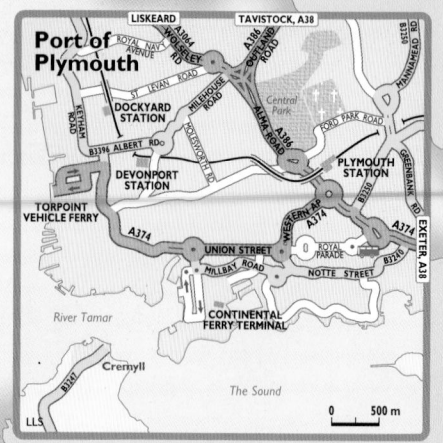

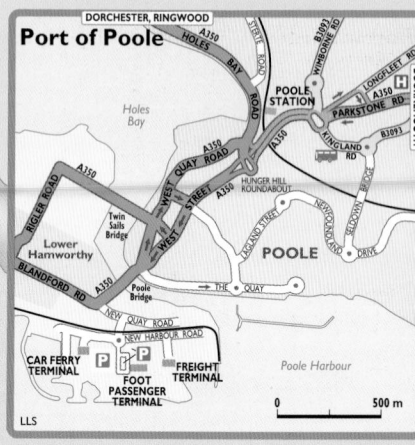

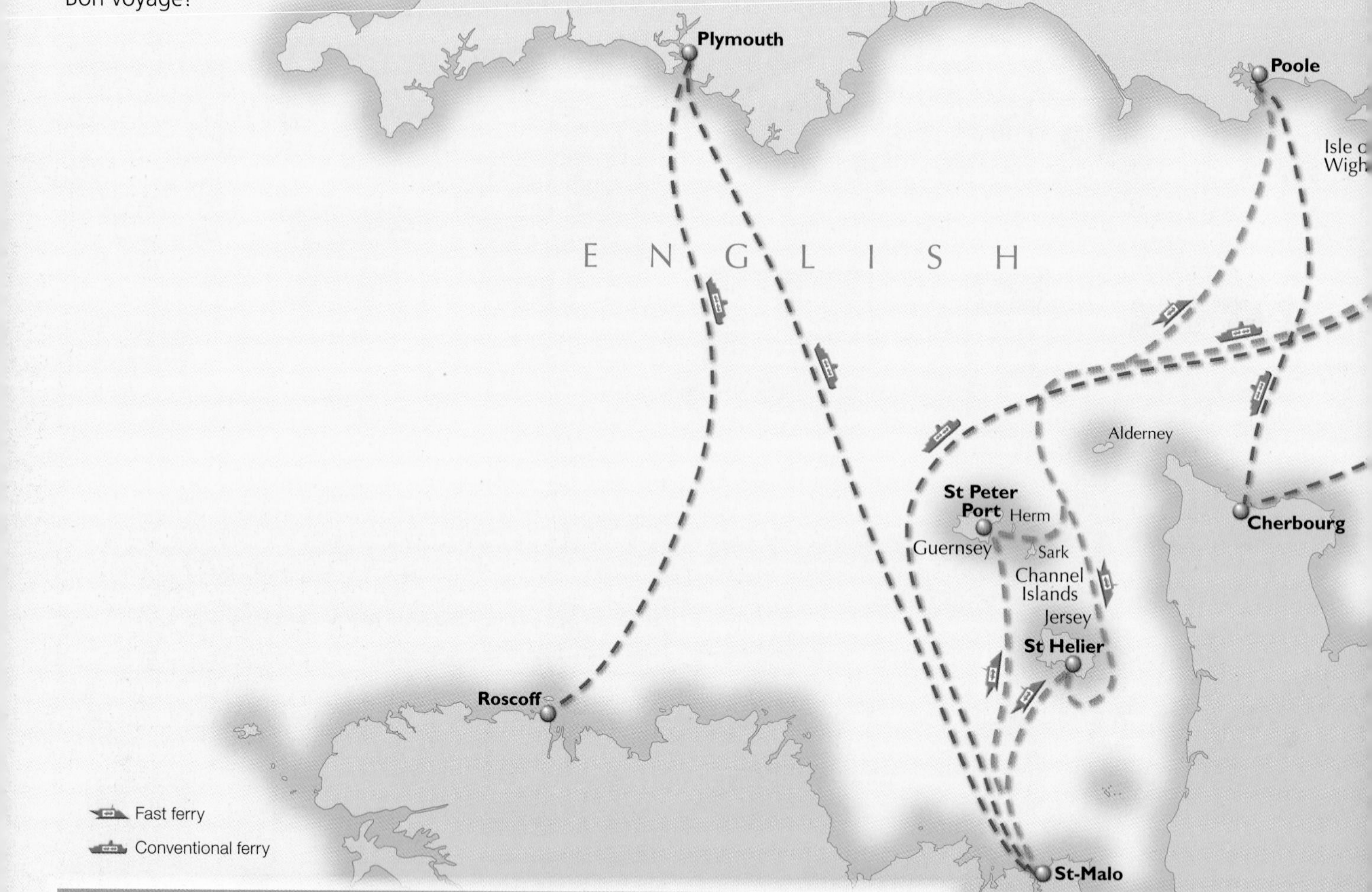

Plymouth

Poole

Isle of Wight

E N G L I S H

Alderney

St Peter Port

Herm

Guernsey

Sark

Channel Islands

Jersey

St Helier

Cherbourg

Roscoff

St-Malo

Fast ferry

Conventional ferry

ENGLISH CHANNEL FERRY CROSSINGS AND OPERATORS

From	To	Journey Time	Operator	Telephone	Website
Dover	Calais	1 hr 30 mins	DFDS Seaways	0871 522 9955	dfdsseaways.co.uk
Dover	Calais	1 hr 30 mins	My Ferry Link	0844 248 2100	myferrylink.com
Dover	Calais	1 hr 30 mins	P&O Ferries	0871 664 2020	poferries.com
Dover	Dunkerque	2 hrs	DFDS Seaways	0871 522 9955	dfdsseaways.co.uk
Folkestone	Calais (Coquelles)	35 mins	Eurotunnel	0844 335 3535	eurotunnel.com
Newhaven	Dieppe	4 hrs	DFDS Seaways	0871 522 9955	dfdsseaways.co.uk
Plymouth	Roscoff	6–8 hrs	Brittany Ferries	0871 244 0744	brittany-ferries.co.uk
Plymouth	St-Malo	10 hrs 15 mins (Nov–Mar)	Brittany Ferries	0871 244 0744	brittany-ferries.co.uk
Poole	Cherbourg	4 hrs 15 mins (Jan–Oct)	Brittany Ferries	0871 244 0744	brittany-ferries.co.uk
Poole	Guernsey	3 hrs	Condor Ferries	0845 609 1024	condorferries.co.uk
Poole	Jersey	4 hrs 30 mins	Condor Ferries	0845 609 1024	condorferries.co.uk
Poole	St-Malo	7–12 hrs (via Channel Is.)	Condor Ferries	0845 609 1024	condorferries.co.uk
Portsmouth	Caen (Ouistreham)	6–7 hrs	Brittany Ferries	0871 244 0744	brittany-ferries.co.uk
Portsmouth	Cherbourg	3 hrs (May–Sept)	Brittany Ferries	0871 244 0744	brittany-ferries.co.uk
Portsmouth	Guernsey	7 hrs	Condor Ferries	0845 609 1024	condorferries.co.uk
Portsmouth	Jersey	8–11 hrs	Condor Ferries	0845 609 1024	condorferries.co.uk
Portsmouth	Le Havre	3 hrs 45 mins (May–Sept)	Brittany Ferries	0871 244 0744	brittany-ferries.co.uk
Portsmouth	Le Havre	8 hrs (Mar–Oct)	Brittany Ferries	0871 244 0744	brittany-ferries.co.uk
Portsmouth	St-Malo	9–11 hrs	Brittany Ferries	0871 244 0744	brittany-ferries.co.uk

Ferry services listed are provided as a guide only and are liable to change at short notice.

Please check sailings before planning your journey.

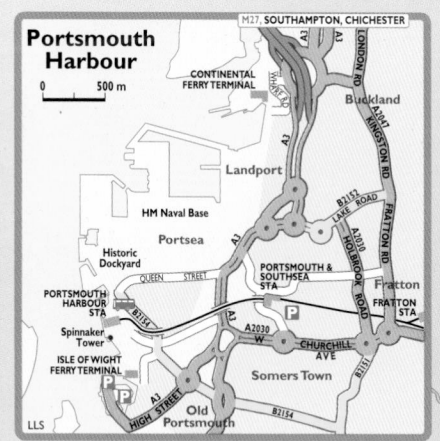

Portsmouth Harbour

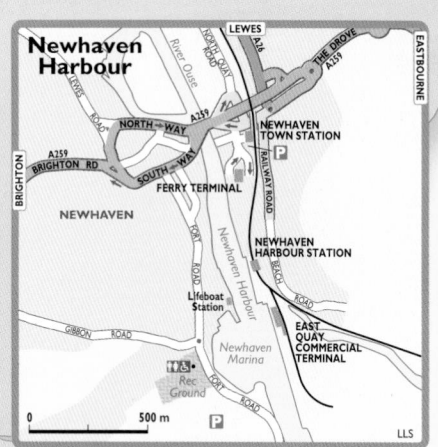

Newhaven Harbour

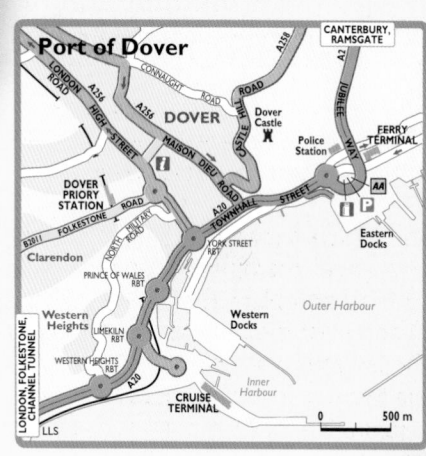

Port of Dover

Portsmouth

Folkestone

Dover

Newhaven

Calais

Calais (Coquelles)

Dunkerque

C H A N N E L

Dieppe

le Havre

Caen (Ouistreham)

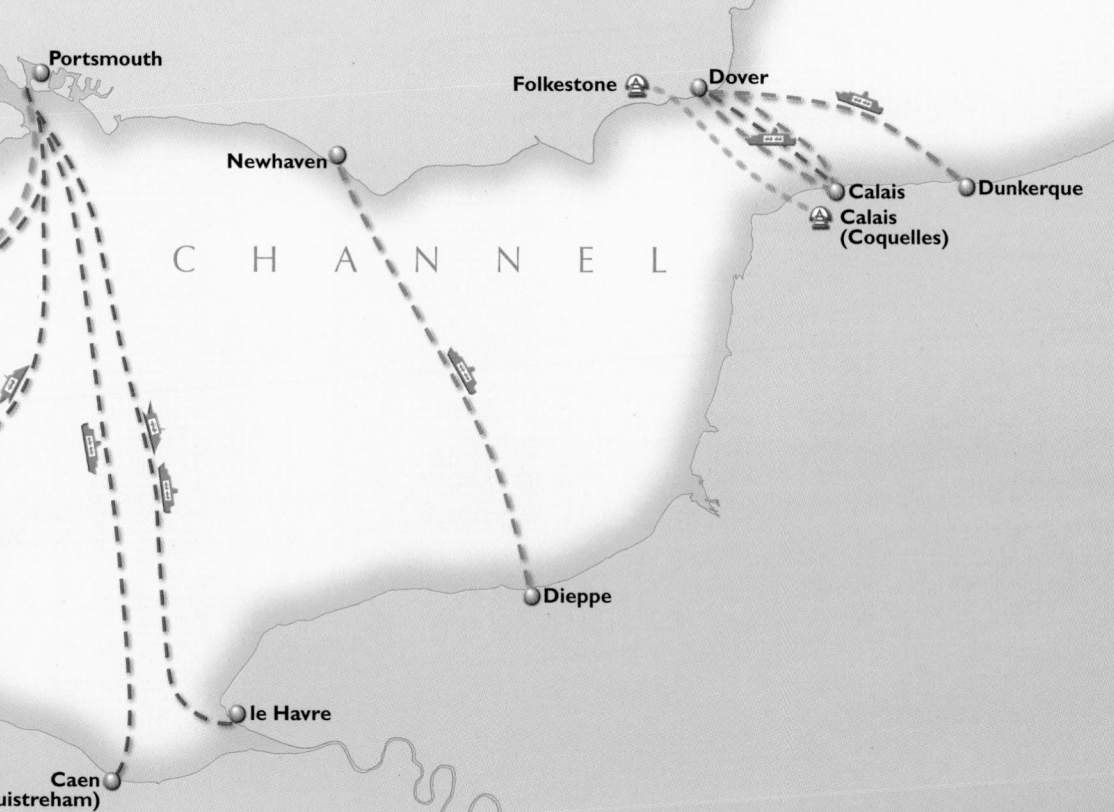

Calais

Ferries to Ireland and the Isle of Man

With so many sea crossings to Ireland and the Isle of Man this map will help you make the right choice.

The vehicle ferry routes shown on this map give you all the options, together with detailed port plans to help you navigate to and from the ferry terminals. Simply choose your preferred route, not forgetting the fast sailings; then check the colour-coded table for ferry operators, crossing times and contact details.

🚢 Fast ferry   🚢 Conventional ferry

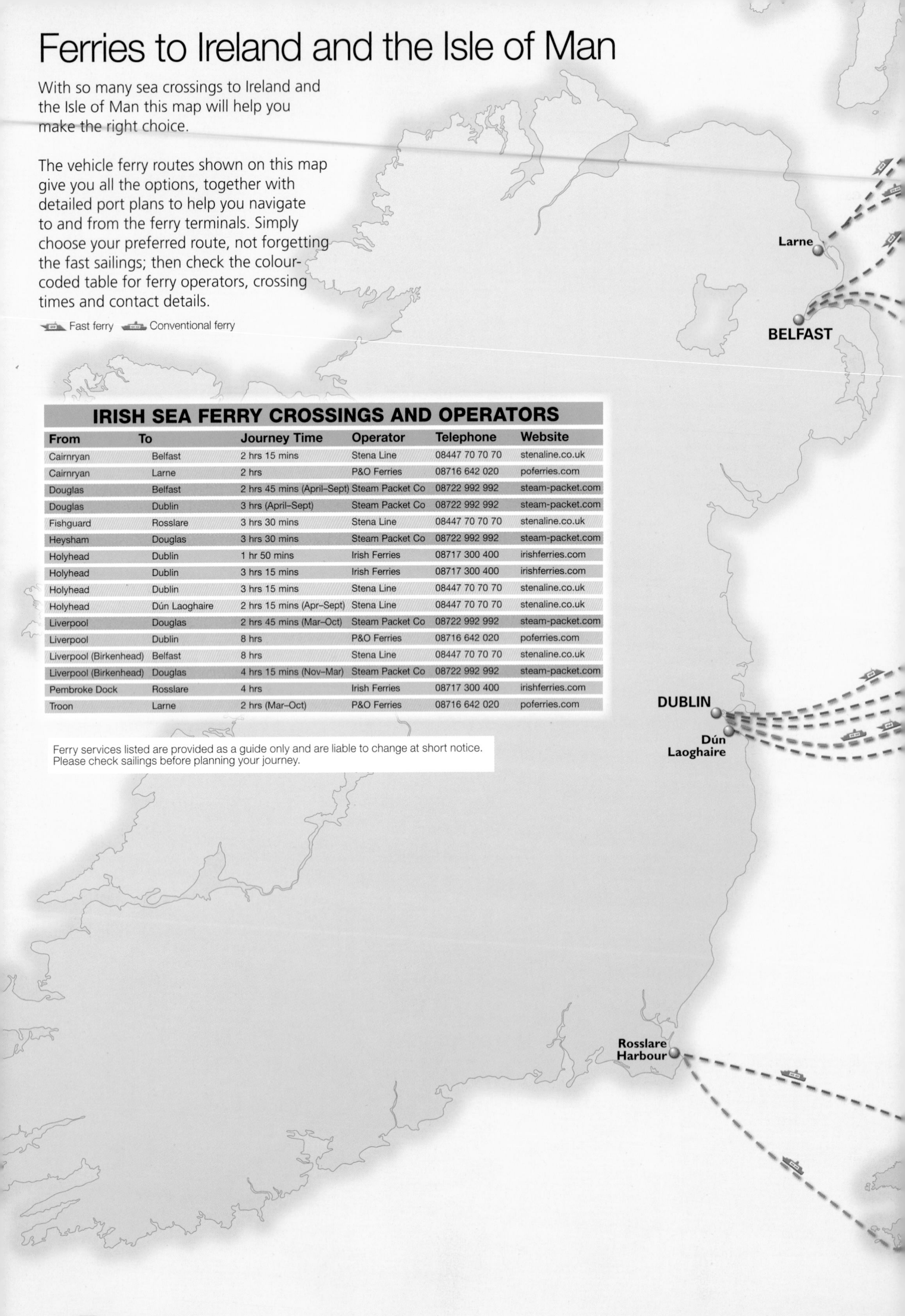

Larne

BELFAST

IRISH SEA FERRY CROSSINGS AND OPERATORS

From	To	Journey Time	Operator	Telephone	Website
Cairnryan	Belfast	2 hrs 15 mins	Stena Line	08447 70 70 70	stenaline.co.uk
Cairnryan	Larne	2 hrs	P&O Ferries	08716 642 020	poferries.com
Douglas	Belfast	2 hrs 45 mins (April–Sept)	Steam Packet Co	08722 992 992	steam-packet.com
Douglas	Dublin	3 hrs (April–Sept)	Steam Packet Co	08722 992 992	steam-packet.com
Fishguard	Rosslare	3 hrs 30 mins	Stena Line	08447 70 70 70	stenaline.co.uk
Heysham	Douglas	3 hrs 30 mins	Steam Packet Co	08722 992 992	steam-packet.com
Holyhead	Dublin	1 hr 50 mins	Irish Ferries	08717 300 400	irishferries.com
Holyhead	Dublin	3 hrs 15 mins	Irish Ferries	08717 300 400	irishferries.com
Holyhead	Dublin	3 hrs 15 mins	Stena Line	08447 70 70 70	stenaline.co.uk
Holyhead	Dún Laoghaire	2 hrs 15 mins (Apr–Sept)	Stena Line	08447 70 70 70	stenaline.co.uk
Liverpool	Douglas	2 hrs 45 mins (Mar–Oct)	Steam Packet Co	08722 992 992	steam-packet.com
Liverpool	Dublin	8 hrs	P&O Ferries	08716 642 020	poferries.com
Liverpool (Birkenhead)	Belfast	8 hrs	Stena Line	08447 70 70 70	stenaline.co.uk
Liverpool (Birkenhead)	Douglas	4 hrs 15 mins (Nov–Mar)	Steam Packet Co	08722 992 992	steam-packet.com
Pembroke Dock	Rosslare	4 hrs	Irish Ferries	08717 300 400	irishferries.com
Troon	Larne	2 hrs (Mar–Oct)	P&O Ferries	08716 642 020	poferries.com

Ferry services listed are provided as a guide only and are liable to change at short notice. Please check sailings before planning your journey.

DUBLIN

Dún Laoghaire

Rosslare Harbour

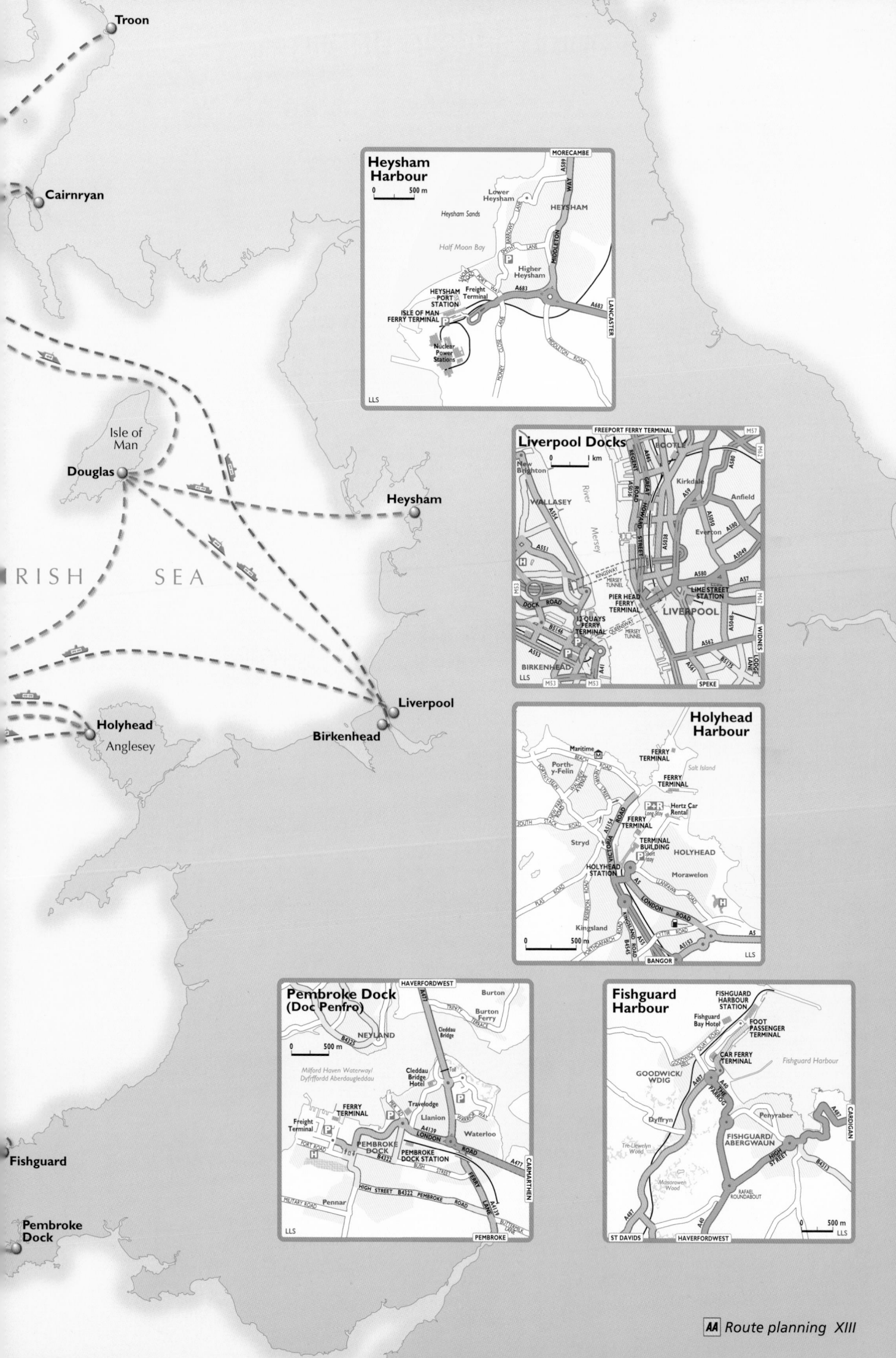

Troon

Cairnryan

Isle of Man

Douglas

I R I S H S E A

Heysham

Liverpool

Birkenhead

Holyhead
Anglesey

Fishguard

Pembroke Dock

Heysham Harbour

0   500 m

MORECAMBE
Lower Heysham
Heysham Sands
Half Moon Bay
HEYSHAM
Higher Heysham
A589
MIDDLETON WAY
LANCASTER
MIDDLETON ROAD
A683
P
HEYSHAM PORT STATION
Freight Terminal
ISLE OF MAN FERRY TERMINAL
P
Nuclear Power Stations
LLS

Liverpool Docks

FREEPORT FERRY TERMINAL
M57
BOOTLE
New Brighton
WALLASEY
River Mersey
Kirkdale
A59
Anfield
A5049
Everton
A5058
A580
A57
KINGSWAY MERSEY TUNNEL
PIER HEAD FERRY TERMINAL
LIME STREET STATION
LIVERPOOL
WIDNES
M62
12 QUAYS FERRY TERMINAL
P
DOCK ROAD
QUEENSWAY MERSEY TUNNEL
A562
LODGE LANE
B5178
BIRKENHEAD
LLS
M53
M53
A41
SPEKE
0   1 km

Holyhead Harbour

Maritime
FERRY TERMINAL
Salt Island
Porth-y-Felin
FERRY TERMINAL
BEACH ROAD
P+R Long Stay
Hertz Car Rental
FERRY TERMINAL
TERMINAL BUILDING
P Short Stay
HOLYHEAD
Stryd
Morawelon
HOLYHEAD STATION
A5
LONDON ROAD
A5
Kingsland
KINGSLAND ROAD
B4545
A5153
A5
LLS
BANGOR
0   500 m

Pembroke Dock (Doc Penfro)

HAVERFORDWEST
Burton
NEYLAND
A477
TRINITY
Burton Ferry TERRACE
Cleddau Bridge
Milford Haven Waterway/ Dyfrffordd Aberdaugleddau
Cleddau Bridge Hotel
Toll
P
Travelodge
Llanion
FERRY TERMINAL
P
Freight Terminal
P
A4139
Waterloo
LONDON ROAD
H
PEMBROKE DOCK
PEMBROKE DOCK STATION
A477
CARMARTHEN
B4322
HIGH STREET
B4322
PEMBROKE ROAD
MILITARY ROAD
Pennar
FERRY LANE
BUTTERMILK LANE
LLS
PEMBROKE
0   500 m

Fishguard Harbour

FISHGUARD HARBOUR STATION
Fishguard Bay Hotel
FOOT PASSENGER TERMINAL
CAR FERRY TERMINAL
GOODWICK/ WDIG
Fishguard Harbour
THE PARROG
A487
A40
Dyffryn
Penyraber
Tre-Llewelyn Wood
FISHGUARD/ ABERGWAUN
CARDIGAN
A487
HIGH STREET
B4313
Manorowen Wood
RAFAEL ROUNDABOUT
A40
A487
ST DAVIDS
HAVERFORDWEST
LLS
0   500 m

Caravan and camping sites in Britain

These pages list the top 300 AA-inspected Caravan and Camping (C & C) sites in the Pennant rating scheme. **Five Pennant Premier sites are shown in green,** **Four Pennant sites are shown in blue.**

Listings include addresses, telephone numbers and websites together with page and grid references to locate the sites in the atlas. The total number of touring pitches is also included for each site, together with the type of pitch available. The following abbreviations are used: **C = Caravan CV = Campervan T = Tent**

To find out more about the AA's Pennant rating scheme and other rated caravan and camping sites not included on these pages please visit **theAA.com**

ENGLAND

Alders Caravan Park
Home Farm, Alne, York
YO61 1RY
Tel: 01347 838722   **97 R7**
alderscaravanpark.co.uk
Total Pitches: 87 (C, CV & T)

Andrewshayes Holiday Park
Dalwood, Axminster
EX13 7DY
Tel: 01404 831225   **10 E5**
andrewshayes.co.uk
Total Pitches: 150 (C, CV & T)

Apple Tree Park
C & C Site
A38, Claypits, Stonehouse
GL10 3AL
Tel: 01452 742362   **32 E3**
appletreepark.co.uk
Total Pitches: 65 (C, CV & T)

Appuldurcombe Gardens
Holiday Park
Appuldurcombe Road, Wroxall,
Isle of Wight
PO38 3EP
Tel: 01983 852597   **14 F10**
appuldurcombegardens.co.uk
Total Pitches: 130 (C, CV & T)

Arrow Bank Holiday Park
Nun House Farm, Eardisland,
Leominster
HR6 9BG
Tel: 01544 388312   **45 N3**
arrowbank.co.uk
Total Pitches: 38 (C, CV & T)

Atlantic Bays Holiday Park
St Merryn, Padstow
PL28 8PY
Tel: 01841 520855   **4 D7**
atlanticbaysholidaypark.co.uk
Total Pitches: 70 (C, CV & T)

Ayr Holiday Park
St Ives, Cornwall
TR26 1EJ
Tel: 01736 795855   **2 E5**
ayrholidaypark.co.uk
Total Pitches: 40 (C, CV & T)

Back of Beyond
Touring Park
234 Ringwood Rd,
St Leonards, Dorset
BH24 2SB
Tel: 01202 876968   **13 J4**
backofbeyondtouringpark.co.uk
Total Pitches: 80 (C, CV & T)

Bagwell Farm Touring Park
Knights in the Bottom,
Chickerell, Weymouth
DT3 4EA
Tel: 01305 782575   **11 N8**
bagwellfarm.co.uk
Total Pitches: 320 (C, CV & T)

Bardsea Leisure Park
Priory Road, Ulverston
LA12 9QE
Tel: 01229 584712   **94 F5**
bardsealeisure.co.uk
Total Pitches: 83 (C & CV)

Barn Farm Campsite
Barn Farm, Birchover,
Matlock
DE4 2BL
Tel: 01629 650245   **84 B8**
barnfarmcamping.com
Total Pitches: 50 (C, CV & T)

Barnstones C & C Site
Great Bourton, Banbury
OX17 1QU
Tel: 01295 750289   **48 E6**
Total Pitches: 49 (C, CV & T)

Bath Chew Valley
Caravan Park
Ham Lane, Bishop Sutton
BS39 5TZ
Tel: 01275 332127   **19 Q3**
bathchewvalley.co.uk
Total Pitches: 45 (C, CV & T)

Bay View Holiday Park
Bolton le Sands, Carnforth
LA5 9TN
Tel: 01524 701508   **95 K7**
holgates.co.uk
Total Pitches: 100 (C, CV & T)

Beaconsfield Farm
Caravan Park
Battlefield, Shrewsbury
SY4 4AA
Tel: 01939 210370   **69 P11**
beaconsfield-farm.co.uk
Total Pitches: 60 (C & CV)

Beech Croft Farm
Beech Croft,
Blackwell in the Peak, Buxton
SK17 9TQ
Tel: 01298 85330   **83 P10**
beechcroftfarm.co.uk
Total Pitches: 30 (C, CV & T)

Bellingham C & C Club Site
Brown Rigg, Bellingham
NE48 2JY
Tel: 01434 220175   **112 B4**
campingandcaravanningclub.
co.uk/bellingham
Total Pitches: 64 (C, CV & T)

Beverley Parks C & C Park
Goodrington Road,
Paignton
TQ4 7JE
Tel: 01803 661979   **7 M7**
beverley-holidays.co.uk
Total Pitches: 172 (C, CV & T)

Bingham Grange
Touring & Camping Park
Melplash, Bridport
DT6 3TT
Tel: 01308 488234   **11 K5**
binghamgrange.co.uk
Total Pitches: 150 (C, CV & T)

Blackmore Vale C & C Park
Sherborne Causeway,
Shaftesbury
SP7 9PX
Tel: 01747 851523   **20 F10**
blackmorevalecaravanpark.co.uk
Total Pitches: 16 (C, CV & T)

Blue Rose Caravan Country Park
Star Carr Lane,
Brandesburton
YO25 8RU
Tel: 01964 543366   **99 N11**
bluerosepark.co.uk
Total Pitches: 58 (C & CV)

Bo Peep Farm Caravan Park
Bo Peep Farm, Aynho Road,
Adderbury, Banbury
OX17 3NP
Tel: 01295 810605   **48 E8**
bo-peep.co.uk
Total Pitches: 104 (C, CV & T)

Briarfields Motel & Touring Park
Gloucester Road, Cheltenham
GL51 0SX
Tel: 01242 235324   **46 H10**
briarfields.net
Total Pitches: 72 (C, CV & T)

Broadhembury C & C Park
Steeds Lane, Kingsnorth, Ashford
TN26 1NQ
Tel: 01233 620859   **26 H4**
broadhembury.co.uk
Total Pitches: 110 (C, CV & T)

Brokerswood Country Park
Brokerswood, Westbury
BA13 4EH
Tel: 01373 822238   **20 F4**
brokerswoodcountrypark.co.uk
Total Pitches: 69 (C, CV & T)

Budemeadows Touring Park
Widemouth Bay, Bude
EX23 0NA
Tel: 01288 361646   **16 C11**
budemeadows.com
Total Pitches: 145 (C, CV & T)

Burrowhayes Farm C & C Site
& Riding Stables
West Luccombe, Porlock, Minehead
TA24 8HT
Tel: 01643 862463   **18 B5**
burrowhayes.co.uk
Total Pitches: 120 (C, CV & T)

Burton Constable
Holiday Park & Arboretum
Old Lodges, Sproatley, Hull
HU11 4LJ
Tel: 01964 562508   **93 L3**
burtonconstable.co.uk
Total Pitches: 140 (C, CV & T)

Cakes & Ale
Abbey Lane, Theberton,
Leiston
IP16 4TE
Tel: 01728 831655   **65 N9**
cakesandale.co.uk
Total Pitches: 55 (C, CV & T)

Calloose C & C Park
Leedstown, Hayle
TR27 5ET
Tel: 01736 850431   **2 F7**
calloose.co.uk
Total Pitches: 109 (C, CV & T)

Camping Caradon
Touring Park
Trelawne, Looe
PL13 2NA
Tel: 01503 272388   **5 L11**
campingcaradon.co.uk
Total Pitches: 75 (C, CV & T)

Capesthorne Hall
Congleton Road, Siddington,
Macclesfield
SK11 9JY
Tel: 01625 861221   **82 H10**
capesthorne.com
Total Pitches: 50 (C & CV)

Carlton Meres Country Park
Rendham Road, Carlton,
Saxmundham
IP17 2QP
Tel: 01728 603344   **65 M8**
carlton-meres.co.uk
Total Pitches: 96 (C, CV & T)

Carlyon Bay C & C Park
Bethesda, Cypress Avenue,
Carlyon Bay
PL25 3RE
Tel: 01726 812735   **3 R3**
carlyonbay.net
Total Pitches: 180 (C, CV & T)

Carnevas Holiday Park &
Farm Cottages
Carnevas Farm, St Merryn
PL28 8PN
Tel: 01841 520230   **4 D7**
carnevasholidaypark.co.uk
Total Pitches: 195 (C, CV & T)

Carnon Downs C & C Park
Carnon Downs, Truro
TR3 6JJ
Tel: 01872 862233   **3 L5**
carnon-downs-caravanpark.co.uk
Total Pitches: 150 (C, CV & T)

Carvynick Country Club
Summercourt, Newquay
TR8 5AF
Tel: 01872 510716   **4 D10**
carvynick.co.uk
Total Pitches: 47 (C & CV)

Castlerigg Hall C & C Park
Castlerigg Hall, Keswick
CA12 4TE
Tel: 017687 74499   **101 J6**
castlerigg.co.uk
Total Pitches: 48 (C, CV & T)

Cayton Village Caravan Park
Mill Lane, Cayton Bay,
Scarborough
YO11 3NN
Tel: 01723 583171   **99 M4**
caytontouring.co.uk
Total Pitches: 310 (C, CV & T)

Cheddar Bridge
Touring Park
Draycott Rd, Cheddar
BS27 3RJ
Tel: 01934 743048   **19 N4**
cheddarbridge.co.uk
Total Pitches: 45 (C, CV & T)

Cheddar Mendip Heights
C & C Club Site
Townsend, Priddy, Wells
BA5 3BP
Tel: 01749 870241   **19 P4**
campingandcaravanningclub.co.uk/
cheddar
Total Pitches: 90 (C, CV & T)

Chiverton Park
East Hill, Blackwater
TR4 8HS
Tel: 01872 560667   **3 J4**
chivertonpark.co.uk
Total Pitches: 12 (C, CV & T)

Church Farm C & C Park
The Bungalow, Church Farm,
High Street, Sixpenny Handley,
Salisbury
SP5 5ND
Tel: 01725 552563   **21 J11**
churchfarmcandcpark.co.uk
Total Pitches: 35 (C, CV & T)

Chy Carne Holiday Park
Kuggar, Ruan Minor,
Helston
TR12 7LX
Tel: 01326 290200   **3 J10**
chycarne.co.uk
Total Pitches: 30 (C, CV & T)

Claylands Caravan Park
Cabus, Garstang
PR3 1AJ
Tel: 01524 791242   **95 K11**
claylands.com
Total Pitches: 30 (C, CV & T)

Clippesby Hall
Hall Lane, Clippesby,
Great Yarmouth
NR29 3BL
Tel: 01493 367800   **77 N9**
clippesby.com
Total Pitches: 120 (C, CV & T)

Cofton Country Holidays
Starcross, Dawlish
EX6 8RP
Tel: 01626 890111   **9 N8**
coftonholidays.co.uk
Total Pitches: 450 (C, CV & T)

Coombe Touring Park
Race Plain, Netherhampton,
Salisbury
SP2 8PN
Tel: 01722 328451   **21 L9**
coombecaravanpark.co.uk
Total Pitches: 50 (C, CV & T)

Corfe Castle C & C Club Site
Bucknowle, Wareham
BH20 5PQ
Tel: 01929 480280   **12 F8**
campingandcaravanningclub.co.uk/
corfecastle
Total Pitches: 80 (C, CV & T)

Cornish Farm Touring Park
Shoreditch, Taunton
TA3 7BS
Tel: 01823 327746   **18 H10**
cornishfarm.com
Total Pitches: 50 (C, CV & T)

Cosawes Park
Perranarworthal, Truro
TR3 7QS
Tel: 01872 863724   **3 K6**
cosaweestouringandcamping.co.uk
Total Pitches: 59 (C, CV & T)

Cote Ghyll C & C Park
Osmotherley, Northallerton
DL6 3AH
Tel: 01609 883425   **104 E11**
coteghyll.com
Total Pitches: 77 (C, CV & T)

Cotswold View
Touring Park
Enstone Road, Charlbury
OX7 3JH
Tel: 01608 810314   **48 C10**
cotswoldview.co.uk
Total Pitches: 125 (C, CV & T)

Country View
Holiday Park
Sand Road, Sand Bay,
Weston-super-Mare
BS22 9UJ
Tel: 01934 627595   **19 K2**
cvhp.co.uk
Total Pitches: 190 (C, CV & T)

Cove C & C Park
Ullswater, Watermillock
CA11 0LS
Tel: 017684 86549   **101 M6**
cove-park.co.uk
Total Pitches: 50 (C, CV & T)

Crealy Meadows C & C Park
Sidmouth Road,
Clyst St Mary, Exeter
EX5 1DR
Tel: 01395 234888   **9 P6**
crealymeadows.co.uk
Total Pitches: 120 (C, CV & T)

Crows Nest Caravan Park
Gristhorpe, Filey
YO14 9PS
Tel: 01723 582206   **99 M4**
crowsnestcaravanpark.com
Total Pitches: 49 (C, CV & T)

Dell Touring Park
Beyton Road, Thurston,
Bury St Edmunds
IP31 3RB
Tel: 01359 270121   **64 C9**
thedellcaravanpark.co.uk
Total Pitches: 50 (C, CV & T)

Diamond Farm C & C Park
Islip Road, Bletchingdon
OX5 3DR
Tel: 01869 350909   **48 F11**
diamondpark.co.uk
Total Pitches: 37 (C, CV & T)

Dibles Park
Dibles Road, Warsash,
Southampton
SO31 9SA
Tel: 01489 575232   **14 F5**
diblespark.co.uk
Total Pitches: 14 (C, CV & T)

Dolbeare Park C & C
St Ive Road, Landrake,
Saltash
PL12 5AF
Tel: 01752 851332   **5 P9**
dolbeare.co.uk
Total Pitches: 60 (C, CV & T)

Dornafield
Dornafield Farm, Two Mile Oak,
Newton Abbot
TQ12 6DD
Tel: 01803 812732   **7 L5**
dornafield.com
Total Pitches: 135 (C, CV & T)

East Fleet Farm
Touring Park
Chickerell, Weymouth
DT3 4DW
Tel: 01305 785768   **11 N9**
eastfleet.co.uk
Total Pitches: 400 (C, CV & T)

Eden Valley Holiday Park
Lanlivery, Nr Lostwithiel
PL30 5BU
Tel: 01208 872277   **4 H10**
edenvalleyholidaypark.co.uk
Total Pitches: 56 (C, CV & T)

Eskdale C & C Club Site
Boot, Holmrook
CA19 1TH
Tel: 019467 23253   **100 G10**
campingandcaravanningclub.co.uk/
eskdale
Total Pitches: 100 (CV & T)

Exe Valley Caravan Site
Mill House, Bridgetown,
Dulverton
TA22 9JR
Tel: 01643 851432   **18 B8**
exevalleycamping.co.uk
Total Pitches: 48 (C, CV & T)

Fernwood Caravan Park
Lyneal, Ellesmere
SY12 0QF
Tel: 01948 710221   **69 N8**
fernwoodpark.co.uk
Total Pitches: 60 (C & CV)

Fields End Water
Caravan Park & Fishery
Benwick Road, Doddington,
March
PE15 0TY
Tel: 01354 740199   **62 E2**
fieldsendcaravans.co.uk
Total Pitches: 52 (C, CV & T)

Fishpool Farm Caravan Park
Fishpool Road, Delamere,
Northwich
CW8 2HP
Tel: 01606 883970   **82 C11**
fishpoolfarmcaravanpark.co.uk
Total Pitches: 50 (C, CV & T)

Flusco Wood
Flusco, Penrith
CA11 0JB
Tel: 017684 80020   **101 N5**
fluscowood.co.uk
Total Pitches: 36 (C & CV)

Globe Vale Holiday Park
Radnor, Redruth
TR16 4BH
Tel: 01209 891183 **3 J5**
globevale.co.uk
Total Pitches: 138 (C, CV & T)

Golden Cap Holiday Park
Seatown, Chideock, Bridport
DT6 6JX
Tel: 01308 422139 **11 J6**
wdlh.co.uk
Total Pitches: 108 (C, CV & T)

**Golden Square Touring
Caravan Park**
Oswaldkirk, Helmsley
YO62 5YQ
Tel: 01439 788269 **98 C5**
goldensquarecaravanpark.com
Total Pitches: 129 (C, CV & T)

Golden Valley C & C Park
Coach Road, Ripley
DE55 4ES
Tel: 01773 513881 **84 F10**
goldenvalleycaravanpark.co.uk
Total Pitches: 45 (C, CV & T)

Goosewood Caravan Park
Sutton-on-the-Forest, York
YO61 1ET
Tel: 01347 810829 **98 B8**
flowerofmay.com
Total Pitches: 100 (C & CV)

Green Acres Caravan Park
High Knells, Houghton, Carlisle
CA6 4JW
Tel: 01228 675418 **110 H8**
caravanpark-cumbria.com
Total Pitches: 30 (C, CV & T)

Greenacres Touring Park
Haywards Lane, Chelston,
Wellington
TA21 9PH
Tel: 01823 652844 **18 G10**
greenacres-wellington.co.uk
Total Pitches: 40 (C & CV)

Greenhill Farm C & C Park
Greenhill Farm, New Road,
Landford, Salisbury
SP5 2AZ
Tel: 01794 324117 **21 Q11**
greenhillholidays.co.uk
Total Pitches: 160 (C, CV & T)

Greenhill Leisure Park
Greenhill Farm, Station Road,
Bletchingdon, Oxford
OX5 3BQ
Tel: 01869 351600 **48 E11**
greenhill-leisure-park.co.uk
Total Pitches: 92 (C, CV & T)

Grouse Hill Caravan Park
Flask Bungalow Farm,
Fylingdales, Robin Hood's Bay
YO22 4QH
Tel: 01947 880543 **105 P10**
grousehill.co.uk
Total Pitches: 175 (C, CV & T)

Gunvenna Caravan Park
St Minver, Wadebridge
PL27 6QN
Tel: 01208 862405 **4 F6**
gunvenna.co.uk
Total Pitches: 75 (C, CV & T)

Gwithian Farm Campsite
Gwithian Farm, Gwithian, Hayle
TR27 5BX
Tel: 01736 753127 **2 F5**
gwithianfarm.co.uk
Total Pitches: 87 (C, CV & T)

Harbury Fields
Harbury Fields Farm, Harbury,
Nr Leamington Spa
CV33 9JN
Tel: 01926 612457 **48 C2**
harburyfields.co.uk
Total Pitches: 59 (C & CV)

Heathfield Farm Camping
Heathfield Road, Freshwater,
Isle of Wight
PO40 9SH
Tel: 01983 407822 **13 P7**
heathfieldcamping.co.uk
Total Pitches: 60 (C, CV & T)

Heathland Beach Caravan Park
London Road, Kessingland
NR33 7PJ
Tel: 01502 740337 **65 Q4**
heathlandbeach.co.uk
Total Pitches: 63 (C, CV & T)

Hele Valley Holiday Park
Hele Bay, Ilfracombe
EX34 9RD
Tel: 01271 862460 **17 J2**
helevalley.co.uk
Total Pitches: 55 (C, CV & T)

Hendra Holiday Park
Newquay
TR8 4NY
Tel: 01637 875778 **4 C9**
hendra-holidays.com
Total Pitches: 548 (C, CV & T)

Herding Hill Farm
Shield Hill, Haltwhistle
NE49 9NW
Tel: 01434 320175 **111 P8**
herdinghillfarm.co.uk
Total Pitches: 44 (C, CV & T)

Hidden Valley Park
West Down, Braunton,
Ilfracombe
EX34 8NU
Tel: 01271 813837 **17 J3**
hiddenvalleypark.com
Total Pitches: 100 (C, CV & T)

**Highfield Farm
Touring Park**
Long Road, Comberton,
Cambridge
CB23 7DG
Tel: 01223 262308 **62 E9**
highfieldfarmtouringpark.co.uk
Total Pitches: 120 (C, CV & T)

**Highlands End
Holiday Park**
Eype, Bridport, Dorset
DT6 6AR
Tel: 01308 422139 **11 K6**
wdlh.co.uk
Total Pitches: 195 (C, CV & T)

**Hill Cottage Farm
C & C Park**
Sandleheath Road, Alderholt,
Fordingbridge
SP6 3EG
Tel: 01425 650513 **13 K2**
hillcottagefarmcampingand
caravanpark.co.uk
Total Pitches: 95 (C, CV & T)

Hill Farm Caravan Park
Branches Lane,
Sherfield English, Romsey
SO51 6FH
Tel: 01794 340402 **21 Q10**
hillfarmpark.com
Total Pitches: 100 (C, CV & T)

Hill of Oaks & Blakeholme
Windermere
LA12 8NR
Tel: 015395 31578 **94 H3**
hillofoaks.co.uk
Total Pitches: 43 (C & CV)

Hillside Caravan Park
Canvas Farm, Moor Road,
Thirsk
YO7 4BR
Tel: 01845 537349 **97 P3**
hillsidecaravanpark.co.uk
Total Pitches: 35 (C & CV)

Hollins Farm C & C
Far Arnside, Carnforth
LA5 0SL
Tel: 01524 701508 **95 J5**
holgates.co.uk
Total Pitches: 12 (C, CV & T)

Homing Park
Church Lane, Seasalter,
Whitstable
CT5 4BU
Tel: 01227 771777 **39 J9**
homingpark.co.uk
Total Pitches: 43 (C, CV & T)

Honeybridge Park
Honeybridge Lane, Dial Post,
Horsham
RH13 8NX
Tel: 01403 710923 **24 E7**
honeybridgepark.co.uk
Total Pitches: 130 (C, CV & T)

Hurley Riverside Park
Park Office, Hurley,
Nr Maidenhead
SL6 5NE
Tel: 01628 824493 **35 M8**
hurleyriversidepark.co.uk
Total Pitches: 200 (C, CV & T)

Hylton Caravan Park
Eden Street, Silloth
CA7 4AY
Tel: 016973 31707 **109 P10**
stanwix.com
Total Pitches: 90 (C, CV & T)

**Jacobs Mount
Caravan Park**
Jacobs Mount, Stepney Road,
Scarborough
YO12 5NL
Tel: 01723 361178 **99 L3**
jacobsmount.com
Total Pitches: 156 (C, CV & T)

Jasmine Caravan Park
Cross Lane, Snainton,
Scarborough
YO13 9BE
Tel: 01723 859240 **99 J4**
jasminepark.co.uk
Total Pitches: 68 (C, CV & T)

Juliot's Well Holiday Park
Camelford, Cornwall
PL32 9RF
Tel: 01840 213302 **4 H5**
juliotswell.com
Total Pitches: 39 (C, CV & T)

**Kenneggy Cove
Holiday Park**
Higher Kenneggy, Rosudgeon,
Penzance
TR20 9AU
Tel: 01736 763453 **2 F8**
kenneggycove.co.uk
Total Pitches: 45 (C, CV & T)

King's Lynn C & C Park
New Road, North Runcton,
King's Lynn
PE33 0RA
Tel: 01553 840004 **75 M7**
kl-cc.co.uk
Total Pitches: 150 (C, CV & T)

Kneps Farm Holiday Park
River Road, Stanah,
Thornton-Cleveleys, Blackpool
FY5 5LR
Tel: 01253 823632 **88 D2**
knepsfarm.co.uk
Total Pitches: 40 (C & CV)

**Ladycross Plantation
Caravan Park**
Egton, Whitby
YO21 1UA
Tel: 01947 895502 **105 M9**
ladycrossplantation.co.uk
Total Pitches: 130 (C, CV & T)

Lady's Mile Holiday Park
Dawlish, Devon
EX7 0LX
Tel: 01626 863411 **9 N9**
ladysmile.co.uk
Total Pitches: 570 (C, CV & T)

**Lamb Cottage
Caravan Park**
Dalefords Lane, Whitegate,
Northwich
CW8 2BN
Tel: 01606 882302 **82 D11**
lambcottage.co.uk
Total Pitches: 45 (C & CV)

**Langstone Manor
C & C Park**
Moortown, Tavistock
PL19 9JZ
Tel: 01822 613371 **6 E4**
langstone-manor.co.uk
Total Pitches: 40 (C, CV & T)

Lebberston Touring Park
Filey Road, Lebberston,
Scarborough
YO11 3PE
Tel: 01723 585723 **99 M4**
lebberstontouring.co.uk
Total Pitches: 125 (C & CV)

Lee Valley C & C Park
Meridian Way, Edmonton,
London
N9 0AR
Tel: 020 8803 6900 **37 J2**
visitleevalley.org.uk
Total Pitches: 100 (C, CV & T)

Lee Valley Campsite
Sewardstone Road, Chingford,
London
E4 7RA
Tel: 020 8529 5689 **51 J11**
visitleevalley.org.uk
Total Pitches: 81 (C, CV & T)

Lickpenny Caravan Site
Lickpenny Lane, Tansley,
Matlock
DE4 5GF
Tel: 01629 583040 **84 D9**
lickpennycaravanpark.co.uk
Total Pitches: 80 (C & CV)

Lime Tree Park
Dukes Drive, Buxton
SK17 9RP
Tel: 01298 22988 **83 N10**
limetreeparkbuxton.co.uk
Total Pitches: 106 (C, CV & T)

**Lincoln Farm Park
Oxfordshire**
High Street, Standlake
OX29 7RH
Tel: 01865 300239 **34 C4**
lincolnfarmpark.co.uk
Total Pitches: 90 (C, CV & T)

Little Cotton Caravan Park
Little Cotton, Dartmouth
TQ6 0LB
Tel: 01803 832558 **7 M8**
littlecotton.co.uk
Total Pitches: 95 (C, CV & T)

Little Lakeland Caravan Park
Wortwell, Harleston
IP20 0EL
Tel: 01986 788646 **65 K4**
littlelakeland.co.uk
Total Pitches: 38 (C, CV & T)

Long Acres Touring Park
Station Road, Old Leake, Boston
PE22 9RF
Tel: 01205 871555 **87 L10**
longacres-caravanpark.co.uk
Total Pitches: 40 (C, CV & T)

Long Hazel Park
High Street, Sparkford, Yeovil
BA22 7JH
Tel: 01963 440002 **20 B9**
longhazelpark.co.uk
Total Pitches: 50 (C, CV & T)

Longnor Wood Holiday Park
Newtown, Longnor,
Nr Buxton
SK17 0NG
Tel: 01298 83648 **71 K2**
longnorwood.co.uk
Total Pitches: 47 (C, CV & T)

Lower Polladras Touring Park
Carleen, Breage, Helston
TR13 9NX
Tel: 01736 762220 **2 G7**
lower-polladras.co.uk
Total Pitches: 39 (C, CV & T)

Lowther Holiday Park
Eamont Bridge, Penrith
CA10 2JB
Tel: 01768 863631 **101 P5**
lowther-holidaypark.co.uk
Total Pitches: 180 (C, CV & T)

Lytton Lawn Touring Park
Lymore Lane, Milford on Sea
SO41 0TX
Tel: 01590 648331 **13 N6**
shorefield.co.uk
Total Pitches: 136 (C, CV & T)

**Manor Wood Country
Caravan Park**
Manor Wood, Coddington,
Chester
CH3 9EN
Tel: 01829 782990 **69 N3**
cheshire-caravan-sites.co.uk
Total Pitches: 45 (C, CV & T)

Meadowbank Holidays
Stour Way, Christchurch
BH23 2PQ
Tel: 01202 483597 **13 K6**
meadowbank-holidays.co.uk
Total Pitches: 41 (C & CV)

Merley Court
Merley, Wimborne Minster
BH21 3AA
Tel: 01590 648331 **12 H5**
shorefield.co.uk
Total Pitches: 160 (C, CV & T)

**Middlewood Farm
Holiday Park**
Middlewood Lane, Fylingthorpe,
Robin Hood's Bay, Whitby
YO22 4UF
Tel: 01947 880414 **105 P10**
middlewoodfarm.com
Total Pitches: 100 (C, CV & T)

Minnows Touring Park
Holbrook Lane,
Sampford Peverell
EX16 7EN
Tel: 01884 821770 **18 D11**
minnowstouringpark.co.uk
Total Pitches: 59 (C, CV & T)

Moon & Sixpence
Newbourn Road, Waldringfield,
Woodbridge
IP12 4PP
Tel: 01473 736650 **53 N2**
moonandsixpence.eu
Total Pitches: 50 (C & CV)

Moss Wood Caravan Park
Crimbles Lane, Cockerham
LA2 0ES
Tel: 01524 791041 **95 K11**
mosswood.co.uk
Total Pitches: 25 (C, CV & T)

Naburn Lock Caravan Park
Naburn
YO19 4RU
Tel: 01904 728697 **98 C11**
naburnlock.co.uk
Total Pitches: 100 (C, CV & T)

Newberry Valley Park
Woodlands,
Combe Martin
EX34 0AT
Tel: 01271 882334 **17 K2**
newberryvalleypark.co.uk
Total Pitches: 110 (C, CV & T)

**Newhaven Caravan &
Camping Park**
Newhaven, Nr Buxton
SK17 0DT
Tel: 01298 84300 **71 M3**
newhavencaravanpark.co.uk
Total Pitches: 125 (C, CV & T)

Newlands C & C Park
Charmouth, Bridport
DT6 6RB
Tel: 01297 560259 **10 H6**
newlandsholidays.co.uk
Total Pitches: 240 (C, CV & T)

Newperran Holiday Park
Rejerrah, Newquay
TR8 5QJ
Tel: 01872 572407 **3 K3**
newperran.co.uk
Total Pitches: 357 (C, CV & T)

Ninham Country Holidays
Ninham, Shanklin,
Isle of Wight
PO37 7PL
Tel: 01983 864243 **14 G10**
ninham-holidays.co.uk
Total Pitches: 150 (C, CV & T)

**North Morte Farm
C & C Park**
North Morte Road,
Mortehoe, Woolacombe
EX34 7EG
Tel: 01271 870381 **16 H2**
northmortefarm.co.uk
Total Pitches: 180 (C, CV & T)

**Northam Farm Caravan &
Touring Park**
Brean, Burnham-on-Sea
TA8 2SE
Tel: 01278 751244 **19 K3**
northamfarm.co.uk
Total Pitches: 350 (C, CV & T)

**Oakdown Country
Holiday Park**
Gatedown Lane,
Sidmouth
EX10 0PT
Tel: 01297 680387 **10 D6**
oakdown.co.uk
Total Pitches: 150 (C, CV & T)

**Oathill Farm Touring and
Camping Site**
Oathill, Crewkerne
TA18 8PZ
Tel: 01460 30234 **11 J3**
oathillfarmleisure.co.uk
Total Pitches: 13 (C, CV & T)

Old Hall Caravan Park
Capernwray, Carnforth
LA6 1AD
Tel: 01524 733276 **95 L6**
oldhallcaravanpark.co.uk
Total Pitches: 38 (C & CV)

Orchard Park
Frampton Lane,
Hubbert's Bridge, Boston
PE20 3QU
Tel: 01205 290328 **74 E2**
orchardpark.co.uk
Total Pitches: 87 (C, CV & T)

Ord House Country Park
East Ord,
Berwick-upon-Tweed
TD15 2NS
Tel: 01289 305288 **129 P9**
ordhouse.co.uk
Total Pitches: 79 (C, CV & T)

Oxon Hall Touring Park
Welshpool Road,
Shrewsbury
SY3 5FB
Tel: 01743 340868 **56 H2**
morris-leisure.co.uk
Total Pitches: 105 (C, CV & T)

Padstow Touring Park
Padstow
PL28 8LE
Tel: 01841 532061 **4 E7**
padstowtouringpark.co.uk
Total Pitches: 150 (C, CV & T)

**Park Cliffe Camping &
Caravan Estate**
Birks Road, Tower Wood,
Windermere
LA23 3PG
Tel: 01539 531344 **94 H2**
parkcliffe.co.uk
Total Pitches: 60 (C, CV & T)

Parkers Farm Holiday Park
Higher Mead Farm,
Ashburton, Devon
TQ13 7LJ
Tel: 01364 654869 **7 K4**
parkersfarmholidays.co.uk
Total Pitches: 100 (C, CV & T)

Parkland C & C Site
Sorley Green Cross, Kingsbridge
TQ7 4AF
Tel: 01548 852723 **7 J9**
parklandsite.co.uk
Total Pitches: 100 (C, CV & T)

Pear Tree Holiday Park
Organford Road, Holton Heath,
Organford, Poole
BH16 6LA
Tel: 01202 622434 **12 F6**
peartreepark.co.uk
Total Pitches: 154 (C, CV & T)

Penrose Holiday Park
Goonhavern, Truro
TR4 9QF
Tel: 01872 573185 **3 K3**
penroseholidaypark.com
Total Pitches: 110 (C, CV & T)

Pentire Haven Holiday Park
Stibb Road, Kilkhampton, Bude
EX23 9QY
Tel: 01288 321601 **16 C9**
pentirehaven.co.uk
Total Pitches: 120 (C, CV & T)

Piccadilly Caravan Park
Folly Lane West, Lacock
SN15 2LP
Tel: 01249 730260 **32 H11**
piccadillylacock.co.uk
Total Pitches: 41 (C, CV & T)

Pilgrims Way C & C Park
Church Green Road, Fishtoft,
Boston
PE21 0QY
Tel: 01205 366646 **74 G2**
pilgrimsway-caravanandcamping.com
Total Pitches: 22 (C, CV & T)

Polmanter Touring Park
Halsetown, St Ives
TR26 3LX
Tel: 01736 795640 **2 E6**
polmanter.com
Total Pitches: 270 (C, CV & T)

Porlock Caravan Park
Porlock, Minehead
TA24 8ND
Tel: 01643 862269 **18 A5**
porlockcaravanpark.co.uk
Total Pitches: 40 (C, CV & T)

Porthtowan Tourist Park
Mile Hill, Porthtowan, Truro
TR4 8TY
Tel: 01209 890256 **2 H4**
porthtowantouristpark.co.uk
Total Pitches: 80 (C, CV & T)

**Quantock Orchard
Caravan Park**
Flaxpool, Crowcombe, Taunton
TA4 4AW
Tel: 01984 618618 **18 F7**
quantock-orchard.co.uk
Total Pitches: 60 (C, CV & T)

Ranch Caravan Park
Station Road, Honeybourne,
Evesham
WR11 7PR
Tel: 01386 830744 **47 M6**
ranch.co.uk
Total Pitches: 120 (C & CV)

Ripley Caravan Park
Knaresborough Road,
Ripley, Harrogate
HG3 3AU
Tel: 01423 770050 **97 L8**
ripleycaravanpark.com
Total Pitches: 100 (C, CV & T)

River Dart Country Park
Holne Park, Ashburton
TQ13 7NP
Tel: 01364 652511 **7 J5**
riverdart.co.uk
Total Pitches: 170 (C, CV & T)

River Valley Holiday Park
London Apprentice, St Austell
PL26 7AP
Tel: 01726 73533 **3 Q3**
rivervalleyholidaypark.co.uk
Total Pitches: 45 (C, CV & T)

Riverside C & C Park
Marsh Lane, North Molton Road,
South Molton
EX36 3HQ
Tel: 01769 579269 **17 N6**
exmoorriverside.co.uk
Total Pitches: 54 (C, CV & T)

Riverside Caravan Park
High Bentham,
Lancaster
LA2 7FJ
Tel: 015242 61272 **95 P7**
riversidecaravanpark.co.uk
Total Pitches: 61 (C & CV)

Riverside Caravan Park
Leigham Manor Drive,
Marsh Mills, Plymouth
PL6 8LL
Tel: 01752 344122 **6 E7**
riversidecaravanpark.com
Total Pitches: 259 (C, CV & T)

**Riverside Meadows Country
Caravan Park**
Ure Bank Top, Ripon
HG4 1JD
Tel: 01765 602964 **97 M6**
flowerofmay.com
Total Pitches: 80 (C, CV & T)

**Rose Farm Touring &
Camping Park**
Stepshort, Belton,
Nr Great Yarmouth
NR31 9JS
Tel: 01493 780896 **77 P11**
rosefarmtouringpark.co.uk
Total Pitches: 145 (C, CV & T)

Ross Park
Park Hill Farm, Ipplepen,
Newton Abbot
TQ12 5TT
Tel: 01803 812983 **7 L5**
rossparkcaravanpark.co.uk
Total Pitches: 110 (C, CV & T)

Rudding Holiday Park
Follifoot, Harrogate
HG3 1JH
Tel: 01423 870439 **97 M10**
ruddingholidaypark.co.uk
Total Pitches: 141 (C, CV & T)

Rutland C & C
Park Lane, Greetham,
Oakham
LE15 7FN
Tel: 01572 813520 **73 N8**
rutlandcaravanandcamping.co.uk
Total Pitches: 130 (C, CV & T)

St Helens Caravan Park
Wykeham, Scarborough
YO13 9QD
Tel: 01723 862771 **99 K4**
sthelenscaravanpark.co.uk
Total Pitches: 250 (C, CV & T)

St Mabyn Holiday Park
Longstone Road, St Mabyn,
Wadebridge
PL30 3BY
Tel: 01208 841677 **4 H7**
stmabynholidaypark.co.uk
Total Pitches: 120 (C, CV & T)

**Sandy Balls
Holiday Village**
Sandy Balls Estate Ltd,
Godshill, Fordingbridge
SP6 2JZ
Tel: 0844 693 1336 **13 L2**
sandyballs.co.uk
Total Pitches: 225 (C, CV & T)

**Seaview International
Holiday Park**
Boswinger, Mevagissey
PL26 6LL
Tel: 01726 843425 **3 P5**
seaviewinternational.com
Total Pitches: 201 (C, CV & T)

Severn Gorge Park
Bridgnorth Road, Tweedale,
Telford
TF7 4JB
Tel: 01952 684789 **57 N3**
severngorgepark.co.uk
Total Pitches: 12 (C & CV)

Shamba Holidays
230 Ringwood Road,
St Leonards, Ringwood
BH24 2SB
Tel: 01202 873302 **13 K4**
shambaholidays.co.uk
Total Pitches: 150 (C, CV & T)

Shaw Hall Holiday Park
Smithy Lane, Scarisbrick,
Ormskirk
L40 8HJ
Tel: 01704 840298 **119 M4**
shawhall.co.uk
Total Pitches: 37 (C, CV & T)

Shrubbery Touring Park
Rousdon, Lyme Regis
DT7 3XW
Tel: 01297 442227 **10 F6**
shrubberypark.co.uk
Total Pitches: 120 (C, CV & T)

Silverbow Park
Perranwell, Goonhavern
TR4 9NX
Tel: 01872 572347 **3 K3**
chycor.co.uk/parks/silverbow
Total Pitches: 90 (C, CV & T)

Silverdale Caravan Park
Middlebarrow Plain, Cove Road,
Silverdale, Nr Carnforth
LA5 0SH
Tel: 01524 701508 **95 K5**
holgates.co.uk
Total Pitches: 80 (C, CV & T)

Skelwith Fold Caravan Park
Ambleside, Cumbria
LA22 0HX
Tel: 015394 32277 **101 L10**
skelwith.com
Total Pitches: 150 (C & CV)

Somers Wood Caravan Park
Somers Road, Meriden
CV7 7PL
Tel: 01676 522978 **59 K8**
somerswood.co.uk
Total Pitches: 48 (C & CV)

**South Lytchett Manor
C & C Park**
Dorchester Road,
Lytchett Minster, Poole
BH16 6JB
Tel: 01202 622577 **12 G6**
southlytchettmanor.co.uk
Total Pitches: 150 (C, CV & T)

South Meadows Caravan Park
South Road, Belford
NE70 7DP
Tel: 01668 213326 **88 D8**
southmeadows.co.uk
Total Pitches: 120 (C, CV & T)

Southfork Caravan Park
Parrett Works, Martock
TA12 6AE
Tel: 01935 825661 **19 M11**
southforkcaravans.co.uk
Total Pitches: 27 (C, CV & T)

Springfield Holiday Park
Tedburn St Mary, Exeter
EX6 6EW
Tel: 01647 24242 **9 K6**
springfieldholidaypark.co.uk
Total Pitches: 48 (C, CV & T)

Stanmore Hall Touring Park
Stourbridge Road, Bridgnorth
WV15 6DT
Tel: 01746 761761 **57 N6**
morris-leisure.co.uk
Total Pitches: 129 (C, CV & T)

Stowford Farm Meadows
Berry Down, Combe Martin
EX34 0PW
Tel: 01271 882476 **17 K3**
stowford.co.uk
Total Pitches: 700 (C, CV & T)

Stroud Hill Park
Fen Road, Pidley
PE28 3DE
Tel: 01487 741333 **62 D5**
stroudhillpark.co.uk
Total Pitches: 60 (C, CV & T)

**Sumners Ponds Fishery &
Campsite**
Chapel Road, Barns Green, Horsham
RH13 0PR
Tel: 01403 732539 **24 D5**
sumnersponds.co.uk
Total Pitches: 86 (C, CV & T)

Sun Valley Resort
Pentewan Road, St Austell
PL26 6DJ
Tel: 01726 843266 **3 Q4**
sunvalleyresort.co.uk
Total Pitches: 29 (C, CV & T)

**Swiss Farm Touring &
Camping**
Marlow Road, Henley-on-Thames
RG9 2HY
Tel: 01491 573419 **35 L8**
swissfarmcamping.co.uk
Total Pitches: 140 (C, CV & T)

**Tanner Farm Touring C & C
Park**
Tanner Farm, Goudhurst Road,
Marden
TN12 9ND
Tel: 01622 832399 **26 B3**
tannerfarmpark.co.uk
Total Pitches: 130 (C, CV & T)

Tattershall Lakes Country Park
Sleaford Road, Tattershall
LN4 4LR
Tel: 01526 348800 **86 H9**
tattershall-lakes.com
Total Pitches: 186 (C, CV & T)

Tehidy Holiday Park
Harris Mill, Illogan, Portreath
TR16 4JQ
Tel: 01209 216489 **2 H5**
tehidy.co.uk
Total Pitches: 18 (C, CV & T)

Teversal C & C Club Site
Silverhill Lane, Teversal
NG17 3JJ
Tel: 01623 551838 **84 G8**
campingandcaravanningclub.co.uk/
teversal
Total Pitches: 126 (C, CV & T)

The Inside Park
Down House Estate,
Blandford Forum
DT11 9AD
Tel: 01258 453719 **12 E4**
theinsidepark.co.uk
Total Pitches: 125 (C, CV & T)

**The Laurels
Holiday Park**
Padstow Road,
Whitecross, Wadebridge
PL27 7JQ
Tel: 01209 313474 **4 F7**
thelaurelsholidaypark.co.uk
Total Pitches: 30 (C, CV & T)

The Old Brick Kilns
Little Barney Lane, Barney,
Fakenham
NR21 0NL
Tel: 01328 878305 **76 E5**
old-brick-kilns.co.uk
Total Pitches: 65 (C, CV & T)

**The Old Oaks
Touring Park**
Wick Farm, Wick,
Glastonbury
BA6 8JS
Tel: 01458 831437 **19 P7**
theoldoaks.co.uk
Total Pitches: 98 (C, CV & T)

**The Orchards Holiday
Caravan Park**
Main Road, Newbridge,
Yarmouth, Isle of Wight
PO41 0TS
Tel: 01983 531331 **14 D9**
orchards-holiday-park.co.uk
Total Pitches: 160 (C, CV & T)

The Quiet Site
Ullswater, Watermillock
CA11 0LS
Tel: 07768 727016 **101 M6**
thequietsite.co.uk
Total Pitches: 100 (C, CV & T)

Tollgate Farm C & C Park
Budnick Hill, Perranporth
TR6 0AD
Tel: 01872 572130 **3 K3**
tollgatefarm.co.uk
Total Pitches: 102 (C, CV & T)

Townsend Touring Park
Townsend Farm, Pembridge,
Leominster
HR6 9HB
Tel: 01544 388527 **45 M3**
townsendfarm.co.uk
Total Pitches: 60 (C, CV & T)

**Treago Farm
Caravan Site**
Crantock, Newquay
TR8 5QS
Tel: 01637 830277 **4 B9**
treagofarm.co.uk
Total Pitches: 90 (C, CV & T)

Trencreek Holiday Park
Hillcrest, Higher Trencreek,
Newquay
TR8 4NS
Tel: 01637 874210 **4 C9**
trencreekholidaypark.co.uk
Total Pitches: 194 (C, CV & T)

**Trethem Mill
Touring Park**
St Just-in-Roseland,
Nr St Mawes, Truro
TR2 5JF
Tel: 01872 580504 **3 M6**
trethem.com
Total Pitches: 84 (C, CV & T)

Trevalgan Touring Park
Trevalgan, St Ives
TR26 3BJ
Tel: 01736 791892 **2 D6**
trevalgantouringpark.co.uk
Total Pitches: 120 (C, CV & T)

Trevarth Holiday Park
Blackwater, Truro
TR4 8HR
Tel: 01872 560266 **3 J4**
trevarth.co.uk
Total Pitches: 30 (C, CV & T)

Trevella Tourist Park
Crantock, Newquay
TR8 5EW
Tel: 01637 830308 **4 C10**
trevella.co.uk
Total Pitches: 171 (C, CV & T)

Trevornick Holiday Park
Holywell Bay, Newquay
TR8 5PW
Tel: 01637 830531 **4 B10**
trevornick.co.uk
Total Pitches: 688 (C, CV & T)

Troutbeck C & C Club Site
Hutton Moor End, Troutbeck,
Penrith
CA11 0SX
Tel: 017687 79149 **101 L5**
campingandcaravanningclub.co.uk/
troutbeck
Total Pitches: 54 (C, CV & T)

Truro C & C Park
Truro
TR4 8QN
Tel: 01872 560274 **3 K4**
trurocaravanandcampingpark.co.uk
Total Pitches: 51 (C, CV & T)

Tudor C & C
Shepherds Patch, Slimbridge,
Gloucester
GL2 7BP
Tel: 01453 890483 **32 D4**
tudorcaravanpark.com
Total Pitches: 75 (C, CV & T)

Two Mills Touring Park
Yarmouth Road, North Walsham
NR28 9NA
Tel: 01692 405829 **77 K6**
twomills.co.uk
Total Pitches: 81 (C, CV & T)

Ulwell Cottage Caravan Park
Ulwell Cottage, Ulwell,
Swanage
BH19 3DG
Tel: 01929 422823 **12 H8**
ulwellcottagepark.co.uk
Total Pitches: 77 (C, CV & T)

Vale of Pickering Caravan Park
Carr House Farm, Allerston,
Pickering
YO18 7PQ
Tel: 01723 859280 **98 H4**
valeofpickering.co.uk
Total Pitches: 120 (C, CV & T)

Wagtail Country Park
Cliff Lane, Marston, Grantham
NG32 2HU
Tel: 01400 251955 **73 M2**
wagtailcountrypark.co.uk
Total Pitches: 76 (C & CV)

Warcombe Farm C & C Park
Station Road, Mortehoe
EX34 7EJ
Tel: 01271 870690 **16 H2**
warcombefarm.co.uk
Total Pitches: 250 (C, CV & T)

**Wareham Forest
Tourist Park**
North Trigon, Wareham
BH20 7NZ
Tel: 01929 551393 **12 E6**
warehamforest.co.uk
Total Pitches: 200 (C, CV & T)

Watergate Bay Touring Park
Watergate Bay, Tregurrian
TR8 4AD
Tel: 01637 860387 **4 C9**
watergatebaytouringpark.co.uk
Total Pitches: 171 (C, CV & T)

Waterrow Touring Park
Wiveliscombe, Taunton
TA4 2AZ
Tel: 01984 623464 **18 E9**
waterrowpark.co.uk
Total Pitches: 45 (C, CV & T)

Waters Edge Caravan Park
Crooklands, Nr Kendal
LA7 7NN
Tel: 015395 67708 **95 L4**
watersedgecaravanpark.co.uk
Total Pitches: 26 (C, CV & T)

Wayfarers C & C Park
Relubbus Lane, St Hilary,
Penzance
TR20 9EF
Tel: 01736 763326 **2 F7**
wayfarerspark.co.uk
Total Pitches: 32 (C, CV & T)

Wells Holiday Park
Haybridge, Wells
BA5 1AJ
Tel: 01749 676869 **19 P5**
wellsholidaypark.co.uk
Total Pitches: 72 (C, CV & T)

Westwood Caravan Park
Old Felixstowe Road,
Bucklesham, Ipswich
IP10 0BN
Tel: 01473 659637 **53 N3**
westwoodcaravanpark.co.uk
Total Pitches: 100 (C, CV & T)

Wheathill Touring Park
Wheathill, Bridgnorth
WV16 6QT
Tel: 01584 823456 **57 L8**
wheathillpark.co.uk
Total Pitches: 25 (C & CV)

Whitefield Forest Touring Park
Brading Road, Ryde,
Isle of Wight
PO33 1QL
Tel: 01983 617069 **14 H9**
whitefieldforest.co.uk
Total Pitches: 90 (C, CV & T)

Widdicombe Farm Touring Park
Marldon, Paignton
TQ3 1ST
Tel: 01803 558325 **7 M6**
widdicombefarm.co.uk
Total Pitches: 180 (C, CV & T)

Widemouth Fields C & C Park
Park Farm, Poundstock,
Bude
EX23 0NA
Tel: 01288 361351 **16 C11**
widemouthbaytouring.co.uk
Total Pitches: 156 (C, CV & T)

Wild Rose Park
Ormside,
Appleby-in-Westmorland
CA16 6EJ
Tel: 017683 51077 **102 C7**
wildrose.co.uk
Total Pitches: 226 (C & CV)

Wilksworth Farm Caravan Park
Cranborne Road,
Wimborne Minster
BH21 4HW
Tel: 01202 885467 **12 H4**
wilksworthfarmcaravanpark.co.uk
Total Pitches: 85 (C, CV & T)

Wood Farm C & C Park
Axminster Road, Charmouth
DT6 6BT
Tel: 01297 560697 **10 H6**
woodfarm.co.uk
Total Pitches: 175 (C, CV & T)

Wooda Farm Holiday Park
Poughill, Bude
EX23 9HJ
Tel: 01288 352069 **16 C10**
wooda.co.uk
Total Pitches: 200 (C, CV & T)

Woodclose Caravan Park
High Casterton,
Kirkby Lonsdale
LA6 2SE
Tel: 01524 271597 **95 N5**
woodclosepark.com
Total Pitches: 29 (C, CV & T)

Woodhall Country Park
Stixwold Road,
Woodhall Spa
LN10 6UJ
Tel: 01526 353710 **86 G8**
woodhallcountrypark.co.uk
Total Pitches: 115 (C, CV & T)

Woodland Springs Adult Touring Park
Venton, Drewsteignton
EX6 6PG
Tel: 01647 231695 **8 G6**
woodlandsprings.co.uk
Total Pitches: 81 (C, CV & T)

Woodlands Grove C & C Park
Blackawton, Dartmouth
TQ9 7DQ
Tel: 01803 712598 **7 L8**
woodlands-caravanpark.com
Total Pitches: 350 (C, CV & T)

Woodovis Park
Gulworthy, Tavistock
PL19 8NY
Tel: 01822 832968 **6 C4**
woodovis.com
Total Pitches: 50 (C, CV & T)

Yeatheridge Farm Caravan Park
East Worlington, Crediton
EX17 4TN
Tel: 01884 860330 **9 J2**
yeatheridge.co.uk
Total Pitches: 103 (C, CV & T)

Zeacombe House Caravan Park
Blackerton Cross, East Anstey,
Tiverton
EX16 9JU
Tel: 01398 341279 **17 R7**
zeacombeadultretreat.co.uk
Total Pitches: 50 (C, CV & T)

SCOTLAND

Beecraigs C & C Site
Beecraigs Country Park,
The Visitor Centre, Linlithgow
EH49 6PL
Tel: 01506 844516 **127 J3**
beecraigs.com
Total Pitches: 36 (C, CV & T)

Blair Castle Caravan Park
Blair Atholl, Pitlochry
PH18 5SR
Tel: 01796 481263 **141 L4**
blaircastlecaravanpark.co.uk
Total Pitches: 226 (C, CV & T)

Brighouse Bay Holiday Park
Brighouse Bay, Borgue,
Kirkcudbright
DG6 4TS
Tel: 01557 870267 **108 D11**
gillespie-leisure.co.uk
Total Pitches: 190 (C, CV & T)

Cairnsmill Holiday Park
Largo Road, St Andrews
KY16 8NN
Tel: 01334 473604 **135 M5**
cairnsmill.co.uk
Total Pitches: 62 (C, CV & T)

Castle Cary Holiday Park
Creetown, Newton Stewart
DG8 7DQ
Tel: 01671 820264 **107 N6**
castlecary-caravans.com
Total Pitches: 50 (C, CV & T)

Craigtoun Meadows Holiday Park
Mount Melville, St Andrews
KY16 8PQ
Tel: 01334 475959 **135 M4**
craigtounmeadows.co.uk
Total Pitches: 57 (C, CV & T)

Drum Mohr Caravan Park
Levenhall, Musselburgh
EH21 8JS
Tel: 0131 665 6867 **128 B5**
drummohr.org
Total Pitches: 120 (C, CV & T)

Gart Caravan Park
The Gart, Callander
FK17 8LE
Tel: 01877 330002 **133 J6**
theholidaypark.co.uk
Total Pitches: 128 (C & CV)

Glenearly Caravan Park
Dalbeattie
DG5 4NE
Tel: 01556 611393 **108 H8**
glenearlycaravanpark.co.uk
Total Pitches: 39 (C, CV & T)

Glen Nevis C & C Park
Glen Nevis, Fort William
PH33 6SX
Tel: 01397 702191 **139 L3**
glen-nevis.co.uk
Total Pitches: 380 (C, CV & T)

Hoddom Castle Caravan Park
Hoddom, Lockerbie
DG11 1AS
Tel: 01576 300251 **110 C6**
hoddomcastle.co.uk
Total Pitches: 200 (C, CV & T)

Huntly Castle Caravan Park
The Meadow, Huntly
AB54 4UJ
Tel: 01466 794999 **158 D9**
huntlycastle.co.uk
Total Pitches: 90 (C, CV & T)

Invercoe C & C Park
Glencoe, Ballachulish
PH49 4HP
Tel: 01855 811210 **139 K6**
invercoe.co.uk
Total Pitches: 60 (C, CV & T)

Linnhe Lochside Holidays
Corpach, Fort William
PH33 7NL
Tel: 01397 772376 **139 K2**
linnhe-lochside-holidays.co.uk
Total Pitches: 85 (C, CV & T)

Loch Ken Holiday Park
Parton, Castle Douglas
DG7 3NE
Tel: 01644 470282 **108 E6**
lochkenholidaypark.co.uk
Total Pitches: 40 (C, CV & T)

Lomond Woods Holiday Park
Old Luss Road, Balloch, Loch
Lomond
G83 8QP
Tel: 01389 755000 **132 D11**
holiday-parks.co.uk
Total Pitches: 100 (C & CV)

Milton of Fonab Caravan Park
Bridge Road, Pitlochry
PH16 5NA
Tel: 01796 472882 **141 M6**
fonab.co.uk
Total Pitches: 154 (C, CV & T)

River Tilt Caravan Park
Blair Atholl, Pitlochry
PH18 5TE
Tel: 01796 481467 **141 L4**
rivertilt.co.uk
Total Pitches: 30 (C, CV & T)

Sands of Luce Holiday Park
Sands of Luce, Sandhead,
Stranraer
DG9 9JN
Tel: 01776 830456 **106 F7**
sandsofluceholidaypark.co.uk
Total Pitches: 100 (C, CV & T)

Seaward Caravan Park
Dhoon Bay, Kirkcudbright
DG6 4TJ
Tel: 01557 870267 **108 E11**
gillespie-leisure.co.uk
Total Pitches: 25 (C, CV & T)

Shieling Holidays
Craignure, Isle of Mull
PA65 6AY
Tel: 01680 812496 **138 C10**
shielingholidays.co.uk
Total Pitches: 90 (C, CV & T)

Silver Sands Leisure Park
Covesea, West Beach,
Lossiemouth
IV31 6SP
Tel: 01343 813262 **157 N3**
silver-sands.co.uk
Total Pitches: 140 (C, CV & T)

Skye C & C Club Site
Loch Greshornish, Borve,
Arnisort, Edinbane, Isle of Skye
IV51 9PS
Tel: 01470 582230 **152 E7**
*campingandcaravanningclub.co.uk/
skye*
Total Pitches: 105 (C, CV & T)

Thurston Manor Leisure Park
Innerwick, Dunbar
EH42 1SA
Tel: 01368 840643 **129 J5**
thurstonmanor.co.uk
Total Pitches: 120 (C, CV & T)

Trossachs Holiday Park
Aberfoyle
FK8 3SA
Tel: 01877 382614 **132 G8**
trossachsholidays.co.uk
Total Pitches: 66 (C, CV & T)

Witches Craig C & C Park
Blairlogie, Stirling
FK9 5PX
Tel: 01786 474947 **133 N8**
witchescraig.co.uk
Total Pitches: 60 (C, CV & T)

WALES

Barcdy Touring C & C Park
Talsarnau
LL47 6YG
Tel: 01766 770736 **67 L7**
barcdy.co.uk
Total Pitches: 80 (C, CV & T)

Bodnant Caravan Park
Nebo Road, Llanrwst,
Conwy Valley
LL26 0SD
Tel: 01492 640248 **67 Q2**
bodnant-caravan-park.co.uk
Total Pitches: 54 (C, CV & T)

Bron Derw Touring Caravan Park
Llanrwst
LL26 0YT
Tel: 01492 640494 **67 P2**
bronderw-wales.co.uk
Total Pitches: 48 (C & CV)

Bron-Y-Wendon Caravan Park
Wern Road, Llanddulas,
Colwyn Bay
LL22 8HG
Tel: 01492 512903 **80 C9**
northwales-holidays.co.uk
Total Pitches: 130 (C & CV)

Caerfai Bay Caravan & Tent Park
Caerfai Bay, St Davids,
Haverfordwest
SA62 6QT
Tel: 01437 720274 **40 E6**
caerfaibay.co.uk
Total Pitches: 106 (C, CV & T)

Cenarth Falls Holiday Park
Cenarth, Newcastle Emlyn
SA38 9JS
Tel: 01239 710345 **41 Q2**
cenarth-holipark.co.uk
Total Pitches: 30 (C, CV & T)

Daisy Bank Caravan Park
Snead, Churchstoke
SY15 6EB
Tel: 01588 620471 **56 E6**
daisy-bank.co.uk
Total Pitches: 80 (C, CV & T)

Dinlle Caravan Park
Dinas Dinlle,
Caernarfon
LL54 5TW
Tel: 01286 830324 **66 G3**
thornleyleisure.co.uk
Total Pitches: 175 (C, CV & T)

Disserth C & C Park
Disserth, Howey,
Llandrindod Wells
LD1 6NL
Tel: 01597 860277 **44 E3**
disserth.biz
Total Pitches: 30 (C, CV & T)

Eisteddfa
Eisteddfa Lodge,
Pentrefelin, Criccieth
LL52 0PT
Tel: 01766 522696 **67 J7**
eisteddfapark.co.uk
Total Pitches: 100 (C, CV & T)

Erwlon C & C Park
Brecon Road, Llandovery
SA20 0RD
Tel: 01550 721021 **43 Q8**
erwlon.co.uk
Total Pitches: 75 (C, CV & T)

Fforest Fields C & C Park
Hundred House,
Builth Wells
LD1 5RT
Tel: 01982 570406 **44 G4**
fforestfields.co.uk
Total Pitches: 80 (C, CV & T)

Hendre Mynach Touring C & C Park
Llanaber Road,
Barmouth
LL42 1YR
Tel: 01341 280262 **67 L11**
hendremynach.co.uk
Total Pitches: 240 (C, CV & T)

Home Farm Caravan Park
Marian-Glas,
Isle of Anglesey
LL73 8PH
Tel: 01248 410614 **78 H8**
homefarm-anglesey.co.uk
Total Pitches: 102 (C, CV & T)

Hunters Hamlet Caravan Park
Sirior Goch Farm,
Betws-yn-Rhos, Abergele
LL22 8PL
Tel: 01745 832237 **80 C10**
huntershamlet.co.uk
Total Pitches: 30 (C & CV)

Islawrffordd Caravan Park
Tal-y-bont, Barmouth
LL43 2AQ
Tel: 01341 247269 **67 K10**
islawrffordd.co.uk
Total Pitches: 105 (C, CV & T)

Llys Derwen C & C Site
Ffordd Bryngwyn, Llanrug,
Caernarfon
LL55 4RD
Tel: 01286 673322 **67 J2**
llysderwen.co.uk
Total Pitches: 20 (C, CV & T)

Moelfryn C & C Park
Ty-Cefn, Pant-y-Bwlch,
Newcastle Emlyn
SA38 9JE
Tel: 01559 371231 **42 F7**
moelfryncaravanpark.co.uk
Total Pitches: 25 (C, CV & T)

Pencelli Castle C & C Park
Pencelli, Brecon
LD3 7LX
Tel: 01874 665451 **44 F10**
pencelli-castle.com
Total Pitches: 80 (C, CV & T)

Penisar Mynydd Caravan Park
Caerwys Road, Rhuallt,
St Asaph
LL17 0TY
Tel: 01745 582227 **80 F9**
penisarmynydd.co.uk
Total Pitches: 71 (C, CV & T)

Plas Farm Caravan Park
Betws-yn-Rhos,
Abergele
LL22 8AU
Tel: 01492 680254 **80 B10**
plasfarmcaravanpark.co.uk
Total Pitches: 54 (C, CV & T)

Plassey Holiday Park
The Plassey, Eyton,
Wrexham
LL13 0SP
Tel: 01978 780277 **69 L5**
plassey.com
Total Pitches: 90 (C, CV & T)

Pont Kemys C & C Park
Chainbridge, Abergavenny
NP7 9DS
Tel: 01873 880688 **31 K3**
pontkemys.com
Total Pitches: 65 (C, CV & T)

River View Touring Park
The Dingle, Llanedi,
Pontarddulais
SA4 0FH
Tel: 01269 844876 **28 G3**
riverviewtouringpark.com
Total Pitches: 60 (C, CV & T)

Riverside Camping
Seiont Nurseries, Pont Rug,
Caernarfon
LL55 2BB
Tel: 01286 678781 **67 J2**
riversidecamping.co.uk
Total Pitches: 73 (C, CV & T)

St David's Park
Red Wharf Bay, Pentraeth,
Isle of Anglesey
LL75 8RJ
Tel: 01248 852341 **79 J8**
stdavidspark.com
Total Pitches: 45 (C, CV & T)

The Little Yurt Meadow
Bay Tree Barns, Mill Road,
Bronington
SY13 3HJ
Tel: 01948 780136 **69 N7**
thelittleyurtmeadow.co.uk
Total Pitches: 3 (T)

Trawsdir Touring C & C Park
Llanaber, Barmouth
LL42 1RR
Tel: 01341 280999 **67 K11**
barmouthholidays.co.uk
Total Pitches: 70 (C, CV & T)

Trefalun Park
Devonshire Drive, St Florence,
Tenby
SA70 8RD
Tel: 01646 651514 **41 L10**
trefalunpark.co.uk
Total Pitches: 90 (C, CV & T)

Tyddyn Isaf Caravan Park
Lligwy Bay, Dulas,
Isle of Anglesey
LL70 9PQ
Tel: 01248 410203 **78 H7**
tyddynisaf.co.uk
Total Pitches: 80 (C, CV & T)

Wernddu Caravan Park
Old Ross Road, Abergavenny
NP7 8NG
Tel: 01873 856223 **45 L11**
wernddu-golf-club.co.uk
Total Pitches: 70 (C, CV & T)

CHANNEL ISLANDS

Beuvelande Camp Site
Beuvelande, St Martin,
Jersey
JE3 6EZ
Tel: 01534 853575 **11 c1**
campingjersey.com
Total Pitches: 150 (CV & T)

Fauxquets Valley Campsite
Castel, Guernsey
GY5 7QL
Tel: 01481 255460 **10 b2**
fauxquets.co.uk
Total Pitches: 120 (CV & T)

Rozel Camping Park
Summerville Farm, St Martin,
Jersey
JE3 6AX
Tel: 01534 855200 **11 c1**
rozelcamping.co.uk
Total Pitches: 100 (C, CV & T)

Road safety cameras

First, the advice you would expect from the AA - we advise drivers to always follow the signed speed limits - breaking the speed limit is illegal and can cost lives.

Both the AA and the Government believe that safety cameras ('speed cameras') should be operated within a transparent system. By providing information relating to road safety and speed hotspots, the AA believes that the driver is better placed to be aware of speed limits and can ensure adherence to them, thus making the roads safer for all users.

Most fixed cameras are installed at accident 'black spots' where four or more fatal or serious road collisions have occurred over the previous three years. It is the policy of both the police and the Department for Transport to make the location of cameras as well known as possible. By showing camera locations in this atlas the AA is identifying the places where extra care should be taken while driving. Speeding is illegal and dangerous and you MUST keep within the speed limit at all times.

Gatso™

Truvelo™

SPECS™

Traffipax™

There are currently more than 3,000 fixed cameras in Britain and the road mapping in this atlas identifies their on-the-road locations.

This symbol is used on the mapping to identify **individual** camera locations - with speed limits (mph)

This symbol is used on the mapping to identify **multiple** cameras on the same stretch of road - with speed limits (mph)

This symbol is used on the mapping to highlight SPECS™ camera systems which calculate your **average speed** along a stretch of road between two or more sets of cameras - with speed limits (mph)

Mobile cameras are also deployed at other sites where speed is perceived to be a problem and mobile enforcement often takes place at the fixed camera sites shown on the maps in this atlas. Additionally, regular police enforcement can take place on any road.

Speed Limits

Types of vehicle	Built up areas* MPH (km/h)	Single carriageways MPH (km/h)	Dual carriageways MPH (km/h)	Motorways MPH (km/h)
Cars & motorcycles (including car derived vans up to 2 tonnes maximum laden weight)	30 (48)	60 (96)	70 (112)	70 (112)
Cars towing caravans or trailers (including car derived vans and motorcycles)	30 (48)	50 (80)	60 (96)	60 (96)
Buses, coaches and minibuses (not exceeding 12 metres (39 feet) in overall length)	30 (48)	50 (80)	60 (96)	70 (112)
Goods vehicles (not exceeding 7.5 tonnes maximum laden weight)	30 (48)	50 (80)	60 (96)	70† (112)
Goods vehicles (exceeding 7.5 tonnes maximum laden weight)	30 (48)	40‡ (64)	50§ (80)	60 (96)

* The 30mph (48km/h) limit usually applies to all traffic on all roads with street lighting unless signs show otherwise.
† 60mph (96km/h) if articulated or towing a trailer.
‡ May increase to 50mph (80km/h) in April 2015. Check www.gov.uk to confirm
§ May increase to 60mph (96km/h) in April 2015. Check www.gov.uk to confirm

Read this before you use the atlas

Safety cameras and speed limits

The fixed camera symbols on the mapping show the maximum speed in mph that applies to that particular stretch of road and above which the camera is set to activate. The actual road speed limit however will vary for different vehicle types and you must ensure that you drive within the speed limit for your particular class of vehicle at all times.

The chart above details the speed limits applying to the different classes. Don't forget that mobile enforcement can take account of vehicle class at any designated site.

Camera locations

1 The camera locations were correct at the time of finalising the information to go to press.

2 Camera locations are approximate due to limitations in the scale of the road mapping used in this atlas.

3 In towns and urban areas camera locations are shown only on roads that appear on the road maps in this atlas.

4 Where two or more cameras appear close together, a special symbol is used to indicate multiple cameras on the same stretch of road.

5 Our symbols do not indicate the direction in which cameras point.

6 On the mapping we symbolise more than 3,000 fixed camera locations. Mobile laser device locations, roadwork cameras and 'fixed red light' cameras cannot be shown.

Map pages

Road map symbols

Motoring information

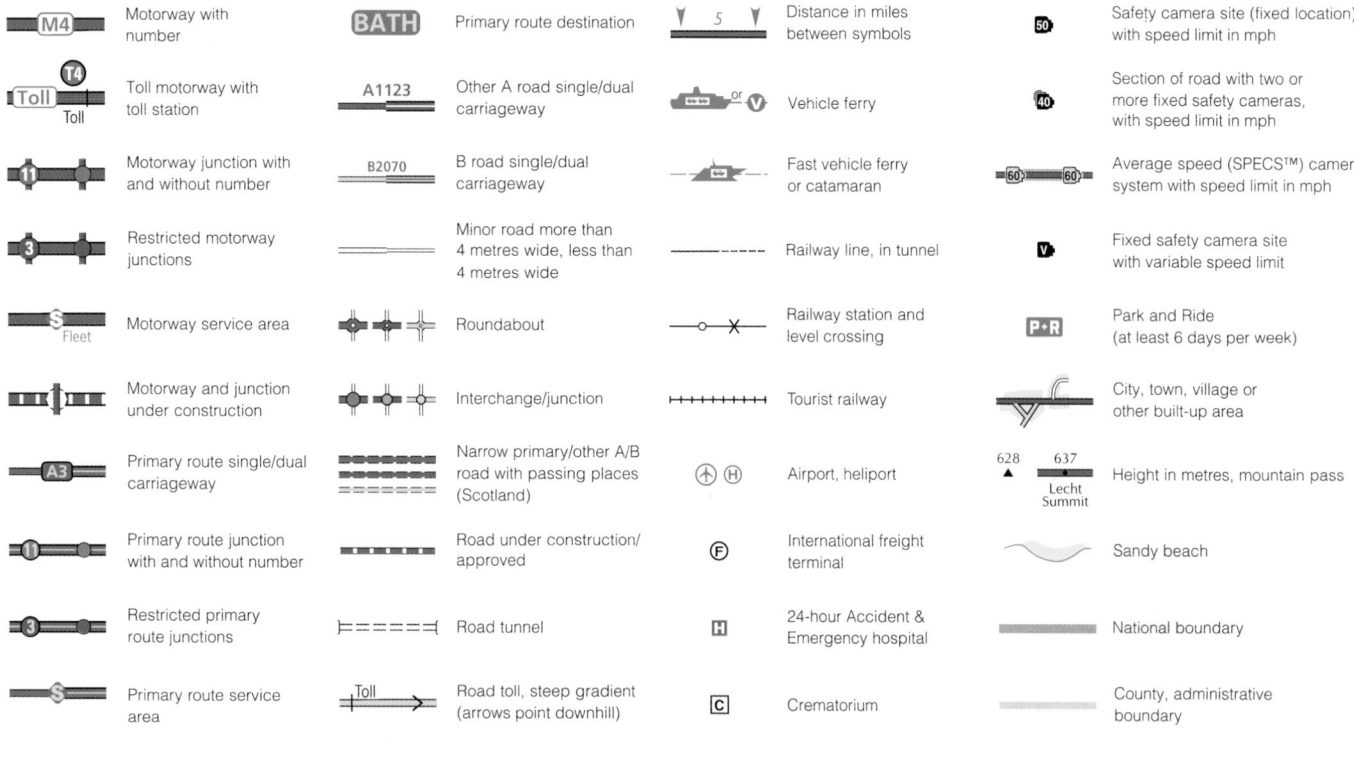

M4 — Motorway with number	BATH — Primary route destination	▼ 5 ▼ — Distance in miles between symbols	50 — Safety camera site (fixed location) with speed limit in mph
Toll T4 — Toll motorway with toll station	A1123 — Other A road single/dual carriageway	or V — Vehicle ferry	40 — Section of road with two or more fixed safety cameras, with speed limit in mph
11 — Motorway junction with and without number	B2070 — B road single/dual carriageway	— Fast vehicle ferry or catamaran	60 — 60 — Average speed (SPECS™) camera system with speed limit in mph
3 — Restricted motorway junctions	— Minor road more than 4 metres wide, less than 4 metres wide	— — — — Railway line, in tunnel	V — Fixed safety camera site with variable speed limit
S Fleet — Motorway service area	— Roundabout	—o—X— Railway station and level crossing	P•R — Park and Ride (at least 6 days per week)
— Motorway and junction under construction	— Interchange/junction	++++++++ Tourist railway	— City, town, village or other built-up area
A3 — Primary route single/dual carriageway	— Narrow primary/other A/B road with passing places (Scotland)	✈ H — Airport, heliport	628 ▲ 637 Lecht Summit — Height in metres, mountain pass
1 — Primary route junction with and without number	— Road under construction/approved	F — International freight terminal	— Sandy beach
3 — Restricted primary route junctions	⊨=====⊨ Road tunnel	H — 24-hour Accident & Emergency hospital	— National boundary
S — Primary route service area	Toll → Road toll, steep gradient (arrows point downhill)	C — Crematorium	— County, administrative boundary

Touring information   To avoid disappointment, check opening times before visiting.

— Scenic route	✳ Garden	— — — — National trail	Air show venue
i Tourist Information Centre	♣ Arboretum	☀ Viewpoint	Ski slope (natural, artificial)
i Tourist Information Centre (seasonal)	❀ Vineyard	Hill-fort	National Trust property
V Visitor or heritage centre	Y Country park	Roman antiquity	National Trust for Scotland property
♣ Picnic site	Agricultural showground	Prehistoric monument	English Heritage site
Caravan site (AA inspected)	Theme park	1066 Battle site with year	Historic Scotland site
▲ Camping site (AA inspected)	Farm or animal centre	Steam railway centre	Cadw (Welsh heritage) site
Caravan & camping site (AA inspected)	Zoological or wildlife collection	Cave	★ Other place of interest
Abbey, cathedral or priory	Bird collection	Windmill, monument	Boxed symbols indicate attractions within urban areas
Ruined abbey, cathedral or priory	Aquarium	Golf course (AA listed)	World Heritage Site (UNESCO)
Castle	RSPB RSPB site	County cricket ground	National Park
Historic house or building	National Nature Reserve (England, Scotland, Wales)	Rugby Union national stadium	National Scenic Area (Scotland)
Museum or art gallery	Local nature reserve	International athletics stadium	Forest Park
Industrial interest	Wildlife Trust reserve	Horse racing, show jumping	Heritage coast
Aqueduct or viaduct	········· Forest drive	Motor-racing circuit	Major shopping centre

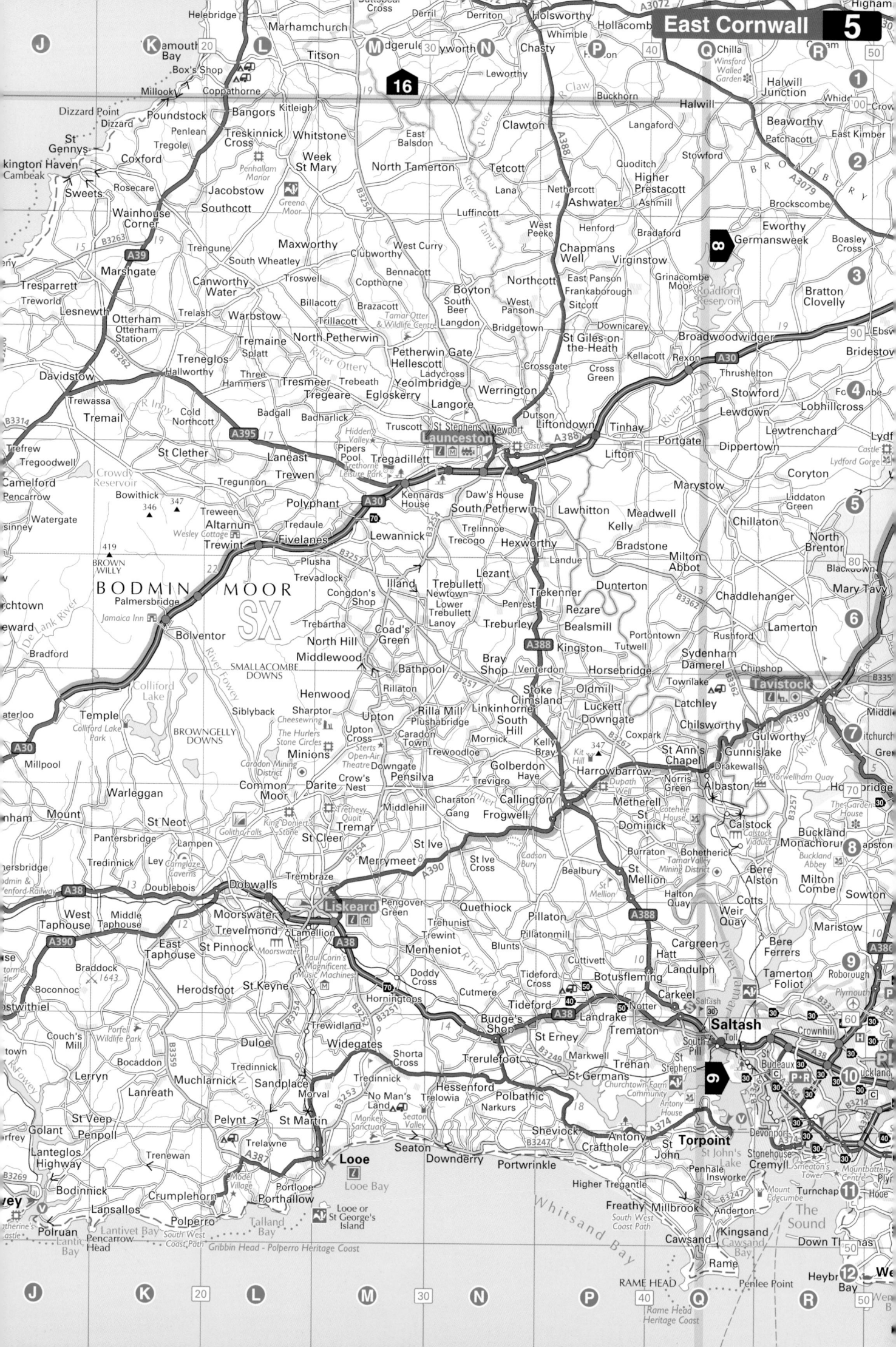

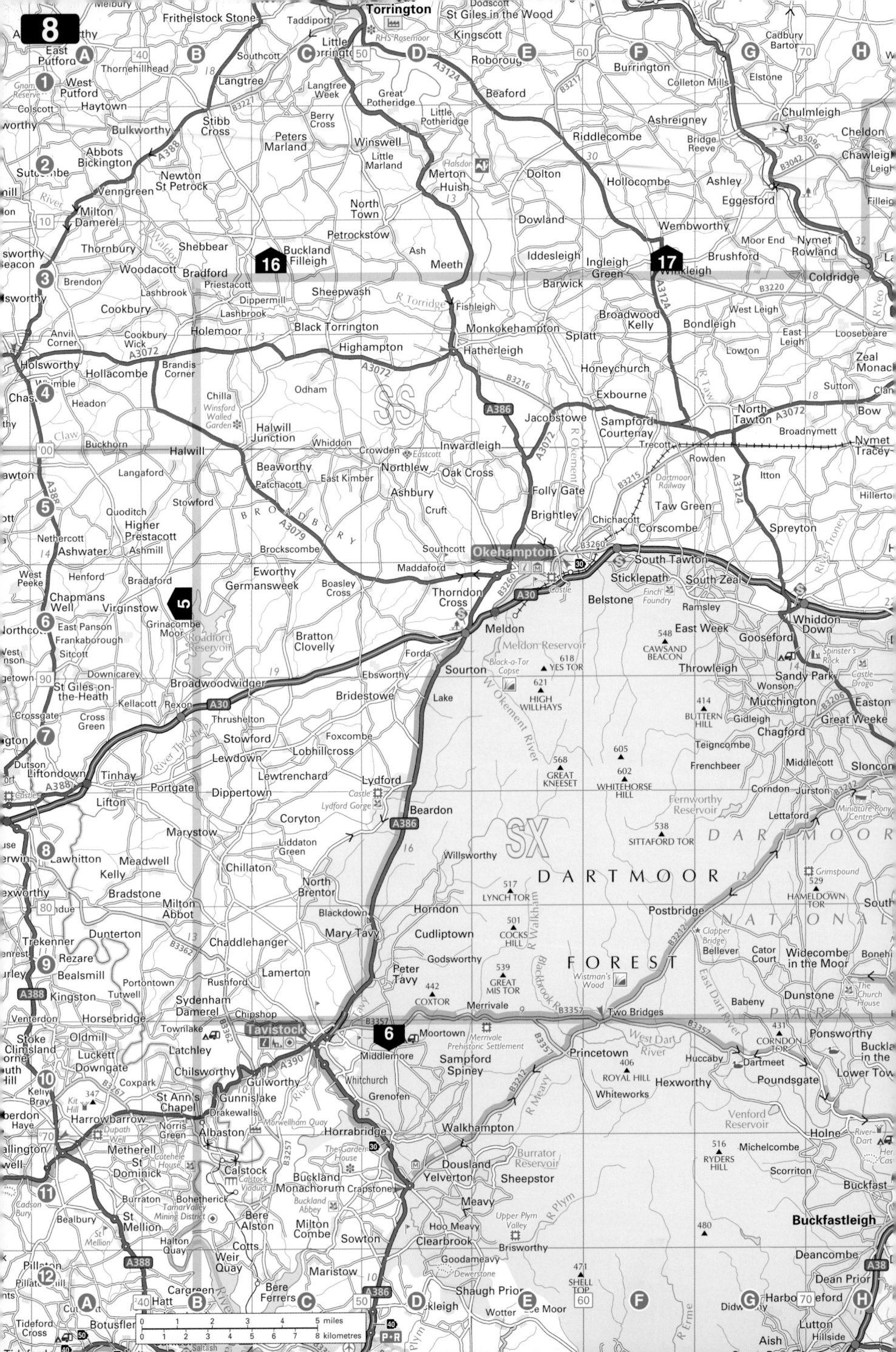

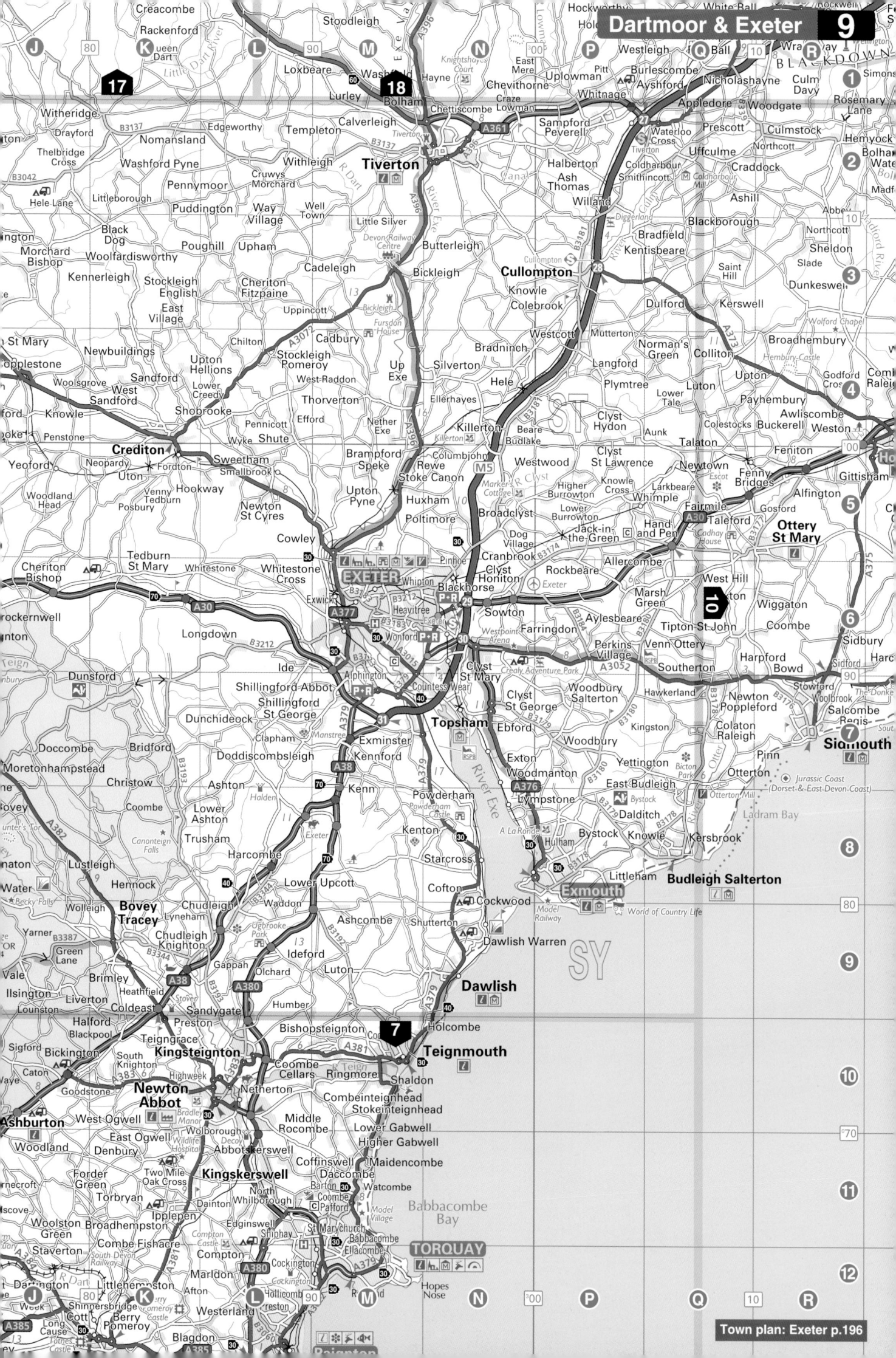

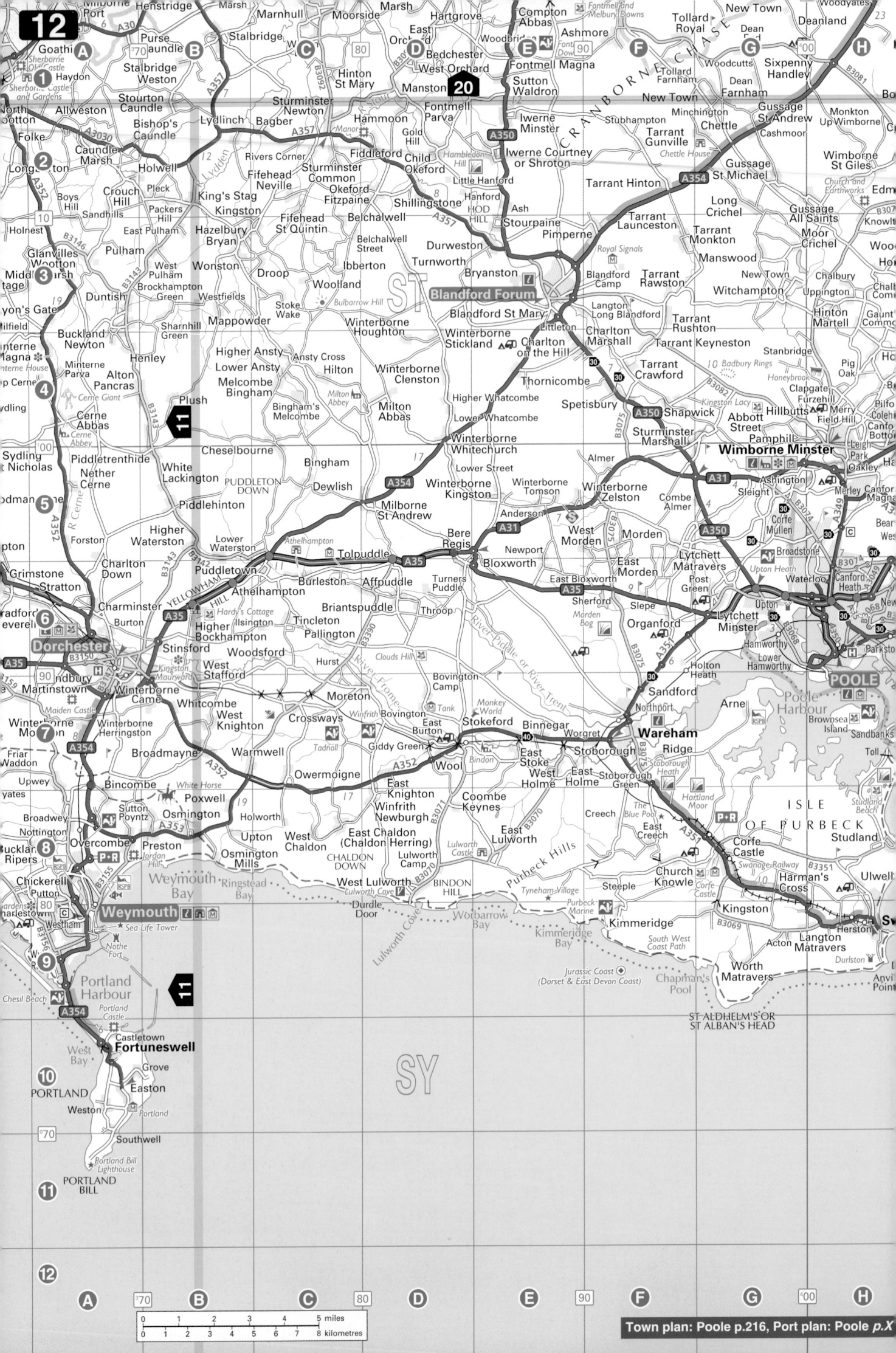

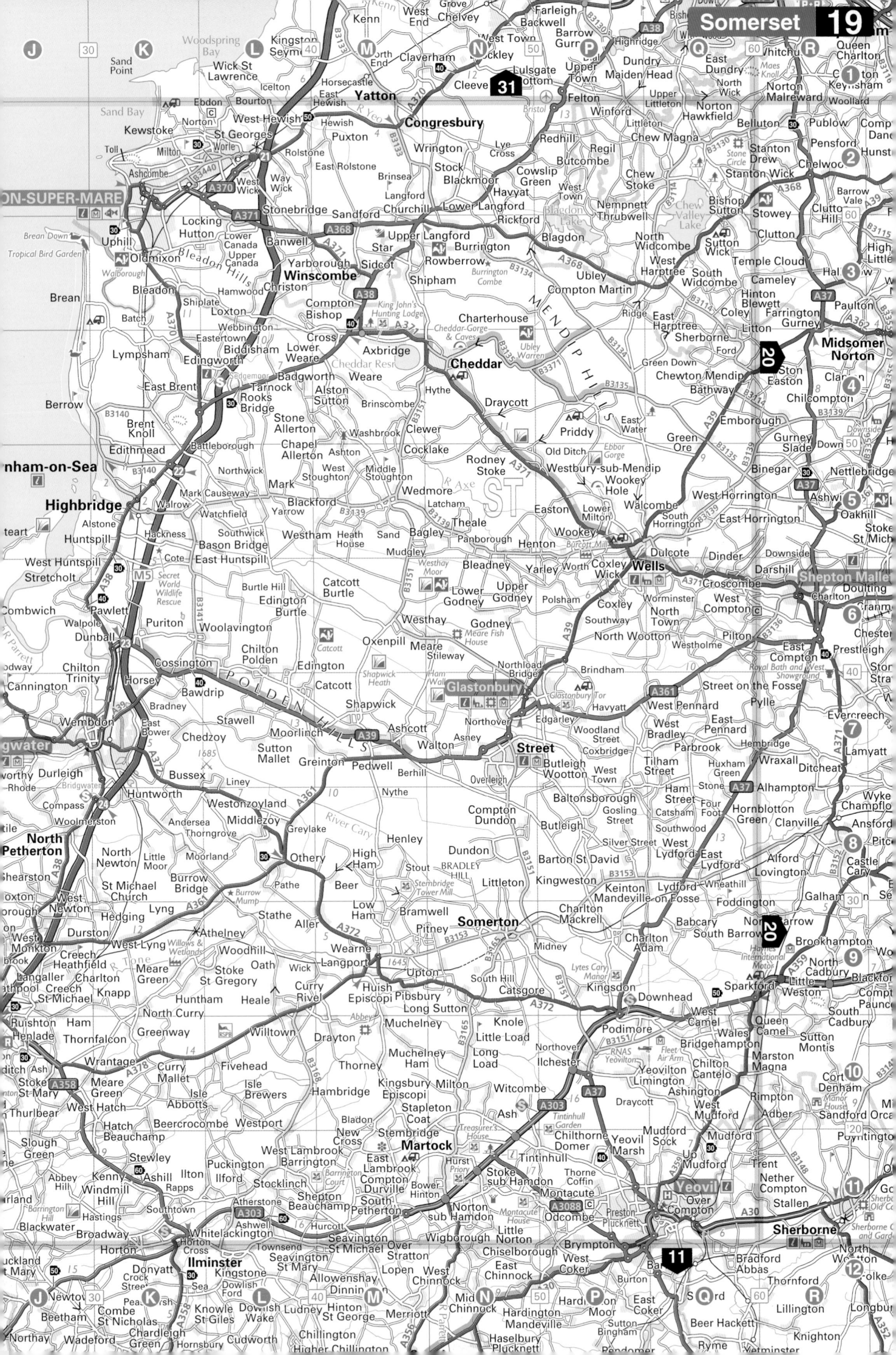

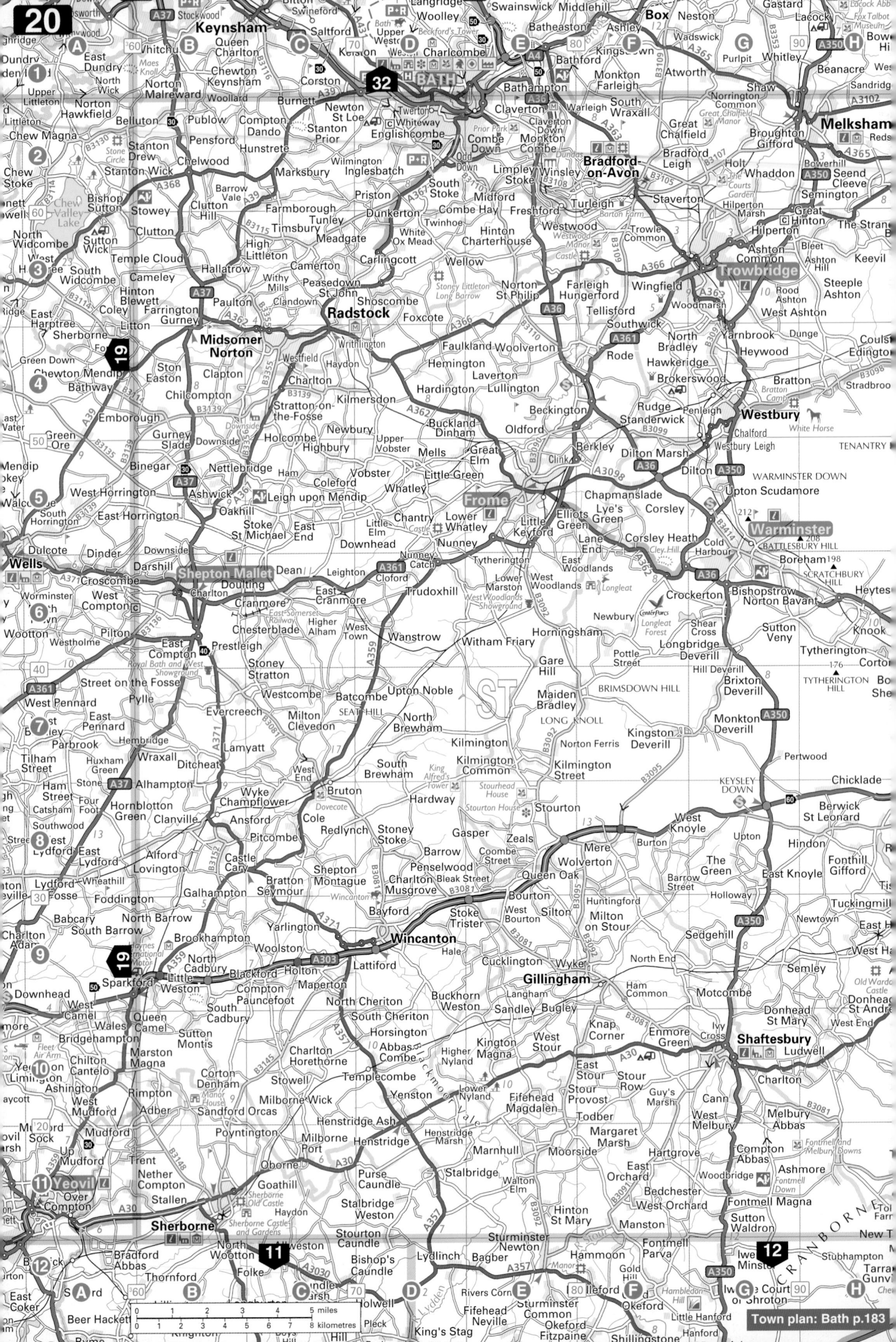

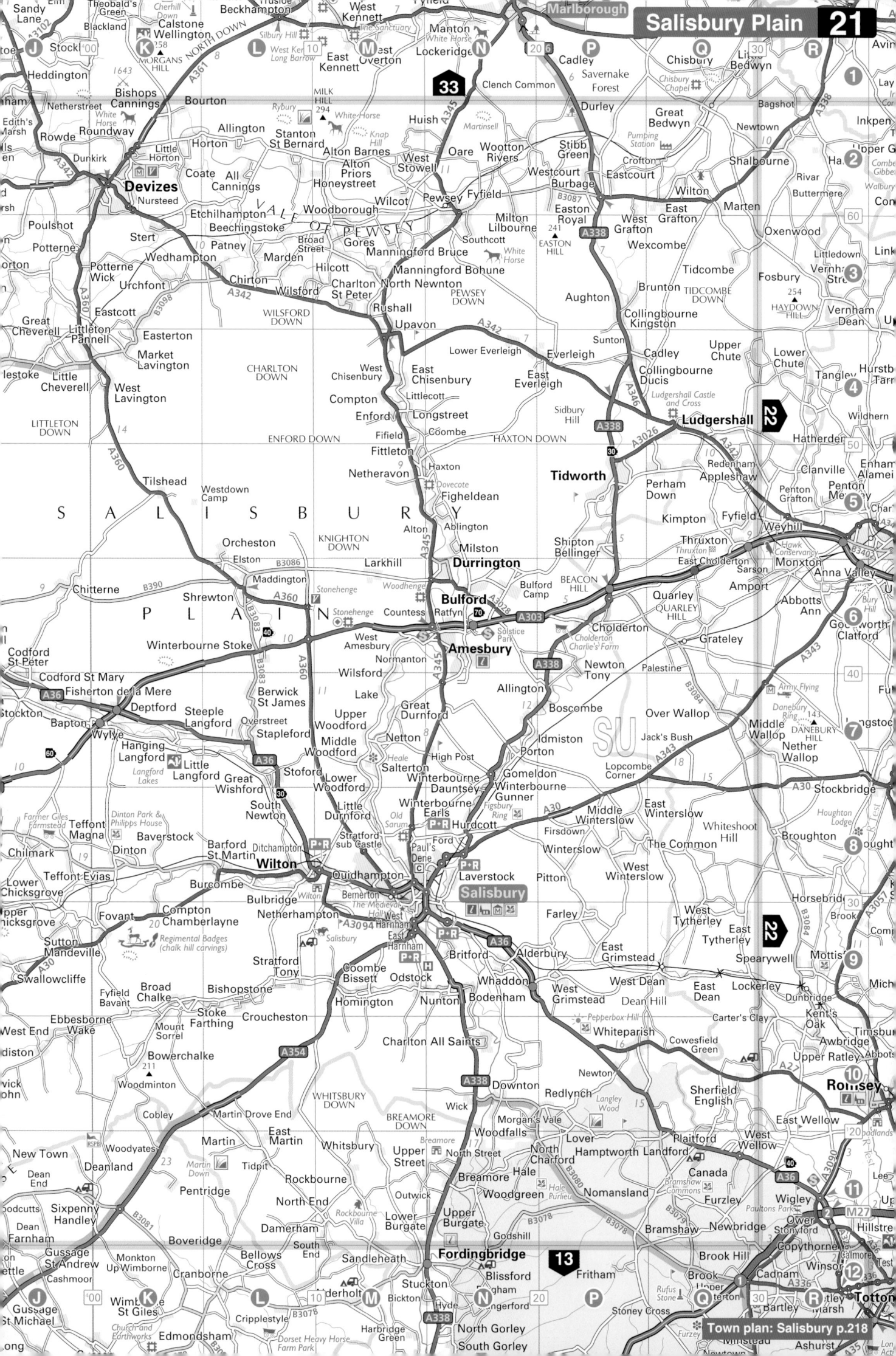

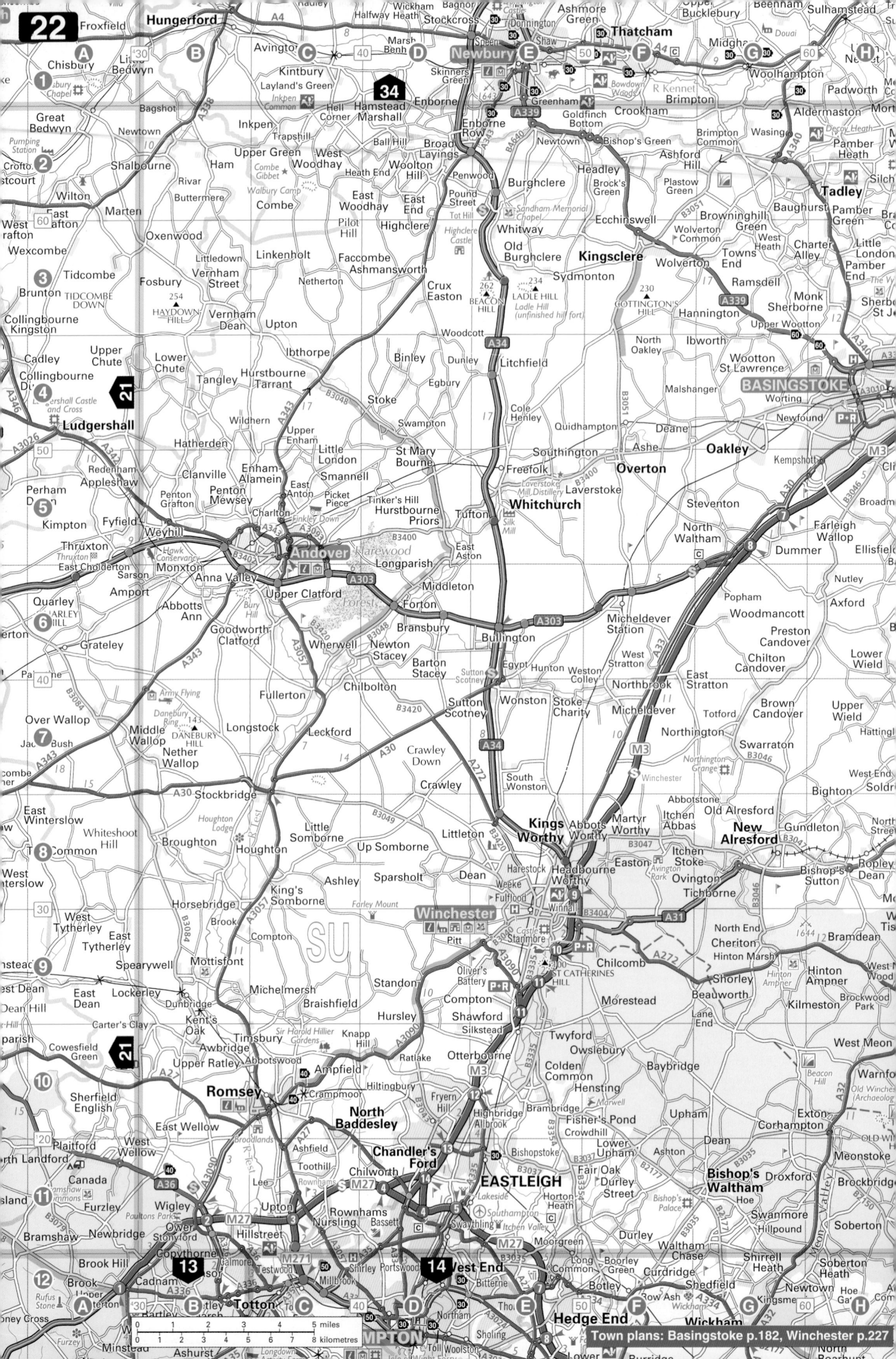

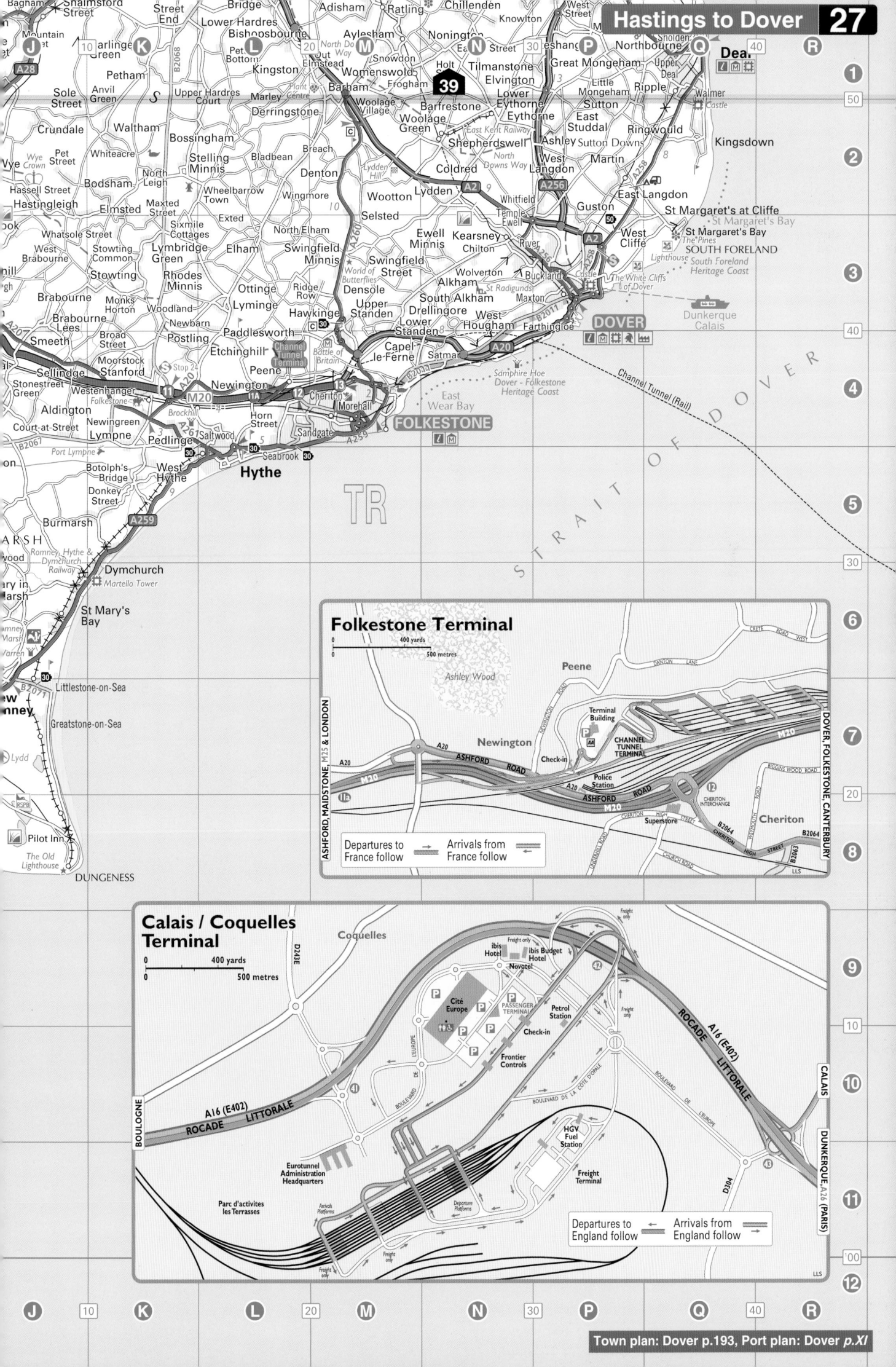

Folkestone Terminal

Departures to France follow →
Arrivals from France follow ←

Calais / Coquelles Terminal

Departures to England follow →
Arrivals from England follow ←

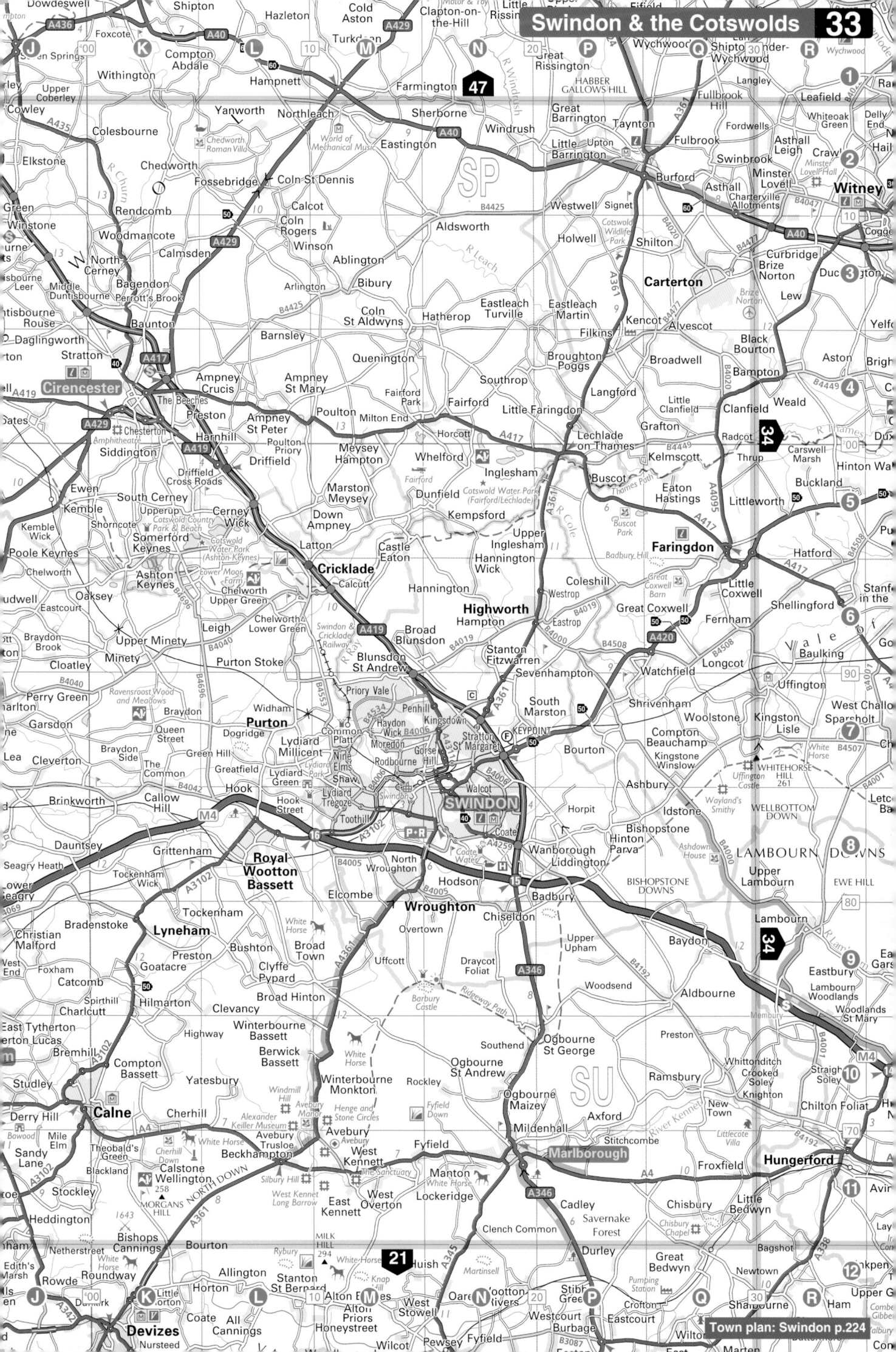

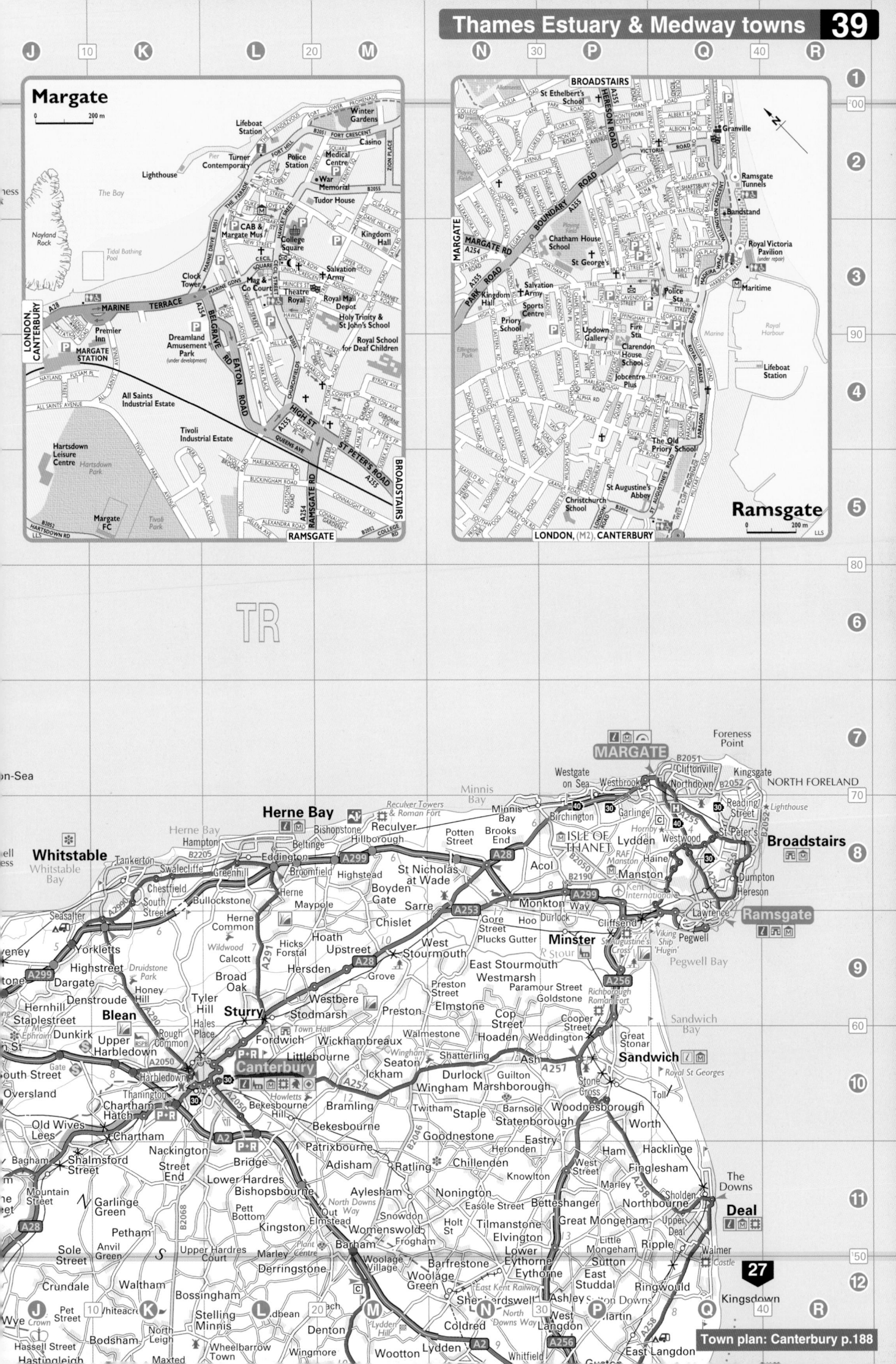

Margate

0 200 m

Lifeboat Station
Fort Lower Promenade
Winter Gardens
Rendezvous
Casino
Turner Contemporary
Police Station
Medical Centre
War Memorial
Tudor House
Lighthouse
The Bay
Pier
CAB & Margate Mus
College Square
Kingdom Hall
Clock Tower
Salvation Army
Mag & Co Court
Theatre Royal
Royal Mail Depot
Holy Trinity & St John's School
Royal School for Deaf Children
Nayland Rock
Tidal Bathing Pool
Premier Inn
MARINE TERRACE
MARGATE STATION
Dreamland Amusement Park (under development)
All Saints Industrial Estate
Tivoli Industrial Estate
Hartsdown Leisure Centre
Hartsdown Park
Margate FC
Tivoli Park
RAMSGATE
BROADSTAIRS
LONDON, CANTERBURY

Ramsgate

0 200 m

BROADSTAIRS
St Ethelbert's School
Allotments
Chatham House School
St George's
Salvation Army
Kingdom Hall
Sports Centre
Priory School
Updown Gallery
Fire Sta
Clarendon House School
Jobcentre Plus
The Old Priory School
St Augustine's Abbey
Christchurch School
Ramsgate Tunnels
Bandstand
Royal Victoria Pavilion (under repair)
Maritime
Marina
Royal Harbour
Lifeboat Station
Police Sta
MARGATE RD
MARGATE
BOUNDARY ROAD
LONDON, (M2), CANTERBURY

TR

MARGATE
Foreness Point
Westgate on Sea
Westbrook
Cliftonville
Northdown
Kingsgate
NORTH FORELAND
Minnis Bay
Birchington
Garlinge
Reading Street
Lighthouse
Herne Bay
Reculver Towers & Roman Fort
Hampton
Bishopstone
Reculver
Beltinge
Hillborough
Potten Street
Brooks End
ISLE OF THANET
Lydden
Hornby
Westwood
St Peter's
Broadstairs
Whitstable
Whitstable Bay
Tankerton
Swalecliffe
Greenhill
Eddington
Broomfield
Highstead
St Nicholas at Wade
Acol
RAF Manston Park
Manston
Haine
Kent International
Dumpton
Hereson
Ramsgate
Seasalter
Chestfield
South Street
Bullockstone
Herne
Maypole
Boyden Gate
Sarre
Chislet
Monkton
Gore Street
Hoo
Durlock
Cliffsend
St Lawrence
Yorkletts
Herne Common
Wildwood Calcott
Hoath
Upstreet
West Stourmouth
Plucks Gutter
Minster
Viking Ship 'Hugin'
St Augustine's Cross
Pegwell
Pegwell Bay
Highstreet
Dargate
Honey Hill
Tyler Hill
Hersden
Grove
East Stourmouth
Westmarsh
Paramour Street
Goldstone
Richborough Roman Fort
Sandwich Bay
Hernhill
Staplestreet
Denstroude
Blean
Sturry
Hales Place
Broad Oak
Westbere
Stodmarsh
Preston
Cop Street
Elmstone
Sandwich
Royal St Georges
Dunkirk
Upper Harbledown
Rough Common
Fordwich
Littlebourne
Wickhambreaux
Walmestone
Hoaden
Weddington
Cooper Street
Great Stonar
Ephraim
Harbledown
Canterbury
Seaton
Ickham
Durlock
Guilton
Ash
Marshborough
Stone Cross
Toll
Oversland
Thanington
Chartham Hatch
Bekesbourne Hill
Bramling
Twitham
Staple
Barnsole
Statenborough
Woodnesborough
Worth
Old Wives Lees
Chartham
Bridge
Bekesbourne
Patrixbourne
Goodnestone
Eastry
Ham
Hacklinge
Finglesham
The Downs
Bagham
Shalmsford Street
Nackington
Street End
Adisham
Ratling
Chillenden
Heronden
West Street
Marley
Northbourne
Deal
Mountain Street
Garlinge Green
Lower Hardres
Bishopsbourne
Aylesham
Nonington
Knowlton
Easole Street
Betteshanger
Great Mongeham
Upper Deal
Ripple
Walmer
Petham
Pett Bottom
Kingston
Elmstead
Womenswold
Snowdon
Holt St
Tilmanstone
Elvington
Little Mongeham
Sutton
East Studdal
Ringwould
Castle
Sole Street
Anvil Green
Upper Hardres Court
Marley
Derringstone
Barham
Woolage Village
Woolage Green
Barfrestone
Lower Eythorne
Eythorne
Sutton
Downs
Kingsdown
Crundale
Waltham
Bossingham
Stelling Minnis
Denton
Lydden Hill
Shepherdswell
Ashley
Martin
West Langdon
East Langdon
Wye
Pet Street
Whiteacre
Bodsham
North Leigh
Wingmore
Wheelbarrow Town
Wootton
Lydden
Coldred
North Downs Way
Whitfield
Hassell Street
Hastingleigh
Maxted

Town plan: Canterbury p.188

27

SM

St David's Head

Whitesands Bay

RAMSEY ISLAND

Ramsey Sound

RSPB

St David's Peninsula Heritage Coast

St David's Head

Treleddyd-fawr

Rhodiad-y-brenin

Bishop's Palace

St Davids (Tyddewi)

Whitchurch

Middle Mill

Nine Wells

Solva

Newgale

Pen-y-cwn

16

PEMBROKESHIRE COAST NATIONAL PARK

Rickets Head

Nolton Haven

Nolton

St Brides Bay Heritage Coast

St Brides Bay

Haroldston West

Broad Haven

Broadway

Little Haven

Walton West

Solbury

Pembrokeshire Coast Path

Talbenny

St Brides

Walwyn's Castle

Tiers Cross

SKOMER ISLAND

Wooltack Point

B4327

Marloes

Hasguard

Sandy Haven

Thornton

Broad Sound

St Ishmael's

Herbrandston

Marloes and Dale Heritage Coast

Dale

Hubberston

Hakin

Westdale Bay

Dale Point

Great Castle Head

Milford Haven

Milford Haven (Aberdaugleddau)

SKOKHOLM ISLAND

St Anns Head

Angle

Angle Bay

Pwllcrochan

Rhoscrowther

Rosslare Harbour

SR

Freshwater West

Castlemartin Brook

B4320

B4319

10

Castlemartin

Warren

Linney Head

Merri

PEMBROKESHIRE CO NATIONAL PARK

Pembrokeshire Coast Path

Rosslare Harbour

STRUMBLE HEAD

Pen Brush

Trefasser

Goodwick

Pwll Deri

Manorowen

Pembrokeshire Coast Path

St Nicholas

Panteg

Ynys Daullyn

Granston

Carreg Sampson

Abercastle

A4071

Porthgain

Trefin

Mathry

16

Llangloffan

Jordans

Castle Morris

B4331

Abereiddy

Llanrhian

A487

Square & Compass

Llangloffan Fen

Berea

Tretio

Croes-goch

Treffynnon

Letterst

W

Carnhedryn

Treglemais

Cerbyd

B4330

Llandeloy

Tancredston

Pont-yr-hafod

River Solva

Caer Farchell

Treffgarne Owen

Hayscastle

Hayscast Cross

Tre

A487

178

DUDWELL MT

Leweston

Roch

Wolfsdale

Roch Gate

Simpson Cross

Cam

Keeston

Pembr

A487

Pelcomb Cross

Pelcom

Lambston

Druidston

Sutton

Pelcomb Bridge

Portfield Gate

B4341

Dreen Hill

A

B4327

Steynton

Honeyborou

Waterston

Llanstadw

Pemb Do

(Doc

0 — 1 — 2 — 3 — 4 — 5 miles
0 — 1 — 2 — 3 — 4 — 5 — 6 — 7 — 8 kilometres

Port plan: Pembroke Dock p.XIII

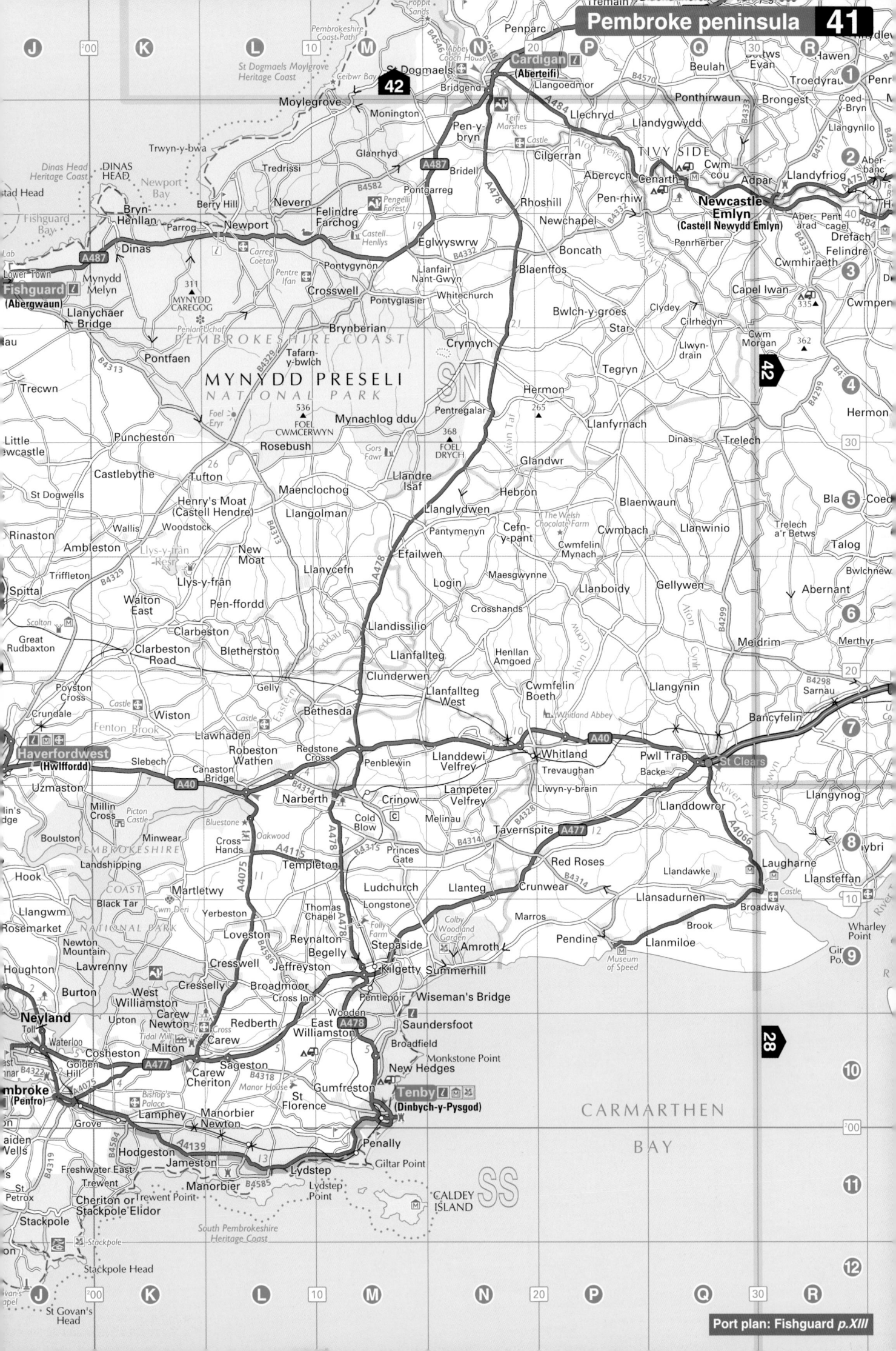

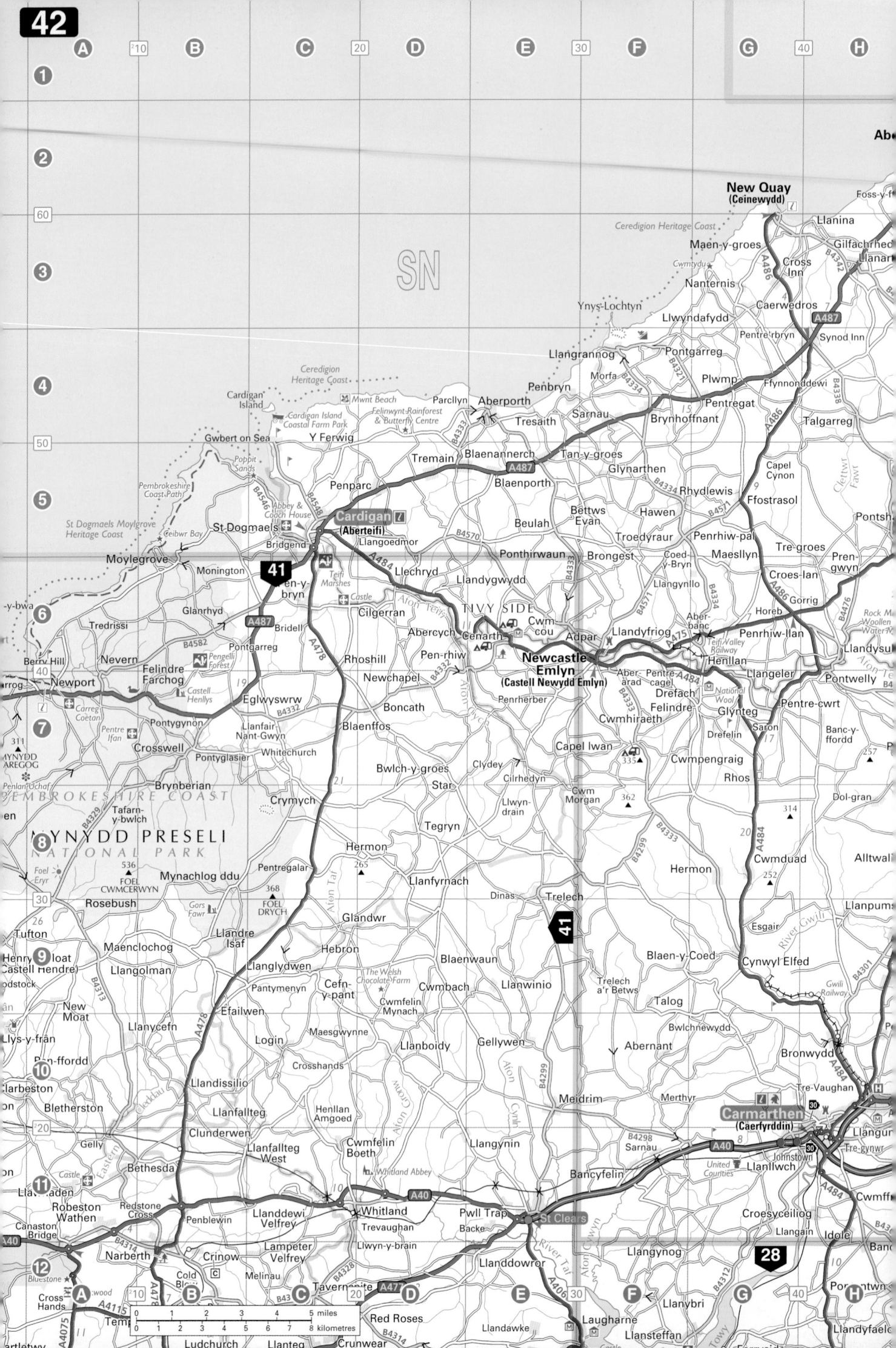

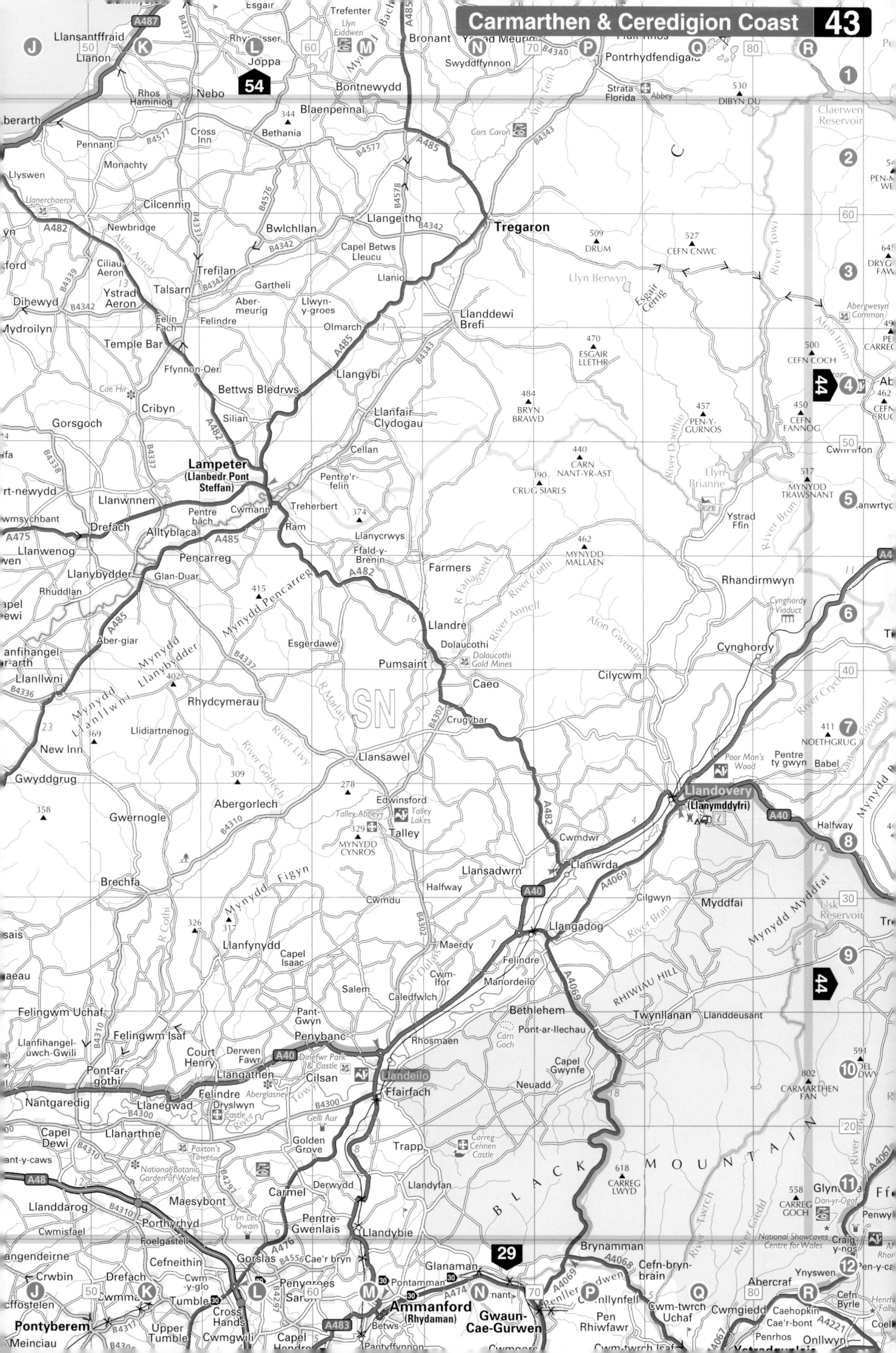

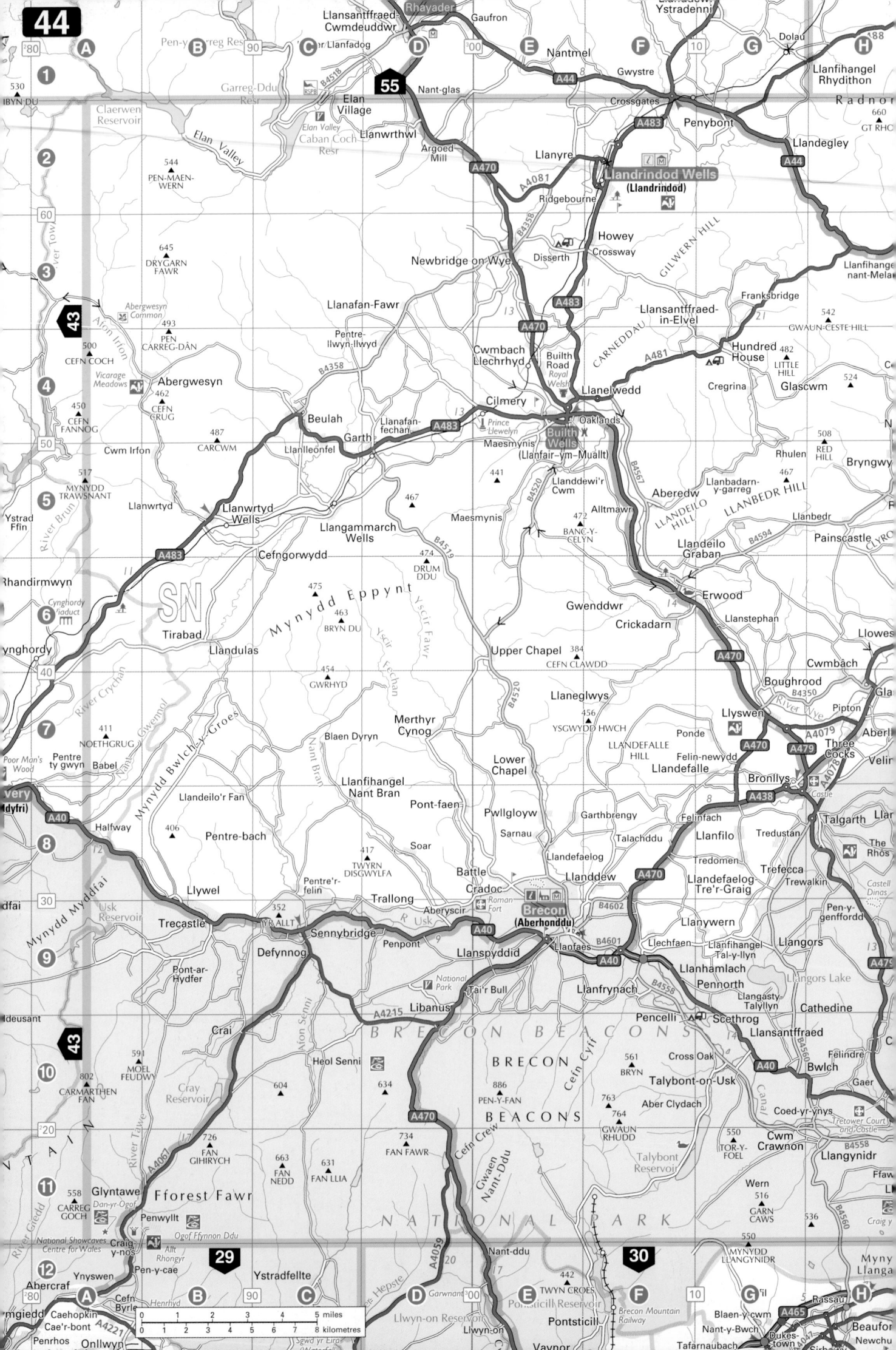

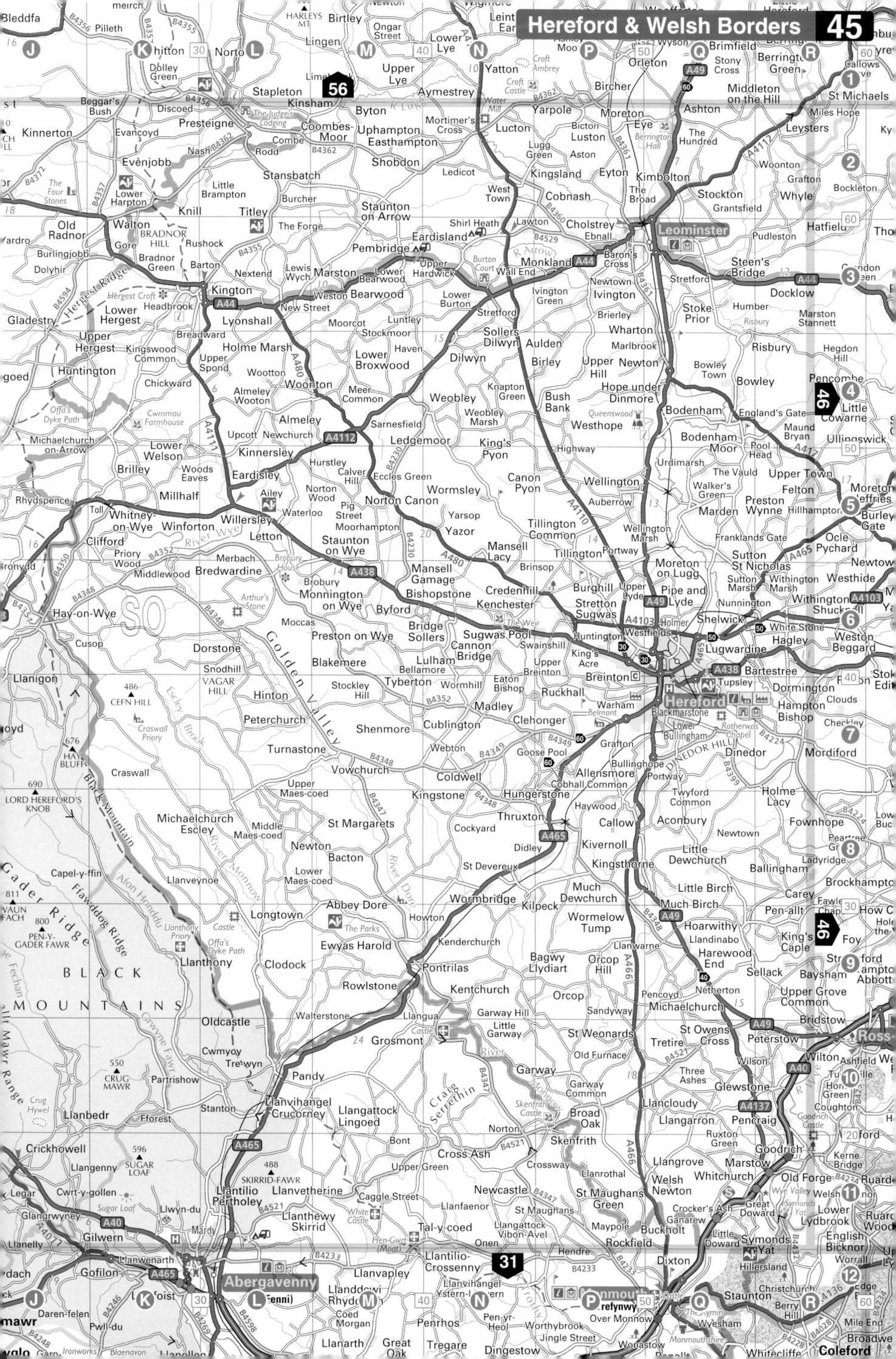

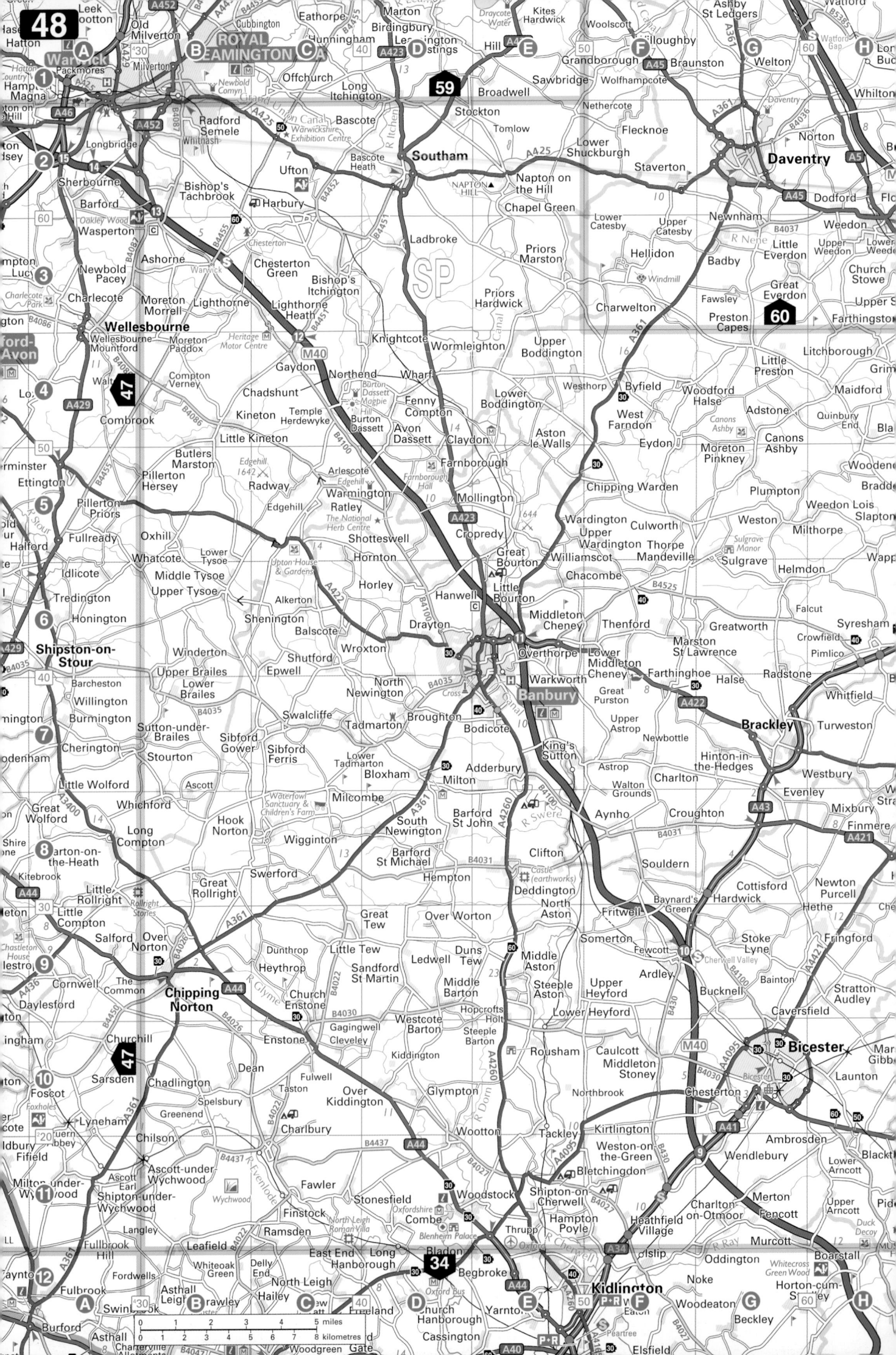

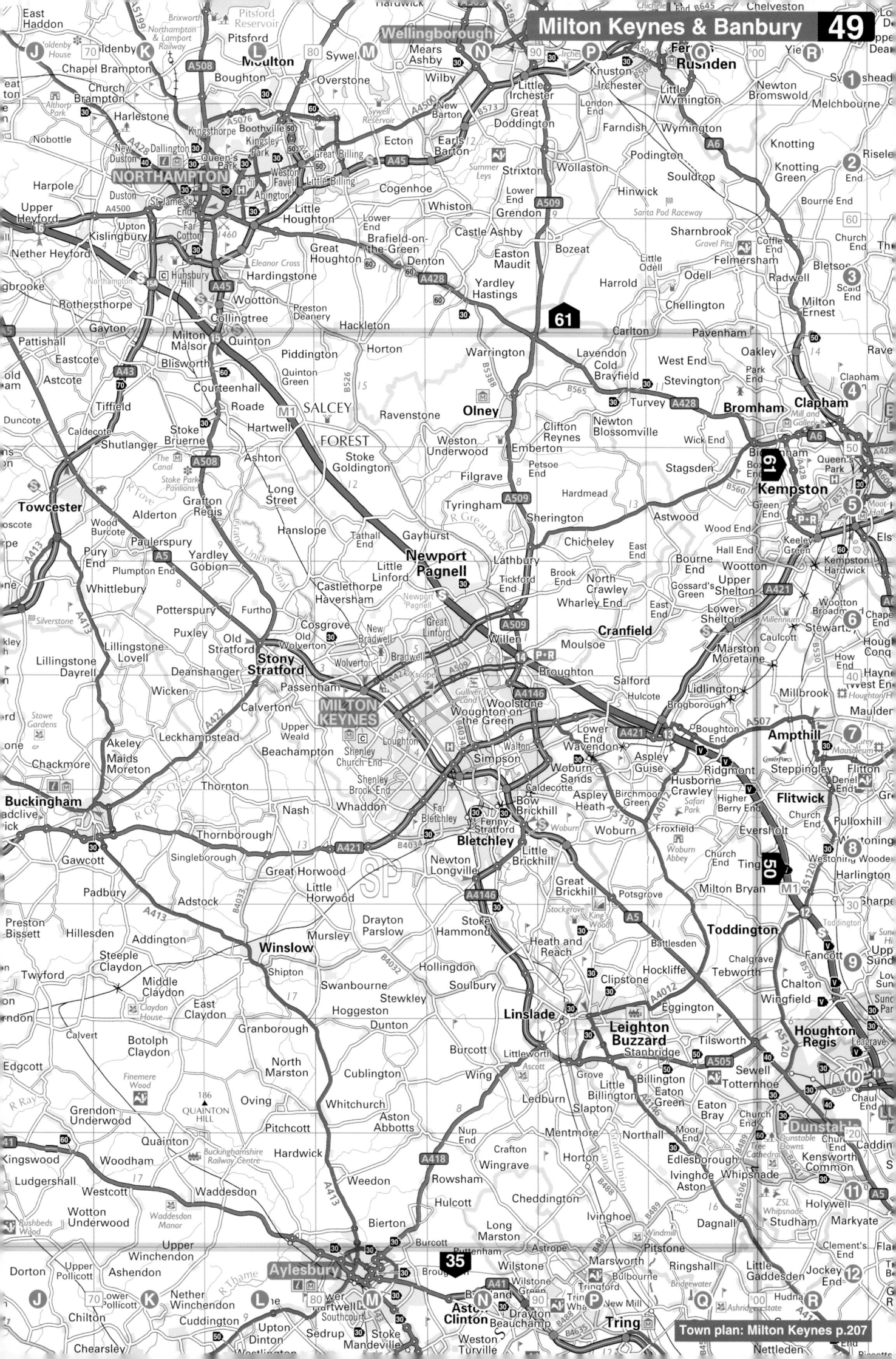

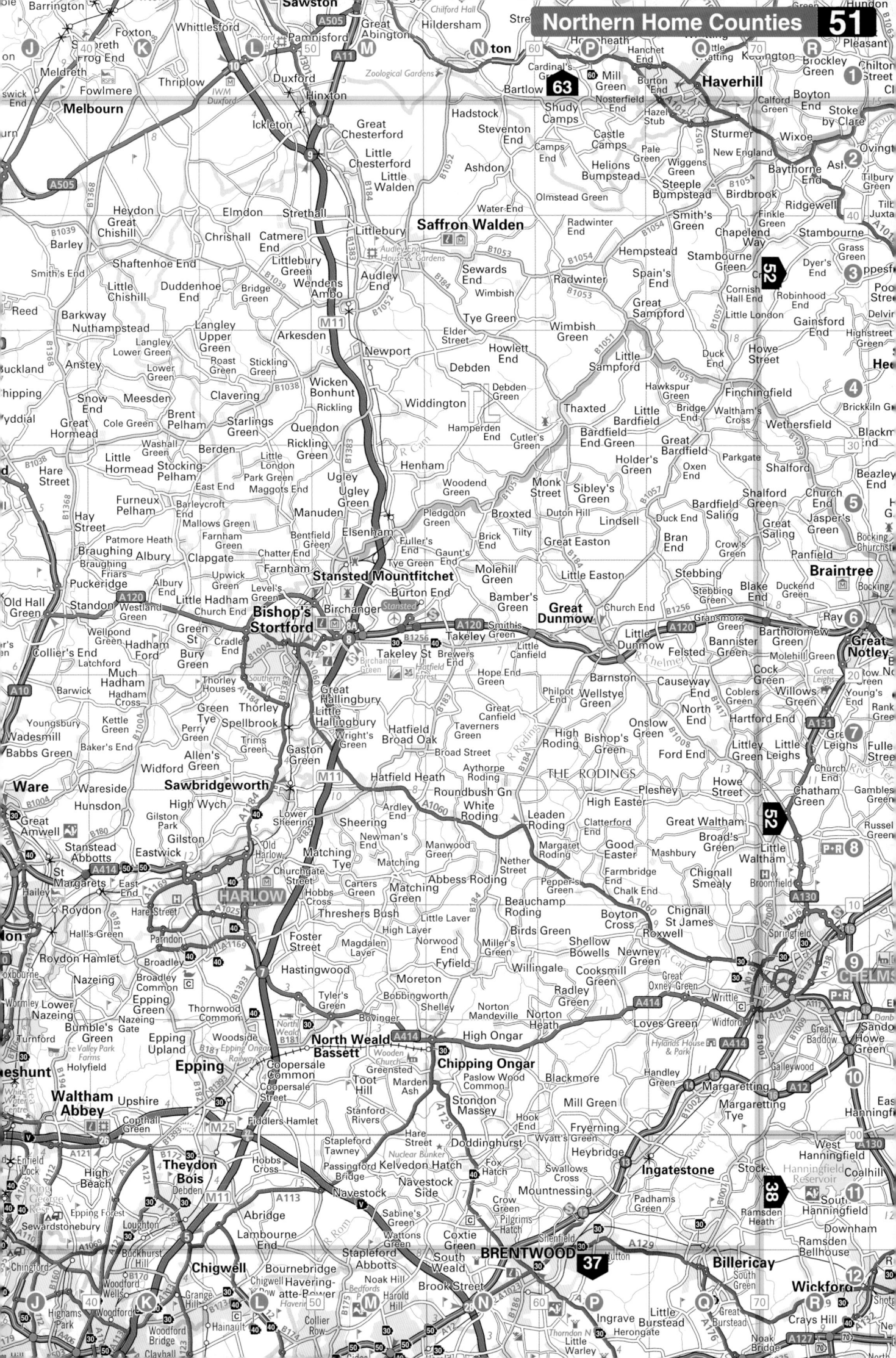

Harwich International Port

PASSENGER & CRUISE TERMINAL

HARWICH INTERNATIONAL STATION

0   400 m

CAR FERRY TERMINAL

EAST DOCK ROAD

WEST DOCK ROAD

REFINERY ROAD

A136

CONTAINER TERMINAL

Parkeston

Harwich Industrial Estate

STATION ROAD

Superstore

PARKESTON ROAD

PARKESTON ROUNDABOUT

ST NICHOLAS ROUNDABOUT

A120

HARWICH

IPSWICH, COLCHESTER

A120

Dovercourt

MAIN ROAD

B1352

HIGH ROAD

MAIN ROAD

Upper Dovercourt

FRONK'S

B1352

LLS

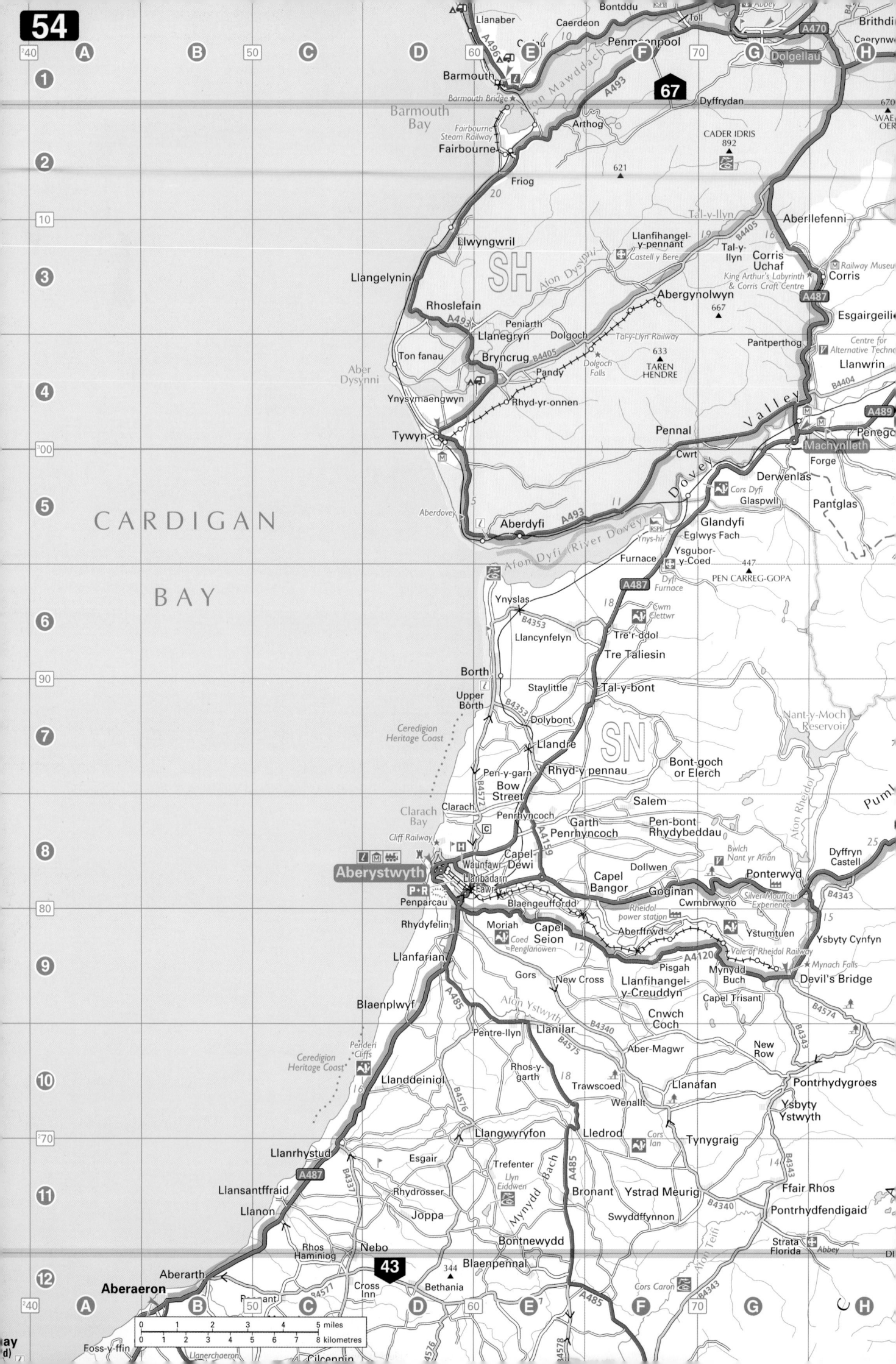

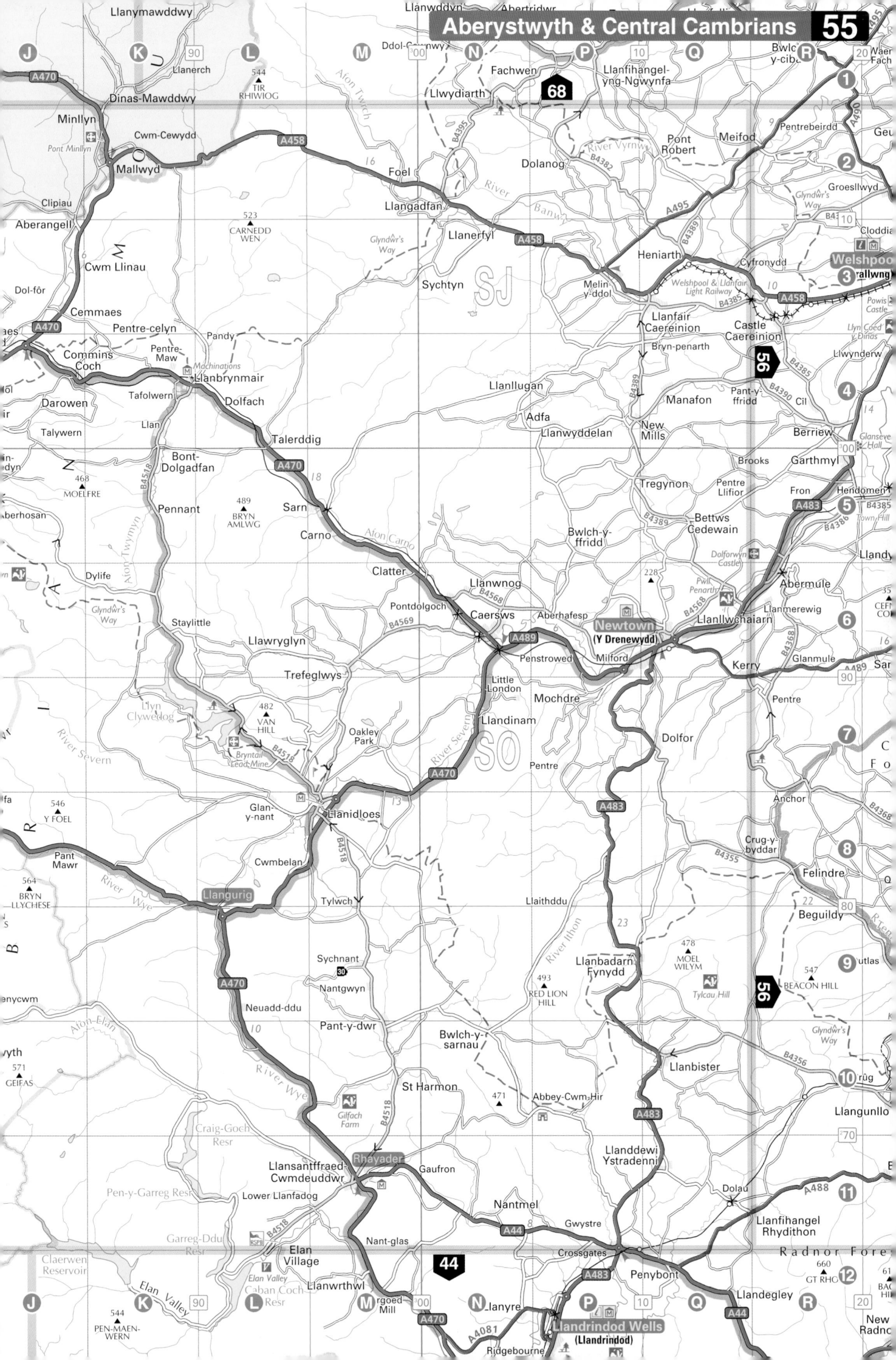

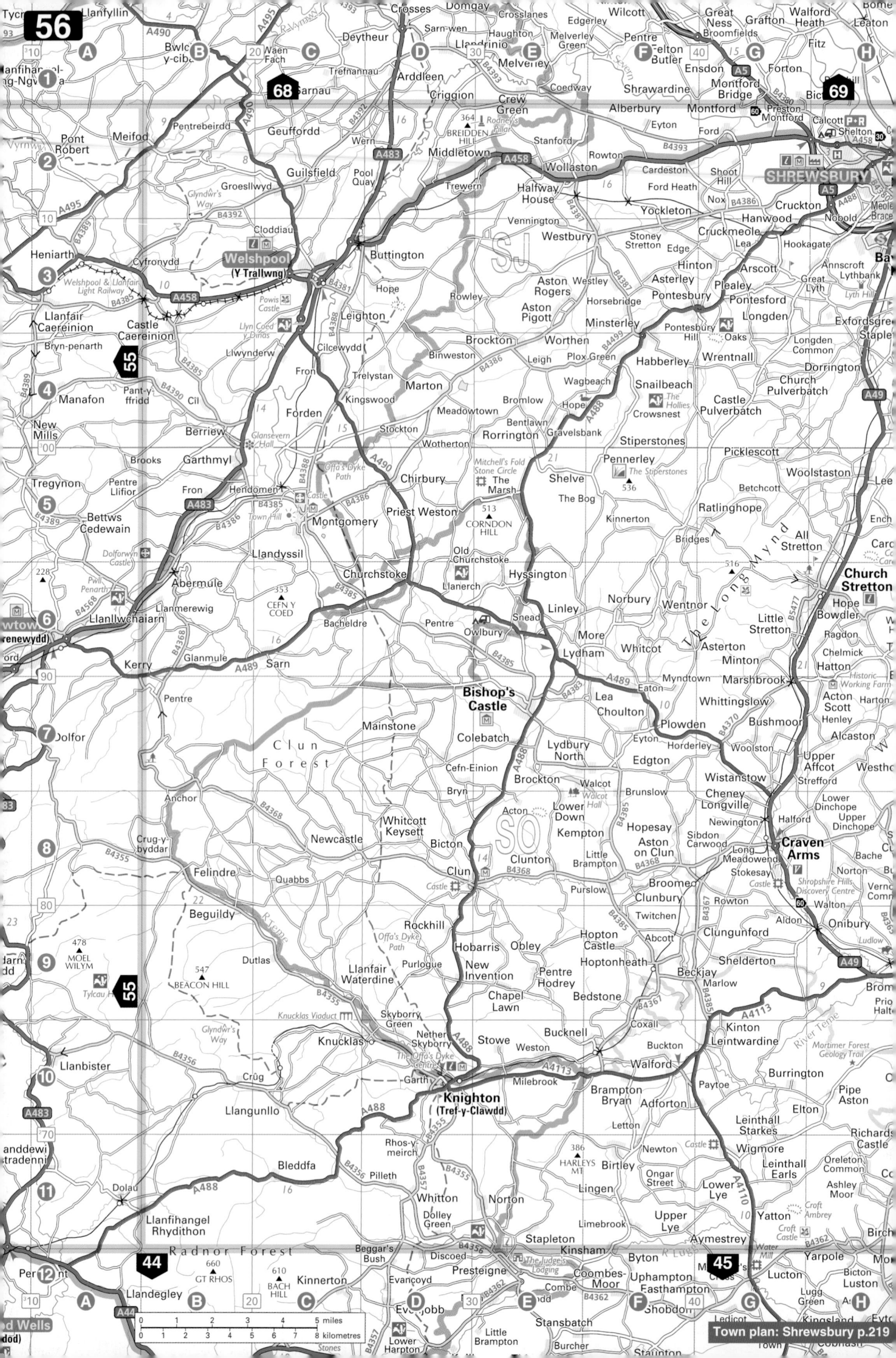

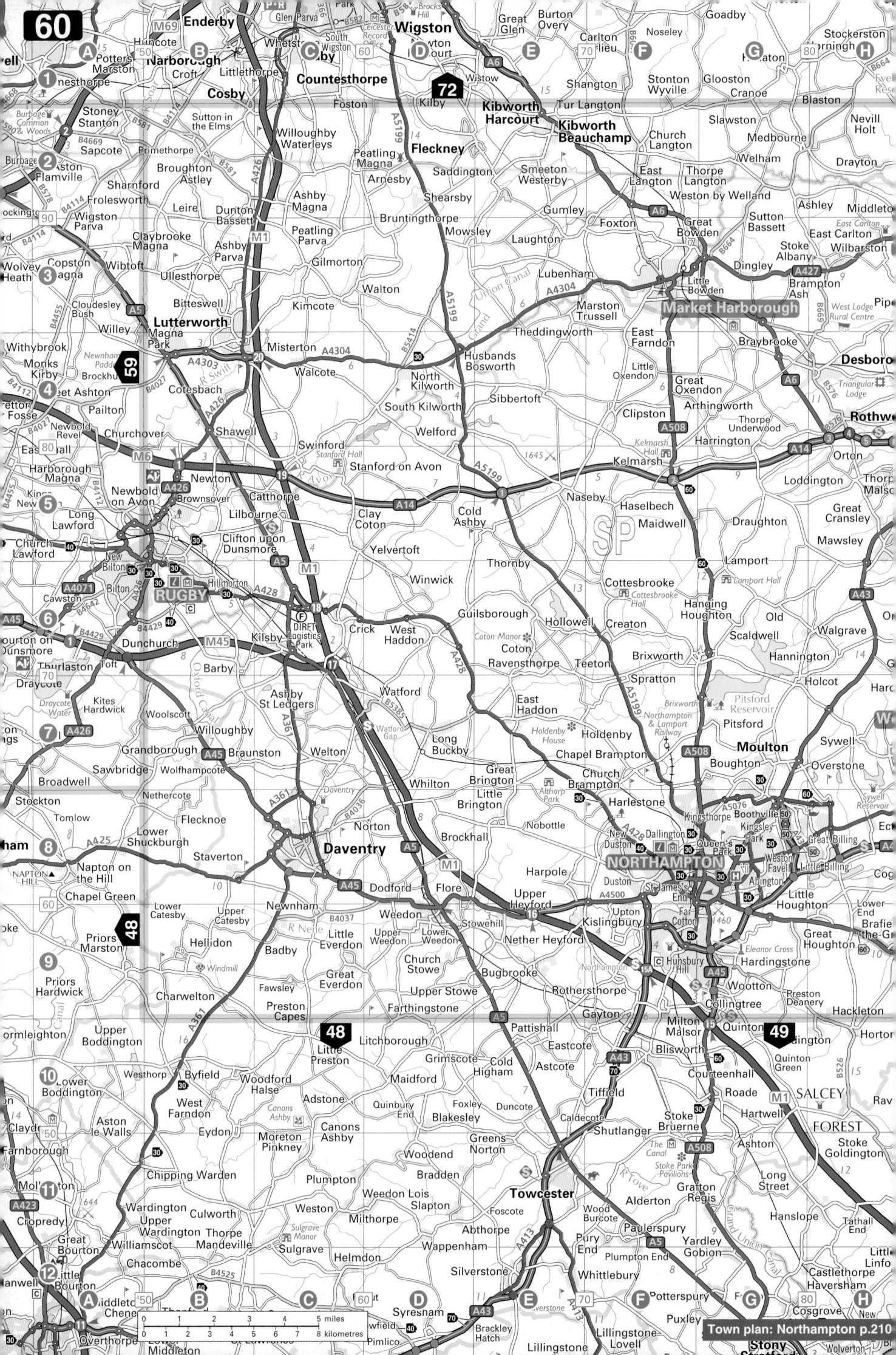

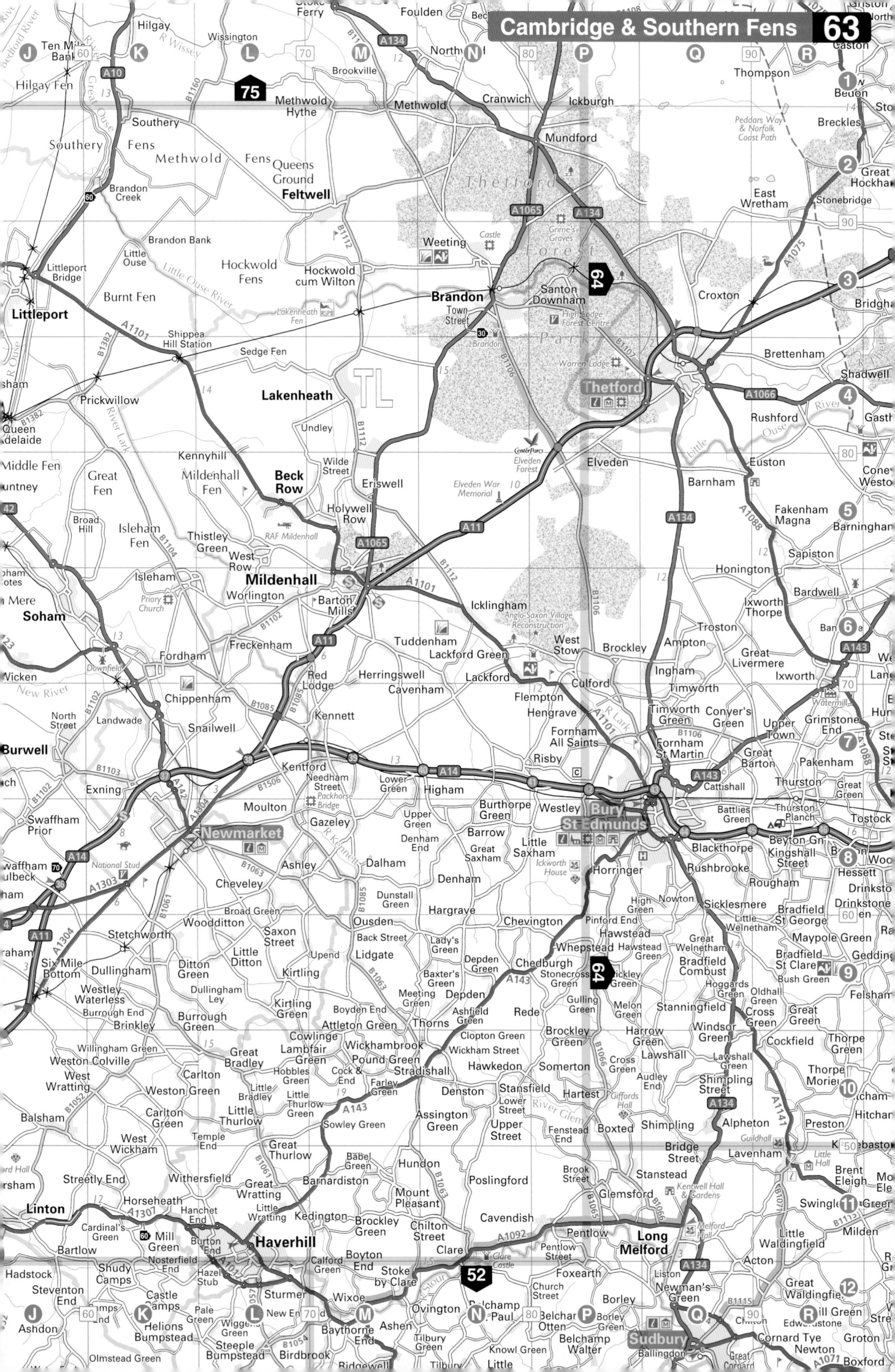

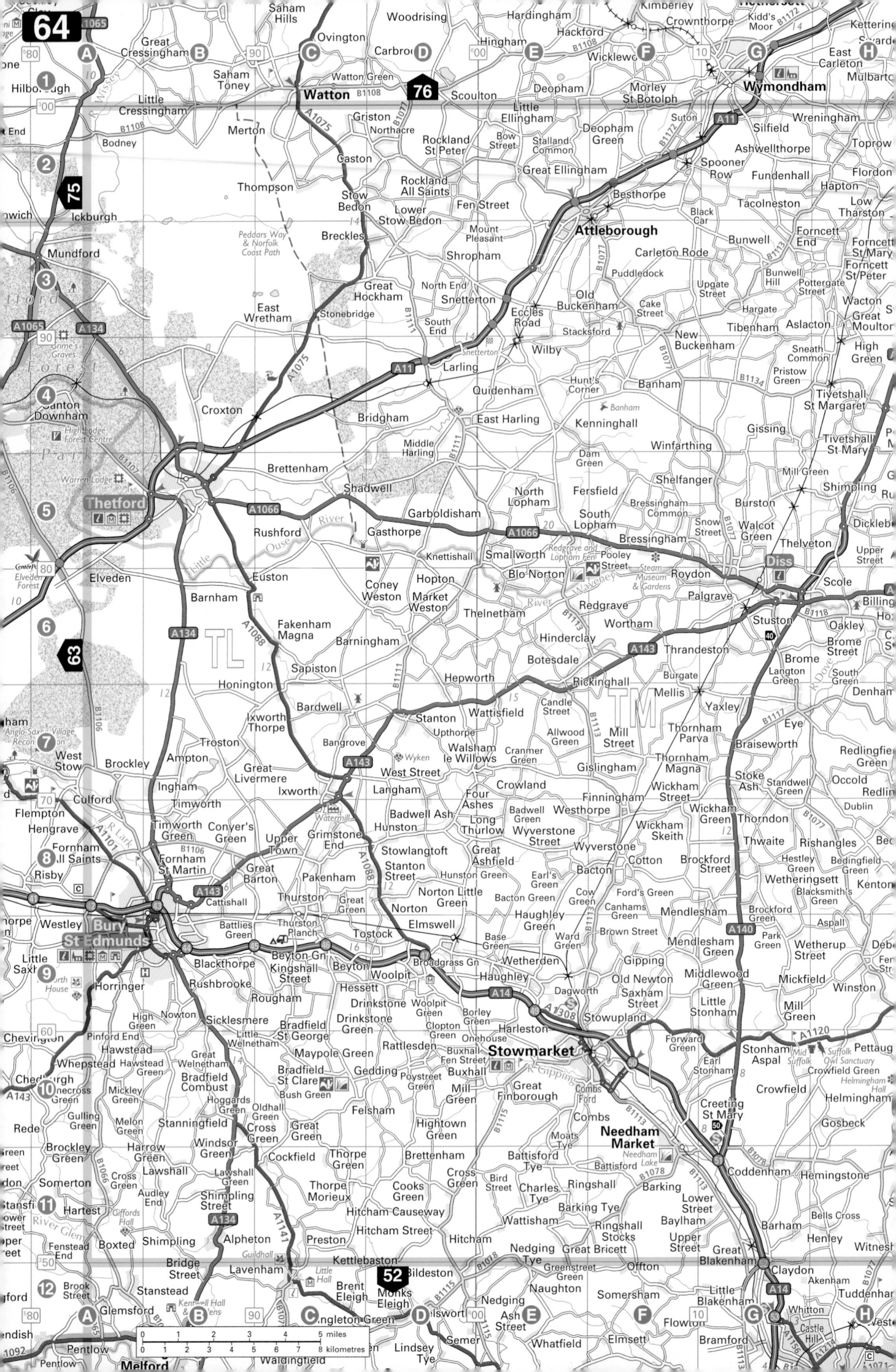

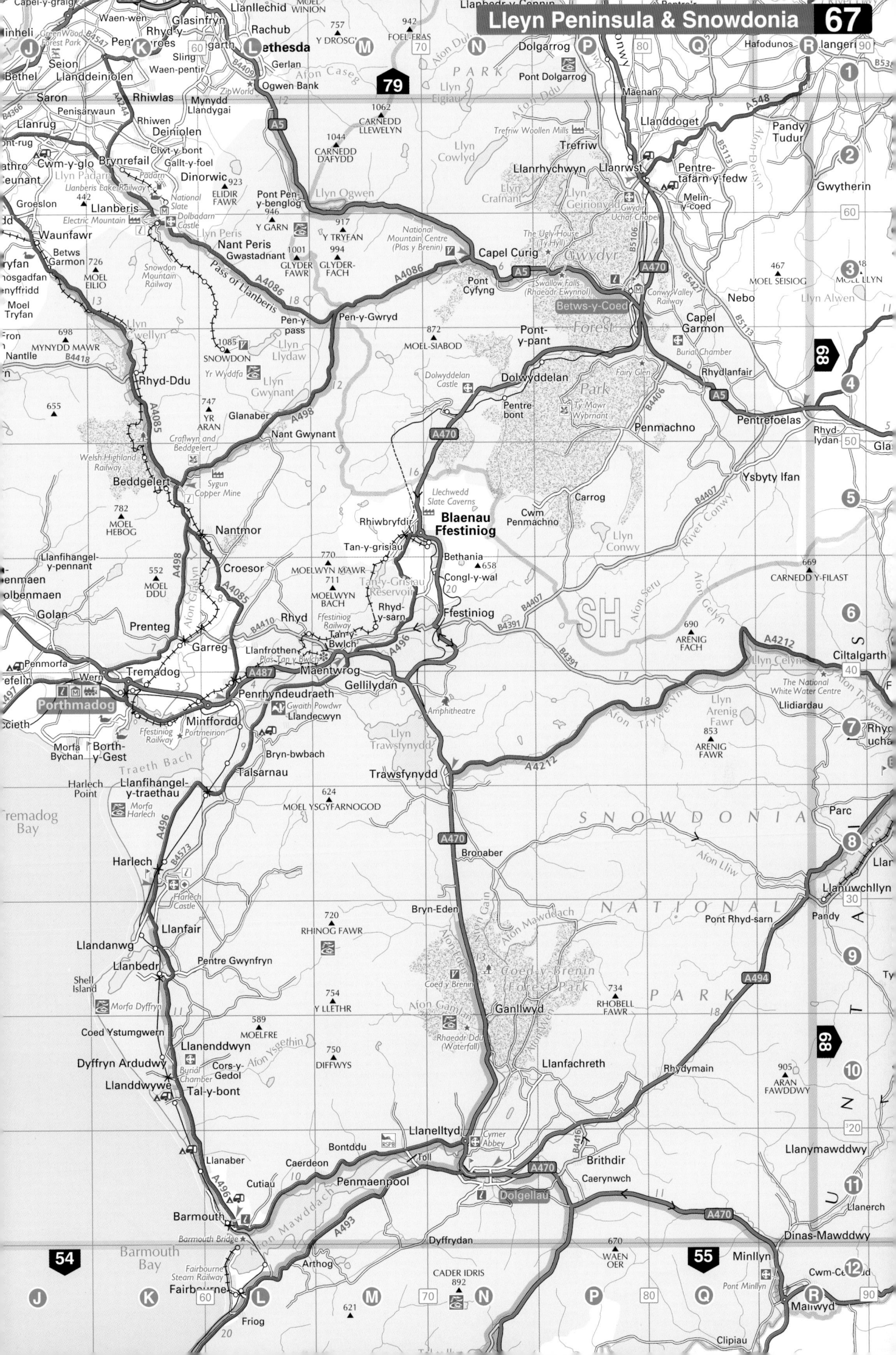

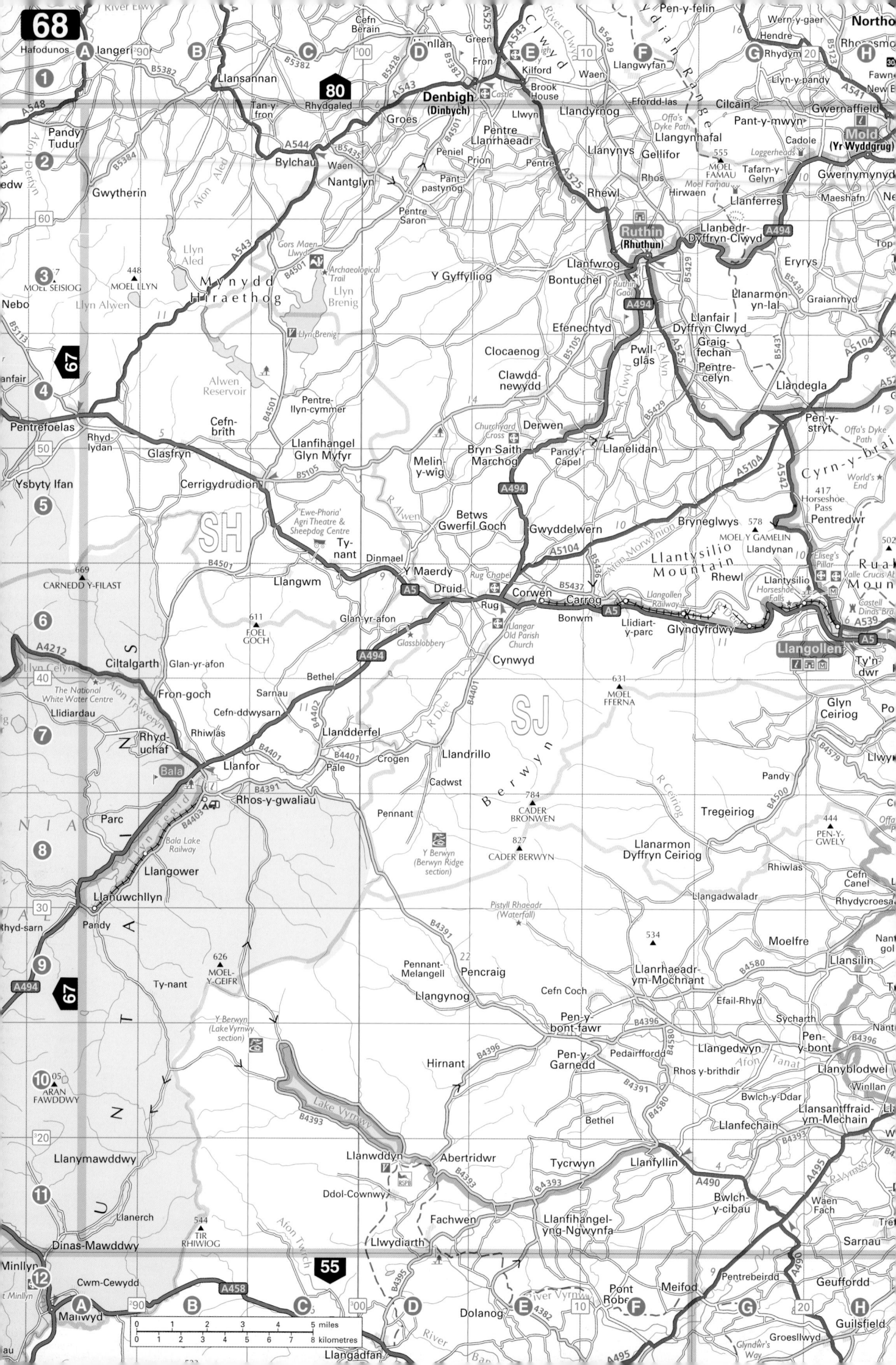

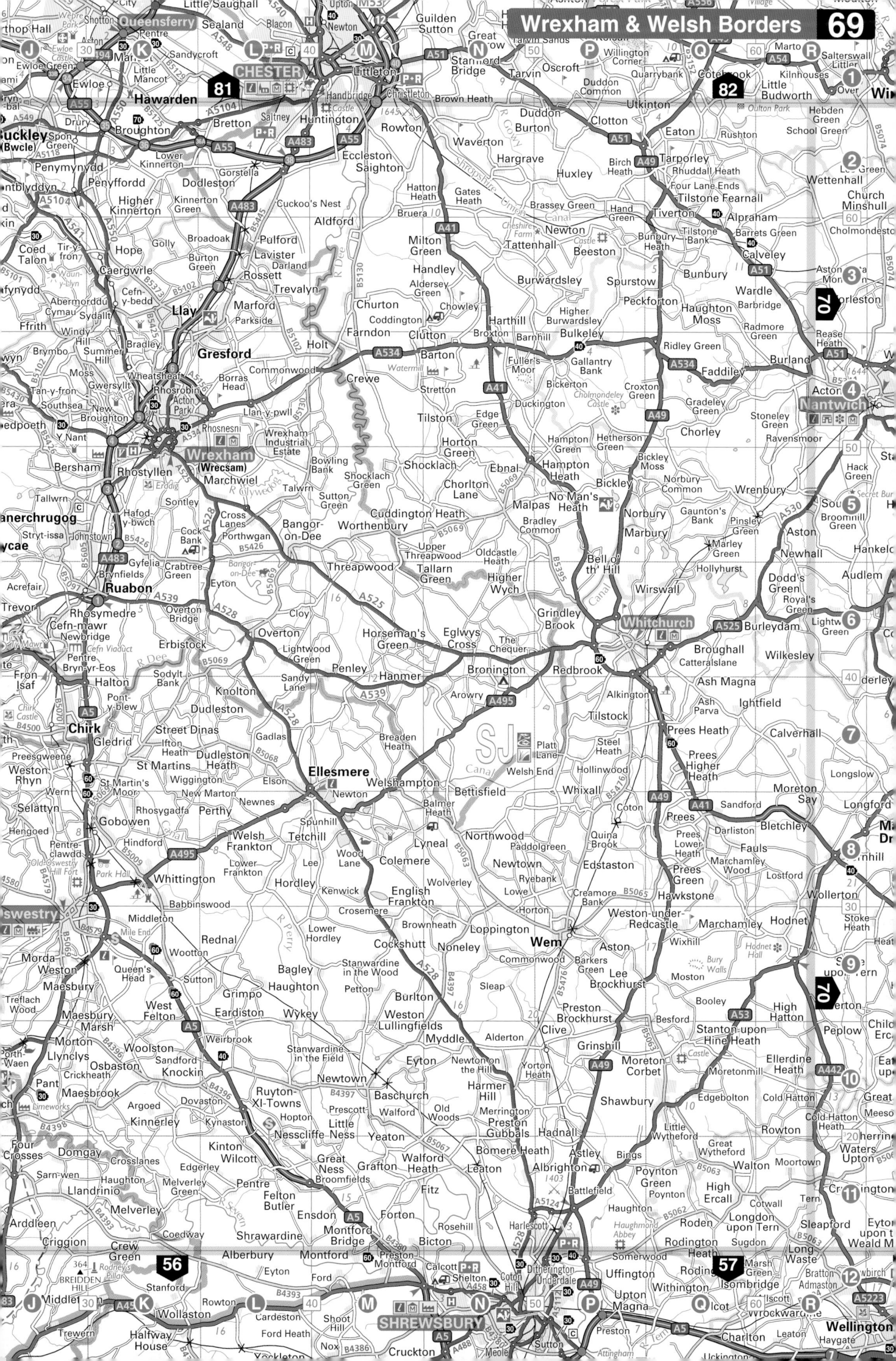

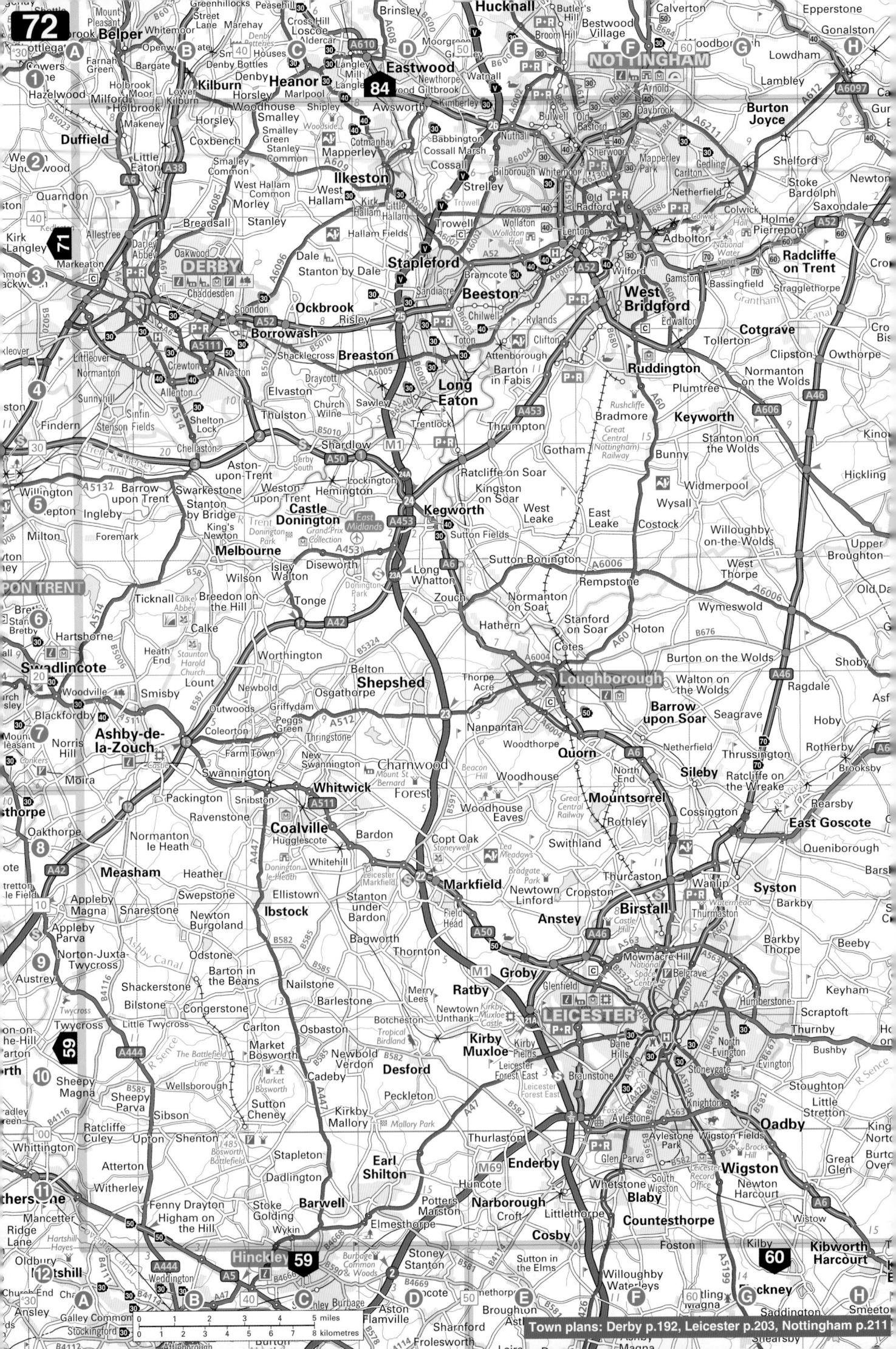

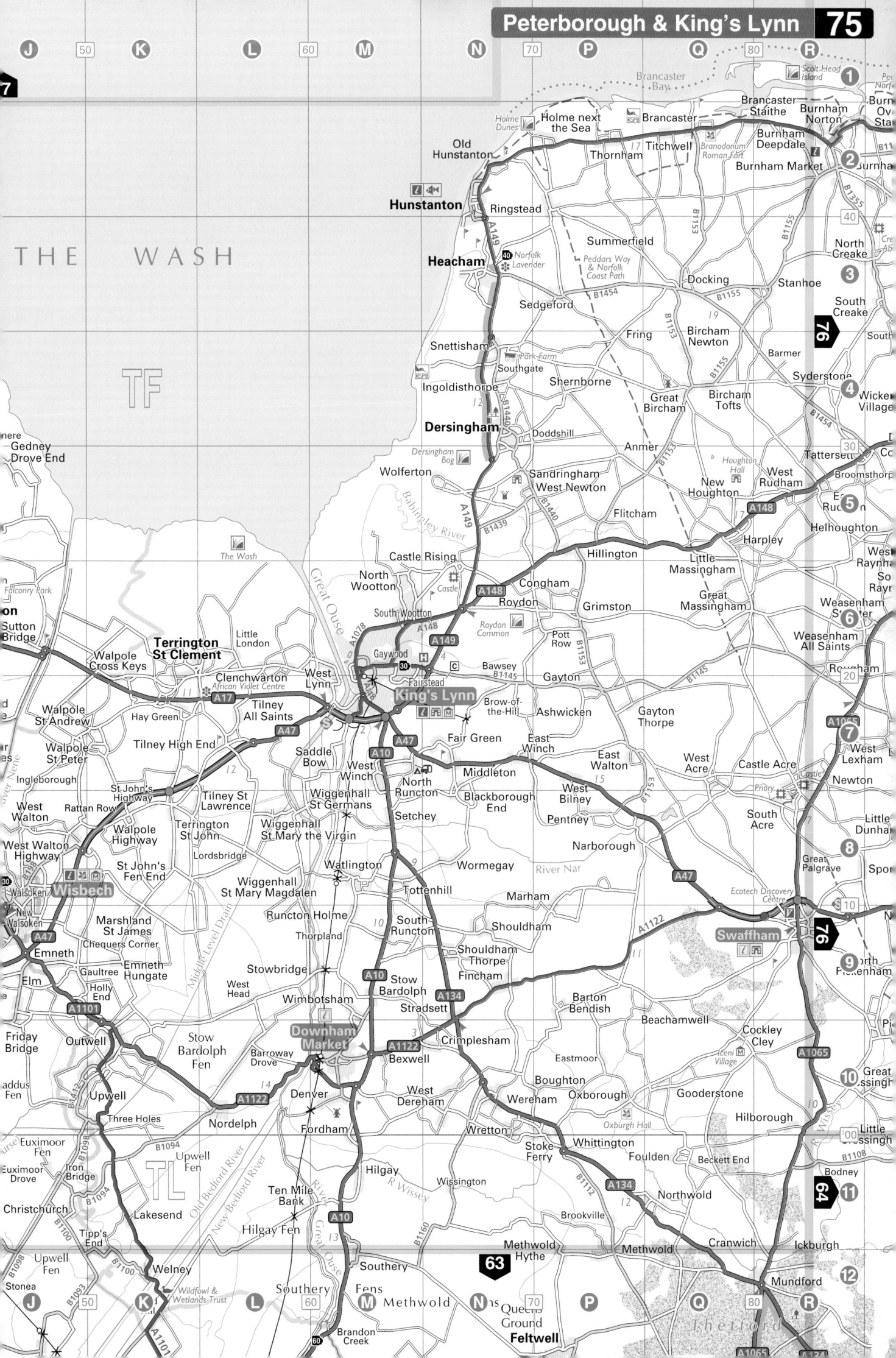

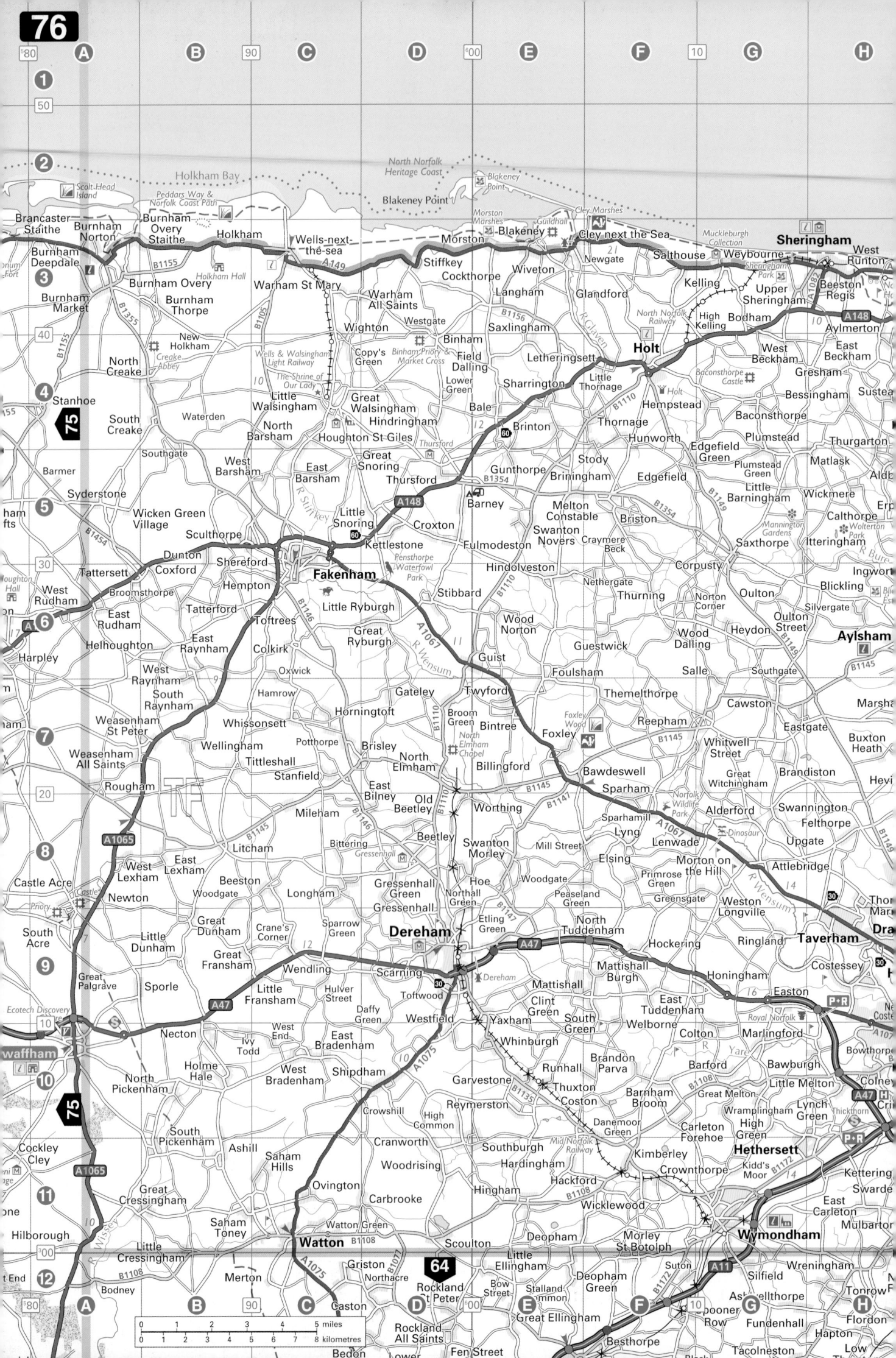

The Skerries

CARMEL HEAD

Holyhead
Bay

Dublin

Dublin
Dún Laoghaire
(Apr-Sept)

North Anglesey
Heritage Coast

Porth
Wen

Bull
Bay

Wylfa
Head

Cemaes
Bay

Cemaes

Llanbadrig

Bull Bay

Amlwch

Pôl

Llaneilian

Pengorff

Nebo

Du

City
Dulas

R

Brynrefail

Din L

Maenaddwyn

Hebron
Bachau

Capel
Coch

Brynte

Tregaian

Llangwyllog

Rhosmeir

Lla

Llangefn

Cein

Cemlyn
Bay

Hen
Borth

Tregele

Burwen

Pentrefelin

Penysarn

Gadfa

Rhosybol

Capel
Parc

Llanfairynghornwy

Llanfechell

Rhosbeirio

Bodewryd

Church
Bay

Swtan Folk

Llanrhyddlad

Penrhos

Llanflewyn

Rhosgoch

Carreglefn

Llanbabo

Llanfaethlu

Porth
Tywynmawr

Llanddeusant

Llynnon Mill

Stryd-y-
Facsen

Elim

Llantrisant

Llanerchymedd

Llyn
Alaw

Gwredog

Llandyfrydog

Llanfwrog

Pen-llyn

B5111

Llanfigael

ANGLESEY

North Stack

Breakwater

Gogarth
Bay

Llaingoch

Holyhead Mountain
Hut Circles

South Stack

Ellins
Tower

Penrhos Feilw

Holyhead Mountain
Heritage Coast

Penrhyn Mawr

**Holyhead
(Caergybi)**

Kingsland

Trefignath

Trearddur Bay

B4545

A55

HOLY ISLAND

Four Mile
Bridge

Llanfair-yn-Neubwll

Rhoscolyn

Rhoscolyn
Head

Cymyran
Bay

SH

Penrhos

Llanynghenedl

Llanfachraeth

Valley

A5025

Bodedern

Llyn
Llywenan

Llechcynfarwy

Presaddfed

B5109

Trefor

B5112

Caergeiliog

Bryngwran

Bodffordd

Gwalchmai

Cefni
Reservoir

Oriel
Ynys Môn

Llanfihangel
yn Nhowyn

Llechylched

RSPB

Capel Gwyn

Dothan

Llynfaes

Heneglwys

18

Anglesey

A5

A55

A5114

Llangristiolus

Pentre Berw

Gaerwen

Llanddaniel

Brynsiency

Ty Newydd

Rhosneigr

A4080

Ty
Croes

Bryn Du

Llanfaelog

Pencarnisiog

Cerrigceinwen

Dir Dryfol

Henblas

Capel Mawr

Trefdraeth

Bethel

B4422

Bodwyr
Burial Chamber

Llanddwyn Island

Llanddwyn
Bay

Porth Trecastell

Aberffraw

Anglesey
Circuit

Llangadwaladr

Hermon

Bodorgan

Malltraeth

Llangaffo

A4080

Castell
Bryn Gwyn

Dwyran

Anglesey
Sea Zoo

B4419

Aberffraw
Bay

Aberffraw Bay
Heritage Coast

Malltraeth Bay

Newborough

Pen-lôn

Foel Farm
Park

Caernarfor

Caernarfor
Castle

66

Port plan: Holyhead *p.XII*

Point

Railway

0 1 2 3 4 5 miles
0 1 2 3 4 5 6 7 8 kilometres

Llandudno

0   200 m

TABOR HILL
Great Orme Tramway
OLD ROAD
PLAS ROAD
TY-COCH ROAD
HILL TERRACE
The Grand Hotel

Llandudno Bay

Victoria Station
CHURCH WALKS
CWLACH ST
CLONMEL ST
NORTH PARADE
HILL PARADE
CLEMENT AVENUE
ST SEIRIOL'S ROAD

The Old Bank Gallery
War Memorial
SOUTH PARADE
The Promenade
MOSTYN STREET
TY ISA ROAD

Travelodge
GLODDAETH STREET
A546
DEGANWY

Town Hall
St John's
Our Lady Star of the Sea
Holy Trinity
Medical Centre
ADELPHI
THE PARADE
A546
B5115

Conwy Archive Service
LLANDUDNO STATION
Mostyn Gallery
CONWY ROAD
A470
MOSTYN BROADWAY
Coach
Parc Llandudno Retail Park
Swimming Pool
Venue Cymru
St Paul's
MOSTYN AVE

AVENUE
Ysgol Tudno
Police Station
Magistrates' Court
CYLCH-TUDUR
Fire & Ambulance Station
Mostyn Champneys Retail Park
Bowling Alley
CLARENCE CRESCENT
MAES CLYD
Ysgol Craig Y Don
CAE C
CLARENCE DRIVE

TRINITY
Superstore
CONWAY ROAD
A470
B5115
KINGSWAY

Ysgol Ffordd Dyffryn
Ysgol Morfa Rhianedd
Coach
Llandudno FC
Ysgol John Bright

BETWS-Y-COED

SH

Seawatch Centre
Moelfre
anallgo
arián-glas

Benllech
Red Wharf Bay
Red Wharf Bay
Puffin Island
Black Point
Penmon Priory
Toll
Caim
Penmon
Glan-yr-afon

Great Orme Heritage Coast
GREAT ORMES HEAD
Great Orme Tramway
Toll
Little Ormes Head
Penrhyn Bay

Llanddona
Llangoed
B5109
Conwy Bay
Llandudno
Penrhynside
Rhôs-on-Sea
Colwyn Bay
(Bae Colwyn)

Pentraeth
Llanfaes
Gaol
Beaumaris Castle
Llanrhos
Deganwy
Pydew
Llandrillo-yn-Rhos
landd
Llysfaen
Rh

Beaumaris
Courthouse
Esgyryn
Mochdre
Old Colwyn
A55
A548

Llansadwrn
Llandegfan
A545
Dwygyfylchi
Conwy
Llandudno Junction
Llanelian-yn-Rhôs
Bryn-y-Maen
Dolwen

Menai Bridge
(Porthaethwy)
Bangor
Penmaenmawr
Conwy Castle
RSPB
Llansanffraid Glan Conwy
A470
80
Dawn
Betws-yn-Rhos

Britannia Column
Plas Newydd
Penrhos garnedd
Capel-y-craig
Llanfairfechan
A55
Garizim
Penmaenan
Capelulo
Henryd
Graig
Eglwysbach
Pentre'r Felin

GreenWood Forest Park
Penrhyn
Abergwyngregyn
Gorddinog
Nant-y-pandy
SNOWDONIA
610
TAL-Y-FAN
Rowen
Caerhun
B5106
Tal-y-Cafn
River Elwy

Waen-wen
Llandygai
Tal-y-bont
Coedydd Aber
Aber Falls
Ty'n-y-Groes
Llanbedr-y-Cennin
Castell
Vale of Conwy
Llangw

Rhyd-y-groes
Glasinfryn
Llanllechid
580
MOEL WNION
NATIONAL
Tal-y-Bont
Dolgarrog
Pentre'r Felin
Hafodunos
Llang

Seion
Llanddeiniolen
Tregarth
Rachub
Gerlan
757
Y DROSGL
942
FOEL-FRAS
PARK
Pont Dolgarrog
Maenan
B5113

Bethesda
Mynydd Llandygai
ZipWorld
Ogwen Bank
Afon Caseg
1062
CARNEDD LLEWELYN
67
Trefriw Woollen Mills
Llanddoget
A548
Pandy Tudur

Saron
Penisarwaun
Rhiwlas
Rhiwen
Deiniolen
1044
CARNEDD DAFYDD
A5
Llyn Ogwen
Llyn Cowly
80
Llanrhychwyn
Llanrwst
Pentre-tafarn-y-fedw
B538

Llanrug
Cwm-y-glo
Brynrefail
Swt-y-b
Gallt-y-foel
Dinorwic
923
Pont Pen-y-benglog
Carnedd
Llyn Cri
Gwytherin

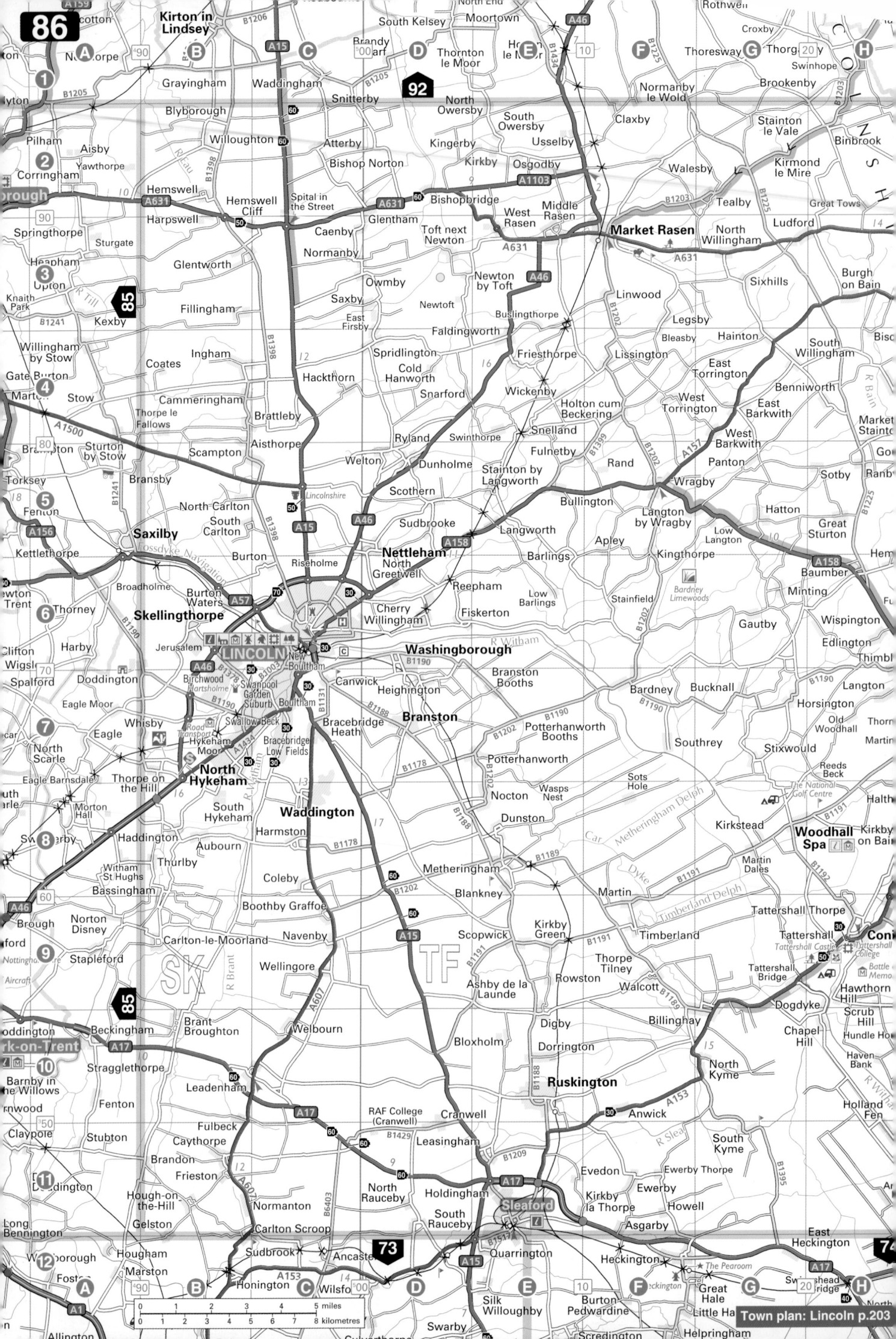

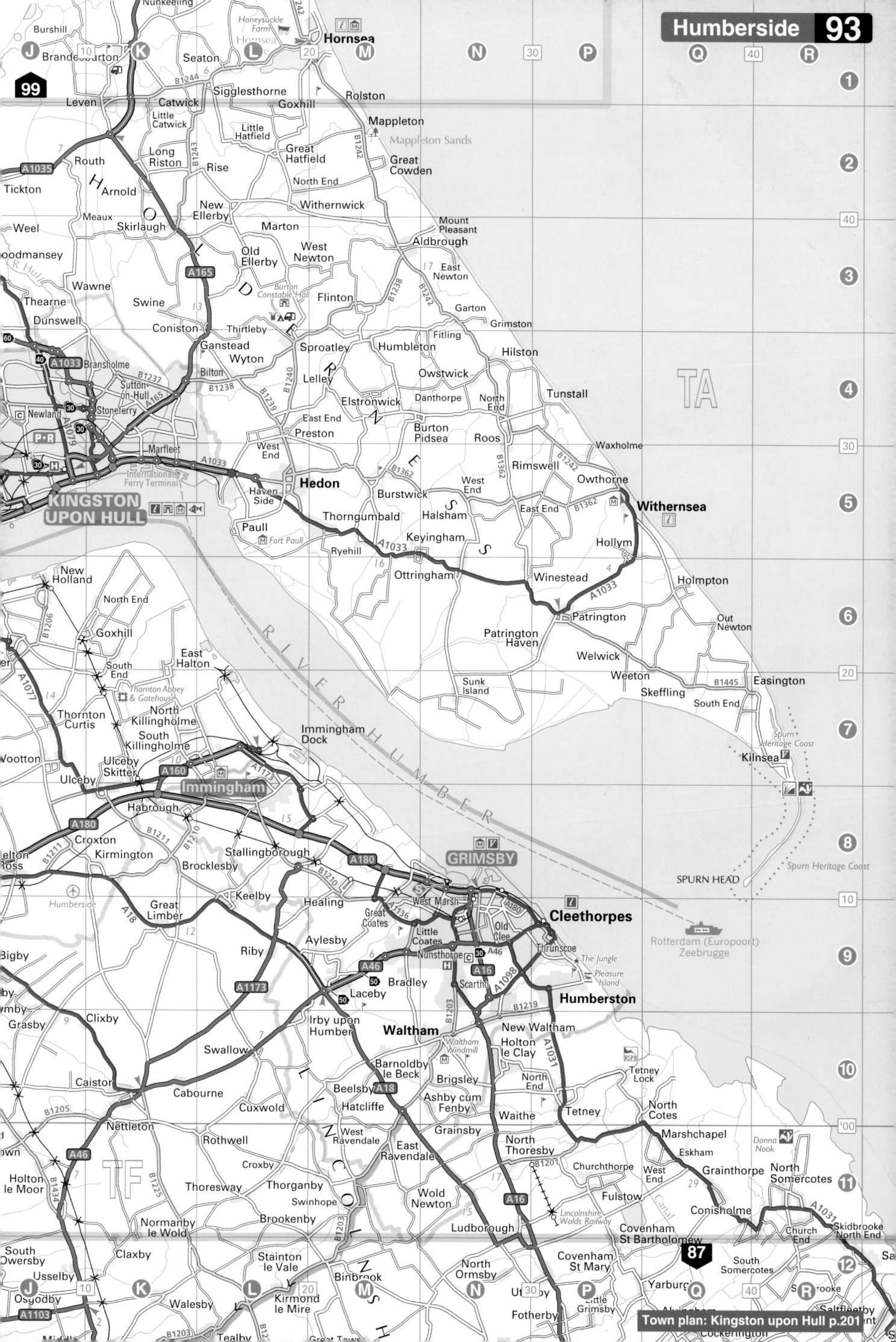

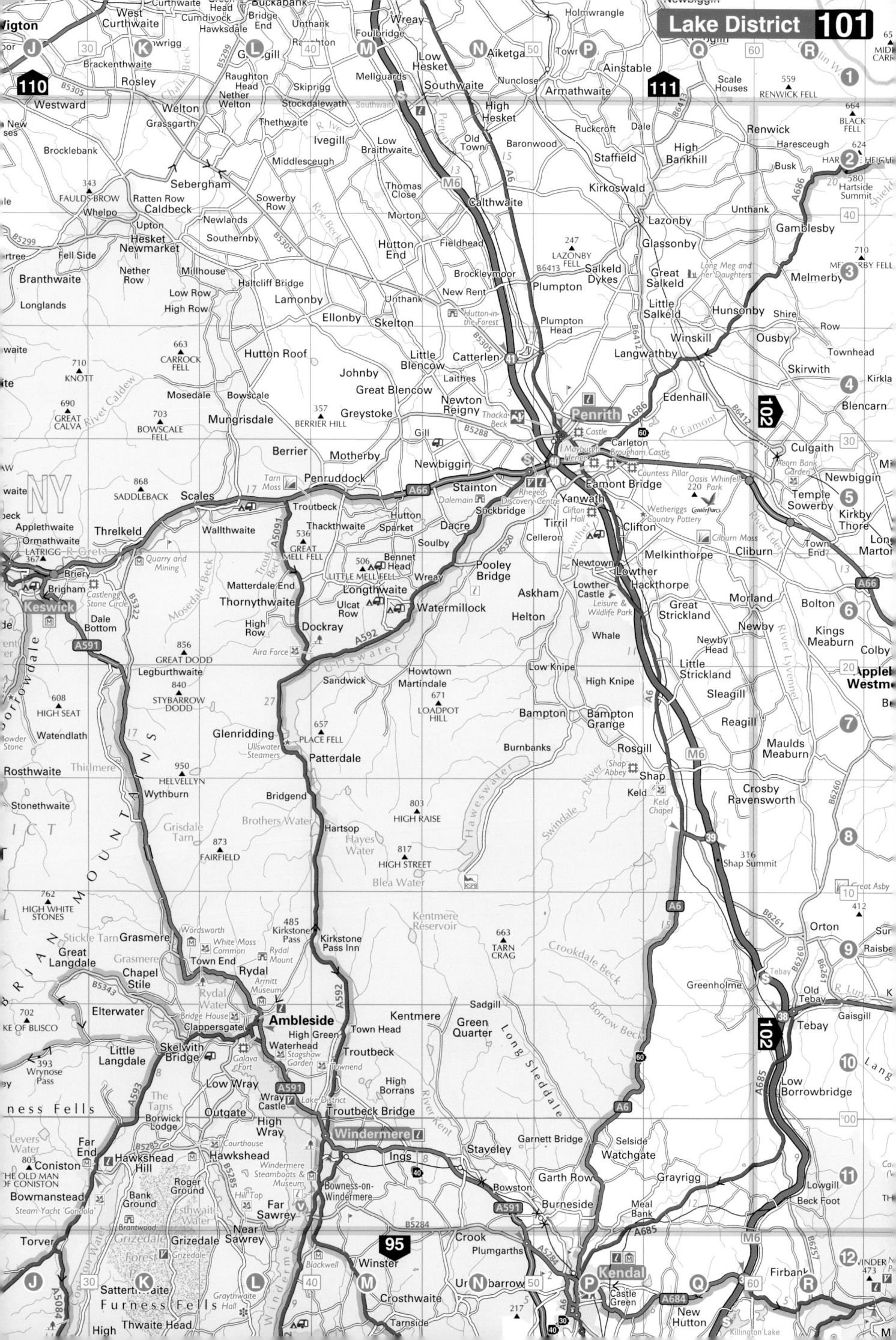

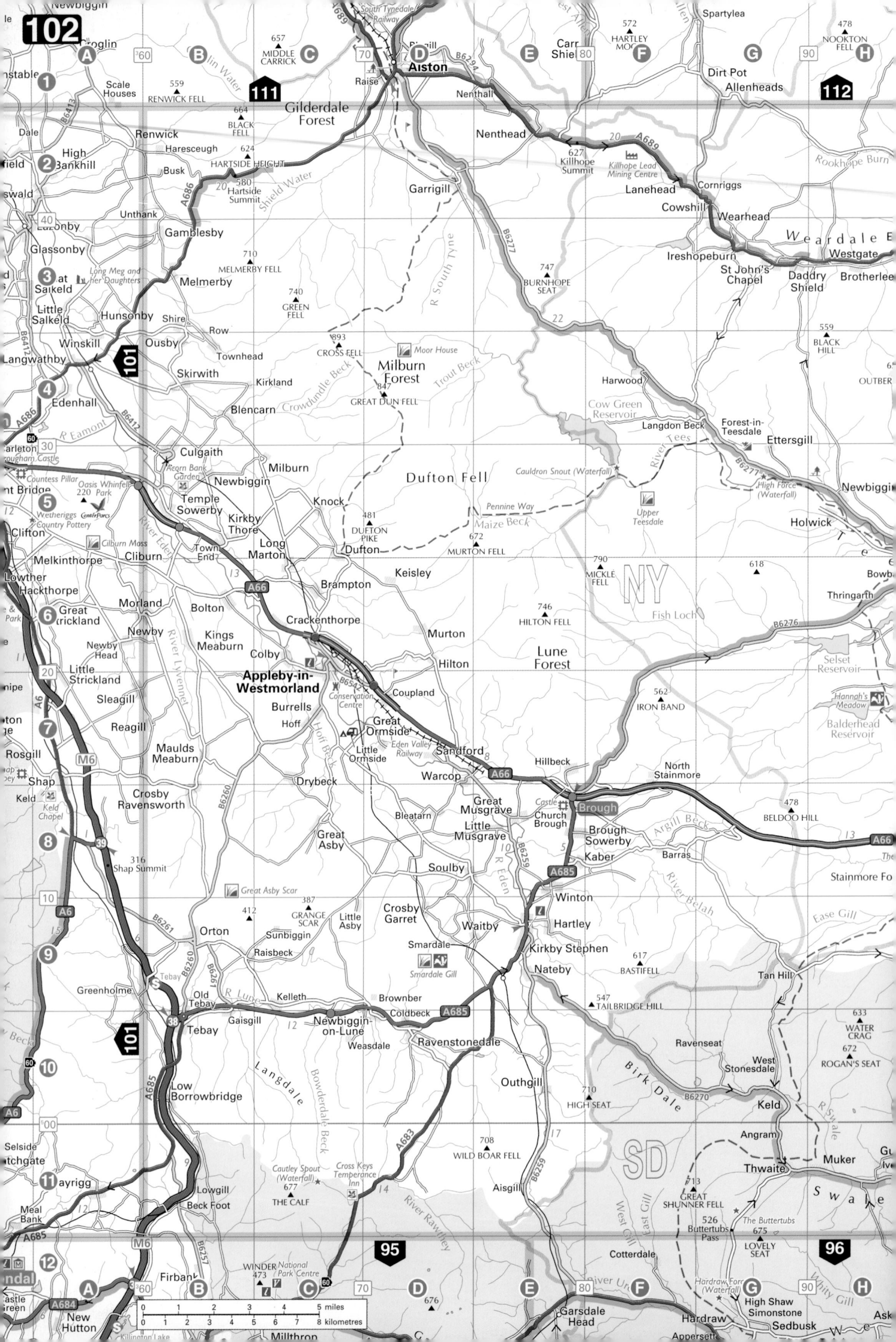

Saltburn-by-the-Sea
New Brotton
Brotton
Skelton
Carlin How
Skinningrove
Kilton
New Skelton
North Skelton
Lingdale
Kilton Thorpe
Stanghow
Woodhill
Liverton
Liverton Mines
Handale
Moorsholm
Scaling
Gerrick
Scaling Dam
Upton
Boulby
Loftus
Staithes
Dalehouse
Easington
Roxby
Borrowby
Hinderwell
Newton Mulgrave
Mickleby
West Barnby
Heritage Centre
Port Mulgrave
Kettleness
Runswick
Ellerby
Goldsborough
Lythe
East Barnby
Sandsend
Raithwaite
Dunsley
Newholm
A174
A171

Hummersea Scar
Runswick Bay
North Yorkshire and Cleveland Heritage Coast
Overdale Wyke
Sandsend Wyke

NZ

The Moors Centre
Danby
Castleton
Ainthorpe
Stonegate
Lealholm
Lealholm Side
The Green
Glaisdale
Egton
Egton Bridge
Street
Danby Bottom
River Esk
Esk Dale
Grosmont
Key Green
Aislaby
Ugthorpe
Hutton Mulgrave
Briggswath
Ruswarp
Sneaton
Ugglebarnby
Sleights
Iburndale
Sneatonthorpe
Littlebeck
Whitby
Abbey
Saltwick Bay
Stainsacre
High Hawsker
Low Hawsker
Ness Point or North Cheek
Robin Hood's Bay
Raw
Fylingthorpe
Robin Hood's Bay
Old Peak or South Cheek
B1416
A171
Ravenscar

NORTH YORK MOORS

301
326
PIKE HILL
369
NATIONAL PARK
Rosedale
Thorgill
Low Bell End
Rosedale Abbey
Mill
Beck Hole
Goathland
North Yorkshire Moors Railway
Wheeldale Roman Road
Newtondale Forest Drive
Stape
Hole of Horcum
292
Eller Beck
Harwood Dale
Staintondale
Cloughton Newlands
Shire Horse Centre
Hayburn Wyke
Cloughton Wyke
Cloughton
Cromer Point
Cleveland Way

TA

NORTH RIDING
Forest
NEW
290

99

Levisham
Lastingham
Kirtoft End
Bickley
Broxa
Silpho
Bu 00ton
Suffield
Hackness
Langdale
Bridestones (Rock Formation)
Newton-on-
Dalby
Toll

NORTH YORK MOORS

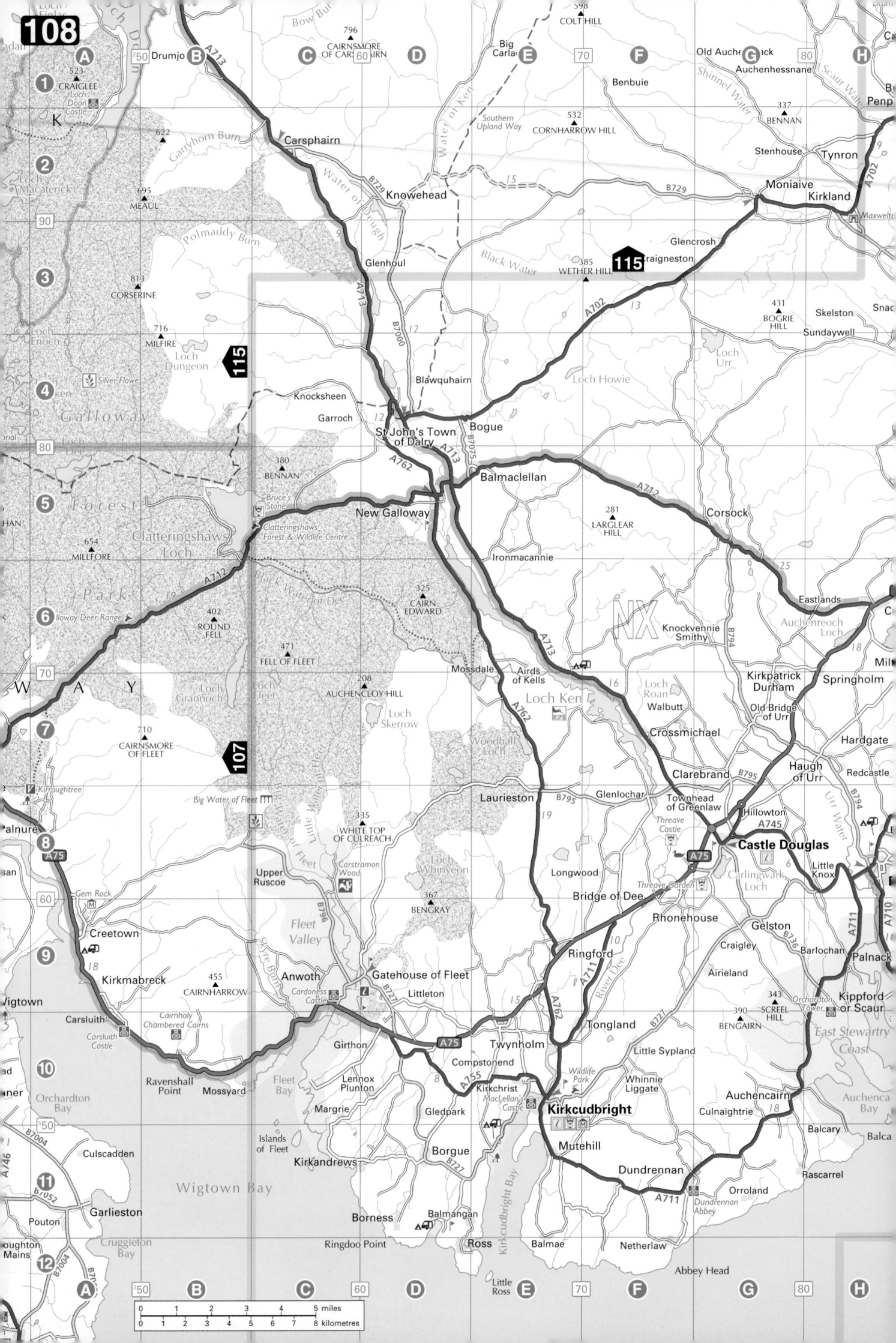

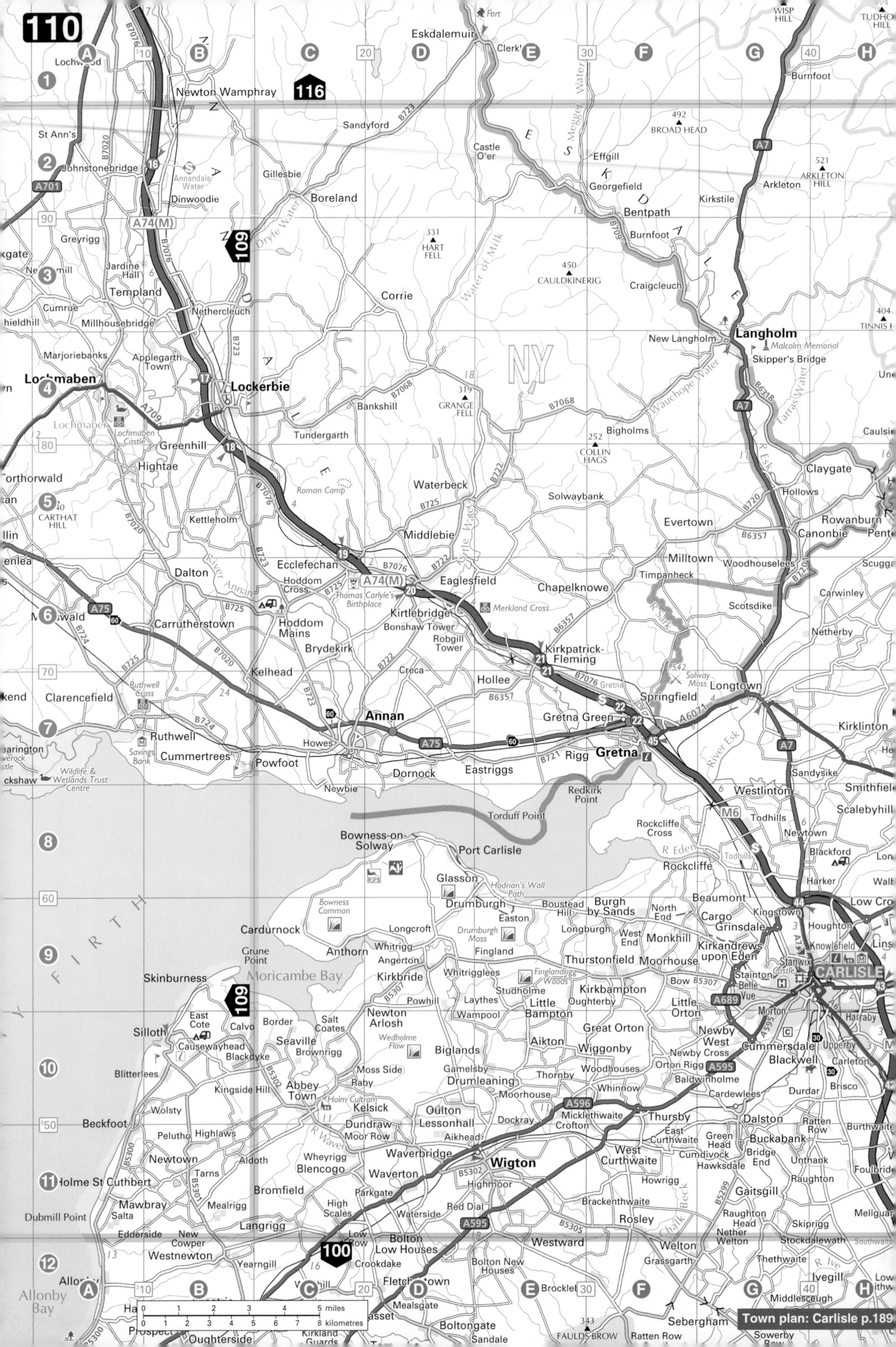

Port of Tyne

TYNEMOUTH
NEWCASTLE THE NORTH
NEWCASTLE
MEADOW WELL
PERCY MAIN
HOWDON ROAD
Wet'n'Wild Water Park
East Howdon
Royal Quays Outlet
Premier Inn
Royal Quays Marina
Check-in
TYNE VIEW
TYNE TUNNEL
INTERNATIONAL PASSENGER TERMINAL
PRIORY ROAD
Jarrow
SUNDERLAND
LLS
River Tyne

0 — 500 m

Place names (map labels)

West Thirston, Eshott, Broomhill, Red Row, Druridge Bay, Druridge
Causey Park, Helm, West Chevington, Druridge, Widdrington, North Northumberland Heritage Coast
Causey Park Bridge, Earsdon, Stobswood, Widdrington Station, Cresswell
Fenrother, Tritlington, Ulgham, Ellington, Lynemouth
Hebron, Longhirst, Linton, A1068, Woodhorn, Beacon Point
Pegswood, Ashington, Woodhorn Demesne
Morpeth, Hepscott, Bothal, Guide Post, Hirst, North Seaton, Newbiggin-by-the-Sea
Tranwell, Clifton, Choppington, Scotland Gate, Stakeford, Sheepwash, Wansbeck Riverside, North Seaton Colliery
Nedderton, Bedlington, Bomarsund, West Sleekburn, Cambois, North Blyth
Stannington Station, East Hartford, Cowpen, Blyth
Saltwick, Stannington, Plessey Woods, Bebside, Newsham
Shotton, Shankhouse, New Delaval, Seaton Sluice
Berwick Hill, Cramlington, New Hartley, Seaton Hartley
Brenkley, Big Waters, Seaton Burn, Annitsford, Seaton Delaval, St Mary's Lighthouse
Dinnington, Brunswick Village, Mason, Dudley, Burradon, Holywell
Prestwick, Wide Open, Camperdown, Earsworth, Monkseaton, Whitley Bay, Cullercoats
High Callerton, Newcastle, Hazlerigg, Killingworth, Backworth, Shiremoor, Murton, Tynemouth
Woolsington, Forest Hall, New York, Tynemouth Priory & Castle, Amsterdam (IJmuiden)
Black Callerton, Kenton Bankfoot, Rising Sun, Willington Quay, North Shields
North Albotle, Fawdon, Gosforth, South Gosforth, Longbenton, Int. Ferry Terminal, SOUTH SHIELDS
Westerhope, Kenton, Jesmond, Wallsend, Heaton, Walker, Tyne Tunnel, Jarrow, Westoe, Harton, Marsden Bay
Newburn, Heaton, NEWCASTLE UPON TYNE, Byker, Felling, Hebburn, Monkton, Marsden, Souter Lighthouse
Stella, Scotswood, Elswick, Dunston, Metro Centre, Wardley, Boldon Colliery, West Boldon, Cleadon, Souter Point
Blaydon, Winlaton, Derwent Walk, GATESHEAD, East Boldon, Whitburn
Whickham, Team Valley, Low Fell, Wrekenton, A194(M), Hylton Castle, Whitburn Bay
Winlaton Mill, Sunniside, Street Gate, Bowes Railway & Museum, Springwell, Usworth, Wildfowl & Wetlands Trust, Fulwell, Southwick, Roker, Seaburn
Gibside, Lamesley, Angel of the North, Castletown, Monkwearmouth
Sheep Hill, Marley Hill, Byermoor, Tanfield Railway, Birtley, Portobello, South Hylton, SUNDERLAND
White-le-Head, Beamish, High Urpeth, Ouston, WASHINGTON, Pennywell, Hendon
Tanfield Lea, West Pelton, Perkinsville, Fatfield, Offerton, High Newport, Grangetown
Stanley, Catchgate, Pelton, Fence Houses, Penshaw, Herrington, New Silksworth, Tunstall, Ryhope
Oxhill, Quaking Houses, Grange Villa, Pelton Fell, Newfield, Shiney Row, New Herrington, Philadelphia, Durham Heritage Coast
Chester-le-Street, Houghton Gate, Bournmoor, High Dubmire, Houghton-le-Spring, Seaham
Lanchester, Sacriston, Witton Gilbert, Great Lumley, West Rainton, Colliery Row, Hetton-le-Hole, Murton, Parkside, Dalton-le-Dale
Holmside, Edmondsley, Nettlesworth, Chester Moor, Plawsworth, East Rainton, Low Moorsley, Cold Hesleden
Ornsby Hill, Burnhope, Waldridge, Kimblesworth, Leamside, High Moorsley, South Hetton, Hawthorn
Maiden Law, Esh Winning, Langley Park, Framwellgate Moor, Pity Me, Crook Hall, Gilesgate Moor, Carville, Hallgarth, Pittington, Easington Colliery
Quebec, Bearpark, Durham, Littletown, Murton, Haswell, Haswell Plough, Easington, Little Thorpe, Durham Heritage Coast
New Brancepeth, Broompark, Shincliffe, Shadforth, Shotton, Easington

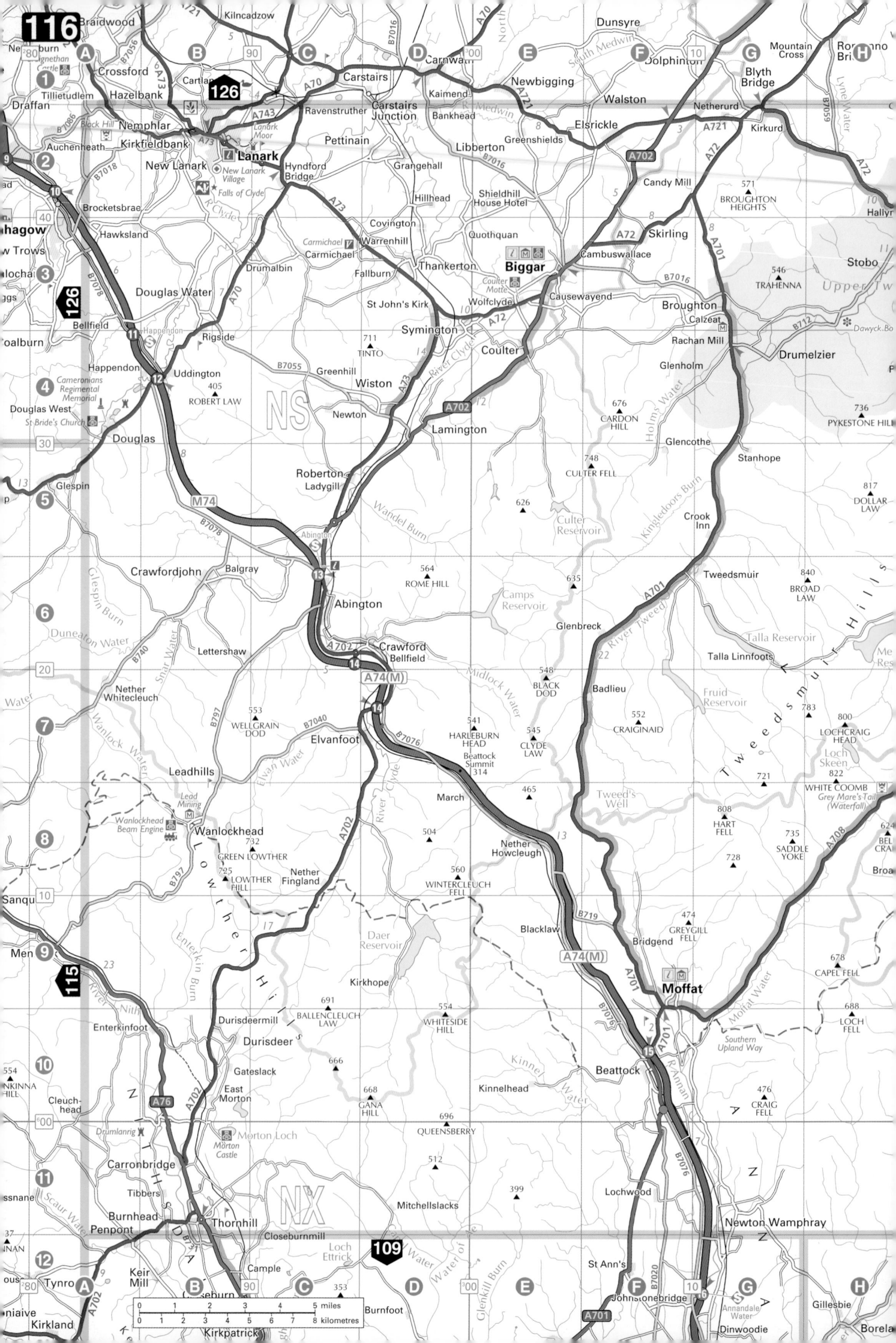

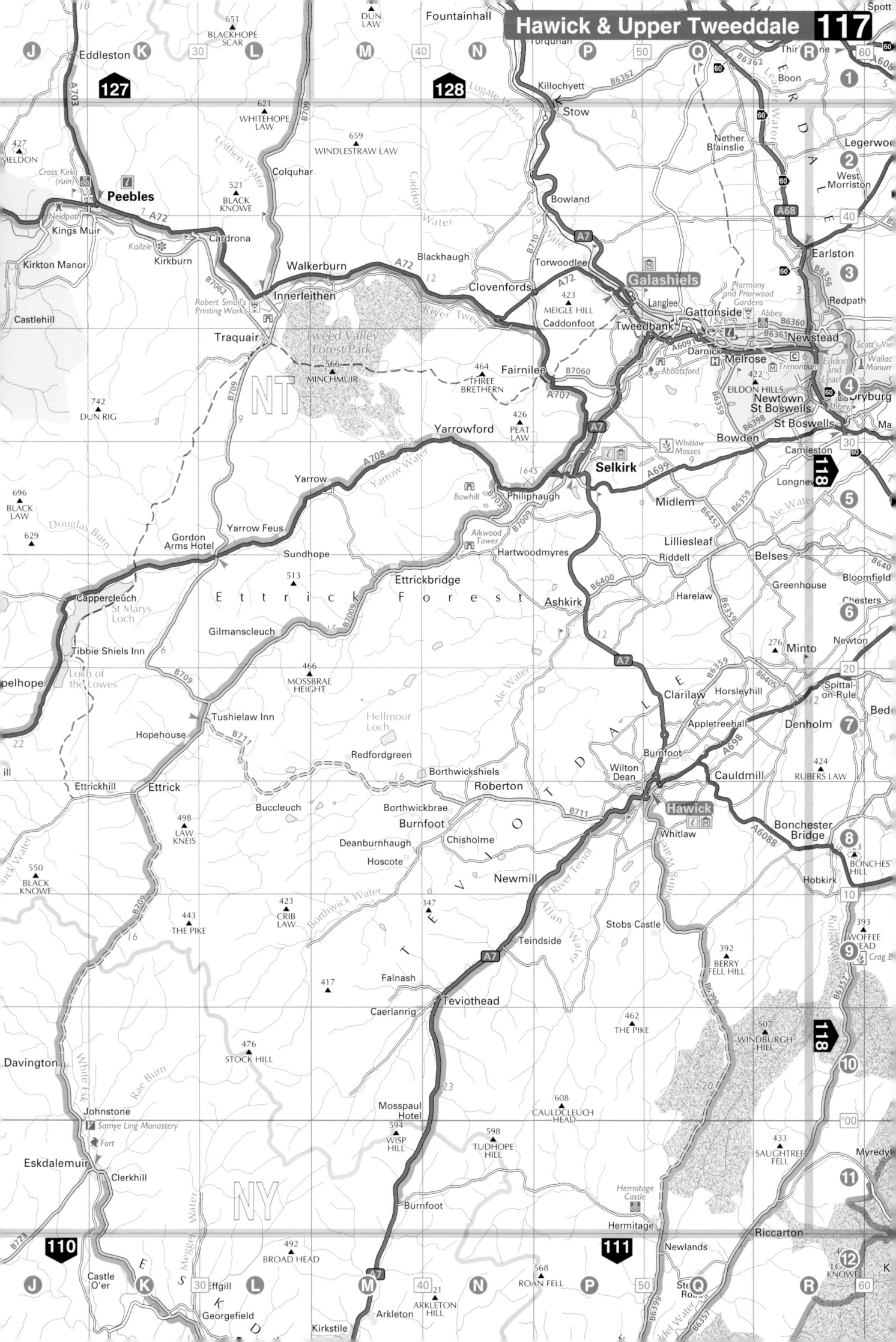

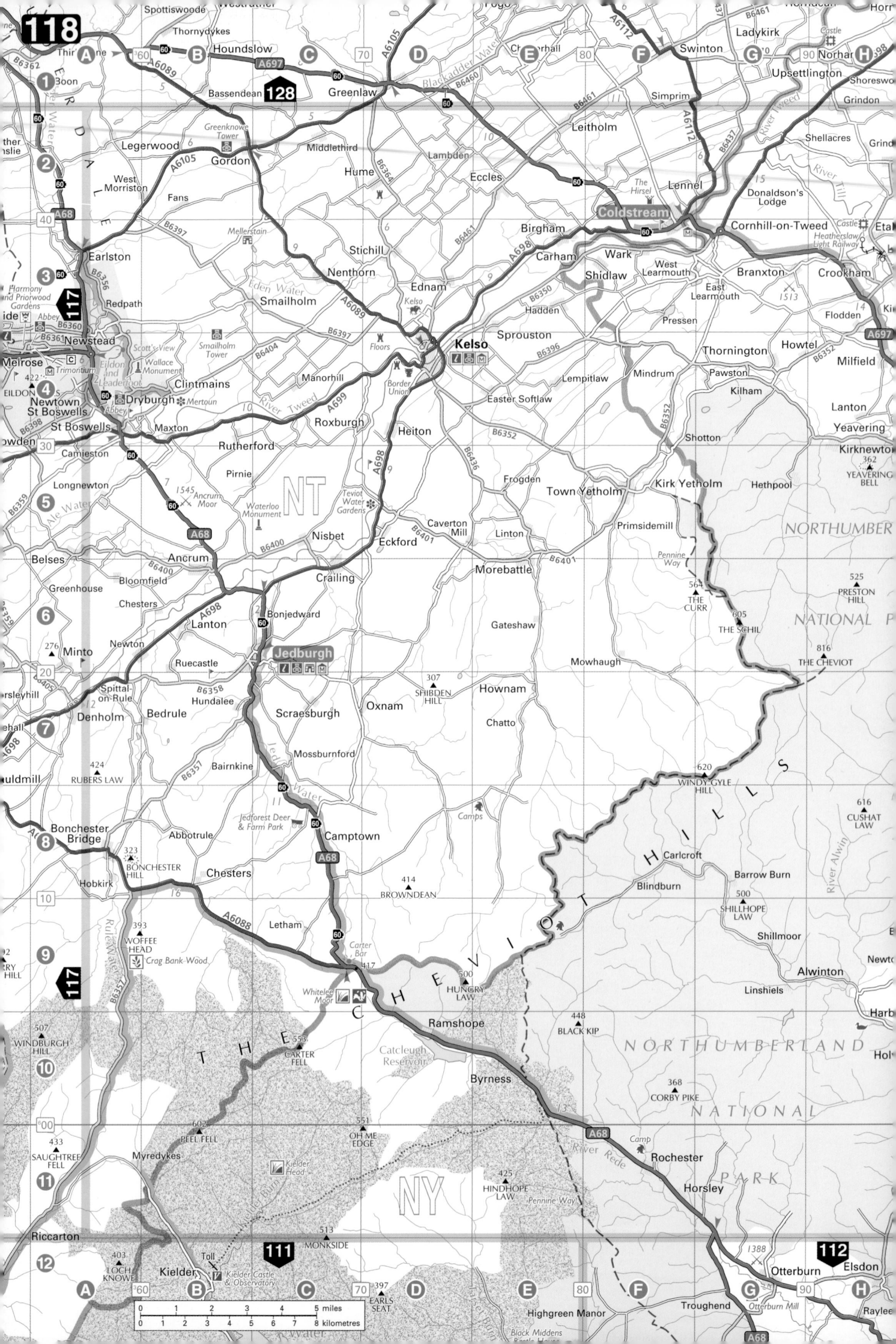

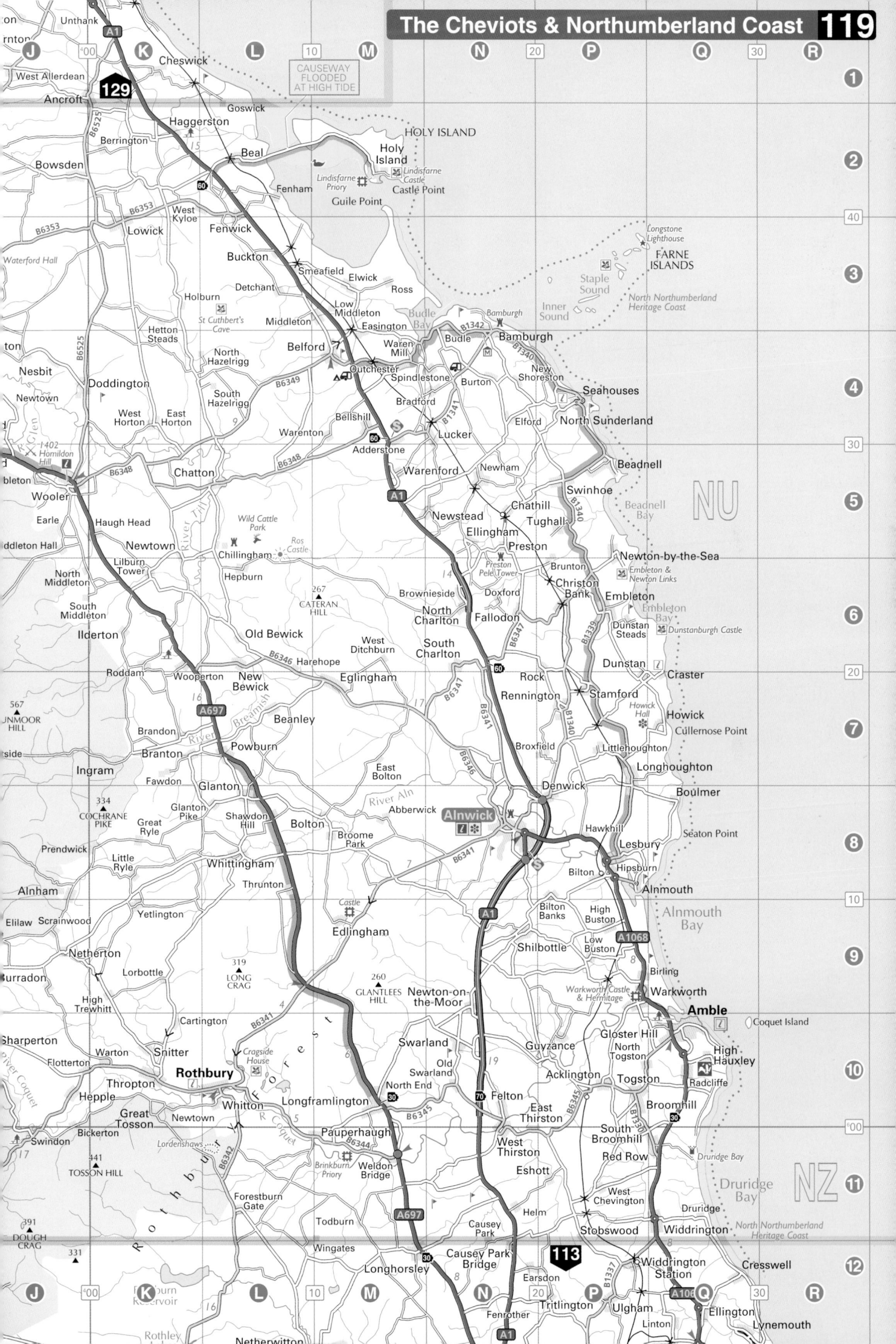

J K 80 L M 90 N P 00 Q R 10

①
90
②
③
80
④

Barns Ness
East Barns
Chapel Point
12
Skateraw
wick
Thorntonloch
60
Crowhill
Reed
Point Cove Pease
Bay Siccar
Point
Fast Castle Head
⑤
319
COCKLAW
HILL Dunglass
Collegiate
Church
60
Oldhamstocks Cockburnspath
A1107
Pease Dean
196
BROWN
RIG Coldingham
Loch
ST ABB'S HEAD
70
⑥
391
HEART
LAW Ecclaw
Southern
Upland Way 60 Grantshouse
Eye Water Butterdean
Houndwood
Coldingham
A1107 22
Coldingham
Bay
St Abbs
21
Quixwood 262
HORSELEY HILL
Heugh
Head 60
Cairncross
60 A1 B6355
Eyemouth
⑦
NU
Abbey St Bathans
Edin's
Hall Broch 14
B6438
Reston
Auchencrow
Ayton 60
Burnmouth
60
emford
325
COCKBURN
LAW
B6355
A6112
Marygold
Lintlaw
B6437
B6355
Lamberton
60
ster B6355 Preston B6355
Chirnside
70
Marshall Meadows Bay
⑧
Primrosehill B6365
Cumledge
Edrom Church
Chirnsidebridge
Foulden
North Northumberland
Heritage Coast
Edrom 15 Broadhaugh Edington Whiteadder Water Foulden
Tithe Barn 1333
A6105
Berwick-upon-Tweed
B6433 Allanton Hutton
Castle
Manderston A6105 Paxton Barracks
Duns Blackadder Paxton Town
Ramparts 70
Tweedmouth
Gavinton B6460 Whitsome Hilton B6461 ⑨
Loanend Spittal
Polwarth Nisbet
Hill Sinclair's
Hill 13 East
Ord A167 Huds
Head 50
7 Fogo A6112 6 Horndean Horncliffe Scremerston
Charterhall Murton Unthank A1
Swinton B6470 Thornton ⑩
B6460 Norham A698 Cheswick
Upsettlington Shoreswood West Allerdean CAUSEWAY
FLOODED
AT HIGH TIDE
A6105 B6461 Simprim 11 Grindon B6354 Ancroft 119 Goswick
118 60 Leitholm Felkington B6525 Berrington Haggerston ⑪
10 Lambden Shellacres Grindonrigg 60 Beal
Eccles 15 River Till Duddo Bowsden West
Kyloe Fenwick 40
Blackadder Water 60 The Hirsel Lennel River Tweed B6353 Lowick
Coldstream Donaldson's
Lodge 6 B6353
Birgham A698 60 Cornhill-on-Tweed Castle Etal West
Kyloe Buckton ⑫
Carham Wark Heatherslaw
Light Railway Heatherslaw
Corn Mill Lady Waters Hall Detchant 10
J K 80 L M 90 N P 00 Q R
Ednam 80 nidlaw West
Learmouth xton Crook Ford Holburn
Kelso East
Learmouth 90
Hadden Flodden 14
Pressen Kimmerston St Cuthbert's

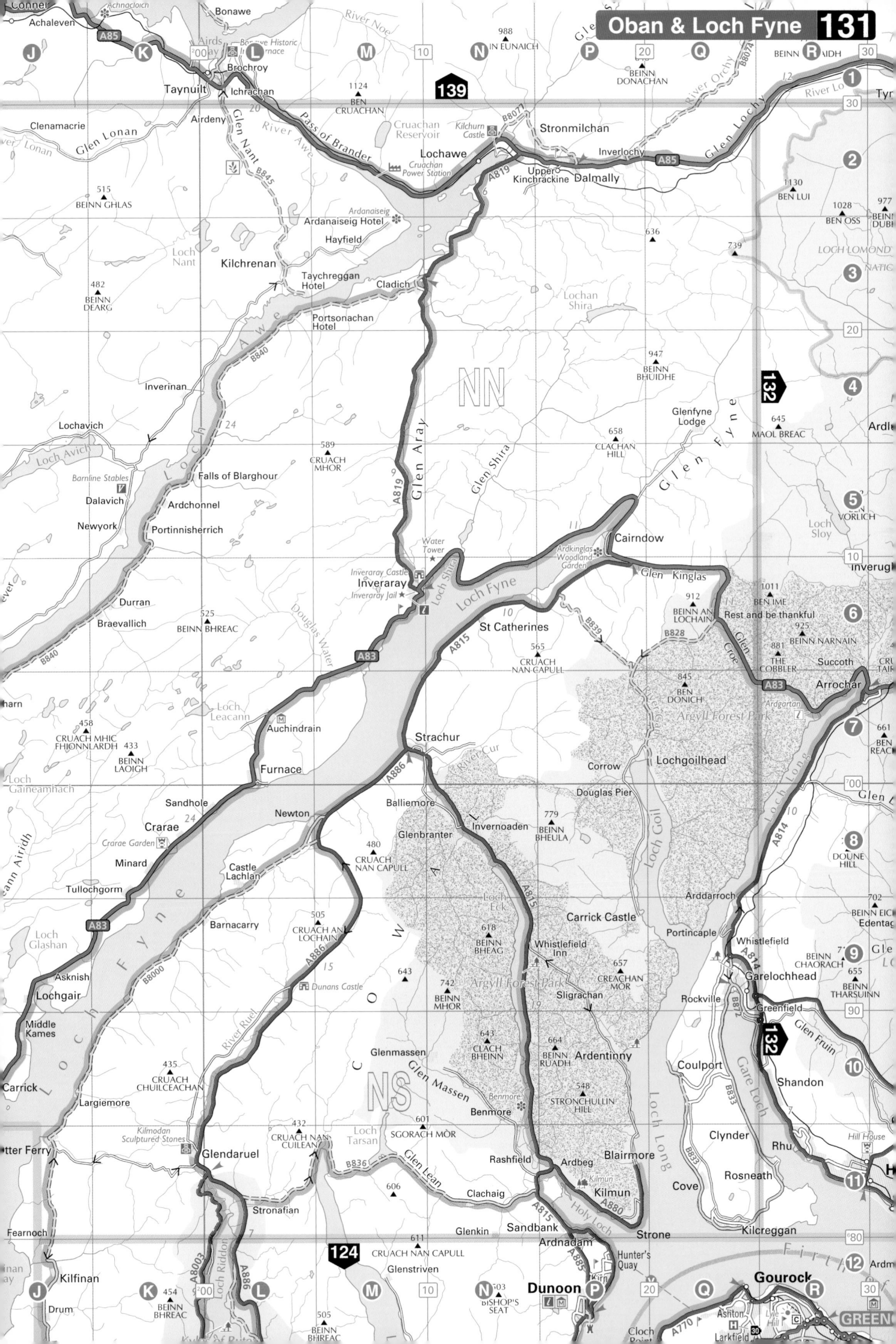

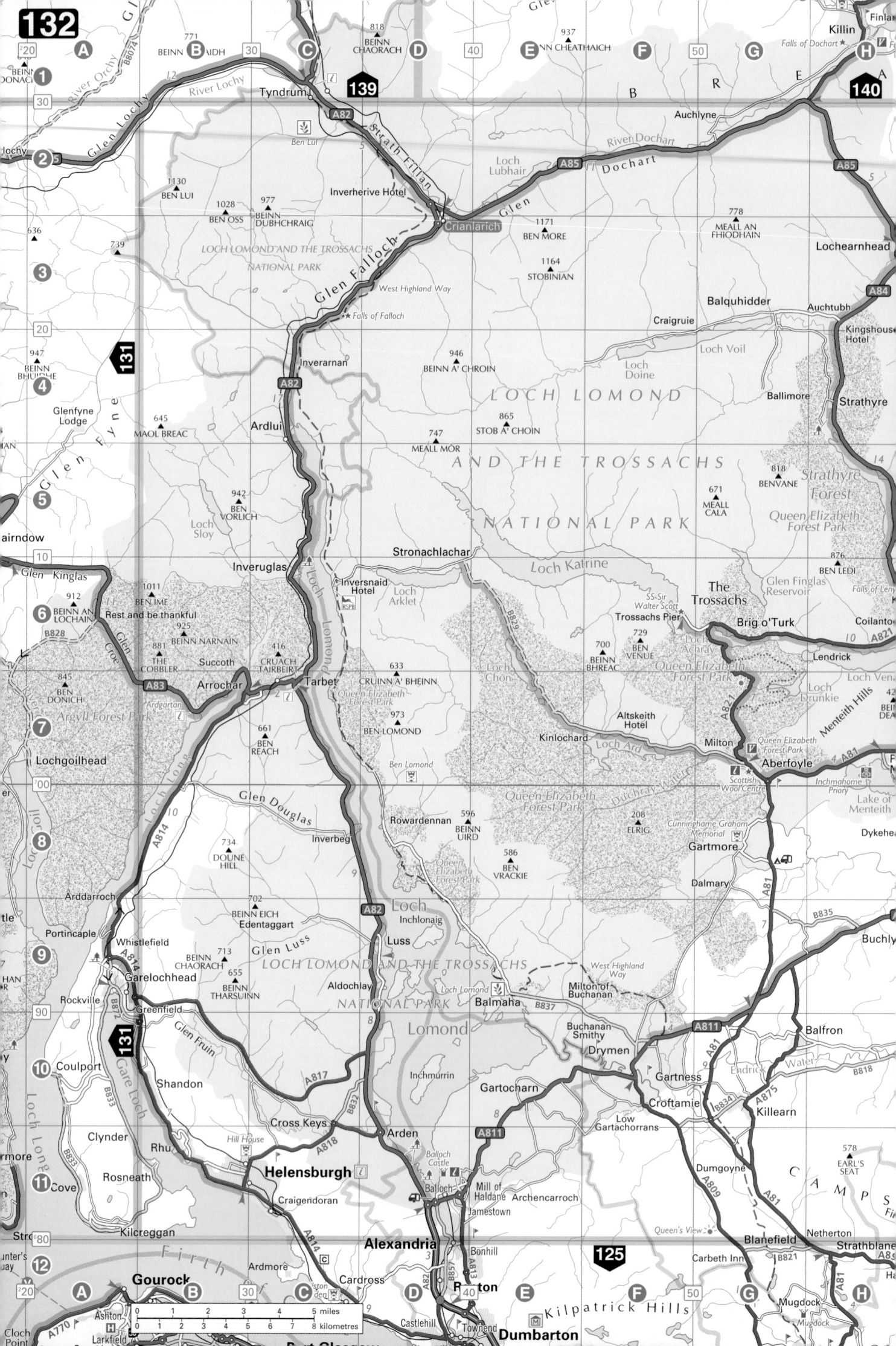

136

A B C D E F G H

1
70
2
3
60
4

NL

5
50
6

COLL

Cliad Bay
Bousd
Sorisd
Eilean Mòr
Rudha Mòr
Rudha Sgor-i
Arnabost
Grishipoll
Clabhach
Loch Cliad
B8071
B8072
Hogh Bay
Ballyhaugh
Arinagour
B8070
Totronald
Coll
Acha
Feall Bay
Arileod
RSPB
Uig
Eilean Ornsay
Calgary Point
Crossapol Bay
Rudha Fàsachd
Loch Breachacha
Gunna

Bagh a Chaisteil
(Castlebay)

(Mar-Oct)

Rudha Port Bhiosd
Clachan Mor
Balephetrish Bay
Caoles
B8069
Rudha Dubh
Loch Bhasapoll
Haugh Bay
Ballevullin
Cornoigmore
Kenovay
B8068
Ruaig
Gott Bay
Kilkenneth
B8068
Tiree
Scarinish
Moss
Heylipoll
B8065
Middleton
Crossapoll
TIREE
Barrapoll
B8065
Hynish Bay
B8067
Balemartine
Loch a Phuill
Mannel
Rinn Thorbhais
Hynish
Balephuil Bay

7
40

8

TRESHNISH ISLES
Lunga
Bac Mòr or Dutchman's
Bac Beag

9

NM

Colonsay

1
'00
2
30
3
'90
4

Eilean Dubh
Balnahard
Rudh' a' Geodha
Kiloran Bay
COLONSAY
Kiloran
Kilchattan
B8087
Scalasaig
B8086
Machrins
Colonsay
B8085
Garvard
Rudha Bàn
Oronsay
Dubh Eilean
Eilean Ghurdmail
ORONSAY

Colonsay - Oban

Colonsay - Port Askaig

NR

0 1 2 3 miles
0 1 2 3 4 5 kilometres

a b c d
'40

IONA
Iona Abbey & Nunnery
Baile Mòr
MacLean's Cross
Sound of C

Soa Island
Erraid

10
30
11
'90
12
'20

A B C D E F G H

0 1 2 3 4 5 miles
0 1 2 3 4 5 6 7 8 kilometres

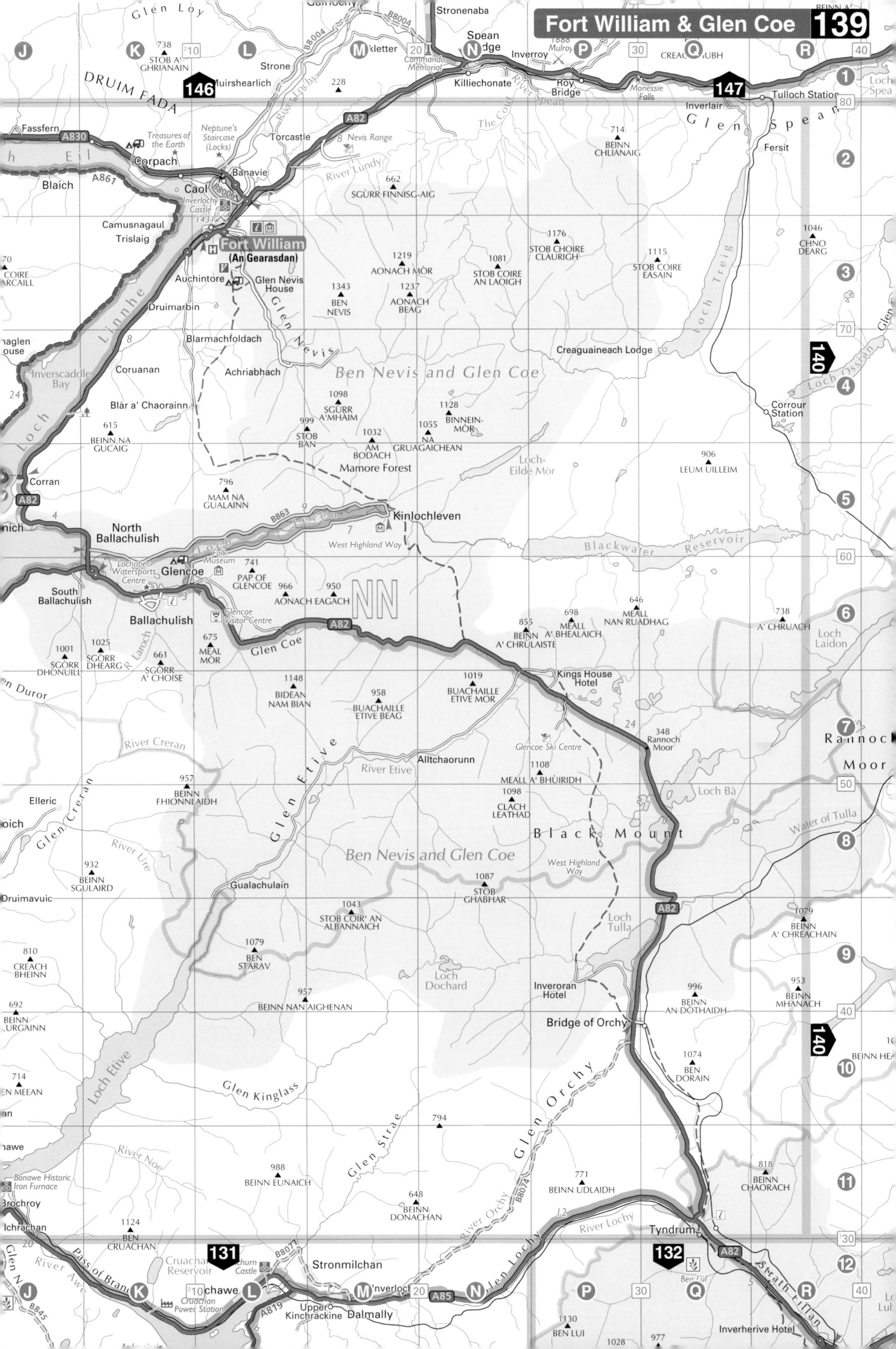

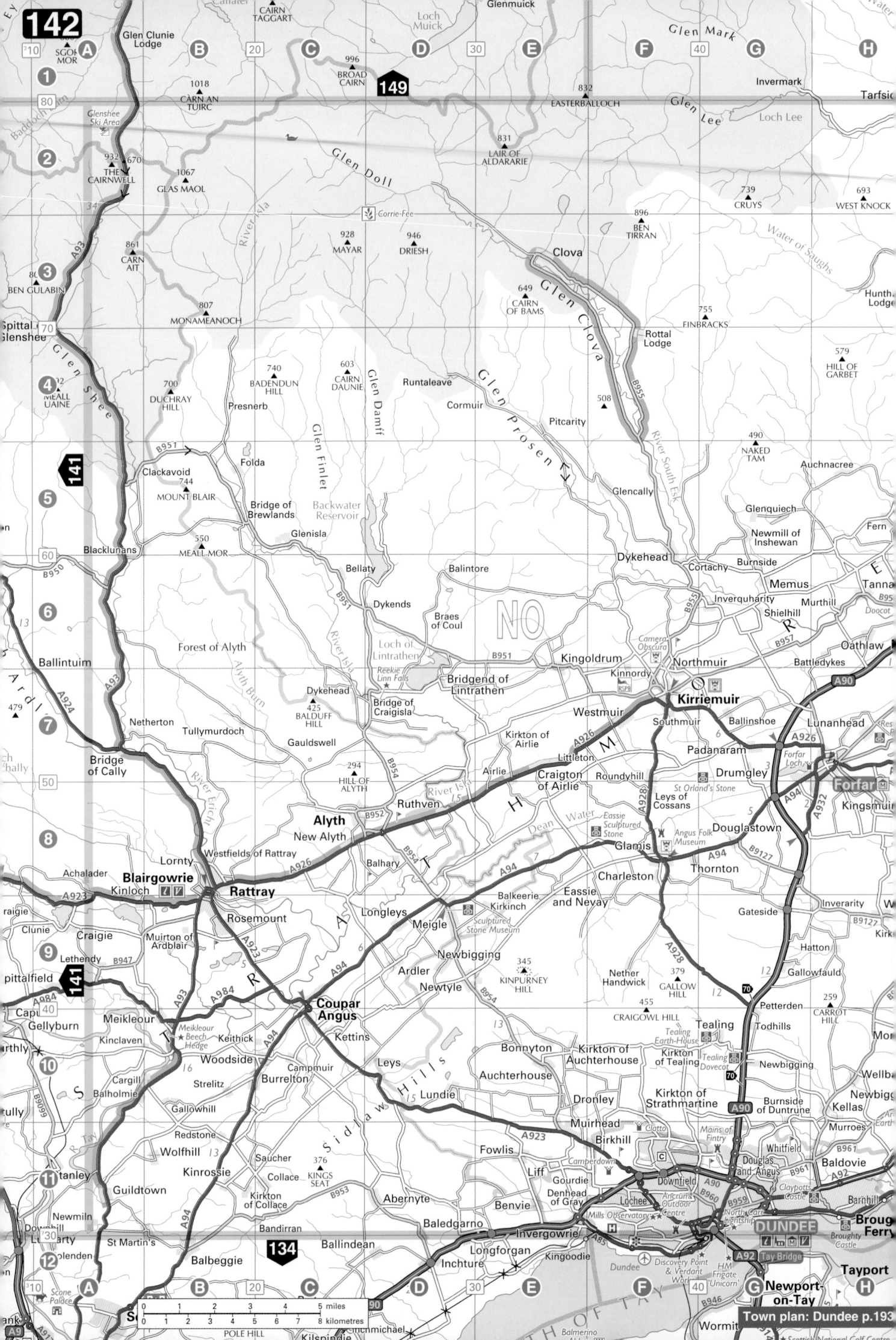

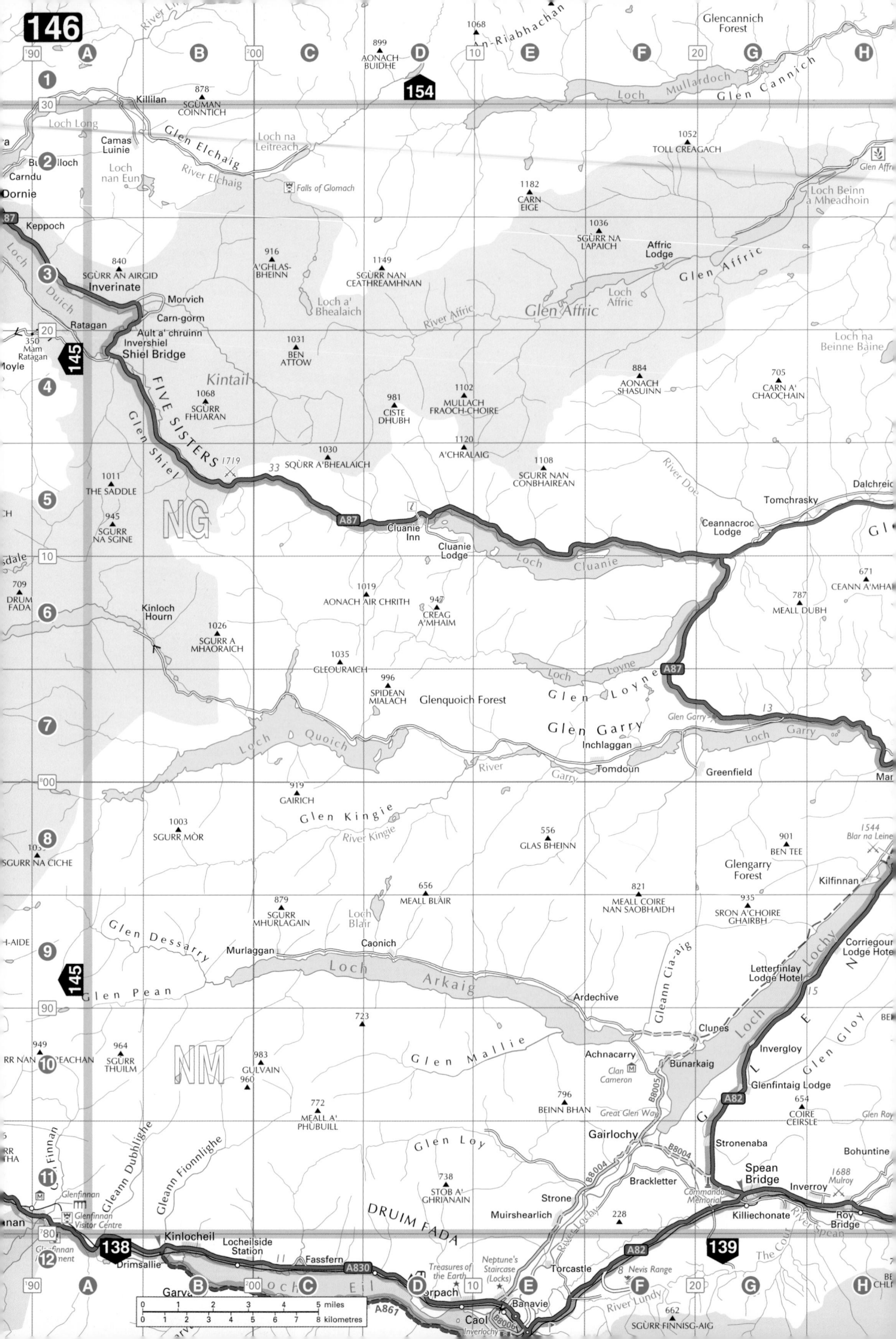

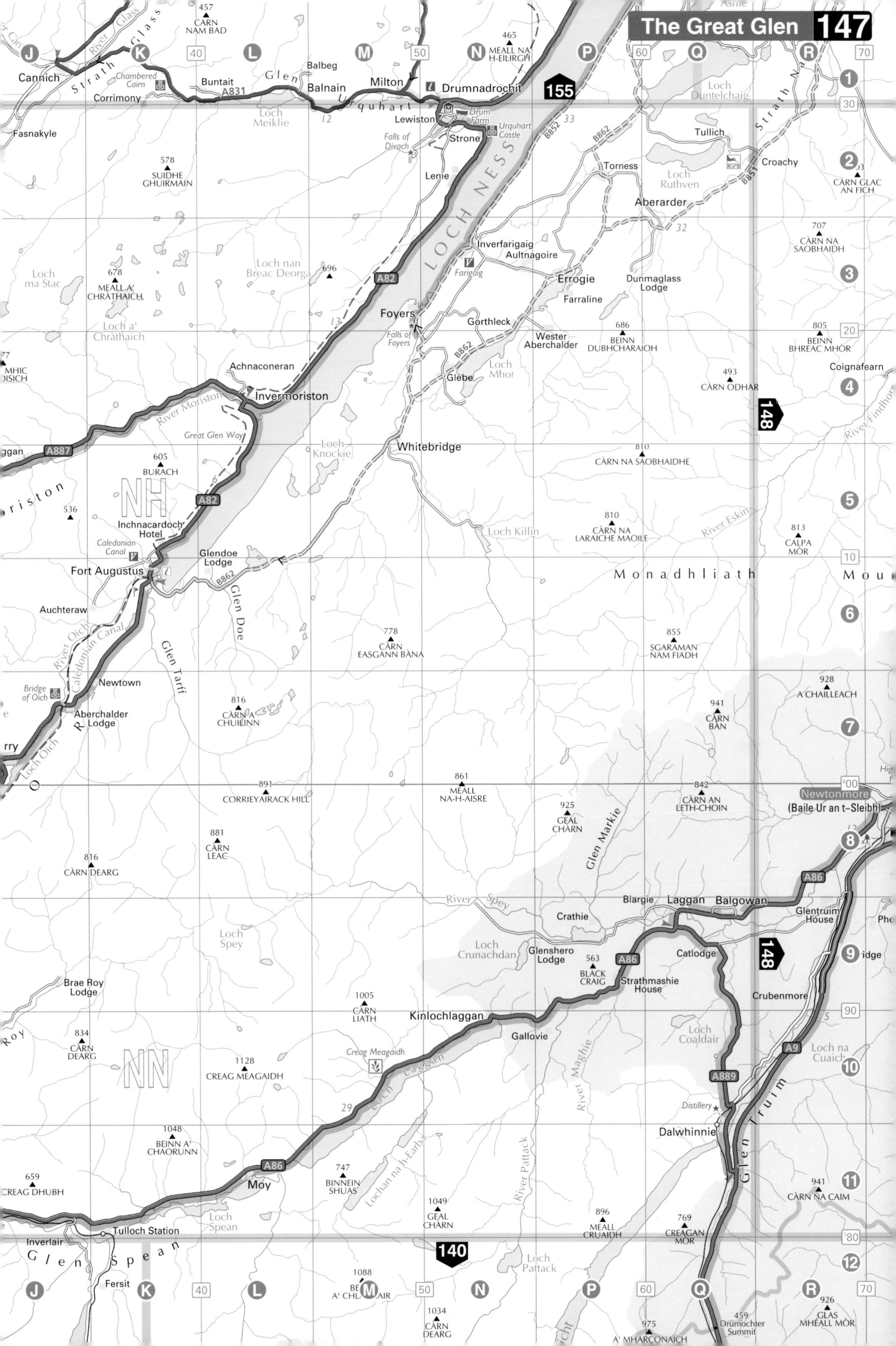

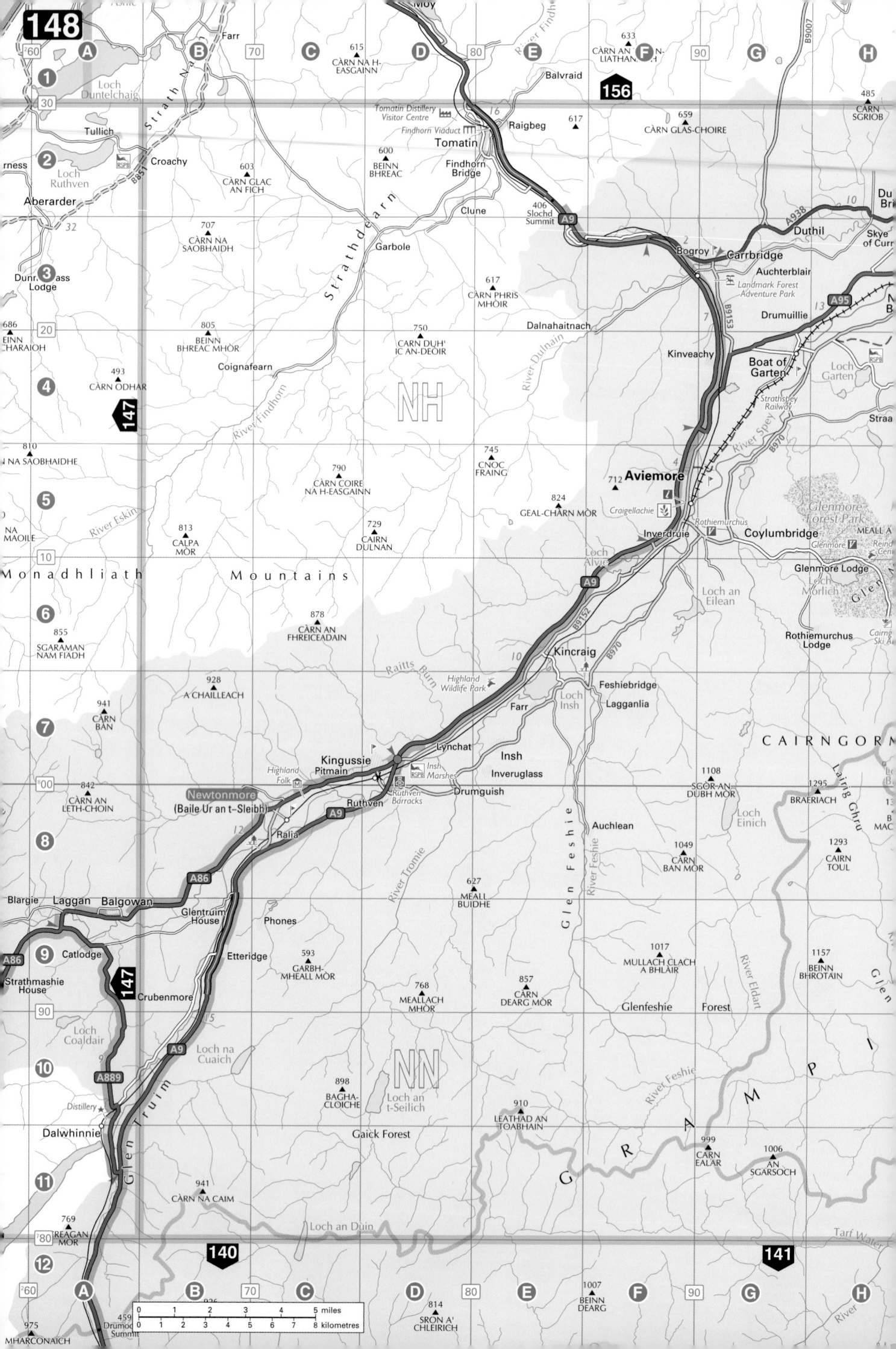

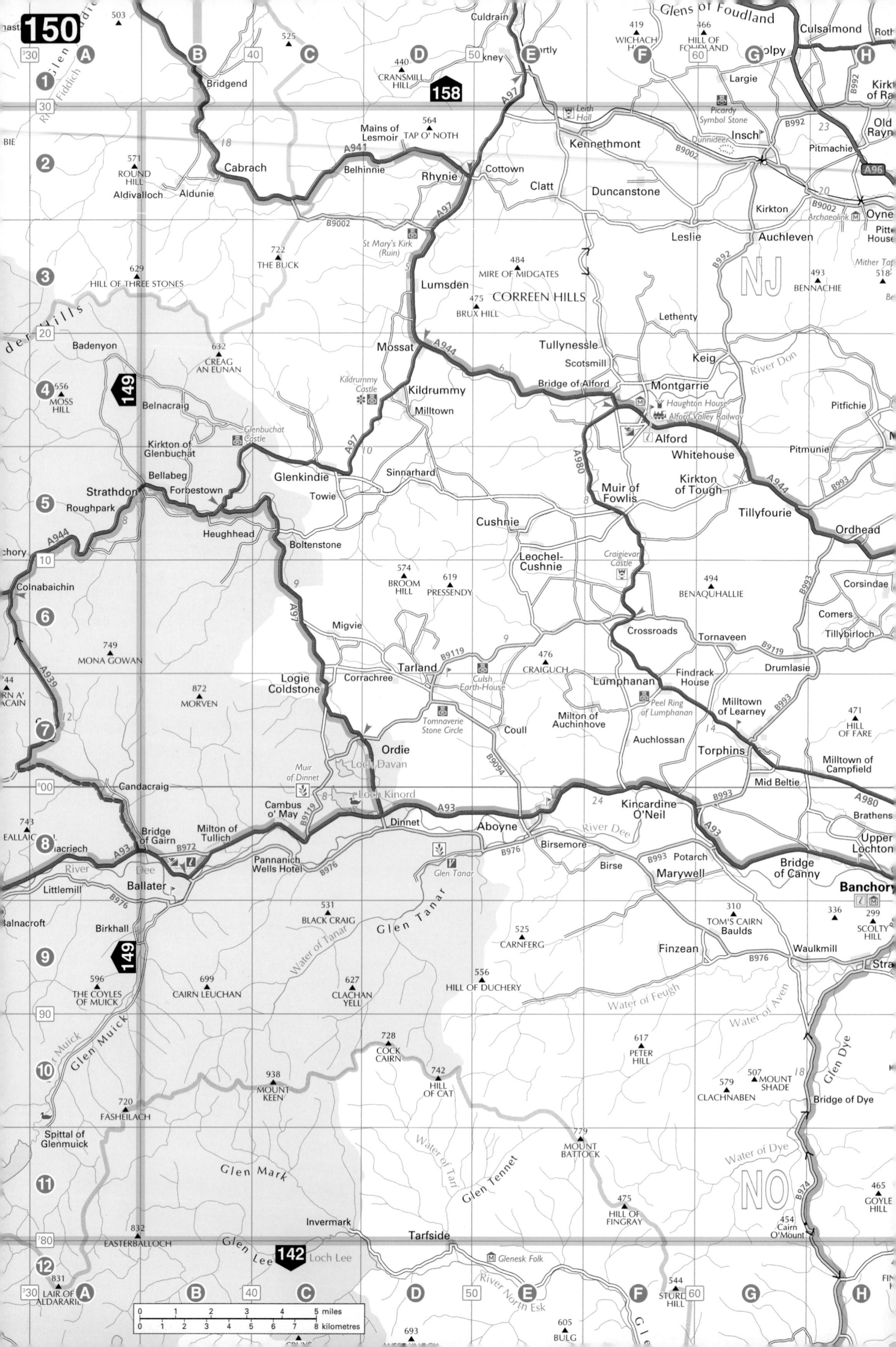

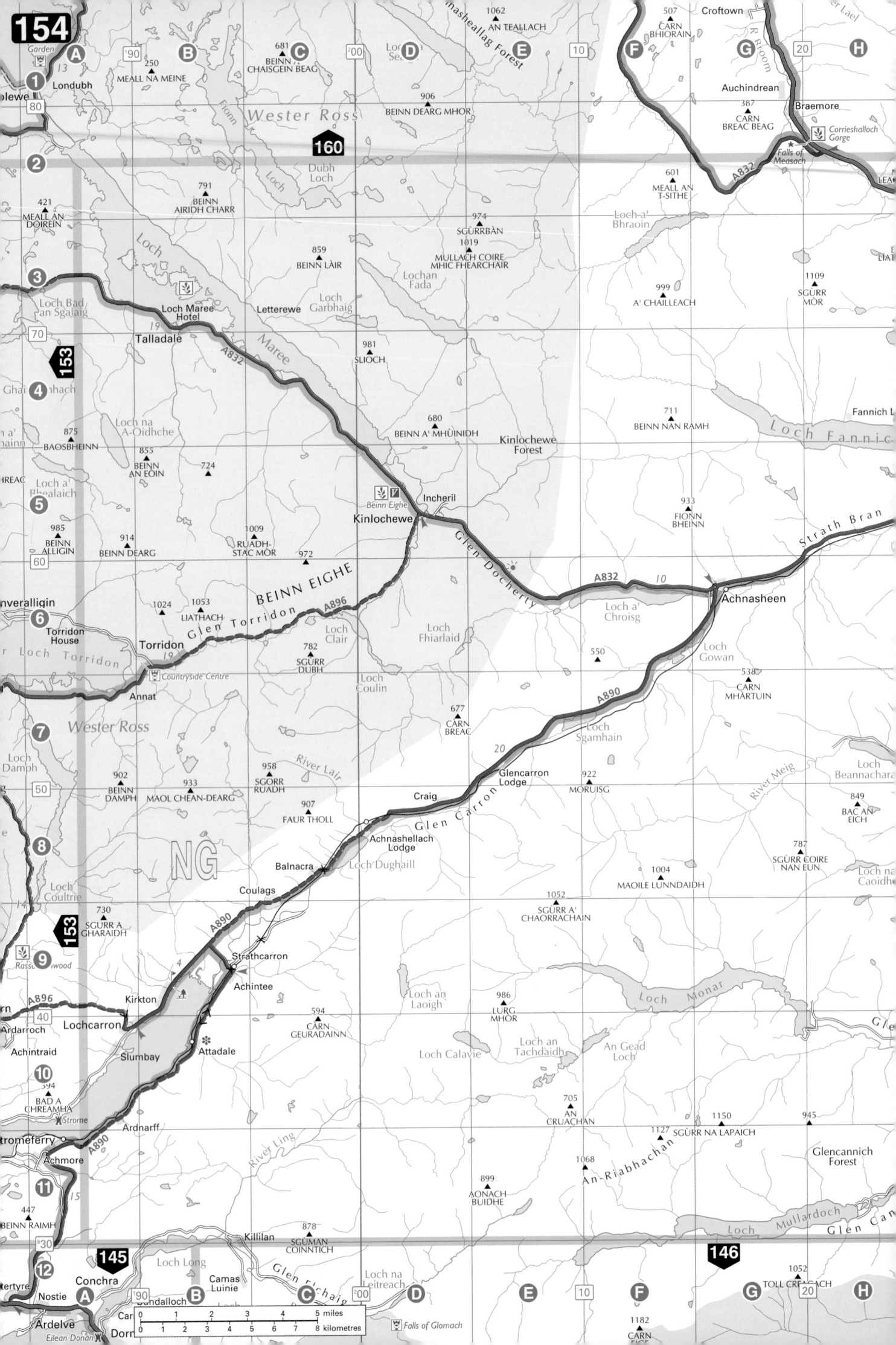

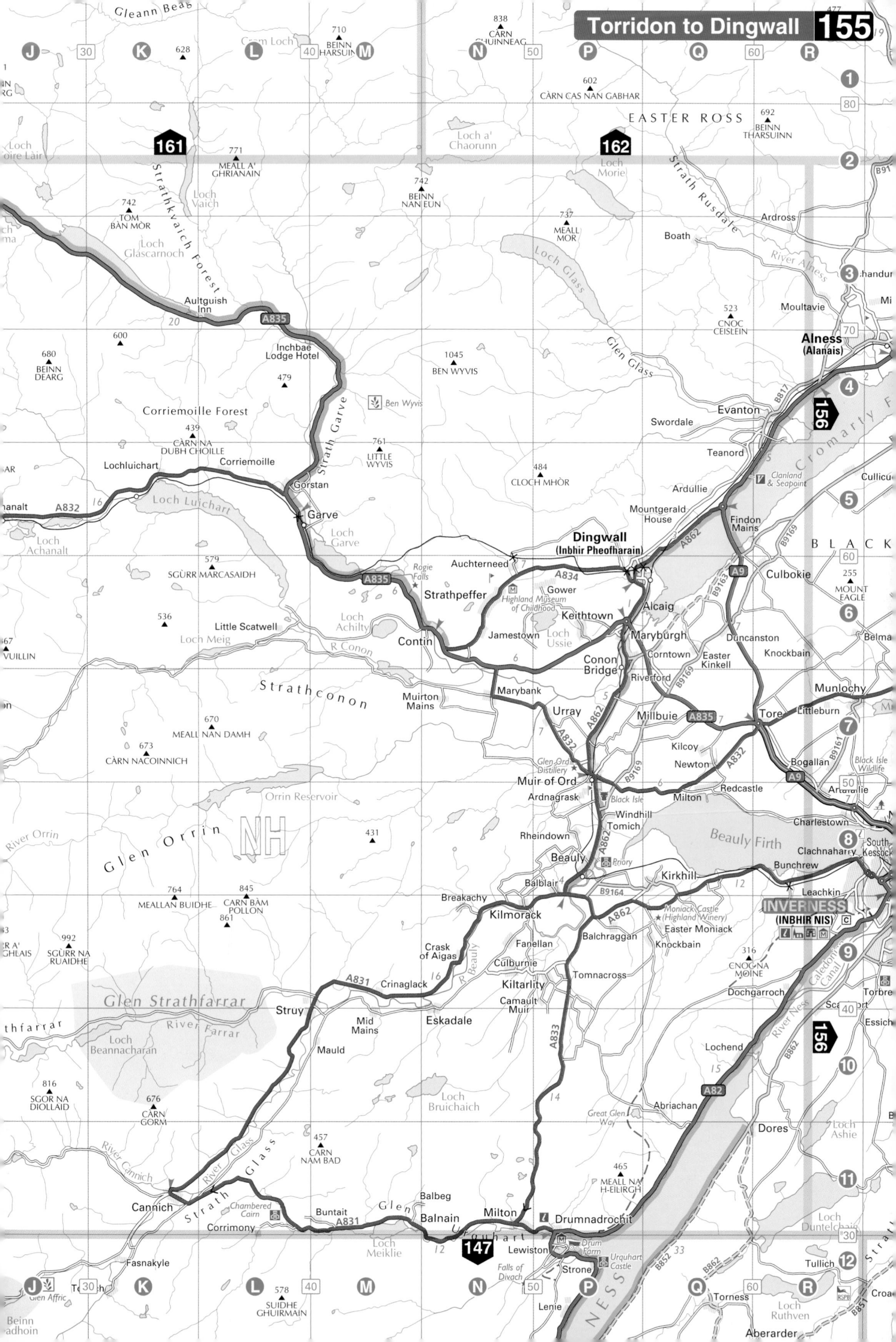

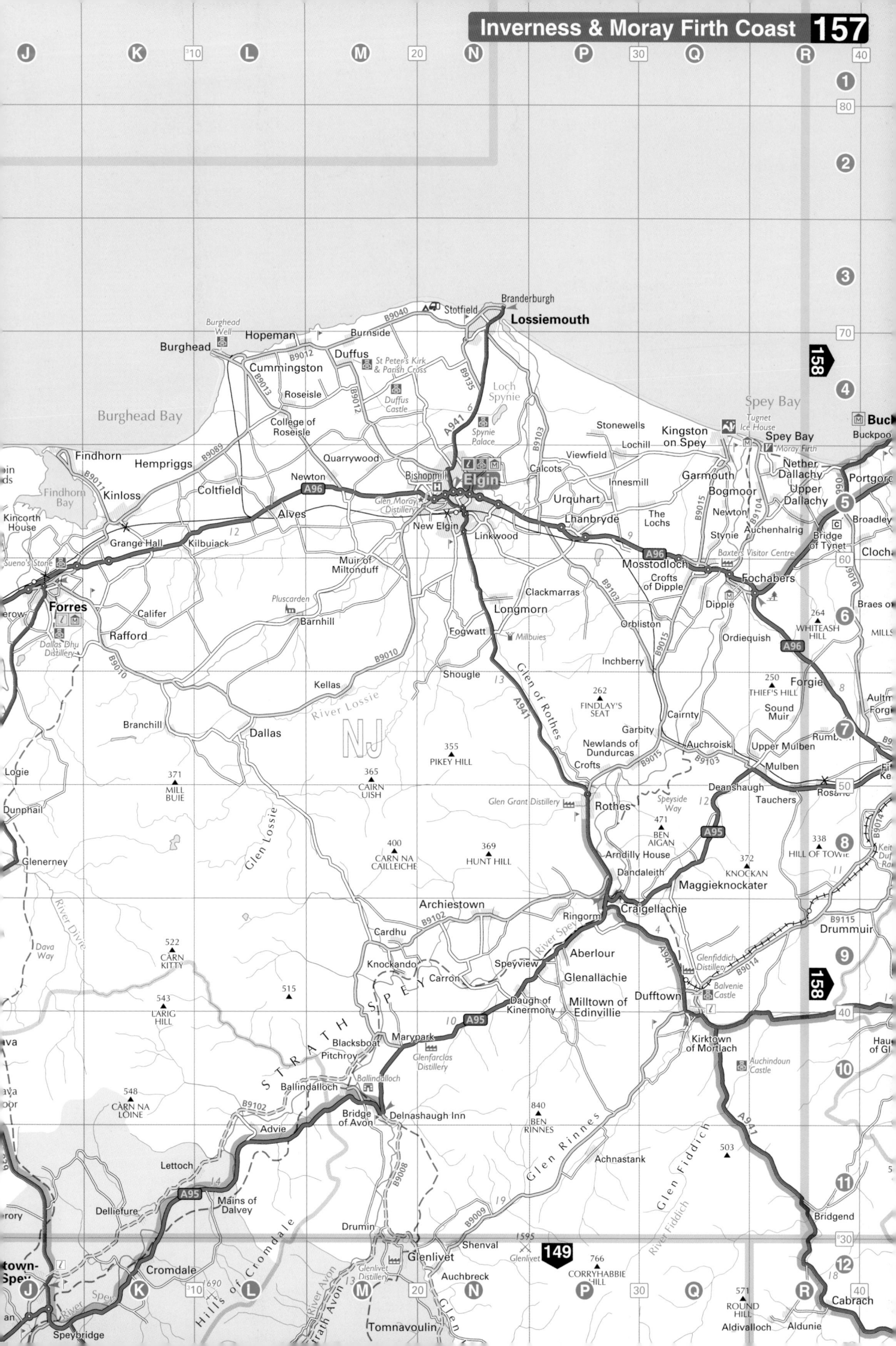

J   K   L   M   N   P   Q   R

1
80
2
3
70
158
4

Branderburgh
B9040   Stotfield
Lossiemouth
Burghead
Well   Hopeman   Burnside
Burghead   Duffus
Cummingston   B9012
St Peter's Kirk
& Parish Cross
Roseisle   Duffus
B9013   Castle   Loch
Spynie
B9135
Burghead Bay   College of
Roseisle   Spynie
Palace   B9103   Stonewells
Quarrywood   Viewfield   Lochill
Findhorn   Hempriggs   B9089   Newton   Bishopmill   Calcots   Innesmill   The
Lochs
Kinloss   Coltfield   A96   H   **Elgin**   Urquhart   Garmouth   Bogmoor
Findhorn
Bay   Alves   Glen Moray   New Elgin   Lhanbryde   B9015   Newton   Auchenhalrig
Kincorth   Distillery   Linkwood   Stynie
House   Grange Hall   Kilbuiack   12   Clackmarras   Baxters Visitor Centre
Sueno's   Muir of   Longmorn   Crofts
Stone   Miltonduff   Fogwatt   of Dipple   Mosstodloch
Forres   Califer   Pluscarden   Millbuies   Orbliston   Dipple
Rafford   Barnhill   B9010   Inchberry   Ordiequish
Dallas Dhu   Kellas   Shougle   13   262   B9015
Distillery   FINDLAY'S   Newlands of
Branchill   B9010   SEAT   Dundurcas   Garbity   Cairnty   Upper Mulben
Dallas   355   Crofts   Auchroisk
Logie   371   PIKEY HILL   Mulben
MILL   365   Glen Grant Distillery   Deanshaugh
Dunphail   BUIE   CAIRN   Rothes   Speyside   Tauchers
UISH   Way   12
Glenerney   400   369   471
CARN NA   HUNT HILL   BEN   Arndilly House   338
CAILLEICHE   AIGAN   HILL OF TOWIE
Dandaleith   372
522   515   KNOCKAN
CARN   Archiestown   Maggieknockater
KITTY   B9102   Ringorm   Craigellachie
Cardhu   Glenfiddich
Knockando   Carron   Speyview   Aberlour   Distillery
543   Glenallachie   A941   Balvenie
LARIG   Glasgow   Milltown of   Castle
HILL   Daugh of   Edinvillie   **Dufftown**
Blacksboat   Kinermony   10   A95
548   Pitchroy   Marypark   Kirkton
CARN NA   Ballindalloch   Glenfarclas   of Mortlach   Auchindoun
LOINE   B9102   Distillery   Castle
Advie   Ballindalloch
Bridge   Delnashaugh Inn
Lettoch   of Avon   840
A95   14   B9008   BEN   Achnastank
Delliefure   Mains of   RINNES   503
Dalvey   B9009
Drumin   1595   149
Glenlivet
Cromdale   690   Shenval   766
Speyside   Distillery   Auchbreck   CORRYHABBIE
HILL
Tomnavoulin   571
ROUND   Cabrach
HILL   Aldivalloch   Aldunie

Spey Bay
Tugnet
Ice House
Kingston   Spey Bay
on Spey
Moray Firth   Nether
Dallachy
Buckpool   **Buck**
Portgord
Upper
Dallachy   **5**
Bridge   60   Broadley
of Tynet   C   Cloch
A96
264   Braes o
WHITEASH   MILLS
HILL   **6**
250   Forgie
THIEF'S HILL   8
Sound   7
Muir   RumbL
B9103
50   Rosarie
A95   Fi
Ke
8
11
B9115
Drummuir   **9**
158
40
B9014   Hau
of Gl
10

J   K   L   M   N   P   Q   R

10   20   30   40

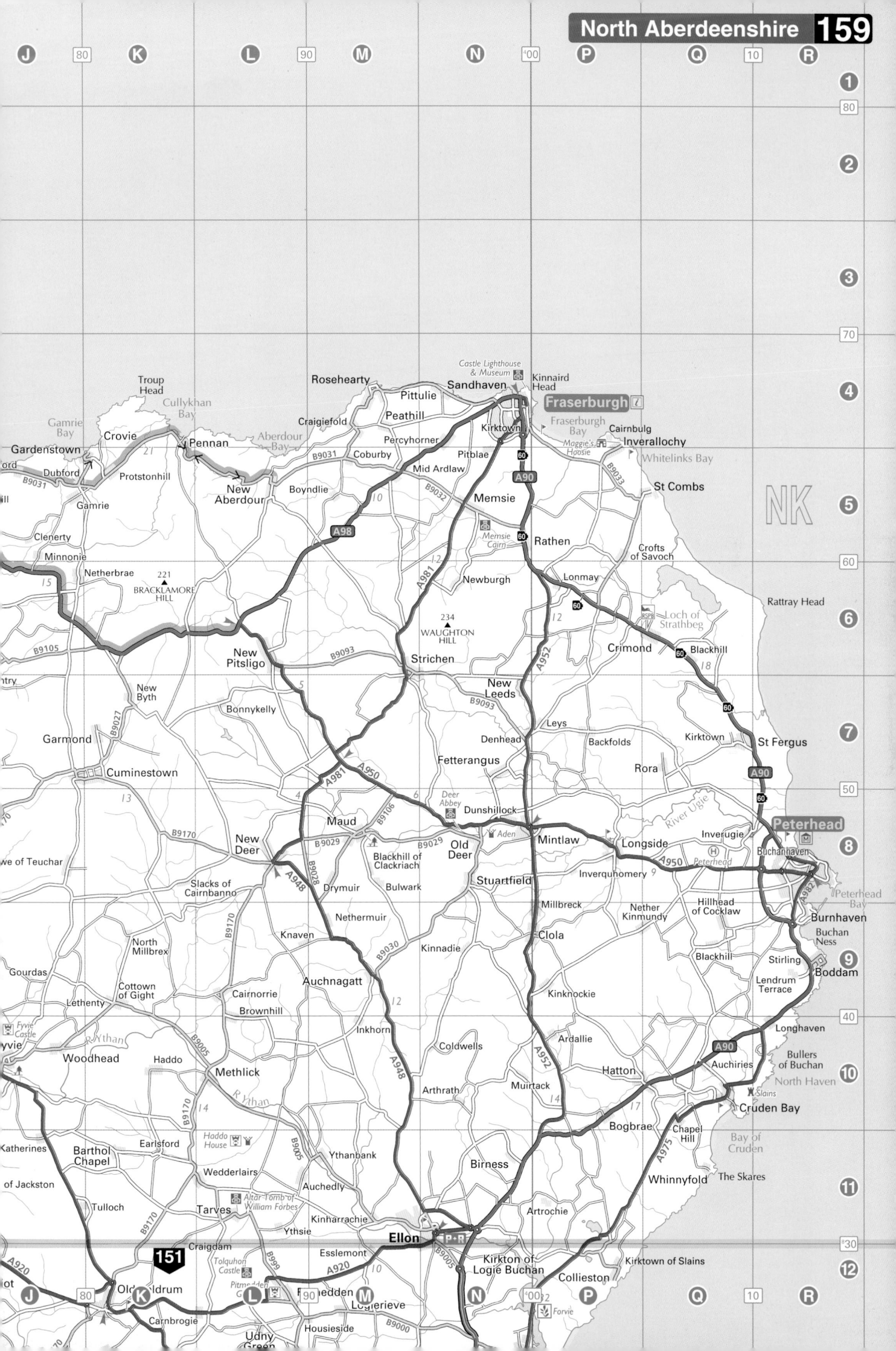

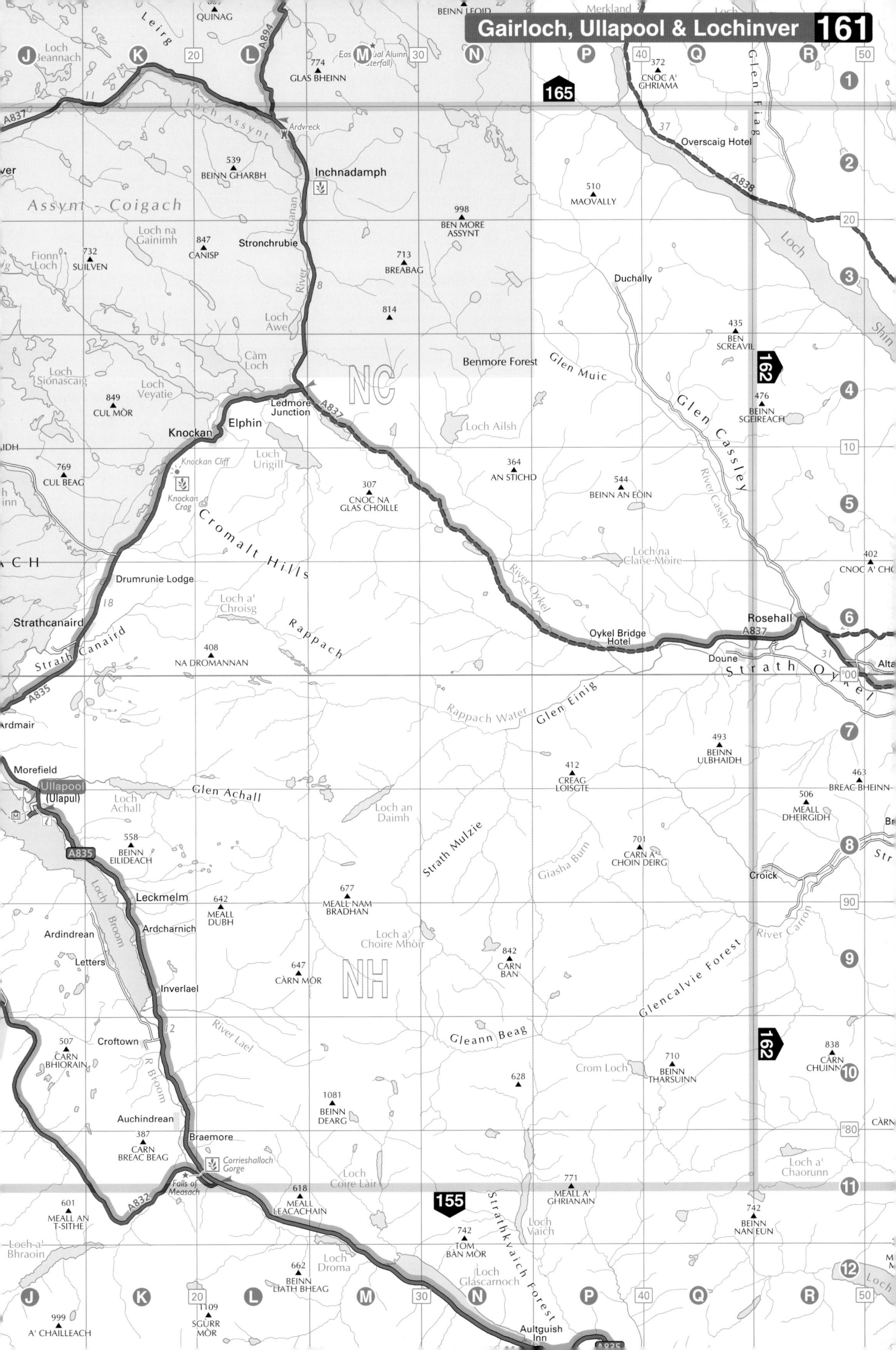

QUINAG

BEINN LEOID

Merkland

J Loch Beannach

K Leirg

L A894

M 774 GLAS BHEINN
Eas **M** Ual Aluinn (Waterfall) 30

N

P

Q 372 CNOC A' GHRIAMA

R 50

1

165

40

162

Loch Assynt

Ardvreck

Inchnadamph

539 BEINN GHARBH

Overscaig Hotel

A838

2

Assynt - Coigach

River Loanan

Stronchrubie

998 BEN MORE ASSYNT

510 MAOVALLY

Loch Shin

20

3

Fionn Loch

732 SUILVEN

847 CANISP

Loch na Gainimh

713 BREABAG

Duchally

Ardvreck

4

814

435 BEN SCREAVIL

476 BEINN SGEIREACH

10

849 CUL MÒR

Loch Veyatie

Càm Loch

Ledmore Junction

A837

Benmore Forest

Glen Muic

Glen Cassley

Loch Sionascaig

NC

Knockan

Elphin

Loch Urigill

307 CNOC NA GLAS CHOILLE

Loch Ailsh

364 AN STICHD

544 BEINN AN EÒIN

River Cassley

5

769 CUL BEAG

Knockan Cliff

Knockan Crag

Loch na Claise-Mòire

402 CNOC A' CHO

IDH

Cromalt Hills

River Oykel

6

Drumrunie Lodge

Rappach

Oykel Bridge Hotel

Rosehall A837

Strathcanaird

Strath Canaird

408 NA DROMANNAN

Doune Strath Oykel

Alt 00

18

A835

Loch a' Chroisg

Rappach Water

Glen Einig

493 BEINN ULBHAIDH

7

Ardmair

Morefield

Glen Achall

Loch Achall

Loch an Daimh

Strath Mulzie

412 CREAG LOISGTE

463 BREAC-BHEINN

506 MEALL DHEIRGIDH

Ullapool (Ulapul)

M Z

558 BEINN EILIDEACH

Giasha Burn

701 CARN A' CHOIN DEIRG

Croick

8

90

A835

Leckmelm

642 MEALL DUBH

677 MEALL NAM BRADHAN

River Carron

Br

Ardindrean

Loch Broom

Ardcharnich

Loch a' Choire Mhòir

842 CARN BAN

Glencalvie Forest

9

Letters

Inverlael

647 CÀRN MÒR

NH

507 CARN BHIORAIN

Croftown

R Broom

River Lael

Gleann Beag

628

710 BEINN THARSUINN

Crom Loch

162

838 CÀRN CHUINN

10

Auchindrean

387 CARN BREAC BEAG

Braemore

1081 BEINN DEARG

771 MEALL A' GHRIANAIN

Loch a' Chaorunn

11

Corrieshalloch Gorge

Falls of Measach

601 MEALL AN T-SITHE

A832

618 MEALL LEACACHAIN

Loch Coire Làir

155

Strathvaich Forest

742 BEINN NAN EUN

Loch-a' Bhraoin

662 BEINN LIATH BHEAG

Loch Droma

742 TOM BÀN MÒR

Loch Vaich

Loch Glascarnoch

12

Loch

J

K 20

L

M 30

N

P 40

Q

R 50

999 A' CHAILLEACH

1109 SGÙRR MÒR

Aultguish Inn

A835

CÀRN

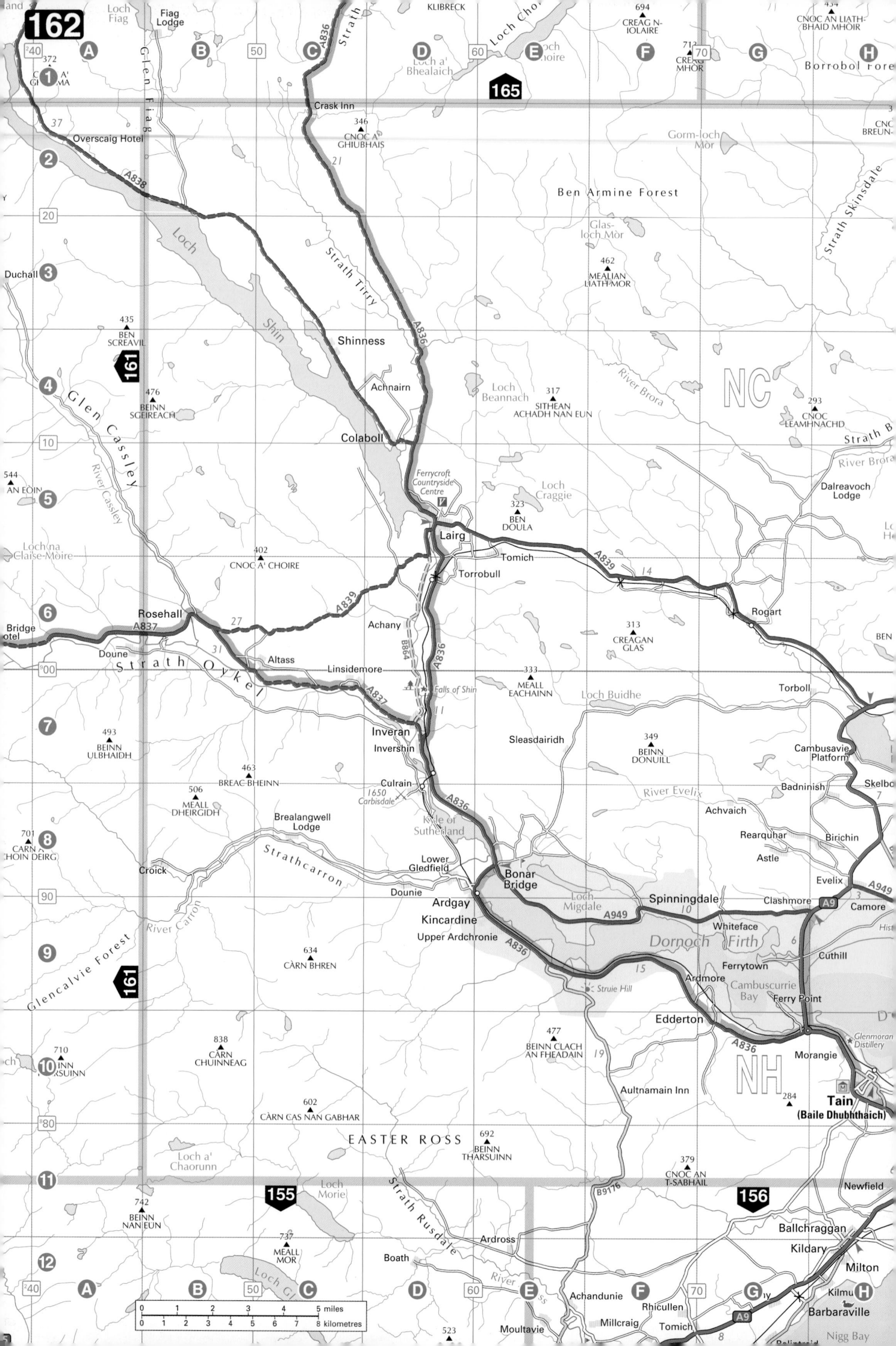

J
K
90
L
Suisgil
M
CNOC AN
EIREANNAICH
'00
N
705
MORVEN
P
626
SCARABEN
10
Q
R
20

▲202
CNOC DAIL-
CHAIRN
Strath Free
Loch
Ascaig
▲518
36

Langwell Forest
167
Borgue

1

Learable Hill
Cairns, Stone Row
& Stone Circles
▲388
CREAG NAM FIADH

Kildonan Lodge
▲554
CREAG
SCALABSDALE
Newport
Langwell
House
Berriedale

2

Strath of Kildonan
Kildonan
416
BEINN
DUBHAIN
A897
River Helmsdale
Torrish
▲401
CNOC NA
MAOILE
A9
CREAG
THORARAIDH
404
Badbea
Historic Village
20

20

▲337
NOC NA H-
NSE MOIRE

▲421
CNOC NAN CRÙBAG MÒR
624
BEINN
DHORAIN
591
BEINN NA
MÈILICH
West
Helmsdale
Gartymore
Portgower
Timespan
Navidale House Hotel
East Helmsdale
Helmsdale
Ord of Caithness

3

Glen Loth
Lothmore
Lothbeg
ND

4

acoil
odge
Loch
Brora
▲539
COL-
BHEINN
21

10

5

Dalchalm
Brora
▲378
CAGAR
FEOSAIG
Doll
Backies
A9
Carn Liath

6

▲383
HRAGGIE
Rhives
Dunrobin Castle
Golspie

'00

7

reet
rpenny
Embo
bo Street

8

oyal Dornoch
rnoch
90

Tarbat Ness

9

Innis Mhor
Brucefield
Wilkhaven
Firth

Portmahomack
Inver
Rockfield
B9165
NJ

10

Arboll
Toulvaddie
Lochslin
'80

Loch
Eye
Rhynie
Hill of
Fearn
Balmuchy
Hilton of Cadboll
Chapel (ruin)

11

Fearn
Tullich
B9166
Arabella
Hilton
Balintore
Shandwick
Ankerville
Shandwick Bay
Pitca.
J
K
90
L
M
'00
N
P
10
Q
R
20
igg
Burghead
B9040
A9

12

J 40 K L 50 M N 60 P Q 70 R

1

2

70

166

3 Ardmore Poin
Kirtomy Point
Farr Point
Kirtom

Faraid
Head

Balnakeil
Bay

Balnakeil ℹ
Durness
Sangomore
Smoo
Keoldale
Sangobeg

Sango
Bay
Smoo Cave

Eilean Hoan

Whiten
Head

Eilean
Nan Ròn

Neave Island

Torrisdale Farr
Bay Bay
Skerray
Achtoty
Torrisdale
Scullomie
Coldbackie

Farr
Bettyhill
Invernaver Achina Swordly
M 60

4

408 ▲
BEN HUTIG

Strathan

Rabbit
Islands

Talmine

Melness
Midtown

Tongue
Bay
Kyle of Tongue

423 ▲
MEALL
MEADHONACH

Loch
Meadaidh

Loch Eriboll

A838

A838

Borgie
13
River Borgie
A836
Skelpick

5

Strath Naver
12

489 ▲
MEALL
NA CRÀ

Laid

230 ▲
BEN
ARNABOLL

Loch Hope

262 ▲
DRUIM
NAN CLIAR

310 ▲
MEALL LEATHAD
NA CRAOIBHE

Tongue

Skelpick Burn

73
INN
NNAIDH

Strath Beag

A838
31

Kinloch

Kyle of Tongue

318 ▲
CNOC
CRAGGIE

Loch
Craggie

6
50

520 ▲
AN LEAN-CHÀRN

Loch na
Seilg

598 ▲
MEALLAN
LIATH

17

527 ▲
BEINN
STUMANADH

213 ▲
CNOC
MALPELLY

213

B871

927 ▲
BEN
HOPE

763 ▲
BEN
LOYAL

A836

Loch
Loyal

NC

7 Loch S
33
MEALL
NA CU

River Hope

Loch an
Deerie

Loyal Lodge

River Naver

Strath More

463 ▲
FEINNE-BHEINN MHÒR

557 ▲
CNOC NAN
CUILEAN

Loch
Syre

Syre

729
SÀBHAL BEAG

Dun Dornaigil
Broch

656 ▲
CNOC AN
DÀIMH MÒR

294 ▲
POLE
HILL

8

Glen Golly

Loch Meadie

259 ▲
BEINN
ROSAIL

B871
40
MF

796 ▲
CÀRN
DEARG

757 ▲
CARN AN
TIONAIL

12
B873

River Mallart

9

Loch Còire na
Saidhe Duibhe

230 ▲
MEALL A'
BHROLLAICH

Strath Naver

270 ▲
BEADAIG

Loch
Rimsdale
Loch
nan Cl

Altnaharra

Loch Naver

166

ch

873 ▲
BEN
HEE

680 ▲
MEALL AN
LIATH MOR

Loch a'
Ghorm-choire

Loch an
Altán Fi na
Loch
Truderscaig

10

13
HEUR LOCH

Loch
Merkland

472 ▲
MEALL AN
FHUARAIN

A836

Strath Bagastie

959 ▲
BEN
KLIBRECK

Loch Choire Forest

694 ▲
CREAG N-
IOLAIRE

434 ▲
CNOC AN
BHAID M

30

11 Borro

Loch
Fiag

Fiag
Lodge

Glen Fiag

372 ▲
CNOC A'
GHRIAMA

Loch a'
Bhealaich

Loch
Choire

713 ▲
CREAG
MHOR

37

Overscaig Hotel

A838

Crask Inn

346 ▲
CNOC A'
GHIUBHAIS

162

12

510
MAOVALLY

Gorm-loch
Mòr

J 40 K 50 L 50 M 21 N 60 P Q 70 R

Ben Armine Forest

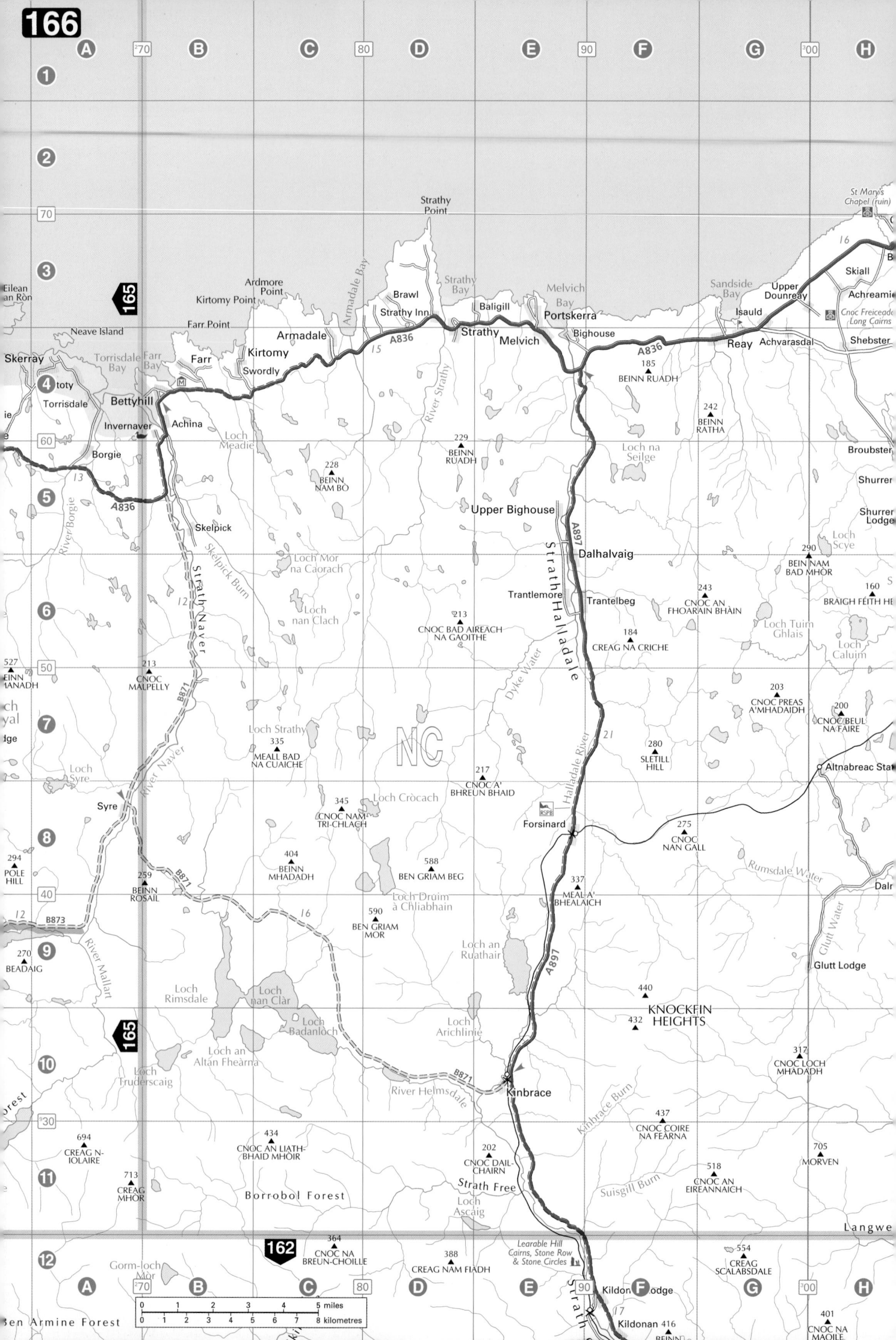

PENTLAND FIRTH

J 10 K L 20 M N 30 P Q 40 R

Langaton Point
Nethertown
Mell Head
Uppertown
ISLAND OF STROMA
St John's Point
St Margaret's Hope

DUNNET HEAD
Briga Head
Stromness
Holborn Head
Scrabster
A836
A9
Thurso
Thurso Bay

DUNNET HILL 121
Brough
St John's Loch
West Dunnet
Dunnet Bay
Dunnet
B855

Castle of Mey
Scarfskerry
Loch Mey
Rattar
Mey
Barrock
Gills Bay
Gills
Kirkstyle
Huna
Canisbay
A836
John o' Groats
DUNCANSBY HEAD
Muckle Stack
Skirza
Freswick Bay
Ness Head

Murkle
Castlehill
Castletown
Olrig House
Weydale
Hilliclay
Sordale
Inkstack
Greenland
Tain
B876
Bowermadden
Bower
Lyth
Sortat
Howe
Brabstermire
Loch Heilen
Slickly
Burn of Lyth
Kirk Burn
Auckengill
Broch
Nybster
Freswick
Brough Head
A99

Glengolly
Westfield
Loch Calder
Roadside
B874
Knockdee
Loch Scarmclate
Clayock
Gillock
Halcro
16
Kirk
B870
Loch of Wester
Killimster
B876
Sinclair Bay
Keiss
Mireland
A99

Halkirk
B870
Georgemas Junction Station
Scotscalder Station
Harpsdale
176 SPITTAL HILL
River Thurso
Spittal
Mybster
21
Watten
Loch Watten
A882
Wick River
Winless
B874
Reiss
Castle Girnigoe & Sinclair
Noss Head

Olgrinmore
132 DRUIM A' MHACAIRNIE
Westerdale
23
Loch of Toftingall
Bilbster
Haster
Milton
Sibster
Ackergill
Wick John o' Groats
Staxigoe
Papigoe
Wick
Wick Bay

BEINN CHÀITEAG 136
Loch Ruard
Loch More
Loch Sand
Loch an Thulachan
Strath Beg
A9
Badlipster
BALLHARN HILL 145
Grey Cairns of Camster
Tannach
HILL OF YARROWS 212
Loch of Yarrows
Janetstown
Newton
Old Wick
Castle of Old Wick
South Head
Whiterow
Loch Hempriggs
ND
Thrumster
A99
17
Sarclet

Achavanich
Loch Stemster
248 STEMSTER HILL
Loch Rangag
226 COIRE NA BEINN
287 BEN-A-CHIELT
Roster
Hill o'Many Stanes
Cairn o'Get
Ulbster
Whaligoe
Whaligoe Steps
Bruan
Upper Lybster
Mid Clyth
Halberry Head

264 CNOCAN CONACHREAG
Houstry
Swiney
Clyth Ness
Occumster
Invershore
Lybster
Lybster Bay
Land-hallow
Smerral
Forse
Latheron
Latheronwheel
Janetstown
A9
Laidhay Croft
Dunbeath
Knockally
626 ARABEN
Dunbeath Water
Langwell House
163
Newport
Ramscraigs
Borgue
20
Langwell House
Berriedale

J 10 K L 20 M N 30 P Q 40 R

1 2 3 4 5 6 7 8 9 10 11 12
70 60 50 40 30
15 16 17 18
5 21 23 20

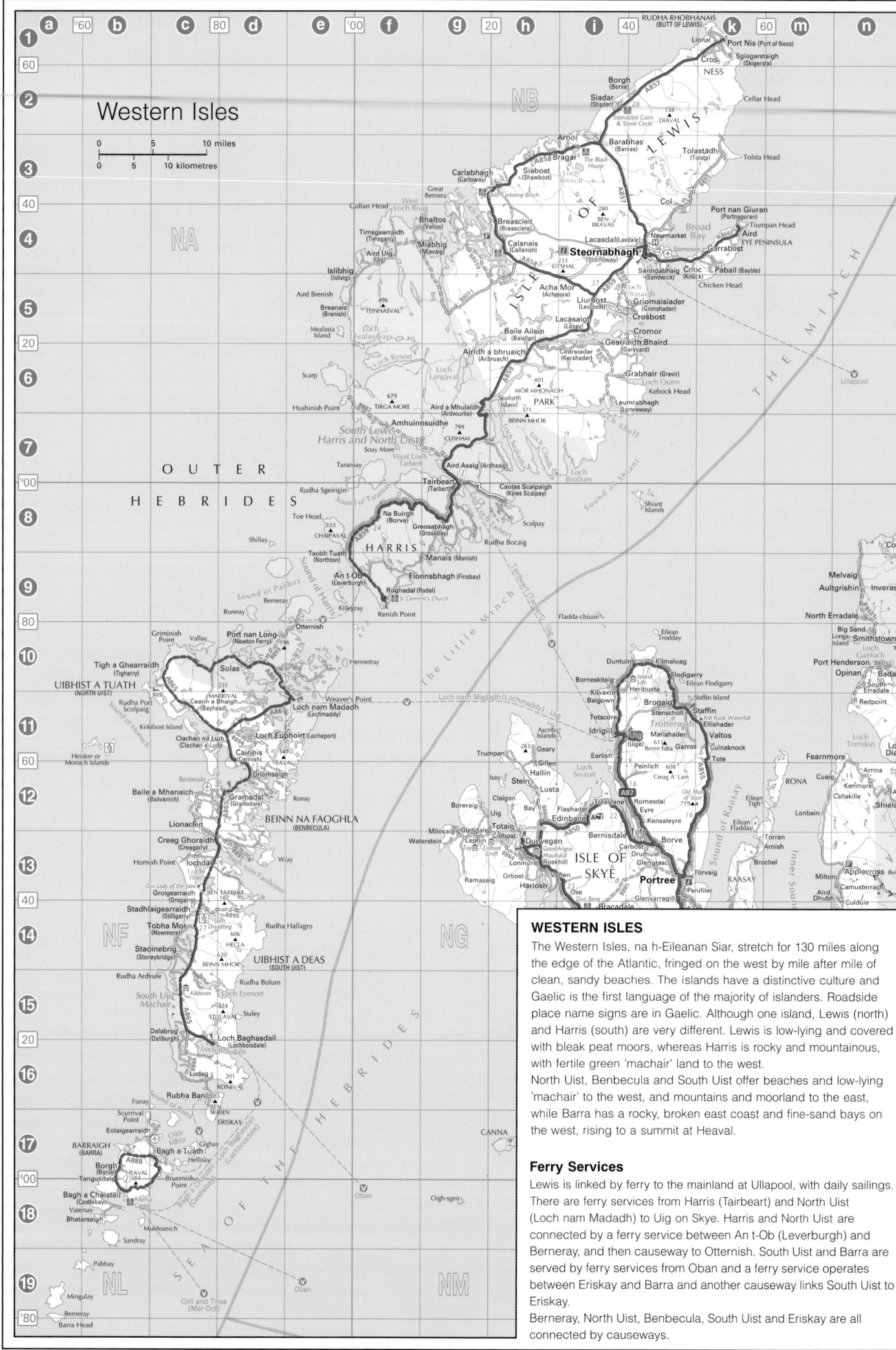

Western Isles

0 ___ 5 ___ 10 miles
0 ___ 5 ___ 10 kilometres

WESTERN ISLES

The Western Isles, na h-Eileanan Siar, stretch for 130 miles along the edge of the Atlantic, fringed on the west by mile after mile of clean, sandy beaches. The islands have a distinctive culture and Gaelic is the first language of the majority of islanders. Roadside place name signs are in Gaelic. Although one island, Lewis (north) and Harris (south) are very different. Lewis is low-lying and covered with bleak peat moors, whereas Harris is rocky and mountainous, with fertile green 'machair' land to the west.

North Uist, Benbecula and South Uist offer beaches and low-lying 'machair' to the west, and mountains and moorland to the east, while Barra has a rocky, broken east coast and fine-sand bays on the west, rising to a summit at Heaval.

Ferry Services

Lewis is linked by ferry to the mainland at Ullapool, with daily sailings. There are ferry services from Harris (Tairbeart) and North Uist (Loch nam Madadh) to Uig on Skye. Harris and North Uist are connected by a ferry service between An t-Ob (Leverburgh) and Berneray, and then causeway to Otternish. South Uist and Barra are served by ferry services from Oban and a ferry service operates between Eriskay and Barra and another causeway links South Uist to Eriskay.

Berneray, North Uist, Benbecula, South Uist and Eriskay are all connected by causeways.

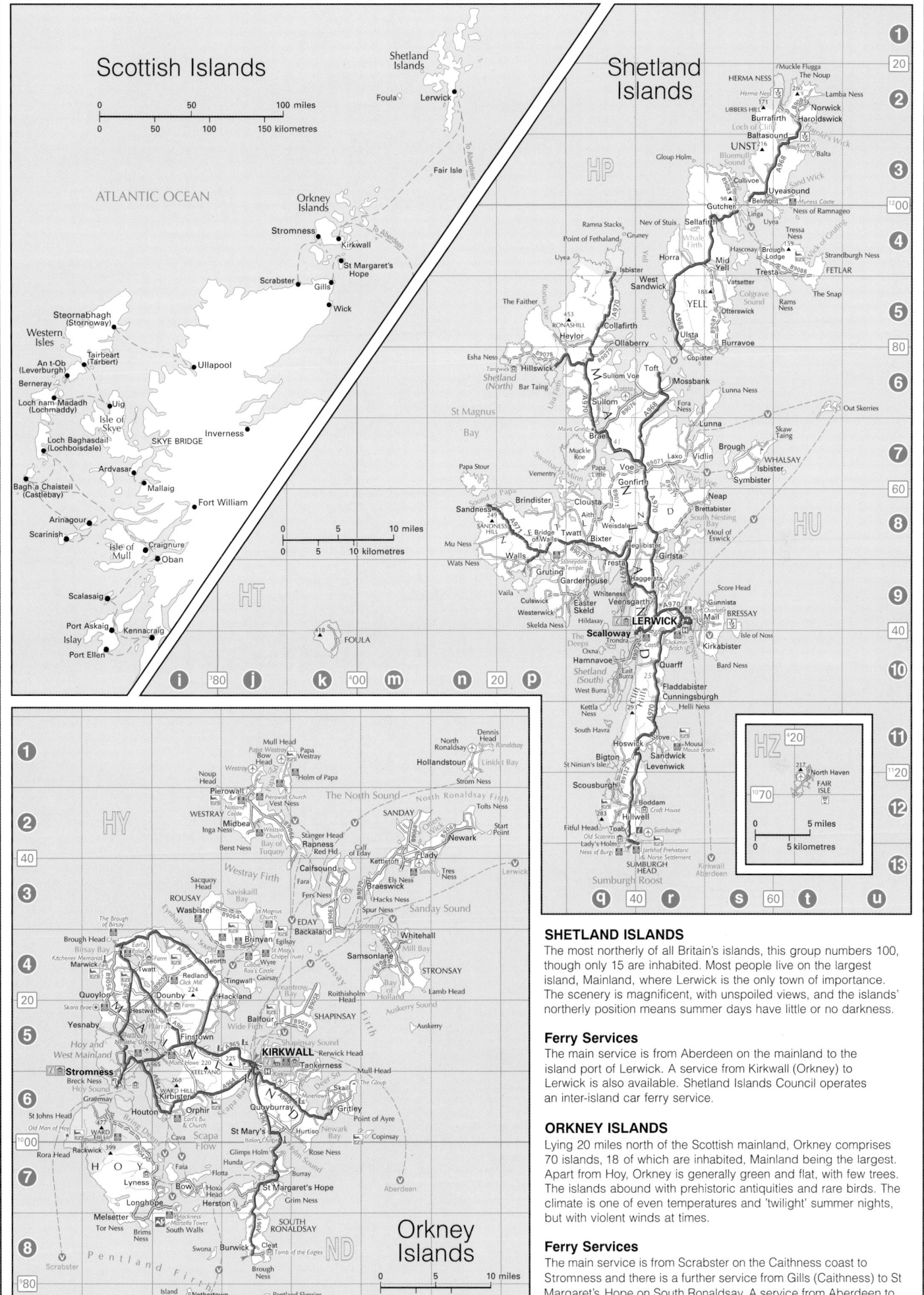

SHETLAND ISLANDS

The most northerly of all Britain's islands, this group numbers 100, though only 15 are inhabited. Most people live on the largest island, Mainland, where Lerwick is the only town of importance. The scenery is magnificent, with unspoiled views, and the islands' northerly position means summer days have little or no darkness.

Ferry Services

The main service is from Aberdeen on the mainland to the island port of Lerwick. A service from Kirkwall (Orkney) to Lerwick is also available. Shetland Islands Council operates an inter-island car ferry service.

ORKNEY ISLANDS

Lying 20 miles north of the Scottish mainland, Orkney comprises 70 islands, 18 of which are inhabited, Mainland being the largest. Apart from Hoy, Orkney is generally green and flat, with few trees. The islands abound with prehistoric antiquities and rare birds. The climate is one of even temperatures and 'twilight' summer nights, but with violent winds at times.

Ferry Services

The main service is from Scrabster on the Caithness coast to Stromness and there is a further service from Gills (Caithness) to St Margaret's Hope on South Ronaldsay. A service from Aberdeen to Kirkwall provides a link to Shetland at Lerwick. Inter-island car ferry services are also operated (advance reservations recommended).

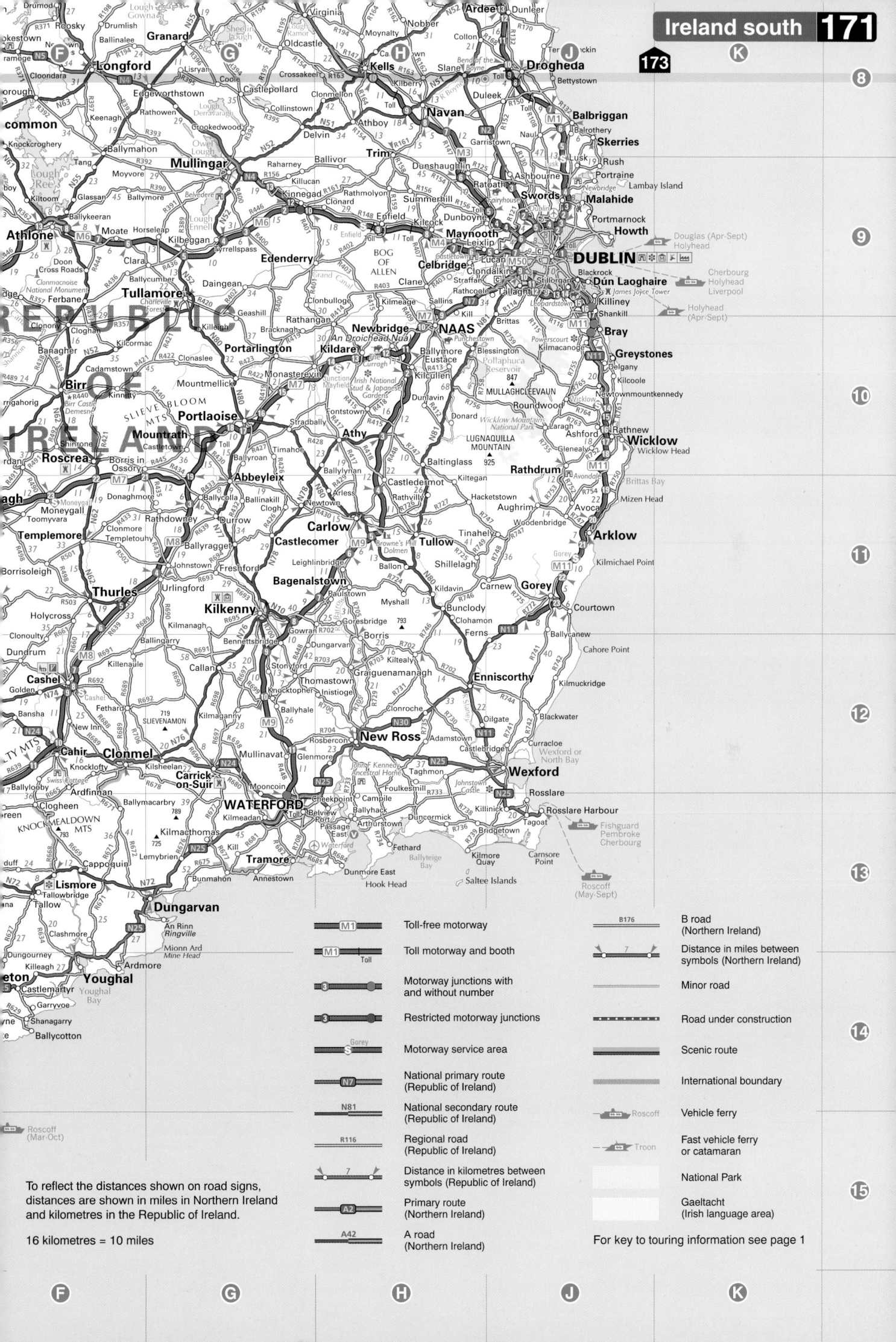

B road
(Northern Ireland)

Toll-free motorway

Distance in miles between
symbols (Northern Ireland)

Toll motorway and booth

Minor road

Motorway junctions with
and without number

Road under construction

Restricted motorway junctions

Scenic route

Motorway service area

International boundary

National primary route
(Republic of Ireland)

Vehicle ferry

National secondary route
(Republic of Ireland)

Fast vehicle ferry
or catamaran

Regional road
(Republic of Ireland)

National Park

Distance in kilometres between
symbols (Republic of Ireland)

Gaeltacht
(Irish language area)

Primary route
(Northern Ireland)

A road
(Northern Ireland)

To reflect the distances shown on road signs,
distances are shown in miles in Northern Ireland
and kilometres in the Republic of Ireland.

16 kilometres = 10 miles

For key to touring information see page 1

Ireland index

| 0 | 10 | 20 miles |
| 0 | 10 | 20 | 30 kilometres |

Restricted junctions

Motorway and Primary Route junctions which have access or exit restrictions are shown on the map pages thus:

M1 London - Leeds

Northbound
Access only from A1
(northbound)

Southbound
Exit only to A1
(southbound)

Northbound
Access only from A41
(northbound)

Southbound
Exit only to A41
(southbound)

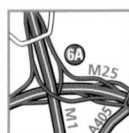
Northbound
Access only from M25
(no link from A405)

Southbound
Exit only to M25 (no link
from A405)

Northbound
Access only from A414

Southbound
Exit only to A414

Northbound
Exit only to M45

Southbound
Access only from M45

Northbound
Exit only to M6
(northbound)
No access restrictions

Southbound
Access only from M6
No exit restrictions

Northbound
Exit only, no access

Southbound
Access only, no exit

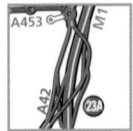
Northbound
Access only from A42

Southbound
No restriction

Northbound
No exit, access only

Southbound
Exit only, no access

Northbound
Exit only, no access

Southbound
Access only, no exit

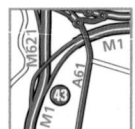
Northbound
Exit only to M621

Southbound
Access only from M621

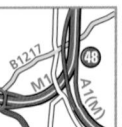
Northbound
Exit only to A1(M)
(northbound)

Southbound
Access only from A1(M)
(southbound)

M2 Rochester - Faversham

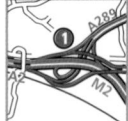
Westbound
No exit to A2
(eastbound)

Eastbound
No access from A2
(westbound)

M3 Sunbury - Southampton

Northeastbound
Access only from A303,
no exit

Southwestbound
Exit only to A303,
no access

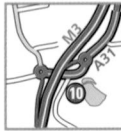
Northbound
Exit only, no access

Southbound
Access only, no exit

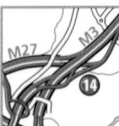
Northeastbound
Access from M27 only.
No exit

Southwestbound
No access to M27
(westbound)

M4 London - South Wales

Westbound
Access only from A4
(westbound)

Eastbound
Exit only to A4
(eastbound)

Westbound
Exit only to M48

Eastbound
Access only from M48

Westbound
Access only from M48

Eastbound
Exit only to M48

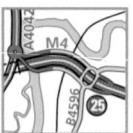
Westbound
Exit only, no access

Eastbound
Access only, no exit

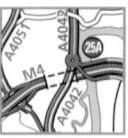
Westbound
Exit only, no access

Eastbound
Access only, no exit

Westbound
Exit only to A48(M)

Eastbound
Access only from A48(M)

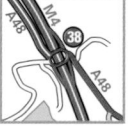
Westbound
Exit only, no access

Eastbound
No restriction

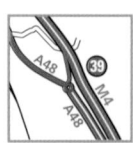
Westbound
Access only, no exit

Eastbound
No access or exit

M5 Birmingham - Exeter

Northeastbound
Access only, no exit

Southwestbound
Exit only, no access

Northeastbound
Access only from A417
(westbound)

Southwestbound
Exit only to A417
(eastbound)

Northeastbound
Exit only to M49

Southwestbound
Access only from M49

Northeastbound
No access, exit only

Southwestbound
No exit, access only

M6 Toll Motorway

See M6 Toll Motorway map on page 179

M6 Rugby - Carlisle

Northbound
Exit only to M6 Toll

Southbound
Access only from M6 Toll

Northbound
Access only from M42
(southbound)

Southbound
Exit only to M42

Northbound
Exit only, no access

Southbound
Access only, no exit

Northbound
Exit only to M54

Southbound
Access only from M54

Northbound
Access only from M6 Toll

Southbound
Exit only to M6 Toll

Northbound
No restriction

Southbound
Access only from M56
(eastbound)

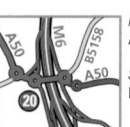
Northbound
Access only, no exit

Southbound
No restriction

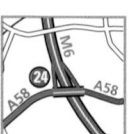
Northbound
Access only, no exit

Southbound
Exit only, no access

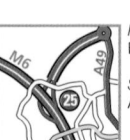
Northbound
Exit only, no access

Southbound
Access only, no exit

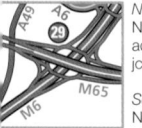

Northbound
No direct access, use adjacent slip road to jct 29A

Southbound
No direct exit, use adjacent slip road from jct 29A

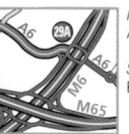

Northbound
Acces only, no exit

Southbound
Exit only, no access

Northbound
Access only from M61

Southbound
Exit only to M61

Northbound
Exit only, no access

Southbound
Access only, no exit

Northbound
Exit only, no access

Southbound
Access only, no exit

M8 Edinburgh - Bishopton

See Glasgow District map on pages 254-255

M9 Edinburgh - Dunblane

Northwestbound
Access only, no exit

Southeastbound
Exit only, no access

Northwestbound
Exit only, no access

Southeastbound
Access only, no exit

Northwestbound
Access only, no exit

Southeastbound
Exit only to A905

Northwestbound
Exit only to M876 (southwestbound)

Southeastbound
Access only from M876 (northeastbound)

M11 London - Cambridge

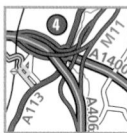

Northbound
Access only from A406 (eastbound)

Southbound
Exit only to A406

Northbound
Exit only, no access

Southbound
Access only, no exit

Northbound
Exit only to A11

Southbound
Access only from A11

Northbound
Exit only, no access

Southbound
Access only, no exit

Northbound
Exit only, no access

Southbound
Access only, no exit

M20 Swanley - Folkestone

Northwestbound
Staggered junction; follow signs - access only

Southeastbound
Staggered junction; follow signs - exit only

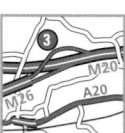

Northwestbound
Exit only to M26 (westbound)

Southeastbound
Access only from M26 (eastbound)

Northwestbound
Access only from A20

Southeastbound
For access follow signs - exit only to A20

Northwestbound
No restriction

Southeastbound
For exit follow signs

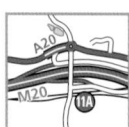

Northwestbound
Access only, no exit

Southeastbound
Exit only, no access

M23 Hooley - Crawley

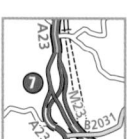

Northbound
Exit only to A23 (northbound)

Southbound
Access only from A23 (southbound)

Northbound
Access only, no exit

Southbound
Exit only, no access

M25 London Orbital Motorway

See M25 London Orbital Motorway map on page 178

M26 Sevenoaks - Wrotham

Westbound
Exit only to clockwise M25 (westbound)

Eastbound
Access only from anti-clockwise M25 (eastbound)

Westbound
Access only from M20 (northwestbound)

Eastbound
Exit only to M20 (southeastbound)

M27 Cadnam - Portsmouth

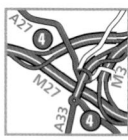

Westbound
Staggered junction; follow signs - access only from M3 (southbound). Exit only to M3 (northbound)

Eastbound
Staggered junction; follow signs - access only from M3 (southbound). Exit only to M3 (northbound)

Westbound
Exit only, no access

Eastbound
Access only, no exit

Westbound
Staggered junction; follow signs - exit only to M275 (southbound)

Eastbound
Staggered junction; follow signs - access only from M275 (northbound)

M40 London - Birmingham

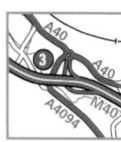

Northwestbound
Exit only, no access

Southeastbound
Access only, no exit

Northwestbound
Exit only, no access

Southeastbound
Access only, no exit

Northwestbound
Exit only to M40/A40

Southeastbound
Access only from M40/A40

Northwestbound
Exit only, no access

Southeastbound
Access only, no exit

Northwestbound
Access only, no exit

Southeastbound
Exit only, no access

Northwestbound
Access only, no exit

Southeastbound
Exit only, no access

M42 Bromsgrove - Measham

See Birmingham District map on pages 252-253

M45 Coventry - M1

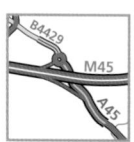

Westbound
Access only from A45 (northbound)

Eastbound
Exit only, no access

Westbound
Access only from M1 (northbound)

Eastbound
Exit only to M1 (southbound)

M53 Mersey Tunnel - Chester

Northbound
Access only from M56 (westbound). Exit only to M56 (eastbound)

Southbound
Access only from M56 (westbound). Exit only to M56 (eastbound)

M54 Telford

Westbound
Access only from M6 (northbound)

Eastbound
Exit only to M6 (southbound)

M56 North Cheshire

For junctions 1,2,3,4 & 7 see Manchester District map on pages 256-257

Westbound
Access only, no exit

Eastbound
No access or exit

Westbound
Exit only to M53

Eastbound
Access only from M53

Westbound
No access or exit

Eastbound
No restriction

M57 Liverpool Outer Ring Road

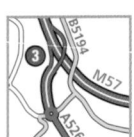

Northwestbound
Access only, no exit

Southeastbound
Exit only, no access

Northwestbound
Access only from A580 (westbound)

Southeastbound
Exit only, no access

M58 Liverpool - Wigan

Westbound
Exit only, no access

Eastbound
Access only, no exit

M60 Manchester Orbital

See Manchester District map on pages 256-257

M61 Manchester - Preston

Northwestbound
No access or exit

Southeastbound
Exit only, no access

Northwestbound
Exit only to M6 (northbound)

Southeastbound
Access only from M6 (southbound)

M62 Liverpool - Kingston upon Hull

Westbound
Access only, no exit

Eastbound
Exit only, no access

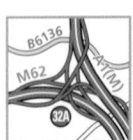

Westbound
No access to A1(M) (southbound)

Eastbound
No restriction

M65 Preston - Colne

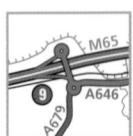

Northeastbound
Exit only, no access

Southwestbound
Access only, no exit

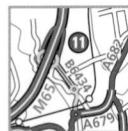

Northeastbound
Access only, no exit

Southwestbound
Exit only, no access

M66 Bury

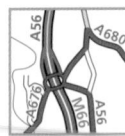

Northbound
Exit only to A56 (northbound)

Southbound
Access only from A56 (southbound)

Northbound
Exit only, no access

Southbound
Access only, no exit

M67 Hyde Bypass

Westbound
Access only, no exit

Eastbound
Exit only, no access

Westbound
Exit only, no access

Eastbound
Access only, no exit

Westbound
Exit only, no access

Eastbound
No restriction

M69 Coventry - Leicester

Northbound
Access only, no exit

Southbound
Exit only, no access

M73 East of Glasgow

Northbound
No access from or exit to A89. No access from M8 (eastbound)

Southbound
No access from or exit to A89. No exit to M8 (westbound)

M74 and A74(M) Glasgow - Gretna

Northbound
Exit only, no access

Southbound
Access only, no exit

Northbound
Access only, no exit

Southbound
Exit only, no access

Northbound
Access only, no exit

Southbound
Exit only, no access

Northbound
No access or exit

Southbound
Exit only, no access

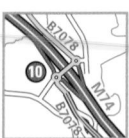

Northbound
No restriction

Southbound
Access only, no exit

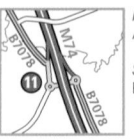

Northbound
Access only, no exit

Southbound
Exit only, no access

Northbound
Exit only, no access

Southbound
Access only, no exit

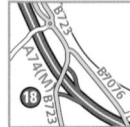

Northbound
Exit only, no access

Southbound
Access only, no exit

M77 South of Glasgow

Northbound
No exit to M8 (westbound)

Southbound
No access from M8 (eastbound)

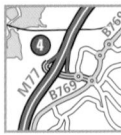

Northbound
Access only, no exit

Southbound
Exit only, no access

Northbound
Access only, no exit

Southbound
Exit only, no access

Northbound
Access only, no exit

Southbound
No restriction

M80 Glasgow - Stirling

For junctions 1 & 4 see Glasgow District map on pages 254-255

Northbound
Exit only, no access

Southbound
Access only, no exit

Northbound
Access only, no exit

Southbound
Exit only, no access

Northbound
Exit only to M876 (northeastbound)

Southbound
Access only from M876 (southwestbound)

M90 Forth Road Bridge - Perth

Northbound
Exit only to A92 (eastbound)

Southbound
Access only from A92 (westbound)

Northbound
Access only, no exit

Southbound
Exit only, no access

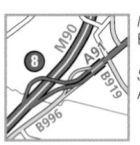

Northbound
Exit only, no access

Southbound
Access only, no exit

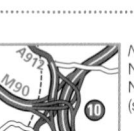

Northbound
No access from A912
No exit to A912 (southbound)

Southbound
No access from A912 (northbound).
No exit to A912

M180 Doncaster - Grimsby

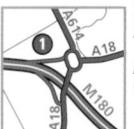

Westbound
Access only, no exit

Eastbound
Exit only, no access

M606 Bradford Spur

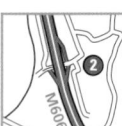

Northbound
Exit only, no access

Southbound
No restriction

M621 Leeds - M1

Clockwise
Access only, no exit

Anticlockwise
Exit only, no access

Clockwise
No exit or access

Anticlockwise
No restriction

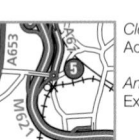

Clockwise
Access only, no exit

Anticlockwise
Exit only, no access

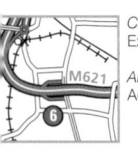
Clockwise
Exit only, no access

Anticlockwise
Access only, no exit

Northbound
No access. Exit only to
A194(M) & A1
(northbound)

Southbound
No exit. Access only from
A194(M) & A1
(southbound)

Northeastbound
Access only, no exit

Southwestbound
Exit only, no access

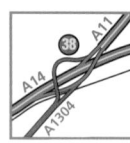
Westbound
Access only from A11

Eastbound
Exit only to A11

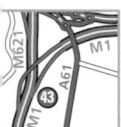
Clockwise
Exit only to M1
(southbound)

Anticlockwise
Access only from M1
(northbound)

M876 Bonnybridge - Kincardine Bridge

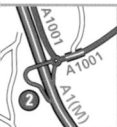
Northeastbound
Access only from M80
(northbound)

Southwestbound
Exit only to M80
(southbound)

Northeastbound
Exit only to M9
(eastbound)

Southwestbound
Access only from M9
(westbound)

A1(M) South Mimms - Baldock

Northbound
Exit only, no access

Southbound
Access only, no exit

Northbound
No restriction

Southbound
Exit only, no access

Northbound
Access only, no exit

Southbound
No access or exit

A1(M) Pontefract - Bedale

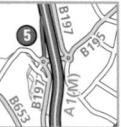
Northbound
No access to M62
(eastbound)

Southbound
No restriction

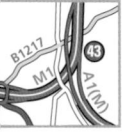
Northbound
Access only from M1
(northbound)

Southbound
Exit only to M1
(southbound)

A1(M) Scotch Corner - Newcastle upon Tyne

Northbound
Exit only to A66(M)
(eastbound)

Southbound
Access only from A66(M)
(westbound)

A3(M) Horndean - Havant

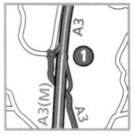
Northbound
Access only from A3

Southbound
Exit only to A3

Northbound
Exit only, no access

Southbound
Access only, no exit

A48(M) Cardiff Spur

Westbound
Access only from M4
(westbound)

Eastbound
Exit only to M4
(eastbound)

Westbound
Exit only to A48
(westbound)

Eastbound
Access only from A48
(eastbound)

A66(M) Darlington Spur

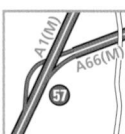
Westbound
Exit only to A1(M)
(southbound)

Eastbound
Access only from A1(M)
(northbound)

A194(M) Newcastle upon Tyne

Northbound
Access only from A1(M)
(northbound)

Southbound
Exit only to A1(M)
(southbound)

A12 M25 - Ipswich

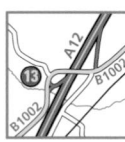
Northeastbound
Access only, no exit

Southwestbound
No restriction

Northeastbound
Exit only, no access

Southwestbound
Access only, no exit

Northeastbound
Exit only, no access

Southwestbound
Access only, no exit

Northeastbound
No restriction

Southwestbound
Access only, no exit

Northeastbound
Exit only, no access

Southwestbound
Access only, no exit

Northeastbound
Access only, no exit

Southwestbound
Exit only, no access

Northeastbound
Exit only, no access

Southwestbound
Access only, no exit

Northeastbound
Exit only (for Stratford
St Mary and Dedham)

Southwestbound
Access only

A14 M1 Felixstowe

Westbound
Exit only to M6 & M1
(northbound)

Eastbound
Access only from M6 &
M1 (southbound)

Westbound
Exit only, no access

Eastbound
Access only, no exit

Westbound
Access only from A1307

Eastbound
Exit only to A1307

Westbound
Access only, no exit

Eastbound
Exit only, no exit

Westbound
Exit only to A11
Access only from A1303

Eastbound
Access only from A11

Westbound
Exit only, no access

Eastbound
Exit only, no access

Westbound
Access only, no exit

Eastbound
Exit only, no access

A55 Holyhead - Chester

Westbound
Exit only, no access

Eastbound
Access only, no exit

Westbound
Access only, no exit

Eastbound
Exit only, no access

Westbound
Exit only, no access

Eastbound
No access or exit.

Westbound
Exit only, no access

Eastbound
No access or exit

Westbound
Exit only, no access

Eastbound
Access only, no exit

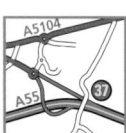
Westbound
Exit only to A5104

Eastbound
Access only from A5104

M25 London Orbital motorway

Refer also to atlas pages 36–37 and 50–51

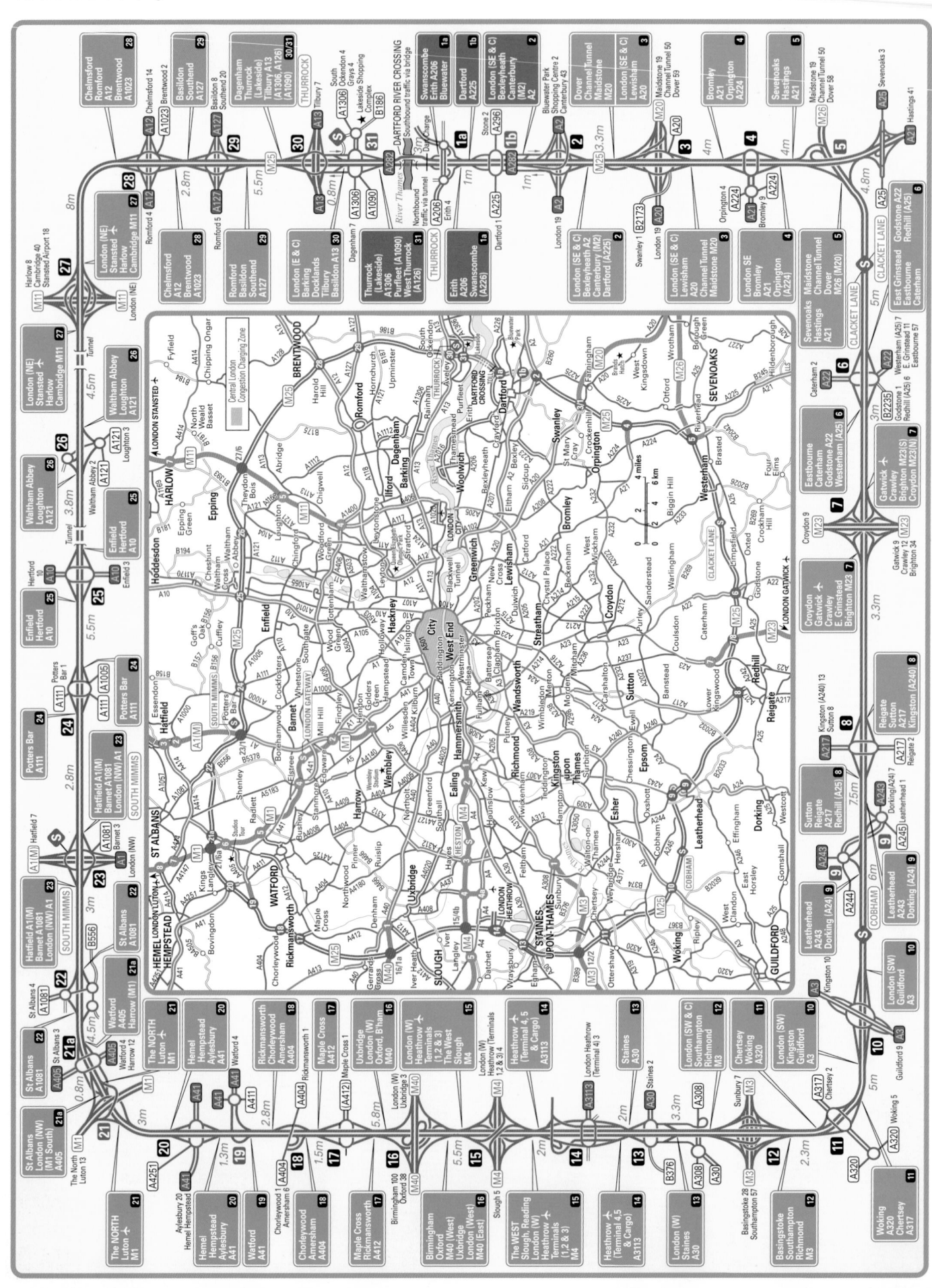

M6 Toll motorway

Refer also to atlas pages 58–59

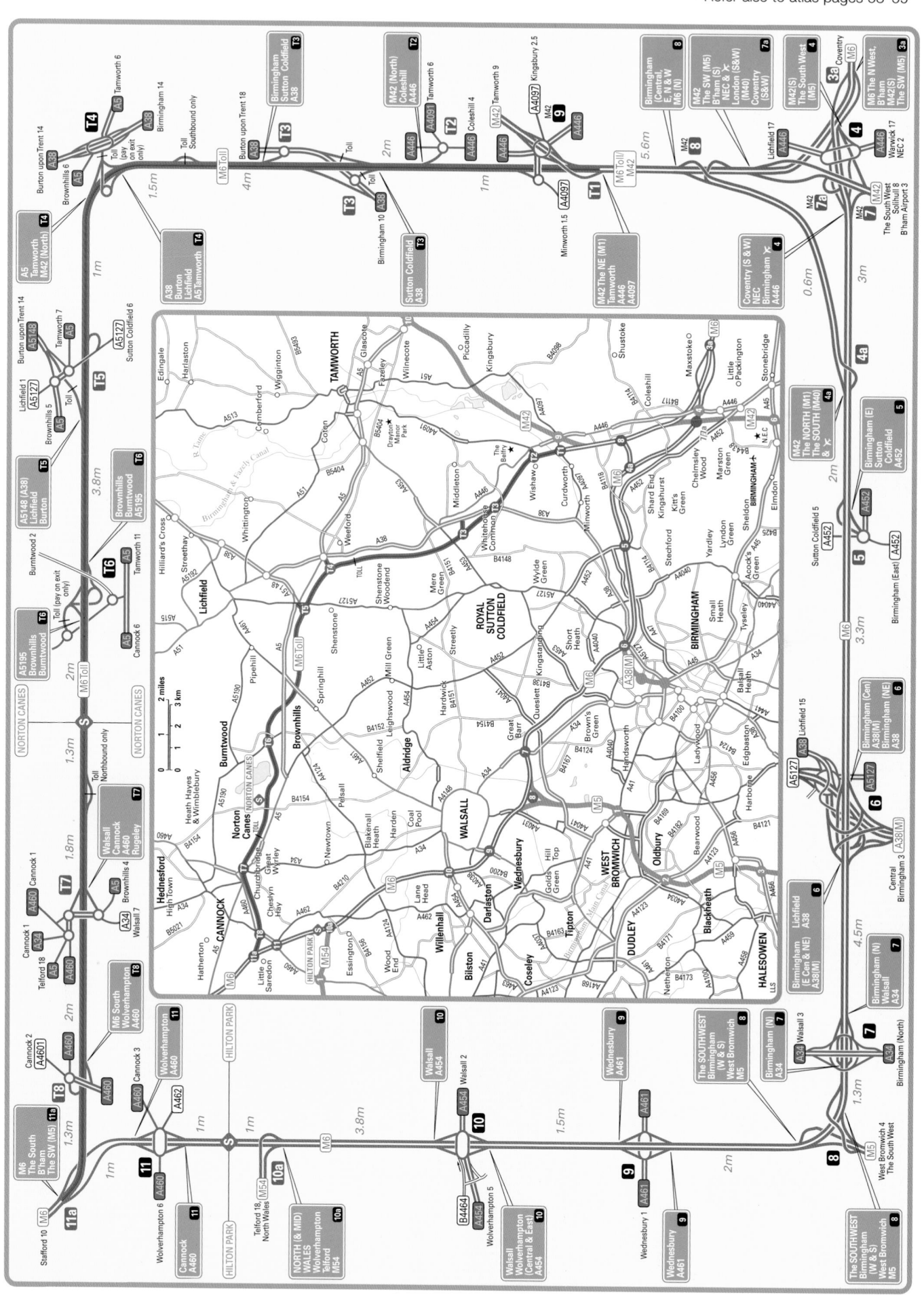

Street map symbols

Town, port and airport plans

Motorway and junction	One-way, gated/closed road	Railway station	Car park
Primary road single/dual carriageway	Restricted access road	Light rapid transit system station	Park and Ride (at least 6 days per week)
A road single/dual carriageway	Pedestrian area	Level crossing	Bus/coach station
B road single/dual carriageway	Footpath	Tramway	Hospital
Local road single/dual carriageway	Road under construction	Ferry route	24-hour Accident & Emergency hospital
Other road single/dual carriageway, minor road	Road tunnel	Airport, heliport	Petrol station, 24 hour Major suppliers only
Building of interest	Museum	Railair terminal	City wall
Ruined building	Castle	Theatre or performing arts centre	Escarpment
Tourist Information Centre	Castle mound	Cinema	Cliff lift
Visitor or heritage centre	Monument, statue	Abbey, chapel, church	River/canal, lake
World Heritage Site (UNESCO)	Post Office	Synagogue	Lock, weir
English Heritage site	Public library	Mosque	Park/sports ground
Historic Scotland site	Shopping centre	Golf Course	Cemetery
Cadw (Welsh heritage) site	Shopmobility	Racecourse	Woodland
National Trust site	Viewpoint	Nature reserve	Built-up area
National Trust Scotland site	Toilet, with facilities for the less able	Aquarium	Beach

Central London street map (see pages 232 – 241)

Safety camera site (fixed location) with speed limit in mph	London Underground station
Section of road with two or more fixed camera sites; speed limit in mph	London Overground station
Average speed (SPECS™) camera system with speed limit in mph	Rail interchange

Docklands Light Railway (DLR) station
Central London Congestion Charging Zone

Royal Parks

Green Park — Park open 24 hours. Constitution Hill and The Mall closed to traffic Sundays and public holidays
Hyde Park — Park open 5am – midnight. Park roads closed to traffic midnight – 5am.
Kensington Gardens — Park open 6am – dusk.
Regent's Park — Park open 5am – dusk. Park roads closed to traffic midnight – 7am.
St James's Park — Park open 5am – midnight. The Mall closed to traffic Sundays and public holidays.

Traffic regulations in the City of London include security checkpoints and restrict the number of entry and exit points.

Note: Oxford Street is closed to through-traffic (except buses & taxis) 7am-7pm Monday-Saturday.

Central London Congestion Charging Zone

The daily charge for driving or parking a vehicle on public roads in the Congestion Charging Zone (CCZ), during operating hours, is £11.50 per vehicle per day in advance or on the day of travel. Alternatively you can pay £10.50 by registering with CC Auto Pay, an automated payment system. Drivers can also pay the next charging day after travelling in the zone but this will cost £14. Payment permits entry, travel within and exit from the CCZ by the vehicle as often as required on that day.

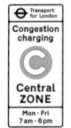

The CCZ operates between 7am and 6pm, Mon–Fri only. There is no charge at weekends, on public holidays or between 25th Dec and 1st Jan inclusive.

For up to date information on the CCZ, exemptions, discounts or ways to pay, telephone 0343 222 2222, visit tfl.gov.uk/modes/driving/congestion-charge or write to Congestion Charging, P.O. Box 4782, Worthing BN11 9PS. Textphone users can call 020 7649 9123.

Towns, ports & airports

Town Plans

Central London

Ferry Ports

Airports

Channel Tunnel

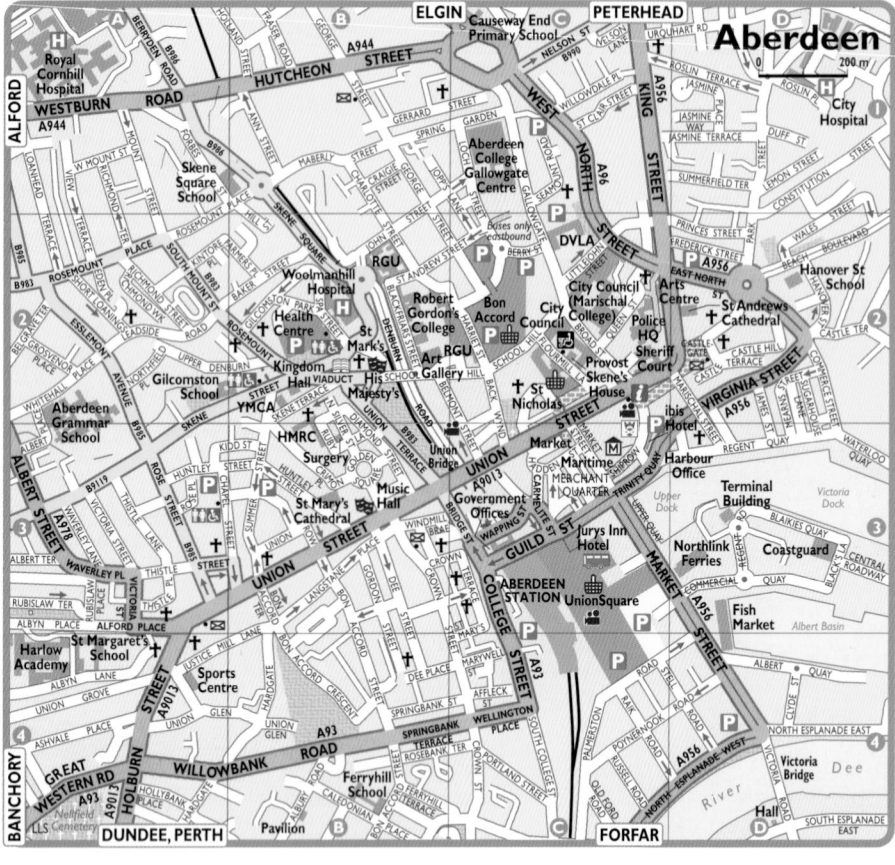

Aberdeen

Aberdeen is found on atlas page **151 N6**

Affleck Street	C4	Maberly Street	B1
Albert Street	A3	Marischal Street	D2
Albury Road	B4	Market Street	C3
Alford Place	A3	Nelson Street	C1
Ann Street	B1	Palmerston Road	C4
Beach Boulevard	D2	Park Street	D1
Belgrave Terrace	A2	Portland Street	C4
Berryden Road	A1	Poynernook Road	C4
Blackfriars Street	B2	Regent Quay	D3
Blaikies Quay	D3	Richmond Street	A2
Bon Accord Crescent	B4	Rose Place	A3
Bon Accord Street	B3	Rose Street	A3
Bridge Street	C3	Rosemount Place	A2
Caledonian Place	B4	Rosemount Viaduct	A2
Carmelite Street	C3	St Andrew Street	B2
Chapel Street	A3	St Clair Street	C1
Charlotte Street	B1	School Hill	C2
College Street	C3	Skene Square	B2
Constitution Street	D1	Skene Street	A3
Crimon Place	B3	Skene Terrace	B2
Crown Street	B3	South College Street	C4
Dee Street	B3	South Esplanade East	D4
Denburn Road	B2	South Mount Street	A2
Diamond Street	B3	Spa Street	B2
East North Street	D2	Springbank Street	B4
Esslemont Avenue	A2	Springbank Terrace	B4
Gallowgate	C1	Summer Street	B3
George Street	B1	Summerfield Terrace	D1
Gilcomston Park	B2	Thistle Lane	A3
Golden Square	B3	Thistle Place	A3
Gordon Street	B3	Thistle Street	A3
Great Western Road	A4	Trinity Quay	C3
Guild Street	C3	Union Bridge	B3
Hadden Street	C3	Union Grove	A4
Hanover Street	D2	Union Street	B3
Hardgate	B4	Union Terrace	B2
Harriet Street	C2	Upper Denburn	A2
Holburn Street	A4	Victoria Road	D4
Huntley Street	A3	Victoria Street	A3
Hutcheon Street	B1	View Terrace	A1
Jasmine Terrace	D1	Virginia Street	C3
John Street	B2	Wapping Street	C3
Justice Mill Lane	A4	Waverley Place	A3
King Street	C1	Wellington Place	C4
Langstane Place	B3	West North Street	C1
Leadside Road	A2	Westburn Road	A1
Loanhead Terrace	A1	Whitehall Place	A2
Loch Street	C1	Willowbank Road	A4

Basingstoke

Basingstoke is found on atlas page **22 H4**

Alencon Link	C1	London Street	C3
Allnutt Avenue	D2	Lower Brook Street	A2
Basing View	C1	Lytton Road	D3
Beaconsfield Road	C4	Market Place	B3
Bounty Rise	A4	May Place	C3
Bounty Road	A4	Montague Place	C4
Bramblys Close	A3	Mortimer Lane	A2
Bramblys Drive	A3	New Road	B3
Budd's Close	A3	New Road	C2
Castle Road	C4	New Street	B3
Chapel Hill	B1	Penrith Road	A3
Chequers Road	C2	Rayleigh Road	A2
Chester Place	A4	Red Lion Lane	C3
Churchill Way	B2	Rochford Road	A2
Churchill Way East	D1	St Mary's Court	C2
Churchill Way West	A2	Sarum Hill	A3
Church Square	B2	Seal Road	C2
Church Street	B2	Solby's Road	A2
Church Street	B3	Southend Road	A2
Cliddesden Road	C4	Southern Road	B4
Clifton Terrace	C1	Stukeley Road	A4
Cordale Road	A4	Sylvia Close	B4
Council Road	B4	Timberlake Road	B2
Crossborough Gardens	D3	Victoria Street	B3
Crossborough Hill	D3	Victory Roundabout	A1
Cross Street	B3	Vyne Road	B1
Devonshire Place	A4	Winchcombe Road	A3
Eastfield Avenue	D2	Winchester Road	A4
Eastrop Lane	D2	Winchester Street	B3
Eastrop Roundabout	C1	Winterthur Way	A1
Eastrop Way	D2	Worting Road	A3
Essex Road	A2	Wote Street	C3
Fairfields Road	B4		
Festival Way	C2		
Flaxfield Court	A2		
Flaxfield Road	A3		
Flaxfield Road	B3		
Frances Road	A4		
Frescade Crescent	A4		
Goat Lane	C2		
Hackwood Road	C4		
Hamelyn Road	A4		
Hardy Lane	A4		
Hawkfield Lane	A4		
Haymarket Yard	C3		
Joices Yard	B3		
Jubilee Road	B4		
London Road	D3		

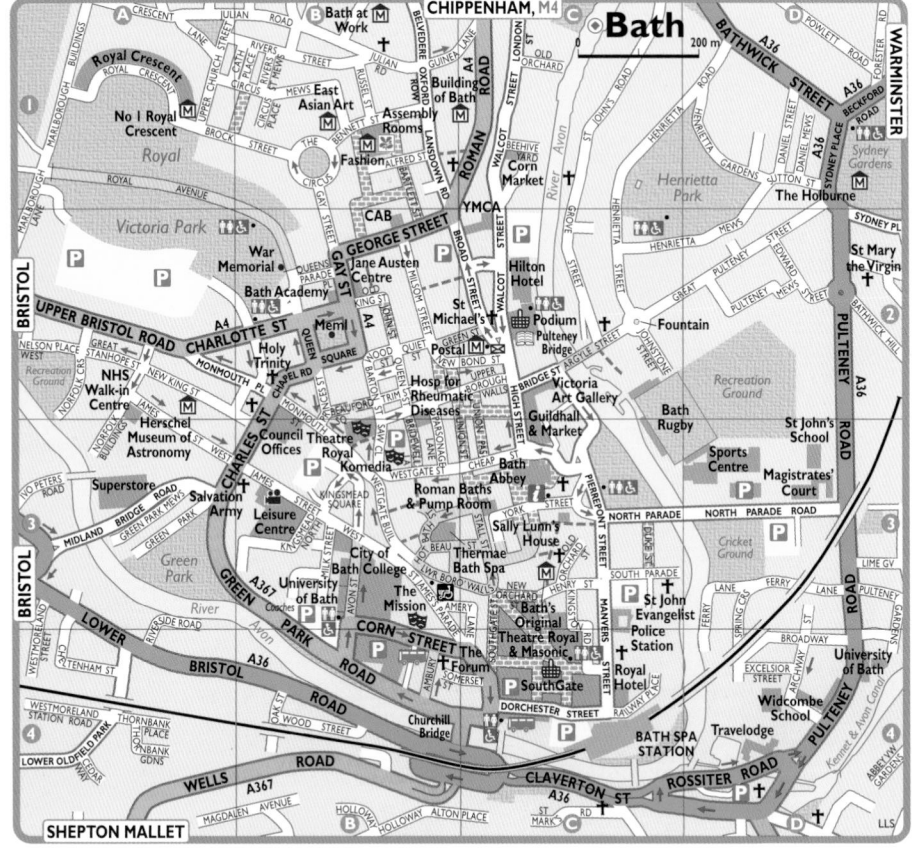

Bath

Bath is found on atlas page **20 D2**

Archway Street	D4	Lower Bristol Road	A3
Argyle Street	C2	Lower Oldfield Park	A4
Avon Street	B3	Manvers Street	C3
Bartlett Street	B1	Midland Bridge Road	A3
Barton Street	B2	Milk Street	B3
Bathwick Street	D1	Milsom Street	B2
Beauford Square	B2	Monmouth Place	A2
Beau Street	B3	Monmouth Street	B2
Beckford Road	D1	New Bond Street	B2
Bennett Street	B1	New King Street	A2
Bridge Street	C2	New Orchard Street	C3
Broad Street	C2	Norfolk Buildings	A3
Broadway	D4	North Parade	C3
Brock Street	A1	North Parade Road	D3
Chapel Road	B2	Old King Street	B2
Charles Street	A3	Oxford Row	B1
Charlotte Street	A2	Pierrepont Street	C3
Cheap Street	C3	Princes Street	B2
Cheltenham Street	A4	Pulteney Road	D2
Circus Mews	B1	Queen Square	B2
Claverton Street	C4	Queen Street	B2
Corn Street	B4	Railway Place	C4
Daniel Street	D1	Rivers Street	B1
Dorchester Street	C4	Roman Road	C1
Edward Street	D2	Rossiter Road	C4
Gay Street	B1	Royal Avenue	A1
George Street	B2	Royal Crescent	A1
Great Pulteney Street	C2	St James's Parade	B3
Great Stanhope Street	A2	St John's Road	C1
Green Park Road	A3	Saw Close	B3
Green Street	B2	Southgate Street	C4
Grove Street	C2	South Parade	C3
Guinea Lane	B1	Stall Street	C3
Henrietta Gardens	D1	Sutton Street	D1
Henrietta Mews	C2	Sydney Place	D1
Henrietta Road	C1	The Circus	B1
Henrietta Street	C2	Thornbank Place	A4
Henry Street	C3	Union Street	B2
High Street	C2	Upper Borough Walls	C2
Hot Bath Street	B3	Upper Bristol Road	A2
James Street West	B3	Upper Church Street	A1
John Street	B2	Walcot Street	C2
Julian Road	B1	Wells Road	A4
Kingsmead North	B3	Westgate Buildings	B3
Kingston Road	C3	Westgate Street	B3
Lansdown Road	B1	Westmoreland Station	
London Street	C1	Road	A4
Lower Borough Walls	B3	York Street	C3

Blackpool

Blackpool is found on atlas page **88 C3**

Abingdon Street	B1	Havelock Street	C4
Adelaide Street	B3	High Street	C1
Albert Road	B3	Hornby Road	B3
Albert Road	C3	Hornby Road	D3
Alfred Street	C2	Hull Road	B3
Ashton Road	D4	Kay Street	C4
Bank Hey Street	B2	Kent Road	C4
Banks Street	B1	King Street	C2
Belmont Avenue	C4	Leamington Road	D2
Bennett Avenue	D3	Leicester Road	D2
Bethesda Road	C4	Leopold Grove	C2
Birley Street	B2	Lincoln Road	D2
Blenheim Avenue	D4	Livingstone Road	C3
Bonny Street	B4	Lord Street	B1
Buchanan Street	C1	Louise Street	C4
Butler Street	C1	Milbourne Street	C1
Caunce Street	D1	Montreal Avenue	D3
Cedar Square	C2	New Bonny Street	B3
Central Drive	C4	New Larkhill Street	C1
Chapel Street	B4	Palatine Road	C4
Charles Street	C1	Palatine Road	D3
Charnley Road	C3	Park Road	D2
Cheapside	B2	Park Road	D4
Church Street	B2	Peter Street	D2
Church Street	C2	Pier Street	B4
Church Street	D2	Princess Parade	B1
Clifton Street	B2	Promenade	B1
Clinton Avenue	D4	Queen Street	B1
Cookson Street	C2	Raikes Parade	D2
Coop Street	B4	Reads Avenue	C3
Coronation Street	C3	Reads Avenue	D3
Corporation Street	B2	Regent Road	C2
Dale Street	B4	Ribble Road	C4
Deansgate	B2	Ripon Road	D3
Dickson Road	B1	Seasiders Way	B4
Edward Street	C2	Selbourne Road	D1
Elizabeth Street	D1	South King Street	C2
Fairhurst Street	D1	Springfield Road	B1
Fisher Street	C1	Stanley Road	C3
Fleet Street	C3	Talbot Road	B2
Foxhall Road	B4	Talbot Road	C1
Freckleton Street	D4	Topping Street	C2
General Street	B1	Vance Road	B3
George Street	C1	Victoria Street	B2
Gorton Street	D1	Victory Road	D1
Granville Road	D2	West Street	B2
Grosvenor Street	C1	Woolman Road	D4
Harrison Street	D4	York Street	B4

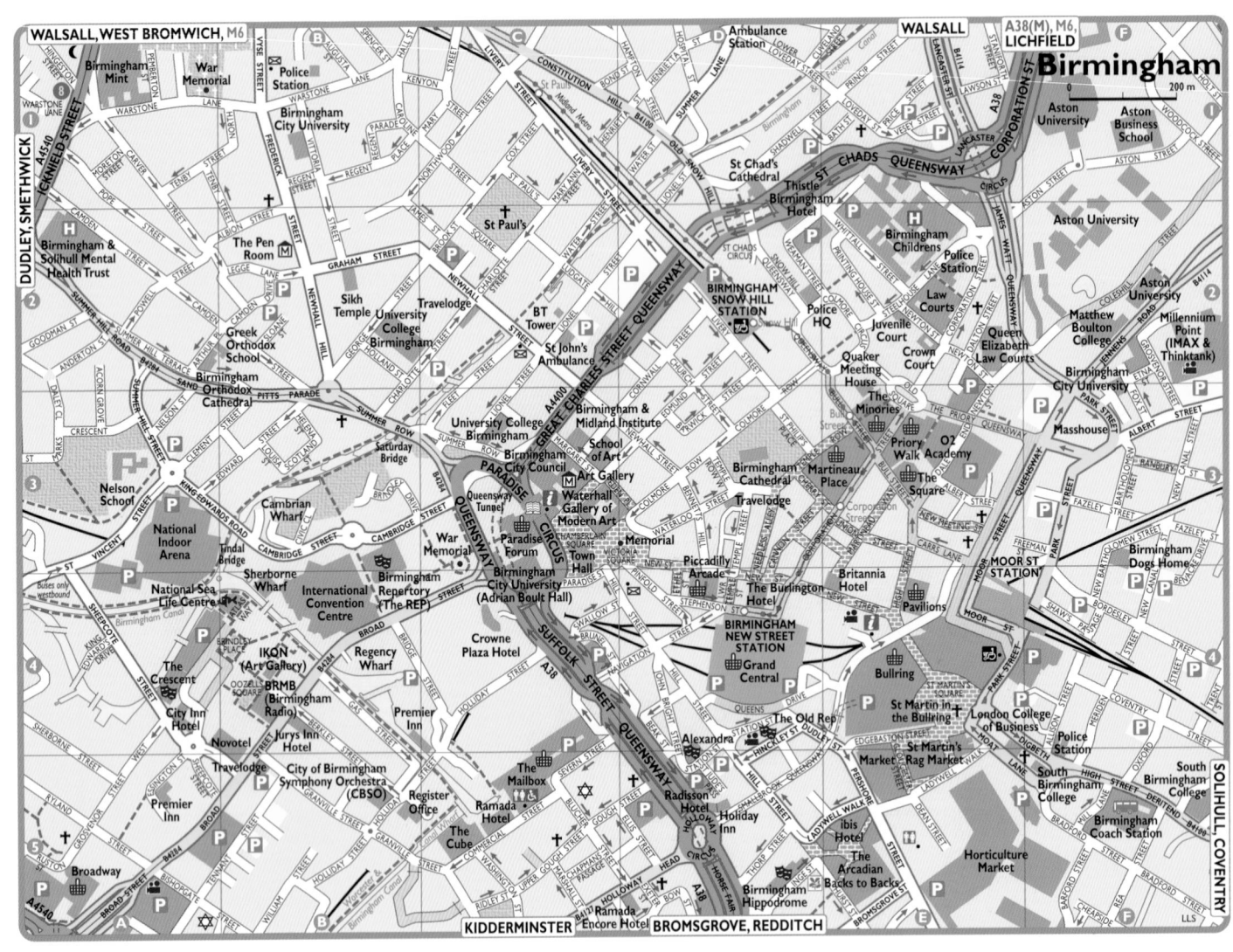

Birmingham

Birmingham is found on atlas page **58 G7**

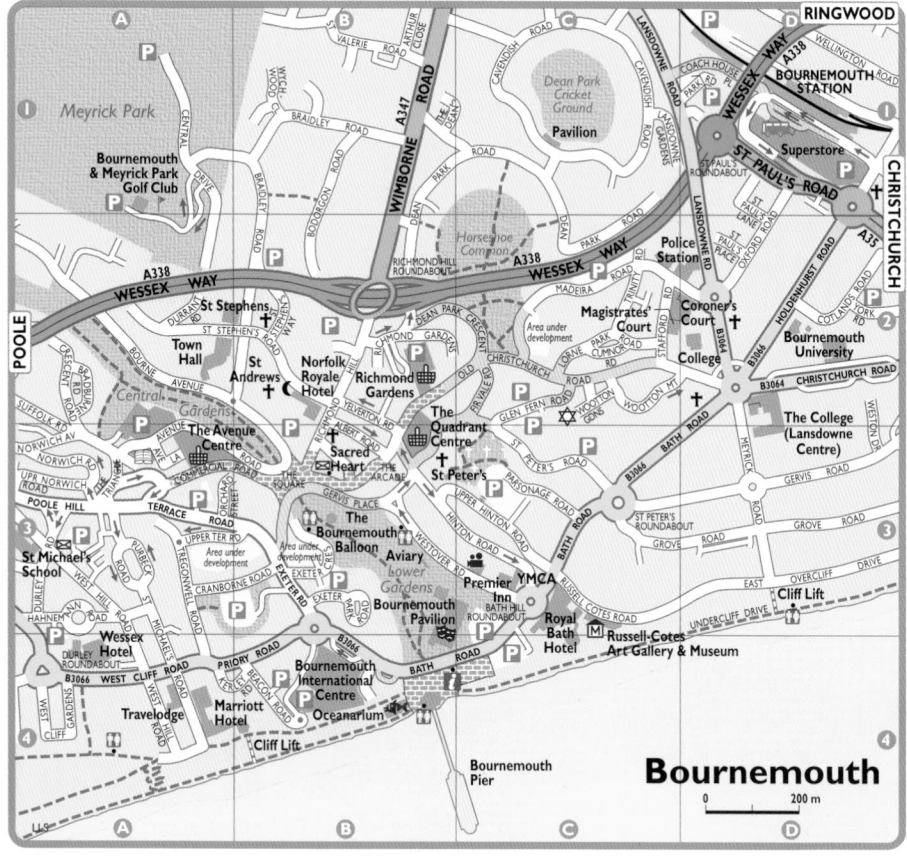

Bournemouth

Bournemouth is found on atlas page **13 J6**

Albert Road	B3		Park Road	D1
Arthur Close	B1		Parsonage Road	C3
Avenue Lane	A3		Poole Hill	A3
Avenue Road	A3		Priory Road	A4
Bath Hill Roundabout	C3		Purbeck Road	A3
Bath Road	B4		Richmond Gardens	B2
Beacon Road	B4		Richmond Hill	B3
Bodorgon Road	B2		Richmond Hill Roundabout	B2
Bourne Avenue	A2		Russell Cotes Road	C3
Bradburne Road	A2		St Michael's Road	A3
Braidley Road	B1		St Paul's Lane	D1
Cavendish Road	C1		St Paul's Place	D2
Central Drive	A1		St Paul's Road	D1
Christchurch Road	D2		St Paul's Roundabout	D1
Coach House Place	D1		St Peter's Road	C3
Commercial Road	A3		St Peter's Roundabout	C3
Cotlands Road	D2		St Stephen's Road	A2
Cranborne Road	A3		St Stephen's Way	B2
Crescent Road	A2		St Valerie Road	B1
Cumnor Road	C2		Stafford Road	C2
Dean Park Crescent	B2		Suffolk Road	A2
Dean Park Road	B2		Terrace Road	A3
Durley Road	A3		The Arcade	B3
Durley Roundabout	A4		The Deans	B1
Durrant Road	A2		The Square	B3
East Overcliff Drive	D3		The Triangle	A3
Exeter Crescent	B3		Tregonwell Road	A3
Exeter Park Road	B3		Trinity Road	C2
Exeter Road	B3		Undercliff Drive	D3
Fir Vale Road	C2		Upper Hinton Road	C3
Gervis Place	B3		Upper Norwich Road	A3
Gervis Road	D3		Upper Terrace Road	A3
Glen Fern Road	C2		Wellington Road	D1
Grove Road	C3		Wessex Way	A2
Hahnemann Road	A3		West Cliff Gardens	A4
Hinton Road	B3		West Cliff Road	A4
Holdenhurst Road	D2		West Hill Road	A3
Kerley Road	A4		Weston Drive	D2
Lansdowne Gardens	C1		Westover Road	B3
Lansdowne Road	C1		Wimborne Road	B1
Lorne Park Road	C2		Wootton Gardens	C2
Madeira Road	C2		Wootton Mount	C2
Meyrick Road	D3		Wychwood Close	B1
Norwich Avenue	A3		Yelverton Road	B2
Norwich Road	A3		York Road	D2
Old Christchurch Road	C2			
Orchard Street	A3			
Oxford Road	D2			

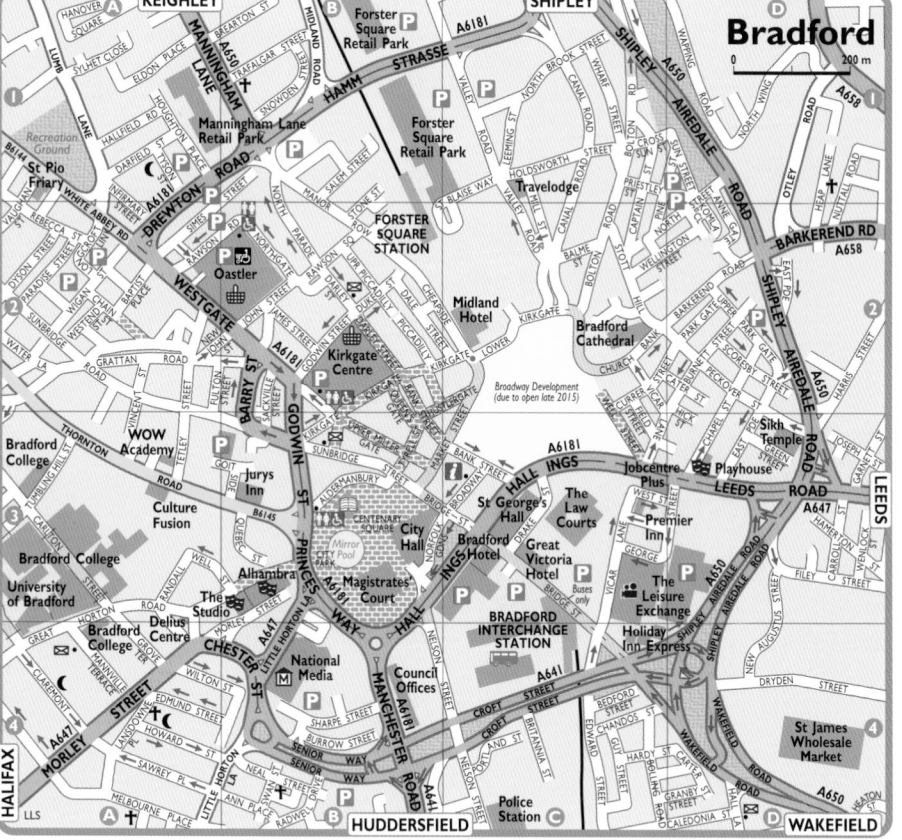

Bradford

Bradford is found on atlas page **90 F4**

Aldermanbury	B3		Lower Kirkgate	C2
Bank Street	B2		Lumb Lane	A1
Barkerend Road	D2		Manchester Road	B4
Barry Street	B2		Manningham Lane	A1
Bolling Road	C4		Manor Row	B1
Bolton Road	C2		Market Street	B3
Bridge Street	C3		Midland Road	B1
Broadway	C3		Morley Street	A4
Burnett Street	D2		Nelson Street	B4
Canal Road	C1		North Brook Street	C1
Carlton Street	A3		Northgate	B2
Centenary Square	B3		North Parade	B1
Chandos Street	C4		North Street	C2
Chapel Street	D3		North Wing	D1
Cheapside	B2		Otley Road	D1
Chester Street	A4		Paradise Street	A2
Church Bank	C2		Peckover Street	D2
Claremont	A4		Piccadilly	B2
Croft Street	C4		Pine Street	C2
Darfield Street	A1		Princes Way	B3
Darley Street	B2		Randall Well Street	A3
Drewton Road	A2		Rawson Road	A2
Dryden Street	D4		Rawson Square	B2
Duke Street	B2		Rebecca Street	A2
East Parade	D3		St Blaise Way	C1
Edmund Street	A4		Sawrey Place	A4
Edward Street	C4		Senior Way	B4
Eldon Place	A1		Shipley Airedale Road	C1
Filey Street	D3		Stott Hill	C2
George Street	C3		Sunbridge Road	A2
Godwin Street	B2		Sunbridge Street	B3
Grattan Road	A2		Tetley Street	A3
Great Horton Road	A4		Thornton Road	A2
Grove Terrace	A4		Trafalgar Street	B1
Hallfield Road	A1		Tyrell Street	B2
Hall Ings	B4		Upper Park Gate	D2
Hamm Strasse	B1		Upper Piccadilly	B2
Holdsworth Street	C1		Valley Road	C1
Houghton Place	A1		Vicar Lane	C3
Howard Street	A4		Wakefield Road	D4
Hustlergate	B3		Wapping Road	D1
Infirmary Street	A1		Water Lane	A2
John Street	B2		Wellington Street	C2
Lansdowne Place	A1		Westgate	A2
Leeds Road	D3		Wharf Street	C1
Little Horton	A4		White Abbey Road	A1
Little Horton Lane	B4		Wigan Street	A2
Longcroft Link	A2		Wilton Street	A4

Brighton

Brighton is found on atlas page **24 H10**

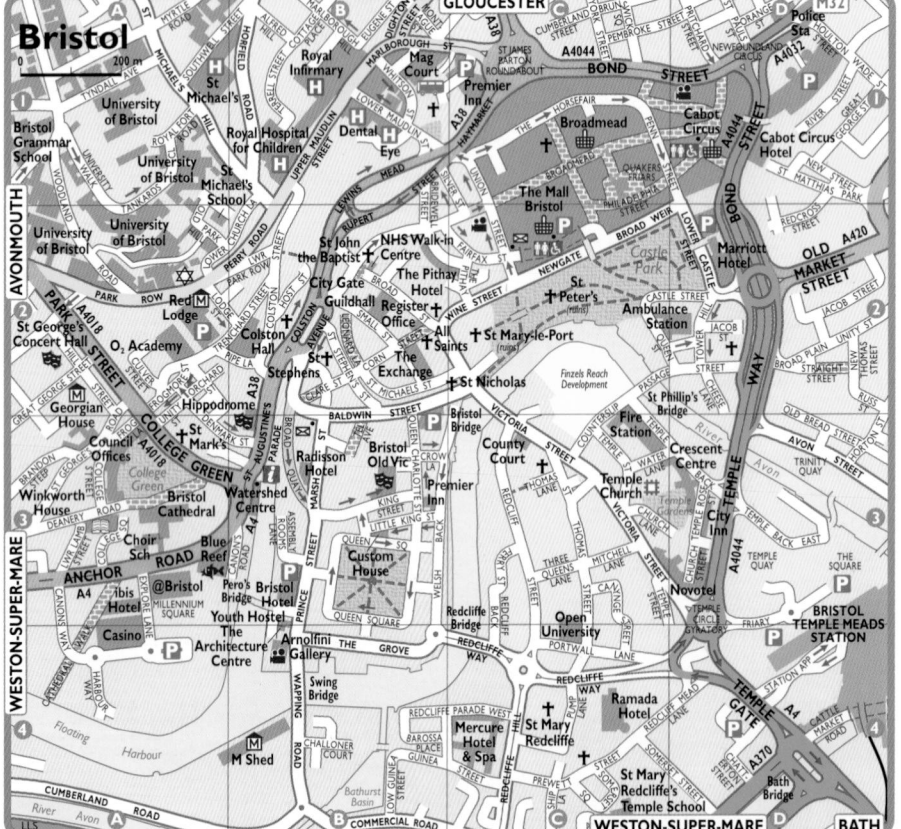

Bristol

Bristol is found on atlas page **31 Q10**

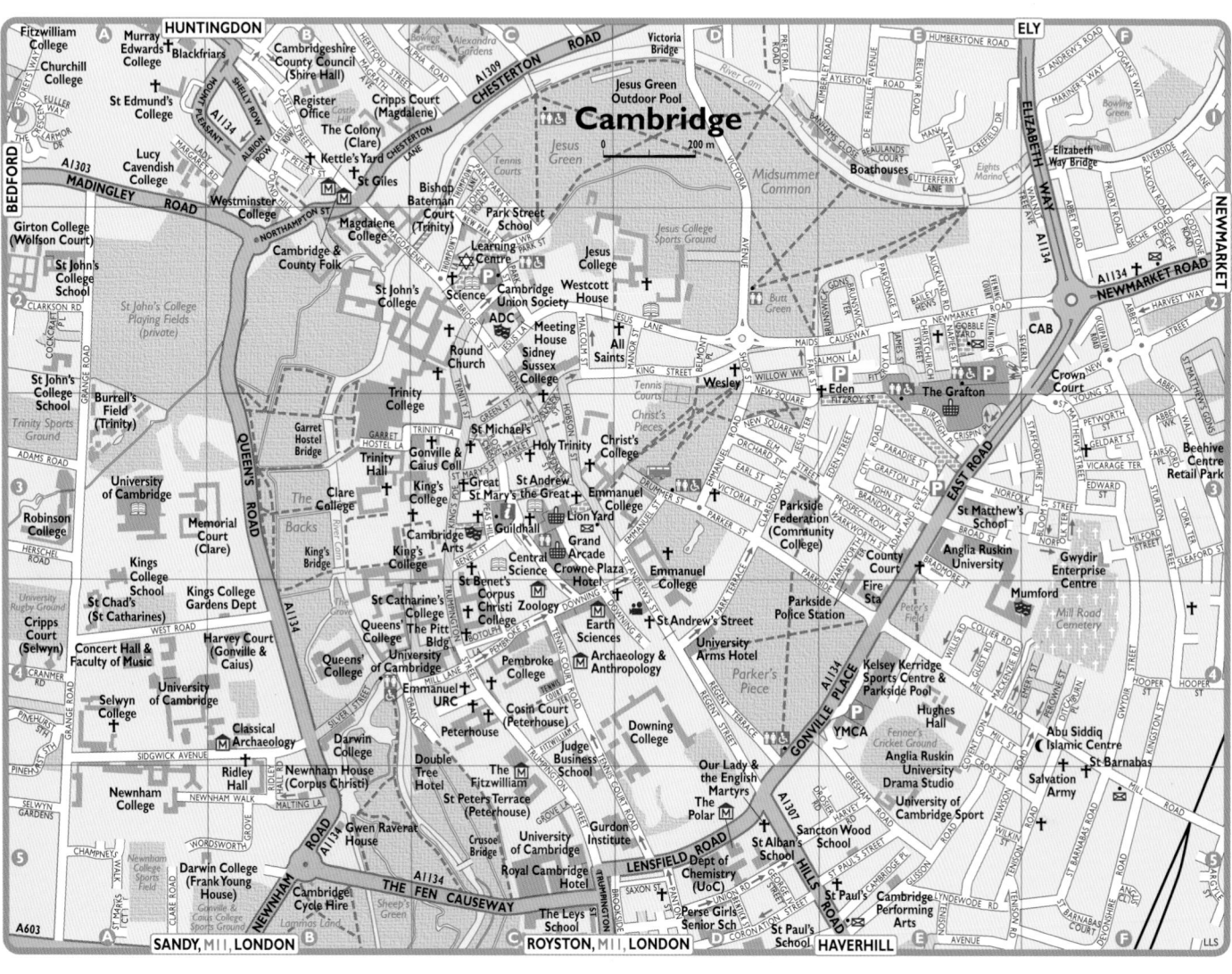

Cambridge

Cambridge is found on atlas page **62 G9**

University Colleges

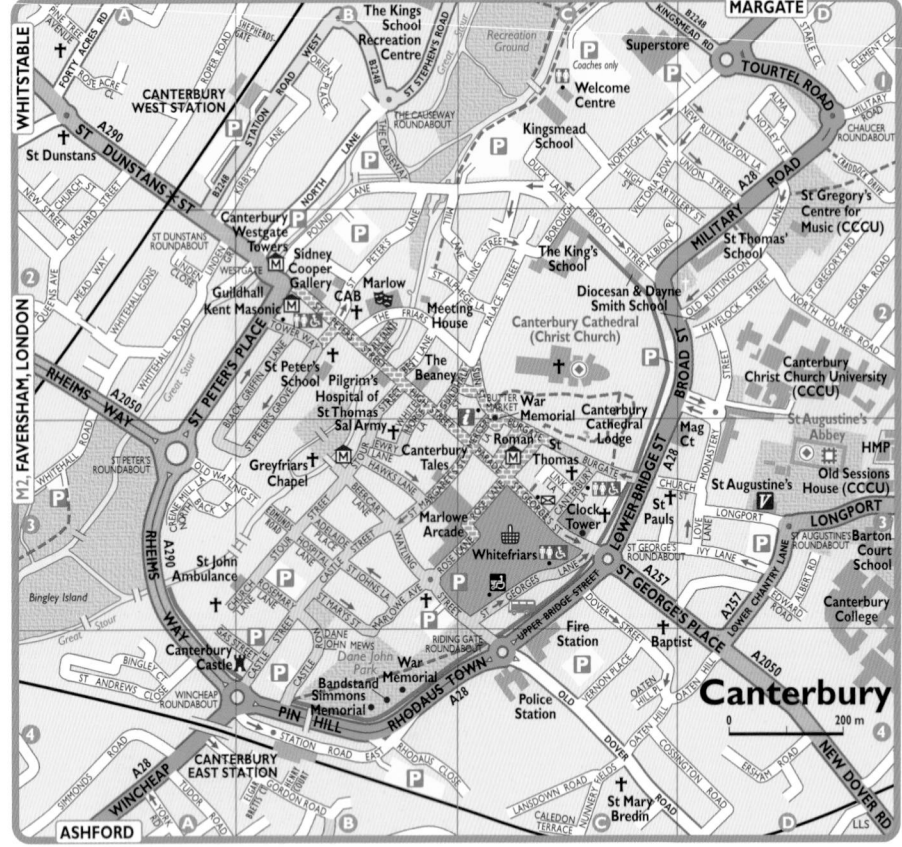

Canterbury

Canterbury is found on atlas page **39 K10**

Cardiff

Cardiff is found on atlas page **30 G9**

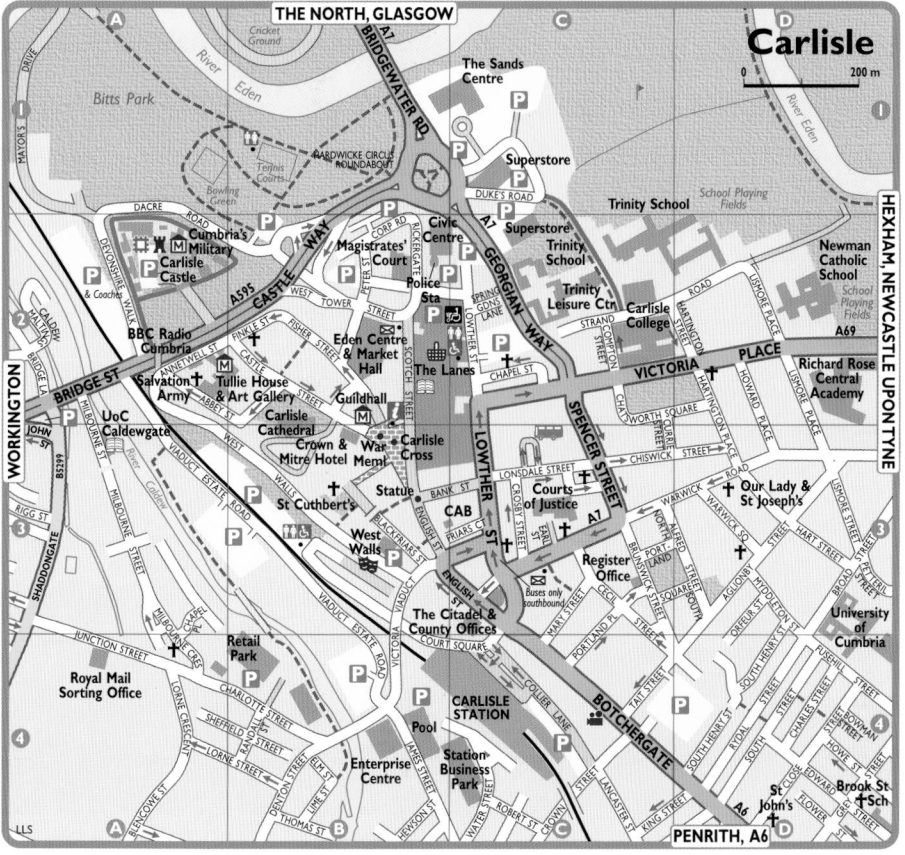

Carlisle

Carlisle is found on atlas page 110 G9

Cheltenham

Cheltenham is found on atlas page 46 H10

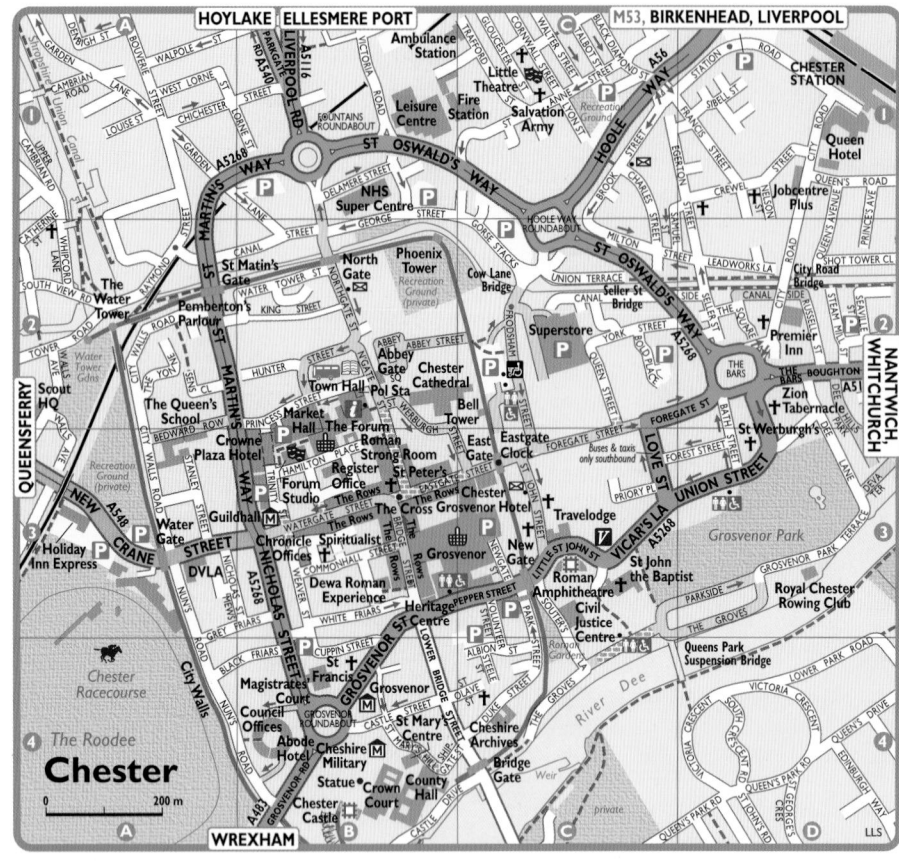

Chester

Chester is found on atlas page **81 N11**

Colchester

Colchester is found on atlas page **52 G6**

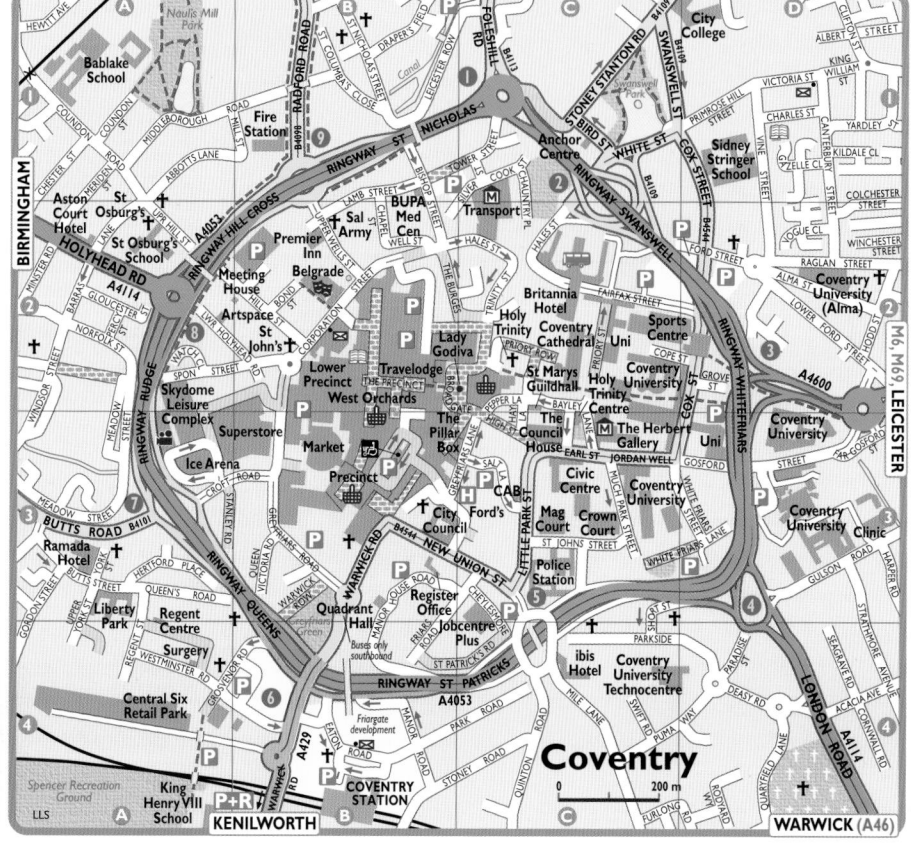

Coventry

Coventry is found on atlas page **59 M9**

Abbotts Lane	A1	Much Park Street	C3
Acacia Avenue	D4	New Union Street	B3
Alma Street	D2	Norfolk Street	A2
Barras Lane	A2	Paradise Street	D4
Bayley Lane	C2	Park Road	B4
Bird Street	C1	Parkside	C4
Bishop Street	B1	Primrose Hill Street	D1
Broadgate	B2	Priory Row	C2
Butts Road	A3	Priory Street	C2
Butts Street	A3	Puma Way	C4
Canterbury Street	D1	Quarryfield Lane	D4
Chester Street	A2	Queen's Road	A3
Cheylesmore	C3	Queen Victoria Road	B3
Cornwall Road	D4	Quinton Road	C4
Corporation Street	B2	Radford Road	B1
Coundon Road	A1	Raglan Street	D2
Cox Street	D1	Regent Street	A4
Cox Street	D2	Ringway Hill Cross	A2
Croft Road	A3	Ringway Queens	A3
Earl Street	C3	Ringway Rudge	A3
Eaton Road	B4	Ringway St Nicholas	B1
Fairfax Street	C2	Ringway St Patricks	B4
Foleshill Road	C1	Ringway Swanswell	C1
Gloucester Street	A2	Ringway Whitefriars	D2
Gosford Street	D3	St Johns Street	C3
Greyfriars Lane	B3	St Nicholas Street	B1
Greyfriars Road	B3	Salt Lane	C3
Grosvenor Road	A4	Seagrave Road	D4
Gulson Road	D3	Spon Street	A2
Hales Street	C2	Stanley Road	A3
Hertford Place	A3	Stoney Road	B4
High Street	C3	Stoney Stanton Road	C1
Hill Street	B2	Strathmore Avenue	D3
Holyhead Road	A2	Swanswell Street	C1
Jordan Well	C3	The Burges	B2
Lamb Street	B2	Tower Street	B1
Leicester Row	B1	Trinity Street	C2
Little Park Street	C3	Upper Hill Street	B2
London Road	D4	Upper Wells Street	A4
Lower Ford Street	D2	Victoria Street	D1
Lower Holyhead Road	A2	Vine Street	D1
Manor House Road	B4	Warwick Road	B3
Manor Road	B4	Warwick Road	B4
Meadow Street	A3	Westminster Road	A4
Meriden Street	A1	White Friars Street	D3
Middleborough Road	A1	White Street	C1
Mile Lane	C4	Windsor Street	A3
Mill Street	A1	Yardley Street	D1

Darlington

Darlington is found on atlas page **103 Q8**

Abbey Road	A3	Maude Street	A2
Albert Street	D4	Neasham Road	D4
Appleby Close	D4	Northgate	C2
Barningham Street	B1	North Lodge Terrace	B2
Bartlett Street	B1	Northumberland Street	B4
Beaumont Street	B3	Oakdene Avenue	A4
Bedford Street	C4	Outram Street	A2
Beechwood Avenue	A4	Parkgate	D3
Blackwellgate	B3	Park Lane	D4
Bondgate	B3	Park Place	C4
Borough Road	D3	Pendower Street	B1
Brunswick Street	C3	Pensbury Street	D4
Brunton Street	D4	Polam Lane	B4
Chestnut Street	C1	Portland Place	A3
Cleveland Terrace	A4	Powlett Street	B3
Clifton Road	C4	Priestgate	C3
Commercial Street	B2	Raby Terrace	B3
Coniscliffe Road	A4	Russell Street	C2
Corporation Road	B1	St Augustine's Way	B2
Crown Street	C2	St Cuthbert's Way	C2
Dodds Street	B1	St Cuthbert's Way	C4
Duke Street	A3	St James Place	D4
Easson Road	B1	Salisbury Terrace	A1
East Mount Road	D1	Salt Yard	B3
East Raby Street	B3	Scarth Street	A4
East Street	C3	Skinnergate	B3
Elms Road	A2	South Arden Street	B4
Feethams	C4	Southend Avenue	A4
Fife Road	A3	Stanhope Road North	A2
Four Riggs	B2	Stanhope Road South	A3
Freemans Place	C2	Stonebridge	C3
Gladstone Street	B2	Sun Street	B2
Grange Road	B4	Swan Street	C4
Greenbank Road	A1	Swinburne Road	A3
Greenbank Road	B2	Trinity Road	A3
Green Street	D3	Tubwell Row	B3
Hargreave Terrace	C4	Uplands Road	A3
Haughton Road	D2	Valley Street North	C2
High Northgate	C1	Vane Terrace	A2
High Row	B3	Victoria Embankment	A2
Hollyhurst Road	A1	Victoria Road	B4
Houndgate	B3	Victoria Road	C4
Jack Way Steeple	D3	West Crescent	A2
John Street	C1	West Powlett Street	A3
Kendrew Street	B2	West Row	B3
Kingston Street	B1	West Street	B4
Langholm Crescent	A4	Woodland Road	A2
Larchfield Street	A3	Yarm Road	D3

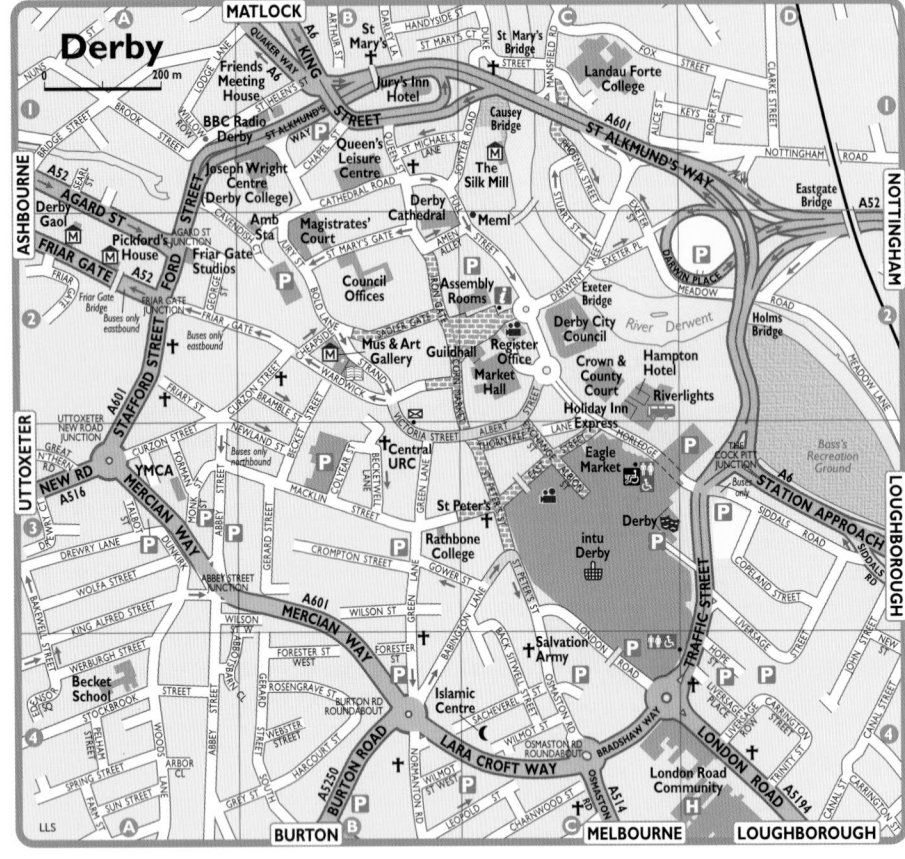

Derby

Derby is found on atlas page **72 B3**

Abbey Street	A4	King Alfred Street	A4
Agard Street	A1	King Street	B1
Albert Street	C3	Lara Croft Way	B4
Babington Lane	B4	Leopold Street	B4
Back Sitwell Street	C4	Liversage Row	D4
Becket Street	B3	Liversage Street	D3
Bold Lane	B2	Lodge Lane	A1
Bradshaw Way	C4	London Road	C3
Bramble Street	B2	Macklin Street	B3
Bridge Street	A1	Mansfield Road	C1
Brook Street	A1	Meadow Lane	D2
Burton Road	B4	Meadow Road	D2
Canal Street	D4	Mercian Way	B3
Carrington Street	D4	Morledge	C3
Cathedral Road	B1	Newland Street	A3
Cavendish Court	A2	New Road	A3
Chapel Street	B1	New Street	D4
Clarke Street	D1	Nottingham Road	D1
Copeland Street	D3	Osmaston Road	C4
Corn Market	B2	Phoenix Street	C1
Crompton Street	B3	Queen Street	B1
Curzon Street	A2	Robert Street	D1
Curzon Street	A3	Rosengrave Street	B4
Darwin Place	C2	Sacheverel Street	C4
Derwent Street	C2	Sadler Gate	B2
Drewry Lane	A3	St Alkmund's Way	C1
Duke Street	C1	St Helen's Street	B1
Dunkirk	A3	St Mary's Gate	B2
East Street	C3	St Peter's Street	C3
Exchange Street	C3	Siddals Road	D3
Exeter Place	C2	Sowter Road	C1
Exeter Street	C2	Spring Street	A4
Ford Street	A2	Stafford Street	A3
Forester Street West	B4	Station Approach	D3
Forman Street	A3	Stockbrook Street	A4
Fox Street	C1	Strand	B2
Friary Street	A2	Stuart Street	C1
Full Street	B1	Sun Street	A4
Gerard Street	B3	The Cock Pitt	D3
Gower Street	B3	Thorntree Lane	C3
Green Lane	B3	Traffic Street	C4
Grey Street	A4	Trinity Street	D4
Handyside Street	B1	Victoria Street	B2
Harcourt Street	B4	Wardwick	B2
Iron Gate	B2	Werburgh Street	A4
John Street	D4	Wilmot Street	C4
Jury Street	B2	Wolfa Street	A3
Keys Street	D1	Woods Lane	A4

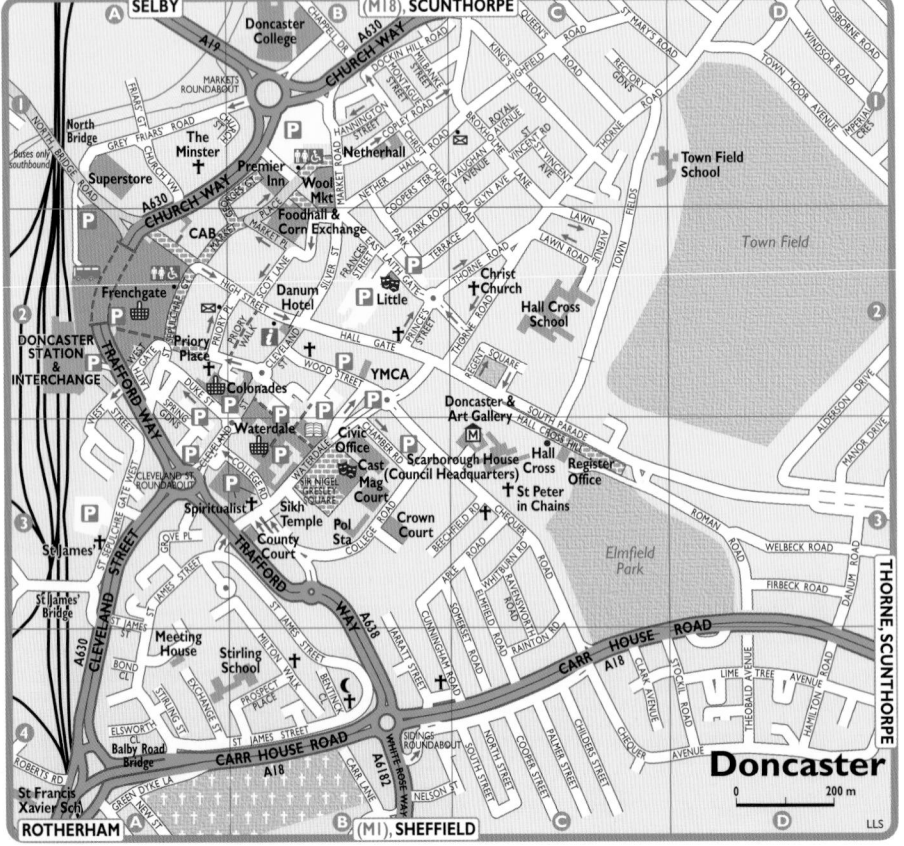

Doncaster

Doncaster is found on atlas page **91 P10**

Alderson Drive	D3	Milton Walk	B4
Apley Road	B3	Montague Street	B1
Balby Road Bridge	A4	Nelson Street	B4
Beechfield Road	B3	Nether Hall Road	B1
Broxholme Lane	C1	North Bridge Road	A1
Carr House Road	C4	North Street	C4
Carr Lane	B4	Palmer Street	C4
Chamber Road	B3	Park Road	B2
Chequer Avenue	C4	Park Terrace	B2
Chequer Road	C3	Prince's Street	B2
Childers Street	C4	Priory Place	A2
Christ Church Road	B1	Prospect Place	B4
Church View	A1	Queen's Road	C1
Church Way	B1	Rainton Road	C4
Clark Avenue	C4	Ravensworth Road	C3
Cleveland Street	A4	Rectory Gardens	C1
College Road	B3	Regent Square	C1
Cooper Street	C4	Roman Road	D3
Coopers Terrace	B2	Royal Avenue	C1
Copley Road	B1	St James Street	B4
Cunningham Road	B3	St Mary's Road	C1
Danum Road	D3	St Sepulchre Gate	A2
Dockin Hill Road	B1	St Sepulchre Gate West	A3
Duke Street	A2	St Vincent Avenue	C1
East Laith Gate	B2	St Vincent Road	C1
Elmfield Road	C3	Scot Lane	B2
Exchange Street	A4	Silver Street	B2
Firbeck Road	D3	Somerset Road	B3
Frances Street	B2	South Parade	C4
Georges Gate	B2	South Street	C4
Glyn Avenue	C1	Spring Gardens	A2
Green Dyke Lane	A4	Stirling Street	A4
Grey Friars' Road	A1	Stockil Road	C4
Hall Cross Hill	C2	Theobald Avenue	D4
Hall Gate	B2	Thorne Road	C1
Hamilton Road	D4	Thorne Road	C2
Hannington Street	B1	Town Fields	C2
High Street	A2	Town Moor Avenue	D1
Highfield Road	C1	Trafford Way	A2
Jarratt Street	B4	Vaughan Avenue	B3
King's Road	C1	Waterdale	B3
Lawn Avenue	C2	Welbeck Road	D3
Lawn Road	C2	West Laith Gate	A2
Lime Tree Avenue	D4	West Street	A2
Manor Drive	D3	Whitburn Road	C3
Market Place	A2	White Rose Way	B4
Market Road	B1	Windsor Road	D1
Milbanke Street	B1	Wood Street	B2

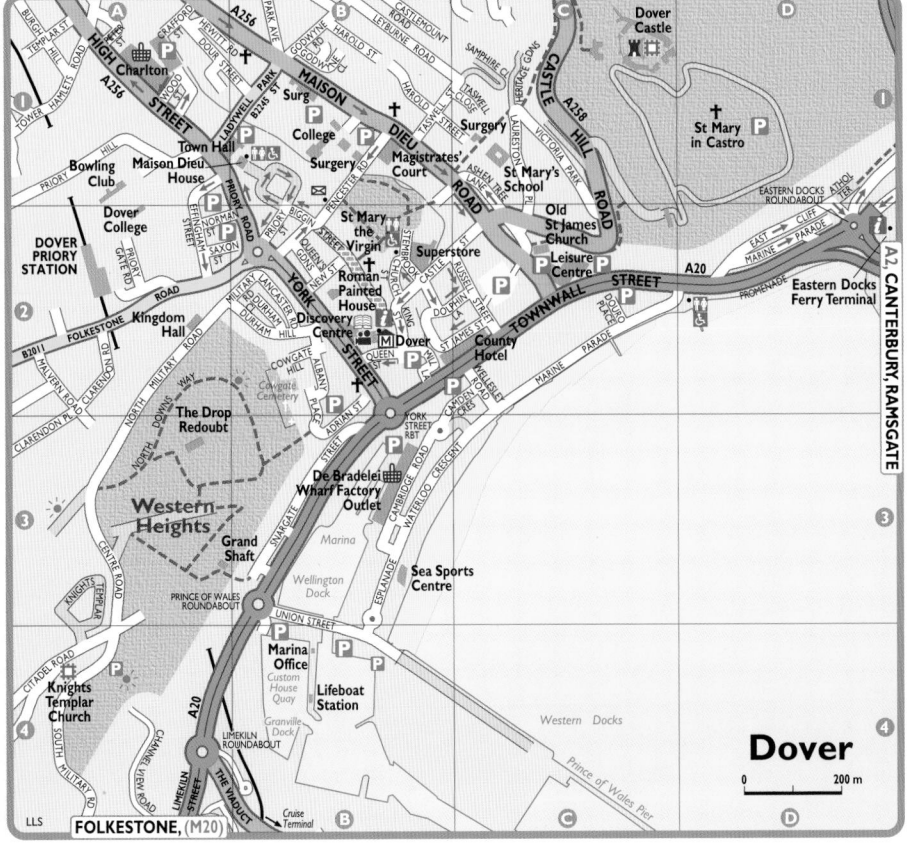

Dover

Dover is found on atlas page **27 P3**

Adrian Street	B3	Marine Parade	D2
Albany Place	B2	Military Road	B2
Ashen Tree Lane	C1	Mill Lane	B2
Athol Terrace	D1	New Street	B2
Biggin Street	B2	Norman Street	A2
Burgh Hill	A1	North Downs Way	A3
Cambridge Road	B3	North Military Road	A3
Camden Crescent	C2	Park Avenue	B1
Castle Hill Road	C1	Park Street	B1
Castlemount Road	B1	Pencester Road	B2
Castle Street	B2	Peter Street	A1
Centre Road	A3	Princes of Wales	
Channel View Road	A4	Roundabout	B3
Church Street	B2	Priory Gate Road	A2
Citadel Road	A4	Priory Hill	A1
Clarendon Place	A3	Priory Road	A1
Clarendon Road	A2	Priory Street	B2
Cowgate Hill	B2	Promenade	D2
Crafford Street	A1	Queen's Gate	B2
Dolphin Lane	B2	Queen Street	B2
Douro Place	C2	Russell Street	B2
Dour Street	A1	St James Street	B2
Durham Close	B2	Samphire Close	C1
Durham Hill	B2	Saxon Street	A2
East Cliff	D2	Snargate Street	B3
Eastern Docks		South Military Road	A4
Roundabout	D2	Stembrook	B2
Effingham Street	A2	Taswell Close	C1
Esplanade	B3	Taswell Street	B1
Folkestone Road	A2	Templar Street	A1
Godwyne Close	B1	The Viaduct	A4
Godwyne Road	B1	Tower Hamlets Road	A1
Harold Street	B1	Townwall Street	C2
Harold Street	B1	Union Street	B3
Heritage Gardens	C1	Victoria Park	C1
Hewitt Road	A1	Waterloo Crescent	B3
High Street	A1	Wellesley Road	C2
King Street	B2	Wood Street	A1
Knights Templar	A3	York Street	B2
Ladywell	A1	York Street Roundabout	B3
Lancaster Road	B2		
Laureston Place	C1		
Leyburne Road	B1		
Limekiln Roundabout	A4		
Limekiln Street	A4		
Maison Dieu Road	B1		
Malvern Road	A2		
Marine Parade	C2		

Dundee

Dundee is found on atlas page **142 G11**

Albert Square	B2	Laburn Street	A1
Bank Street	B2	Ladywell Avenue	C1
Barrack Road	A1	Laurel Bank	B1
Barrack Road	B2	Lochee Road	A1
Bell Street	B2	McDonald Street	D2
Blackscroft	D1	Meadowside	B2
Blinshall Street	A1	Miln Street	A2
Blinshall Street	A2	Murraygate	C2
Bonnybank Road	C1	Nethergate	A4
Brown Street	A2	Nicoll Street	B2
Candle Lane	C2	North Lindsay Street	B2
Castle Street	C2	North Marketgait	B1
Chandlers Lane	D3	North Victoria Road	C1
Chapel Street	C2	Old Hawkhill	A3
City Square	C3	Panmure Street	B2
Commercial Street	C2	Park Place	A3
Constable Street	D1	Perth Road	A4
Constitution Crescent	A1	Princes Street	D1
Constitution Road	A1	Prospect Place	B1
Constitution Road	B2	Queen Street	C1
Court House Square	A2	Rattray Street	B2
Cowgate	C1	Reform Street	B2
Cowgate	D1	Riverside Drive	B4
Crighton Street	C3	Roseangle	A4
Dens Street	D1	St Andrews Street	C1
Dock Street	C3	Scrimgeour Place	A1
Douglas Street	A2	Seabraes Lane	A4
Dudhope Street	B1	Seagate	C2
East Dock Street	D2	Session Street	A2
East Marketgait	C1	Shore Terrace	C3
East Whale Lane	D1	South Marketgait	C3
Euclid Crescent	B2	South Tay Street	B3
Euclid Street	B2	South Victoria Dock Road	D3
Forebank Road	C1	South Ward Road	B2
Forester Street	B2	Sugarhouse Wynd	C2
Foundry Lane	D1	Tay Road Bridge	D3
Gellatly Street	C2	Tay Square	B3
Greenmarket	B4	Trades Lane	C2
Guthrie Street	A2	Union Street	B3
Hawkhill	A3	Union Terrace	B1
High Street	C3	Ward Road	B2
Hilltown	B1	Weavers Yard	D1
Hilltown Terrace	B1	West Bell Street	A2
Hunter Street	A3	West Marketgait	A2
Infirmary Brae	A1	West Port	A3
Johnston Street	B2	West Victoria Dock Road	D2
King Street	C1	Whitehall Place	C3
Kirk Lane	C1	Whitehall Street	C3

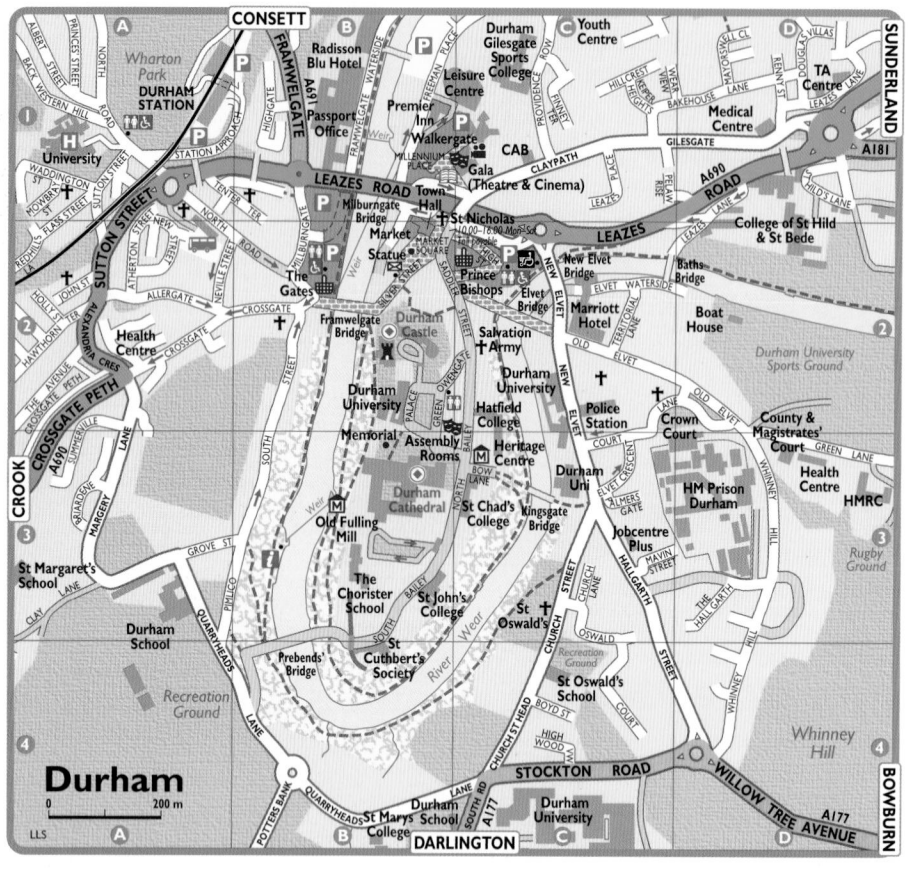

Durham

Durham

Durham is found on atlas page 103 Q2

Albert Street	A1	Mayorswell Close	D1
Alexandria Crescent	A2	Milburngate Bridge	B1
Allergate	A2	Millburngate	B2
Atherton Street	A2	Millennium Place	B1
Back Western Hill	A1	Mowbray Street	A1
Bakehouse Lane	C1	Neville Street	A2
Baths Bridge	C2	New Elvet	C2
Bow Lane	C3	New Elvet Bridge	C2
Boyd Street	C4	New Street	A2
Briardene	A3	North Bailey	C3
Church Lane	C3	North Road	A1
Church Street	C4	Old Elvet	C3
Church Street Head	C4	Oswald Court	C2
Clay Lane	A3	Owengate	B2
Claypath	C1	Palace Green	B2
Court Lane	C3	Palmers Gate	C3
Crossgate	A2	Pelaw Rise	C1
Crossgate Peth	A3	Pimlico	A3
Douglas Villas	D1	Potters Bank	B4
Elvet Bridge	C2	Prebends' Bridge	B4
Elvet Crescent	C3	Princes' Street	A1
Elvet Waterside	C2	Providence Row	C1
Finney Terrace	C1	Quarryheads Lane	A3
Flass Street	A2	Redhills Lane	A2
Framwelgate	B1	Renny Street	D1
Framwelgate Bridge	B2	Saddler Street	B2
Framwelgate Waterside	B1	St Hild's Lane	D1
Freeman Place	B1	Silver Street	B2
Gilesgate	C1	South Bailey	B3
Green Lane	D3	South Road	C4
Grove Street	A3	South Street	B3
Hallgarth Street	C3	Station Approach	A1
Hawthorn Terrace	A2	Stockton Road	C4
Highgate	B1	Summerville	A3
High Road View	C4	Sutton Street	A2
High Street	C2	Tenter Terrace	A1
Hillcrest	C1	Territorial Lane	C1
Holly Street	A2	The Avenue	A2
John Street	A2	The Hall Garth	D3
Keiper Heights	C1	Waddington Street	A1
Kingsgate Bridge	C3	Wear View	D1
Leazes Lane	D1	Whinney Hill	D3
Leazes Lane	D2	Willow Tree Avenue	D4
Leazes Place	C1		
Leazes Road	B1		
Margery Lane	A3		
Market Square	B2		
Mavin Street	C3		

Eastbourne

Eastbourne is found on atlas page 25 P11

Arlington Road	A2	Langney Road	D1
Ashford Road	B2	Langney Road	C2
Ashford Road	C1	Lascelles Terrace	B4
Ashford Square	B1	Latimer Road	D1
Avenue Lane	A1	Leaf Road	B1
Belmore Road	C1	Lismore Road	B2
Blackwater Road	A4	Longstone Road	C1
Bolton Road	B3	Lushington Road	B3
Bourne Street	C1	Marine Parade	D2
Burlington Place	B3	Marine Road	D1
Burlington Road	C3	Mark Lane	B2
Camden Road	A3	Meads Road	A3
Carew Road	B1	Melbourne Road	C1
Carlisle Road	A4	Old Orchard Road	B2
Carlisle Road	B4	Old Wish Road	A4
Cavendish Avenue	C1	Pevensey Road	C2
Cavendish Place	C1	Promenade	C3
Ceylon Place	C2	Queen's Gardens	D2
Chiswick Place	B3	Saffrons Road	A2
College Road	B3	St Anne's Road	A1
Colonnade Gardens	D2	St Aubyn's Road	D1
Commercial Road	B1	St Leonard's Road	B1
Compton Street	B4	Seaside	D1
Compton Street	C3	Seaside Road	C2
Cornfield Lane	B3	Southfields Road	A2
Cornfield Road	B2	South Street	A3
Cornfield Terrace	B3	South Street	B3
Devonshire Place	B3	Spencer Road	B3
Dursley Road	C1	Station Street	B2
Elms Road	C3	Susan's Road	C2
Enys Road	A1	Sutton Road	B2
Eversfield Road	A1	Sydney Road	C1
Furness Road	A3	Terminus Road	B2
Gildredge Road	B2	Terminus Road	C3
Grand Parade	C3	The Avenue	A1
Grange Road	A3	Tideswell Road	C2
Grassington Road	A3	Trinity Place	C3
Grove Road	A3	Trinity Trees	C2
Hardwick Road	B3	Upper Avenue	B1
Hartfield Lane	A1	Upperton Gardens	A1
Hartfield Road	A1	Upperton Lane	A1
Hartington Place	C3	Upperton Road	A1
Howard Square	C4	West Street	A3
Hyde Gardens	B2	West Terrace	A2
Hyde Road	A2	Willowfield Road	D1
Ivy Terrace	A2	Wilmington Square	B4
Jevington Gardens	A4	Wish Road	B3
Junction Road	B2	York Road	A3

Eastbourne

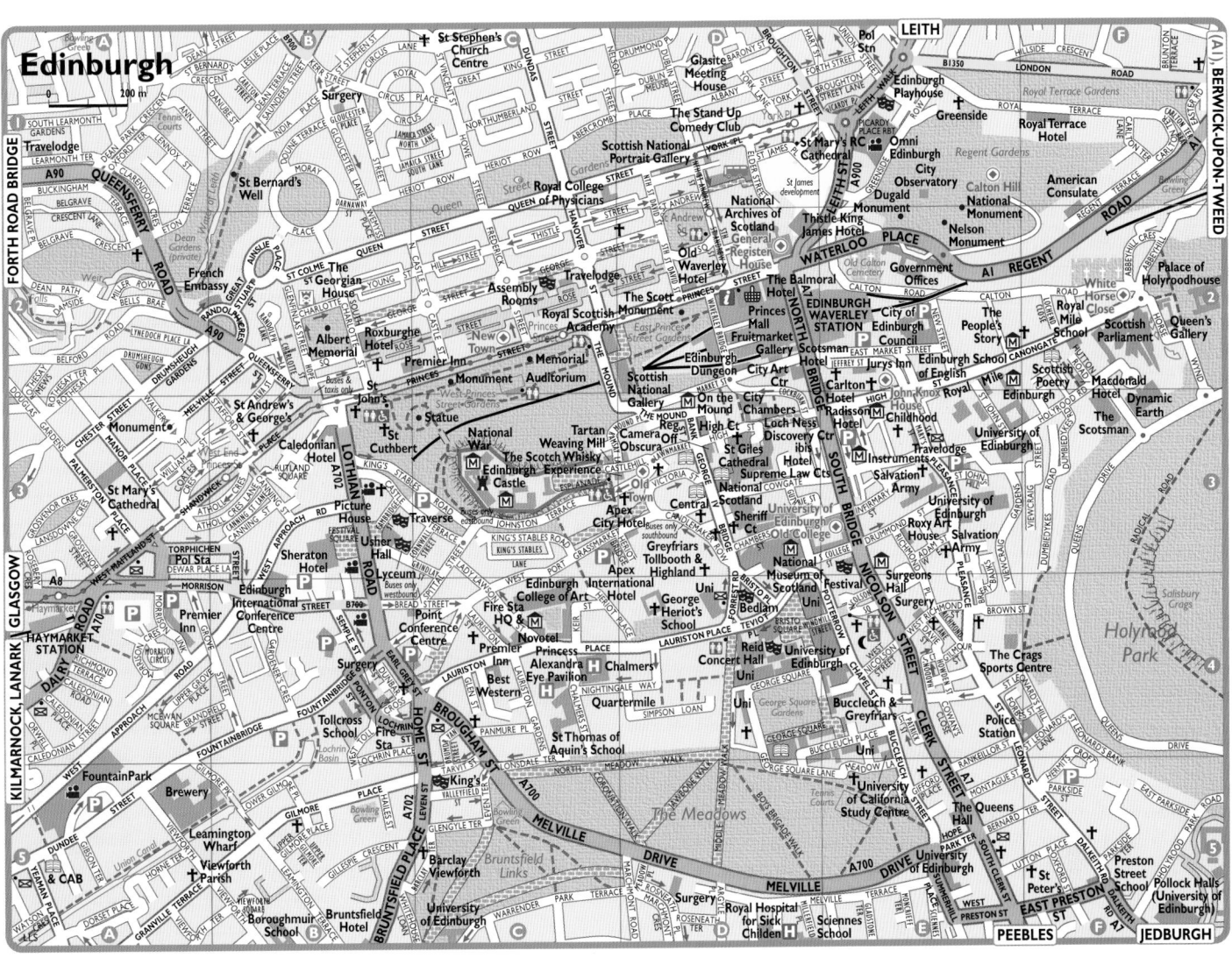

Edinburgh

Edinburgh is found on atlas page **127 P3**

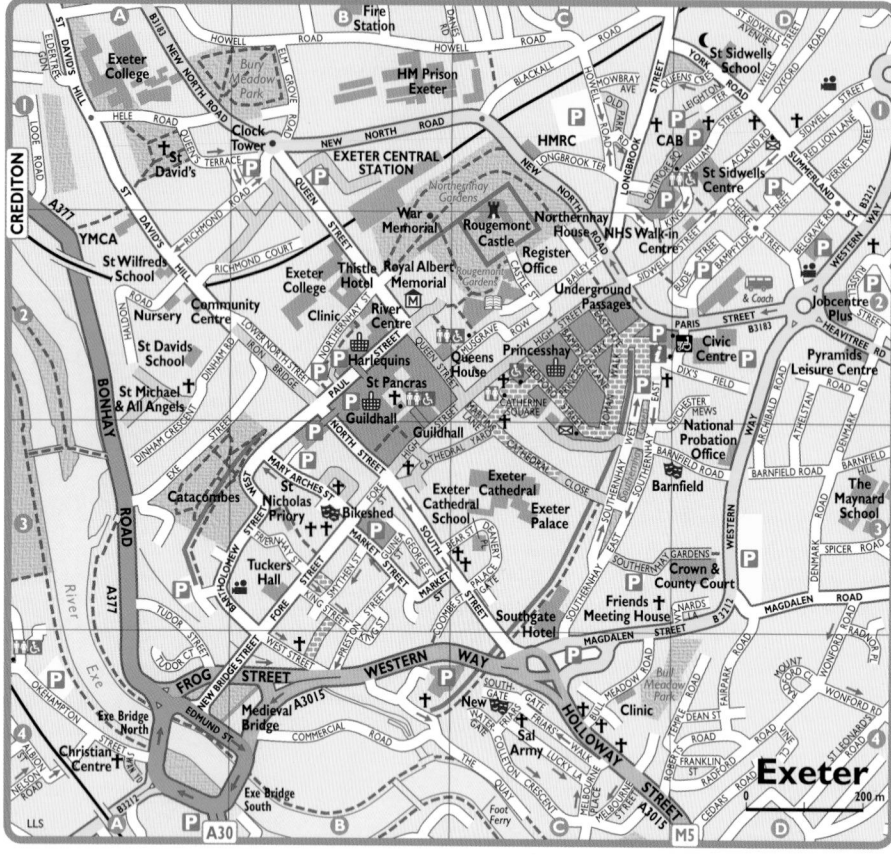

Exeter

Exeter is found on atlas page **9 M6**

Acland Road D1	King William Street D1
Archibald Road D3	Longbrook Street C1
Athelstan Road D3	Lower North Street B2
Bailey Street C2	Magdalen Road D3
Bampfylde Lane C2	Magdalen Street C4
Bampfylde Street D2	Market Street B3
Barnfield Road D3	Martins Lane C2
Bartholomew Street West ... B3	Mary Arches Street B3
Bear Street C3	Musgrave Row C2
Bedford Street C2	New Bridge Street A4
Belgrave Road D2	New North Road A1
Blackall Road C1	Northernhay Street B2
Bonhay Road A2	North Street C2
Bude Street D2	Old Park Road C1
Bull Meadow Road C4	Oxford Road D1
Castle Street C2	Palace Gate C3
Cathedral Close C3	Paris Street D2
Cathedral Yard B3	Paul Street B2
Cedars Road D4	Preston Street B4
Cheeke Street D1	Princesshay C2
Chichester Mews C3	Queens Crescent C1
Commercial Road B4	Queen's Terrace A1
Coombe Street B3	Queen Street B1
Deanery Place C3	Radford Road D4
Dean Street D4	Red Lion Lane D1
Denmark Road D3	Richmond Court B2
Dinham Crescent A3	Richmond Road A2
Dinham Road A2	Roberts Road C4
Dix's Field D2	Roman Walk C2
Eastgate C2	St David's Hill A1
Edmund Street A4	Sidwell Street C2
Elm Grove Road B1	Sidwell Street D1
Exe Street A3	Smythen Street B3
Fairpark Road D4	Southernhay East C3
Fore Street B3	Southernhay Gardens C3
Franklin Street D4	Southernhay West C3
Friernhay Street B3	South Street B3
Frog Street A4	Spicer Road D3
George Street B3	Summerland Street D1
Guinea Street B3	Temple Road D4
Haldon Road A2	Tudor Court A3
Heavitree Road D2	Tudor Street A3
Hele Road A1	Verney Street D1
High Street C2	Wells Street D1
Holloway Street C4	Western Way B4
Howell Road B1	West Street B4
Iron Bridge B2	Wonford Road D4
King Street B3	York Road D1

Gloucester

Gloucester is found on atlas page **46 F11**

Albert Street D4	Montpellier B4
Albion Street B4	Napier Street D4
All Saints' Road D4	Nettleton Road C3
Alvin Street C2	New Inn Lane B3
Archdeacon Street B2	New Inn Lane C3
Arthur Street C4	Norfolk Street B4
Barbican Road B3	Northgate Street C3
Barrack Square B3	Old Tram Road B4
Barton Street D4	Over Causeway A1
Bedford Street C3	Oxford Road D1
Belgrave Road C4	Oxford Street D2
Berkeley Street B3	Park Road C4
Black Dog Way C2	Park Street C2
Blenheim Road D4	Parliament Street C4
Brunswick Road B4	Pembroke Street C4
Brunswick Square B4	Pitt Street B2
Bruton Way D3	Priory Road B1
Bull Lane B3	Quay Street B2
Castle Meads Way A2	Royal Oak Road A2
Clarence Street C3	Russell Street C3
Clare Street B2	St Aldate Street C2
College Court B2	St Catherine Street C1
Commercial Road B3	St John's Lane B3
Cromwell Street C4	St Mark Street C1
Deans Walk C1	St Mary's Square B2
Eastgate Street C3	St Mary's Street B2
Gouda Way B1	St Michael's Square C4
Great Western Road D2	St Oswald's Road B1
Greyfriars B3	Sebert Street C1
Hampden Way C3	Severn Road A3
Hare Lane C2	Sherborne Street D2
Heathville Road D2	Sinope Street D4
Henry Road D1	Southgate Street B4
Henry Street D2	Spa Road B4
High Orchard Street A4	Station Road C3
Honyatt Road D1	Swan Road C1
King Barton Street C4	Sweetbriar Street C1
Kingsholm Road C1	The Cross C3
King's Square C3	The Oxbode C3
Ladybellegate Street B3	The Quay A2
Llanthony Road A4	Union Street C1
London Road D2	Upper Quay Street B2
Longsmith Street B3	Vauxhall Road D4
Market Parade C3	Wellington Street C4
Merchants' Road A4	Westgate Street A2
Mercia Road B1	Widden Street D4
Metz Way D3	Worcester Parade C2
Millbrook Street D4	Worcester Street C2

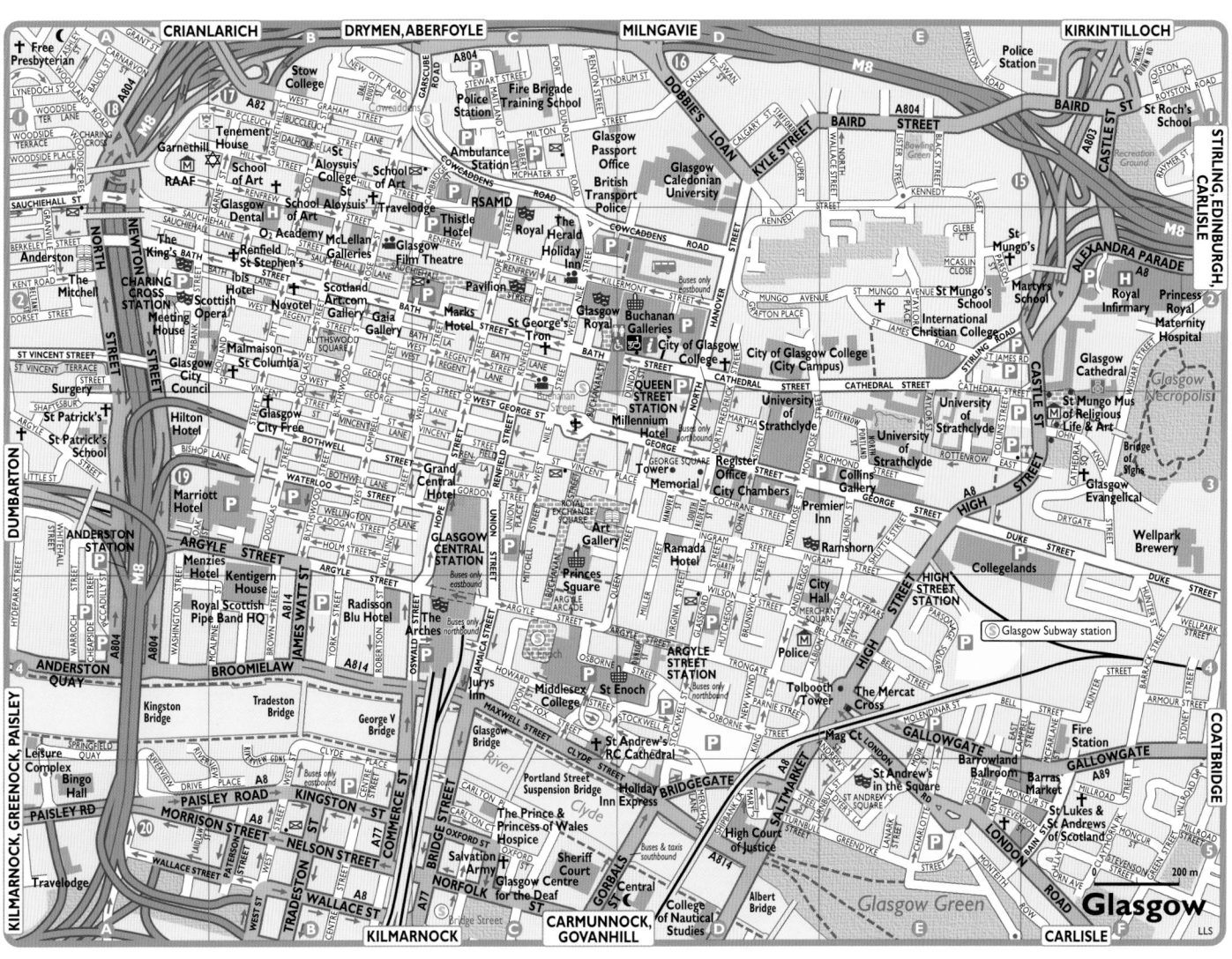

Glasgow

Glasgow is found on atlas page **125 P4**

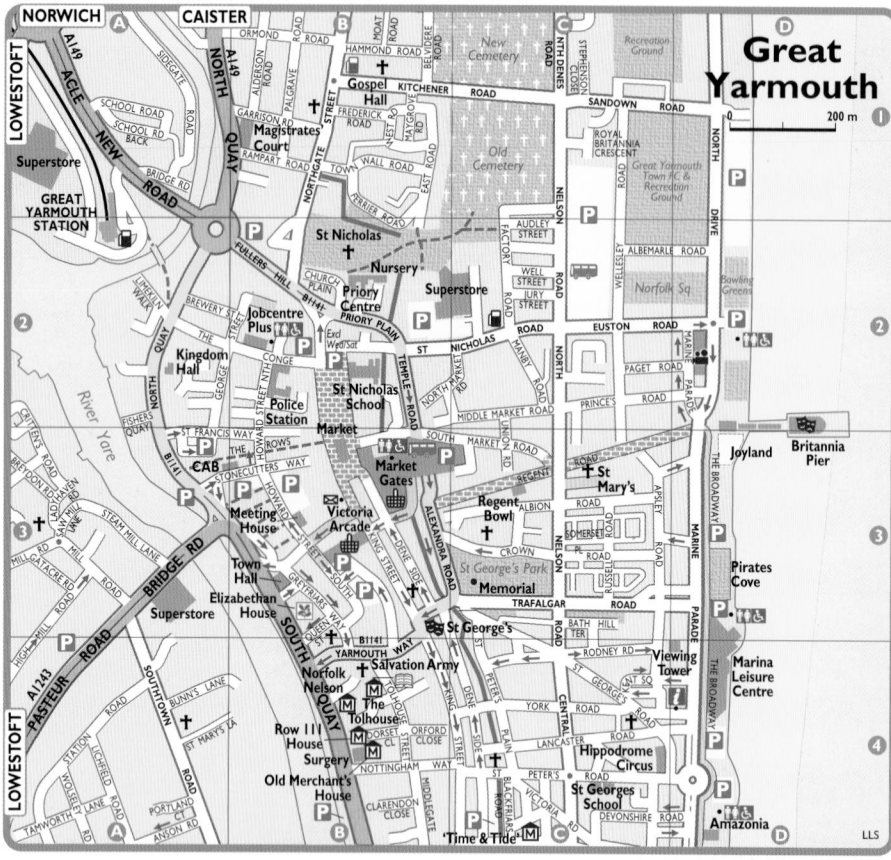

Great Yarmouth

Great Yarmouth is found on atlas page **77 Q10**

Acle New Road	A1	North Drive	D1
Albemarle Road	C2	North Market Road	C2
Albion Road	C3	North Quay	A2
Alderson Road	B1	Northgate Street	B1
Alexandra Road	B3	Nottingham Way	B4
Apsley Road	C3	Ormond Road	B1
Belvidere Road	B1	Paget Road	C2
Blackfriars Road	C4	Palgrave Road	B1
Brewery Street	A2	Pasteur Road	A4
Breydon Road	A3	Prince's Road	C2
Bridge Road	A1	Priory Plain	B2
Bridge Road	A3	Queen Street	B2
Bunn's Lane	A4	Rampart Road	B1
Church Plain	B2	Regent Road	C3
Critten's Road	A3	Rodney Road	C4
Crown Road	C3	Russell Road	C3
Dene Side	B3	St Francis Way	A3
Devonshire Road	C4	St George's Road	C4
East Road	B1	St Nicholas Road	B2
Euston Road	C2	St Peter's Plain	C4
Factory Road	C2	St Peter's Road	C4
Ferrier Road	B1	Sandown Road	C1
Fishers Quay	A2	Saw Mill Lane	A3
Frederick Road	B1	School Road	A1
Fullers Hill	B2	School Road Back	A1
Garrison Road	B1	Sidegate Road	A1
Gatacre Road	A3	South Market Road	C3
George Street	A2	South Quay	B3
Greyfriars Way	B3	Southtown Road	A4
Hammond Road	B1	Station Road	A4
High Mill Road	A3	Steam Mill Lane	A3
Howard Street North	B2	Stephenson Close	C1
Howard Street South	B3	Stonecutters Way	A2
King Street	B3	Tamworth Lane	A4
Kitchener Road	B1	Temple Road	B2
Ladyhaven Road	A3	The Broadway	D3
Lancaster Road	C4	The Conge	A2
Lichfield Road	A4	The Rows	B3
Limekiln Walk	A2	Tolhouse Street	B4
Manby Road	C2	Town Wall Road	B1
Marine Parade	D3	Trafalgar Road	C3
Maygrove Road	B1	Union Road	C3
Middle Market Road	C2	Victoria Road	C4
Middlegate	B4	Wellesley Road	C2
Moat Road	B1	West Road	B1
Nelson Road Central	C3	Wolseley Road	A4
Nelson Road North	C1	Yarmouth Way	B2
North Denes Road	C1	York Road	C4

Guildford

Guildford is found on atlas page **23 Q5**

Abbot Road	C4	Millmead Terrace	B4
Angel Gate	B3	Mount Pleasant	A4
Artillery Road	B1	Nightingale Road	D1
Artillery Terrace	C1	North Street	B3
Bedford Road	A2	Onslow Road	C1
Bridge Street	A3	Onslow Street	B3
Bright Hill	C3	Oxford Road	C3
Brodie Road	D3	Pannells Court	C2
Bury Fields	B4	Park Street	B3
Bury Street	B4	Pewley Bank	D3
Castle Hill	C4	Pewley Fort Inner Court	D4
Castle Street	C3	Pewley Hill	C4
Chapel Street	B3	Pewley Way	D3
Chertsey Street	C2	Phoenix Court	B3
Cheselden Road	D2	Porridge Pot Alley	B4
Church Road	B1	Portsmouth Road	A4
College Road	B2	Poyle Road	D4
Commercial Road	B2	Quarry Street	B3
Dene Road	D2	Sandfield Terrace	D2
Denmark Road	D2	Semaphore Road	D3
Drummond Road	B1	South Hill	C3
Eagle Road	C1	Springfield Road	C1
Epsom Road	D2	Station Approach	D1
Falcon Road	C1	Stoke Fields	C1
Fort Road	C4	Stoke Grove	C1
Foxenden Road	D1	Stoke Road	C1
Friary Bridge	A3	Swan Lane	B3
Friary Street	B3	Sydenham Road	C3
George Road	B1	Testard Road	A3
Guildford Park Road	A2	The Bars	C2
Harvey Road	D3	The Mount	A4
Haydon Place	C2	The Shambles	B3
High Pewley	D4	Tunsgate	C3
High Street	B3	Upperton Road	A3
Jeffries Passage	C2	Victoria Road	D1
Jenner Road	D2	Walnut Tree Close	A1
Laundry Road	B2	Ward Street	C2
Leapale Lane	B2	Warwicks Bench	C4
Leapale Road	B2	Wherwell Road	A3
Leas Road	B1	William Road	B1
London Road	D2	Wodeland Avenue	A3
Mareschal Road	A4	Woodbridge Road	B1
Market Street	C3	York Road	B1
Martyr Road	C2		
Mary Road	A1		
Millbrook	B3		
Mill Lane	B3		
Millmead	B3		

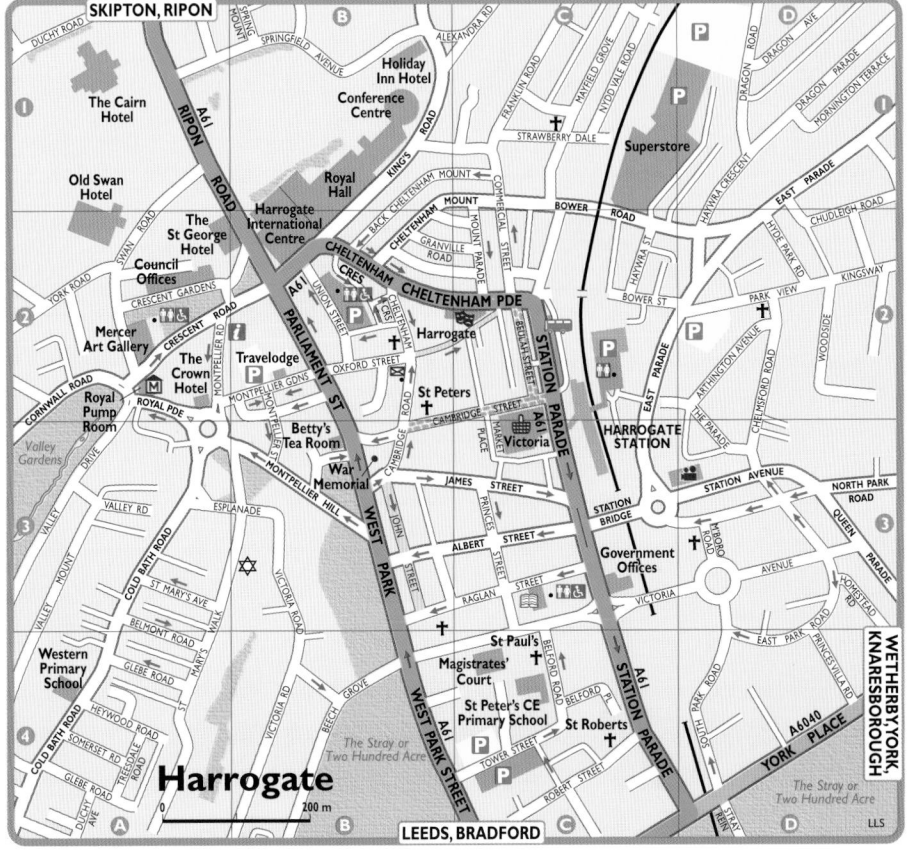

Harrogate

Harrogate is found on atlas page **97 M9**

Albert Street	C3	Montpellier Road	A2
Alexandra Road	B1	Montpellier Street	B2
Arthington Avenue	D2	Mornington Terrace	D1
Back Cheltenham Mount	B2	Mount Parade	C2
Beech Grove	B4	North Park Road	D3
Belford Place	C4	Nydd Vale Road	C1
Belford Road	C4	Oxford Street	B2
Belmont Road	A3	Park View	D2
Beulah Street	C2	Parliament Street	B2
Bower Road	C1	Princes Street	C3
Bower Street	C2	Princes Villa Road	D4
Cambridge Road	B3	Queen Parade	D3
Cambridge Street	C2	Raglan Street	C3
Chelmsford Road	D3	Ripon Road	A1
Cheltenham Crescent	B2	Robert Street	C4
Cheltenham Mount	B2	Royal Parade	A2
Cheltenham Parade	B2	St Mary's Avenue	A3
Chudleigh Road	D2	St Mary's Walk	A4
Cold Bath Road	A3	Somerset Road	A4
Commercial Street	C1	South Park Road	D4
Cornwall Road	A2	Springfield Avenue	B1
Crescent Gardens	A2	Spring Mount	B1
Crescent Road	A2	Station Avenue	D3
Dragon Avenue	D1	Station Bridge	C3
Dragon Parade	D1	Station Parade	C2
Dragon Road	D1	Strawberry Dale	C1
Duchy Avenue	A4	Stray Rein	D4
Duchy Road	A1	Swan Road	A2
East Parade	C2	The Parade	D2
East Park Road	D4	Tower Street	C4
Esplanade	A3	Treesdale Road	A4
Franklin Road	C1	Union Street	B2
Glebe Road	A4	Valley Drive	A3
Granville Road	B2	Valley Mount	A3
Haywra Street	C2	Valley Road	A3
Heywood Road	A4	Victoria Avenue	C3
Homestead Road	D3	Victoria Road	B3
Hyde Park Road	D2	West Park	B3
Hywra Crescent	D2	West Park Street	B4
James Street	B3	Woodside	D2
John Street	B3	York Place	D4
King's Road	B1	York Road	A2
Kingsway	D2		
Market Place	C3		
Marlborough Road	D3		
Mayfield Grove	C1		
Montpellier Gardens	B2		
Montpellier Hill	B3		

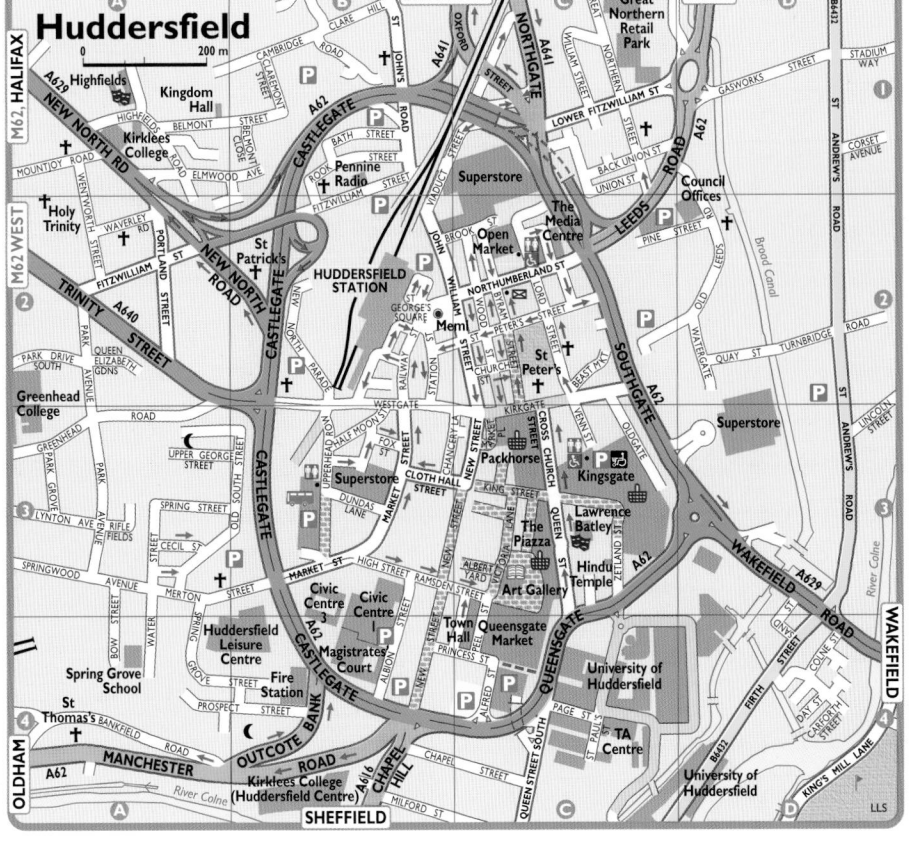

Huddersfield

Huddersfield is found on atlas page **90 E7**

Albion Street	B4	New North Road	A2
Alfred Street	C4	New Street	B4
Back Union Street	C1	Northgate	C1
Bankfield Road	A4	Northumberland Street	C2
Bath Street	B1	Old Leeds Road	D2
Belmont Street	A1	Old South Street	B3
Brook Street	C2	Outcote Bank	B4
Byram Street	C2	Oxford Street	C1
Cambridge Road	B1	Park Avenue	A2
Carforth Street	D4	Park Drive South	A2
Castlegate	B1	Peel Street	C4
Chancery Lane	B3	Pine Street	C2
Chapel Hill	B4	Portland Street	A2
Chapel Street	B4	Princess Street	B4
Church Street	C2	Prospect Street	A4
Clare Hill	B1	Quay Street	D2
Claremont Street	B1	Queen Street	C3
Cloth Hall Street	B3	Queen Street South	C4
Cross Church Street	C3	Queensgate	C4
Dundas Lane	B3	Railway Street	B2
Elizabeth Queen Gardens	A2	Ramsden Street	B3
Elmwood Avenue	A1	Rook Street	B1
Firth Street	D4	St Andrew's Road	D2
Fitzwilliam Street	A2	St George's Square	B2
Fitzwilliam Street	B2	St John's Road	B1
Gasworks Street	D1	St Peter's Street	C2
Great Northern Street	C1	Southgate	C2
Greenhead Road	A3	Spring Grove Street	A4
Half Moon Street	B3	Spring Street	A3
High Street	B3	Springwood Avenue	A3
Highfields Road	A1	Stadium Way	D1
John William Street	B2	Station Street	B2
King Street	C3	Trinity Street	A2
King's Mill Lane	D4	Turnbridge Road	D2
Kirkgate	C3	Union Street	C1
Leeds Road	C2	Upper George Street	A3
Lincoln Street	D3	Upperhead Row	B3
Lord Street	C2	Viaduct Street	B2
Lower Fitzwilliam Street	C1	Victoria Lane	C3
Lynton Avenue	A3	Wakefield Road	D3
Manchester Road	A4	Water Street	A3
Market Place	C3	Watergate	D2
Market Street	B3	Waverley Road	A2
Merton Street	A3	Wentworth Street	A2
Milford Street	B4	Westgate	B3
Mountjoy Road	A1	William Street	C1
New North Parade	B2	Wood Street	C2
New North Road	A1	Zetland Street	C3

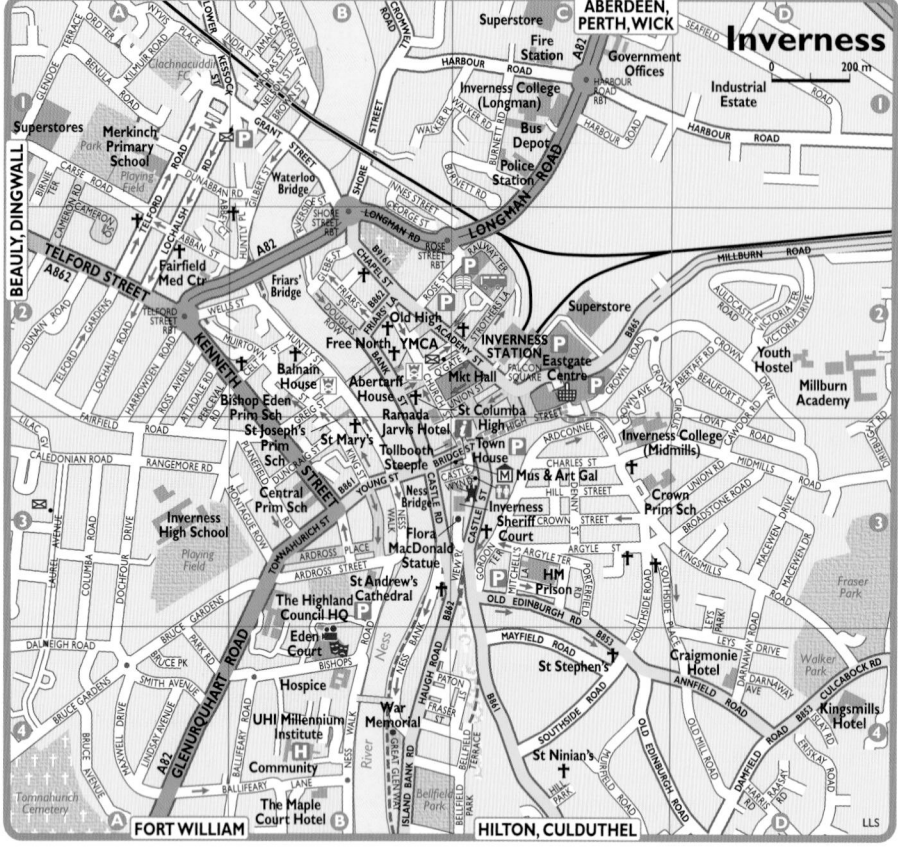

Inverness

Inverness is found on atlas page **156 B8**

Abertaff Road	D2	Gordon Terrace	C3
Academy Street	B2	Grant Street	B1
Anderson Street	B1	Great Glen Way	B4
Annfield Road	D4	Harbour Road	C1
Ardconnel Terrace	C3	Harris Road	D4
Ardross Street	B3	Harrowden Road	A2
Argyle Street	C3	Haugh Road	B4
Argyle Terrace	C3	High Street	C3
Ballifeary Lane	A4	Hill Park	C4
Ballifeary Road	B4	Hill Street	C4
Bank Street	B2	Huntly Street	B2
Bellfield Terrace	C4	Innes Street	B1
Benula Road	A1	Islay Road	D4
Birnie Terrace	A1	Kenneth Street	B2
Bishops Road	B4	King Street	B3
Bridge Street	B3	Kingsmills Road	D3
Broadstone Road	D3	Laurel Avenue	A3
Bruce Gardens	A4	Lindsay Avenue	A4
Bruce Park	A4	Lochalsh Road	A2
Burnett Road	C1	Longman Road	C1
Caledonian Road	A3	Lovat Road	D3
Cameron Road	A2	Lower Kessock Street	A1
Cameron Square	A2	Maxwell Drive	A4
Carse Road	A1	Mayfield Road	C4
Castle Road	B3	Midmills Road	D3
Castle Street	C3	Millburn Road	D2
Chapel Street	B2	Mitchell's Lane	C3
Charles Street	C3	Muirfield Road	C4
Columba Road	A3	Ness Bank	B4
Crown Circus	C2	Old Edinburgh Road	C3
Crown Drive	D2	Park Road	A4
Crown Road	C2	Planefield Road	B3
Crown Street	C3	Porterfield Road	C4
Culcabock Road	D4	Raasay Road	D4
Dalneigh Road	A4	Rangemore Road	A3
Damfield Road	D4	Ross Avenue	A2
Darnaway Road	D4	Seafield Road	D1
Denny Street	C3	Shore Street	B1
Dochfour Drive	A3	Smith Avenue	A4
Dunabban Road	A1	Southside Place	C4
Dunain Road	A2	Southside Road	C4
Duncraig Street	B3	Telford Gardens	A2
Eriskay Road	D4	Telford Road	A2
Fairfield Road	A3	Telford Street	A2
Falcon Square	C2	Tomnahurich Street	B3
Friars' Lane	B2	Union Road	D3
Glendoe Terrace	A1	Walker Road	C1
Glenurquhart Road	A4	Young Street	B3

Ipswich

Ipswich is found on atlas page **53 L3**

Alderman Road	A3	Key Street	C3
Anglesea Road	B1	King Street	B2
Argyle Street	D2	London Road	A2
Austin Street	C4	Lower Brook Street	C3
Barrack Lane	A1	Lower Orwell Street	C3
Belstead Road	B4	Museum Street	B2
Berners Street	B1	Neale Street	C1
Black Horse Lane	B2	Neptune Quay	D3
Blanche Street	D2	New Cardinal Street	B3
Bolton Lane	C1	Newson Street	A1
Bond Street	D3	Northgate Street	C2
Bramford Road	A1	Norwich Road	A1
Bridge Street	C4	Old Foundry Road	C2
Burlington Road	A2	Orchard Street	C2
Burrell Road	B4	Orford Street	A1
Cardigan Street	A1	Orwell Place	C3
Carr Street	C2	Orwell Quay	D4
Cecil Road	B1	Portman Road	A3
Cemetery Road	D1	Princes Street	A3
Chancery Road	A4	Quadling Street	B3
Charles Street	B1	Queen Street	B2
Christchurch Street	D1	Ranelagh Road	A4
Civic Drive	B2	Russell Road	A3
Clarkson Street	A1	St George's Street	B1
Cobbold Street	C2	St Helen's Street	D2
College Street	C3	St Margaret's Street	B2
Commercial Road	A4	St Matthews Street	B2
Constantine Road	A3	St Nicholas Street	B3
Crown Street	B2	St Peter's Street	B3
Cumberland Street	A1	Silent Street	B3
Dalton Road	A2	Sir Alf Ramsey Way	A3
Dock Street	C4	Soane Street	C2
Duke Street	D4	South Street	A1
Eagle Street	C3	Star Lane	C3
Elm Street	B2	Stoke Quay	C4
Falcon Street	B3	Suffolk Road	D1
Fonnereau Road	B1	Tacket Street	C3
Foundation Street	C3	Tavern Street	B3
Franciscan Way	B3	Tower Ramparts	B2
Geneva Road	A1	Tuddenham Avenue	D1
Grafton Way	B3	Turret Lane	C3
Great Gipping Street	A2	Upper Orwell Street	C3
Great Whip Street	C4	Vernon Street	C4
Grey Friars Road	B3	West End Road	A3
Grimwade Street	D3	Westgate Street	B2
Handford Road	A2	Willoughby Road	B4
Hervey Street	D1	Wolsey Street	B3
High Street	B1	Woodbridge Road	D2

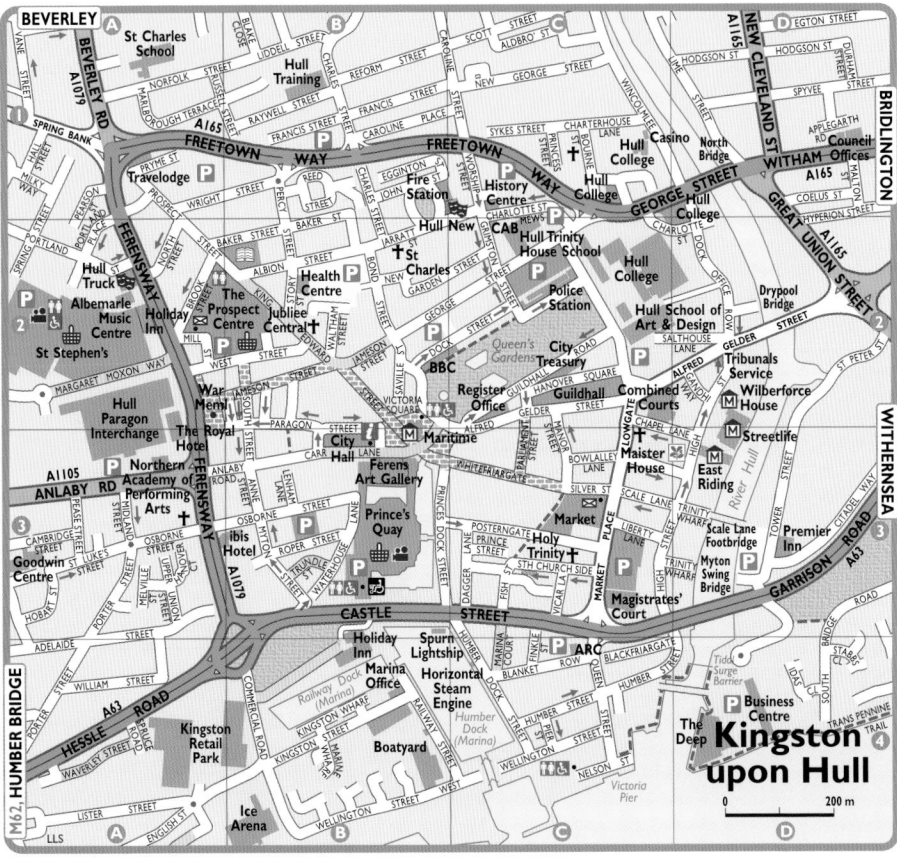

Kingston upon Hull

Kingston upon Hull is found on atlas page **93 J5**

Adelaide Street	A4	Market Place	C3
Albion Street	B2	Mill Street	A2
Alfred Gelder Street	C2	Myton Street	B3
Anlaby Road	A3	New Cleveland Street	D1
Baker Street	B2	New Garden Street	B2
Beverley Road	A1	New George Street	C1
Blackfriargate	C4	Norfolk Street	A1
Blanket Row	C4	Osborne Street	B3
Bond Street	B2	Osborne Street	A3
Brook Street	A2	Paragon Street	B2
Caroline Street	B1	Pease Street	A3
Carr Lane	B3	Percy Street	B1
Castle Street	B3	Porter Street	A3
Chapel Lane	C2	Portland Place	A2
Charles Street	B1	Portland Street	A2
Charterhouse Lane	C1	Posterngate	C3
Citadel Way	D3	Princes Dock Street	B3
Commercial Road	B4	Prospect Street	A1
Dagger Lane	C3	Queen Street	C4
Dock Office Row	D2	Railway Street	B4
Dock Street	B2	Raywell Street	B1
Durham Street	D1	Reform Street	B1
Egginton Street	B1	Russell Street	A1
Ferensway	A2	St Luke's Street	A3
Freetown Way	A1	St Peter Street	D2
Gandhi Way	D2	Saville Street	B2
Garrison Road	D3	Scale Lane	C3
George Street	B2	Scott Street	C1
George Street	D1	Silver Street	C3
Great Union Street	D1	South Bridge Road	D4
Grimston Street	C2	South Church Side	C3
Guildhall Road	C2	South Street	B2
Hanover Square	C2	Spring Bank	A1
Hessle Road	A4	Spyvee Street	D1
High Street	C3	Sykes Street	C1
Hodgson Street	D1	Tower Street	D3
Humber Dock Street	C4	Upper Union Street	A3
Humber Street	C4	Victoria Square	B2
Hyperion Street	D1	Waterhouse Lane	B3
Jameson Street	B2	Wellington Street	C4
Jarratt Street	B2	Wellington Street West	B4
King Edward Street	B2	West Street	A2
Kingston Street	B4	Whitefriargate	C3
Liddell Street	B1	William Street	A4
Lime Street	C1	Wincolmlee	C1
Lister Street	A4	Witham	D1
Lowgate	C3	Worship Street	C1
Margaret Moxon Way	A2	Wright Street	A1

Lancaster

Lancaster is found on atlas page **95 K8**

Aberdeen Road	D4	Lincoln Road	A3
Aldcliffe Road	B4	Lindow Street	B4
Alfred Street	C2	Lodge Street	C2
Ambleside Road	D1	Long Marsh Lane	A2
Balmoral Road	D4	Lune Street	B1
Bath Street	D3	Market Street	B3
Blades Street	A3	Meeting House Lane	A3
Bond Street	D3	Middle Street	B3
Borrowdale Road	D2	Moor Gate	D3
Brewery Lane	C3	Moor Lane	C3
Bridge Lane	B2	Morecambe Road	B1
Brock Street	C3	Nelson Street	C3
Bulk Road	D2	North Road	C2
Bulk Street	C3	Owen Road	C1
Cable Street	B2	Park Road	D3
Castle Hill	B3	Parliament Street	C2
Castle Park	A3	Patterdale Road	D2
Caton Road	C2	Penny Street	B4
Cheapside	C3	Portland Street	B4
China Street	B3	Primrose Street	D4
Church Street	B2	Prospect Street	D4
Common Garden Street	B3	Quarry Road	C4
Dale Street	D4	Queen Street	B4
Dallas Road	B3	Regent Street	B4
Dalton Road	D2	Ridge Lane	D1
Dalton Square	C3	Ridge Street	D1
Damside Street	B2	Robert Street	C3
Derby Road	C1	Rosemary Lane	C2
De Vitre Street	C2	St George's Quay	A1
Dumbarton Road	D4	St Leonard's Gate	C2
East Road	D3	St Peter's Road	C4
Edward Street	C3	Sibsey Street	A3
Fairfield Road	A3	South Road	C4
Fenton Street	B3	Station Road	A3
Gage Street	C3	Stirling Road	D4
Garnet Street	D2	Sulyard Street	C3
George Street	C3	Sun Street	B3
Grasmere Road	D3	Thurnham Street	C3
Great John Street	C3	Troutbeck Road	D2
Gregson Road	D4	Ulleswater Road	D3
Greyhound Bridge Road	B1	West Road	A3
High Street	B4	Westbourne Road	A3
Kelsey Street	A3	Wheatfield Street	A3
Kentmere Road	D2	Williamson Road	D3
King Street	B3	Wingate-Saul Road	A3
Kingsway	C1	Wolseley Street	D3
Kirkes Road	D4	Woodville Street	D2
Langdale Road	D1	Wyresdale Road	D3

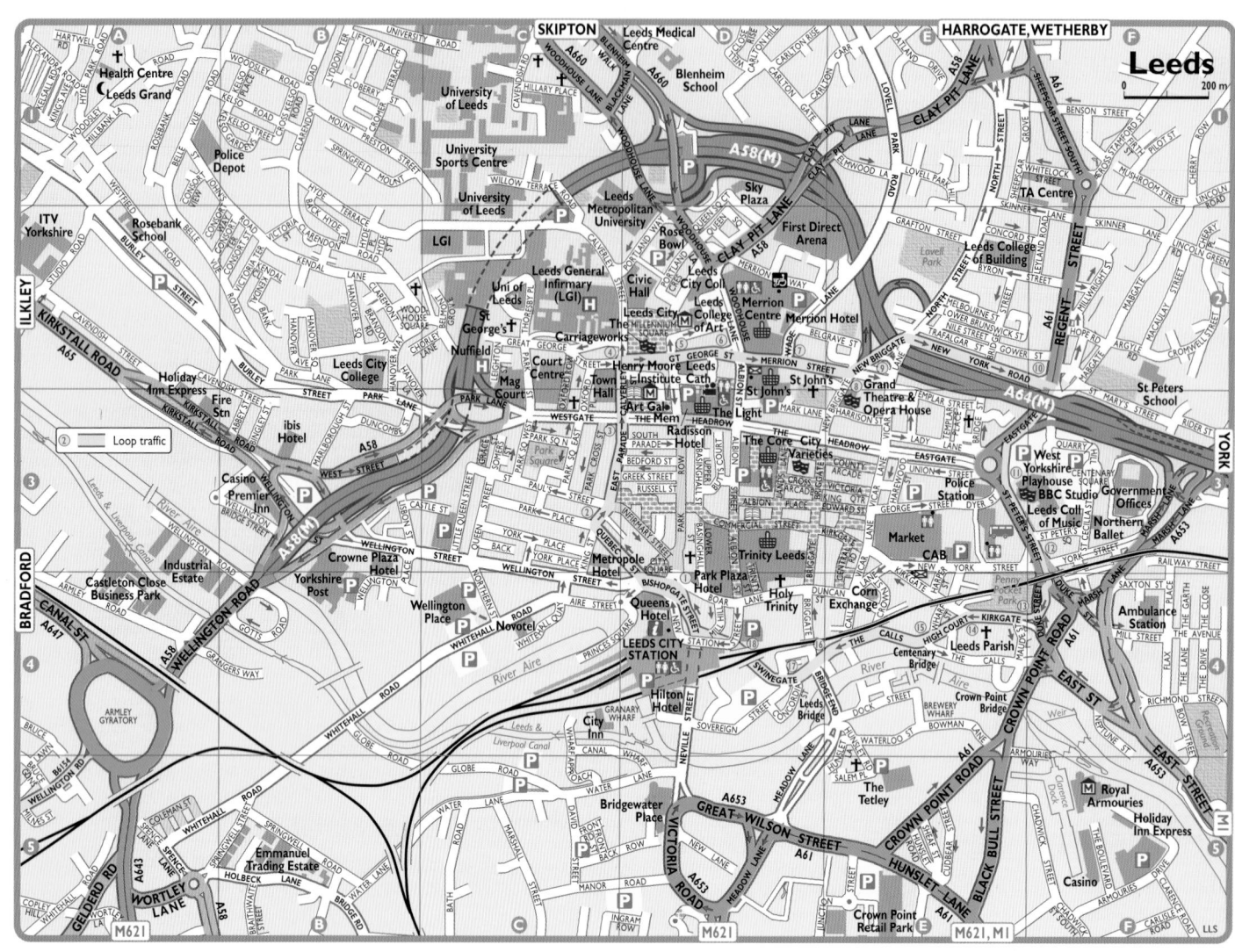

Leeds

Leeds is found on atlas page **90 H4**

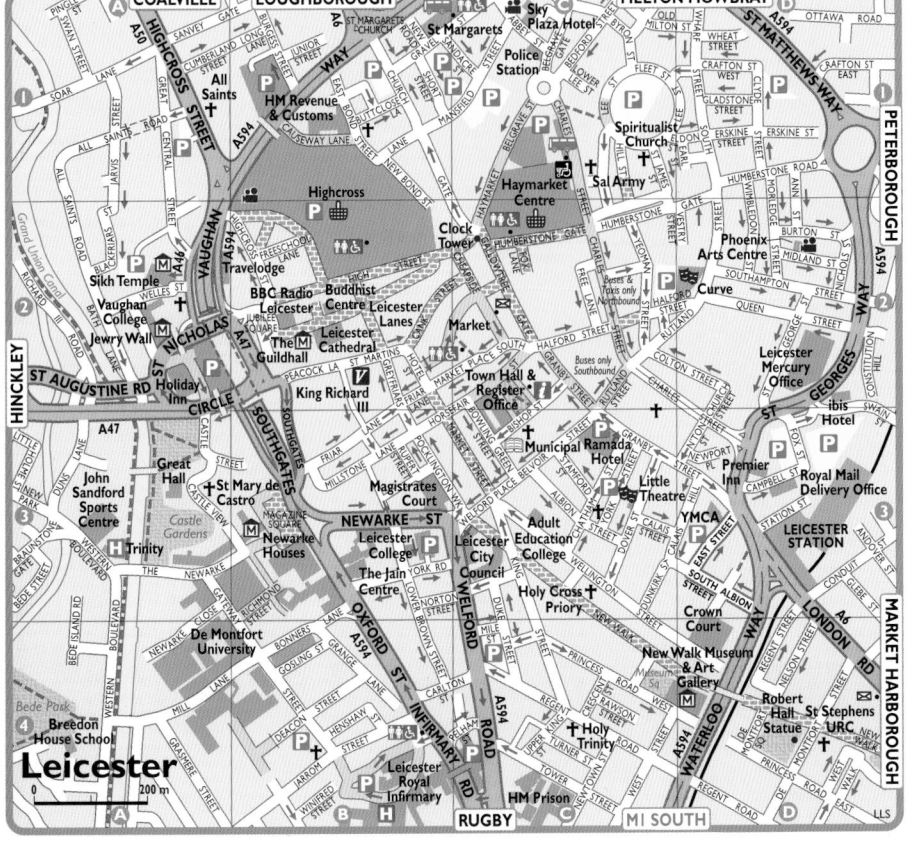

Leicester

Leicester is found on atlas page **72 F10**

Lincoln

Lincoln is found on atlas page **86 C6**

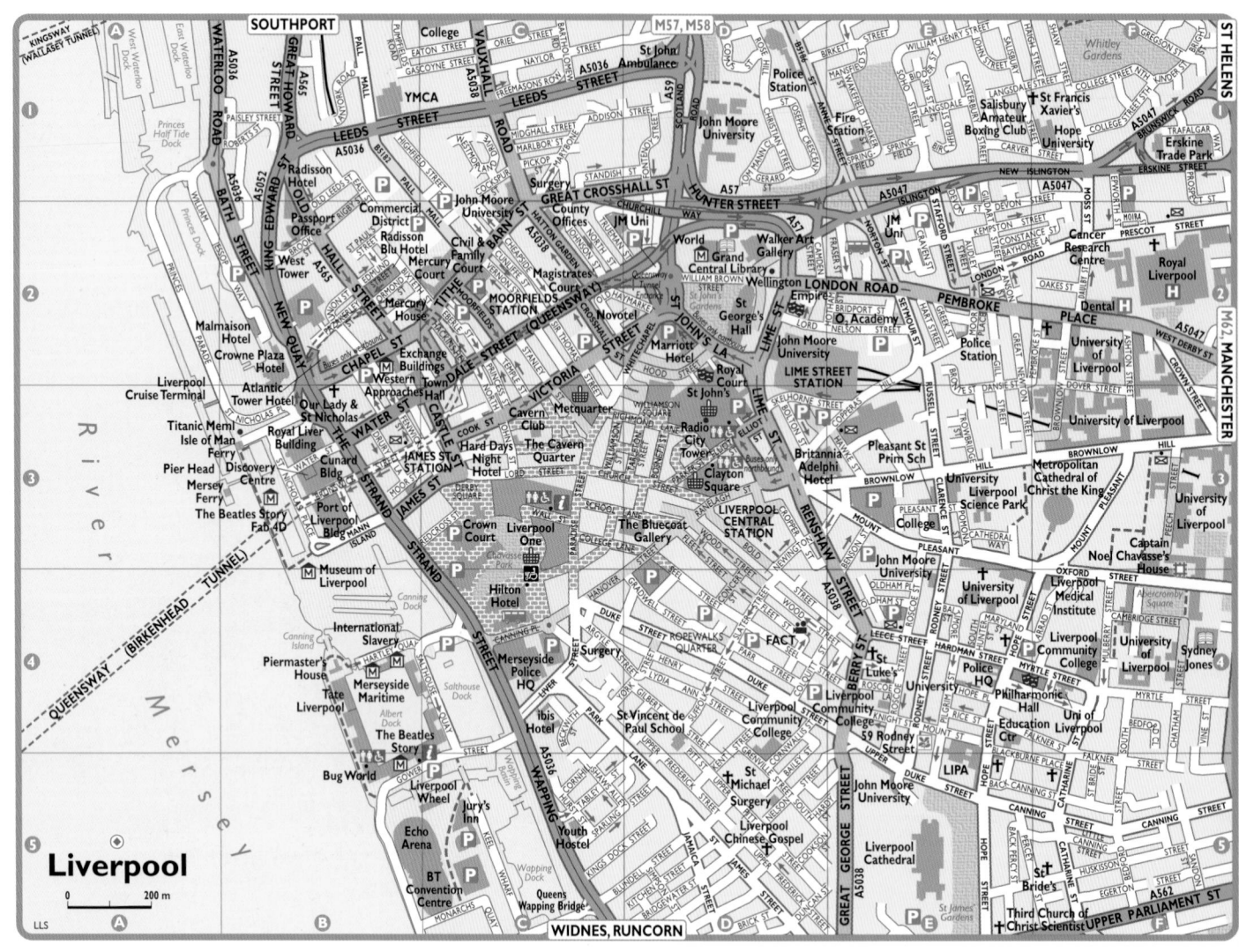

Liverpool

Liverpool is found on atlas page **81 L6**

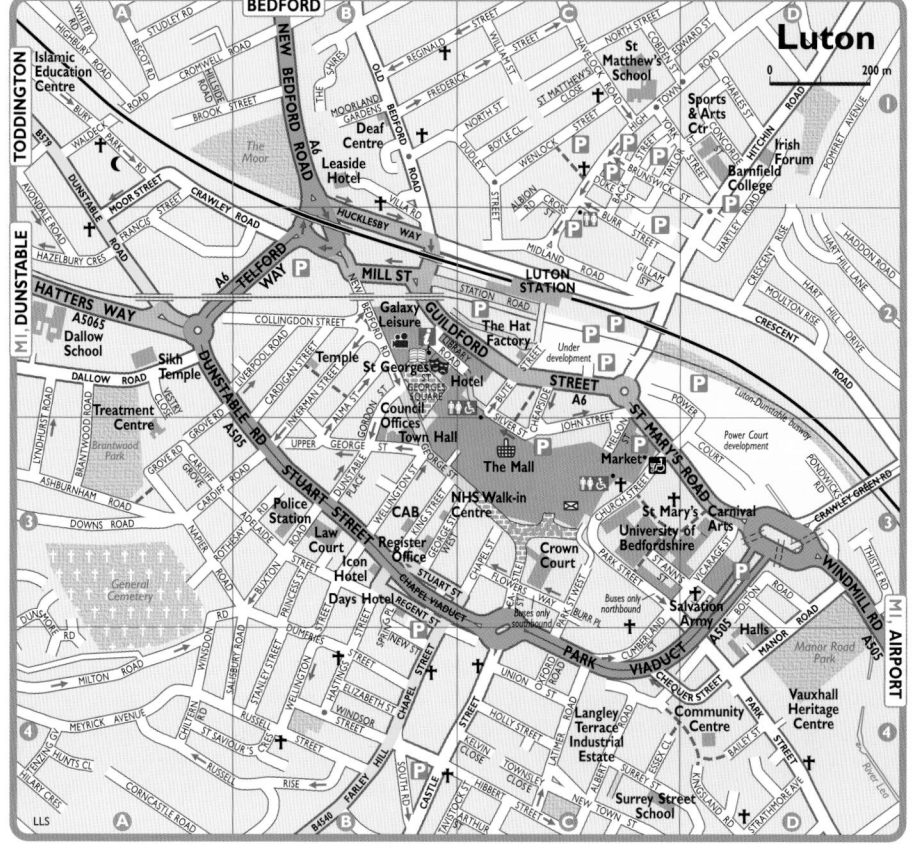

Luton

Luton is found on atlas page **50 C6**

Adelaide Street	B3	Hibbert Street	C4
Albert Road	C4	Highbury Road	A1
Alma Street	B2	High Town Road	C1
Arthur Street	C4	Hitchin Road	D1
Ashburnham Road	A3	Holly Street	C4
Biscot Road	A1	Hucklesby Way	B2
Brantwood Road	A3	Inkerman Street	B3
Brunswick Street	C1	John Street	C3
Burr Street	C2	King Street	B3
Bury Park Road	A1	Latimer Road	C4
Buxton Road	B3	Liverpool Road	B2
Cardiff Road	A3	Manor Road	D4
Cardigan Street	B2	Meyrick Avenue	A4
Castle Street	B4	Midland Road	C2
Chapel Street	B4	Mill Street	B2
Chapel Viaduct	B3	Milton Road	A4
Charles Street	D1	Moor Street	A1
Chequer Street	C4	Napier Road	A3
Chiltern Road	A4	New Bedford Road	B1
Church Street	C2	New Town Street	C4
Church Street	C3	Old Bedford Road	B1
Cobden Street	C1	Park Street	C3
Collingdon Street	B2	Park Street West	C3
Concorde Street	D1	Park Viaduct	C4
Crawley Green Road	D3	Princess Street	B3
Crawley Road	A1	Regent Street	B3
Crescent Road	D2	Reginald Street	B1
Cromwell Road	A1	Rothesay Road	A3
Cumberland Street	C4	Russell Rise	A4
Dallow Road	A2	Russell Street	B4
Dudley Street	C1	St Mary's Road	C3
Dumfries Street	B4	Salisbury Road	A4
Dunstable Road	A1	Stanley Street	B4
Farley Hill	B4	Station Road	C2
Flowers Way	C3	Strathmore Ave	D4
Frederick Street	B1	Stuart Street	B3
George Street	B3	Surrey Street	C4
George Street West	B3	Tavistock Street	B4
Gordon Street	B3	Telford Way	B2
Grove Road	A3	Upper George Street	B3
Guildford Street	B2	Vicarage Street	D3
Hart Hill Drive	D2	Waldeck Road	A1
Hart Hill Lane	D2	Wellington Street	B4
Hartley Road	D2	Wenlock Street	C1
Hastings Street	B4	Windmill Road	D3
Hatters Way	A2	Windsor Street	B4
Havelock Road	C1	Winsdon Road	A4
Hazelbury Crescent	A2	York Street	C1

Maidstone

Maidstone is found on atlas page **38 C10**

Albany Street	D1	Market Buildings	B2
Albion Place	D2	Marsham Street	C2
Allen Street	D1	Meadow Walk	D4
Ashford Road	D3	Medway Street	B3
Bank Street	B3	Melville Road	C4
Barker Road	B4	Mill Street	B3
Bedford Place	A3	Mote Avenue	D3
Bishops Way	B3	Mote Road	D3
Brewer Street	C2	Old School Place	D2
Broadway	A3	Orchard Street	C3
Broadway	B3	Padsole Lane	C3
Brunswick Street	C4	Palace Avenue	B3
Buckland Hill	A2	Princes Street	D1
Buckland Road	A2	Priory Road	C4
Camden Street	C1	Pudding Lane	B2
Chancery Lane	D3	Queen Anne Road	D2
Charles Street	A4	Reginald Road	A4
Church Street	C2	Rocky Hill	A3
College Avenue	B4	Romney Place	C3
College Road	C4	Rose Yard	B2
County Road	C1	Rowland Close	A4
Crompton Gardens	D4	St Anne Court	A2
Cromwell Road	D2	St Faith's Street	B2
Douglas Road	A4	St Luke's Avenue	D1
Earl Street	B2	St Luke's Road	D1
Elm Grove	D4	St Peters Street	A2
Fairmeadow	B1	Sandling Road	B1
Florence Road	A4	Sittingbourne Road	D1
Foley Street	D1	Square Hill Road	D3
Foster Street	C4	Stacey Street	B1
Gabriel's Hill	C3	Station Road	B1
George Street	C4	Terrace Road	A3
Greenside	D4	Tonbridge Road	A4
Hart Street	A4	Tufton Street	C3
Hastings Road	D4	Union Street	C2
Hayle Road	C4	Upper Stone Street	C4
Heathorn Street	D1	Victoria Street	A3
Hedley Street	C1	Vinters Road	D2
High Street	B3	Wat Tyler Way	C3
Holland Road	D1	Week Street	B2
James Street	C1	Well Road	C1
Jeffrey Street	C1	Westree Road	A4
King Street	C3	Wheeler Street	C1
Kingsley Road	D4	Woollett Street	C1
Knightrider Street	C4	Wyatt Street	C2
Lesley Place	A1		
London Road	A3		
Lower Stone Street	C3		

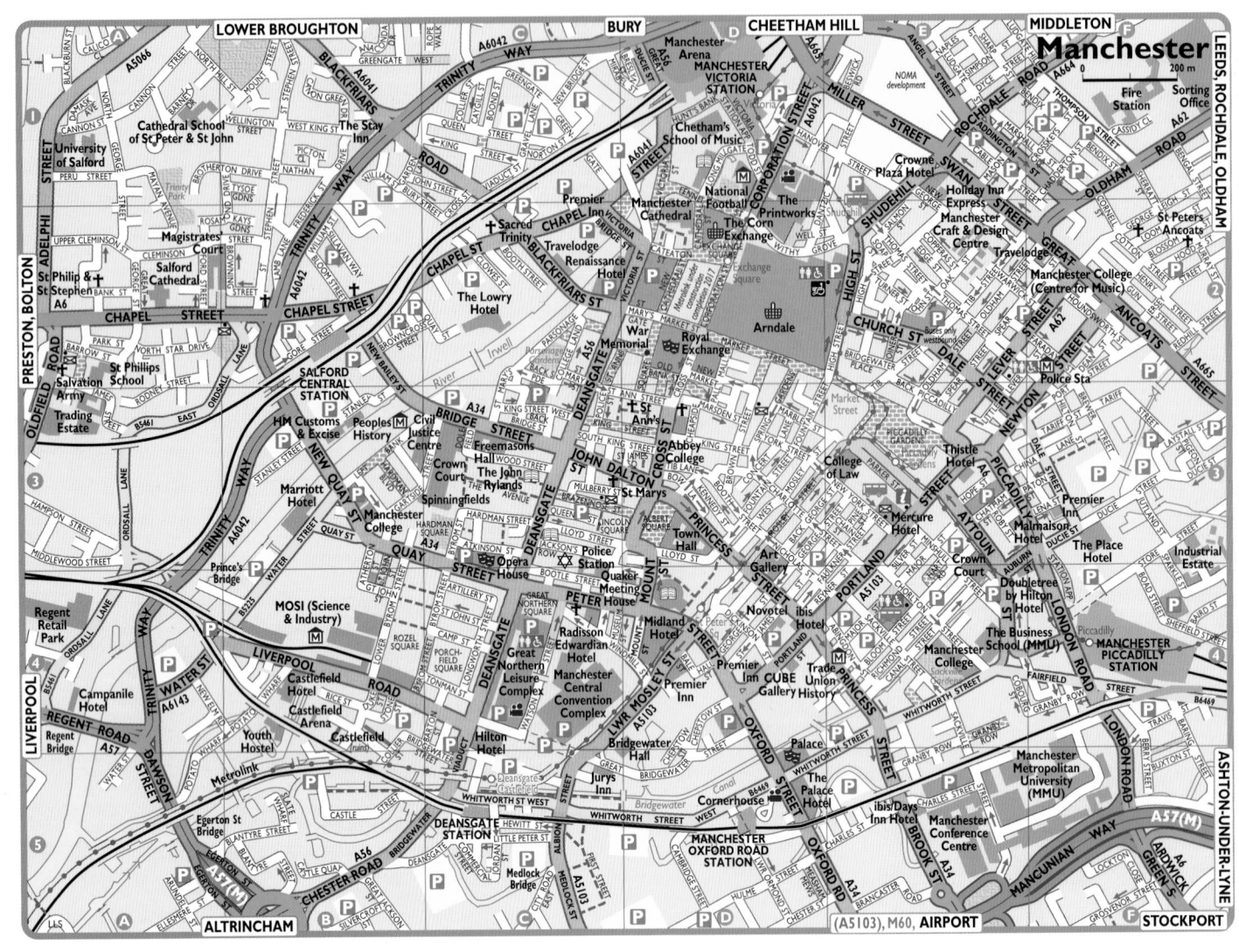

Manchester

Manchester is found on atlas page **82 H5**

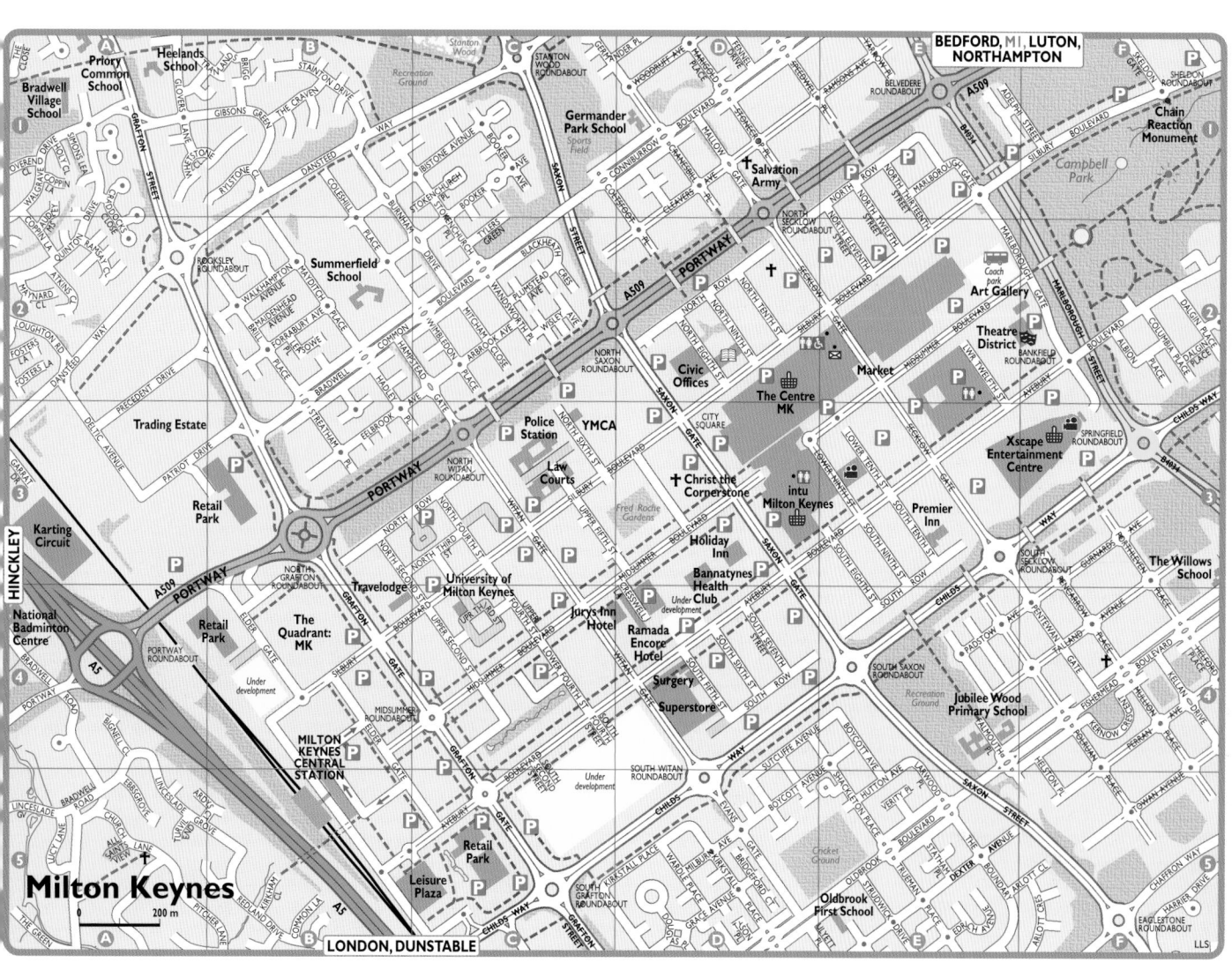

Milton Keynes

Milton Keynes is found on atlas page **49 N7**

Adelphi Street	E1	Craddocks Close	A1	Kellan Drive	F4	North Secklow		Simons Lea	A1	Tyson Place	D5
Albion Place	F2	Cranesbill Place	D1	Kernow Crescent	F4	Roundabout	D1	Skeldon Gate	F1	Ulyett Place	D5
All Saints View	A5	Cresswell Lane	D3	Kirkham Close	B5	North Second Street	B3	South Eighth Street	E3	Upper Fifth Street	C3
Arbrook Avenue	C2	Dalgin Place	F2	Kirkstall Place	C5	North Sixth Street	C3	South Fifth Street	D4	Upper Fourth Street	C4
Ardys Court	A5	Dansteed Way	A2	Larwood Place	E5	North Tenth Street	D2	South Fourth Street	C4	Upper Second Street	C4
Arlott Close	E5	Deltic Avenue	A3	Leasowe Place	B2	North Third Street	C3	South Grafton Roundabout	C5	Upper Third Street	C4
Arlott Crescent	F5	Dexter Avenue	E5	Linceslade Grove	A5	North Thirteenth Street	E1	South Ninth Street	E3	Verity Place	E5
Atkins Close	A2	Douglas Place	D5	Loughton Road	A2	North Twelfth Street	E1	South Row	D4	Walgrave Drive	A1
Audley Mews	A2	Ebbsgrove	A5	Lower Fourth Street	C4	North Witan Roundabout	C2	South Saxon Roundabout	E4	Walkhampton Avenue	B2
Avebury Boulevard	C5	Edrich Avenue	E5	Lower Ninth Street	E3	Oldbrook Boulevard	E5	South Secklow Roundabout	F3	Wandsworth Place	C2
Bankfield Roundabout	E2	Eelbrook Avenue	B3	Lower Tenth Street	E3	Overend Close	A1	South Second Street	C5	Wardle Place	D5
Belvedere Roundabout	E1	Elder Gate	B4	Lower Twelfth Street	E2	Padstow Avenue	E4	South Seventh Street	D4	Whetstone Close	A1
Bignell Close	A4	Evans Gate	D5	Lucy Lane	A5	Patriot Drive	A3	South Sixth Street	D4	Wimbledon Place	C2
Blackheath Crescent	C2	Falmouth Place	E4	Maidenhead Avenue	B2	Pencarrow Place	F3	South Tenth Street	E3	Wisely Avenue	C2
Booker Avenue	C1	Fennel Drive	D1	Mallow Gate	D1	Pentewan Gate	F4	South Witan Roundabout	D5	Witan Gate	C3
Boycott Avenue	D5	Fishermead Boulevard	F4	Marigold Place	D1	Perran Avenue	F4	Speedwell Place	D1	Woodruff Avenue	D1
Boycott Avenue	E4	Forrabury Avenue	B2	Marlborough Gate	E1	Pitcher Lane	A5	Springfield Roundabout	F3	Yarrow Place	E1
Bradwell Common		Fosters Lane	A2	Marlborough Gate	E2	Plumstead Avenue	C2	Stainton Drive	B1		
Boulevard	B2	Garrat Drive	A3	Marlborough Street	F2	Polruan Place	F4	Stanton Wood			
Bradwell Road	A4	Germander Place	C1	Mayditch Place	B2	Porthleven Place	F3	Roundabout	C1		
Bradwell Road	A5	Gibsons Green	B1	Maynard Close	A2	Portway	A4	Statham Place	E5		
Bridgeford Court	D5	Glovers Lane	A1	Midsummer Boulevard	C4	Portway Roundabout	A4	Stokenchurch Place	C1		
Brill Place	B2	Grace Avenue	D5	Midsummer Boulevard	E2	Precedent Drive	A3	Stonecrop Place	D1		
Burnham Drive	B1	Grafton Gate	B4	Midsummer Roundabout	B4	Quinton Drive	A2	Streatham Place	B3		
Chaffron Way	F5	Grafton Street	A1	Milburn Avenue	D5	Ramsay Close	A2	Strudwick Drive	E5		
Childs Way	C5	Grafton Street	C5	Mitcham Close	C2	Ramsons Avenue	E1	Sutcliffe Avenue	D4		
Childs Way	F3	Gurnards Avenue	F3	Mullion Place	F4	Redland Drive	B5	Talland Avenue	F4		
Church Lane	A5	Hadley Place	B2	North Eighth Street	D2	Rooksley Roundabout	B2	The Boundary	E5		
City Square	D3	Hampstead Gate	B2	North Eleventh Street	E1	Rylstone Close	B1	The Close	A1		
Cleavers Avenue	D1	Harrier Drive	F5	North Fourth Street	C3	Saxon Gate	D2	The Craven	B1		
Coleshill Place	B1	Helford Place	F4	North Grafton		Saxon Street	C1	The Green	A5		
Coltsfoot Avenue	C1	Helston Place	F4	Roundabout	B3	Secklow Gate	D2	Towan Avenue	F5		
Columbia Place	F2	Holy Close	A1	North Ninth Street	D2	Shackleton Place	E5	Tranlands Brigg	B1		
Common Lane	B5	Hutton Avenue	E5	North Row	B3	Sheldon Roundabout	F1	Trueman Place	E5		
Conniburrow Boulevard	C1	Ibistone Avenue	C1	North Row	D2	Silbury Boulevard	B4	Turvil End	A5		
Coppin Lane	A2			North Saxon Roundabout	C2	Silbury Roundabout	B4	Tylers Green	C2		

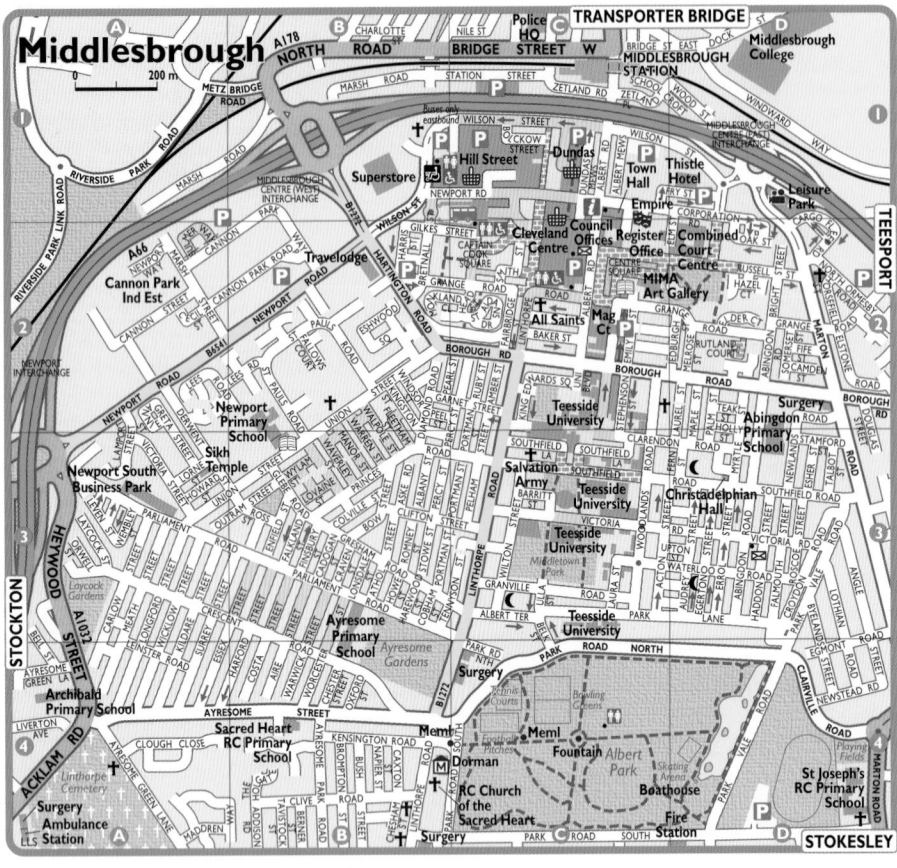

Middlesbrough

Middlesbrough is found on atlas page **104 E7**

Acklam Road	A4	Heywood Street	A3
Acton Street	C3	Kensington Road	B4
Aire Street	B4	Kildare Street	A4
Albany Street	B3	Laurel Street	D3
Albert Road	C2	Lees Road	A2
Amber Street	C2	Linthorpe Road	B4
Athol Street	B3	Longford Street	A3
Audrey Street	D3	Lorne Street	A3
Ayresome Park Road	B4	Lothian Road	D3
Ayresome Street	A4	Marsh Street	A2
Borough Road	C2	Marton Road	D2
Bretnall Street	B2	Melrose Street	D2
Bridge Street East	C1	Metz Bridge Road	A1
Bridge Street West	C1	Myrtle Street	D3
Bush Street	B4	Newlands Road	D3
Camden Street	D2	Newport Road	D3
Cannon Park Road	A2	Palm Street	D3
Cannon Park Way	A2	Park Lane	C3
Cannon Street	A2	Park Road North	C4
Carlow Street	A3	Park Road South	C4
Centre Square	C2	Park Vale Road	D4
Clairville Road	D4	Parliament Road	A3
Clarendon Road	C3	Pearl Street	C3
Clifton Street	B3	Pelham Street	C3
Corporation Road	D1	Portman Street	B3
Costa Street	B4	Princes Road	B3
Craven Street	B3	Riverside Park Road	A1
Crescent Road	A3	Ruby Street	C3
Croydon Road	D3	Russell Street	D2
Derwent Street	A2	St Pauls Road	B2
Diamond Road	B3	Southfield Road	C3
Egmont Road	D4	Station Street	C1
Emily Street	C2	Stowe Street	B4
Errol Street	D3	Tavistock Street	B4
Essex Street	A4	Tennyson Street	B4
Fairbridge Street	C2	Union Street	A3
Falmouth Street	D3	Victoria Road	A3
Finsbury Street	B3	Victoria Street	A3
Fleetham Street	B2	Warren Street	B3
Garnet Street	B2	Waterloo Road	D3
Glebe Road	B3	Waverley Street	A3
Grange Road	B2	Wembley Street	A3
Grange Road	D2	Wilson Street	B2
Granville Road	C3	Wilton Street	C3
Gresham Road	B3	Windsor Street	B2
Harewood Street	B3	Woodlands Road	C3
Harford Street	B4	Worcester Street	B4
Hartington Road	B2	Zetland Road	C1

Newport

Newport is found on atlas page **31 K7**

Albert Terrace	B3	Jones Street	B3
Allt-Yr-Yn Avenue	A2	Keynsham Avenue	C4
Bailey Street	B3	King Street	C4
Bedford Road	D2	Kingsway	C2
Blewitt Street	B3	Kingsway	C4
Bond Street	C1	Llanthewy Road	A3
Bridge Street	B2	Locke Street	B1
Bryngwyn Road	A3	Lower Dock Street	C4
Brynhyfryd Avenue	A4	Lucas Street	B1
Brynhyfryd Road	A4	Market Street	B2
Caerau Crescent	A4	Mellon Street	C4
Caerau Road	A3	Mill Street	B2
Cambrian Road	B2	North Street	B3
Caroline Street	D3	Oakfield Road	A3
Cedar Road	D2	Park Square	B3
Charles Street	C3	Pugsley Street	C1
Chepstow Road	D1	Queen's Hill	B1
Clarence Place	C1	Queen's Hill Crescent	A1
Clifton Place	B4	Queen Street	C4
Clifton Road	B4	Queensway	B2
Clyffard Crescent	A3	Risca Road	A4
Clytha Park Road	A2	Rodney Road	C2
Clytha Square	C4	Rudry Street	D1
Colts Foot Close	A1	Ruperra Lane	D4
Commercial Street	C4	Ruperra Street	D4
Corelli Street	D1	St Edward Street	B3
Corn Street	C2	St Julian Street	B4
Corporation Road	D2	St Mark's Crescent	A2
Devon Place	B2	St Mary Street	C2
Dewsland Park Road	B4	St Vincent Road	C2
Dumfries Place	D4	St Woolos Road	B4
East Street	B3	School Lane	C3
East Usk Road	C1	Serpentine Road	A2
Factory Road	B1	Skinner Street	C2
Fields Road	A2	Sorrel Drive	A1
Friars Field	B4	Spencer Road	A3
Friars Road	B4	Stow Hill	B3
Friar Street	C3	Stow Hill	C4
George Street	D4	Stow Park Avenue	A4
Godfrey Road	A2	Talbot Lane	C3
Gold Tops	A2	Tregare Street	D1
Grafton Road	C2	Tunnel Terrace	A3
Granville Lane	D4	Upper Dock Street	C2
Granville Street	D4	Upper Dock Street	C3
High Street	B2	Usk Way	D3
Hill Street	C3	Victoria Crescent	B3
John Frost Square	C3	West Street	B3
John Street	D4	York Place	A4

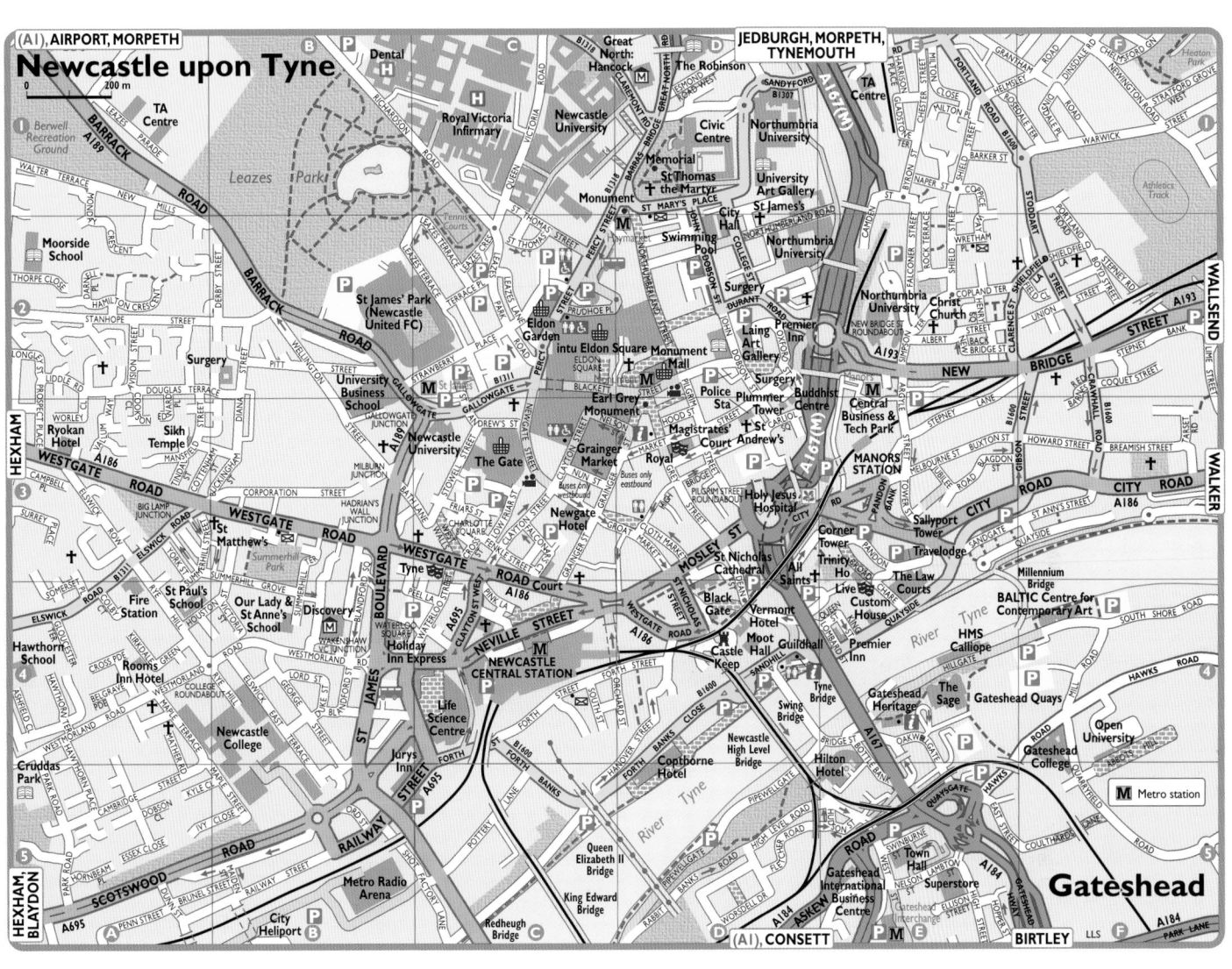

Newcastle upon Tyne

Newcastle upon Tyne is found on atlas page **113 K8**

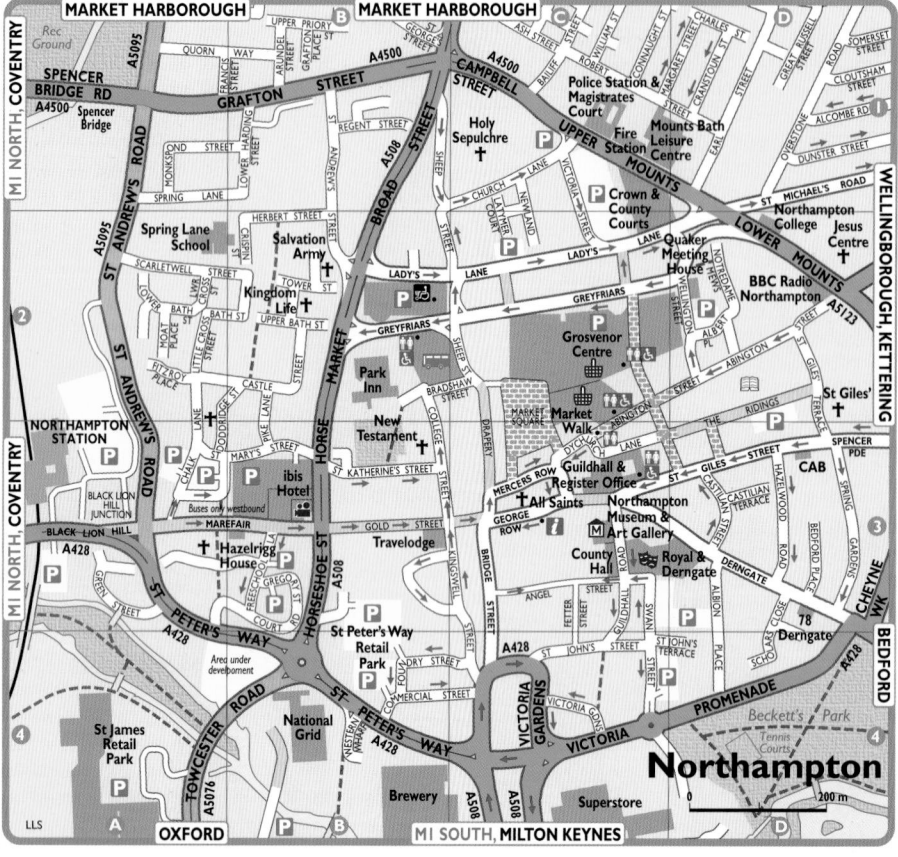

Northampton

Northampton is found on atlas page **60 G8**

Norwich

Norwich is found on atlas page **77 J10**

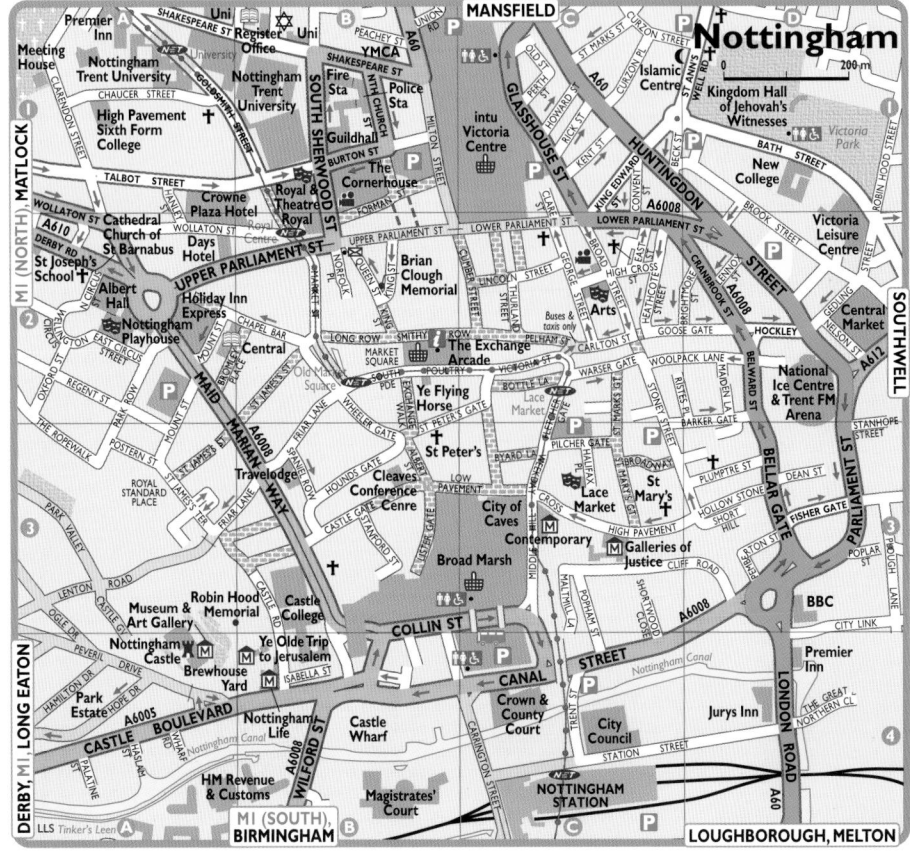

Nottingham

Nottingham is found on atlas page **72 F3**

Albert Street	B3	Lenton Road	A3
Barker Gate	D2	Lincoln Street	C2
Bath Street	D1	Lister Gate	B3
Bellar Gate	D3	London Road	D4
Belward Street	D2	Long Row	B2
Broad Street	C2	Lower Parliament Street	C2
Broadway	C3	Low Pavement	B3
Bromley Place	A2	Maid Marian Way	A2
Brook Street	D1	Market Street	B2
Burton Street	B1	Middle Hill	C3
Canal Street	C4	Milton Street	B1
Carlton Street	C2	Mount Street	A3
Carrington Street	C4	Norfolk Place	B2
Castle Boulevard	A4	North Circus Street	A2
Castle Gate	B3	Park Row	A3
Castle Road	B3	Parliament Street	D3
Chapel Bar	B2	Pelham Street	C2
Chaucer Street	A1	Peveril Drive	A4
Clarendon Street	A1	Pilcher Gate	C3
Cliff Road	C3	Popham Street	C3
Collin Street	B4	Poultry	B2
Cranbrook Street	D2	Queen Street	B2
Cumber Street	C2	Regent Street	A2
Curzon Place	C1	St Ann's Well Road	D1
Derby Road	A2	St James's Street	A3
Exchange Walk	B2	St Marks Gate	C3
Fisher Gate	D3	St Marks Street	C1
Fletcher Gate	C3	St Mary's Gate	C3
Forman Street	B1	St Peter's Gate	B3
Friar Lane	A3	Shakespeare Street	A1
Gedling Street	D2	Smithy Row	B2
George Street	C2	South Parade	B2
Glasshouse Street	C1	South Sherwood Street	B1
Goldsmith Street	A1	Spaniel Row	B3
Goose Gate	C2	Station Street	C4
Halifax Place	C3	Stoney Street	C2
Heathcote Street	C2	Talbot Street	A1
High Cross Street	C2	Thurland Street	C2
High Pavement	C3	Trent Street	C4
Hockley	D2	Upper Parliament Street	A2
Hollow Stone	D3	Victoria Street	C2
Hope Drive	A4	Warser Gate	C2
Hounds Gate	B3	Weekday Cross	C3
Howard Street	C1	Wellington Circus	A2
Huntingdon Street	C1	Wheeler Gate	B2
Kent Street	C1	Wilford Street	B4
King Edward Street	C1	Wollaton Street	A1
King Street	B2	Woolpack Lane	C2

Oldham

Oldham is found on atlas page **83 K4**

Ascroft Street	B3	Mortimer Street	D1
Bar Gap Road	B1	Napier Street East	A4
Barlow Street	D4	New Radcliffe Street	A2
Barn Street	B3	Oldham Way	A3
Beever Street	D2	Park Road	B4
Bell Street	D2	Park Street	A4
Belmont Street	B1	Peter Street	B3
Booth Street	A3	Prince Street	D3
Bow Street	C3	Queen Street	C3
Brook Street	D2	Radcliffe Street	B1
Brunswick Street	B3	Raleigh Close	B1
Cardinal Street	C2	Ramsden Street	A1
Chadderton Way	A1	Regent Street	D2
Chaucer Street	B3	Rhodes Bank	C3
Clegg Street	C3	Rhodes Street	C2
Coldhurst Road	B1	Rifle Street	B1
Cromwell Street	B4	Rochdale Road	A1
Crossbank Street	B4	Rock Street	B2
Curzon Street	B2	Roscoe Street	C3
Dunbar Street	A1	Ruskin Street	A1
Eden Street	B2	St Hilda's Drive	A1
Egerton Street	C2	St Marys Street	B1
Emmett Way	C4	St Mary's Way	B2
Firth Street	C3	Shaw Road	D1
Fountain Street	B2	Shaw Street	C1
Franklin Street	B1	Siddall Street	C1
Gower Street	D2	Silver Street	B3
Grange Street	A2	Southgate Street	C3
Greaves Street	C3	South Hill Street	D4
Greengate Street	B2	Spencer Street	D2
Hardy Street	D4	Sunfield Road	B1
Harmony Street	C4	Thames Street	D1
Henshaw Street	B2	Trafalgar Street	A1
Higginshaw Road	C1	Trinity Street	B1
Highfield Street	A2	Tulbury Street	A1
High Street	B3	Union Street	B3
Hobson Street	B3	Union Street West	A4
Hooper Street	D4	Union Street West	B3
Horsedge Street	C1	Wallshaw Street	D2
John Street	A3	Wall Street	B4
King Street	B3	Ward Street	A1
Lemnos Street	D2	Waterloo Street	C3
Malby Street	C1	Wellington Street	B4
Malton Street	A4	West End Street	A2
Manchester Street	A3	West Street	B3
Market Place	B3	Willow Street	D2
Marlborough Street	C4	Woodstock Street	C4
Middleton Road	A3	Yorkshire Street	C3

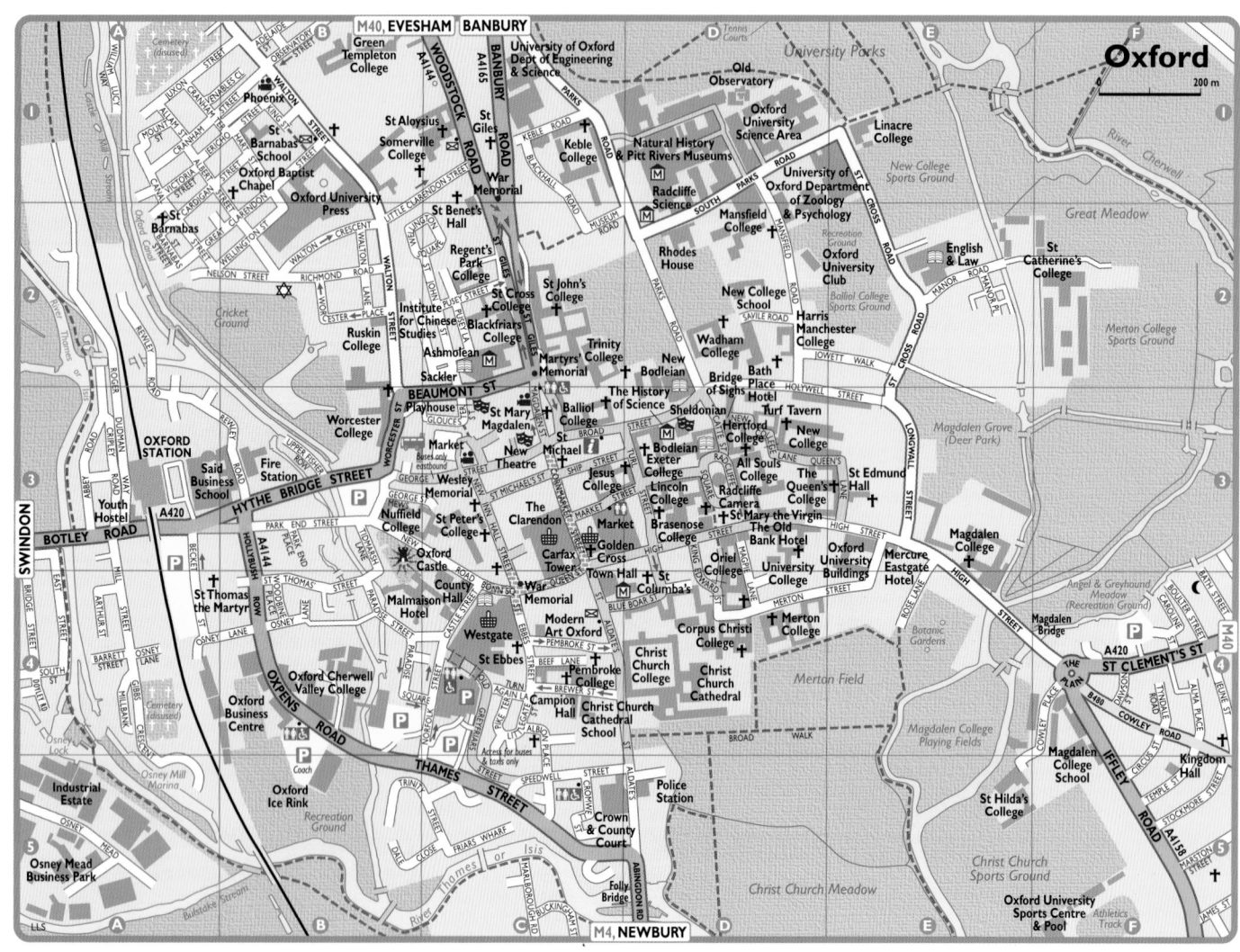

Oxford

Oxford is found on atlas page **34 F3**

University Colleges

Perth

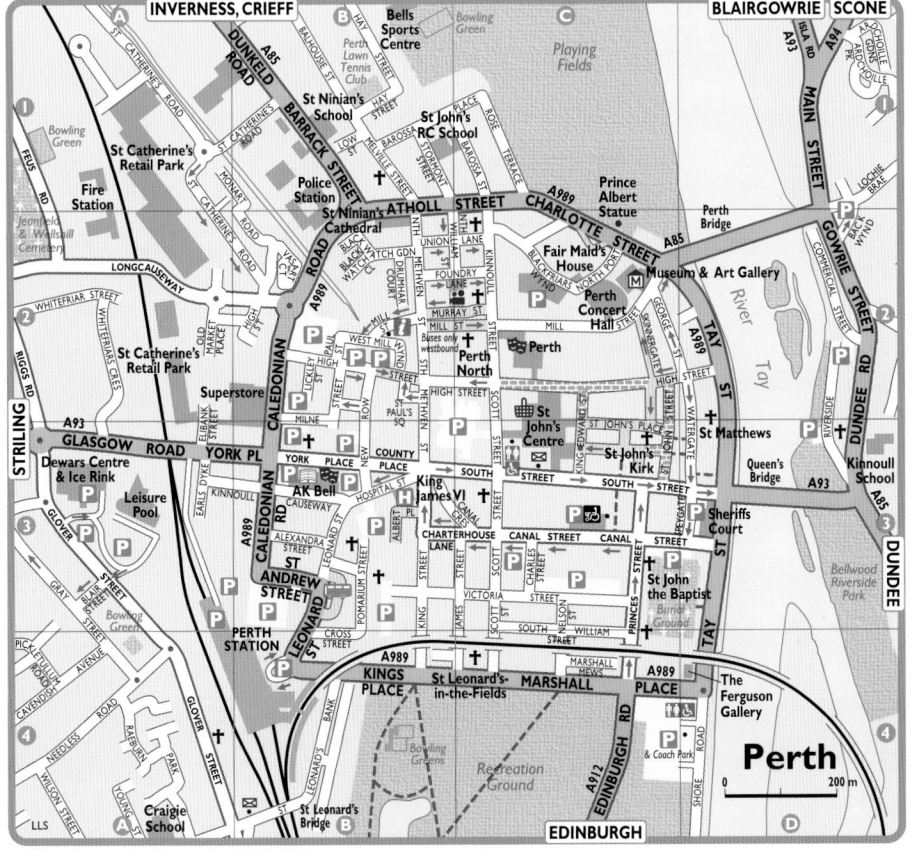

Perth is found on atlas page **134 E3**

Albert Place	B3	Marshall Place	C4
Alexandra Street	B3	Melville Street	B1
Ardchoille Park	D1	Mill Street	B2
Atholl Street	B1	Mill Street	C2
Back Wynd	D2	Milne Street	B2
Balhousie Street	B1	Monart Road	A1
Barossa Place	B1	Murray Street	B2
Barrack Street	B1	Needless Road	A4
Blackfriars Wynd	C2	New Row	B3
Black Watch Garden	B2	North Methven Street	B2
Caledonian Road	B2	North Port	C2
Caledonian Road	B3	North William Street	B2
Canal Street	C3	Old Market Place	A2
Cavendish Avenue	A4	Paul Street	B2
Charles Street	C3	Perth Bridge	D2
Charlotte Street	C2	Pickletullum Road	A4
Charterhouse Lane	B3	Pomarium Street	B3
Commercial Street	D2	Princes Street	C3
County Place	B3	Queen's Bridge	D3
Cross Street	B4	Raeburn Park	A4
Dundee Road	D3	Riggs Road	A2
Dunkeld Road	B1	Riverside	D3
Earls Dyke	A3	Rose Terrace	C1
Edinburgh Road	C4	St Andrew Street	B3
Elibank Street	A3	St Catherine's Road	A1
Feus Road	A1	St John's Place	C3
Foundry Lane	B2	St John Street	C3
George Street	C2	St Leonard's Bank	B4
Glasgow Road	A3	St Paul's Square	B2
Glover Street	A3	Scott Street	C3
Glover Street	A4	Shore Road	D4
Gowrie Street	D2	Skinnergate	C2
Gray Street	A3	South Methven Street	B2
Hay Street	B1	South Street	C3
High Street	B2	South William Street	C4
High Street	C2	Speygate	D3
Hospital Street	B3	Stormont Street	B1
Isla Road	D1	Tay Street	C3
James Street	C3	Tay Street	D4
King Edward Street	C3	Union Lane	B2
Kings Place	B4	Victoria Street	C3
King Street	B3	Watergate	D2
Kinnoull Causeway	A3	West Mill Wynd	B2
Kinnoull Street	C2	Whitefriars Crescent	A2
Leonard Street	B3	Whitefriar Street	A2
Lochie Brae	D1	Wilson Street	A4
Longcauseway	A2	York Place	A3
Main Street	D1	York Place	B3

Peterborough

Peterborough is found on atlas page **74 C11**

Albert Place	B3	New Road	C1
Bishop's Road	C3	Northminster	C1
Boongate	D1	North Street	B1
Bourges Boulevard	A1	Oundle Road	B4
Bridge Street	B3	Park Road	B1
Bright Street	A1	Peet Street	B1
Broadway	B2	Pipe Lane	D2
Brook Street	C1	Priestgate	A2
Cathedral Square	B2	Rivergate	B3
Cattle Market Street	B1	River Lane	A2
Chapel Street	C1	Russell Street	A1
Church Street	B2	St John's Street	C2
Church Walk	C1	St Peters Road	B3
City Road	C2	South Street	D2
Cowgate	B2	Star Road	D1
Craig Street	B1	Station Road	A2
Crawthorne Road	C1	Thorpe Lea Road	A3
Cripple Sidings Lane	B4	Thorpe Road	A2
Cromwell Road	A1	Trinity Street	B3
Cross Street	B2	Viersen Platz	B3
Cubitt Way	B4	Vineyard Road	C3
Deacon Street	A1	Wake Road	D2
Dickens Street	D1	Wareley Road	A4
Eastfield Road	D1	Wellington Street	D1
Eastgate	D2	Wentworth Street	B3
East Station Road	C4	Westgate	A1
Embankment Road	C3		
Exchange Street	B2		
Fengate Close	D2		
Field Walk	D1		
Fitzwilliam Street	B1		
Frank Perkins Parkway	D4		
Geneva Street	B1		
Gladstone Street	A1		
Granby Street	C2		
Hereward Close	D2		
Hereward Road	D2		
King Street	B2		
Laxton Square	C2		
Lea Gardens	A3		
Lincoln Road	B1		
London Road	B4		
Long Causeway	B2		
Manor House Street	B1		
Mayor's Walk	A1		
Midgate	B2		
Morris Street	D1		
Nene Street	D2		

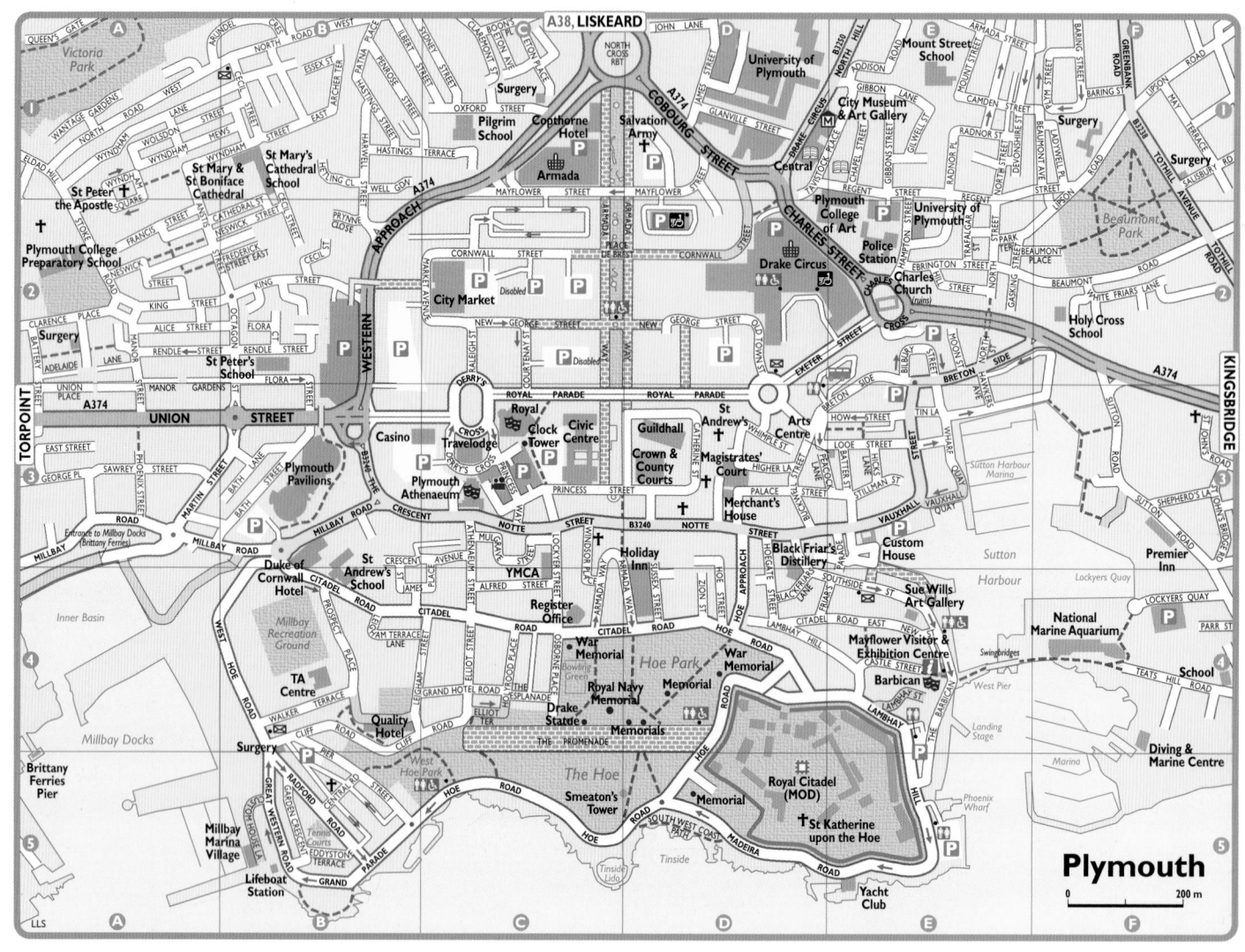

Plymouth

Plymouth is found on atlas page **6 D8**

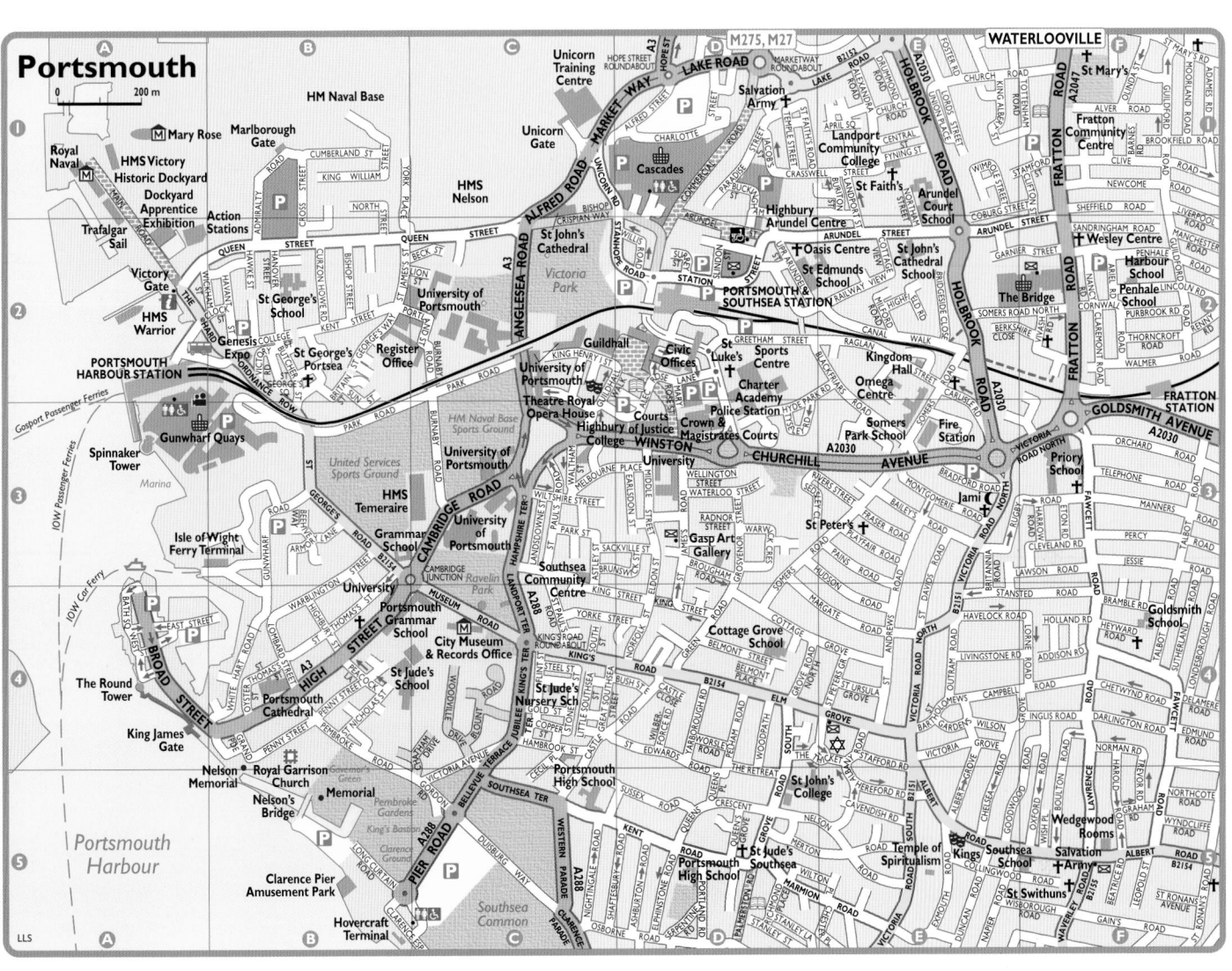

Portsmouth

Portsmouth is found on atlas page **14 H7**

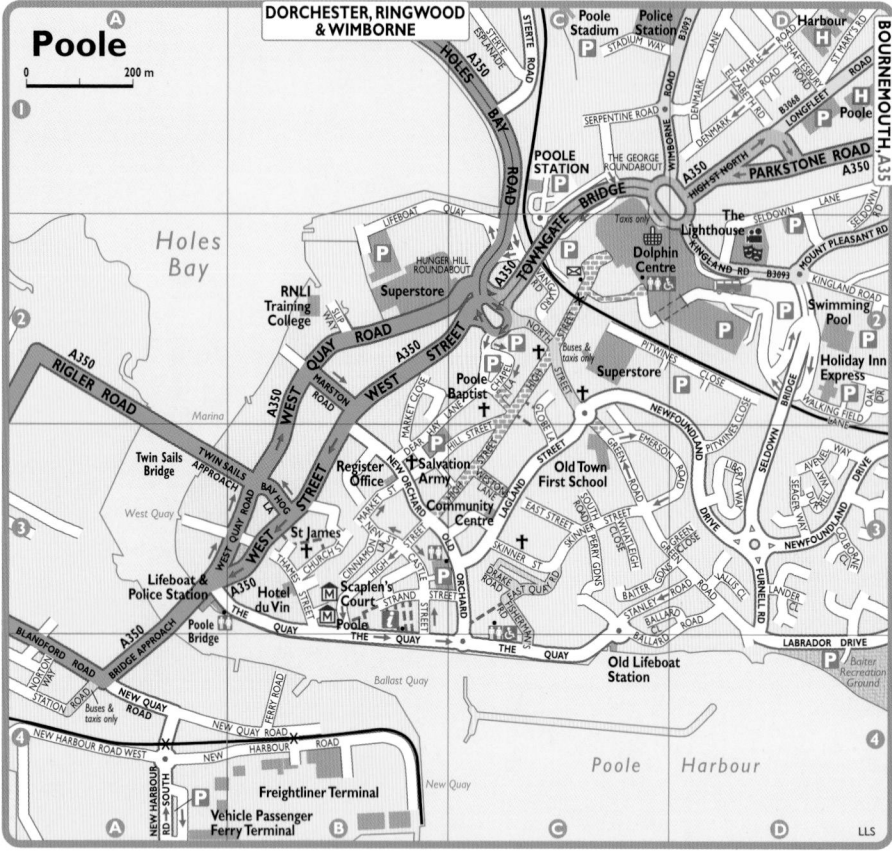

Poole

Poole is found on atlas page **12 H6**

Preston

Preston is found on atlas page **88 G5**

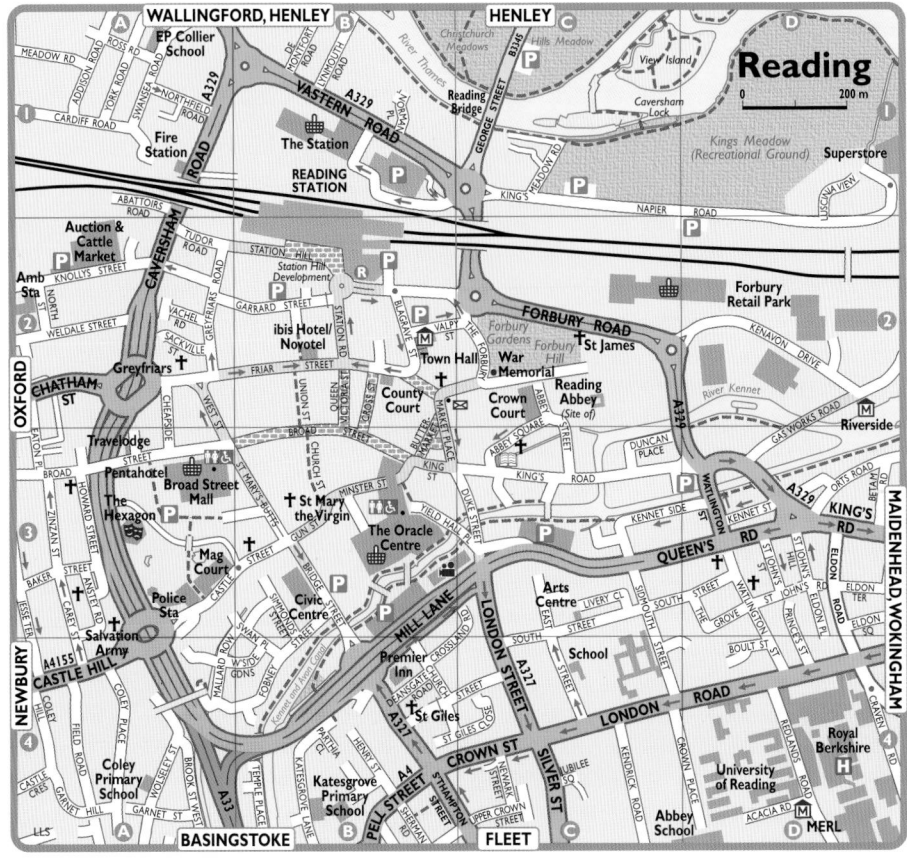

Reading

Reading is found on atlas page **35 K10**

Abbey Square	C3	King's Road	D3
Abbey Street	C2	King Street	B3
Addison Road	A1	Knollys Street	A2
Anstey Road	A3	Livery Close	C3
Baker Street	A3	London Road	C4
Blagrave Street	B2	London Street	C3
Boult Street	D4	Mallard Row	A4
Bridge Street	B3	Market Place	B2
Broad Street	A3	Mill Lane	B4
Brook Street West	A4	Minster Street	B3
Buttermarket	B3	Napier Road	C1
Cardiff Road	A1	Newark Street	C4
Carey Street	A3	Northfield Road	A1
Castle Hill	A4	Parthia Close	B4
Castle Street	A3	Pell Street	B4
Caversham Road	A2	Prince's Street	D3
Chatham Street	A2	Queen's Road	C3
Cheapside	A2	Queen Victoria Street	B2
Church Street	B3	Redlands Road	D4
Church Street	B4	Ross Road	A1
Coley Place	A4	Sackville Street	A2
Craven Road	D4	St Giles Close	B4
Crossland Road	B4	St John's Road	D3
Cross Street	B2	St Mary's Butts	B3
Crown Street	C4	Sidmouth Street	C3
Deansgate Road	B4	Silver Street	C4
Duke Street	C3	Simmonds Street	B3
Duncan Place	C3	Southampton Street	B4
East Street	C3	South Street	C3
Eldon Road	D3	Station Hill	B2
Field Road	A4	Station Road	B2
Fobney Street	B4	Swan Place	B3
Forbury Road	C2	Swansea Road	A1
Friar Street	B2	The Forbury	C2
Garnet Street	A4	Tudor Road	A2
Garrard Street	B2	Union Street	B2
Gas Works Road	D3	Upper Crown Street	C4
George Street	C1	Vachel Road	A2
Greyfriars Road	A2	Valpy Street	B2
Gun Street	B3	Vastern Road	B1
Henry Street	B4	Waterside Gardens	B4
Howard Street	A3	Watlington Street	D3
Katesgrove Lane	B4	Weldale Street	A2
Kenavon Drive	D2	West Street	A2
Kendrick Road	C4	Wolseley Street	A4
Kennet Side	C3	Yield Hall Place	B3
Kennet Street	D3	York Road	A1
King's Meadow Road	C1	Zinzan Street	A3

Royal Tunbridge Wells

Royal Tunbridge Wells is found on atlas page **25 N3**

Albert Street	C1	High Street	B4
Arundel Road	C4	Lansdowne Road	C2
Bayhall Road	D2	Lime Hill Road	B1
Belgrave Road	C1	Linden Park Road	A4
Berkeley Road	B4	Little Mount Sion	B4
Boyne Park	A1	London Road	A2
Buckingham Road	C4	Lonsdale Gardens	B2
Calverley Gardens	C3	Madeira Park	B4
Calverley Park	C2	Major York's Road	A4
Calverley Park Gardens	D2	Meadow Road	B1
Calverley Road	C2	Molyneux Park Road	A1
Calverley Street	C1	Monson Road	C2
Cambridge Gardens	D4	Monson Way	B2
Cambridge Street	D3	Mount Edgcumbe Road	A3
Camden Hill	D3	Mount Ephraim	A2
Camden Park	D3	Mount Ephraim Road	B1
Camden Road	C1	Mountfield Gardens	C3
Carlton Road	D2	Mountfield Road	C3
Castle Road	A2	Mount Pleasant Avenue	B2
Castle Street	B3	Mount Pleasant Road	B2
Chapel Place	B4	Mount Sion	B4
Christchurch Avenue	B3	Nevill Street	B4
Church Road	A2	Newton Road	B1
Civic Way	B2	Norfolk Road	C4
Claremont Gardens	C4	North Street	D2
Claremont Road	C4	Oakfield Court Road	D3
Clarence Road	B2	Park Street	D3
Crescent Road	B2	Pembury Road	D2
Culverden Street	B1	Poona Road	D3
Dale Street	C1	Prince's Street	D3
Dudley Road	B1	Prospect Road	D3
Eden Road	B4	Rock Villa Road	B1
Eridge Road	A4	Royal Chase	A1
Farmcombe Lane	C4	St James' Road	D1
Farmcombe Road	C4	Sandrock Road	D1
Ferndale	D1	Somerville Gardens	A1
Frant Road	B4	South Green	B3
Frog Lane	B4	Station Approach	B3
Garden Road	C1	Stone Street	D1
Garden Street	C1	Sutherland Road	C3
George Street	D3	Tunnel Road	C1
Goods Station Road	B1	Upper Grosvenor Road	B1
Grecian Road	C4	Vale Avenue	B3
Grosvenor Road	B1	Vale Road	B3
Grove Hill Gardens	C3	Victoria Road	C1
Grove Hill Road	C3	Warwick Park	B4
Guildford Road	C3	Wood Street	C1
Hanover Road	B1	York Road	B2

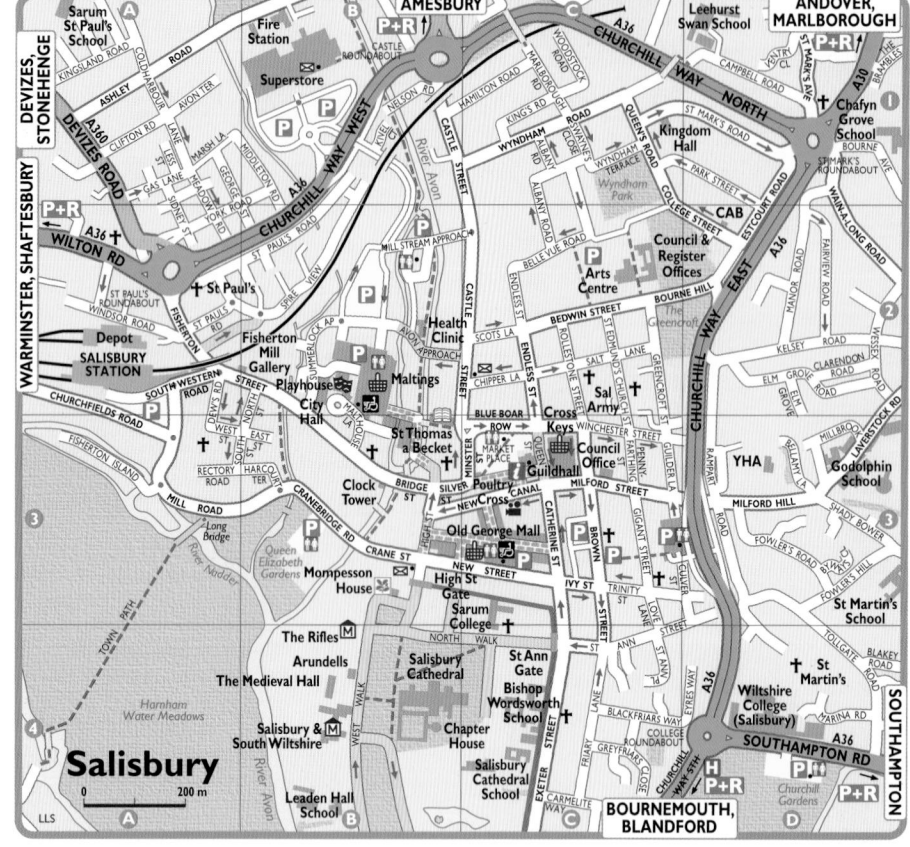

Salisbury

Salisbury is found on atlas page **21 M9**

Albany Road	C1	Kingsland Road	A1
Ashley Road	A1	King's Road	C1
Avon Approach	B2	Laverstock Road	D3
Bedwin Street	C2	Malthouse Lane	B3
Belle Vue Road	C2	Manor Road	D2
Blackfriars Way	C4	Marlborough Road	C1
Blue Boar Row	C3	Meadow Road	A1
Bourne Avenue	D1	Middleton Road	A1
Bourne Hill	C2	Milford Hill	D3
Bridge Street	B3	Milford Street	C3
Brown Street	C3	Mill Road	A3
Campbell Road	D1	Minster Street	C3
Castle Street	B1	Nelson Road	B1
Catherine Street	C3	New Canal	B3
Chipper Lane	C2	New Street	B3
Churchfields Road	A2	North Street	B3
Churchill Way East	D3	Park Street	D1
Churchill Way North	C1	Pennyfarthing Street	C2
Churchill Way South	C4	Queen's Road	C1
Churchill Way West	B2	Queen Street	C3
Clarendon Road	D2	Rampart Road	D3
Clifton Road	A1	Rectory Road	A1
Coldharbour Lane	A1	Rollestone Street	C2
College Street	C1	St Ann Street	C4
Cranebridge Road	B3	St Edmund's Church Street	C2
Crane Street	B3	St Mark's Avenue	D1
Devizes Road	A1	St Mark's Road	D1
Dew's Road	A3	St Paul's Road	B2
East Street	B3	Salt Lane	C2
Elm Grove	D2	Scots Lane	C2
Elm Grove Road	D2	Sidney Street	A1
Endless Street	C2	Silver Street	B3
Estcourt Road	D2	Southampton Road	D4
Exeter Street	C4	South Street	A3
Eyres Way	D4	South Western Road	A2
Fairview Road	D2	Spire View	B2
Fisherton Street	A2	Summerlock Approach	B2
Fowler's Road	D3	Tollgate Road	D4
Friary Lane	C4	Trinity Street	C3
Gas Lane	A1	Wain-A-Long Road	D1
George Street	A1	Wessex Road	D2
Gigant Street	C3	West Street	A3
Greencroft Street	C2	Wilton Road	A2
Guilder Lane	C3	Winchester Street	C3
Hamilton Road	C1	Windsor Road	A2
High Street	B3	Woodstock Road	C1
Ivy Street	C3	Wyndham Road	C1
Kelsey Road	D2	York Road	A2

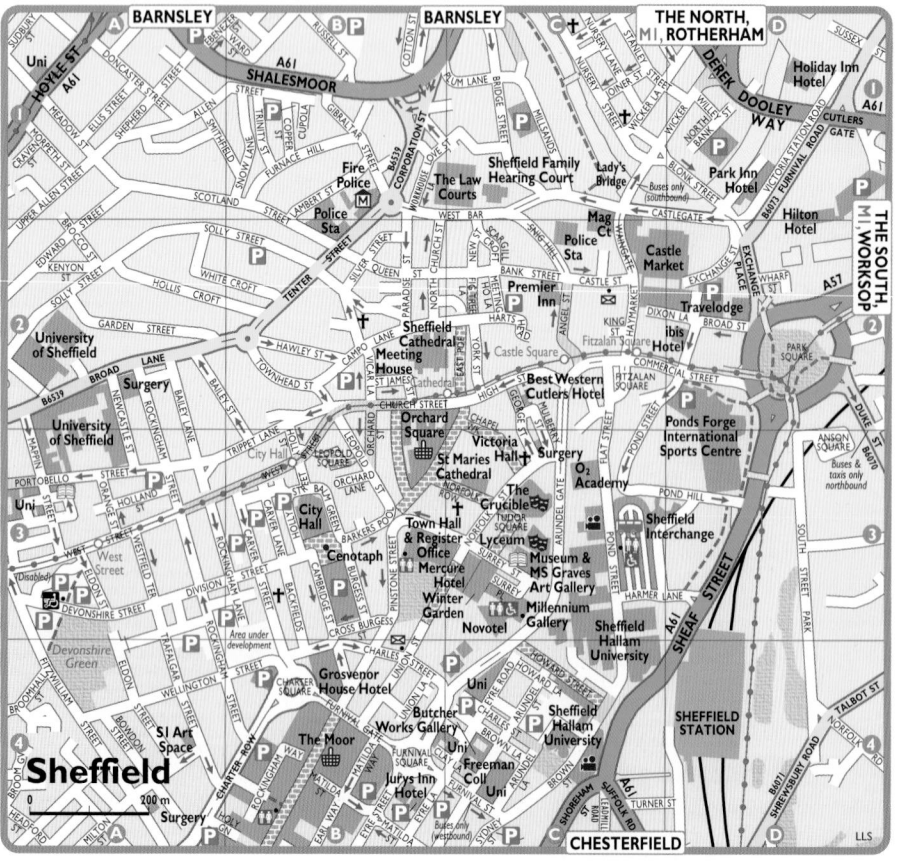

Sheffield

Sheffield is found on atlas page **84 E3**

Angel Street	C2	Howard Street	C4
Arundel Gate	C3	Hoyle Street	A1
Arundel Street	C4	King Street	C2
Backfields	B3	Lambert Street	B1
Bailey Street	A2	Leopold Street	B3
Balm Green	B3	Mappin Street	A3
Bank Street	C2	Matilda Street	B4
Barkers Pool	B3	Meetinghouse Lane	C2
Broad Lane	A2	Mulberry Street	C2
Broad Street	D2	Newcastle Street	A2
Brown Street	C4	New Street	C2
Cambridge Street	B3	Norfolk Street	C3
Campo Lane	B2	North Church Street	B2
Carver Street	B3	Orchard Street	B3
Castlegate	C1	Paradise Street	B2
Castle Street	C2	Pinstone Street	B3
Charles Street	B4	Pond Hill	C3
Charter Row	A4	Pond Street	C3
Church Street	B2	Portobello Street	A3
Commercial Street	C2	Queen Street	B2
Corporation Street	B1	Rockingham Street	A2
Cross Burgess Street	B3	St James Street	B2
Cutlers Gate	D1	Scargill Croft	C2
Derek Dooley Way	D1	Scotland Street	A1
Devonshire Street	A3	Shalesmoor	B1
Division Street	A3	Sheaf Street	D4
Dixon Lane	C2	Shoreham Street	C4
Duke Street	D2	Shrewsbury Road	D4
Exchange Street	D2	Silver Street	B2
Eyre Street	B4	Smithfield	A1
Fig Tree Lane	C2	Snig Hill	C2
Fitzwilliam Street	A4	Solly Street	A2
Flat Street	C3	Suffolk Road	C4
Furnace Hill	B1	Surrey Street	C3
Furnival Gate	B4	Talbot Street	D4
Furnival Road	D1	Tenter Street	B2
Furnival Street	C4	Townhead Street	B2
Garden Street	A2	Trafalgar Street	A4
George Street	C2	Trippet Lane	B3
Gibralter Street	B1	Union Street	B4
Harmer Lane	C3	Vicar Lane	B2
Harts Head	C2	Victoria Station Road	D1
Hawley Street	B2	Waingate	C2
Haymarket	C2	Wellington Street	A4
High Street	C2	West Bar	B2
Holland Street	A3	West Street	A3
Hollis Croft	A2	White Croft	A2
Holly Street	B3	York Street	C2

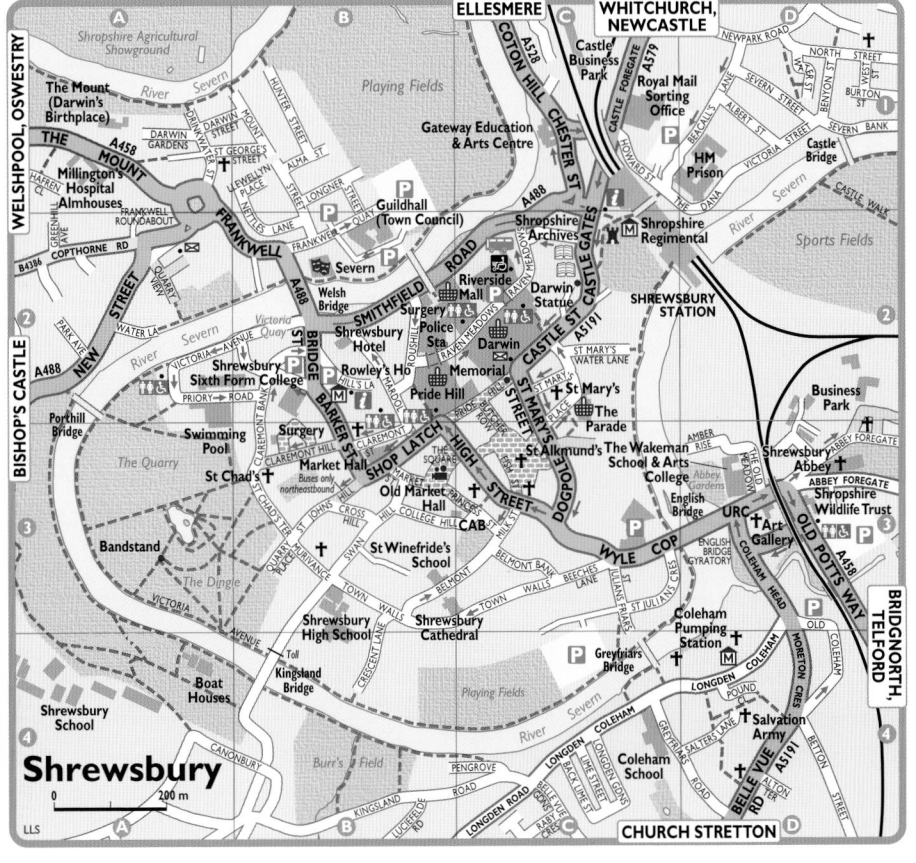

Shrewsbury

Shrewsbury is found on atlas page **56 H2**

Abbey Foregate	D3	Longner Street	B1
Albert Street	D1	Mardol	B2
Alma Street	B1	Market Street	B3
Amber Rise	D3	Milk Street	C3
Barker Street	B2	Moreton Crescent	D4
Beacall's Lane	D1	Mount Street	B1
Beeches Lane	C3	Murivance	B3
Belle Vue Gardens	C4	Nettles Lane	B1
Belle Vue Road	D4	Newpark Road	D1
Belmont	B3	New Street	A2
Belmont Bank	C3	North Street	D1
Benyon Street	D1	Old Coleham	D3
Betton Street	D4	Old Potts Way	D3
Bridge Street	B2	Park Avenue	A2
Burton Street	D1	Pengrove	C4
Butcher Row	C2	Pound Close	D4
Canonbury	A4	Pride Hill	C2
Castle Foregate	C1	Princess Street	B3
Castle Gates	C2	Priory Road	A2
Castle Street	C2	Quarry Place	B3
Chester Street	C1	Quarry View	A2
Claremont Bank	B3	Raven Meadows	B2
Claremont Hill	B3	Roushill	B2
Claremont Street	B3	St Chad's Terrace	B3
Coleham Head	D3	St George's Street	A1
College Hill	B3	St Johns Hill	B3
Copthorne Road	A2	St Julians Friars	C3
Coton Hill	C1	St Julians Crescent	C3
Crescent Lane	B4	St Mary's Place	C2
Cross Hill	B3	St Mary's Street	C2
Darwin Gardens	A1	St Mary's Water Lane	D4
Darwin Street	A1	Salters Lane	D4
Dogpole	C3	Severn Bank	D1
Drinkwater Street	A1	Severn Street	D1
Fish Street	C3	Shop Latch	B3
Frankwell	A2	Smithfield Road	B2
Frankwell Quay	B2	Swan Hill	B3
Greenhill Avenue	A2	The Dana	D1
Greyfriars Road	C4	The Mount	A1
High Street	C3	The Old Meadow	D3
Hill's Lane	B2	The Square	B3
Howard Street	C1	Town Walls	B3
Hunter Street	B1	Victoria Avenue	A2
Kingsland Road	B4	Victoria Street	D1
Lime Street	C4	Water Lane	A2
Longden Coleham	C4	Water Street	D1
Longden Gardens	C4	West Street	D1
Longden Road	C4	Wyle Cop	C3

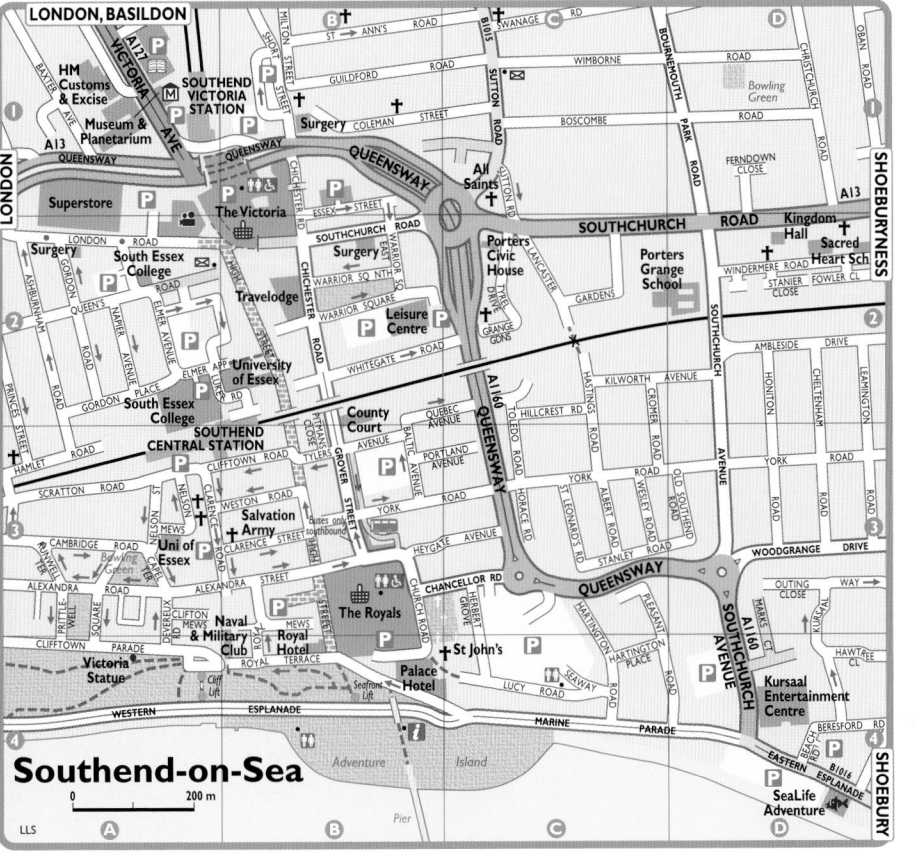

Southend-on-Sea

Southend-on-Sea is found on atlas page **38 E4**

Albert Road	C3	Kursaal Way	D4
Alexandra Road	A3	Lancaster Gardens	C2
Alexandra Street	A3	Leamington Road	D2
Ambleside Drive	D2	London Road	A2
Ashburnham Road	A2	Lucy Road	C4
Baltic Avenue	B3	Luker Road	A2
Baxter Avenue	A1	Marine Parade	C4
Beach Road	D4	Milton Street	B1
Beresford Road	D4	Napier Avenue	A2
Boscombe Road	C1	Nelson Street	A3
Bournemouth Park Road	D1	Oban Road	D1
Cambridge Road	A3	Old Southend Road	D3
Capel Terrace	A3	Outing Close	D3
Chancellor Road	B3	Pitmans Close	B2
Cheltenham Road	D2	Pleasant Road	C3
Chichester Road	B1	Portland Avenue	B3
Christchurch Road	D1	Princes Street	A2
Church Road	B3	Prittlewell Square	A3
Clarence Road	A3	Quebec Avenue	B2
Clarence Street	B3	Queen's Road	A2
Clifftown Parade	A4	Queensway	A1
Clifftown Road	B3	Royal Terrace	B4
Coleman Street	B1	Runwell Terrace	A3
Cromer Road	C2	St Ann's Road	B1
Devereux Road	A4	St Leonard's Road	C3
Eastern Esplanade	D4	Scratton Road	A3
Elmer Approach	A2	Short Street	B1
Elmer Avenue	A2	Southchurch Avenue	C2
Essex Street	B1	Southchurch Road	B2
Ferndown Close	D1	Stanier Close	D2
Fowler Close	D2	Stanley Road	C3
Gordon Place	A2	Sutton Road	C1
Gordon Road	A2	Swanage Road	C1
Grange Gardens	C2	Toledo Road	D2
Grover Street	B3	Tylers Avenue	B2
Guildford Road	B1	Tyrel Drive	C2
Hamlet Road	A3	Victoria Avenue	A1
Hartington Place	C4	Warrior Square East	B2
Hartington Road	C3	Warrior Square North	B2
Hastings Road	C2	Warrior Square	B2
Hawtree Close	D4	Wesley Road	C3
Herbert Grove	C3	Western Esplanade	A4
Heygate Avenue	B3	Weston Road	B3
High Street	B2	Whitegate Road	B2
Hillcrest Road	C2	Wimborne Road	C1
Honiton Road	D2	Windermere Road	D2
Horace Road	C3	Woodgrange Drive	D3
Kilworth Avenue	C2	York Road	B3

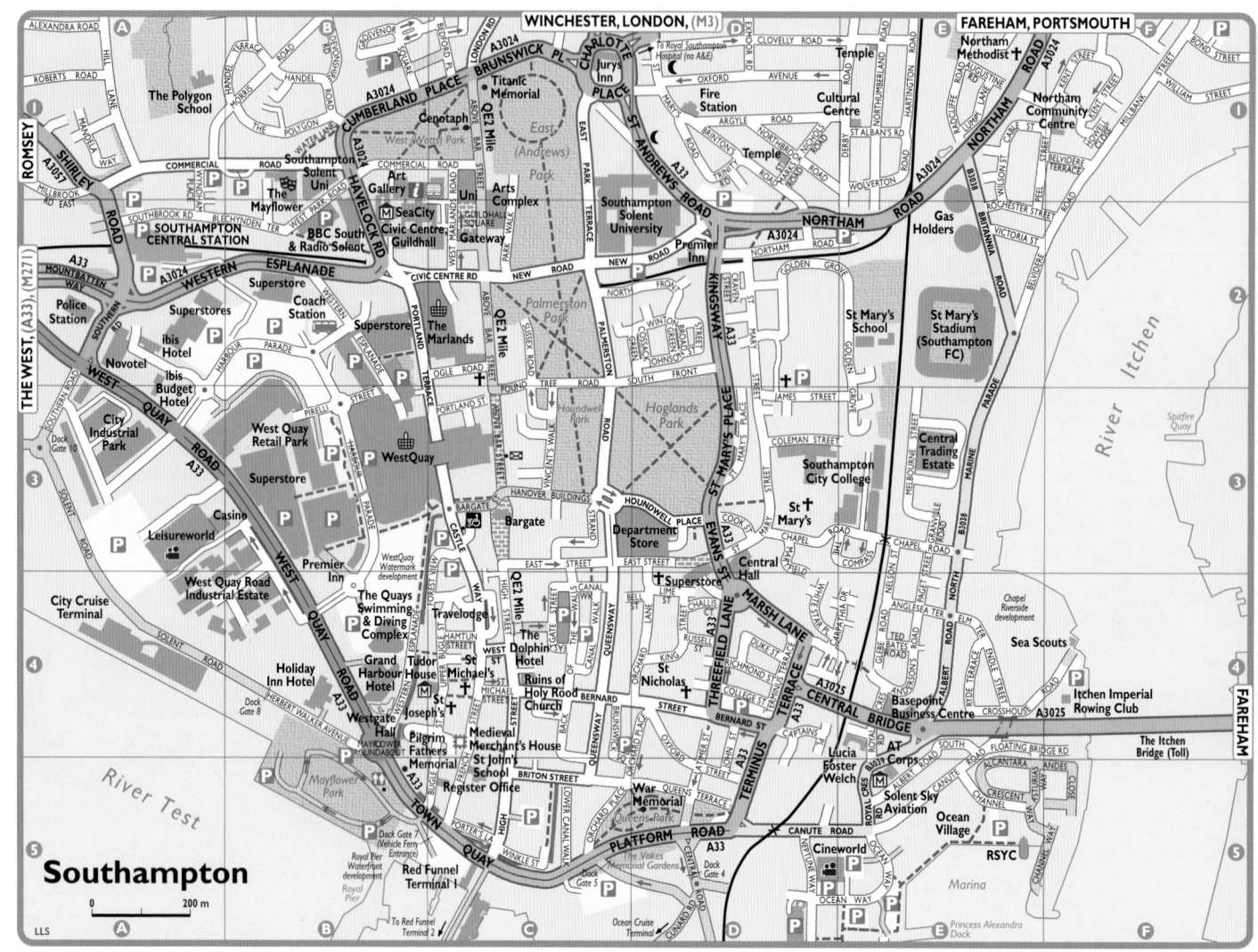

Southampton

Southampton is found on atlas page **14 D4**

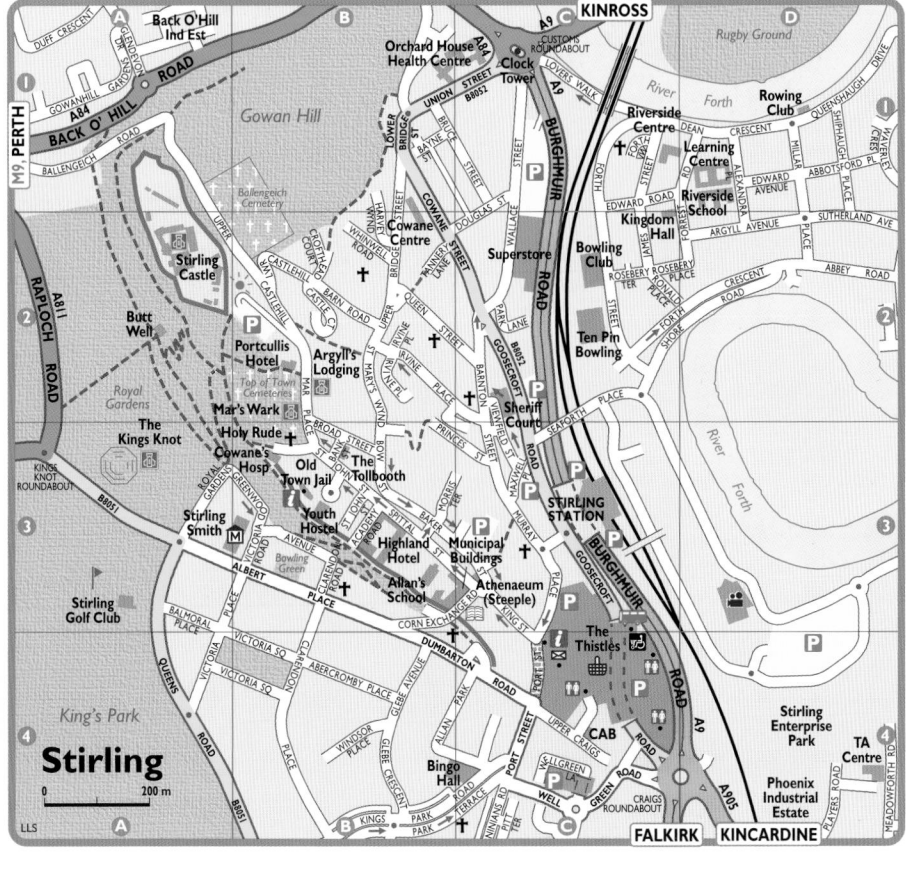

Stirling

Stirling is found on atlas page **133 M9**

Abbey Road	D2	Kings Park Road	B4
Abbotsford Place	D1	King Street	C3
Abercromby Place	B4	Lovers Walk	C1
Academy Road	B3	Lower Bridge Street	B1
Albert Place	A3	Lower Castlehill	B2
Alexandra Place	D1	Mar Place	B2
Allan Park	B4	Maxwell Place	C3
Argyll Avenue	D2	Meadowforth Road	D4
Back O' Hill Road	A1	Millar Place	D1
Baker Street	B3	Morris Terrace	B3
Ballengeich Road	A1	Murray Place	C3
Balmoral Place	A3	Ninians Road	C4
Bank Street	B3	Park Lane	C2
Barn Road	B2	Park Terrace	B4
Barnton Street	C2	Pitt Terrace	C4
Bayne Street	B1	Players Road	D4
Bow Street	B3	Port Street	C4
Broad Street	B3	Princes Street	B3
Bruce Street	B1	Queenshaugh Drive	D1
Burghmuir Road	C1	Queens Road	A4
Castle Court	B2	Queen Street	B2
Clarendon Place	B4	Raploch Road	A2
Clarendon Road	B3	Ronald Place	C2
Corn Exchange Road	B3	Rosebery Place	C2
Cowane Street	B1	Rosebery Terrace	C2
Craigs Roundabout	C4	Royal Gardens	A3
Crofthead Court	B2	St John Street	B3
Customs Roundabout	C1	St Mary's Wynd	B2
Dean Crescent	D1	Seaforth Place	C3
Douglas Street	C2	Shiphaugh Place	D1
Duff Crescent	A1	Shore Road	C2
Dumbarton Road	B4	Spittal Street	B3
Edward Avenue	D1	Sutherland Avenue	D2
Edward Road	C1	Tannery Lane	B2
Forrest Road	D2	Union Street	B1
Forth Crescent	C2	Upper Bridge Street	B2
Forth Street	C1	Upper Castlehill	A2
Forth View	C1	Upper Craigs	C4
Glebe Avenue	B4	Victoria Place	A4
Glebe Crescent	B4	Victoria Road	B3
Glendevon Drive	A1	Victoria Square	A4
Goosecroft Road	C2	Viewfield Street	C2
Gowanhill Gardens	A1	Wallace Street	C2
Greenwood Avenue	A3	Waverley Crescent	D1
Harvey Wynd	B1	Wellgreen Lane	C4
Irvine Place	B2	Wellgreen Road	C4
James Street	C2	Whinwell Road	B2
Kings Knot Roundabout	A3	Windsor Place	B4

Stockton-on-Tees

Stockton-on-Tees is found on atlas page **104 D7**

1825 Way	B4	Massey Road	D3
Allison Street	B1	Melbourne Street	A2
Alma Street	B1	Middle Street	B2
Bath Lane	C1	Mill Street West	A2
Bedford Street	A1	Nelson Terrace	B2
Bishop Street	B2	North Shore Road	D2
Bishopton Lane	A1	Northport Road	D1
Bishopton Road	A1	Northshore Link	C2
Bowesfield Lane	A4	Norton Road	B1
Bridge Road	B3	Palmerston Street	A2
Bridge Road	C4	Park Road	A4
Bright Street	B2	Park Terrace	C3
Britannia Road	A1	Parkfield Road	B4
Brunswick Street	B3	Parliament Street	B4
Bute Street	A2	Portrack Lane	D1
Church Road	D1	Prince Regent Terrace	B3
Clarence Row	C1	Princess Avenue	C1
Corporation Street	A2	Princeton Drive	D4
Council of Europe		Quayside Road	C3
Boulevard	C2	Raddcliffe Crescent	D3
Cromwell Avenue	B1	Ramsgate	B3
Dixon Street	A2	Riverside	C3
Dovecot Street	A3	Russell Street	B2
Dugdale Street	D1	St Paul's Street	A1
Durham Road	A1	Silver Street	B2
Durham Street	A2	Skinner Street	B3
Edwards Street	A4	Station Street	D4
Farrer Street	B1	Sydney Street	B2
Finkle Street	C3	The Square	D2
Frederick Street	B1	Thistle Green	C2
Fudan Way	D3	Thomas Street	B1
Gooseport Road	D1	Thompson Street	B1
Hartington Road	A3	Tower Street	B4
Harvard Avenue	D3	Union Street East	C1
High Street	B2	University Boulevard	C3
Hill Street East	D1	Vane Street	B2
Hume Street	B1	Vicarage Avenue	A1
Hutchinson Street	A2	Wellington Street	B2
John Street	B2	West Row	B3
King Street	B2	Westbourne Street	A4
Knightport Road	D1	Westpoint Road	C3
Knowles Street	C2	Wharf Street	B4
Laing Street	B1	William Street	B3
Leeds Street	B2	Woodland Street	A4
Lobdon Street	B2	Worthing Street	A3
Lodge Street	B3	Yale Crescent	C4
Mandale Road	D4	Yarm Lane	A4
Maritime Road	C1	Yarm Road	A4

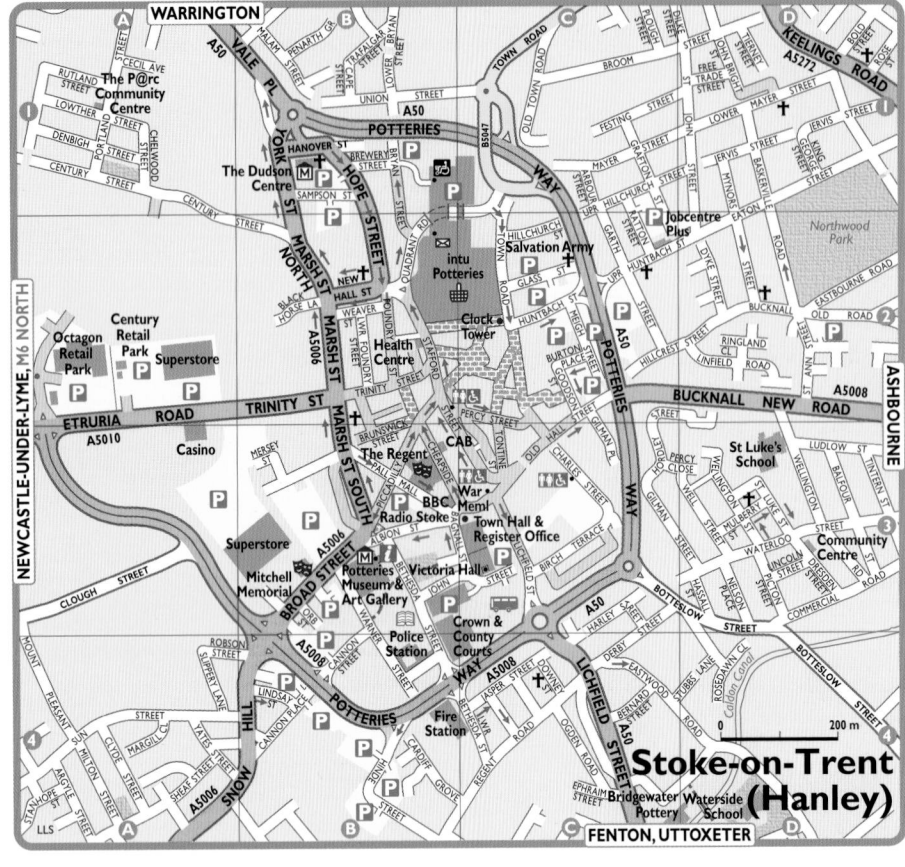

Stoke-on-Trent (Hanley)

Stoke-on-Trent (Hanley) is found on atlas page **70 F5**

Albion Street	B3	Lichfield Street	C3
Bagnall Street	B3	Linfield Road	D2
Balfour Street	D3	Lower Mayer Street	D1
Baskerville Road	D1	Lowther Street	A1
Bathesda Street	B4	Ludlow Street	D3
Bernard Street	C4	Malam Street	B1
Bethesda Street	B3	Marsh Street	B2
Birch Terrace	C3	Marsh Street North	B2
Botteslow Street	C3	Marsh Street South	B3
Broad Street	B3	Mayer Street	C1
Broom Street	C1	Mersey Street	B3
Brunswick Street	B3	Milton Street	C1
Bryan Street	B1	Mount Pleasant	A4
Bucknall New Road	C2	Mynors Street	D1
Bucknall Old Road	D2	New Hall Street	B2
Cardiff Grove	B4	Ogden Road	C4
Century Street	A1	Old Hall Street	C3
Charles Street	C3	Old Town Road	C1
Cheapside	B3	Pall Mall	B3
Chelwood Street	A1	Percy Street	C2
Clough Street	A3	Piccadilly	B3
Clyde Street	A4	Portland Street	A1
Commercial Road	D3	Potteries Way	B1
Denbigh Street	A1	Quadrant Road	B2
Derby Street	C4	Regent Road	C4
Dyke Street	D2	Rutland Street	A1
Eastwood Road	C4	St John Street	D1
Eaton Street	D2	St Luke Street	D3
Etruria Road	A2	Sampson Street	B1
Festing Street	C1	Sheaf Street	A4
Foundry Street	B2	Slippery Lane	A4
Garth Street	C2	Snow Hill	A4
Gilman Street	C3	Stafford Street	B2
Goodson Street	C2	Sun Street	A4
Grafton Street	C1	Tontine Street	C3
Hanover Street	B1	Town Road	C2
Harley Street	C4	Trafalgar Street	B1
Hillchurch	C2	Trinity Street	B2
Hillcrest Street	C2	Union Street	B1
Hinde Street	B4	Upper Hillchurch Street	C2
Hope Street	B1	Upper Huntbach Street	C2
Hordley Street	C3	Warner Street	B3
Huntbach Street	C2	Waterloo Street	D3
Jasper Street	C4	Well Street	D3
Jervis Street	D1	Wellington Road	D3
John Bright Street	D1	Wellington Street	D3
John Street	B3	Yates Street	A4
Keelings Road	D1	York Street	C3

Stratford-upon-Avon

Stratford-upon-Avon is found on atlas page **47 P3**

Albany Road	A3	Old Red Hen Court	C2
Alcester Road	A2	Old Town	C4
Arden Street	B2	Orchard Way	A4
Avenue Road	C1	Payton Street	C2
Bancroft Place	C2	Percy Street	C1
Birmingham Road	B1	Rother Street	B3
Brewery Street	B1	Rowley Crescent	D1
Bridge Foot	D2	Ryland Street	B4
Bridge Street	C2	St Andrew's Crescent	A3
Bridgeway	D2	St Gregory's Road	C1
Broad Street	B4	St Martin's Close	C1
Brookvale Road	A4	Sanctus Drive	B4
Bull Street	B4	Sanctus Road	A4
Cedar Close	D1	Sanctus Street	B4
Chapel Lane	C3	Sandfield Road	A4
Chapel Street	C3	Scholars Lane	B3
Cherry Orchard	A4	Seven Meadows Road	A4
Cherry Street	B4	Shakespeare Street	B1
Chestnut Walk	B3	Sheep Street	C3
Church Street	B3	Shipston Road	D4
Clopton Road	B1	Shottery Road	A3
College Lane	B4	Shrieves Walk	C3
College Mews	B4	Southern Lane	C3
College Street	B4	Station Road	A2
Ely Gardens	B3	Swan's Nest	D3
Ely Street	B3	The Willows	A3
Evesham Place	B3	Tiddington Road	D3
Evesham Road	A4	Town Square	C2
Garrick Way	A4	Tramway Bridge	D3
Great William Street	C1	Tyler Street	C2
Greenhill Street	B2	Union Street	C2
Grove Road	B3	Warwick Court	C1
Guild Street	C2	Warwick Crescent	D1
Henley Street	B2	Warwick Road	C2
High Street	C3	Waterside	C3
Holtom Street	B4	Welcombe Road	D1
John Street	C2	Wellesbourne Grove	B3
Kendall Avenue	B1	Western Road	B1
Lock Close	C2	West Street	B4
Maidenhead Road	C1	Willows Drive North	A2
Mansell Street	B2	Windsor Street	B2
Mayfield Avenue	C1	Wood Street	B2
Meer Street	B2		
Mill Lane	C4		
Mulberry Street	C1		
Narrow Lane	B4		
New Broad Street	B4		
New Street	B4		

Sunderland

Sunderland is found on atlas page **113 N9**

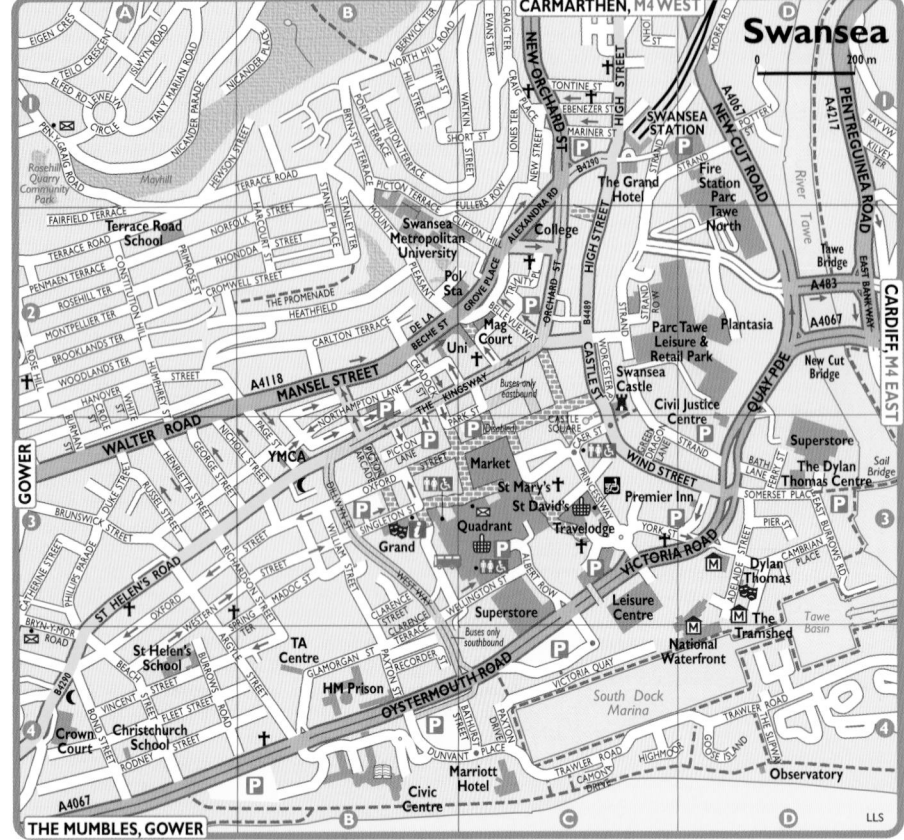

Swansea

Swansea is found on atlas page **29 J6**

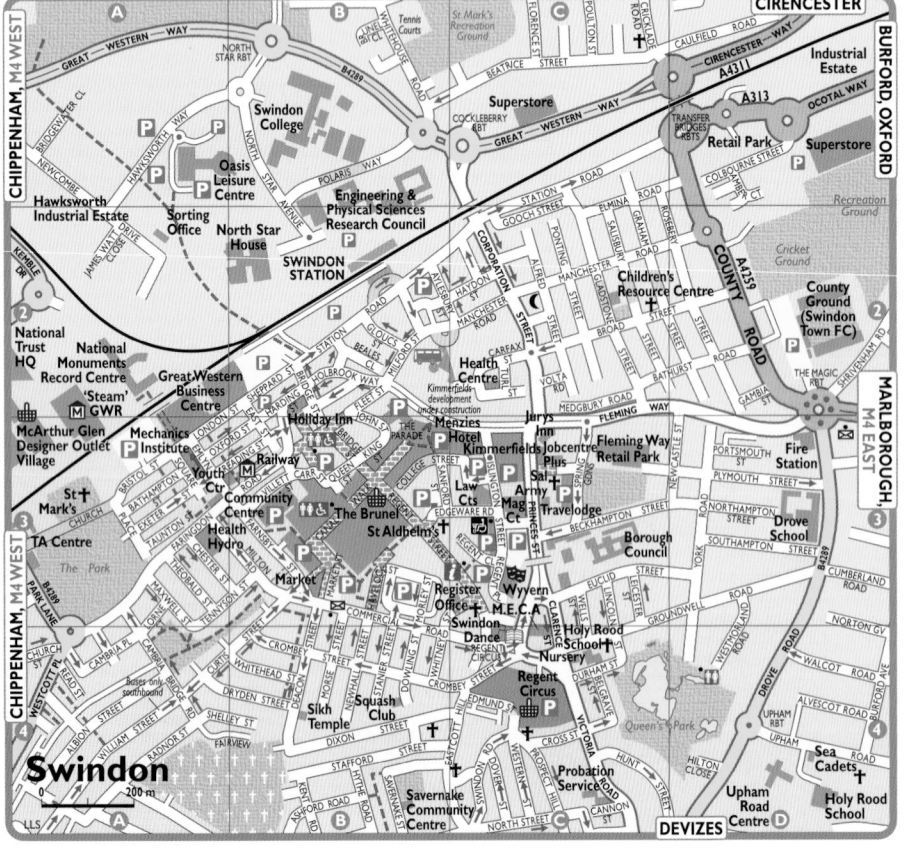

Swindon

Swindon is found on atlas page **33 M8**

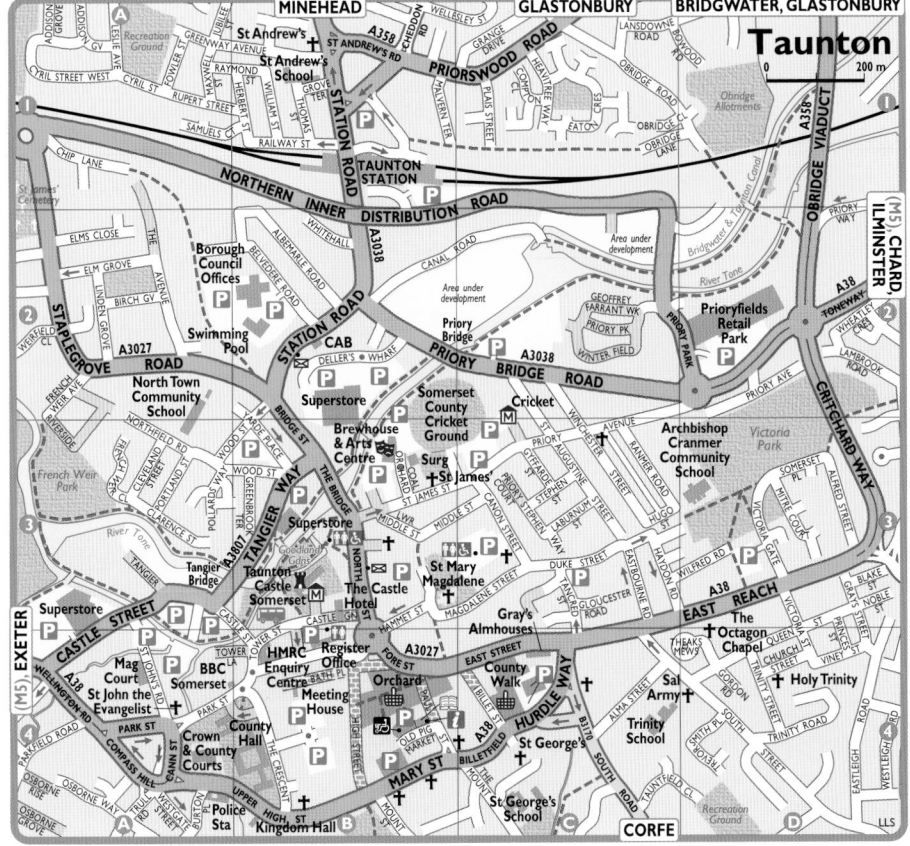

Taunton

Taunton is found on atlas page **18 H10**

Albemarle Road	B2		Middle Street	B3	
Alfred Street	D3		Northfield Road	A3	
Alma Street	C4		North Street	B3	
Belvedere Road	B2		Obridge Road	C1	
Billetfield	C4		Obridge Viaduct	D2	
Billet Street	C4		Old Pig Market	B4	
Bridge Street	B2		Parkfield Road	A4	
Canal Road	B2		Park Street	A4	
Cann Street	A4		Paul Street	B4	
Canon Street	C3		Plais Street	C1	
Castle Street	A4		Portland Street	A3	
Cheddon Road	B1		Priorswood Road	B1	
Chip Lane	A1		Priory Avenue	C3	
Church Street	D4		Priory Bridge Road	C2	
Clarence Street	A3		Queen Street	D4	
Cleveland Street	A3		Railway Street	B1	
Compass Hill	A4		Ranmer Road	C3	
Critchard Way	D2		Raymond Street	A1	
Cyril Street	A1		Rupert Street	A1	
Deller's Wharf	B2		St Andrew's Road	B1	
Duke Street	C3		St Augustine Street	C3	
Eastbourne Road	C3		St James Street	B3	
Eastleigh Road	D4		St John's Road	A4	
East Reach	D3		Samuels Court	A1	
East Street	C4		South Road	C4	
Fore Street	B4		South Street	D4	
Fowler Street	A1		Staplegrove Road	A2	
French Weir Avenue	A2		Station Road	B2	
Gloucester Road	C3		Stephen Street	C3	
Grange Drive	C1		Stephen Way	C3	
Grays Street	D3		Tancred Street	C3	
Greenway Avenue	A1		The Avenue	A2	
Gyffarde Street	C3		The Bridge	B3	
Hammet Street	B4		The Crescent	B4	
Haydon Road	C3		Thomas Street	B1	
Herbert Street	B1		Toneway	D2	
High Street	B4		Tower Street	B4	
Hugo Street	C3		Trinity Road	D4	
Hurdle Way	C4		Trinity Street	D4	
Laburnum Street	C3		Upper High Street	B4	
Lambrook Road	D2		Victoria Gate	D3	
Lansdowne Road	C1		Victoria Street	D3	
Leslie Avenue	A1		Viney Street	D4	
Linden Grove	A2		Wellington Road	A4	
Lower Middle Street	B3		Wilfred Road	C3	
Magdalene Street	B3		William Street	B1	
Mary Street	B4		Winchester Street	C2	
Maxwell Street	A1		Wood Street	B3	

Torquay

Torquay is found on atlas page **7 N6**

Abbey Road	B1		Middle Warbury Road	D1	
Alexandra Road	C1		Mill Lane	A1	
Alpine Road	C2		Montpellier Road	D3	
Ash Hill Road	C1		Morgan Avenue	B1	
Avenue Road	A1		Museum Road	D3	
Bampfylde Road	A2		Palm Road	B1	
Beacon Hill	D4		Parkhill Road	D4	
Belgrave Road	A1		Pembroke Road	C1	
Braddons Hill Road East	D3		Pennsylvania Road	D1	
Braddons Hill Road West	C2		Pimlico	C2	
Braddons Street	D2		Potters Hill	C1	
Bridge Road	A1		Princes Road	C1	
Camden Road	D1		Queen Street	C2	
Cary Parade	C3		Rathmore Road	A2	
Cary Road	C3		Rock Road	C2	
Castle Lane	C1		Rosehill Road	D1	
Castle Road	C1		St Efride's Road	A1	
Cavern Road	D1		St Luke's Road	B2	
Chestnut Avenue	A2		St Marychurch Road	C1	
Church Lane	A1		Scarborough Road	B2	
Church Street	A1		Seaway Lane	A4	
Cleveland Road	A1		Shedden Hill Road	B3	
Croft Hill	B2		Solbro Road	A3	
Croft Road	B2		South Hill Road	D3	
East Street	A1		South Street	A1	
Ellacombe Road	C1		Stentiford Hill Road	C2	
Falkland Road	A2		Strand	D3	
Fleet Street	C3		Sutherland Road	D1	
Grafton Road	D2		Temperance Street	C2	
Hennapyn Road	A4		The Terrace	D3	
Higher Union Lane	B1		Torbay Road	A4	
Hillesdon Road	D2		Tor Church Road	A1	
Hoxton Road	D1		Tor Hill Road	B1	
Hunsdon Road	D3		Torwood Street	D3	
King's Drive	A3		Trematon Ave	B1	
Laburnum Street	A1		Trinity Hill	D3	
Lime Avenue	A2		Union Street	B1	
Lower Ellacombe			Upper Braddons Hill	D2	
Church Road	D1		Vanehill Road	D4	
Lower Union Lane	C2		Vansittart Road	A1	
Lower Warbury Road	D2		Vaughan Parade	C3	
Lucius Street	A1		Victoria Parade	D4	
Lymington Road	B1		Victoria Road	C1	
Magdalene Road	B1		Vine Road	A1	
Market Street	C2		Walnut Road	A2	
Meadfoot Lane	D4		Warberry Road West	C1	
Melville Lane	C2		Warren Road	B2	
Melville Street	C2		Wellington Road	C1	

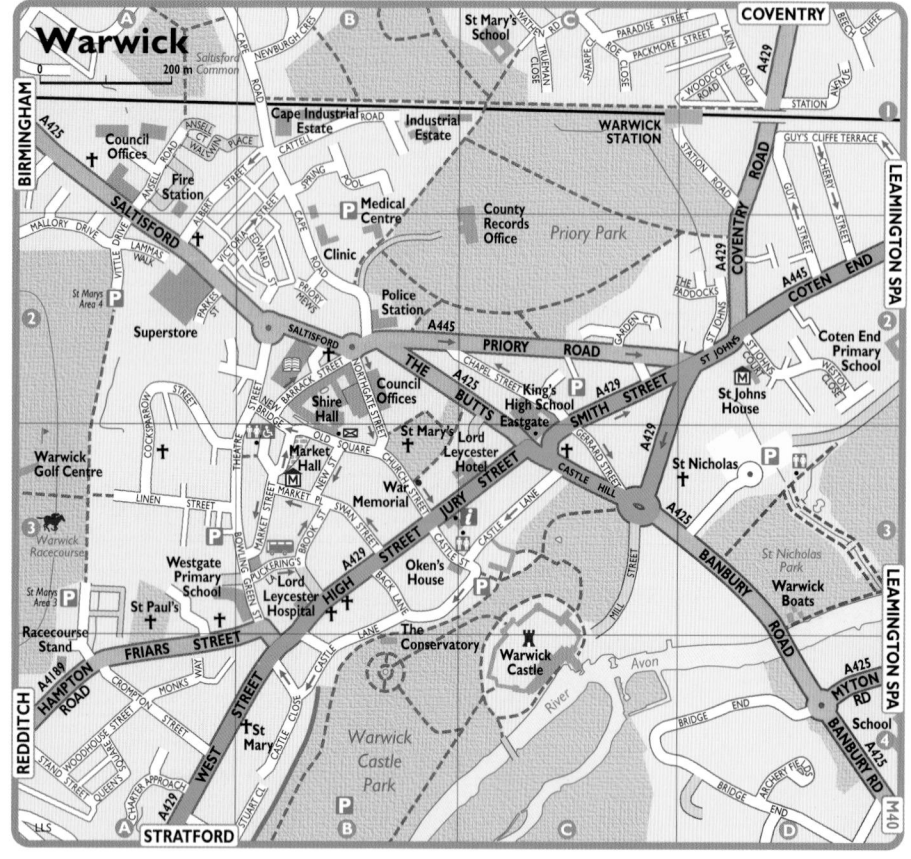

Warwick

Warwick is found on atlas page **59 L11**

Albert Street	A2	Packmore Street	C1
Ansell Court	A1	Paradise Street	C1
Ansell Road	A1	Parkes Street	A2
Archery Fields	D4	Priory Mews	B2
Back Lane	B3	Priory Road	C2
Banbury Road	D3	Puckering's Lane	B3
Barrack Street	B2	Queen's Square	A4
Beech Cliffe	D1	Roe Close	C1
Bowling Green Street	B3	St Johns	D2
Bridge End	D4	St Johns Court	D2
Brook Street	B3	Saltisford	A1
Cape Road	B1	Sharpe Close	C1
Castle Close	B4	Smith Street	C2
Castle Hill	C3	Spring Pool	B1
Castle Lane	B4	Stand Street	A4
Castle Street	B3	Station Avenue	D1
Cattell Road	B1	Station Road	D1
Chapel Street	C2	Stuart Close	B4
Charter Approach	A4	Swan Street	B3
Cherry Street	D1	Theatre Street	B3
Church Street	B3	The Butts	B2
Cocksparrow Street	A3	The Paddocks	D2
Coten End	D2	Trueman Close	C1
Coventry Road	D2	Victoria Street	A2
Crompton Street	A4	Vittle Drive	A2
Edward Street	B2	Wallwin Place	A1
Friars Street	A4	Wathen Road	C1
Garden Court	C2	Weston Close	D2
Gerrard Street	C3	West Street	A4
Guy's Cliffe Terrace	D1	Woodcote Road	D1
Guy Street	D1	Woodhouse Street	A4
Hampton Road	A4		
High Street	B3		
Jury Street	B3		
Lakin Road	D1		
Lammas Walk	A2		
Linen Street	A3		
Mallory Drive	A2		
Market Place	B3		
Market Street	B3		
Mill Street	C3		
Monks Way	A4		
Myton Road	D4		
New Bridge	B2		
Newburgh Crescent	B1		
New Street	B3		
Northgate Street	B2		
Old Square	B3		

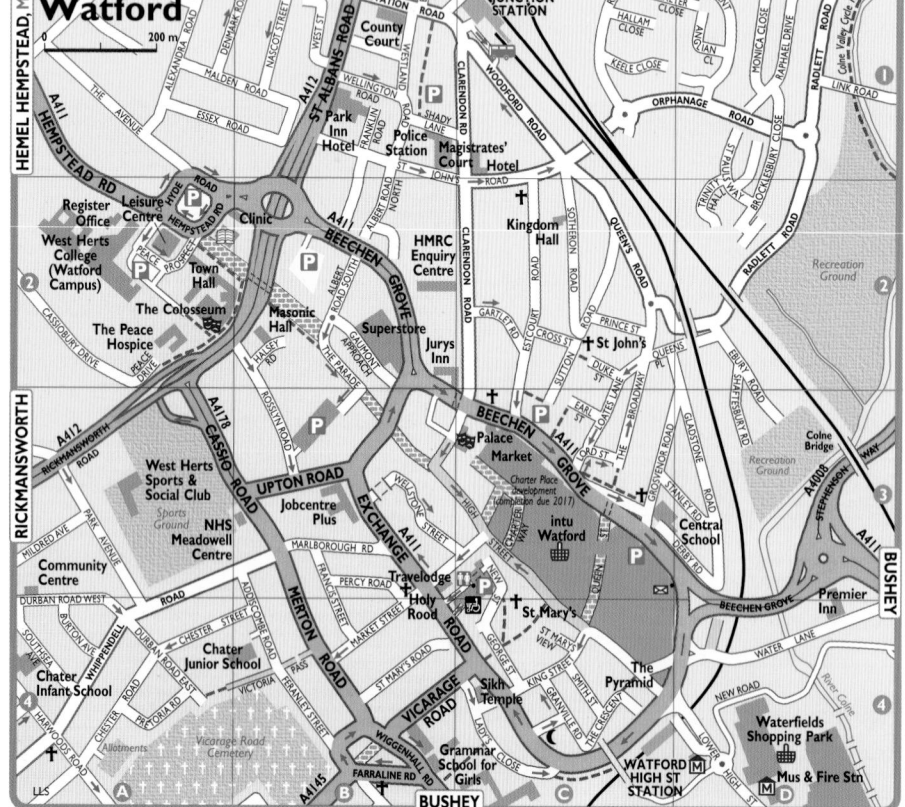

Watford

Watford is found on atlas page **50 D11**

Addiscombe Road	B3	Market Street	B4
Albert Road North	B2	Marlborough Road	B3
Albert Road South	B2	Merton Road	B3
Alexandra Road	A1	Mildred Avenue	A3
Anglian Close	D1	Monica Close	D1
Beechen Grove	C3	Nascot Street	B1
Brocklesbury Close	D2	New Road	D4
Burton Avenue	A4	New Street	C3
Cassiobury Drive	A2	Orphanage Road	C1
Cassio Road	A3	Park Avenue	A3
Charter Way	C3	Peace Prospect	A2
Chester Road	A4	Percy Road	B3
Chester Street	A4	Pretoria Road	A4
Clarendon Road	C1	Prince Street	C2
Cross Street	C2	Queen's Road	C2
Denmark Road	A1	Queen Street	C3
Derby Road	C3	Radlett Road	D2
Duke Street	C2	Raphael Drive	D1
Durban Road East	A4	Reeds Crescent	C1
Durban Road West	A4	Rickmansworth Road	A3
Earl Street	C3	Rosslyn Road	B3
Ebury Road	D2	St Albans Road	B1
Essex Road	A1	St John's Road	B1
Estcourt Road	C2	St Mary's Road	B4
Exchange Road	B3	St Pauls Way	D1
Farraline Road	B4	Shady Lane	B1
Feranley Street	B4	Shaftesbury Road	D2
Francis Street	B3	Smith Street	C4
Franklin Road	B1	Sotheron Road	C2
Gartlet Road	C2	Southsea Avenue	A4
Gaumont Approach	B2	Stanley Road	C3
George Street	C4	Station Road	B1
Gladstone Road	D3	Stephenson Way	D3
Granville Road	C4	Sutton Road	C2
Grosvenor Road	C3	The Avenue	A1
Halsey Road	B2	The Broadway	C4
Harwoods Road	A4	The Crescent	C4
Hempstead Road	A1	The Parade	B2
High Street	C4	Upton Road	B3
Hyde Road	A2	Vicarage Road	B4
Keele Close	C1	Water Lane	D4
King Street	C4	Wellington Road	B1
Lady's Close	C4	Wellstone Street	B3
Link Road	D1	Westland Road	B1
Loates Lane	C3	West Street	B1
Lord Street	C3	Whippendell Road	A4
Lower High Street	D4	Wiggenhall Road	B4
Malden Road	A1	Woodford Road	C1

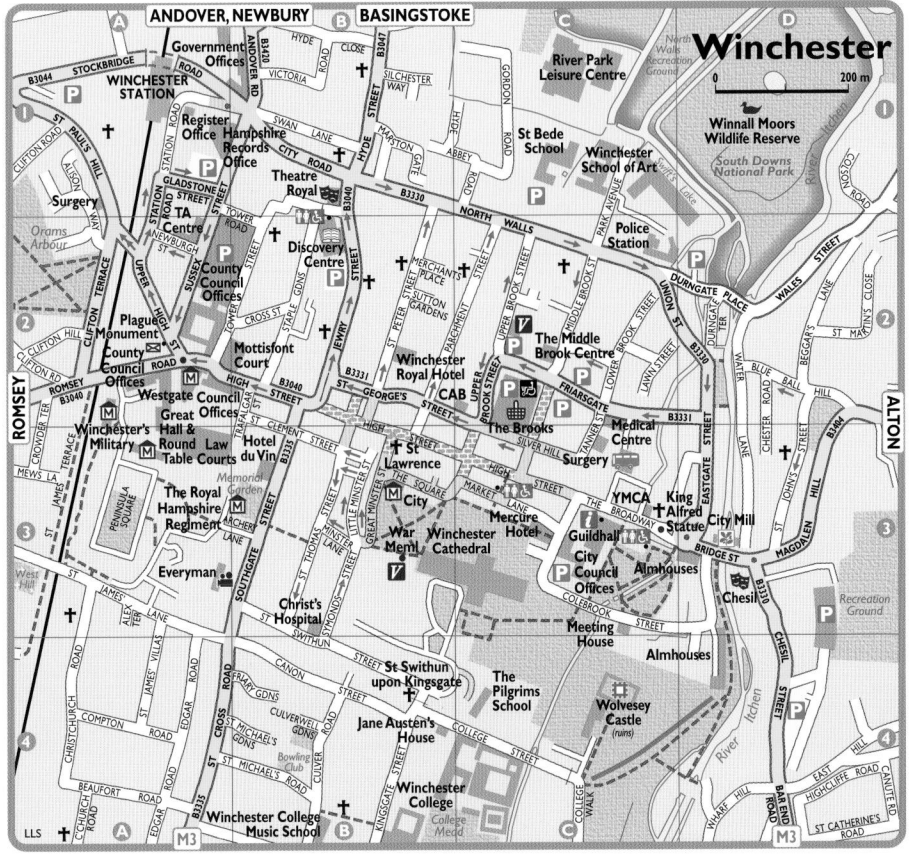

Winchester

Winchester is found on atlas page **22 E9**

Alex Terrace	A3	Market Lane	C3
Alison Way	A1	Marston Gate	B1
Andover Road	B1	Merchants Place	B2
Archery Lane	A3	Mews Lane	A3
Bar End Road	D4	Middle Brook Street	C2
Beaufort Road	A4	Minster Lane	B3
Beggar's Lane	D2	Newburgh Street	A2
Blue Ball Hill	D2	North Walls	B1
Bridge Street	D3	Parchment Street	B2
Canon Street	B4	Park Avenue	C2
Canute Road	D4	Romsey Road	A2
Chesil Street	D3	St Clement Street	B2
Chester Road	D2	St Cross Road	A4
Christchurch Road	A4	St George's Street	B2
City Road	B1	St James' Lane	A3
Clifton Hill	A2	St James Terrace	A3
Clifton Road	A1	St James' Villas	A4
Clifton Terrace	A2	St John's Street	D3
Colebrook Street	C3	St Martin's Close	D2
College Street	B4	St Michael's Gardens	B4
College Walk	C4	St Michael's Road	B4
Colson Road	D1	St Paul's Hill	A1
Compton Road	A4	St Peter Street	B2
Cross Street	B2	St Swithun Street	B3
Crowder Terrace	A3	St Thomas Street	B3
Culver Road	B4	Silchester Way	B1
Culverwell Gardens	B4	Silver Hill	C3
Durngate Place	D2	Southgate Street	B3
Durngate Terrace	D2	Staple Gardens	B2
Eastgate Street	D3	Station Road	A1
East Hill	D4	Stockbridge Road	A1
Edgar Road	A4	Sussex Street	A2
Friarsgate	C2	Sutton Gardens	B2
Friary Gardens	B4	Swan Lane	B1
Gladstone Street	A1	Symonds Street	B3
Gordon Road	C1	Tanner Street	C3
Great Minster Street	B3	The Broadway	C3
Highcliffe Road	D3	The Square	B3
High Street	B2	Tower Road	A1
Hyde Abbey Road	B1	Tower Street	A2
Hyde Close	B1	Trafalgar Street	B3
Hyde Street	B1	Union Street	C2
Jewry Street	B2	Upper Brook Street	C2
Kingsgate Street	B4	Upper High Street	A2
Lawn Street	C2	Victoria Road	B1
Little Minster Street	B3	Wales Street	D2
Lower Brook Street	C2	Water Lane	D3
Magdalen Hill	D3	Wharf Hill	D4

Wolverhampton

Wolverhampton is found on atlas page **58 D5**

Bath Avenue	A1	Penn Road	B4
Bath Road	A2	Piper's Row	D2
Bell Street	B3	Pitt Street	B3
Bilston Road	D3	Powlett Street	D4
Bilston Street	C3	Princess Street	C2
Birch Street	B2	Queen Square	B2
Broad Street	C2	Queen Street	C2
Castle Street	C3	Raby Street	D4
Chapel Ash	A3	Raglan Street	A3
Church Lane	B4	Railway Drive	D2
Church Street	B4	Red Lion Street	B2
Clarence Road	B2	Retreat Street	A4
Clarence Street	B2	Ring Road St Andrews	A2
Cleveland Road	D4	Ring Road St Davids	D2
Cleveland Street	B3	Ring Road St Georges	C4
Corn Street	D2	Ring Road St Johns	B4
Culwell Street	D1	Ring Road St Marks	B3
Dale Street	A4	Ring Road St Patricks	C1
Darlington Street	B3	Ring Road St Peters	B2
Dudley Road	C4	Russell Street	B4
Dudley Street	C2	St George's Parade	C3
Fold Street	B3	St John's Square	C4
Fryer Street	C2	St Mark's Road	A3
Garrick Street	C3	St Mark's Street	A3
Graiseley Street	A4	Salop Street	B3
Great Brickkiln Street	A4	School Street	B3
Great Western Street	C1	Skinner Street	B3
Grimstone Street	D1	Snow Hill	C3
Horseley Fields	D2	Stafford Street	C1
Hospital Street	D4	Stephenson Street	A3
Lansdown Road	A1	Stewart Street	B4
Lever Street	C4	Summer Row	B3
Lichfield Street	C2	Tempest Street	B3
Little's Lane	C1	Temple Street	B3
Long Street	C2	Thomas Street	B4
Lord Street	A3	Tower Street	C2
Mander Street	A4	Vicarage Road	D4
Market Street	C3	Victoria Street	B3
Merridale Street	A4	Warwick Street	D3
Middle Cross	D3	Waterloo Road	B1
Mitre Fold	B2	Wednesfield Road	D1
Molineux Street	B1	Westbury Street	C2
New Hampton Road East	A1	Whitemore Hill	B1
North Street	B2	Whitmore Street	C2
Park Avenue	A1	Worcester Street	B4
Park Road East	B1	Wulfruna Street	C2
Park Road West	A2	Zoar Street	A4
Peel Street	B3		

Worcester

Worcester is found on atlas page **46 G4**

Albert Road	D4	Middle Street	B1
Angel Street	B2	Midland Road	D2
Arboretum Road	B1	Mill Street	B4
Back Lane South	A1	Moor Street	A1
Blockhouse Close	C3	Newport Street	A2
Britannia Road	A1	New Road	A3
Broad Street	B2	New Street	C3
Byfield Rise	D2	Northfield Street	B1
Carden Street	C3	North Parade	A3
Castle Street	A1	Padmore Street	C1
Cathedral Ferry	A4	Park Street	C2
Cecil Road	D3	Pheasant Street	C2
Charles Street	C3	Pierpoint Street	B1
Charter Place	A1	Providence Street	B2
Church Street	B2	Pump Street	B3
City Walls Road	C3	Quay Street	A3
Cole Hill	C4	Queen Street	B2
College Street	B3	Richmond Road	D4
Commandery Road	C4	Rose Hill	D4
Compton Road	D3	Rose Terrace	D4
Copenhagen Street	B3	St Martin's Gate	B2
Croft Road	A2	St Nicholas Street	B2
Cromwell Street	D2	St Paul's Street	C3
Deansway	B3	St Swithin Street	B2
Dent Close	C3	Sansome Walk	B1
Derby Road	C4	Severn Street	B4
Dolday	A2	Severn Terrace	A1
East Street	B1	Shaw Street	B2
Edgar Street	B4	Shrub Hill Road	D2
Farrier Street	B1	Sidbury	C4
Fish Street	B3	Southfield Street	C1
Foregate Street	B1	Spring Hill	D2
Fort Royal Hill	C4	Stanley Road	D3
Foundry Street	C3	Tallow Hill	D2
Friar Street	C3	Taylor's Lane	B1
George Street	C2	The Butts	A2
Grandstand Road	A2	The Cross	B2
Hamilton Road	C3	The Moors	A1
High Street	B3	The Shambles	B2
Hill Street	D2	The Tything	B1
Hylton Road	A3	Tolladine Road	C1
King Street	B4	Trinity Street	B2
Little Southfield Street	B1	Union Street	C3
Lock Street	C3	Upper Park Street	D4
London Road	C4	Vincent Road	D3
Love's Grove	A1	Wellington Close	C3
Lowesmoor	C2	Westbury Street	C1
Lowesmoor Terrace	C1	Wyld's Lane	C4

York

York is found on atlas page **98 C10**

Aldwark	C2	Lower Ousegate	C3
Barbican Road	D4	Lower Priory Street	B3
Bishopgate Street	B4	Low Petergate	C2
Bishophill Senior	B3	Margaret Street	D3
Black Horse Lane	D2	Market Street	C2
Blake Street	B2	Micklegate	A3
Blossom Street	A4	Minster Yard	B1
Bootham	B1	Monkgate	C1
Bridge Street	B3	Museum Street	B2
Buckingham Street	B3	Navigation Road	D3
Cemetery Road	D4	New Street	B2
Church Street	C2	North Street	B2
Clifford Street	C3	Nunnery Lane	A3
College Street	C1	Ogleforth	C1
Colliergate	C2	Palmer Lane	D2
Coney Street	B2	Palmer Street	D2
Coppergate	C3	Paragon Street	D4
Cromwell Road	B4	Parliament Street	C2
Davygate	B2	Pavement	C2
Deangate	C1	Peasholme Green	D2
Dove Street	B4	Percy's Lane	D3
Duncombe Place	B1	Piccadilly	C3
Dundas Street	D2	Price's Lane	B4
Fairfax Street	B3	Priory Street	B3
Fawcett Street	D4	Queen Street	A3
Feasegate	C2	Rougier Street	B2
Fetter Lane	B3	St Andrewgate	C2
Finkle Street	C2	St Denys' Road	D3
Fishergate	C4	St Leonard's Place	B1
Foss Bank	D1	St Martins Lane	B3
Fossgate	C2	St Maurice's Road	C1
Foss Islands Road	D2	St Saviourgate	C2
George Street	D3	St Saviours Place	C2
Gillygate	B1	Scarcroft Road	A4
Goodramgate	C2	Shambles	C2
Hampden Street	B4	Skeldergate	B3
High Ousegate	C3	Spen Lane	C2
High Petergate	B1	Spurriergate	C3
Holgate Road	A4	Station Road	A3
Hope Street	D4	Stonegate	B2
Hungate	D2	Swinegate	C2
Jewbury	D1	The Stonebow	C2
Kent Street	D4	Toft Green	A3
King Street	C3	Tower Street	C3
Kyme Street	B4	Trinity Lane	B3
Lendal	B2	Victor Street	B4
Long Close Lane	D4	Walmgate	D2
Lord Mayor's Walk	C1	Wellington Road	B2

Major airports

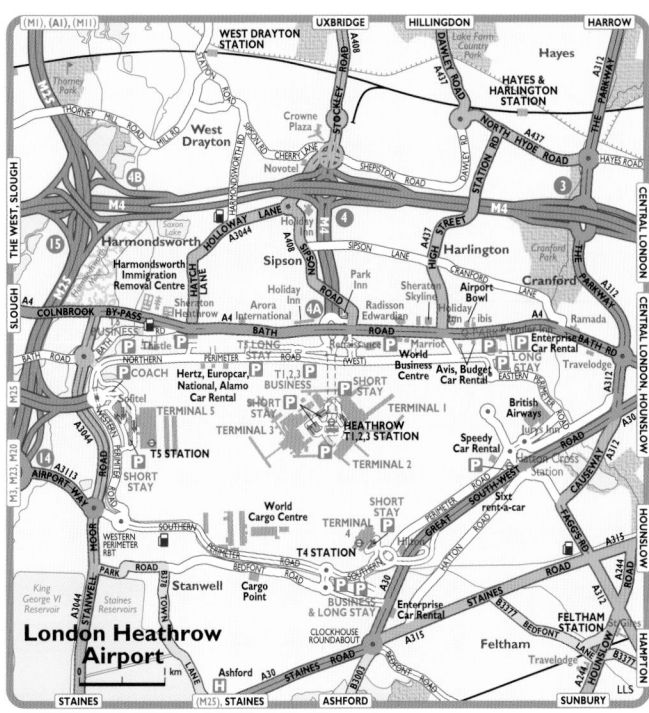

London Heathrow Airport – 16 miles west of London

Telephone: 0844 335 1801 or visit *www.heathrowairport.com*
Parking: short-stay, long-stay and business parking is available.
For booking and charges tel: 0844 335 1000
Public Transport: coach, bus, rail and London Underground.
There are several 4-star and 3-star hotels within easy reach of the airport.
Car hire facilities are available.

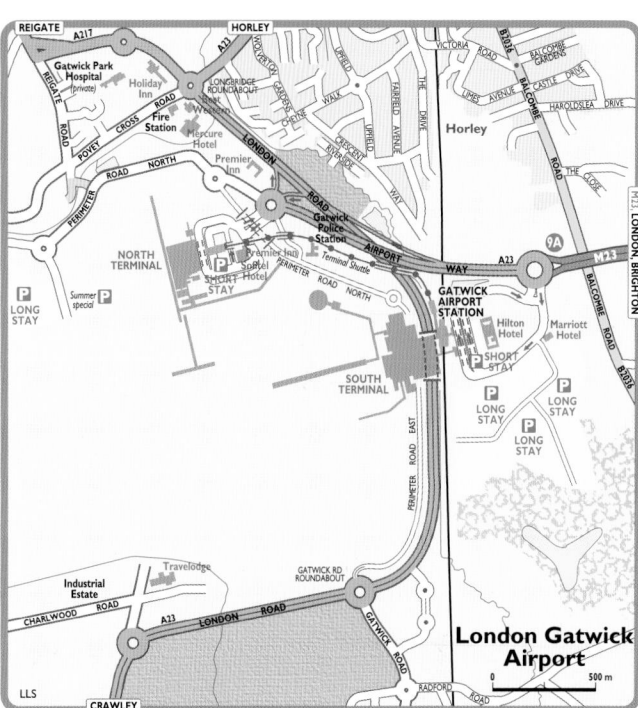

London Gatwick Airport – 35 miles south of London

Telephone: 0844 892 0322 or visit *www.gatwickairport.com*
Parking: short and long-stay parking is available at both the North and South terminals.
For booking and charges tel: 0844 811 8311
Public Transport: coach, bus and rail.
There are several 4-star and 3-star hotels within easy reach of the airport.
Car hire facilities are available.

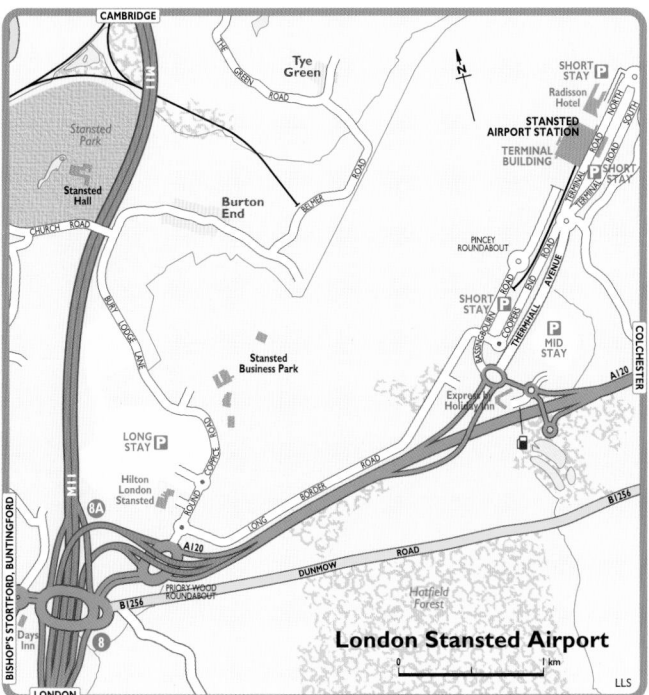

London Stansted Airport – 36 miles north east of London

Telephone: 0844 335 1803 or visit *www.stanstedairport.com*
Parking: short, mid and long-stay open-air parking is available.
For booking and charges tel: 0871 310 4111
Public Transport: coach, bus and direct rail link to London on the Stansted Express.
There are several hotels within easy reach of the airport.
Car hire facilities are available.

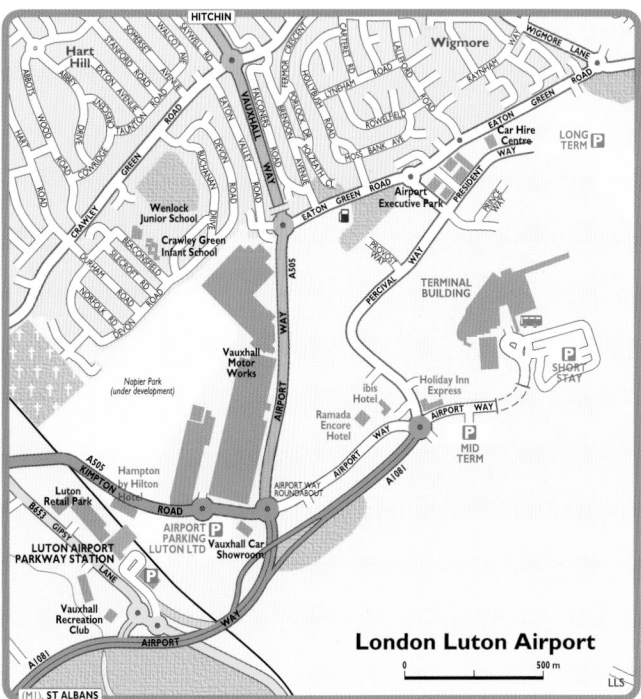

London Luton Airport – 33 miles north of London

Telephone: 01582 405 100 or visit *www.london-luton.co.uk*
Parking: short-term, mid-term and long-stay parking is available.
For booking and charges tel: 0345 303 7397
Public Transport: coach, bus and rail.
There are several hotels within easy reach of the airport.
Car hire facilities are available.

London City Airport – 7 miles east of London

Telephone: 020 7646 0088 or visit *www.londoncityairport.com*
Parking: short and long-stay open-air parking is available.
For booking and charges tel: 0844 332 1237
Public Transport: easy access to the rail network, Docklands Light Railway and the London Underground.
There are 5-star, 4-star and 3-star hotels within easy reach of the airport.
Car hire facilities are available.

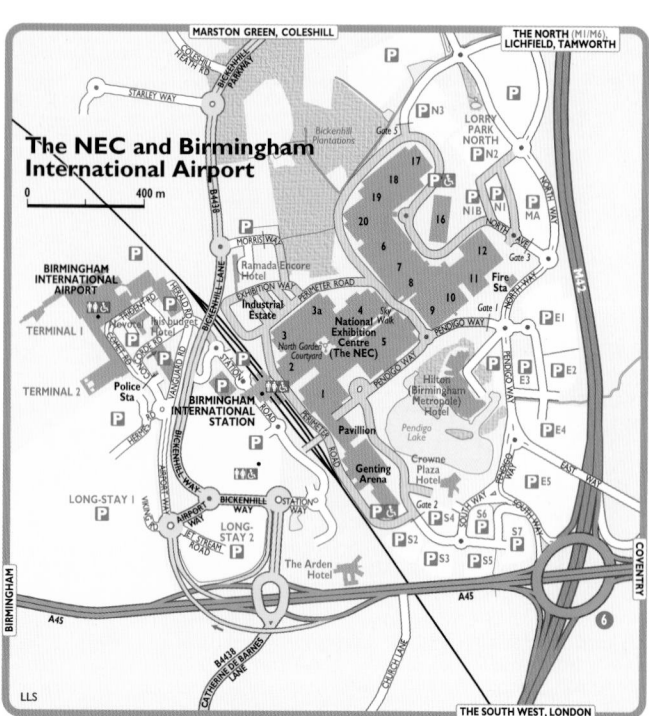

Birmingham International Airport – 8 miles east of Birmingham

Telephone: 0871 222 0072 or visit *www.birminghamairport.co.uk*
Parking: short, mid-term and long-stay parking is available.
For booking and charges tel: 0871 222 0072
Public Transport: Air-Rail Link service operates every 2 minutes to and from Birmingham International Railway Station & Interchange.
There is one 3-star hotel adjacent to the airport and several 4 and 3-star hotels within easy reach of the airport. Car hire facilities are available.

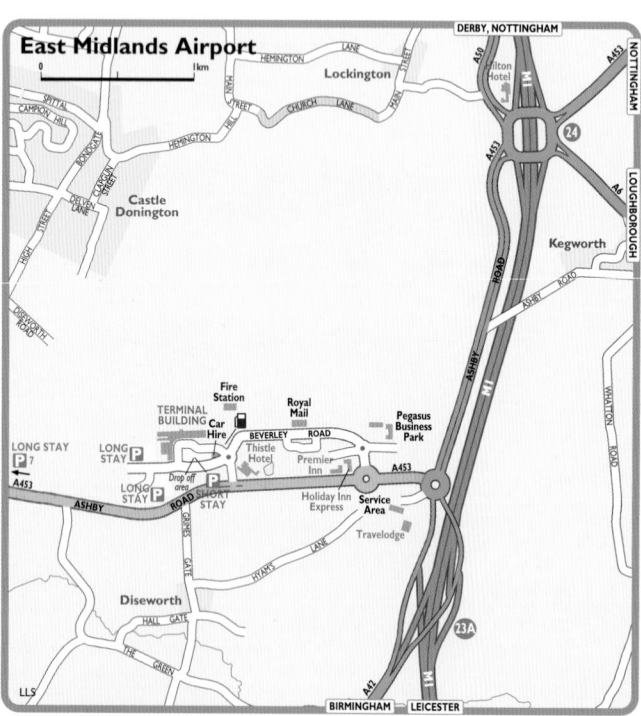

East Midlands Airport – 15 miles south west
of Nottingham, next to the M1 at junctions 23A and 24

Telephone: 0871 919 9000 or visit *www.eastmidlandsairport.com*
Parking: short and long-stay parking is available.
For booking and charges tel: 0871 310 3300
Public Transport: bus and coach services to major towns and cities in the East Midlands.
There are several 3-star hotels within easy reach of the airport.
Car hire facilities are available.

Manchester Airport – 10 miles south of Manchester

Telephone: 0871 271 0711 or visit *www.manchesterairport.co.uk*
Parking: short and long-stay parking is available.
For booking and charges tel: 0871 310 2200
Public Transport: coach, bus and rail.
There are several 4-star and 3-star hotels within easy reach of the airport.
Car hire facilities are available.

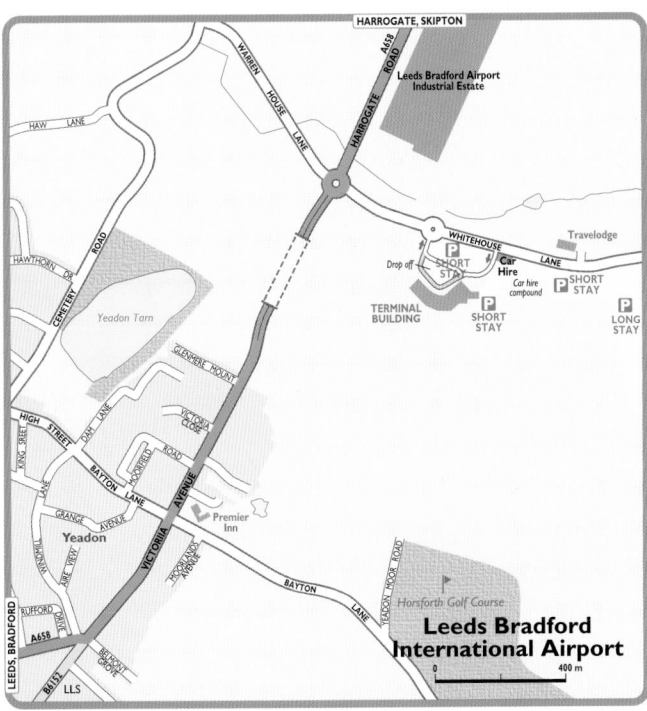

Leeds Bradford International Airport – 7 miles north east of Bradford and 9 miles north west of Leeds

Telephone: 0871 288 2288 or visit www.leedsbradfordairport.co.uk
Parking: short, mid-term and long-stay parking is available.
For booking and charges tel: 0844 414 3295
Public Transport: bus service operates every 30 minutes from Bradford, Leeds and Otley.
There are several 4-star and 3-star hotels within easy reach of the airport.
Car hire facilities are available.

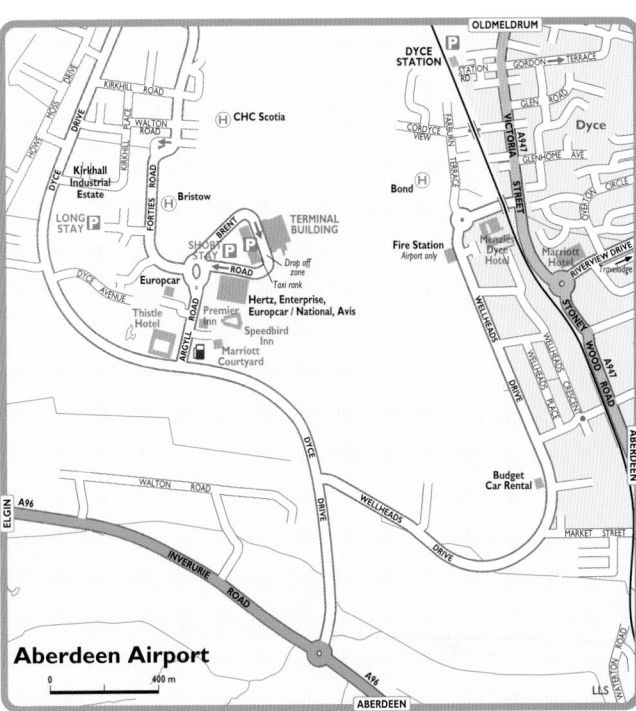

Aberdeen Airport – 7 miles north west of Aberdeen

Telephone: 0844 481 6666 or visit www.aberdeenairport.com
Parking: short and long-stay parking is available.
For booking and charges tel: 0844 335 1000
Public Transport: regular bus service to central Aberdeen.
There are several 4-star and 3-star hotels within easy reach of the airport.
Car hire facilities are available.

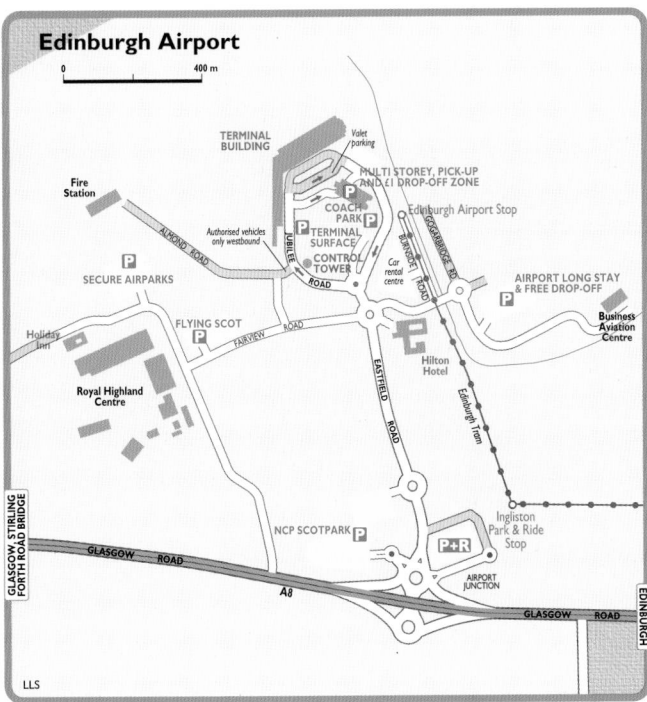

Edinburgh Airport – 7 miles west of Edinburgh

Telephone: 0844 448 8833 or visit www.edinburghairport.com
Parking: short and long-stay parking is available.
For booking and charges tel: 0844 770 3040
Public Transport: regular bus services to central Edinburgh, Glasgow and Fife
and a tram service to Edinburgh.
There are several 4-star and 3-star hotels within easy reach of the airport.
Car hire and valet parking facilities are available.

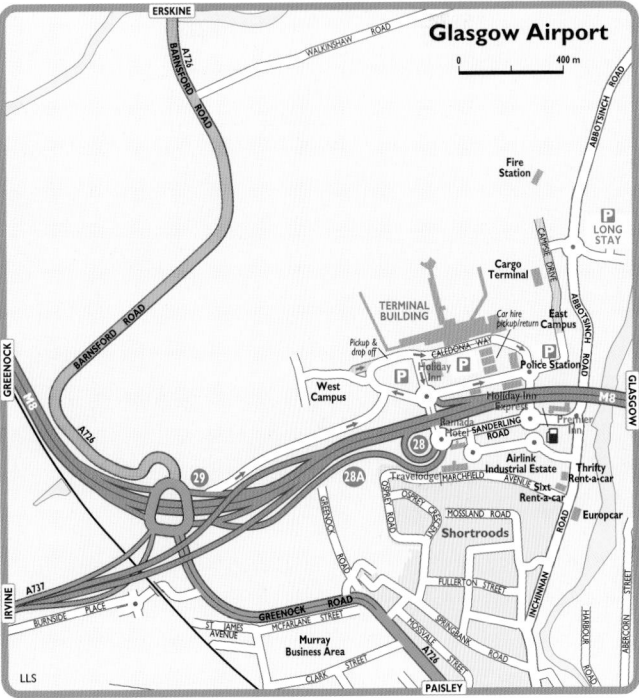

Glasgow Airport – 8 miles west of Glasgow

Telephone: 0844 481 5555 or visit www.glasgowairport.com
Parking: short and long-stay parking is available.
For booking and charges tel: 0844 335 1000
Public Transport: regular coach services operate direct to central Glasgow and Edinburgh.
There are several 3-star hotels within easy reach of the airport.
Car hire facilities are available.

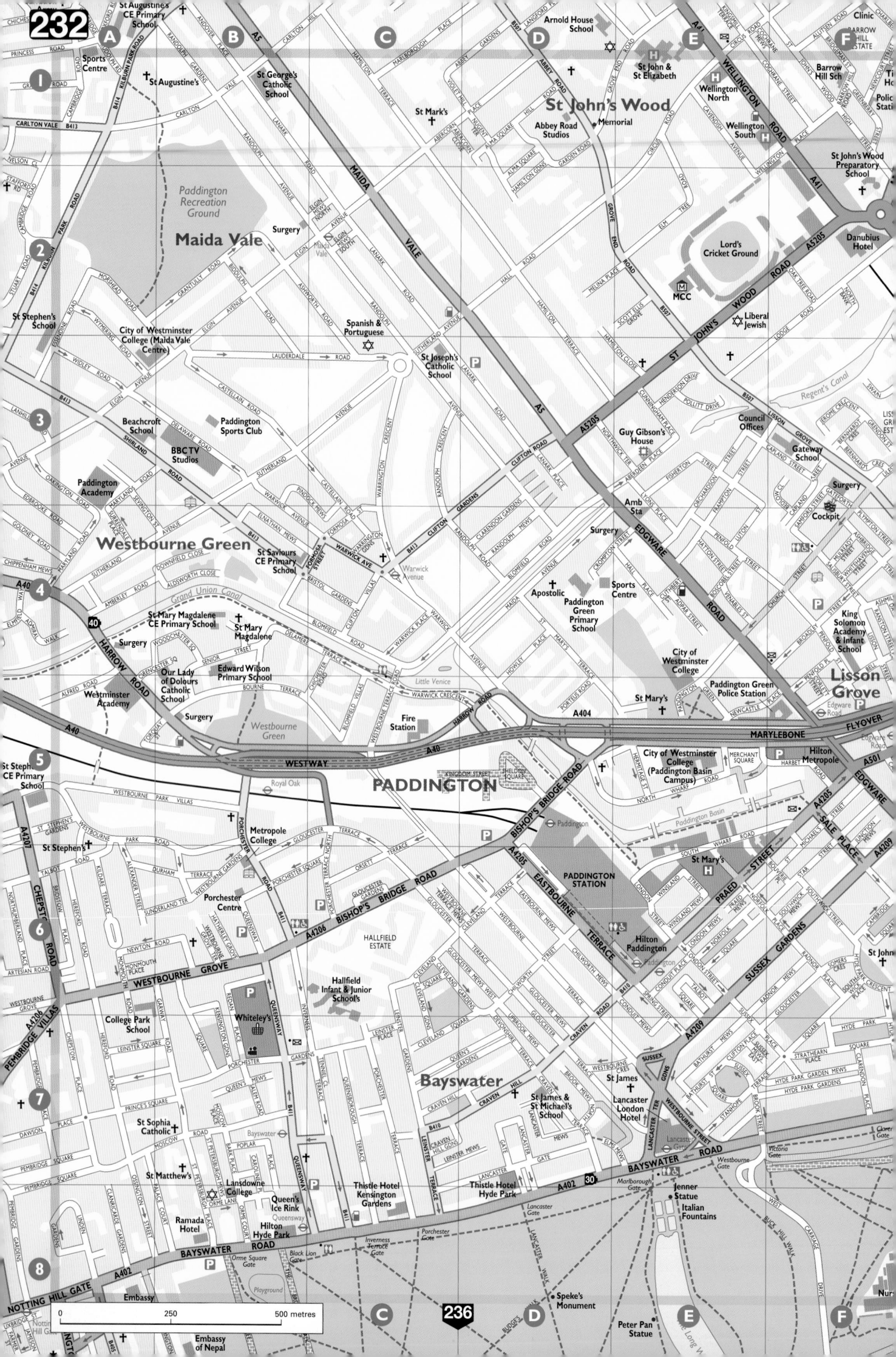

A · B · C · **232** · D · E · F

Embassy of Slovak Republic
'Time Flies' Clock Tower
Speke's Monument
Peter Pan Statue
Serpentine Bridge
Embassy of Nepal
Playground
Embassy of Russia
Kensington Gardens
Physical Energy Statue
Isis Statue
The Lido
Hawkesdown House School
Embassy of Lebanon
Sunken Gardens
Round Pond
Serpentine Gallery
Diana Princess of Wales Memorial Fountain
Mount Gate
Romanian Embassy
Kensington Palace Green
Kensington Palace
Bandstand
St Govor's Well
Tennis Courts
Bowling Green
Prince of Wales Gate
Israel Embassy
Fire Station
Royal Garden Hotel
Albert Memorial
Queen's Gate
Alexandra Gate
KENSINGTON ROAD A315
Kensington & Chelsea Town Hall
St Mary Abbots
St Mary Abbots CE Primary School
Milestone Hotel
HYDE PARK GATE
KENSINGTON GORE
Royal College of Art
Royal Albert Hall
Royal Geographical Society
Knightsbridge
KENSINGTON
High Street Kensington
Heythrop College
Albert Place
DOURO PLACE
PRINCE CONSORT ROAD
Royal College of Music
Imperial College London
Prince's Gardens
Imperial College London
Thomas's Day School
ST ALBAN'S GROVE
CANNING PLACE
KENSINGTON GATE
QUEEN'S GATE MEWS
Imperial College London
COTTESMORE GARDENS
QUEEN'S GATE TERRACE
PETERSHAM PLACE
Imperial College London
KELSO PLACE
ELDON ROAD
PETERSHAM MEWS
Science
South Kensington
Royal College of Art
CHANTRY SQUARE
KYNANCE PLACE MEWS
ELVASTON PLACE
Victoria & Albert
The Oratory
KYNANCE
CORNWALL GARDENS
Darwin Centre
Natural History
CORNWALL GARDENS
Health Centre
CORNWALL MS SOUTH
QUEEN'S GATE GDNS
Baden Powell House
LEXHAM GDNS
SOUTHWELL GDNS
QUEEN'S GATE PLACE MEWS
Superstore
EMPEROR'S GATE
Radisson Edwardian
CROMWELL ROAD 30
Institut Francais
Cromwell
PENNANT MEWS
A4 30 **CROMWELL** 30 **ROAD**
Holiday Inn
Emirates Hotel
Lycée Francais
Ampersand Hotel
THURLOE PLACE
BROMPTON ROAD
Marriott Hotel
Gloucester Road
South Kensington
Our Lady of Victories RC Primary School
PELHAM STREET
West Cromwell Road
REDFIELD LANE
ASHBURN GARDENS
COURTFIELD
HARRINGTON
Earl's Court Road
CHILD'S STREET
COLBECK MEWS
MANSON PLACE
HARRINGTON
EARL'S COURT GARDENS
COLLINGHAM GARDENS
HARRINGTON
OLD BROMPTON ROAD
ONSLOW SQUARE
SUMNER PLACE
EARL'S COURT STATION
HESPER MEWS
BRAMHAM GARDENS
WETHERBY
BINA
ROSARY GARDENS
HEREFORD SQ
GLOUCESTER GROVE
A3218
ONSLOW GARDENS
NEVILLE TERRACE
FULHAM ROAD
Royal Marsden
Warwick
Earl's Court
BOLTON GARDENS
BRECHIN PLACE
DRAYTON GARDENS
CRANLEY
Royal Marsden
A3220
St Cuthbert & St Matthais CE Primary School
EARL'S COURT SQUARE
OLD BROMPTON ROAD
Bousfield Primary School
THE BOLTONS
SELWOOD PL
Royal Cancer
Royal Brompton & Harefield
St Luke's
CHELSEA
THE LITTLE BOLTONS
EVELYN GDNS
ELM PARK GARDENS
Gems Hampshire School
WHARFEDALE ST
St Luke's
REDCLIFFE GARDENS
HARCOURT TERRACE
PRIORY WALK
GILSTON ROAD
KING'S
Fire Station
WEST BROMPTON STATION
FINBOROUGH ROAD
REDCLIFFE GARDENS
CATHCART ROAD
FULHAM ROAD
ELM PARK LANE
West Brompton
LILLIE ROAD
Serbite RC Primary School
Brompton Cemetery
Chelsea & Westminster
Park Walk Primary School
Fulham Primary School
Ambulance
A3220
EDITH GROVE
A308
BEAUFORT ST A3220

0 · 250 · 500 metres

I · 2 · 3 · 4 · 5 · 6 · 7 · 8

Central London index

This index lists street and station names, and top places of tourist interest shown in **red**. Names are listed in alphabetical order and written in full, but may be abbreviated on the map. Each entry is followed by its Postcode District and then the page number and grid reference to the square in which the name is found. Names are asterisked (*) in the index where there is insufficient space to show them on the map.

King's Stairs Close - Paddington Street 245

King's Stairs Close SE16 240 F6
King Street WC2E 234 D7
King Street SW1Y 238 A1
King Street EC2V 235 K6
Kingsway WC2B 234 E6
King William Street EC4N 235 L7
Kinnerton Place North * SW1X 237 J3
Kinnerton Place South * SW1X 237 J3
Kinnerton Street SW1X 237 J3
Kinnerton Yard * SW1X 237 J3
Kipling Estate SE1 239 L3
Kipling Street SE1 239 L3
Kirby Estate SE16 240 D7
Kirby Grove SE1 239 M3
Kirby Street EC1N 235 G4
Knaresborough Place SW5 236 B5
Knightrider Street EC4V 235 H7
Knightsbridge SW1X 237 H3
Knightsbridge ⊖ SW3 237 H3
Knox Street W1H 233 H4
Kynance Mews SW7 236 C4
Kynance Place SW7 236 C4

L

Lackington Street EC2A 235 L4
Lafone Street SE1 240 B6
Lagado Mews SE16 241 H5
Lambeth Bridge SW1P 238 D5
Lambeth High Street SE1 238 E5
Lambeth Hill EC4V 235 J7
Lambeth North ⊖ SE1 238 F3
Lambeth Palace Road SE1 238 E4
Lambeth Road SE1 238 F4
Lambeth Walk SE11 238 F5
Lamb's Conduit Street WC1N 234 E4
Lamb's Passage EC1Y 235 K4
Lamb Street E1 240 B1
Lamb Way SE1 240 A7
Lamlash Street SE11 239 H5
Lanark Place W9 232 D3
Lanark Road W9 232 B1
Lancaster Gate W2 232 D7
Lancaster Gate W2 232 D8
Lancaster Gate ⊖ W2 232 E7
Lancaster Mews W2 232 D7
Lancaster Place WC2E 234 E7
Lancaster Street SE1 239 H3
Lancaster Terrace W2 232 E7
Lancaster Walk W2 232 D8
Lancelot Place SW7 237 G3
Lancing Street NW1 234 B2
Lanesborough Place * SW1X 237 J3
Langdale Street E1 240 E3
Langford Place NW8 232 D1
Langham Place W1B 233 L5
Langham Street W1W 233 L5
Langham Street W1W 233 M5
Langley Lane SW8 238 D8
Langley Street WC2H 234 C7
Langton Close WC1X 234 E3
Lanhill Road W9 232 A3
Lansdowne Place SE1 239 L4
Lant Street SE1 239 J3
Larcom Street SE17 239 K6
Lauderdale Road W9 232 B3
Laud Street SE11 238 E7
Launcelot Street SE1 238 F3
Launceston Place W8 236 C4
Laurence Pountney Lane EC4V 235 L7
Lavender Road SE16 241 K5
Lavender Wharf SE16 241 K4
Lavington Street SE1 239 J1
Lawn Lane SW8 238 D8
Lawrence Street SW3 236 F8
Lawrence Wharf SE16 241 L6
Law Street SE1 239 L4
Laxton Place NW1 233 L3
Laystall Street EC1R 234 F4
Leadenhall Street EC3A 240 A3
Leadenhall Street EC3V 235 M6
Leake Street SE1 238 E2
Leather Lane EC1N 235 G4
Leathermarket Street SE1 239 M3
Leeke Street WC1X 234 E2
Lees Place W1K 233 J7
Leicester Square ⊖ WC2H 234 C7
Leicester Square WC2H 234 C7
Leicester Street WC2H 234 B7
Leigh Street WC1H 234 C3
Leinster Gardens W2 232 C6
Leinster Mews W2 232 C7
Leinster Place W2 232 C7
Leinster Square W2 232 A7
Leinster Terrace W2 232 C7
Leman Street E1 240 C3
Lennox Gardens SW1X 237 G4
Lennox Gardens Mews SW1X 237 G5
Leonard Street EC2A 235 L3
Leopold Estate E3 241 M1
Leopold Street E3 241 L1
Leroy Street SE1 239 M5
Lever Street EC1V 235 J2
Lewisham Street SW1H 238 B3
Lexham Gardens W8 236 A5
Lexham Mews W8 236 A5
Lexington Street W1F 234 A7
Leyden Street E1 240 B2
Leydon Close SE16 241 H5
Library Street SE1 239 H3
Lidlington Place NW1 234 A1
Lilestone Street NW8 232 F3
Lilley Close E1W 240 D5
Lillie Road SW6 236 A7
Lillie Yard SW6 236 A7
Limeburner Lane EC4M 235 H6
Lime Close E1W 240 D5
Limehouse Causeway E14 241 L4
Limehouse Link E14 241 L3
Limehouse ⇌ ⊖ E14 241 J3
Limerston Street SW10 236 D8
Lime Street EC3M 235 M7
Lincoln's Inn Fields WC2A 234 E6
Linden Gardens W2 232 A8
Lindley Street E1 240 F1
Lindsay Square SW1V 238 B7
Lindsey Street EC1A 235 H4
Linhope Street NW1 233 G3
Linsey Street SE16 240 D8
Lisle Street WC2H 234 B7
Lisson Green Estate NW8 232 F3
Lisson Grove NW1 233 G4
Lisson Grove NW8 232 F3
Lisson Street NW1 232 F4
Litchfield Street WC2H 234 C7
Little Argyll Street W1F 233 M6
Little Britain EC1A 235 J5
Little Chester Street SW1X 237 K4
Little George Street SW1P 238 C3
Little Marlborough Street W1F 234 A7
Little New Street EC4A 235 G6
Little Portland Street W1G 233 L6
Little Russell Street WC1A 234 C5
Little St James's Street SW1A 237 M2
Little Sanctuary SW1A 238 C3
Little Somerset Street E1 240 B3
Little Titchfield Street W1W 233 M5
Liverpool Grove SE17 239 K7
Liverpool Street EC2M 235 M5
Liverpool Street ⇌ ⊖ EC2M 235 M5
Lizard Street EC1V 235 K3
Llewellyn Street SE16 240 D7
Lloyd Baker Street WC1X 234 F2
Lloyd's Avenue EC3N 240 B3
Lloyd Square WC1X 234 F2
Lloyds Row EC1R 235 G2
Lloyd's Street WC1X 234 F2
Locksley Estate E14 241 L2
Locksley Street E14 241 L1
Lockyer Street SE1 239 L3
Lodge Road NW8 232 F3
Loftie Street SE16 240 D7
Logan Place W8 236 A5
Lolesworth Close E1 240 B1
Lollard Street SE11 238 F5
Lollard Street SE11 238 F6
Loman Street SE1 239 J2
Lomas Street E1 240 D1
Lombard Lane EC4Y 235 G6
Lombard Street EC3V 235 L7
London Bridge EC4R 235 L8
London Bridge ⇌ ⊖ SE1 239 L1
London Bridge Street SE1 239 L1
London Dungeon SE1 238 E2
London Eye SE1 238 E2
London Mews W2 232 E6
London Road SE1 239 H4
London Street EC3R 240 A3
London Street W2 232 E6
London Transport Museum WC2E 234 D7
London Wall EC2M 235 K5
London Zoo ZSL NW1 233 J1
Long Acre WC2E 234 D7
Longford Street NW1 233 L3
Long Lane EC1A 235 J5
Long Lane SE1 239 L3
Longmoore Street SW1V 237 M5
Longridge Road SW5 236 A5
Longville Road SE11 239 H5
Long Walk SE1 240 A8
Long Yard WC1N 234 E4
Lord North Street SW1P 238 C4
Lord's Cricket Ground NW8 232 E2
Lorenzo Street WC1X 234 E1
Lorrimore Road SE17 239 J8
Lorrimore Square SE17 239 H8
Lothbury EC2R 235 L6
Loughborough Street SE11 238 F7
Lovat Lane EC3R 235 M7
Love Lane EC2V 235 K6
Lovell Place SE16 241 K7
Lowell Street E14 241 K2
Lower Belgrave Street SW1W 237 K4
Lower Grosvenor Place SW1W 237 L4
Lower James Street W1F 234 A7
Lower John Street W1F 234 A7
Lower Marsh SE1 238 F3
Lower Road SE16 241 G7
Lower Sloane Street SW1W 237 J6
Lower Thames Street EC3R 240 A4
Lowndes Close * SW1X 237 J4
Lowndes Place SW1X 237 J4
Lowndes Square SW1X 237 H3
Lowndes Street SW1X 237 J4
Lucan Place SW3 236 F5
Lucey Road SE16 240 C8
Ludgate Circus EC4M 235 H6
Ludgate Hill EC4M 235 H6
Luke Street EC2A 235 M3
Lukin Street E1 241 G3
Lumley Street W1K 233 K7
Lupus Street SW1V 237 L7
Lupus Street SW1V 238 B7
Luton Street NW8 232 E4
Luxborough Street W1U 233 J4
Lyall Mews SW1X 237 J4
Lyall Street SW1X 237 J4
Lyons Place NW8 232 E3
Lytham Street SE17 239 K7

M

Macclesfield Road EC1V 235 J2
Macclesfield Street * W1D 234 B7
Mace Close E1W 240 E5
Macklin Street WC2B 234 D6
Mackworth Street NW1 233 M2
Macleod Street SE17 239 K7
Madame Tussauds NW1 233 J4
Maddox Street W1S 233 M7
Magdalen Street SE1 239 M2
Magee Street SE11 238 F8
Maguire Street SE1 240 C6
Maida Avenue W9 232 D4
Maida Vale W9 232 C2
Maida Vale ⊖ W9 232 C1
Maiden Lane SE1 239 K1
Maiden Lane WC2E 234 D7
Major Road SE16 240 D7
Makins Street SW3 237 G6
Malet Street WC1E 234 B4
Mallord Street SW3 236 E8
Mallory Street NW8 232 F3
Mallow Street EC1Y 235 L3
Malta Street EC1V 235 H3
Maltby Street SE1 240 B7
Manchester Square W1U 233 J6
Manchester Street W1U 233 J5
Manciple Street SE1 239 L3
Mandeville Place W1U 233 K6
Manette Street W1D 234 B6
Manilla Street E14 241 M6
Manningford Close EC1V 235 H2
Manor Place SE17 239 J7
Manresa Road SW3 236 F7
Mansell Street E1 240 C3
Mansfield Mews W1G 233 L5
Mansfield Street W1G 233 L5
Mansion House ⊖ EC4V 235 K7
Manson Mews SW7 236 D5
Manson Place SW7 236 D6
Mapleleaf Square SE16 241 J6
Maples Place E1 240 F1
Maple Street W1T 233 M4
Marble Arch ⊖ W1C 233 H7
Marchmont Street WC1H 234 C3
Margaret Street W1W 233 L6
Margaretta Terrace SW3 236 F7
Margery Street WC1X 234 F3
Marigold Street SE16 240 E7
Marine Street SE16 240 C7
Market Mews W1J 237 K1
Market Place W1W 233 M6
Markham Square SW3 237 G6
Markham Street SW3 237 G6
Mark Lane EC3R 240 A4
Marlborough Gate W2 232 E7
Marlborough Place NW8 232 C1
Marlborough Road SW1A 238 A2
Marlborough Street SW3 236 F6
Marloes Road W8 236 B4
Marlow Way SE16 241 H6
Maroon Street E14 241 K2
Marshall Street W1F 234 A7
Marshalsea Road SE1 239 J2
Marsham Street SW1P 238 C5
Marsh Wall E14 241 M5
Martha's Buildings EC1V 235 K3
Martha Street E1 240 F3
Martin Lane EC4V 235 L7
Maryland Road W9 232 A4
Marylands Road W9 232 A4
Marylebone ⇌ ⊖ NW1 233 G4
Marylebone Flyover W2 232 E5
Marylebone High Street W1U 233 K5
Marylebone Lane W1U 233 K6
Marylebone Road NW1 233 G4
Marylebone Street W1G 233 K5
Marylee Way SE11 238 F6
Masjid Lane E14 241 M2
Mason Street SE17 239 M5
Massinger Street SE17 239 M6
Masters Street E1 241 J1
Matlock Street E14 241 J2
Matthew Parker Street SW1H 238 C3
Maunsel Street SW1P 238 B5
Mayfair Place W1J 237 L1
Mayflower Street SE16 240 F7
Mayford Estate NW1 234 A1
Maynards Quay E1W 240 F4
May's Street WC2N 234 C8
McAuley Close SE1 238 F4
McLeod's Mews SW7 236 C5
Meadcroft Road SE11 239 G8
Meadcroft Road SE11 239 H8
Meadow Road SW8 238 E8
Meadow Row SE1 239 J5
Mead Row SE1 238 F4
Meakin Estate SE1 239 M4
Mecklenburgh Square WC1N 234 E3
Medway Street SW1P 238 B5
Meeting House Alley E1W 240 E5
Melcombe Place NW1 233 G4
Melcombe Street W1U 233 H4
Melina Place NW8 232 D2
Melior Street SE1 239 M2
Melton Street NW1 234 A2
Memorial Gates SW1W 237 K3
Mepham Street SE1 238 F2
Mercer Street WC2H 234 C7
Merchant Square W2 232 E5
Merlin Street EC1R 234 F2
Mermaid Court SE1 239 K2
Merrick Square SE1 239 K4
Merrington Road SW6 236 A8
Merrow Street SE17 239 L7
Methley Street SE11 239 G7
Meymott Street SE1 239 G2
Micawber Street N1 235 K1
Micklethwaite Lane SW6 236 A8
Middlesex Street E1 240 A1
Middlesex Street E1 240 B2
Middle Street EC1A 235 J5
Middle Temple WC2R 234 F7
Middle Temple Lane EC4Y 234 F7
Middleton Drive SE16 241 H6
Midland Road NW1 234 C1
Midship Close SE16 241 H6
Milborne Grove SW10 236 D7
Milcote Street SE1 239 H3
Miles Street SW8 238 D8
Milford Lane WC2R 234 F7
Milk Street EC2V 235 K6
Milk Yard E1W 241 G4
Millbank SW1P 238 D4
Millennium Bridge SE1 235 J8
Millennium Harbour E14 241 M6
Milligan Street E14 241 L4
Millman Mews WC1N 234 E4
Millman Street WC1N 234 E4
Mill Place E14 241 K3
Millstream Road SE1 240 B7
Mill Street SE1 240 C6
Mill Street W1S 233 L7
Milner Street SW3 237 G5
Milton Street EC2Y 235 K4
Milverton Street SE11 239 G7
Mincing Lane EC3M 240 A4
Minera Mews SW1W 237 J5
Minories EC3N 240 B3
Mitchell Street EC1V 235 J3
Mitre Road SE1 239 G2
Mitre Street EC3A 240 A3
Molyneux Street W1H 233 G5
Monck Street SW1P 238 C4
Monkton Street SE11 239 G5
Monkwell Square EC2Y 235 K5
Monmouth Place W2 232 A6
Monmouth Road W2 232 A6
Monmouth Street WC2H 234 C6
Montague Close SE1 239 L1
Montague Place EC3R 234 C5
Montague Street WC1B 234 C5
Montagu Mansions W1U 233 H5
Montagu Mews North W1H 233 H5
Montagu Mews West W1H 233 H6
Montagu Place W1H 233 H5
Montagu Row W1U 233 H5
Montagu Square W1H 233 H5
Montagu Street W1H 233 H6
Montford Place SE11 238 F7
Monthorpe Road E1 240 C1
Montpelier Square SW7 237 G3
Montpelier Street SW7 237 G3
Montpelier Walk SW7 236 G3
Montrose Place SW1X 237 K3
Monument ⊖ EC4R 235 L7
Monument Street EC3R 235 L7
Monument Street EC3R 235 M7
Monza Street E1W 241 G4
Moodkee Street SE16 241 G7
Moore Street SW3 237 H5
Moorfields EC2Y 235 L5
Moorgate EC2R 235 L6
Moorgate ⇌ ⊖ EC2Y 235 L5
Moor Lane EC2Y 235 K5
Moor Street W1D 234 C7
Mora Street EC1V 235 K2
Morecambe Street SE17 239 K6
Moreland Street EC1V 235 H2
More London SE1 240 A5
Moreton Place SW1V 238 A6
Moreton Street SW1V 238 B6
Moreton Terrace SW1V 238 A6
Morgan's Lane SE1 239 M2
Morgan's Lane SE1 240 A5
Morley Street SE1 239 G3
Mornington Crescent NW1 233 M1
Mornington Place NW1 233 L1
Mornington Terrace NW1 233 L1
Morocco Street SE1 240 A7
Morpeth Terrace SW1P 237 M5
Morris Street E1 240 F3
Morshead Road W9 232 A2
Mortimer Market WC1E 234 A4
Mortimer Street W1T 234 A5
Mortimer Street W1W 233 M5
Morton Place SE1 238 F4
Morwell Street WC1B 234 B5
Moscow Place W2 232 B7
Moscow Road W2 232 B7
Mossop Street SW3 237 G5
Motcomb Street SW1X 237 J4
Mount Gate W2 236 E2
Mount Mills EC1V 235 J3
Mount Pleasant WC1X 234 F4
Mount Row W1K 233 K8
Mount Street W1K 233 K8
Mount Street Mews W1K 233 K8
Mount Terrace E1 240 E1
Moxon Street W1U 233 J5
Mulberry Street E1 240 D2
Mulberry Walk SW3 236 E8
Mulready Street NW8 232 F4
Mundy Street N1 235 M2
Munster Square NW1 233 L3
Munton Road SE17 239 K5
Murphy Street SE1 238 F3
Murray Grove N1 235 K1
Musbury Street E1 241 G2
Muscovy Street EC3N 240 A4
Museum of London EC2Y 235 J5
Museum Street WC1A 234 C5
Myddelton Passage EC1R 235 G2
Myddelton Square EC1R 235 G1
Myddelton Street EC1R 235 G3
Myrdle Street E1 240 D2

N

Naoroji Street WC1X 234 F2
Napier Grove N1 235 K1
Narrow Street E14 241 K4
Nash Street NW1 233 L2
Nassau Street W1W 233 M5
Nathaniel Close * E1 240 C2
National Portrait Gallery WC2H 234 C8
Natural History Museum SW7 236 E4
Neal Street WC2H 234 C6
Neckinger SE1 240 C8
Needleman Street SE16 241 H7
Nelson Close NW6 232 A1
Nelson Place N1 235 H1
Nelson's Column WC2N 234 C8
Nelson Square SE1 239 H2
Nelson Street E1 240 E2
Nelson Terrace N1 235 H1
Neptune Street SE16 241 G7
Nesham Street E1W 240 D4
Netherton Grove SW10 236 D8
Netley Street NW1 233 M2
Nevern Place SW5 236 A6
Nevern Square SW5 236 A6
Neville Street SW7 236 E6
Newark Street E1 240 E2
New Atlas Wharf E14 241 M8
New Bond Street W1S 233 L7
New Bond Street W1S 233 L8
New Bridge Street EC4V 235 H6
New Broad Street EC2M 235 M5
New Burlington Street W1S 233 M7
Newburn Street SE11 238 F7
Newbury Street EC1A 235 J5
Newcastle Place W2 232 E5
New Cavendish Street W1G 233 K5
New Change EC4M 235 J6
New Church Road SE5 239 L8
Newcomen Street SE1 239 K2
Newcourt Street NW8 232 F1
Newell Street E14 241 L3
New Fetter Lane EC4A 235 G6
Newgate Street WC1A 235 H6
New Goulston Street E1 240 B2
Newham's Row SE1 240 A7
Newington Butts SE1 239 H6
Newington Causeway SE1 239 J4
New Kent Road SE1 239 K5
Newlands Quay E1W 240 F4
Newman Street W1T 234 A5
New North Place EC2A 235 M3
New North Road N1 235 L1
New North Street WC1N 234 D4
New Oxford Street WC1A 234 C6
Newport Street SE11 238 E5
New Quebec Street W1H 233 H6
New Ride SW7 236 E3
New Road E1 240 E2
New Row WC2N 234 C7
New Spring Gardens Walk SE1 238 D7
New Square WC2A 234 F6
New Street EC2M 240 A2
New Street Square EC4A 235 G6
Newton Road W2 232 A6
Newton Street WC2B 234 D5
New Union Street EC2Y 235 K5
Nicholas Lane EC3V 235 L7
Nicholson Street SE1 239 H1
Nightingale Place SW10 236 D8
Nile Street N1 235 K2
Nine Elms Lane SW8 238 C8
Noble Street EC2V 235 J6
Noel Road N1 235 J1
Noel Street W1F 234 A6
Norbiton Road E14 241 L2
Norfolk Crescent W2 233 G6
Norfolk Place W2 232 E6
Norfolk Square W2 232 E6
Norman Street EC1V 235 J3
Norris Street SW1Y 234 B8
Northampton Road EC1R 235 G3
Northampton Square EC1V 235 H2
North Audley Street W1K 233 J7
North Bank NW8 232 F2
Northburgh Street EC1V 235 H3
North Carriage Drive W2 232 F7
Northdown Street N1 234 D1
Northey Street E14 241 K4
North Gower Street NW1 234 A2
Northington Street WC1N 234 E4
North Mews WC1N 234 E4
North Ride W2 233 G7
North Row W1K 233 J7
North Tenter Street E1 240 C3
North Terrace SW3 236 F5
Northumberland Alley EC3N 240 B3
Northumberland Avenue WC2N 238 C1
Northumberland Place W2 232 A6
Northumberland Street WC2N 238 C1
North Wharf Road W2 232 E5
Northwick Terrace NW8 232 D3
Norway Gate SE16 241 K7
Norway Place E14 241 L3
Norwich Street EC4A 234 F5
Nottingham Place W1U 233 J4
Nottingham Street W1U 233 J4
Notting Hill Gate W11 232 A8
Notting Hill Gate ⊖ W11 236 A1
Nugent Terrace NW8 232 D1
Nutford Place W1H 233 G6

O

Oakden Street SE11 239 G5
Oakington Road W9 232 A3
Oak Lane E14 241 L3
Oakley Close EC1V 235 H1
Oakley Gardens SW3 237 G8
Oakley Square NW1 234 A1
Oakley Street SW3 236 F8
Oak Tree Road NW8 232 F2
Oat Lane EC2V 235 J5
Occupation Road SE17 239 J6
Ocean Square E1 241 J1
Odessa Street SE16 241 L7
Ogle Street W1W 233 M5
Old Bailey EC4M 235 H6
Old Barrack Yard SW1X 237 J3
Old Bond Street W1S 233 M8
Old Broad Street EC2N 235 M6
Old Brompton Road SW5 236 B6
Old Brompton Road SW7 236 D6
Old Burlington Street W1S 233 M7
Oldbury Place W1U 233 J4
Old Castle Street E1 240 B2
Old Cavendish Street W1G 233 L6
Old Church Road E1 241 H2
Old Church Street SW3 236 E7
Old Compton Street W1D 234 B7
Old Court Place W8 236 B3
Old Gloucester Street WC1N 234 D4
Old Jamaica Road SE16 240 C7
Old Jewry EC2R 235 K6
Old Kent Road SE1 239 M5
Old Marylebone Road NW1 233 G5
Old Montague Street E1 240 C1
Old North Street WC1X 234 E5
Old Paradise Street SE11 238 E5
Old Park Lane W1J 237 K2
Old Pye Street SW1P 238 B4
Old Queen Street SW1H 238 B3
Old Square WC2A 234 F6
Old Street EC1V 235 J3
Old Street ⇌ ⊖ EC1Y 235 L3
Old Street Junction EC1Y 235 L3
Oliver's Yard EC1Y 235 L3
Olney Road SE17 239 J8
O'Meara Street SE1 239 K2
Omega Place N1 234 D1
Onega Gate SE16 241 J8
Ongar Road SW6 236 A8
Onslow Gardens SW7 236 D6
Onslow Square SW7 236 E5
Onslow Square SW7 236 E6
Ontario Street SE1 239 J4
Ontario Way E14 241 M4
Opal Street SE1 239 H6
Orange Place SE16 241 G8
Orange Square SW1W 237 K6
Orange Street E1W 240 D5
Orange Street WC2H 234 B8
Orb Street SE17 239 L6
Orchardson Street NW8 232 E4
Orchard Street W1H 233 J6
Ordehall Street WC1N 234 E4
Orient Street SE11 239 H5
Orme Court W2 232 B8
Orme Lane W2 232 B8
Orme Square Gate W2 232 B8
Ormond Close WC1N 234 D4
Ormonde Gate SW3 237 H7
Ormond Yard SW1Y 234 A8
Orsett Street SE11 238 E6
Orsett Terrace W2 232 C6
Orton Street E1W 240 D5
Osbert Street SW1V 238 B6
Osborn Street E1 240 C2
Oslo Square SE16 241 K7
Osnaburgh Street NW1 233 L3
Osnaburgh Terrace NW1 233 L3
Ossington Buildings W1U 233 J5
Ossington Street W2 232 A7
Ossulston Street NW1 234 B1
Oswin Street SE11 239 H5
Othello Close SE1 239 H6
Otto Street SE17 239 H8
Outer Circle NW1 233 H3
Outer Circle NW1 233 K1
Oval ⊖ SE11 238 F8
Oval Way SE11 238 E7
Ovington Square SW3 237 G4
Ovington Street SW3 237 G5
Owen Street EC1V 235 G1
Oxendon Street SW1Y 234 B8
Oxford Circus ⊖ W1B 233 M6
Oxford Road NW6 232 A1
Oxford Square W2 232 F6
Oxford Street W1C 233 L6
Oxford Street WC1A 234 A6

P

Pace Place E1 240 E3
Pacific Wharf SE16 241 H5
Paddington ⇌ ⊖ W2 232 D6
Paddington Green W2 232 E5
Paddington Street W1U 233 J5

246 Pageant Crescent - Stainer Street

Pageant Crescent SE16 241 K5
Page Street SW1P 238 B5
Paget Street EC1V 235 H2
Pakenham Street WC1X 234 E3
Palace Avenue W8 236 B2
Palace Court W2 232 A7
Palace Gardens Terrace W8 236 A1
Palace Gate W8 236 C3
Palace Green W8 236 B2
Palace Place SW1E 237 M4
Palace Street SW1E 237 M4
Pall Mall SW1Y 238 A1
Pall Mall East SW1Y 238 B1
Palmer Street SW1H 238 B3
Pancras Lane EC4N 235 K6
Pancras Road N1C 234 C1
Panton Street SW1Y 234 B8
Paradise Street SE16 240 E7
Paradise Walk SW3 237 H8
Pardoner Street SE1 239 L4
Pardon Street EC1V 235 H3
Parfett Street E1 240 D2
Paris Garden SE1 239 G1
Park Crescent W1B 233 K4
Parker's Row SE1 240 C7
Parker Street WC2B 234 D6
Park Lane W1K 233 H7
Park Lane W2 237 J1
Park Place SW1A 237 M1
Park Road NW1 233 H3
Park Square East NW1 233 L3
Park Square Mews NW1 233 K3
Park Square West NW1 233 K3
Park Street SE1 239 K1
Park Street W1K 233 J7
Park Village East NW1 233 L1
Park Walk SW10 236 D8
Park West Place W2 233 G6
Parliament Street SW1A 238 C2
Parry Street SW8 238 D8
Passmore Street SW1W 237 J6
Paternoster Square 235 J6
Pater Street W8 236 A4
Pattina Walk SE16 241 K5
Paul Street EC2A 235 M3
Paultons Square SW3 236 E8
Paveley Street NW1 233 G3
Pavilion Road SW1X 237 H3
Pavilion Street SW1X 237 H4
Paxton Terrace SW1V 237 L7
Peabody Avenue SW1V 237 L7
Peabody Estate SE1 239 J1
Peacock Street SE17 239 J6
Pearl Street E1W 240 F5
Pearman Street SE1 239 G3
Pear Tree Court EC1R 235 G3
Peartree Lane E1W 241 G4
Pear Tree Street EC1V 235 J3
Peel Street W8 236 A1
Peerless Street EC1V 235 K2
Pelham Crescent SW7 236 F6
Pelham Place SW7 236 F5
Pelham Street SW7 236 F5
Pelier Street SE17 239 K8
Pemberton Row EC4A 235 G6
Pembridge Gardens W2 232 A8
Pembridge Place W2 232 A7
Pembridge Square W2 232 A7
Pembridge Villas W11 232 A7
Pembroke Close SW1X 237 J3
Penang Street E1W 240 F5
Penfold Place NW8 232 F5
Penfold Street NW8 232 E4
Pennant Mews W8 236 B5
Pennington Street E1W 240 D4
Pennyfields E14 241 M4
Penrose Grove SE17 239 J7
Penrose Street SE17 239 J7
Penryn Road SE16 240 E7
Penton Place SE17 239 H6
Penton Rise WC1X 234 E2
Penton Street N1 234 F1
Pentonville Road N1 234 E1
Penywern Road SW5 236 A6
Pepper Street SE1 239 J2
Pepys Street EC3N 240 A4
Percival Street EC1V 235 H3
Percy Circus WC1X 234 F2
Percy Street W1T 234 B5
Perkin's Rent SW1P 238 B4
Petersham Mews SW7 236 D4
Petersham Place SW7 236 C4
Peter Street W1F 234 B7
Peto Place NW1 233 L3
Petticoat Lane E1 240 B2
Petty France SW1H 238 A3
Petty Wales EC3R 240 A4
Petyward SW3 237 G6
Phelp Street SE17 239 L7
Phene Street SW3 237 G8
Phillimore Walk W8 236 A3
Philpot Lane EC3M 235 M7
Philpot Street E1 240 E2
Phipp's Mews SW1W 237 L5
Phipp Street EC2A 235 M3
Phoenix Place WC1X 234 F3
Phoenix Road NW1 234 B1
Phoenix Street WC2H 234 C6
Piccadilly W1J 237 L2
Piccadilly Arcade SW1Y 237 M1
Piccadilly Circus W1B 234 A8
Piccadilly Circus ⊖ W1J 234 B8
Pickard Street EC1V 235 J2
Picton Place W1U 233 K6
Pier Head E1W 240 E6
Pigott Street E14 241 M3
Pilgrimage Street SE1 239 L3
Pimlico ⊖ SW1V 238 B6
Pimlico Road SW1W 237 J6
Pinchin Street E1 240 D3
Pindar Street EC2A 235 M4
Pindock Mews W9 232 B3
Pine Street EC1R 234 F3
Pitfield Street N1 235 M1
Pitsea Street E1 241 H3
Pitt's Head Mews W1J 237 K2
Pitt Street W8 236 A2
Pixley Street E14 241 L2
Platina Street * EC2A 235 L3
Plover Way SE16 241 K8
Plumbers Row E1 240 D2
Plumtree Court EC4A 235 G5
Plympton Street NW8 232 F4
Pocock Street SE1 239 H2
Poland Street W1F 234 A6
Pollen Street W1S 233 L7
Pollitt Drive NW8 232 E3
Polperron SE11 239 G5
Polygon Road NW1 234 B1
Pond Place SW3 236 F6
Ponler Street E1 240 E3
Ponsonby Place SW1P 238 C6
Ponsonby Terrace SW1P 238 C6
Ponton Road SW1V 238 B8
Pont Street SW1X 237 H4
Poolmans Street SE16 241 H6
Pope Street SE1 240 B7
Poplar Place W2 232 B7
Poppin's Court EC4A 235 H6
Porchester Gardens W2 232 B7
Porchester Gate W2 232 C8
Porchester Place W2 233 G6
Porchester Road W2 232 B5
Porchester Square W2 232 B6
Porchester Terrace W2 232 C7
Porchester Terrace North W2 232 C6
Porlock Street SE1 239 L3
Porter Street NW1 233 H4
Porteus Road W2 232 D5
Portland Place W1B 233 L4
Portland Place W1B 233 L5
Portland Square E1W 240 E5
Portland Street SE17 239 L7
Portman Close W1H 233 J6
Portman Mews South W1H 233 J6
Portman Square W1H 233 J6
Portman Street W1H 233 J6
Portpool Lane EC1N 234 F4
Portsea Place W2 233 G6
Portsmouth Street WC2A 234 E6
Portsoken Street E1 240 B3
Portugal Street WC2A 234 E6
Potier Street SE1 239 L4
Potters Fields SE1 240 B6
Pottery Street SE16 240 E7
Poultry EC2V 235 K6
Powis Place WC1N 234 D4
Praed Mews W2 232 E6
Praed Street W2 232 E6
Pratt Walk SE1 238 E5
Premier Place E14 241 M4
Prescot Street E1 240 C3
Preston Close SE1 239 M5
Price's Street SE1 239 H1
Prideaux Place WC1X 234 F2
Primrose Street EC2A 240 A1
Prince Albert Road NW8 232 F1
Prince Consort Road SW7 236 D3
Princelet Street E1 240 C1
Prince of Wales Gate SW7 236 F3
Princes Arcade SW1Y 234 A8
Prince's Gardens SW7 236 E3
Prince's Gate Mews SW7 236 E4
Princes Riverside Road SE16 241 H5
Prince's Square W2 232 A7
Princess Road NW6 232 A1
Princess Street SE1 239 H4
Princes Street W1B 233 L6
Prince's Street EC2R 235 L6
Princeton Street WC1R 234 E5
Prioress Street SE1 239 L4
Priory Green Estate N1 234 E1
Priory Walk SW10 236 D7
Proctor Street WC1V 234 E5
Prospect Place E1W 241 G5
Prospect Street SE16 240 E7
Provident Court W1K 233 J7
Provost Street N1 235 L1
Prusom Street E1W 240 F5
Pudding Lane EC3R 235 M7
Pumphouse Mews E1 240 D3
Purbrook Street SE1 240 A7
Purcell Street N1 235 M1
Purchese Street NW1 234 B1

Q

Quebec Way SE16 241 J7
Queen Anne's Gate SW1H 238 B3
Queen Anne Street W1G 233 K5
Queen Elizabeth Street SE1 240 B6
Queen Mother Gate W2 237 J2
Queensborough Terrace W2 232 C7
Queensberry Place SW7 236 E5
Queen's Gardens W2 232 C7
Queen's Gate SW7 236 D3
Queen's Gate SW7 236 D4
Queen's Gate Gardens SW7 236 D5
Queen's Gate Mews SW7 236 D4
Queen's Gate Place SW7 236 D4
Queen's Gate Place Mews SW7 236 D4
Queen's Gate Terrace SW7 236 C4
Queen's Head Yard SE1 239 L2
Queen's Mews W2 232 B7
Queen Square WC1N 234 D4
Queen's Row SE17 239 K7
Queen Street EC4N 235 K7
Queen Street W1J 237 L1
Queen Street Place EC4R 235 K7
Queen's Walk SE1 240 A5
Queen's Walk SW1A 237 M2
Queensway W2 232 B6
Queensway ⊖ W2 232 B8
Queen Victoria Street EC4V 235 J7
Quick Street N1 235 H1

R

Raby Street E14 241 K2
Radcliffe Road SE1 240 B8
Radcot Street SE11 239 G7
Radnor Mews W2 232 E6
Radnor Place W2 232 F6
Radnor Street EC1V 235 K3
Radnor Walk SW3 237 G7
Railway Approach SE1 239 L1
Railway Avenue SE16 241 G6
Railway Street N1 234 D1
Raine Street E1W 240 F5
Ralston Street SW3 237 H7
Ramillies Place W1F 233 M6
Ramillies Street W1F 233 M6
Rampart Street E1 240 E2
Rampayne Street SW1V 238 B6
Randall Road SE11 238 D6
Randall Row SE11 238 E6
Randolph Avenue W9 232 B1
Randolph Crescent W9 232 C3
Randolph Gardens NW6 232 B1
Randolph Mews W9 232 D4
Randolph Road W9 232 C4
Ranelagh Grove SW1W 237 K6
Ranelagh Road SW1V 238 A7
Rangoon Street * EC3N 240 B3
Ranston Street NW8 232 F4
Raphael Street SW7 237 G3
Ratcliffe Cross Street E1W 241 J3
Ratcliffe Lane E14 241 J3
Rathbone Place W1T 234 B5
Rathbone Street W1T 234 A5
Raven Row E1 240 F1
Ravensdon Street SE11 239 G7
Ravey Street EC2A 235 M3
Rawlings Street SW3 237 G5
Rawstone Street EC1V 235 H2
Ray Street EC1R 235 G4
Reardon Place E1W 240 E5
Reardon Street E1W 240 E5
Rectory Square E1 241 H1
Redan Place W2 232 B6
Redburn Street SW3 237 G7
Redcastle Close E1W 241 G4
Redcliffe Gardens SW10 236 B7
Redcliffe Mews SW10 236 C7
Redcliffe Place SW10 236 C8
Redcliffe Road SW10 236 D7
Redcliffe Square SW10 236 B7
Redcliffe Street SW10 236 B8
Redcross Way SE1 239 K2
Redesdale Street SW3 237 G7
Redfield Lane SW5 236 A5
Redhill Street NW1 233 L1
Red Lion Row SE5 239 K8
Red Lion Square WC1R 234 E5
Red Lion Street WC2B 234 E5
Redman's Road E1 241 G1
Red Place W1K 233 J7
Redriff Road SE16 241 J8
Reedworth Street SE11 239 G6
Reeves Mews W1K 233 J8
Regal Close E1 240 D1
Regan Way N1 235 M1
Regency Street SW1P 238 B5
Regent Place W1B 234 A7
Regent's Park ⊖ W1B 233 L4
Regent's Park NW1 233 J1
Regent's Park Estate NW1 233 L2
Regent Square WC1H 234 D2
Regent Street SW1Y 234 B8
Regent Street W1S 233 M7
Relton Mews SW7 237 G4
Remington Street N1 235 H1
Remnant Street WC2A 234 E6
Renforth Street SE16 241 G7
Renfrew Road SE11 239 H5
Rennie Street SE1 239 H1
Rephidim Street SE1 239 M4
Repton Street E14 241 K2
Reveley Square SE16 241 K7
Rex Place W1K 233 J8
Rhodeswell Road E14 241 L2
Rich Street E14 241 M3
Rickett Street SW6 236 A8
Ridgemount Street WC1E 234 B4
Ridgemount Gardens WC1E 234 B4
Riding House Street W1W 233 M5
Riley Road SE1 240 B7
Ripley's Believe It or Not! W1J 234 B8
Risborough Street SE1 239 J2
Risdon Street SE16 241 G7
Rissinghill Street N1 234 F1
River Street EC1R 234 F2
Rivington Street EC2A 235 M3
Robert Adam Street W1U 233 J6
Roberts Close SE16 241 J7
Robert Street NW1 233 L2
Rochester Row SW1P 238 A5
Rochester Street SW1P 238 B5
Rockingham Street SE1 239 J4
Rocliffe Street N1 235 H1
Roding Mews E1W 240 D5
Rodmarton Street W1U 233 H5
Rodney Place SE17 239 K5
Rodney Road SE17 239 K5
Rodney Street N1 234 E1
Roger Street WC1N 234 E4
Roland Gardens SW7 236 D6
Roland Way SE17 239 L7
Romford Street E1 240 E2
Romilly Street W1D 234 B7
Romney Street SW1P 238 C5
Rood Lane EC3M 235 M7
Ropemaker Road SE16 241 K7
Ropemaker Street EC2Y 235 L4
Roper Lane SE1 240 B7
Rope Street SE16 241 K8
Rope Walk Gardens E1 240 E2
Rosary Gardens SW7 236 D6
Roscoe Street EC1Y 235 K3
Rose Alley SE1 235 K8
Rosebery Avenue EC1R 234 F3
Rosemoor Street SW3 237 G6
Rose Street WC2E 234 C7
Rossmore Road NW1 233 G3
Rotary Street SE1 239 H3
Rotherhithe ⊖ SE16 241 G6
Rotherhithe Street SE16 241 G6
Rotherhithe Street SE16 241 J4
Rotherhithe Tunnel SE16 241 H5
Rothsay Street SE1 239 M4
Rotten Row W2 236 F2
Rouel Road SE16 240 C8
Roupell Street SE1 239 G2
Royal Albert Hall SW7 236 E3
Royal Avenue SW3 237 H6
Royal Hospital Road SW3 237 H7
Royal Mint Street E1 240 C4
Royal Oak ⊖ W2 232 B5
Royal Oak Yard SE1 240 A7
Royal Opera House WC2E 234 D7
Royal Road SE17 239 H8
Royal Street SE1 238 E3
Rudolph Road NW6 232 A1
Rugby Street WC1N 234 E4
Rum Close E1W 240 F4
Rupack Street SE16 240 F7
Rupert Street W1D 234 B7
Rushworth Street SE1 239 H2
Russell Court SW1A 238 A2
Russell Square WC1B 234 C4
Russell Square ⊖ WC1B 234 D4
Russell Street WC2B 234 D7
Russia Dock Road SE16 241 K6
Rutherford Street SW1P 238 B5
Rutland Gardens SW7 237 G3
Rutland Gate SW7 236 F3
Rutland Mews SW7 236 F4
Rutland Street SW7 236 F4
Ryder Street SW1Y 238 A1

S

Sackville Street W1S 234 A8
Saffron Hill EC1N 235 G4
Saffron Street EC1N 235 G4
Sail Street SE11 238 F5
St Agnes Place SE11 239 G8
St Alban's Grove W8 236 B4
St Alban's Street SW1Y 234 B8
St Alphage Garden EC2Y 235 K5
St Andrews Hill EC4V 235 H7
St Andrew's Place NW1 233 L3
St Andrew Street EC4A 235 G5
St Anne's Court W1F 234 B6
St Ann's Street SW1P 238 C4
St Anselm's Place W1K 233 K7
St Barnabas Street SW1W 237 K6
St Botolph Street EC3N 240 B2
St Bride Street EC4A 235 G6
St Chad's Street WC1H 234 D2
St Clare Street EC3N 240 B3
St Clements Lane WC2A 234 E6
St Cross Street EC1N 235 G4
St Dunstan's Hill EC3R 235 M8
St Dunstan's Lane EC3R 235 M7
St Elmos Road SE16 241 J7
St Ermin's Hill SW1H 238 B3
St George's Circus SE1 239 H3
St George's Drive SW1V 237 M6
St George's Estate E1 240 D3
St George's Lane * EC3R 235 M7
St George's Road SE1 239 G4
St George's Square SW1V 238 B7
St George Street W1S 233 L7
St Giles High Street WC2H 234 C6
St Helen's Place EC3A 235 M6
St James Market * SW1Y 234 B8
St James's Park ⊖ SW1H 238 B3
St James's Park SW1A 238 B3
St James's Place SW1A 237 M2
St James's Road SE16 240 D8
St James's Square SW1Y 238 A1
St James's Street SW1A 237 M1
St James Walk EC1R 235 G3
St John's Lane EC1M 235 H4
St John's Place EC1M 235 H4
St John's Square EC1V 235 H4
St John Street EC1V 235 H2
St John's Wood High Street NW8 232 F1
St John's Wood Road NW8 232 E3
St Katharine's Way E1W 240 C5
St Leonard's Terrace SW3 237 H7
St Loo Avenue SW3 237 G8
St Luke's Close EC1V 235 K3
St Luke's Street SW3 236 F6
St Manningtree E1 240 C2
St Mark Street E1 240 C3
St Martin's Lane WC2N 234 C7
St Martin's le Grand EC1A 235 J6
St Mary at Hill EC3R 235 M8
St Mary Axe EC3A 240 A3
St Mary Church Street SE16 240 F7
St Mary's Gardens SE11 239 G5
St Mary's Terrace W2 232 D4
St Mary's Walk SE11 239 G5
St Matthew Street SW1P 238 B4
St Michael's Street W2 232 F6
St Olav's Square SE16 240 F7
St Oswald's Place SE11 238 E7
St Pancras International ⇌ N1C 234 C1
St Paul's ⊖ EC1A 235 J6
St Paul's Avenue SE16 241 J5
St Paul's Cathedral EC4M 235 J6
St Paul's Churchyard EC4M 235 J6
St Paul's Way E3 241 L1
St Petersburgh Mews W2 232 B7
St Petersburgh Place W2 232 B7
St Saviours Wharf SE1 240 C6
St Stephen's Gardens W2 232 A5
St Swithin's Lane EC4N 235 L7
St Thomas Street SE1 239 L2
St Vincent Street W1U 233 J5
Salamanca Street SE1 238 D6
Salem Road W2 232 B7
Sale Place W2 232 F5
Salisbury Court EC4Y 235 G6
Salisbury Place W1H 233 H4
Salisbury Street NW8 232 F4
Salmon Lane E14 241 J2
Salter Road SE16 241 J5
Salter Street E14 241 M4
Samford Street NW8 232 F4
Sampson Street E1W 240 D5
Sancroft Street SE11 238 F6
Sandford Row SE17 239 L6
Sandland Street WC1R 234 E5
Sandpiper Close SE16 241 L6
Sandwich Street WC1H 234 C2
Sandy's Row E1 240 B1
Sans Walk EC1R 235 G3
Sardinia Street WC2A 234 E6
Savage Gardens EC3N 240 B3
Savile Row W1S 233 M7
Savoy Hill WC2R 234 E8
Savoy Place WC2R 234 D8
Savoy Street WC2E 234 E7
Sawyer Street SE1 239 J2
Scala Street W1T 234 A5
Scandrett Street E1W 240 E5
Scarborough Street E1 240 C3
Scarsdale Villas W8 236 A4
Schooner Close * SE16 241 H6
Science Museum SW7 236 E4
Scoresby Street SE1 239 H2
Scotch House Junction SW1X 237 H3
Scotland Place SW1A 238 C1
Scott Ellis Grove NW8 232 E2
Scott Lidgett Crescent SE16 240 D7
Scrutton Street EC2A 235 M3
Seaford Street WC1H 234 D2
Seagrave Road SW6 236 A8
Sea Life London Aquarium SE1 238 E3
Searles Road SE1 239 L5
Sebastian Street EC1V 235 H2
Secker Street SE1 238 F2
Sedan Way SE17 239 M6
Sedding Street SW1X 237 J5
Seddon Street WC1X 234 E3
Seething Lane EC3N 240 A4
Sekforde Street EC1R 235 H3
Selfridges W1A 233 J6
Selsey Street E14 241 M1
Selwood Place SW7 236 E6
Semley Place SW1W 237 K6
Senior Street W2 232 B4
Senrab Street E1 241 H2
Serle Street WC2A 234 F6
Serpentine Bridge W2 236 E1
Serpentine Road W2 236 F2
Seth Street SE16 241 G7
Settles Street E1 240 D2
Seven Dials WC2H 234 C6
Seville Street SW1X 237 H3
Sevington Street W9 232 A3
Seward Street EC1V 235 J3
Seymour Mews W1H 233 J6
Seymour Place W1H 233 G5
Seymour Street W1H 233 H6
Seymour Street W2 233 G7
Seymour Walk SW10 236 C7
Shad Thames SE1 240 B6
Shad Thames SE1 240 C6
Shadwell ⊖ ⊖ E1 240 F3
Shadwell Gardens E1 240 F3
Shaftesbury Avenue W1D 234 B7
Shaftesbury Avenue WC2H 234 C6
Shaftesbury Street N1 235 K1
Shakespeare's Globe SE1 235 J8
Shand Street SE1 240 A6
Sharsted Street SE17 239 H7
Shaw Crescent E14 241 K2
Shawfield Street SW3 237 G7
Sheffield Terrace W8 236 A2
Sheldon Square W2 232 D5
Shelmerdine Close E3 241 M1
Shelton Street WC2H 234 D6
Shepherdess Walk N1 235 K1
Shepherd Street W1J 237 K1
Sheraton Street W1F 234 B6
Sherborne Lane EC4N 235 L7
Ship and Mermaid Row SE1 239 M2
Shipwright Road SE16 241 K7
Shirland Road W9 232 A3
Shoe Lane EC4A 235 G5
Shorter Street EC3N 240 B4
Shorts Gardens WC2H 234 C6
Short Street SE1 239 G2
Shoulder of Mutton Alley E14 241 K4
Shouldham Street W1H 233 G5
Shroton Street NW1 232 F4
Siddons Lane W1H 233 H4
Sidmouth Street WC1N 234 D3
Sidney Square E1 240 F2
Sidney Street E1 240 F1
Silex Street SE1 239 H3
Silk Street EC2Y 235 K4
Silver Walk SE16 241 K5
Silvester Street SE1 239 K3
Singer Street EC2A 235 L3
Sir John Soane's Museum WC2A 234 E5
Skinner Place * SW1W 237 J6
Skinners Lane EC4V 235 K7
Skinner Street EC1R 235 G3
Slippers Place SE16 240 F8
Sloane Avenue SW3 237 G6
Sloane Court SW3 237 J6
Sloane Court East SW3 237 J6
Sloane Gardens SW1W 237 J6
Sloane Square SW1W 237 J5
Sloane Square ⊖ SW1W 237 J6
Sloane Street SW1X 237 H3
Sloane Terrace SW1X 237 J5
Smeaton Street E1W 240 E5
Smithfield Street EC1A 235 H5
Smith Square SW1P 238 C4
Smith Street SW3 237 G7
Smith Terrace SW3 237 G7
Smithy Street E1 241 G1
Snowden Street EC2A 235 M4
Snow Hill EC1A 235 H5
Snowsfields SE1 239 L2
Soho Square W1D 234 B6
Soho Street W1D 234 B6
Somerford Way SE16 241 K7
Somers Crescent W2 232 F6
Somerset House WC2R 234 E7
Somerstown Estate NW1 234 A1
Sondes Street SE17 239 L7
South & West Africa Gate SW1A 238 A3
Southall Place SE1 239 L3
Southampton Buildings WC2A 234 F5
Southampton Place WC1A 234 D5
Southampton Row WC1B 234 D4
Southampton Street WC2E 234 D7
South Audley Street W1K 233 K8
South Carriage Drive SW1X 237 H3
South Carriage Drive SW7 236 F3
South Eaton Place SW1W 237 J5
Southern Street N1 234 E1
South Kensington ⊖ SW7 236 E4
South Kensington ⊖ SW7 236 E5
South Lambeth Road SW8 238 D8
South Molton Lane W1K 233 K7
South Molton Street W1K 233 K7
South Parade SW3 236 E7
South Place EC2M 235 L5
South Sea Street SE16 241 L8
South Square WC1R 234 F5
South Street W1K 237 J1
South Tenter Street E1 240 C3
South Terrace SW7 236 F5
Southwark ⊖ SE1 239 H2
Southwark Bridge SE1 235 K8
Southwark Bridge Road SE1 239 J3
Southwark Park Road SE16 240 E8
Southwark Street SE1 239 H1
Southwell Gardens SW7 236 C5
South Wharf Road W2 232 E6
Southwick Mews W2 232 F6
Southwick Place W2 232 F6
Southwick Street W2 232 F6
Sovereign Close E1W 240 F4
Sovereign Crescent SE16 241 J4
Spanish Place W1U 233 J5
Spa Road SE16 240 C8
Spear Mews SW5 236 A6
Spelman Street E1 240 C1
Spence Close SE16 241 K7
Spencer Street EC1V 235 H2
Spenser Street SW1E 238 A4
Spert Street E14 241 J4
Spital Square E1 240 A1
Spring Gardens SW1A 238 C1
Spring Street W2 232 E6
Spurgeon Street SE1 239 L4
Spur Road SE1 238 F3
Stables Way SE11 238 F7
Stable Yard Road SW1A 238 A2
Stacey Street WC2H 234 C6
Stafford Place SW1E 237 M3
Stafford Road NW6 232 A2
Stafford Street W1S 233 M8
Stafford Terrace W8 236 A3
Stainer Street SE1 239 L2

Town plans: Manchester p.206, Oldham p.211

NORTH

SEA

Index to place names

This index lists places appearing in the main-map section of the atlas in alphabetical order. The reference following each name gives the atlas page number and grid reference of the square in which the place appears. The map shows counties, unitary authorities and administrative areas, together with a list of the abbreviated name forms used in the index. The top 100 places of tourist interest are indexed in **red**, World Heritage sites in **green**, motorway service areas in **blue**, airports in *blue italic* and National Parks in *green italic*.

Scotland

Abers	**Aberdeenshire**
Ag & B	**Argyll and Bute**
Angus	**Angus**
Border	**Scottish Borders**
C Aber	**City of Aberdeen**
C Dund	**City of Dundee**
C Edin	**City of Edinburgh**
C Glas	**City of Glasgow**
Clacks	**Clackmannanshire (1)**
D & G	**Dumfries & Galloway**
E Ayrs	**East Ayrshire**
E Duns	**East Dunbartonshire (2)**
E Loth	**East Lothian**
E Rens	**East Renfrewshire (3)**
Falk	**Falkirk**
Fife	**Fife**
Highld	**Highland**
Inver	**Inverclyde (4)**
Mdloth	**Midlothian (5)**
Moray	**Moray**
N Ayrs	**North Ayrshire**
N Lans	**North Lanarkshire (6)**
Ork	**Orkney Islands**
P & K	**Perth & Kinross**
Rens	**Renfrewshire (7)**
S Ayrs	**South Ayrshire**
Shet	**Shetland Islands**
S Lans	**South Lanarkshire**
Stirlg	**Stirling**
W Duns	**West Dunbartonshire (8)**
W Isls	**Western Isles (Na h-Eileanan an Iar)**
W Loth	**West Lothian**

Wales

Blae G	**Blaenau Gwent (9)**
Brdgnd	**Bridgend (10)**
Caerph	**Caerphilly (11)**
Cardif	**Cardiff**
Carmth	**Carmarthenshire**
Cerdgn	**Ceredigion**
Conwy	**Conwy**
Denbgs	**Denbighshire**
Flints	**Flintshire**
Gwynd	**Gwynedd**
IoA	**Isle of Anglesey**
Mons	**Monmouthshire**
Myr Td	**Merthyr Tydfil (12)**
Neath	**Neath Port Talbot (13)**
Newpt	**Newport (14)**
Pembks	**Pembrokeshire**
Powys	**Powys**
Rhondd	**Rhondda Cynon Taff (15)**
Swans	**Swansea**
Torfn	**Torfaen (16)**
V Glam	**Vale of Glamorgan (17)**
Wrexhm	**Wrexham**

Channel Islands & Isle of Man

Guern	**Guernsey**
Jersey	**Jersey**
IoM	**Isle of Man**

England

BaNES	**Bath & N E Somerset (18)**
Barns	**Barnsley (19)**
Bed	**Bedford**
Birm	**Birmingham**
Bl w D	**Blackburn with Darwen (20)**
Bmouth	**Bournemouth**
Bolton	**Bolton (21)**
Bpool	**Blackpool**
Br & H	**Brighton & Hove (22)**
Br For	**Bracknell Forest (23)**
Bristl	**City of Bristol**
Bucks	**Buckinghamshire**
Bury	**Bury (24)**
C Beds	**Central Bedfordshire**
C Brad	**City of Bradford**
C Derb	**City of Derby**
C KuH	**City of Kingston upon Hull**
C Leic	**City of Leicester**
C Nott	**City of Nottingham**
C Pete	**City of Peterborough**
C Plym	**City of Plymouth**
C Port	**City of Portsmouth**
C Sotn	**City of Southampton**
C Stke	**City of Stoke-on-Trent**
C York	**City of York**
Calder	**Calderdale (25)**
Cambs	**Cambridgeshire**
Ches E	**Cheshire East**
Ches W	**Cheshire West and Chester**
Cnwll	**Cornwall**
Covtry	**Coventry**
Cumb	**Cumbria**
Darltn	**Darlington (26)**
Derbys	**Derbyshire**
Devon	**Devon**
Donc	**Doncaster (27)**
Dorset	**Dorset**
Dudley	**Dudley (28)**
Dur	**Durham**
E R Yk	**East Riding of Yorkshire**
E Susx	**East Sussex**
Essex	**Essex**
Gatesd	**Gateshead (29)**
Gloucs	**Gloucestershire**
Gt Lon	**Greater London**
Halton	**Halton (30)**
Hants	**Hampshire**
Hartpl	**Hartlepool (31)**
Herefs	**Herefordshire**
Herts	**Hertfordshire**
IoS	**Isles of Scilly**
IoW	**Isle of Wight**
Kent	**Kent**
Kirk	**Kirklees (32)**
Knows	**Knowsley (33)**
Lancs	**Lancashire**
Leeds	**Leeds**
Leics	**Leicestershire**
Lincs	**Lincolnshire**
Lpool	**Liverpool**
Luton	**Luton**
M Keyn	**Milton Keynes**
Manch	**Manchester**
Medway	**Medway**
Middsb	**Middlesbrough**
NE Lin	**North East Lincolnshire**
N Linc	**North Lincolnshire**
N Som	**North Somerset (34)**
N Tyne	**North Tyneside (35)**
N u Ty	**Newcastle upon Tyne**
N York	**North Yorkshire**
Nhants	**Northamptonshire**
Norfk	**Norfolk**
Notts	**Nottinghamshire**
Nthumb	**Northumberland**
Oldham	**Oldham (36)**
Oxon	**Oxfordshire**
Poole	**Poole**
R & Cl	**Redcar & Cleveland**
Readg	**Reading**
Rochdl	**Rochdale (37)**
Rothm	**Rotherham (38)**
Rutlnd	**Rutland**
S Glos	**South Gloucestershire (39)**
S on T	**Stockton-on-Tees (40)**
S Tyne	**South Tyneside (41)**
Salfd	**Salford (42)**
Sandw	**Sandwell (43)**
Sefton	**Sefton (44)**
Sheff	**Sheffield**
Shrops	**Shropshire**
Slough	**Slough (45)**
Solhll	**Solihull (46)**
Somset	**Somerset**
St Hel	**St Helens (47)**
Staffs	**Staffordshire**
Sthend	**Southend-on-Sea**
Stockp	**Stockport (48)**
Sundld	**Sunderland**
Surrey	**Surrey**
Swindn	**Swindon**
Tamesd	**Tameside (49)**
Thurr	**Thurrock (50)**
Torbay	**Torbay**
Traffd	**Trafford (51)**
W & M	**Windsor and Maidenhead (52)**
W Berk	**West Berkshire**
W Susx	**West Sussex**
Wakefd	**Wakefield (53)**
Warrtn	**Warrington (54)**
Warwks	**Warwickshire**
Wigan	**Wigan (55)**
Wilts	**Wiltshire**
Wirral	**Wirral (56)**
Wokham	**Wokingham (57)**
Wolves	**Wolverhampton (58)**
Worcs	**Worcestershire**
Wrekin	**Telford & Wrekin (59)**
Wsall	**Walsall (60)**

Abbas Combe - Ansford 261

A

Abbas Combe Somset 20 D10
Abberley Worcs 57 P11
Abberley Common Worcs 57 N11
Abberton Essex 52 H8
Abberton Worcs 47 J4
Abberwick Nthumb 119 M8
Abbess Roding Essex 51 N8
Abbey Devon 10 C2
Abbey-Cwm-Hir Powys 55 P10
Abbeydale Sheff 84 D4
Abbey Dore Herefs 45 M8
Abbey Green Staffs 70 H3
Abbey Hill Somset 19 J11
Abbey St Bathans Border 129 K7
Abbeystead Lancs 95 M10
Abbey Town Cumb 110 C10
Abbey Village Lancs 89 J6
Abbey Wood Gt Lon 37 L5
Abbotrule Border 118 B8
Abbots Bickington Devon 16 F9
Abbots Bromley Staffs 71 K10
Abbotsbury Dorset 11 M7
Abbot's Chair Derbys 83 M6
Abbots Deuglie P & K 134 E5
Abbotsham Devon 16 G6
Abbotskerswell Devon 7 M5
Abbots Langley Herts 50 C10
Abbotsleigh Devon 7 L9
Abbots Leigh N Som 31 P10
Abbotsley Cambs 62 B9
Abbots Morton Worcs 47 K3
Abbots Ripton Cambs 62 B5
Abbot's Salford Warwks 47 L4
Abbotstone Hants 22 G8
Abbotswood Hants 22 C10
Abbots Worthy Hants 22 E8
Abbotts Ann Hants 22 B6
Abbott Street Dorset 12 G4
Abcott Shrops 56 F9
Abdon Shrops 57 K7
Abenhall Gloucs 46 C11
Aberaeron Cerdgn 43 J2
Aberaman Rhondd 30 D4
Aberangell Gwynd 55 J2
Aber-arad Carmth 42 F6
Aberarder Highld 147 Q2
Aberargie P & K 134 F4
Aberarth Cerdgn 43 J2
Aberavon Neath 29 K7
Aber-banc Cerdgn 42 G6
Aberbargoed Caerph 30 G4
Aberbeeg Blae G 30 H4
Abercanaid Myr Td 30 E4
Abercarn Caerph 30 H6
Abercastle Pembks 40 G4
Abercegir Powys 55 J4
Aberchalder Lodge Highld 147 J7
Aberchirder Abers 158 F7
Aber Clydach Powys 44 G10
Abercraf Powys 29 M2
Abercregan Neath 29 M5
Abercwmboi Rhondd 30 D5
Abercych Pembks 41 P2
Abercynon Rhondd 30 E6
Aberdalgie P & K 134 D3
Aberdare Rhondd 30 D4
Aberdaron Gwynd 66 B9
Aberdeen C Aber 151 N6
Aberdeen Airport C Aber 151 M5
Aberdeen Crematorium C Aber 151 M6
Aberdesach Gwynd 66 G4
Aberdour Fife 134 F10
Aberdulais Neath 29 L5
Aberdyfi Gwynd 54 E5
Aberedw Powys 44 F5
Abereiddy Pembks 40 E4
Abererch Gwynd 66 F7
Aberfan Myr Td 30 E4
Aberfeldy P & K 141 L8
Aberffraw IoA 78 F11
Aberffrwd Cerdgn 54 F9
Aberford Leeds 91 L3
Aberfoyle Stirlg 132 G7
Abergarw Brdgnd 29 P8
Abergarwed Neath 29 M4
Abergavenny Mons 31 J2
Abergele Conwy 80 C9
Aber-giar Carmth 43 K6
Abergorlech Carmth 43 L8
Abergwesyn Powys 44 B4
Abergwili Carmth 42 H10
Abergwydol Powys 54 H4
Abergwynfi Neath 29 N5
Abergwyngregyn Gwynd 79 M10
Abergynolwyn Gwynd 54 F3
Aberhafesp Powys 55 P6
Aberhosan Powys 55 J5
Aberkenfig Brdgnd 29 N8
Aberlady E Loth 128 D4
Aberlemno Angus 143 J6
Aberllefenni Gwynd 54 H3
Aberllynfi Powys 44 H7
Aberlour Moray 157 P9
Aber-Magwr Cerdgn 54 F10
Aber-meurig Cerdgn 43 L3
Abermorddu Flints 69 K3
Abermule Powys 56 B6
Abernant Carmth 42 F10
Aber-nant Rhondd 30 D4
Abernethy P & K 134 F4
Abernyte P & K 142 D11
Aberporth Cerdgn 42 E4
Abersoch Gwynd 66 E9
Abersychan Torfn 31 J4
Aberthin V Glam 30 D10
Abertillery Blae G 30 H4
Abertridwr Caerph 30 F7
Abertridwr Powys 68 D11
Abertysswg Caerph 30 F3
Aberuthven P & K 134 B4
Aberyscir Powys 44 D9
Aberystwyth Cerdgn 54 D8
Aberystwyth Crematorium Cerdgn 54 E8
Abingdon-on-Thames Oxon 34 E5
Abinger Common Surrey 36 D11
Abinger Hammer Surrey 36 C11
Abington Nhants 60 G8
Abington S Lans 116 C6
Abington Pigotts Cambs 50 H2
Abington Services S Lans 116 C6
Abingworth W Susx 24 D7
Ab Kettleby Leics 73 J6
Ab Lench Worcs 47 K4
Ablington Gloucs 33 M3
Ablington Wilts 21 N5
Abney Derbys 83 Q8
Above Church Staffs 71 J4
Aboyne Abers 150 E8
Abram Wigan 82 D4
Abriachan Highld 155 Q10
Abridge Essex 51 L11
Abronhill N Lans 126 D2
Abson S Glos 32 D10
Abthorpe Nhants 48 H5
Aby Lincs 87 M5
Acaster Malbis C York 98 B11
Acaster Selby N York 91 P2
Accrington Lancs 89 M5
Accrington Crematorium Lancs 89 M5
Acha Ag & B 136 F5
Achahoish Ag & B 123 N4
Achalader P & K 141 R8
Achaleven Ag & B 138 G11
Acha Mor W Isls 168 i5
Achanalt Highld 155 J5
Achandunie Highld 156 A3
Achany Highld 162 D6
Acharacle Highld 138 B4
Acharn Highld 138 C7
Acharn P & K 141 J9
Achavanich Highld 167 L8
Achduart Highld 160 G6
Achfary Highld 164 G9
A'Chill Highld 144 C6
Achiltibuie Highld 160 G5
Achina Highld 166 B4
Achinhoan Ag & B 120 E8
Achintee Highld 154 B9
Achintraid Highld 153 Q10
Achmelvich Highld 160 H2
Achmore Highld 153 R11
Achmore W Isls 168 i5
Achnacarnin Highld 164 B10
Achnacarry Highld 146 F10
Achnacloich Highld 145 J6
Achnaconeran Highld 147 L4
Achnacroish Ag & B 138 F9
Achnadrish House Ag & B 137 M5
Achnafauld P & K 141 L10
Achnagarron Highld 156 B3
Achnaha Highld 137 M2
Achnahaird Highld 160 G4
Achnairn Highld 162 D4
Achnalea Highld 138 F5
Achnamara Ag & B 130 F10
Achnasheen Highld 154 G6
Achnashellach Lodge Highld 154 D8
Achnastank Moray 157 P11
Achosnich Highld 137 L2
Achranich Highld 138 C8
Achreamie Highld 166 H3
Achriabhach Highld 139 L4
Achriesgill Highld 164 G6
Achtoty Highld 165 Q4
Achurch Nhants 61 M4
Achvaich Highld 162 G8
Achvarasdal Highld 166 G4
Ackergill Highld 167 Q6
Acklam Middsb 104 E7
Acklam N York 98 F8
Ackleton Shrops 57 P5
Acklington Nthumb 119 P10
Ackton Wakefd 91 L6
Ackworth Moor Top Wakefd 91 L7
Acle Norfk 77 N9
Acock's Green Birm 58 H8
Acol Kent 39 P8
Acomb C York 98 B10
Acomb Nthumb 112 D7
Acombe Somset 10 D2
Aconbury Herefs 45 Q8
Acre Lancs 89 M6
Acrefair Wrexhm 69 J6
Acton Ches E 70 A4
Acton Dorset 12 G9
Acton Gt Lon 36 F4
Acton Shrops 56 E8
Acton Staffs 70 E6
Acton Suffk 52 E2
Acton Worcs 58 B11
Acton Beauchamp Herefs 46 C4
Acton Bridge Ches W 82 C9
Acton Burnell Shrops 57 J4
Acton Green Herefs 46 C4
Acton Park Wrexhm 69 K4
Acton Pigott Shrops 57 J4
Acton Round Shrops 57 L5
Acton Scott Shrops 56 H7
Acton Trussell Staffs 70 G11
Acton Turville S Glos 32 F8
Adbaston Staffs 70 D9
Adber Dorset 19 Q10
Adbolton Notts 72 F3
Adderbury Oxon 48 E7
Adderley Shrops 70 B7
Adderstone Nthumb 119 M4
Addiewell W Loth 126 H5
Addingham C Brad 96 G11
Addington Bucks 49 K9
Addington Gt Lon 37 J8
Addington Kent 37 Q9
Addiscombe Gt Lon 36 H7
Addlestone Surrey 36 C8
Addlestonemoor Surrey 36 C7
Addlethorpe Lincs 87 P7
Adeney Wrekin 70 B11
Adeyfield Herts 50 C9
Adfa Powys 55 P4
Adforton Herefs 56 G10
Adisham Kent 39 M11
Adlestrop Gloucs 47 P9
Adlingfleet E R Yk 92 D6
Adlington Ches E 83 K8
Adlington Lancs 89 J8
Admaston Staffs 71 J10
Admaston Wrekin 57 L2
Admington Warwks 47 P5
Adpar Cerdgn 42 F6
Adsborough Somset 19 J9
Adscombe Somset 18 G7
Adstock Bucks 49 K8
Adstone Nhants 48 G4
Adswood Stockp 83 J7
Adversane W Susx 24 C6
Advie Highld 157 L11
Adwalton Leeds 90 G5
Adwell Oxon 35 J5
Adwick Le Street Donc 91 N9
Adwick upon Dearne Donc 91 M10
Ae D & G 109 L3
Ae Bridgend D & G 109 M3
Afan Forest Park Neath 29 N5
Affetside Bury 89 M8
Affleck Abers 158 E9
Affpuddle Dorset 12 D6
Affric Lodge Highld 146 F3
Afon-wen Flints 80 G10
Afton Devon 7 L6
Afton IoW 13 P7
Agecroft Crematorium Salfd 82 H4
Agglethorpe N York 96 G3
Aigburth Lpool 81 M7
Aike E R Yk 99 L11
Aiketgate Cumb 111 J11
Aikhead Cumb 110 D11
Aikton Cumb 110 E10
Ailby Lincs 87 M5
Ailey Herefs 45 L5
Ailsworth C Pete 74 B11
Ainderby Quernhow N York 97 M4
Ainderby Steeple N York 97 M2
Aingers Green Essex 53 K7
Ainsdale Sefton 88 C8
Ainsdale-on-Sea Sefton 88 B8
Ainstable Cumb 111 K11
Ainsworth Bury 89 M8
Ainthorpe N York 105 K9
Aintree Sefton 81 M5
Ainville W Loth 127 L5
Aird Ag & B 130 F7
Aird D & G 106 E5
Aird W Isls 168 k4
Aird a Mhulaidh W Isls 168 g6
Aird Asaig W Isls 168 g7
Aird Dhubh Highld 153 N9
Airdeny Ag & B 131 K2
Aird of Kinloch Ag & B 137 N10
Aird of Sleat Highld 145 J7
Airdrie N Lans 126 D4
Airdriehill N Lans 126 D4
Airds of Kells D & G 108 E6
Aird Uig W Isls 168 f4
Airidh a bhruaich W Isls 168 h6
Airieland D & G 108 G9
Airlie Angus 142 E7
Airmyn E R Yk 92 B6
Airntully P & K 141 Q10
Airor Highld 145 M6
Airth Falk 133 Q10
Airton N York 96 D9
Aisby Lincs 73 Q3
Aisby Lincs 85 Q2
Aisgill Cumb 102 E11
Aish Devon 6 H6
Aish Devon 7 L7
Aisholt Somset 18 G7
Aiskew N York 97 L3
Aislaby N York 98 F3
Aislaby N York 105 N9
Aislaby S on T 104 D8
Aisthorpe Lincs 86 B4
Aith Shet 169 q8
Akeld Nthumb 119 J5
Akeley Bucks 49 K7
Akenham Suffk 53 K2
Albaston Cnwll 5 Q7
Alberbury Shrops 56 F2
Albourne W Susx 24 G7
Albourne Green W Susx 24 G7
Albrighton Shrops 57 Q4
Albrighton Shrops 69 N11
Alburgh Norfk 65 K4
Albury Herts 51 K6
Albury Oxon 35 J3
Albury Surrey 36 B11
Albury End Herts 51 K6
Albury Heath Surrey 36 C11
Alby Hill Norfk 76 H5
Alcaig Highld 155 Q6
Alcaston Shrops 56 H7
Alcester Warwks 47 L3
Alcester Lane End Birm 58 G8
Alciston E Susx 25 M9
Alcombe Somset 18 C5
Alcombe Wilts 32 F11
Alconbury Cambs 61 Q5
Alconbury Weston Cambs 61 Q5
Aldborough N York 97 P7
Aldborough Norfk 76 H5
Aldbourne Wilts 33 Q9
Aldbrough E R Yk 93 M3
Aldbrough St John N York 103 P8
Aldbury Herts 35 Q2
Aldcliffe Lancs 95 K8
Aldclune P & K 141 L5
Aldeburgh Suffk 65 P10
Aldeby Norfk 65 N3
Aldenham Herts 50 D11
Alderbury Wilts 21 N9
Aldercar Derbys 84 F11
Alderford Norfk 76 G8
Alderholt Dorset 13 K2
Alderley Gloucs 32 E6
Alderley Edge Ches E 82 H9
Aldermans Green Covtry 59 N8
Aldermaston W Berk 34 G11
Alderminster Warwks 47 P5
Alder Moor Staffs 71 N9
Aldersey Green Ches W 69 N3
Aldershot Hants 23 N4
Alderton Gloucs 47 K8
Alderton Nhants 49 K5
Alderton Shrops 69 N10
Alderton Suffk 53 P3
Alderton Wilts 32 F8
Alderwasley Derbys 71 Q4
Aldfield N York 97 L7
Aldford Ches W 69 M3
Aldgate Rutlnd 73 P10
Aldham Essex 52 F6
Aldham Suffk 52 J2
Aldingbourne W Susx 15 P5
Aldingham Cumb 94 F6
Aldington Kent 27 J4
Aldington Worcs 47 L6
Aldington Corner Kent 27 J4
Aldivalloch Moray 150 B2
Aldochlay Ag & B 132 D9
Aldon Shrops 56 G9
Aldoth Cumb 109 P11
Aldreth Cambs 62 F6
Aldridge Wsall 58 G4
Aldringham Suffk 65 N9
Aldro N York 98 G8
Aldsworth Gloucs 33 N3
Aldsworth W Susx 15 L5
Aldunie Moray 150 B2
Aldwark Derbys 84 B9
Aldwark N York 97 Q8
Aldwick W Susx 15 P7
Aldwincle Nhants 61 M4
Aldworth W Berk 34 G9
Alexandria W Duns 125 K2
Aley Somset 18 G7
Alfardisworthy Devon 16 D9
Alfington Devon 10 C5
Alfold Surrey 24 B4
Alfold Bars W Susx 24 B4
Alfold Crossways Surrey 24 B3
Alford Abers 150 F4
Alford Lincs 87 N5
Alford Somset 20 B8
Alford Crematorium Lincs 87 M5
Alfreton Derbys 84 F9
Alfrick Worcs 46 D4
Alfrick Pound Worcs 46 D4
Alfriston E Susx 25 M10
Algarkirk Lincs 74 E3
Alhampton Somset 20 B8
Alkborough N Linc 92 E6
Alkerton Gloucs 32 E3
Alkerton Oxon 48 C6
Alkham Kent 27 N3
Alkington Shrops 69 P7
Alkmonton Derbys 71 M7
Allaleigh Devon 7 L8
Allanaquoich Abers 149 L9
Allanbank N Lans 126 E6
Allanton Border 129 M9
Allanton N Lans 126 E6
Allanton S Lans 126 C7
Allaston Gloucs 32 B4
Allbrook Hants 22 E10
All Cannings Wilts 21 L2
Allendale Nthumb 112 B9
Allen End Warwks 59 J5
Allenheads Nthumb 112 C11
Allensford Dur 112 G10
Allen's Green Herts 51 L7
Allensmore Herefs 45 P7
Allenton C Derb 72 B4
Aller Devon 17 P6
Aller Somset 19 M9
Allerby Cumb 100 E3
Allercombe Devon 9 P6
Allerford Somset 18 B5
Allerston N York 98 H4
Allerthorpe E R Yk 98 F11
Allerton C Brad 90 E4
Allerton Highld 156 D4
Allerton Lpool 81 M7
Allerton Bywater Leeds 91 L5
Allerton Mauleverer N York 97 P9
Allesley Covtry 59 M8
Allestree C Derb 72 A3
Allet Common Cnwll 3 K4
Allexton Leics 73 L10
Allgreave Ches E 83 L11
Allhallows Medway 38 D6
Allhallows-on-Sea Medway 38 D6
Alligin Shuas Highld 153 Q6
Allimore Green Staffs 70 F11
Allington Dorset 11 K6
Allington Kent 38 C10
Allington Lincs 73 M2
Allington Wilts 21 L2
Allington Wilts 21 P7
Allington Wilts 32 G9
Allithwaite Cumb 94 H5
Alloa Clacks 133 P9
Allonby Cumb 100 E2
Allostock Ches W 82 F10
Alloway S Ayrs 114 F4
Allowenshay Somset 10 H2
All Saints South Elmham Suffk 65 L5
Allscott Shrops 57 N5
Allscott Wrekin 57 L2
All Stretton Shrops 56 H5
Alltami Flints 81 K11
Alltchaorunn Highld 139 M7
Alltmawr Powys 44 F5
Alltwalis Carmth 42 H8
Alltwen Neath 29 K4
Alltyblaca Cerdgn 43 K5
Allweston Dorset 11 P2
Allwood Green Suffk 64 E7
Almeley Herefs 45 L4
Almeley Wooton Herefs 45 L4
Almer Dorset 12 F5
Almholme Donc 91 P9
Almington Staffs 70 C8
Almodington W Susx 15 M7
Almondbank P & K 134 D2
Almondbury Kirk 90 F8
Almondsbury S Glos 32 B8
Alne N York 97 Q7
Alness Highld 156 B4
Alnham Nthumb 119 J8
Alnmouth Nthumb 119 P8
Alnwick Nthumb 119 N8
Alperton Gt Lon 36 E4
Alphamstone Essex 52 E4
Alpheton Suffk 64 B11
Alphington Devon 9 M6
Alpington Norfk 77 K11
Alport Derbys 84 B8
Alpraham Ches E 69 Q3
Alresford Essex 53 J7
Alrewas Staffs 59 J2
Alsager Ches E 70 D3
Alsagers Bank Staffs 70 D5
Alsop en le Dale Derbys 71 M4
Alston Cumb 111 P11
Alston Devon 10 G4
Alstone Gloucs 47 J8
Alstone Somset 19 K5
Alstonefield Staffs 71 L3
Alston Sutton Somset 19 M4
Alswear Devon 17 N7
Alt Oldham 83 K4
Altandhu Highld 160 F4
Altarnun Cnwll 5 L5
Altass Highld 162 C6
Altcreich Ag & B 138 B10
Altgaltraig Ag & B 124 C3
Altham Lancs 89 M4
Althorne Essex 38 F2
Althorpe N Linc 92 D9
Altnabreac Station Highld 166 H7
Altnaharra Highld 165 N9
Altofts Wakefd 91 K6
Alton Derbys 84 E8
Alton Hants 23 K7
Alton Staffs 71 K6
Alton Wilts 21 N5
Alton Barnes Wilts 21 M2
Alton Pancras Dorset 11 Q4
Alton Priors Wilts 21 M2
Alton Towers Staffs 71 K6
Altrincham Traffd 82 G7
Altrincham Crematorium Traffd 82 F7
Altskeith Hotel Stirlg 132 F7
Alva Clacks 133 P8
Alvanley Ches W 81 P10
Alvaston C Derb 72 B4
Alvechurch Worcs 58 F10
Alvecote Warwks 59 K4
Alvediston Wilts 21 J10
Alveley Shrops 57 P8
Alverdiscott Devon 17 J6
Alverstoke Hants 14 H7
Alverstone IoW 14 G9
Alverthorpe Wakefd 91 J6
Alverton Notts 73 K2
Alves Moray 157 L5
Alvescot Oxon 33 Q4
Alveston S Glos 32 B7
Alveston Warwks 47 P3
Alvingham Lincs 87 L2
Alvington Gloucs 32 B4
Alwalton C Pete 74 B11
Alwinton Nthumb 118 H9
Alwoodley Leeds 90 H2
Alwoodley Gates Leeds 91 J2
Alyth P & K 142 C8
Ambergate Derbys 84 D10
Amber Hill Lincs 86 H11
Amberley Gloucs 32 G4
Amberley W Susx 24 B8
Amber Row Derbys 84 E9
Amberstone E Susx 25 N8
Amble Nthumb 119 Q10
Amblecote Dudley 58 C7
Ambler Thorn C Brad 90 D5
Ambleside Cumb 101 L10
Ambleston Pembks 41 K5
Ambrosden Oxon 48 H11
Amcotts N Linc 92 E8
America Cambs 62 F5
Amersham Bucks 35 Q5
Amersham Common Bucks 35 Q5
Amersham Old Town Bucks 35 Q5
Amersham on the Hill Bucks 35 Q5
Amerton Staffs 70 H9
Amerton Railway & Farm Staffs 70 H9
Amesbury Wilts 21 N6
Amhuinnsuidhe W Isls 168 f7
Amington Staffs 59 K4
Amisfield Town D & G 109 M4
Amlwch IoA 78 G6
Ammanford Carmth 28 H2
Amotherby N York 98 E6
Ampfield Hants 22 D10
Ampleforth N York 98 B5
Ampney Crucis Gloucs 33 L4
Ampney St Mary Gloucs 33 L4
Ampney St Peter Gloucs 33 L4
Amport Hants 22 B6
Ampthill C Beds 50 B3
Ampton Suffk 64 B7
Amroth Pembks 41 N9
Amulree P & K 141 L10
Amwell Herts 50 E8
Anaheilt Highld 138 E5
Ancaster Lincs 73 P2
Anchor Shrops 56 B7
Ancroft Nthumb 129 P11
Ancrum Border 118 B6
Ancton W Susx 15 Q6
Anderby Lincs 87 P5
Andersea Somset 19 K8
Andersfield Somset 18 H8
Anderson Dorset 12 E5
Anderton Ches W 82 D9
Anderton Cnwll 6 C8
Andover Hants 22 C5
Andoversford Gloucs 47 K11
Andreas IoM 80 f2
Anelog Gwynd 66 B9
Anerley Gt Lon 36 H7
Anfield Lpool 81 M6
Anfield Crematorium Lpool 81 M6
Angarrack Cnwll 2 F6
Angarrick Cnwll 3 K6
Angelbank Shrops 57 K9
Angersleigh Somset 18 G11
Angerton Cumb 110 D9
Angle Pembks 40 G10
Anglesey IoA 78 G8
Anglesey Abbey Cambs 62 H8
Angmering W Susx 24 C10
Angram N York 97 R11
Angram N York 102 G11
Angrouse Cnwll 2 H10
Anick Nthumb 112 D7
Ankerville Highld 156 E3
Ankle Hill Leics 73 K7
Anlaby E R Yk 92 H5
Anmer Norfk 75 P5
Anmore Hants 15 J4
Annan D & G 110 C7
Annandale Water Services D & G 109 P2
Annaside Cumb 94 B3
Annat Highld 154 A7
Annathill N Lans 126 C3
Anna Valley Hants 22 C6
Annbank S Ayrs 114 H3
Anne Hathaway's Cottage Warwks 47 N4
Annesley Notts 84 H10
Annesley Woodhouse Notts 84 G10
Annfield Plain Dur 113 J10
Anniesland C Glas 125 N4
Annitsford N Tyne 113 L6
Annscroft Shrops 56 H3
Ansdell Lancs 88 C5
Ansford Somset 20 B8

262 Ansley - Babell

Ansley Warwks 59 M6
Anslow Staffs 71 N9
Anslow Gate Staffs 71 M10
Anslow Lees Staffs 71 N10
Ansteadbrook Surrey 23 P8
Anstey Hants 23 K6
Anstey Herts 51 K4
Anstey Leics 72 F9
Anstruther Fife 135 P7
Ansty W Susx 24 G6
Ansty Warwks 59 P8
Ansty Wilts 21 J9
Ansty Cross Dorset 12 C4
Anthill Common Hants 14 H4
Anthonys Surrey 36 B8
Anthorn Cumb 110 C9
Antingham Norfk 77 K5
An t-Ob W Isls 168 f9
Antonine Wall Falk 126 E2
Anton's Gowt Lincs 87 K11
Antony Cnwll 5 Q11
Antrobus Ches W 82 D9
Anvil Corner Devon 16 F11
Anvil Green Kent 27 K2
Anwick Lincs 86 F10
Anwoth D & G 108 C9
Aperfield Gt Lon 37 K9
Apes Dale Worcs 58 E10
Apethorpe Nhants 73 Q11
Apeton Staffs 70 F11
Apley Lincs 86 F5
Apperknowle Derbys 84 E5
Apperley Gloucs 46 G9
Apperley Bridge C Brad 90 F3
Apperley Dene Nthumb 112 G9
Appersett N York 96 C2
Appin Ag & B 138 G8
Appleby N Linc 92 G8
Appleby-in-Westmorland Cumb 102 C6
Appleby Magna Leics 59 M3
Appleby Parva Leics 59 M3
Appleby Street Herts 50 H10
Applecross Highld 153 N9
Appledore Devon 9 Q2
Appledore Devon 16 H5
Appledore Kent 26 G6
Appledore Heath Kent 26 G5
Appleford Oxon 34 F6
Applegarth Town D & G 109 P4
Applehaigh Wakefd 91 K8
Appleshaw Hants 22 B5
Applethwaite Cumb 101 J5
Appleton Halton 81 Q7
Appleton Oxon 34 D4
Appleton Warrtn 82 D8
Appleton-le-Moors N York 98 E3
Appleton-le-Street N York 98 E6
Appleton Roebuck N York 91 P2
Appleton Thorn Warrtn 82 D8
Appleton Wiske N York 104 C10
Appletreehall Border 117 Q7
Appletreewick N York 96 G8
Appley Somset 18 E10
Appley Bridge Lancs 88 G9
Apse Heath IoW 14 G10
Apsley End C Beds 50 D4
Apuldram W Susx 15 M6
Arabella Highld 156 E2
Arbirlot Angus 143 L9
Arboll Highld 163 K10
Arborfield Wokham 35 L11
Arborfield Cross Wokham 35 L11
Arbourthorne Sheff 84 E3
Arbroath Angus 143 L9
Arbuthnott Abers 143 P2
Arcadia Kent 26 E4
Archddu Carmth 28 D4
Archdeacon Newton Darltn 103 Q7
Archencarroch W Duns 132 E11
Archiestown Moray 157 N9
Archirondel Jersey 11 c1
Arclid Green Ches E 70 D2
Ardallie Abers 159 P10
Ardanaiseig Hotel Ag & B 131 M3
Ardaneaskan Highld 153 Q10
Ardarroch Highld 153 Q10
Ardbeg Ag & B 122 F10
Ardbeg Ag & B 124 D4
Ardbeg Ag & B 131 P11
Ardcharnich Highld 161 K9
Ardchiavaig Ag & B 137 K12
Ardchonnel Ag & B 131 K5
Ardchullarie More Stirlg 132 H5
Arddarroch Ag & B 131 Q9
Arddleen Powys 69 J11
Ardechive Highld 146 E9
Ardeer N Ayrs 124 H9
Ardeley Herts 50 H5
Ardelve Highld 145 Q2
Arden Ag & B 132 D11
Ardens Grafton Warwks 47 M4
Ardentallen Ag & B 130 G3
Ardentinny Ag & B 131 P10
Ardentraive Ag & B 124 C3
Ardeonaig Stirlg 140 G10
Ardersier Highld 156 D7
Ardessie Highld 160 H9
Ardfern Ag & B 130 G7
Ardfernal Ag & B 123 J5
Ardgay Highld 162 D8
Ardgour Highld 139 J5
Ardgowan Inver 124 G3
Ardhallow Ag & B 124 F3
Ardhasig W Isls 168 g7
Ardheslaig Highld 153 P6
Ardindrean Highld 161 K9
Ardingly W Susx 24 H5
Ardington Oxon 34 D7
Ardington Wick Oxon 34 D7
Ardlamont Ag & B 124 B4
Ardleigh Essex 53 J6
Ardleigh Heath Essex 52 H5
Ardler P & K 142 D9
Ardley Oxon 48 F9
Ardley End Essex 51 M8
Ardlui Ag & B 132 C4
Ardlussa Ag & B 130 C10
Ardmair Highld 161 J7
Ardmaleish Ag & B 124 D4
Ardminish Ag & B 123 K10
Ardmolich Highld 138 C3
Ardmore Ag & B 125 J2
Ardmore Highld 162 G9
Ardnadam Ag & B 131 P11
Ardnagrask Highld 155 P8
Ardnarff Highld 154 A10
Ardnastang Highld 138 E5
Ardpatrick Ag & B 123 N8
Ardrishaig Ag & B 130 H10
Ardross Highld 155 R3
Ardrossan N Ayrs 124 G9
Ardsley Barns 91 K9
Ardsley East Leeds 91 J5
Ardslignish Highld 137 P3
Ardtalla Ag & B 122 G9
Ardtoe Highld 138 A3
Arduaine Ag & B 130 F5
Ardullie Highld 155 Q5
Ardvasar Highld 145 K7
Ardvorlich P & K 133 J3
Ardvourlie W Isls 168 g6
Ardwell D & G 106 F8
Ardwick Manch 83 J5
Areley Kings Worcs 57 P10
Arevegaig Highld 138 B4
Arford Hants 23 M7
Arglam E R Yk 92 C3
Argoed Caerph 30 G5
Argoed Shrops 69 K10
Argoed Mill Powys 44 D2
Argos Hill E Susx 25 N5
Argyll Forest Park Ag & B 131 Q7
Aribruach W Isls 168 h6
Aridhglas Ag & B 137 J11
Arileod Ag & B 136 F5
Arinagour Ag & B 136 G4
Ariogan Ag & B 130 H2
Arisaig Highld 145 L10
Arisaig House Highld 145 L11
Arkendale N York 97 N8
Arkesden Essex 51 L4
Arkholme Lancs 95 M6
Arkleby Cumb 100 F3
Arkleton D & G 110 G2
Arkle Town N York 103 K10
Arkley Gt Lon 50 F11
Arksey Donc 91 P9
Arkwright Town Derbys 84 F6
Arle Gloucs 46 H10
Arlecdon Cumb 100 D7
Arlescote Warwks 48 C5
Arlesey C Beds 50 E3
Arleston Wrekin 57 M2
Arley Ches E 82 E8
Arley Warwks 59 L6
Arlingham Gloucs 32 D2
Arlington Devon 17 L3
Arlington E Susx 25 M9
Arlington Gloucs 33 M3
Arlington Beccott Devon 17 L3
Armadale Highld 145 K7
Armadale Highld 166 C4
Armadale W Loth 126 G4
Armaside Cumb 100 G5
Armathwaite Cumb 111 K11
Arminghall Norfk 77 K11
Armitage Staffs 71 K11
Armitage Bridge Kirk 90 E8
Armley Leeds 90 H4
Armscote Warwks 47 P6
Armshead Staffs 70 G5
Armston Nhants 61 N3
Armthorpe Donc 91 Q10
Arnabost Ag & B 136 G3
Arnaby Cumb 94 D4
Arncliffe N York 96 D6
Arncliffe Cote N York 96 D6
Arncroach Fife 135 N6
Arndilly House Moray 157 P8
Arne Dorset 12 G7
Arnesby Leics 60 D2
Arngask P & K 134 E5
Arnisdale Highld 145 P5
Arnish Highld 153 K8
Arniston Mdloth 127 Q5
Arnol W Isls 168 i3
Arnold E R Yk 93 K2
Arnold Notts 85 J11
Arnprior Stirlg 133 J9
Arnside Cumb 95 K5
Aros Ag & B 137 P6
Arowry Wrexhm 69 N7
Arrad Foot Cumb 94 G4
Arram E R Yk 92 H2
Arran N Ayrs 120 H4
Arrathorne N York 97 K2
Arreton IoW 14 F9
Arrina Highld 153 N6
Arrington Cambs 62 D10
Arrochar Ag & B 132 B7
Arrow Warwks 47 L3
Arrowfield Top Worcs 58 F10
Arscott Shrops 56 G3
Artafallie Highld 156 A8
Arthington Leeds 90 H2
Arthingworth Nhants 60 G4
Arthog Gwynd 54 E2
Arthrath Abers 159 N10
Arthursdale Leeds 91 K3
Artrochie Abers 159 P11
Arundel W Susx 24 B9
Asby Cumb 100 E6
Ascog Ag & B 124 E5
Ascot W & M 35 P11
Ascott Warwks 48 B8
Ascott Earl Oxon 48 B11
Ascott-under-Wychwood Oxon 48 B11
Asenby N York 97 N5
Asfordby Leics 73 J7
Asfordby Hill Leics 73 J7
Asgarby Lincs 86 F11
Asgarby Lincs 87 K7
Ash Devon 7 L9
Ash Devon 17 J10
Ash Dorset 12 E2
Ash Kent 37 P8
Ash Kent 39 N10
Ash Somset 19 J10
Ash Somset 19 N10
Ash Surrey 23 P4
Ashampstead W Berk 34 G9
Ashampstead Green W Berk 34 G9
Ashbocking Suffk 64 H11
Ashbourne Derbys 71 M5
Ashbrittle Somset 18 E10
Ashburnham Place E Susx 25 Q8
Ashburton Devon 7 K4
Ashbury Devon 8 D5
Ashbury Oxon 33 Q7
Ashby N Linc 92 E9
Ashby by Partney Lincs 87 M7
Ashby cum Fenby NE Lin 93 N10
Ashby de la Launde Lincs 86 E9
Ashby-de-la-Zouch Leics 72 B7
Ashby Folville Leics 73 J8
Ashby Magna Leics 60 C2
Ashby Parva Leics 60 B3
Ashby Puerorum Lincs 87 K6
Ashby St Ledgers Nhants 60 C7
Ashby St Mary Norfk 77 L11
Ashchurch Gloucs 46 H8
Ashcombe Devon 9 M9
Ashcombe N Som 19 K2
Ashcott Somset 19 M7
Ashdon Essex 51 N2
Ashe Hants 22 F4
Asheldham Essex 52 G11
Ashen Essex 52 B3
Ashendon Bucks 35 K2
Asheridge Bucks 35 P4
Ashfield Hants 22 C11
Ashfield Herefs 46 A10
Ashfield Stirlg 133 M7
Ashfield cum Thorpe Suffk 65 J9
Ashfield Green Suffk 63 N9
Ashfield Green Suffk 65 K7
Ashfold Crossways W Susx 24 F5
Ashford Devon 6 H9
Ashford Devon 17 J4
Ashford Kent 26 H3
Ashford Surrey 36 C6
Ashford Bowdler Shrops 57 J10
Ashford Carbonell Shrops 57 J10
Ashford Hill Hants 22 G2
Ashford in the Water Derbys 83 Q11
Ashgill S Lans 126 D7
Ash Green Surrey 23 P5
Ash Green Warwks 59 M8
Ashill Devon 10 B2
Ashill Norfk 76 B11
Ashill Somset 19 K11
Ashingdon Essex 38 E3
Ashington Nthumb 113 L3
Ashington Poole 12 H5
Ashington Somset 19 Q10
Ashington W Susx 24 D7
Ashkirk Border 117 P6
Ashlett Hants 14 E6
Ashleworth Gloucs 46 F9
Ashleworth Quay Gloucs 46 F9
Ashley Cambs 63 L8
Ashley Ches E 82 G8
Ashley Devon 17 M9
Ashley Dorset 13 K4
Ashley Gloucs 32 H6
Ashley Hants 13 N5
Ashley Hants 22 C8
Ashley Kent 27 P2
Ashley Nhants 60 G2
Ashley Staffs 70 D7
Ashley Wilts 32 F11
Ashley Green Bucks 35 Q3
Ashleyhay Derbys 71 P4
Ashley Heath Dorset 13 K4
Ashley Moor Herefs 56 H11
Ash Magna Shrops 69 Q7
Ashmansworth Hants 22 D3
Ashmansworthy Devon 16 E8
Ashmead Green Gloucs 32 E5
Ashmill Devon 5 P2
Ash Mill Devon 17 P7
Ashmore Dorset 20 H11
Ashmore Green W Berk 34 F11
Ashorne Warwks 48 B3
Ashover Derbys 84 D8
Ashover Hay Derbys 84 D8
Ashow Warwks 59 M10
Ash Parva Shrops 69 Q7
Ashperton Herefs 46 B6
Ashprington Devon 7 L7
Ash Priors Somset 18 G9
Ashreigney Devon 17 L9
Ash Street Suffk 52 H2
Ashtead Surrey 36 E9
Ash Thomas Devon 9 P2
Ashton C Pete 74 B9
Ashton Ches W 81 Q11
Ashton Cnwll 2 G8
Ashton Devon 9 L8
Ashton Hants 22 F11
Ashton Herefs 45 Q2
Ashton Inver 124 G2
Ashton Nhants 49 L5
Ashton Nhants 61 N3
Ashton Somset 19 M5
Ashton Common Wilts 20 G3
Ashton Hill Wilts 20 H3
Ashton-in-Makerfield Wigan 82 C5
Ashton Keynes Wilts 33 K6
Ashton under Hill Worcs 47 J7
Ashton-under-Lyne Tamesd 83 K5
Ashton upon Mersey Traffd 82 G6
Ashurst Hants 13 P2
Ashurst Kent 25 M3
Ashurst Lancs 88 F9
Ashurst W Susx 24 E7
Ashurstwood W Susx 25 K3
Ash Vale Surrey 23 N4
Ashwater Devon 5 P2
Ashwell Herts 50 G3
Ashwell Rutlnd 73 M8
Ashwell Somset 19 L11
Ashwell End Herts 50 G2
Ashwellthorpe Norfk 64 G2
Ashwick Somset 20 B5
Ashwicken Norfk 75 P7
Ashwood Staffs 58 C7
Askam in Furness Cumb 94 E5
Askern Donc 91 P8
Askerswell Dorset 11 L6
Askett Bucks 35 M3
Askham Cumb 101 P6
Askham Notts 85 M6
Askham Bryan C York 98 B11
Askham Richard C York 98 A11
Asknish Ag & B 131 J9
Askrigg N York 96 D2
Askwith N York 97 J11
Aslackby Lincs 74 A4
Aslacton Norfk 64 H3
Aslockton Notts 73 J3
Asney Somset 19 N7
Aspall Suffk 64 H9
Aspatria Cumb 100 F2
Aspenden Herts 51 J5
Aspenshaw Derbys 83 M7
Asperton Lincs 74 E3
Aspley Staffs 70 E8
Aspley Guise C Beds 49 P7
Aspley Heath C Beds 49 P8
Aspley Heath Warwks 58 G10
Aspull Wigan 89 J9
Aspull Common Wigan 82 D5
Asselby E R Yk 92 B5
Asserby Lincs 87 N5
Asserby Turn Lincs 87 N5
Assington Suffk 52 F4
Assington Green Suffk 63 N10
Astbury Ches E 70 E2
Astcote Nhants 49 J4
Asterby Lincs 87 J5
Asterley Shrops 56 F3
Asterton Shrops 56 F6
Asthall Oxon 33 Q2
Asthall Leigh Oxon 34 B2
Astle Highld 162 G8
Astley Shrops 69 P11
Astley Warwks 59 M7
Astley Wigan 82 F4
Astley Worcs 57 P11
Astley Abbots Shrops 57 N5
Astley Bridge Bolton 89 L8
Astley Cross Worcs 57 Q11
Astley Green Wigan 82 F5
Aston Birm 58 G7
Aston Ches E 69 R5
Aston Ches W 82 C9
Aston Derbys 83 Q8
Aston Flints 81 L11
Aston Herefs 45 P2
Aston Herts 50 G6
Aston Oxon 34 B4
Aston Rothm 84 G3
Aston Shrops 57 Q6
Aston Shrops 69 P9
Aston Staffs 70 D6
Aston Staffs 70 F10
Aston Wokham 35 L8
Aston Wrekin 57 L3
Aston Abbotts Bucks 49 M10
Aston Botterell Shrops 57 L8
Aston-by-Stone Staffs 70 G8
Aston Cantlow Warwks 47 M2
Aston Clinton Bucks 35 N2
Aston Crews Herefs 46 C10
Aston Cross Gloucs 46 H8
Aston End Herts 50 G6
Aston-Eyre Shrops 57 M6
Aston Fields Worcs 58 E11
Aston Flamville Leics 59 Q6
Aston Heath Ches W 82 C9
Aston Ingham Herefs 46 C10
Aston juxta Mondrum Ches E 70 A3
Aston le Walls Nhants 48 E4
Aston Magna Gloucs 47 N7
Aston Munslow Shrops 57 J7
Aston on Clun Shrops 56 F8
Aston Pigott Shrops 56 E3
Aston Rogers Shrops 56 E3
Aston Rowant Oxon 35 K5
Aston Sandford Bucks 35 L3
Aston Somerville Worcs 47 K7
Aston-sub-Edge Gloucs 47 M6
Aston Tirrold Oxon 34 G7
Aston-upon-Trent Derbys 72 C5
Aston Upthorpe Oxon 34 G7
Astrop Nhants 48 F7
Astrope Herts 35 N2
Astwick C Beds 50 F3
Astwith Derbys 84 F8
Astwood M Keyn 49 Q5
Astwood Worcs 58 D11
Astwood Bank Worcs 47 K2
Aswarby Lincs 73 R3
Aswardby Lincs 87 L6
Atcham Shrops 57 J3
Atch Lench Worcs 47 K4
Athelhampton Dorset 12 C6
Athelington Suffk 65 J7
Athelney Somset 19 K9
Athelstaneford E Loth 128 E4
Atherfield Green IoW 14 E11
Atherington Devon 17 K7
Atherington W Susx 24 B10
Atherstone Somset 19 L11
Atherstone Warwks 59 M5
Atherstone on Stour Warwks 47 P4
Atherton Wigan 82 E4
Atley Hill N York 103 Q10
Atlow Derbys 71 N5
Attadale Highld 154 B10
Attenborough Notts 72 E4
Atterby Lincs 86 C2
Attercliffe Sheff 84 E3
Atterley Shrops 57 L5
Atterton Leics 72 B11
Attingham Park Shrops 57 J3
Attleborough Norfk 64 E2
Attleborough Warwks 59 N6
Attlebridge Norfk 76 G8
Attleton Green Suffk 63 M10
Atwick E R Yk 99 P10
Atworth Wilts 32 G11
Auberrow Herefs 45 P5
Aubourn Lincs 86 B8
Auchbreck Moray 149 N2
Auchedly Abers 159 L11
Auchenblae Abers 143 N2
Auchenbowie Stirlg 133 M10
Auchencairn D & G 108 G10
Auchencairn D & G 109 L4
Auchencairn N Ayrs 121 K6
Auchencrow Border 129 M7
Auchendinny Mdloth 127 P5
Auchengray S Lans 126 H7
Auchenhalrig Moray 157 R5
Auchenheath S Lans 126 E9
Auchenhessnane D & G 115 R8
Auchenlochan Ag & B 124 B3
Auchenmade N Ayrs 125 K8
Auchenmalg D & G 106 H7
Auchentiber N Ayrs 125 K8
Auchindrain Ag & B 131 L7
Auchindrean Highld 161 K10
Auchininna Abers 158 G8
Auchinleck E Ayrs 115 L3
Auchinloch N Lans 126 B3
Auchinstarry N Lans 126 C2
Auchintore Highld 139 K3
Auchiries Abers 159 Q10
Auchlean Highld 148 F8
Auchlee Abers 151 M8
Auchleven Abers 150 G3
Auchlochan S Lans 126 E10
Auchlossan Abers 150 F7
Auchlyne Stirlg 132 G2
Auchmillan E Ayrs 115 K2
Auchmithie Angus 143 M9
Auchmuirbridge Fife 134 G7
Auchnacree Angus 142 H5
Auchnagatt Abers 159 N9
Auchnarrow Moray 149 N3
Auchnotteroch D & G 106 C5
Auchroisk Moray 157 Q7
Auchterarder P & K 133 Q5
Auchteraw Highld 147 K6
Auchterblair Highld 148 G3
Auchtercairn Highld 153 Q2
Auchterderran Fife 134 G8
Auchterhouse Angus 142 E10
Auchterless Abers 158 H9
Auchtermuchty Fife 134 G5
Auchterneed Highld 155 N6
Auchtertool Fife 134 G9
Auchtertyre Highld 145 P2
Auchtubh Stirlg 132 H3
Auckengill Highld 167 Q3
Auckley Donc 91 Q10
Audenshaw Tamesd 83 K5
Audlem Ches E 70 B6
Audley Staffs 70 D4
Audley End Essex 51 M3
Audley End Essex 52 D4
Audley End Suffk 64 B11
Audley End House & Gardens Essex 51 M3
Audmore Staffs 70 E10
Audnam Dudley 58 C7
Aughertree Cumb 101 J3
Aughton E R Yk 92 B3
Aughton Lancs 88 D9
Aughton Lancs 95 M7
Aughton Rothm 84 G3
Aughton Wilts 21 P3
Aughton Park Lancs 88 E9
Auldearn Highld 156 G6
Aulden Herefs 45 P4
Auldgirth D & G 109 K3
Auldhouse S Lans 125 Q7
Ault a' chruinn Highld 146 A3
Aultbea Highld 160 D9
Aultgrishin Highld 160 A9
Aultguish Inn Highld 155 L3
Ault Hucknall Derbys 84 G7
Aultmore Moray 158 B7
Aultnagoire Highld 147 N3
Aultnamain Inn Highld 162 F10
Aunby Lincs 73 Q8
Aunk Devon 9 P4
Aunsby Lincs 73 Q3
Aust S Glos 31 Q7
Austendike Lincs 74 E6
Austerfield Donc 85 L2
Austerlands Oldham 90 B9
Austhorpe Leeds 91 K4
Austonley Kirk 90 E9
Austrey Warwks 59 L3
Austwick N York 95 R7
Authorpe Lincs 87 L4
Authorpe Row Lincs 87 P6
Avebury Wilts 33 M11
Avebury Wilts 33 M11
Avebury Trusloe Wilts 33 L11
Aveley Thurr 37 N4
Avening Gloucs 32 G5
Averham Notts 85 N10
Aveton Gifford Devon 6 H9
Aviemore Highld 148 F5
Avington W Berk 34 C11
Avoch Highld 156 C6
Avon Hants 13 K5
Avonbridge Falk 126 G3
Avon Dassett Warwks 48 D4
Avonmouth Bristl 31 P9
Avonwick Devon 7 J7
Awbridge Hants 22 B10
Awkley S Glos 31 Q7
Awliscombe Devon 10 C4
Awre Gloucs 32 D3
Awsworth Notts 72 D2
Axborough Worcs 58 C9
Axbridge Somset 19 M4
Axford Hants 22 H6
Axford Wilts 33 P10
Axminster Devon 10 F5
Axmouth Devon 10 F6
Axton Flints 80 G8
Aycliffe Dur 103 Q6
Aydon Nthumb 112 F7
Aylburton Gloucs 32 B4
Ayle Nthumb 111 P11
Aylesbeare Devon 9 P6
Aylesbury Bucks 35 M2
Aylesby NE Lin 93 M9
Aylesford Kent 38 B10
Aylesham Kent 39 M11
Aylestone C Leic 72 F10
Aylestone Park C Leic 72 F10
Aylmerton Norfk 76 H4
Aylsham Norfk 76 H6
Aylton Herefs 46 C7
Aylworth Gloucs 47 M10
Aymestrey Herefs 56 G11
Aynho Nhants 48 F8
Ayot Green Herts 50 F8
Ayot St Lawrence Herts 50 E7
Ayot St Peter Herts 50 F7
Ayr S Ayrs 114 F3
Aysgarth N York 96 F3
Ayshford Devon 18 D11
Ayside Cumb 94 H4
Ayston Rutlnd 73 M10
Aythorpe Roding Essex 51 N7
Ayton Border 129 N7
Azerley N York 97 L6

B

Babbacombe Torbay 7 N5
Babbington Notts 72 D2
Babbinswood Shrops 69 K9
Babbs Green Herts 51 J7
Babcary Somset 19 Q9
Babel Carmth 44 A7
Babel Green Suffk 63 M11
Babell Flints 80 H10

Babeny - Beardwood 263

Babeny Devon 8 G9
Bablock Hythe Oxon 34 D4
Babraham Cambs 62 H10
Babworth Notts 85 L4
Bachau IoA 78 G8
Bache Shrops 56 H8
Bacheldre Powys 56 C6
Bachelor's Bump E Susx 26 D9
Backaland Ork 169 e3
Backbarrow Cumb 94 H4
Backe Carmth 41 Q7
Backfolds Abers 159 P7
Backford Ches W 81 M10
Backford Cross Ches W 81 M10
Backies Highld 163 J6
Back of Keppoch Highld 145 L10
Back o' th' Brook Staffs 71 K4
Back Street Suffk 63 M9
Backwell N Som 31 N11
Backworth N Tyne 113 M6
Bacon's End Solhll 59 J7
Baconsthorpe Norfk 76 G4
Bacton Herefs 45 M8
Bacton Norfk 77 L5
Bacton Suffk 64 F8
Bacton Green Suffk 64 E8
Bacup Lancs 89 P6
Badachro Highld 153 P3
Badbury Swindn 33 N8
Badby Nhants 60 C9
Badcall Highld 164 E8
Badcall Highld 164 F5
Badcaul Highld 160 G8
Baddeley Edge C Stke 70 G4
Baddeley Green C Stke 70 G4
Baddesley Clinton Warwks 59 K10
Baddesley Ensor Warwks 59 L5
Baddidarrach Highld 160 H2
Baddinsgill Border 127 L7
Badenscoth Abers 158 G10
Badentarbet Highld 160 G5
Badenyon Abers 149 Q4
Badgall Cnwll 5 L4
Badgeney Cambs 74 H11
Badger Shrops 57 P5
Badger's Cross Cnwll 2 D7
Badgers Mount Kent 37 L8
Badgeworth Gloucs 46 H11
Badgworth Somset 19 L4
Badharlick Cnwll 5 M4
Badicaul Highld 145 N2
Badingham Suffk 65 L8
Badlesmere Kent 38 H11
Badlieu Border 116 F7
Badlipster Highld 167 M7
Badluarach Highld 160 F8
Badninish Highld 162 H8
Badrallach Highld 160 H8
Badsey Worcs 47 L6
Badshot Lea Surrey 23 N5
Badsworth Wakefd 91 M8
Badwell Ash Suffk 64 D8
Badwell Green Suffk 64 E8
Bagber Dorset 12 C2
Bagby N York 97 Q4
Bag Enderby Lincs 87 L6
Bagendon Gloucs 33 K3
Bagginswood Shrops 57 M8
Baggrow Cumb 100 G2
Bagh a Chaisteil W Isls 168 b18
Bagham Kent 39 J11
Bagh a Tuath W Isls 168 c17
Bagillt Flints 81 J9
Baginton Warwks 59 M10
Baglan Neath 29 K6
Bagley Leeds 90 G3
Bagley Shrops 69 M9
Bagley Somset 19 N5
Bagmore Hants 23 J6
Bagnall Staffs 70 G4
Bagnor W Berk 34 E11
Bagshot Surrey 23 P2
Bagshot Wilts 34 B11
Bagstone S Glos 32 C7
Bagthorpe Notts 84 G10
Bagworth Leics 72 C9
Bagwy Llydiart Herefs 45 N9
Baildon C Brad 90 F3
Baildon Green C Brad 90 E3
Baile Ailein W Isls 168 h5
Baile a Mhanaich W Isls 168 c12
Baile Mor Ag & B 136 H11
Bailey Green Hants 23 J9
Baileyhead Cumb 111 K5
Bailiff Bridge Calder 90 E5
Baillieston C Glas 126 B5
Bailrigg Lancs 95 K9
Bainbridge N York 96 D2
Bainshole Abers 158 F10
Bainton C Pete 74 A9
Bainton E R Yk 99 K10
Bainton Oxon 48 G9
Baintown Fife 135 K7
Bairnkine Border 118 C7
Baker's End Herts 51 J7
Baker Street Thurr 37 P4
Bakewell Derbys 84 B7
Bala Gwynd 68 B7
Balallan W Isls 168 h5
Balbeg Highld 155 M11
Balbeggie P & K 134 F2
Balblair Highld 155 P8
Balblair Highld 156 C4
Balby Donc 91 P10
Balcary D & G 108 H11
Balchraggan Highld 155 P9
Balchreick Highld 164 E4
Balcombe W Susx 24 H4
Balcombe Lane W Susx 24 H4
Balcomie Links Fife 135 Q6
Baldersby N York 97 N5
Baldersby St James N York 97 N5
Balderstone Lancs 89 J4
Balderstone Rochdl 89 Q8
Balderton Notts 85 P10
Baldhu Cnwll 3 K5
Baldinnie Fife 135 L5
Baldinnies P & K 134 C4
Baldock Herts 50 F4
Baldock Services Herts 50 F3
Baldovie C Dund 142 H11
Baldrine IoM 80 f5
Baldslow E Susx 26 D9
Baldwin IoM 80 e5
Baldwinholme Cumb 110 F10
Baldwin's Gate Staffs 70 D7
Baldwin's Hill W Susx 25 J3
Bale Norfk 76 E4
Baledgarno P & K 142 D11
Balemartine Ag & B 136 B7
Balerno C Edin 127 M4
Balfarg Fife 134 H7
Balfield Angus 143 J4
Balfour Ork 169 d5
Balfron Stirlg 132 G10
Balgaveny Abers 158 G9
Balgonar Fife 134 C9
Balgowan D & G 106 F9
Balgowan Highld 147 Q9
Balgown Highld 152 F4
Balgracie D & G 106 C5
Balgray S Lans 116 B6
Balham Gt Lon 36 G6
Balhary P & K 142 D8
Balholmie P & K 142 A10
Baligill Highld 166 E3
Balintore Angus 142 D6
Balintore Highld 156 F2
Balintraid Highld 156 C3
Balivanich W Isls 168 c12
Balk N York 97 Q4
Balkeerie Angus 142 E9
Balkholme E R Yk 92 C5
Ballabeg IoM 80 c7
Ballachulish Highld 139 K6
Ballafesson IoM 80 b7
Ballajora IoM 80 g3
Ballakilpheric IoM 80 b7
Ballamodha IoM 80 c7
Ballanlay Ag & B 124 C5
Ballantrae S Ayrs 114 A11
Ballards Gore Essex 38 F3
Ballards Green Warwks 59 L6
Ballasalla IoM 80 c7
Ballater Abers 150 B8
Ballaugh IoM 80 d3
Ballchraggan Highld 156 D2
Ballencrieff E Loth 128 D4
Ballevullin Ag & B 136 B6
Ball Green C Stke 70 F4
Ball Haye Green Staffs 70 H3
Ball Hill Hants 22 D2
Ballidon Derbys 71 N4
Balliekine N Ayrs 120 G4
Balliemore Ag & B 131 N8
Balligmorrie S Ayrs 114 D9
Ballimore Stirlg 132 G4
Ballindalloch Moray 157 M10
Ballindean P & K 134 H2
Ballingdon Suffk 52 E3
Ballinger Common Bucks 35 P4
Ballingham Herefs 46 A8
Ballingry Fife 134 F8
Ballinluig P & K 141 N7
Ballinshoe Angus 142 G7
Ballintuim P & K 141 R6
Balloch Highld 156 C8
Balloch N Lans 126 C3
Balloch P & K 133 N4
Balloch S Ayrs 114 F8
Balloch W Duns 132 D11
Balls Cross W Susx 23 Q9
Balls Green E Susx 25 L3
Ball's Green Gloucs 32 G5
Ballygown Ag & B 137 L7
Ballygrant Ag & B 122 E6
Ballyhaugh Ag & B 136 F4
Balmacara Highld 145 P2
Balmaclellan D & G 108 E5
Balmae D & G 108 E12
Balmaha Stirlg 132 E9
Balmalcolm Fife 135 J6
Balmangan D & G 108 D11
Balmedie Abers 151 P4
Balmer Heath Shrops 69 M8
Balmerino Fife 135 K3
Balmerlawn Hants 13 P4
Balmichael N Ayrs 120 H5
Balmore E Duns 125 P3
Balmuchy Highld 163 K11
Balmule Fife 134 G10
Balmullo Fife 135 L3
Balnacoil Lodge Highld 163 J4
Balnacra Highld 154 C8
Balnacroft Abers 149 P9
Balnafoich Highld 156 B10
Balnaguard P & K 141 M7
Balnahard Ag & B 136 c2
Balnahard Ag & B 137 M9
Balnain Highld 155 M11
Balnakeil Highld 165 J3
Balne N York 91 P7
Balquharn P & K 141 P10
Balquhidder Stirlg 132 G3
Balsall Common Solhll 59 K9
Balsall Heath Birm 58 G8
Balsall Street Solhll 59 K9
Balscote Oxon 48 C6
Balsham Cambs 63 J10
Baltasound Shet 169 t3
Balterley Staffs 70 D4
Balterley Green Staffs 70 D4
Balterley Heath Staffs 70 C4
Baltersan D & G 107 M5
Baltonsborough Somset 19 P8
Balvicar Ag & B 130 F4
Balvraid Highld 145 P4
Balvraid Highld 156 E11
Balwest Cnwll 2 F7
Bamber Bridge Lancs 88 H5
Bamber's Green Essex 51 N6
Bamburgh Nthumb 119 N4
Bamburgh Castle Nthumb 119 N3
Bamford Derbys 84 B4
Bamford Rochdl 89 P8
Bampton Cumb 101 P7
Bampton Devon 18 C10
Bampton Oxon 34 B4
Bampton Grange Cumb 101 P7
Banavie Highld 139 L2
Banbury Oxon 48 E6
Banbury Crematorium Oxon 48 E6
Bancffosfelen Carmth 28 E2
Banchory Abers 151 H8
Banchory-Devenick Abers 151 N7
Bancycapel Carmth 28 D2
Bancyfelin Carmth 42 F11
Banc-y-ffordd Carmth 42 H7
Bandirran P & K 142 C11
Bandrake Head Cumb 94 G3
Banff Abers 158 G5
Bangor Gwynd 79 K10
Bangor Crematorium Gwynd 79 K10
Bangor-on-Dee Wrexhm 69 L5
Bangors Cnwll 5 L2
Bangor's Green Lancs 88 D9
Bangrove Suffk 64 C7
Banham Norfk 64 F4
Bank Hants 13 N3
Bankend D & G 109 M7
Bankfoot P & K 141 Q10
Bankglen E Ayrs 115 L5
Bank Ground Cumb 101 K11
Bankhead C Aber 151 N6
Bankhead S Lans 116 D2
Bank Newton N York 96 D10
Banknock Falk 126 D2
Banks Cumb 111 L8
Banks Lancs 88 D6
Banks Green Worcs 58 E11
Bankshill D & G 110 C4
Bank Street Worcs 46 B2
Bank Top Calder 90 E6
Bank Top Lancs 88 G9
Banningham Norfk 77 J6
Bannister Green Essex 51 Q6
Bannockburn Stirlg 133 N9
Banstead Surrey 36 G9
Bantham Devon 6 H10
Banton N Lans 126 C2
Banwell N Som 19 L3
Bapchild Kent 38 F9
Bapton Wilts 21 J7
Barabhas W Isls 168 i3
Barassie S Ayrs 125 J11
Barbaraville Highld 156 C3
Barber Booth Derbys 83 P8
Barber Green Cumb 94 H4
Barbieston S Ayrs 114 H4
Barbon Cumb 95 N4
Barbridge Ches E 69 R3
Barbrook Devon 17 N2
Barby Nhants 60 B6
Barcaldine Ag & B 138 H9
Barcheston Warwks 47 Q7
Barclose Cumb 110 H8
Barcombe E Susx 25 K8
Barcombe Cross E Susx 25 K7
Barcroft C Brad 90 C3
Barden N York 96 H2
Barden Park Kent 37 N11
Bardfield End Green Essex 51 P4
Bardfield Saling Essex 51 Q5
Bardney Lincs 86 F7
Bardon Leics 72 C8
Bardon Mill Nthumb 111 Q8
Bardowie E Duns 125 P3
Bardown E Susx 25 Q5
Bardrainney Inver 125 J3
Bardsea Cumb 94 G6
Bardsey Leeds 91 K2
Bardsey Island Gwynd 66 A10
Bardsley Oldham 83 K4
Bardwell Suffk 64 C7
Bare Lancs 95 K8
Bareppa Cnwll 3 K8
Barfad D & G 107 K4
Barford Norfk 76 G10
Barford Warwks 47 Q2
Barford St John Oxon 48 D8
Barford St Martin Wilts 21 L8
Barford St Michael Oxon 48 D8
Barfrestone Kent 39 N11
Bargate Derbys 84 E11
Bargeddie N Lans 126 B5
Bargoed Caerph 30 G5
Bargrennan D & G 107 L2
Barham Cambs 61 P5
Barham Kent 39 M11
Barham Suffk 64 G11
Barham Crematorium Kent 27 M2
Bar Hill Cambs 62 E8
Barholm Lincs 74 A8
Barkby Leics 72 G9
Barkby Thorpe Leics 72 G9
Barkers Green Shrops 69 P9
Barkestone-le-Vale Leics 73 K4
Barkham Wokham 35 L11
Barking Gt Lon 37 K4
Barking Suffk 64 F11
Barkingside Gt Lon 37 K3
Barking Tye Suffk 64 F11
Barkisland Calder 90 D7
Barkla Shop Cnwll 3 J3
Barkston Lincs 73 N2
Barkston Ash N York 91 M3
Barkway Herts 51 J3
Barlanark C Glas 126 B5
Barlaston Staffs 70 F7
Barlavington W Susx 23 Q11
Barlborough Derbys 84 G5
Barlby N York 91 Q4
Barlestone Leics 72 C9
Barley Herts 51 K3
Barley Lancs 89 N2
Barleycroft End Herts 51 K5
Barley Hole Rothm 91 K11
Barleythorpe Rutlnd 73 L9
Barling Essex 38 F4
Barlings Lincs 86 E6
Barlochan D & G 108 H9
Barlow Derbys 84 D6
Barlow Gatesd 113 J8
Barlow N York 91 Q5
Barmby Moor E R Yk 98 F11
Barmby on the Marsh E R Yk 92 A5
Barmer Norfk 75 R4
Barming Heath Kent 38 B10
Barmollack Ag & B 120 F3
Barmouth Gwynd 67 L11
Barmpton Darltn 104 B7
Barmston E R Yk 99 P9
Barnaby Green Suffk 65 P5
Barnacarry Ag & B 131 L9
Barnack C Pete 74 A9
Barnacle Warwks 59 N8
Barnard Castle Dur 103 L7
Barnard Gate Oxon 34 D2
Barnardiston Suffk 63 M11
Barnbarroch D & G 108 H9
Barnburgh Donc 91 M10
Barnby Suffk 65 P4
Barnby Dun Donc 91 Q9
Barnby in the Willows Notts 85 Q10
Barnby Moor Notts 85 L4
Barncorkrie D & G 106 E10
Barnehurst Gt Lon 37 L5
Barnes Gt Lon 36 F5
Barnes Street Kent 37 P11
Barnet Gt Lon 50 F11
Barnetby le Wold N Linc 93 J9
Barnet Gate Gt Lon 50 F11
Barney Norfk 76 D5
Barnham Suffk 64 B6
Barnham W Susx 15 Q6
Barnham Broom Norfk 76 F10
Barnhead Angus 143 M6
Barnhill C Dund 142 H11
Barnhill Ches W 69 N4
Barnhill Moray 157 L6
Barnhills D & G 106 C3
Barningham Dur 103 L8
Barningham Suffk 64 D6
Barnoldby le Beck NE Lin 93 M10
Barnoldswick Lancs 96 C11
Barnsdale Bar Donc 91 N8
Barns Green W Susx 24 D5
Barnsley Barns 91 J9
Barnsley Gloucs 33 L4
Barnsley Crematorium Barns 91 K9
Barnsole Kent 39 N10
Barnstaple Devon 17 K5
Barnston Essex 51 P7
Barnston Wirral 81 K8
Barnstone Notts 73 J3
Barnt Green Worcs 58 F10
Barnton C Edin 127 M3
Barnton Ches W 82 D10
Barnwell All Saints Nhants 61 M4
Barnwell St Andrew Nhants 61 N4
Barnwood Gloucs 46 G11
Baron's Cross Herefs 45 P3
Baronwood Cumb 101 P2
Barr S Ayrs 114 E9
Barra W Isls 168 b17
Barra Airport W Isls 168 c17
Barrachan D & G 107 L8
Barraigh W Isls 168 b17
Barrapoll Ag & B 136 A7
Barras Cumb 102 F8
Barrasford Nthumb 112 D6
Barregarrow IoM 80 d4
Barrets Green Ches E 69 Q3
Barrhead E Rens 125 M6
Barrhill S Ayrs 114 D11
Barrington Cambs 62 E11
Barrington Somset 19 L11
Barripper Cnwll 2 G6
Barrmill N Ayrs 125 K7
Barrock Highld 167 N2
Barrow Gloucs 46 G10
Barrow Lancs 89 L3
Barrow Rutlnd 73 M7
Barrow Shrops 57 M4
Barrow Somset 20 D8
Barrow Suffk 63 N8
Barroway Drove Norfk 75 L10
Barrow Bridge Bolton 89 K8
Barrow Burn Nthumb 118 G8
Barrowby Lincs 73 M3
Barrowden Rutlnd 73 N10
Barrowford Lancs 89 P3
Barrow Gurney N Som 31 P11
Barrow Haven N Linc 93 J6
Barrow Hill Derbys 84 F5
Barrow-in-Furness Cumb 94 E7
Barrow Island Cumb 94 D7
Barrow Nook Lancs 81 N4
Barrow's Green Ches E 70 B3
Barrow Street Wilts 20 F8
Barrow-upon-Humber N Linc 93 J6
Barrow upon Soar Leics 72 F7
Barrow upon Trent Derbys 72 B5
Barrow Vale BaNES 20 B2
Barry Angus 143 J11
Barry V Glam 30 F11
Barry Island V Glam 30 F11
Barsby Leics 72 H8
Barsham Suffk 65 M4
Barston Solhll 59 K9
Bartestree Herefs 45 R6
Barthol Chapel Abers 159 K11
Bartholomew Green Essex 52 B7
Barthomley Ches E 70 D4
Bartley Hants 13 P2
Bartley Green Birm 58 F8
Bartlow Cambs 63 J11
Barton Cambs 62 F9
Barton Ches W 69 M4
Barton Gloucs 47 L9
Barton Herefs 45 K3
Barton Lancs 88 D9
Barton Lancs 88 G3
Barton N York 103 P9
Barton Oxon 34 G3
Barton Torbay 7 N5
Barton Warwks 47 M4
Barton Bendish Norfk 75 P9
Barton End Gloucs 32 F5
Barton Green Staffs 71 M11
Barton Hartshorn Bucks 48 H8
Barton Hill N York 98 E8
Barton in Fabis Notts 72 E4
Barton in the Beans Leics 72 B9
Barton-le-Clay C Beds 50 C4
Barton-le-Street N York 98 E6
Barton-le-Willows N York 98 E8
Barton Mills Suffk 63 M6
Barton-on-Sea Hants 13 M6
Barton-on-the-Heath Warwks 47 Q8
Barton St David Somset 19 P8
Barton Seagrave Nhants 61 J5
Barton Stacey Hants 22 D6
Barton Town Devon 17 M3
Barton Turf Norfk 77 M7
Barton-under-Needwood Staffs 71 M11
Barton-upon-Humber N Linc 92 H6
Barton upon Irwell Salfd 82 G5
Barton Waterside N Linc 92 H6
Barugh Barns 91 J9
Barugh Green Barns 91 J9
Barvas W Isls 168 i3
Barway Cambs 63 J5
Barwell Leics 72 C11
Barwick Devon 17 K10
Barwick Herts 51 J7
Barwick Somset 11 M2
Barwick in Elmet Leeds 91 L3
Baschurch Shrops 69 M10
Bascote Warwks 48 D2
Bascote Heath Warwks 48 C2
Base Green Suffk 64 E9
Basford Green Staffs 70 H4
Bashall Eaves Lancs 89 K2
Bashall Town Lancs 89 L2
Bashley Hants 13 M5
Basildon Essex 38 B4
Basildon & District Crematorium Essex 38 C4
Basingstoke Hants 22 H4
Basingstoke Crematorium Hants 22 G5
Baslow Derbys 84 C6
Bason Bridge Somset 19 K5
Bassaleg Newpt 31 J7
Bassendean Border 128 G10
Bassenthwaite Cumb 100 H4
Bassett C Sotn 22 D11
Bassingbourn Cambs 50 H2
Bassingfield Notts 72 G3
Bassingham Lincs 86 B9
Bassingthorpe Lincs 73 P5
Bassus Green Herts 50 H5
Basted Kent 37 P9
Baston Lincs 74 B8
Bastwick Norfk 77 N8
Batch Somset 19 K3
Batchworth Herts 36 C2
Batchworth Heath Herts 36 C2
Batcombe Dorset 11 N4
Batcombe Somset 20 C7
Bate Heath Ches E 82 E9
Batford Herts 50 D7
Bath BaNES 20 D2
Bathampton BaNES 32 E11
Bath, City of BaNES 20 E2
Bathealton Somset 18 E10
Batheaston BaNES 32 E11
Bathford BaNES 32 E11
Bathgate W Loth 126 H4
Bathley Notts 85 N9
Bathpool Cnwll 5 M7
Bathpool Somset 19 J9
Bath Side Essex 53 N5
Bathville W Loth 126 G4
Bathway Somset 19 Q4
Batley Kirk 90 G6
Batsford Gloucs 47 N8
Batson Devon 7 J11
Battersby N York 104 G9
Battersea Gt Lon 36 G5
Battisborough Cross Devon 6 F9
Battisford Suffk 64 F11
Battisford Tye Suffk 64 E11
Battle E Susx 26 C8
Battle Powys 44 E8
Battleborough Somset 19 K4
Battledown Gloucs 47 J10
Battledykes Angus 142 H6
Battlefield Shrops 69 P11
Battlesbridge Essex 38 C3
Battlesden C Beds 49 Q9
Battleton Somset 18 B9
Battlies Green Suffk 64 C9
Battramsley Cross Hants 13 P5
Batt's Corner Hants 23 M6
Baughton Worcs 46 G6
Baughurst Hants 22 G2
Baulds Abers 150 G9
Baulking Oxon 34 B6
Baumber Lincs 86 H6
Baunton Gloucs 33 K4
Baveney Wood Shrops 57 M9
Baverstock Wilts 21 K8
Bawburgh Norfk 76 H10
Bawdeswell Norfk 76 E7
Bawdrip Somset 19 K7
Bawdsey Suffk 53 P3
Bawsey Norfk 75 N6
Bawtry Donc 85 K2
Baxenden Lancs 89 M5
Baxterley Warwks 59 L5
Baxter's Green Suffk 63 N9
Bay Highld 152 D7
Bayble W Isls 168 k4
Baybridge Hants 22 F10
Baybridge Nthumb 112 E10
Baycliff Cumb 94 F6
Baydon Wilts 33 Q9
Bayford Herts 50 H9
Bayford Somset 20 D9
Bayhead W Isls 168 c11
Bay Horse Lancs 95 K10
Bayley's Hill Kent 37 M10
Baylham Suffk 64 G11
Baynard's Green Oxon 48 F9
Baysdale Abbey N York 104 H9
Baysham Herefs 45 R9
Bayston Hill Shrops 56 H3
Baythorne End Essex 52 B3
Bayton Worcs 57 M10
Bayton Common Worcs 57 N10
Bayworth Oxon 34 E4
Beach S Glos 32 D10
Beachampton Bucks 49 L7
Beachamwell Norfk 75 Q9
Beachley Gloucs 31 Q6
Beachy Head E Susx 25 N11
Beacon Devon 10 D3
Beacon End Essex 52 G7
Beacon Hill E Susx 25 M4
Beacon Hill Kent 26 D5
Beacon Hill Notts 85 P10
Beacon Hill Surrey 23 N7
Beacon's Bottom Bucks 35 L5
Beaconsfield Bucks 35 P6
Beaconsfield Services Bucks 35 Q7
Beadlam N York 98 D4
Beadlow C Beds 50 D3
Beadnell Nthumb 119 P5
Beaford Devon 17 K8
Beal N York 91 N5
Beal Nthumb 119 L2
Bealbury Cnwll 5 P8
Bealsmill Cnwll 5 P6
Beam Hill Staffs 71 N9
Beamhurst Staffs 71 K7
Beaminster Dorset 11 K4
Beamish Dur 113 K10
Beamish Museum Dur 113 K10
Beamsley N York 96 G10
Bean Kent 37 N6
Beanacre Wilts 32 H11
Beanley Nthumb 119 L7
Beardon Devon 8 D8
Beardwood Bl w D 89 K5

Catterlen - Church End

269

Catterlen Cumb 101 N4
Catterline Abers 143 R2
Catterton N York 97 R11
Catteshall Surrey 23 Q6
Catthorpe Leics 60 C5
Cattishall Suffk 64 B8
Cattistock Dorset 11 M5
Catton N York 97 N5
Catton Nthumb 112 B9
Catwick E R Yk 99 N11
Catworth Cambs 61 N6
Caudle Green Gloucs 32 H2
Caulcott C Beds 50 B2
Caulcott Oxon 48 F10
Cauldcots Angus 143 M8
Cauldhame Stirlg 133 J9
Cauldmill Border 117 Q7
Cauldon Staffs 71 K5
Cauldon Lowe Staffs 71 K5
Cauldwell Derbys 71 P11
Caulkerbush D & G 109 K9
Caulside D & G 110 H4
Caundle Marsh Dorset 11 P2
Caunsall Worcs 58 C8
Caunton Notts 85 M8
Causeway Hants 23 K10
Causeway End Cumb 95 K3
Causeway End D & G 107 M6
Causeway End Essex 51 Q7
Causewayend S Lans 116 E3
Causewayhead Cumb 109 P10
Causewayhead Stirlg 133 N8
Causeyend Abers 151 N4
Causey Park Nthumb 113 J2
Causey Park Bridge Nthumb 113 J2
Cavendish Suffk 63 P11
Cavenham Suffk 63 N6
Caversfield Oxon 48 G9
Caversham Readg 35 K10
Caverswall Staffs 70 H6
Caverton Mill Border 118 D5
Cavil E R Yk 92 C4
Cawdor Highld 156 E7
Cawkwell Lincs 87 J5
Cawood N York 91 P3
Cawsand Cnwll 6 C8
Cawston Norfk 76 G7
Cawston Warwks 59 Q10
Cawthorn N York 98 F3
Cawthorne Barns 90 H9
Cawton N York 98 C5
Caxton Cambs 62 D9
Caxton End Cambs 62 D9
Caxton Gibbet Cambs 62 C8
Caynham Shrops 57 K10
Caythorpe Lincs 86 B11
Caythorpe Notts 85 L11
Cayton N York 99 M4
Ceann a Bhaigh W Isls 168 c11
Ceannacroc Lodge Highld 146 G5
Cearsiadar W Isls 168 i5
Ceciliford Mons 31 P4
Cefn Newpt 31 J7
Cefn Berain Conwy 80 D11
Cefn-brith Conwy 68 B4
Cefn-bryn-brain Carmth 29 K2
Cefn Byrle Powys 29 M2
Cefn Canel Powys 68 H8
Cefn Coch Powys 68 F9
Cefn-coed-y-cymmer Myr Td 30 D3
Cefn Cribwr Brdgnd 29 N8
Cefn Cross Brdgnd 29 N8
Cefn-ddwysarn Gwynd 68 C7
Cefn-Einion Shrops 56 D7
Cefneithin Carmth 28 G2
Cefngorwydd Powys 44 C5
Cefn-mawr Wrexhm 69 J6
Cefnpennar Rhondd 30 D4
Cefn-y-bedd Flints 69 K3
Cefn-y-pant Carmth 41 N5
Ceint IoA 78 H9
Cellan Cerdgn 43 M5
Cellardyke Fife 135 P7
Cellarhead Staffs 70 H5
Celleron Cumb 101 N5
Celynen Caerph 30 H5
Cemaes IoA 78 F6
Cemmaes Powys 55 J3
Cemmaes Road Powys 55 J4
Cenarth Cerdgn 41 Q2
Cerbyd Pembks 40 F5
Ceres Fife 135 L5
Cerne Abbas Dorset 11 P4
Cerney Wick Gloucs 33 L5
Cerrigceinwen IoA 78 G10
Cerrigydrudion Conwy 68 C5
Cess Norfk 77 N8
Ceunant Gwynd 67 J2
Chaceley Gloucs 46 G8
Chacewater Cnwll 3 K5
Chackmore Bucks 49 J7
Chacombe Nhants 48 E6
Chadbury Worcs 47 K5
Chadderton Oldham 89 Q9
Chadderton Fold Oldham 89 Q9
Chaddesden C Derb 72 B3
Chaddesley Corbett Worcs 58 C10
Chaddlehanger Devon 8 C9
Chaddleworth W Berk 34 D9
Chadlington Oxon 48 B10
Chadshunt Warwks 48 B4
Chadwell Leics 73 K6
Chadwell Shrops 57 P2
Chadwell End Bed 61 N7
Chadwell Heath Gt Lon 37 L3
Chadwell St Mary Thurr 37 P5
Chadwick Worcs 58 B11
Chadwick End Solhll 59 K10
Chadwick Green St Hel 82 B5
Chaffcombe Somset 10 H2
Chafford Hundred Thurr 37 P5
Chagford Devon 8 H7
Chailey E Susx 25 J7
Chainbridge Cambs 74 H10
Chainhurst Kent 26 B2
Chalbury Dorset 12 H3
Chalbury Common Dorset 12 H3
Chaldon Surrey 36 H9
Chale IoW 14 E11
Chale Green IoW 14 E11
Chalfont Common Bucks 36 B2
Chalfont St Giles Bucks 35 Q6
Chalfont St Peter Bucks 36 B2
Chalford Gloucs 32 G4
Chalford Oxon 35 K4
Chalford Wilts 20 G4
Chalgrave C Beds 50 B5
Chalgrove Oxon 34 H5
Chalk Kent 37 Q6
Chalk End Essex 51 P8
Chalkhouse Green Oxon 35 K9
Chalkway Somset 10 H3
Chalkwell Kent 38 E9
Challaborough Devon 6 H10
Challacombe Devon 17 M3
Challoch D & G 107 L4
Challock Kent 38 H11
Chalmington Dorset 11 M4
Chalton C Beds 50 B5
Chalton C Beds 61 P10
Chalton Hants 23 K11
Chalvey Slough 35 Q9
Chalvington E Susx 25 M9
Chambers Green Kent 26 F3
Chandler's Cross Herts 50 C11
Chandlers Cross Worcs 46 E7
Chandler's Ford Hants 22 D11
Channel's End Bed 61 P9
Chanterlands Crematorium C KuH 93 J4
Chantry Somset 20 D5
Chantry Suffk 53 K3
Chapel Cumb 100 H4
Chapel Fife 134 H9
Chapel Allerton Leeds 91 J3
Chapel Allerton Somset 19 M4
Chapel Amble Cnwll 4 F6
Chapel Brampton Nhants 60 F7
Chapelbridge Cambs 62 C2
Chapel Chorlton Staffs 70 E7
Chapel Cross E Susx 25 P6
Chapel End Bed 61 P9
Chapel End C Beds 50 C2
Chapel End Cambs 61 P4
Chapel End Warwks 59 M6
Chapelend Way Essex 52 B4
Chapel-en-le-Frith Derbys 83 N8
Chapel Field Bury 89 M9
Chapelgate Lincs 74 H6
Chapel Green Warwks 48 E2
Chapel Green Warwks 59 L7
Chapel Haddlesey N York 91 P5
Chapelhall N Lans 126 D5
Chapel Hill Abers 159 Q10
Chapel Hill Lincs 86 H10
Chapel Hill Mons 31 P5
Chapel Hill N York 97 M11
Chapelhope Border 117 J7
Chapelknowe D & G 110 F6
Chapel Lawn Shrops 56 E9
Chapel-le-Dale N York 95 Q5
Chapel Leigh Somset 18 F9
Chapel Milton Derbys 83 N8
Chapel of Garioch Abers 151 J3
Chapel Rossan D & G 106 F9
Chapel Row E Susx 25 P8
Chapel Row Essex 52 C11
Chapel Row W Berk 34 G11
Chapels Cumb 94 E4
Chapel St Leonards Lincs 87 Q6
Chapel Stile Cumb 101 K9
Chapelton Angus 143 L8
Chapelton Devon 17 K6
Chapelton S Lans 126 B8
Chapeltown Bl w D 89 L7
Chapel Town Cnwll 4 D10
Chapeltown Moray 149 N3
Chapeltown Sheff 91 K11
Chapmanslade Wilts 20 F5
Chapmans Well Devon 5 P3
Chapmore End Herts 50 H7
Chappel Essex 52 E6
Charaton Cnwll 5 N8
Chard Somset 10 G3
Chard Junction Somset 10 G4
Chardleigh Green Somset 10 G2
Chardstock Devon 10 G4
Charfield S Glos 32 D6
Chargrove Gloucs 46 H11
Charing Kent 26 G2
Charing Crematorium Kent 26 G2
Charing Heath Kent 26 F2
Charing Hill Kent 38 G11
Charingworth Gloucs 47 N7
Charlbury Oxon 48 C11
Charlcombe BaNES 32 D11
Charlcutt Wilts 33 J9
Charlecote Warwks 47 Q3
Charlemont Sandw 58 F6
Charles Devon 17 M5
Charleshill Surrey 23 N6
Charleston Angus 142 F8
Charlestown C Aber 151 N7
Charlestown C Brad 90 F3
Charlestown Calder 90 B5
Charlestown Cnwll 3 Q3
Charlestown Cnwll 3 Q3
Charlestown Derbys 83 M6
Charlestown Dorset 11 P9
Charlestown Fife 134 D11
Charlestown Highld 153 Q3
Charlestown Highld 156 A8
Charlestown Salfd 82 H4
Charles Tye Suffk 64 E11
Charlesworth Derbys 83 M6
Charlinch Somset 18 H7
Charlottetown Fife 134 H5
Charlton Gt Lon 37 K5
Charlton Hants 22 C5
Charlton Herts 50 E5
Charlton Nhants 48 F7
Charlton Nthumb 112 B4
Charlton Oxon 34 D7
Charlton Somset 19 J9
Charlton Somset 20 B6
Charlton Somset 20 C4
Charlton Surrey 36 C7
Charlton W Susx 15 N4
Charlton Wilts 20 H10
Charlton Wilts 33 J7
Charlton Worcs 47 K5
Charlton Worcs 58 B10
Charlton Wrekin 57 K2
Charlton Abbots Gloucs 47 K10
Charlton Adam Somset 19 P9
Charlton All Saints Wilts 21 N10
Charlton Down Dorset 11 P5
Charlton Hill Shrops 57 K3
Charlton Horethorne Somset 20 C10
Charlton Kings Gloucs 47 J10
Charlton Mackrell Somset 19 P9
Charlton Marshall Dorset 12 F4
Charlton Musgrove Somset 20 D9
Charlton-on-Otmoor Oxon 48 G11
Charlton on the Hill Dorset 12 E4
Charlton St Peter Wilts 21 M3
Charlwood Hants 23 J8
Charlwood Surrey 24 F2
Charminster Dorset 11 P6
Charmouth Dorset 10 H6
Charndon Bucks 49 J10
Charney Bassett Oxon 34 C6
Charnock Green Lancs 88 H7
Charnock Richard Lancs 88 H7
Charnock Richard Crematorium Lancs 88 H7
Charnock Richard Services Lancs 88 G7
Charsfield Suffk 65 K10
Chart Corner Kent 38 C11
Charter Alley Hants 22 G3
Charterhall Border 129 K10
Charterhouse Somset 19 N3
Chartershall Stirlg 133 M9
Charterville Allotments Oxon 34 B2
Chartham Kent 39 K11
Chartham Hatch Kent 39 K10
Chart Hill Kent 26 C2
Chartridge Bucks 35 P4
Chart Sutton Kent 26 D2
Chartway Street Kent 38 D11
Charvil Wokham 35 L9
Charwelton Nhants 60 B9
Chase Terrace Staffs 58 F3
Chasetown Staffs 58 F3
Chastleton Oxon 47 P9
Chasty Devon 16 E11
Chatburn Lancs 89 M2
Chatcull Staffs 70 D8
Chatham Caerph 30 H7
Chatham Medway 38 C8
Chatham Green Essex 52 B8
Chathill Nthumb 119 N5
Chatley Worcs 46 G2
Chatsworth House Derbys 84 C6
Chattenden Medway 38 C7
Chatter End Essex 51 L5
Chatteris Cambs 62 E3
Chatterton Lancs 89 M7
Chattisham Suffk 53 J3
Chatto Border 118 E7
Chatton Nthumb 119 L5
Chaul End C Beds 50 C6
Chawleigh Devon 17 N9
Chawley Oxon 34 E4
Chawston Bed 61 Q9
Chawton Hants 23 K7
Chaxhill Gloucs 32 D2
Chazey Heath Oxon 35 J9
Cheadle Staffs 71 J6
Cheadle Stockp 83 J7
Cheadle Heath Stockp 83 J7
Cheadle Hulme Stockp 83 J7
Cheam Gt Lon 36 F8
Cheapside W & M 35 P11
Chearsley Bucks 35 K2
Chebsey Staffs 70 F9
Checkendon Oxon 35 J8
Checkley Ches E 70 C5
Checkley Herefs 46 A7
Checkley Staffs 71 J7
Checkley Green Ches E 70 C5
Chedburgh Suffk 63 N9
Cheddar Somset 19 N4
Cheddington Bucks 49 P11
Cheddleton Staffs 70 H4
Cheddleton Heath Staffs 70 H4
Cheddon Fitzpaine Somset 18 H9
Chedglow Wilts 32 H6
Chedgrave Norfk 65 M2
Chedington Dorset 11 K3
Chediston Suffk 65 M6
Chediston Green Suffk 65 M6
Chedworth Gloucs 33 L2
Chedzoy Somset 19 K7
Cheeseman's Green Kent 26 H4
Cheetham Hill Manch 82 H4
Cheldon Devon 8 H2
Chelford Ches E 82 H10
Chellaston C Derb 72 B4
Chellington Bed 61 L9
Chelmarsh Shrops 57 N7
Chelmick Shrops 56 H6
Chelmondiston Suffk 53 M4
Chelmorton Derbys 83 P11
Chelmsford Essex 52 B10
Chelmsford Crematorium Essex 51 Q9
Chelmsley Wood Solhll 59 J7
Chelsea Gt Lon 36 G5
Chelsfield Gt Lon 37 L8
Chelsham Surrey 37 J9
Chelston Somset 18 G10
Chelsworth Suffk 52 G2
Cheltenham Gloucs 46 H10
Cheltenham Crematorium Gloucs 47 J10
Chelveston Nhants 61 L7
Chelvey N Som 31 N11
Chelwood BaNES 20 B2
Chelwood Common E Susx 25 K5
Chelwood Gate E Susx 25 K4
Chelworth Wilts 33 J6
Chelworth Lower Green Wilts 33 L6
Chelworth Upper Green Wilts 33 L6
Cheney Longville Shrops 56 G8
Chenies Bucks 50 B11
Chepstow Mons 31 P6
Chequerbent Bolton 89 K9
Chequers Corner Norfk 75 J9
Cherhill Wilts 33 K10
Cherington Gloucs 32 H5
Cherington Warwks 47 Q7
Cheriton Devon 17 N2
Cheriton Hants 22 G9
Cheriton Kent 27 M4
Cheriton Swans 28 E6
Cheriton Bishop Devon 9 J6
Cheriton Fitzpaine Devon 9 L3
Cheriton or Stackpole Elidor Pembks 41 J11
Cherrington Wrekin 70 B11
Cherry Burton E R Yk 92 G2
Cherry Hinton Cambs 62 G9
Cherry Orchard Worcs 46 G4
Cherry Willingham Lincs 86 D6
Chertsey Surrey 36 B7
Cherwell Valley Services Oxon 48 F9
Cheselbourne Dorset 12 C5
Chesham Bucks 35 Q4
Chesham Bury 89 N8
Chesham Bois Bucks 35 Q5
Cheshire Farm Ice Cream Ches W 69 P3
Cheshunt Herts 51 J10
Chesil Beach Dorset 11 N9
Chesley Kent 38 E9
Cheslyn Hay Staffs 58 E3
Chessetts Wood Warwks 59 J10
Chessington Gt Lon 36 E8
Chessington World of Adventures Gt Lon 36 E8
Chester Ches W 81 N11
Chesterblade Somset 20 C6
Chester Crematorium Ches W 81 M11
Chesterfield Derbys 84 E6
Chesterfield Staffs 58 G3
Chesterfield Crematorium Derbys 84 E6
Chesterhill Mdloth 128 B7
Chester-le-Street Dur 113 L10
Chester Moor Dur 113 L11
Chesters Border 118 B6
Chesters Border 118 B8
Chester Services Ches W 81 P10
Chesterton Cambs 62 G8
Chesterton Cambs 74 B11
Chesterton Gloucs 33 K4
Chesterton Oxon 48 G10
Chesterton Shrops 57 P5
Chesterton Staffs 70 E5
Chesterton Green Warwks 48 C3
Chesterwood Nthumb 112 B7
Chester Zoo Ches W 81 N10
Chestfield Kent 39 K8
Chestnut Street Kent 38 E9
Cheston Devon 6 H7
Cheswardine Shrops 70 C8
Cheswick Nthumb 129 Q10
Cheswick Green Solhll 58 H9
Chetnole Dorset 11 N3
Chettiscombe Devon 9 N2
Chettisham Cambs 62 H4
Chettle Dorset 12 G2
Chetton Shrops 57 M6
Chetwode Bucks 48 H9
Chetwynd Wrekin 70 C10
Chetwynd Aston Wrekin 70 D11
Cheveley Cambs 63 L8
Chevening Kent 37 L9
Cheverton IoW 14 E10
Chevington Suffk 63 N9
Cheviot Hills 118 E9
Chevithorne Devon 18 C11
Chew Magna BaNES 19 Q2
Chew Moor Bolton 89 K9
Chew Stoke BaNES 19 Q2
Chewton Keynsham BaNES 32 C11
Chewton Mendip Somset 19 Q4
Chichacott Devon 8 F5
Chicheley M Keyn 49 P5
Chichester W Susx 15 N6
Chichester Crematorium W Susx 15 N5
Chickerell Dorset 11 N8
Chickering Suffk 65 J6
Chicklade Wilts 20 H8
Chickward Herefs 45 K4
Chidden Hants 23 J11
Chiddingfold Surrey 23 Q7
Chiddingly E Susx 25 M8
Chiddingstone Kent 25 M2
Chiddingstone Causeway Kent 37 M11
Chideock Dorset 11 J6
Chidham W Susx 15 L6
Chidswell Kirk 90 H6
Chieveley W Berk 34 E10
Chieveley Services W Berk 34 E10
Chignall St James Essex 51 Q8
Chignall Smealy Essex 51 Q8
Chigwell Essex 37 K2
Chigwell Row Essex 37 L2
Chilbolton Hants 22 C6
Chilcomb Hants 22 F9
Chilcombe Dorset 11 L6
Chilcompton Somset 20 B4
Chilcote Leics 59 L2
Childer Thornton Ches W 81 M9
Child Okeford Dorset 12 D2
Childrey Oxon 34 C7
Child's Ercall Shrops 70 B9
Childswickham Worcs 47 L7
Childwall Lpool 81 N7
Childwick Bury Herts 50 D8
Childwick Green Herts 50 D8
Chilfrome Dorset 11 M5
Chilgrove W Susx 15 M4
Chilham Kent 39 J11
Chilla Devon 8 B4
Chillaton Devon 8 B8
Chillenden Kent 39 N11
Chillerton IoW 14 E10
Chillesford Suffk 65 M11
Chillingham Nthumb 119 L5
Chillington Devon 7 K10
Chillington Somset 10 H2
Chilmark Wilts 21 J8
Chilmington Green Kent 26 G3
Chilson Oxon 48 B11
Chilsworthy Cnwll 5 Q7
Chilsworthy Devon 16 E10
Chiltern Green C Beds 50 D7
Chiltern Hills 35 L5
Chilterns Crematorium Bucks 35 P5
Chilthorne Domer Somset 19 P11
Chilton Bucks 35 J2
Chilton Devon 9 L4
Chilton Dur 103 Q5
Chilton Kent 27 N3
Chilton Oxon 34 E7
Chilton Suffk 52 E3
Chilton Candover Hants 22 G6
Chilton Cantelo Somset 19 Q10
Chilton Foliat Wilts 34 B10
Chilton Polden Somset 19 L6
Chilton Street Suffk 63 N11
Chilton Trinity Somset 19 J7
Chilwell Notts 72 E3
Chilworth Hants 22 D11
Chilworth Surrey 36 B11
Chimney Oxon 34 C4
Chineham Hants 23 J3
Chingford Gt Lon 37 J2
Chinley Derbys 83 M8
Chinnor Oxon 35 L4
Chipchase Castle Nthumb 112 C5
Chipnall Shrops 70 C8
Chippenham Cambs 63 L7
Chippenham Wilts 32 H10
Chipperfield Herts 50 B10
Chipping Herts 51 J4
Chipping Lancs 89 J2
Chipping Campden Gloucs 47 N7
Chipping Hill Essex 52 D8
Chipping Norton Oxon 48 B9
Chipping Ongar Essex 51 N10
Chipping Sodbury S Glos 32 D8
Chipping Warden Nhants 48 E5
Chipshop Devon 8 B9
Chipstable Somset 18 D9
Chipstead Kent 37 M9
Chipstead Surrey 36 G9
Chirbury Shrops 56 D5
Chirk Wrexhm 69 J7
Chirnside Border 129 M8
Chirnsidebridge Border 129 M8
Chirton Wilts 21 L3
Chisbury Wilts 33 Q11
Chiselborough Somset 11 K2
Chiseldon Swindn 33 N8
Chiselhampton Oxon 34 G5
Chisholme Border 117 N8
Chislehurst Gt Lon 37 K6
Chislet Kent 39 M9
Chisley Calder 90 C5
Chiswell Green Herts 50 D10
Chiswick Gt Lon 36 F5
Chiswick End Cambs 62 E11
Chisworth Derbys 83 L6
Chitcombe E Susx 26 D7
Chithurst W Susx 23 M10
Chittering Cambs 62 G7
Chitterne Wilts 21 J6
Chittlehamholt Devon 17 M7
Chittlehampton Devon 17 L6
Chittoe Wilts 33 J11
Chivelstone Devon 7 K11
Chivenor Devon 17 J5
Chlenry D & G 106 F5
Chobham Surrey 23 Q2
Cholderton Wilts 21 P6
Cholesbury Bucks 35 P3
Chollerford Nthumb 112 D6
Chollerton Nthumb 112 D6
Cholmondeston Ches E 70 A3
Cholsey Oxon 34 G7
Cholstrey Herefs 45 P3
Chop Gate N York 104 G11
Choppington Nthumb 113 L4
Chopwell Gatesd 112 H9
Chorley Ches E 69 Q4
Chorley Lancs 88 H7
Chorley Shrops 57 M8
Chorley Staffs 58 G2
Chorleywood Herts 50 B11
Chorleywood West Herts 50 B11
Chorlton Ches E 70 C4
Chorlton-cum-Hardy Manch 82 H6
Chorlton Lane Ches W 69 N5
Choulton Shrops 56 F7
Chowley Ches W 69 N3
Chrishall Essex 51 K3
Chrisswell Inver 124 G3
Christchurch Cambs 75 J11
Christchurch Dorset 13 L6
Christchurch Gloucs 31 Q2
Christchurch Newpt 31 K7
Christian Malford Wilts 33 J9
Christleton Ches W 81 N11
Christmas Common Oxon 35 K6
Christon N Som 19 L3
Christon Bank Nthumb 119 P6
Christow Devon 9 K7
Christ's Hospital W Susx 24 D5
Chuck Hatch E Susx 25 L4
Chudleigh Devon 9 L9
Chudleigh Knighton Devon 9 K9
Chulmleigh Devon 17 M9
Chunal Derbys 83 M6
Church Lancs 89 L5
Churcham Gloucs 46 E11
Church Aston Wrekin 70 C11
Church Brampton Nhants 60 F7
Church Brough Cumb 102 E8
Church Broughton Derbys 71 N8
Church Cove Cnwll 3 J11
Church Crookham Hants 23 M4
Churchdown Gloucs 46 G11
Church Eaton Staffs 70 E11
Church End Bed 61 N9
Church End Bed 61 P9
Church End Bucks 35 K3
Church End C Beds 49 Q10
Church End C Beds 49 Q8
Church End C Beds 50 B4
Church End C Beds 50 B7
Church End C Beds 50 E3
Church End C Beds 61 Q10
Church End Cambs 61 N6
Church End Cambs 62 B4
Church End Cambs 62 D5
Church End Cambs 62 G9
Churchend Essex 38 H3
Church End Essex 51 P6
Church End Essex 52 B6
Church End Essex 52 B8
Church End Gloucs 46 G7
Church End Gt Lon 36 F2
Church End Herts 50 D8
Church End Herts 50 G4

270 Church End - Combe Hay

Church End Herts 51 K6
Church End Lincs 74 D4
Church End Lincs 93 R11
Church End Warwks 59 K6
Church End Warwks 59 L6
Church Enstone Oxon 48 C9
Church Fenton N York 91 N3
Churchfield Sandw 58 F6
Churchgate Herts 50 H10
Churchgate Street Essex 51 L8
Church Green Devon 10 D5
Church Gresley Derbys 71 P11
Church Hanborough Oxon 34 D2
Church Hill Staffs 58 F2
Church Houses N York 105 J11
Churchill Devon 10 F4
Churchill Devon 17 K3
Churchill N Som 19 M3
Churchill Oxon 47 Q10
Churchill Worcs 46 H4
Churchill Worcs 58 C9
Churchinford Somset 10 E2
Church Knowle Dorset 12 F8
Church Laneham Notts 85 P5
Church Langton Leics 60 F2
Church Lawford Warwks 59 Q9
Church Lawton Ches E 70 E3
Church Leigh Staffs 71 J7
Church Lench Worcs 47 K4
Church Mayfield Staffs 71 M6
Church Minshull Ches E 70 B2
Church Norton W Susx 15 N7
Churchover Warwks 60 B4
Church Preen Shrops 57 J5
Church Pulverbatch Shrops 56 G4
Churchstanton Somset 10 D2
Churchstoke Powys 56 D6
Churchstow Devon 7 J9
Church Stowe Nhants 60 D9
Church Street Essex 52 C3
Church Street Kent 38 B7
Church Street Suffk 65 P5
Church Stretton Shrops 56 H6
Churchthorpe Lincs 93 P11
Churchtown Bpool 88 C2
Churchtown Cnwll 4 H6
Churchtown Derbys 84 C8
Churchtown Devon 17 M3
Churchtown IoM 80 f3
Churchtown Lancs 88 F2
Church Town N Linc 92 C9
Churchtown Sefton 88 D7
Church Village Rhondd 30 E7
Church Warsop Notts 85 J7
Church Wilne Derbys 72 C4
Churnsike Lodge Nthumb 111 N5
Churston Ferrers Torbay 7 N7
Churt Surrey 23 N7
Churton Ches W 69 M3
Churwell Leeds 90 H5
Chwilog Gwynd 66 G7
Chyandour Cnwll 2 D7
Chyanvounder Cnwll 2 H9
Chyeowling Cnwll 3 K5
Chyvarloe Cnwll 2 H9
Cil Powys 56 B4
Cilcain Flints 80 H11
Cilcennin Cerdgn 43 K2
Cilcewydd Powys 56 C4
Cilfrew Neath 29 L4
Cilfynydd Rhondd 30 E6
Cilgerran Pembks 41 N2
Cilgwyn Carmth 43 P9
Cilgwyn Gwynd 66 H4
Ciliau-Aeron Cerdgn 43 K3
Cilmaengwyn Neath 29 K3
Cilmery Powys 44 E4
Cilrhedyn Pembks 41 Q4
Cilsan Carmth 43 L10
Ciltalgarth Gwynd 68 A6
Cilycwm Carmth 43 Q7
Cimla Neath 29 L5
Cinderford Gloucs 32 C2
Cinder Hill Wolves 58 D6
Cippenham Slough 35 Q8
Cirencester Gloucs 33 K4
Citadilla N York 103 P11
City Gt Lon 36 H4
City V Glam 30 C9
City Airport Gt Lon 37 K4
City Dulas IoA 78 H7
City of London Crematorium Gt Lon 37 K3
Clabhach Ag & B 136 F4
Clachaig Ag & B 131 N11
Clachan Ag & B 123 N8
Clachan Ag & B 130 F4
Clachan Ag & B 138 F9
Clachan Highld 153 J10
Clachan-a-Luib W Isls 168 d11
Clachan Mor Ag & B 136 B6
Clachan na Luib W Isls 168 d11
Clachan of Campsie E Duns 125 Q2
Clachan-Seil Ag & B 130 F4
Clachnaharry Highld 156 A8
Clachtoll Highld 164 B11
Clackavoid P & K 142 A5
Clacket Lane Services Surrey 37 K10
Clackmannan Clacks 133 Q9
Clackmarras Moray 157 N6
Clacton-on-Sea Essex 53 L8
Cladich Ag & B 131 M3
Cladswell Worcs 47 L3
Claggan Highld 138 C8
Claigan Highld 152 C7
Clandown BaNES 20 C3
Clanfield Hants 23 J11
Clanfield Oxon 33 Q4
Clannaborough Devon 8 H4
Clanville Hants 22 B5
Clanville Somset 20 B8
Claonaig Ag & B 123 Q8
Clapgate Dorset 12 H4
Clapgate Herts 51 K6
Clapham Bed 61 M10
Clapham Devon 9 L7
Clapham Gt Lon 36 G5
Clapham N York 95 Q7
Clapham W Susx 24 C9
Clapham Green Bed 61 M10
Clap Hill Kent 27 J4
Clappersgate Cumb 101 L10
Clapton Somset 11 J3
Clapton Somset 20 B4
Clapton-in-Gordano N Som 31 N10
Clapton-on-the-Hill Gloucs 47 N11
Clapworthy Devon 17 M7
Clarach Cerdgn 54 E8
Claravale Gatesd 112 H8
Clarbeston Pembks 41 L6
Clarbeston Road Pembks 41 K6
Clarborough Notts 85 M4
Clare Suffk 63 N11
Clarebrand D & G 108 G7
Clarencefield D & G 109 N7
Clarewood Nthumb 112 F7
Clarilaw Border 117 Q7
Clark's Green Surrey 24 E3
Clarkston E Rens 125 P6
Clashmore Highld 162 G9
Clashmore Highld 164 B10
Clashnessie Highld 164 C10
Clashnoir Moray 149 N3
Clathy P & K 134 B3
Clathymore P & K 134 C3
Clatt Abers 150 E2
Clatter Powys 55 M6
Clatterford End Essex 51 P8
Clatworthy Somset 18 E8
Claughton Lancs 88 G2
Claughton Lancs 95 M7
Claughton Wirral 81 L7
Clavelshay Somset 19 J8
Claverdon Warwks 59 J11
Claverham N Som 31 N11
Clavering Essex 51 L4
Claverley Shrops 57 P6
Claverton BaNES 20 E2
Claverton Down BaNES 20 E2
Clawdd-coch V Glam 30 E9
Clawdd-newydd Denbgs 68 E4
Clawthorpe Cumb 95 L5
Clawton Devon 5 P2
Claxby Lincs 86 F2
Claxby Lincs 87 N6
Claxton N York 98 D9
Claxton Norfk 77 L11
Claybrooke Magna Leics 59 Q7
Clay Common Suffk 65 P5
Clay Coton Nhants 60 C5
Clay Cross Derbys 84 E8
Claydon Oxon 48 E5
Claydon Suffk 53 K2
Clay End Herts 50 H6
Claygate D & G 110 G5
Claygate Kent 26 B3
Claygate Surrey 36 E8
Claygate Cross Kent 37 P9
Clayhall Gt Lon 37 K2
Clayhanger Devon 18 D10
Clayhanger Wsall 58 F4
Clayhidon Devon 18 G11
Clayhill E Susx 26 D7
Clayhill Hants 13 P3
Clayhithe Cambs 62 H8
Clayock Highld 167 L5
Claypit Hill Cambs 62 E10
Claypits Gloucs 32 E3
Claypole Lincs 85 P11
Claythorpe Lincs 87 M5
Clayton C Brad 90 E4
Clayton Donc 91 M9
Clayton W Susx 24 G8
Clayton Green Lancs 88 H6
Clayton-le-Moors Lancs 89 M4
Clayton-le-Woods Lancs 88 H6
Clayton West Kirk 90 H8
Clayworth Notts 85 M3
Cleadale Highld 144 G10
Cleadon S Tyne 113 N8
Clearbrook Devon 6 E5
Clearwell Gloucs 31 Q3
Clearwell Meend Gloucs 31 Q3
Cleasby N York 103 Q8
Cleat Ork 169 d8
Cleatlam Dur 103 M7
Cleator Cumb 100 D8
Cleator Moor Cumb 100 D7
Cleckheaton Kirk 90 F5
Cleedownton Shrops 57 K8
Cleehill Shrops 57 K9
Cleekhimin N Lans 126 D6
Clee St Margaret Shrops 57 K8
Cleestanton Shrops 57 K9
Cleethorpes NE Lin 93 P9
Cleeton St Mary Shrops 57 L9
Cleeve N Som 31 N11
Cleeve Oxon 34 H8
Cleeve Hill Gloucs 47 J9
Cleeve Prior Worcs 47 L5
Cleghornie E Loth 128 F3
Clehonger Herefs 45 N7
Cleish P & K 134 D8
Cleland N Lans 126 D6
Clement's End C Beds 50 B8
Clement Street Kent 37 M6
Clenamacrie Ag & B 131 J2
Clench Common Wilts 33 N11
Clenchwarton Norfk 75 L6
Clenerty Abers 159 J5
Clent Worcs 58 D9
Cleobury Mortimer Shrops 57 M9
Cleobury North Shrops 57 L7
Cleongart Ag & B 120 C5
Clephanton Highld 156 E7
Clerkhill D & G 117 K11
Cleuch-head D & G 115 R7
Clevancy Wilts 33 L9
Clevedon N Som 31 M10
Cleveley Oxon 48 C10
Cleveleys Lancs 88 C2
Cleverton Wilts 33 J7
Clewer Somset 19 M4
Cley next the Sea Norfk 76 E3
Cliburn Cumb 101 Q6
Cliddesden Hants 22 H5
Cliff Warwks 59 K5
Cliffe Lancs 89 L4
Cliffe Medway 38 B6
Cliffe N York 91 R4
Cliffe N York 103 P7
Cliff End E Susx 26 E9
Cliffe Woods Medway 38 B7
Clifford Herefs 45 J5
Clifford Leeds 91 L2
Clifford Chambers Warwks 47 N4
Clifford's Mesne Gloucs 46 D10
Cliffsend Kent 39 P9
Clifton Bristl 31 Q10
Clifton C Beds 50 E3
Clifton C Nott 72 E4
Clifton C York 98 B10
Clifton Calder 90 F6
Clifton Cumb 101 P5
Clifton Derbys 71 M6
Clifton Devon 17 L3
Clifton Donc 91 N11
Clifton Lancs 88 F4
Clifton N York 97 J11
Clifton Nthumb 113 K4
Clifton Oxon 48 E8
Clifton Salfd 82 G4
Clifton Worcs 46 F5
Clifton Campville Staffs 59 L2
Clifton Hampden Oxon 34 F5
Clifton Reynes M Keyn 49 P4
Clifton upon Dunsmore Warwks 60 B5
Clifton upon Teme Worcs 46 D2
Cliftonville Kent 39 Q7
Climping W Susx 15 Q6
Clink Somset 20 E5
Clint N York 97 L9
Clinterty C Aber 151 L5
Clint Green Norfk 76 E9
Clintmains Border 118 B4
Clipiau Gwynd 55 J2
Clippesby Norfk 77 N9
Clipsham Rutlnd 73 P7
Clipston Nhants 60 F4
Clipston Notts 72 G4
Clipstone C Beds 49 P9
Clipstone Notts 85 J8
Clitheroe Lancs 89 L2
Clive Shrops 69 P10
Cliveden Bucks 35 P7
Clixby Lincs 93 J10
Cloatley Wilts 33 J6
Clocaenog Denbgs 68 E4
Clochan Moray 158 B5
Clock Face St Hel 82 B6
Cloddiau Powys 56 C3
Clodock Herefs 45 L9
Cloford Somset 20 D6
Clola Abers 159 P9
Clophill C Beds 50 C3
Clopton Nhants 61 N4
Clopton Suffk 65 J11
Clopton Corner Suffk 65 J11
Clopton Green Suffk 63 N10
Clopton Green Suffk 64 D10
Clos du Valle Guern 10 c1
Closeburn D & G 109 J2
Closeburnmill D & G 109 K2
Closeclark IoM 80 c6
Closworth Somset 11 M2
Clothall Herts 50 G4
Clotton Ches W 69 P2
Cloudesley Bush Warwks 59 Q7
Clouds Herefs 46 A7
Clough Oldham 89 Q9
Clough Foot Calder 89 Q6
Clough Head Calder 90 D7
Cloughton N York 99 L2
Cloughton Newlands N York 105 R11
Clousta Shet 169 q8
Clova Angus 142 E3
Clovelly Devon 16 E7
Clovenfords Border 117 P3
Clovulin Highld 139 J5
Clow Bridge Lancs 89 N5
Clowne Derbys 84 G5
Clows Top Worcs 57 N10
Cloy Wrexhm 69 L6
Cluanie Inn Highld 146 D5
Cluanie Lodge Highld 146 D5
Clubworthy Cnwll 5 M3
Clugston D & G 107 L6
Clun Shrops 56 E8
Clunas Highld 156 F8
Clunbury Shrops 56 F8
Clunderwen Carmth 41 M7
Clune Highld 148 D2
Clunes Highld 146 F10
Clungunford Shrops 56 F9
Clunie P & K 141 R9
Clunton Shrops 56 E8
Cluny Fife 134 G8
Clutton BaNES 20 B3
Clutton Ches W 69 N4
Clutton Hill BaNES 20 B3
Clwt-y-bont Gwynd 67 K2
Clydach Mons 30 H2
Clydach Swans 29 J4
Clydach Vale Rhondd 30 C6
Clydebank W Duns 125 M3
Clydebank Crematorium W Duns 125 M3
Clydey Pembks 41 Q3
Clyffe Pypard Wilts 33 L9
Clynder Ag & B 131 Q11
Clyne Neath 29 M4
Clynnog-fawr Gwynd 66 G5
Clyro Powys 45 J6
Clyst Honiton Devon 9 N6
Clyst Hydon Devon 9 P4
Clyst St George Devon 9 N7
Clyst St Lawrence Devon 9 P4
Clyst St Mary Devon 9 N6
Cnoc W Isls 168 j4
Cnwch Coch Cerdgn 54 F10
Coad's Green Cnwll 5 M6
Coal Aston Derbys 84 E5
Coalbrookvale Blae G 30 G3
Coalburn S Lans 126 E11
Coalburns Gatesd 112 H8
Coaley Gloucs 32 E4
Coalhill Essex 38 C2
Coalmoor Wrekin 57 M3
Coalpit Heath S Glos 32 C8
Coal Pool Wsall 58 F5
Coalport Wrekin 57 M4
Coalsnaughton Clacks 133 Q8
Coal Street Suffk 65 J7
Coaltown of Balgonie Fife 134 H8
Coaltown of Wemyss Fife 135 J8
Coalville Leics 72 C8
Coanwood Nthumb 111 N9
Coat Somset 19 N10
Coatbridge N Lans 126 C4
Coatdyke N Lans 126 C4
Coate Swindn 33 N8
Coate Wilts 21 K2
Coates Cambs 74 F11
Coates Gloucs 33 J4
Coates Lincs 86 B4
Coates Notts 85 P4
Coates W Susx 23 Q11
Coatham R & Cl 104 G5
Coatham Mundeville Darltn 103 Q6
Cobbaton Devon 17 L6
Coberley Gloucs 47 J11
Cobhall Common Herefs 45 P7
Cobham Kent 37 Q7
Cobham Surrey 36 D8
Cobham Services Surrey 36 D9
Coblers Green Essex 51 Q7
Cobley Dorset 21 K10
Cobnash Herefs 45 P2
Cobo Guern 10 b1
Cobridge C Stke 70 F5
Coburby Abers 159 M5
Cock Alley Derbys 84 F6
Cockayne N York 104 H11
Cockayne Hatley C Beds 62 C11
Cock Bank Wrexhm 69 L5
Cock Bevington Warwks 47 L4
Cock Bridge Abers 149 P6
Cockburnspath Border 129 K5
Cock Clarks Essex 52 D11
Cock & End Suffk 63 M10
Cockenzie and Port Seton E Loth 128 C4
Cocker Bar Lancs 88 G6
Cocker Brook Lancs 89 L5
Cockerham Lancs 95 K10
Cockermouth Cumb 100 F4
Cockernhoe Herts 50 D6
Cockersdale Leeds 90 G5
Cockett Swans 28 H6
Cockfield Dur 103 M6
Cockfield Suffk 64 C11
Cockfosters Gt Lon 50 G11
Cock Green Essex 51 Q7
Cocking W Susx 23 N11
Cocking Causeway W Susx 23 N11
Cockington Torbay 7 M6
Cocklake Somset 19 M5
Cockley Beck Cumb 100 H10
Cockley Cley Norfk 75 Q10
Cock Marling E Susx 26 E8
Cockpole Green Wokham 35 L8
Cocks Cnwll 3 K3
Cockshutford Shrops 57 K7
Cockshutt Shrops 69 M9
Cock Street Kent 38 C11
Cockthorpe Norfk 76 D3
Cockwells Cnwll 2 E7
Cockwood Devon 9 N8
Cockwood Somset 18 H6
Cockyard Derbys 83 M9
Cockyard Herefs 45 N8
Coddenham Suffk 64 G11
Coddington Ches W 69 N3
Coddington Herefs 46 D6
Coddington Notts 85 P10
Codford St Mary Wilts 21 J7
Codford St Peter Wilts 21 J7
Codicote Herts 50 F7
Codmore Hill W Susx 24 C6
Codnor Derbys 84 F11
Codrington S Glos 32 D9
Codsall Staffs 58 C4
Codsall Wood Staffs 58 B4
Coedely Rhondd 30 D7
Coedkernew Newpt 31 J8
Coed Morgan Mons 31 L2
Coedpoeth Wrexhm 69 J4
Coed Talon Flints 69 J3
Coedway Powys 69 K11
Coed-y-Bryn Cerdgn 42 G5
Coed-y-caerau Newpt 31 L6
Coed-y-paen Mons 31 K5
Coed-yr-ynys Powys 44 H10
Coed Ystumgwern Gwynd 67 K10
Coelbren Powys 29 N2
Coffinswell Devon 7 M5
Coffle End Bed 61 M9
Cofton Devon 9 N8
Cofton Hackett Worcs 58 F9
Cogan V Glam 30 G10
Cogenhoe Nhants 60 H8
Cogges Oxon 34 C3
Coggeshall Essex 52 E7
Coggin's Mill E Susx 25 N5
Coignafearn Highld 148 C4
Coilacriech Abers 149 Q8
Coilantogle Stirlg 132 H6
Coillore Highld 152 F10
Coity Brdgnd 29 P8
Col W Isls 168 j4
Colaboll Highld 162 D4
Colan Cnwll 4 D9
Colaton Raleigh Devon 10 B7
Colbost Highld 152 C8
Colburn N York 103 N11
Colby Cumb 102 C6
Colby IoM 80 b7
Colby Norfk 77 J5
Colchester Essex 52 G6
Colchester Crematorium Essex 52 G7
Colchester Zoo Essex 52 G7
Cold Ash W Berk 34 F11
Cold Ashby Nhants 60 E5
Cold Ashton S Glos 32 E10
Cold Aston Gloucs 47 M11
Coldbackie Highld 165 P4
Coldbeck Cumb 102 D10
Cold Blow Pembks 41 M8
Cold Brayfield M Keyn 49 P4
Cold Cotes N York 95 Q6
Coldean Br & H 24 H9
Coldeast Devon 7 L4
Colden Calder 90 B5
Colden Common Hants 22 E10
Coldfair Green Suffk 65 N9
Coldham Cambs 74 H10
Cold Hanworth Lincs 86 D4
Coldharbour Cnwll 3 K4
Coldharbour Devon 9 Q2
Coldharbour Gloucs 31 Q4
Cold Harbour Herts 50 D7
Cold Harbour Oxon 34 H9
Coldharbour Surrey 24 D2
Cold Harbour Wilts 20 G5
Cold Hatton Wrekin 70 A10
Cold Hatton Heath Wrekin 70 A10
Cold Hesledon Dur 113 P11
Cold Hiendley Wakefd 91 K8
Cold Higham Nhants 49 J4
Coldingham Border 129 N6
Cold Kirby N York 98 A4
Coldmeece Staffs 70 F8
Cold Newton Leics 73 J9
Cold Northcott Cnwll 5 L4
Cold Norton Essex 52 E11
Cold Overton Leics 73 L8
Coldred Kent 27 N2
Coldridge Devon 17 M10
Coldstream Border 118 F3
Coldwaltham W Susx 24 B7
Coldwell Herefs 45 N7
Coldwells Abers 159 N10
Cold Weston Shrops 57 K8
Cole Somset 20 C8
Colebatch Shrops 56 E7
Colebrook C Plym 6 E7
Colebrook Devon 9 P3
Colebrooke Devon 9 J5
Coleby Lincs 86 C8
Coleby N Linc 92 E7
Cole End Warwks 59 K7
Coleford Devon 9 J4
Coleford Gloucs 31 Q2
Coleford Somset 20 C5
Coleford Water Somset 18 F8
Colegate End Norfk 64 H4
Cole Green Herts 50 G8
Cole Green Herts 51 K4
Cole Henley Hants 22 E4
Colehill Dorset 12 H4
Coleman Green Herts 50 E8
Coleman's Hatch E Susx 25 K4
Colemere Shrops 69 M8
Colemore Hants 23 K8
Colemore Green Shrops 57 N5
Colenden P & K 134 E2
Coleorton Leics 72 C7
Colerne Wilts 32 F10
Colesbourne Gloucs 33 K2
Cole's Cross Devon 7 K9
Coles Cross Dorset 10 H4
Colesden Bed 61 P9
Coles Green Suffk 53 K3
Coleshill Bucks 35 P5
Coleshill Oxon 33 P6
Coleshill Warwks 59 K7
Colestocks Devon 10 B4
Coley BaNES 19 Q3
Colgate W Susx 24 F4
Colinsburgh Fife 135 M7
Colinton C Edin 127 N4
Colintraive Ag & B 124 C3
Colkirk Norfk 76 C6
Coll Ag & B 136 G4
Collace P & K 142 C11
Collafirth Shet 169 q5
Coll Airport Ag & B 136 F4
Collaton Devon 7 J11
Collaton St Mary Torbay 7 M6
College of Roseisle Moray 157 L4
College Town Br For 23 N2
Collessie Fife 134 H5
Colleton Mills Devon 17 M8
Collier Row Gt Lon 37 M2
Collier's End Herts 51 J6
Collier's Green E Susx 26 C7
Colliers Green Kent 26 C4
Collier Street Kent 26 B2
Colliery Row Sundld 113 M11
Collieston Abers 151 Q2
Collin D & G 109 M5
Collingbourne Ducis Wilts 21 P4
Collingbourne Kingston Wilts 21 P3
Collingham Leeds 97 N11
Collingham Notts 85 P8
Collington Herefs 46 B2
Collingtree Nhants 60 G9
Collins Green Warrtn 82 C6
Collins Green Worcs 46 D3
Colliston Angus 143 L8
Colliton Devon 10 B4
Collyweston Nhants 73 P10
Colmonell S Ayrs 114 B10
Colmworth Bed 61 P9
Colnabaichin Abers 149 P6
Colnbrook Slough 36 B5
Colne Cambs 62 E5
Colne Lancs 89 P3
Colne Bridge Kirk 90 F6
Colne Edge Lancs 89 P2
Colne Engaine Essex 52 D5
Colney Norfk 76 H10
Colney Heath Herts 50 F9
Colney Street Herts 50 E10
Coln Rogers Gloucs 33 L3
Coln St Aldwyns Gloucs 33 M3
Coln St Dennis Gloucs 33 L2
Colonsay Ag & B 136 b2
Colonsay Airport Ag & B 136 b3
Colpy Abers 158 F11
Colquhar Border 117 L2
Colquite Cnwll 4 H7
Colscott Devon 16 F9
Colsterdale N York 96 H4
Colsterworth Lincs 73 N6
Colston Bassett Notts 73 J4
Coltfield Moray 157 L5
Colt Hill Hants 23 L4
Coltishall Norfk 77 K8
Colton Cumb 94 G3
Colton Leeds 91 K4
Colton N York 91 N2
Colton Norfk 76 G10
Colton Staffs 71 J10
Colt's Hill Kent 25 P2
Columbjohn Devon 9 N5
Colva Powys 44 H4
Colvend D & G 109 J10
Colwall Herefs 46 E6
Colwell Nthumb 112 E5
Colwich Staffs 71 J10
Colwick Notts 72 G2
Colwinston V Glam 29 P9
Colworth W Susx 15 P6
Colwyn Bay Conwy 80 B9
Colyford Devon 10 F6
Colyton Devon 10 E6
Combe Devon 7 J11
Combe Herefs 45 L2
Combe Oxon 48 D11
Combe W Berk 22 C2
Combe Almer Dorset 12 G5
Combe Common Surrey 23 P7
Combe Down BaNES 20 E2
Combe Fishacre Devon 7 L5
Combe Florey Somset 18 G8
Combe Hay BaNES 20 D3

272 Crindledyke - Dawn

Crindledyke N Lans 126 E6
Cringleford Norfk 76 H10
Cringles C Brad 96 F11
Crinow Pembks 41 M8
Cripplesease Cnwll 2 E6
Cripplestyle Dorset 13 J2
Cripp's Corner E Susx 26 C7
Croachy Highld 148 B2
Croanford Cnwll 4 G7
Crockenhill Kent 37 M7
Crocker End Oxon 35 K7
Crockerhill W Susx 15 P5
Crockernwell Devon 9 J6
Crocker's Ash Herefs 45 Q11
Crockerton Wilts 20 G6
Crocketford D & G 108 H6
Crockey Hill C York 98 C11
Crockham Hill Kent 37 K10
Crockhurst Street Kent 37 P11
Crockleford Heath Essex 52 H6
Crock Street Somset 10 G2
Croeserw Neath 29 N5
Croes-goch Pembks 40 F4
Croes-lan Cerdgn 42 G6
Croesor Gwynd 67 L6
Croesyceiliog Carmth 42 H11
Croesyceiliog Torfn 31 K5
Croes-y-mwyalch Torfn 31 K6
Croes-y-pant Mons 31 K4
Croft Leics 72 E11
Croft Lincs 87 P8
Croft Warrtn 82 D6
Croftamie Stirlg 132 F10
Croft Mitchell Cnwll 2 H6
Crofton Cumb 110 F10
Crofton Wakefd 91 K7
Crofton Wilts 21 Q2
Croft-on-Tees N York 103 Q9
Croftown Highld 161 K10
Crofts Moray 157 P7
Crofts Bank Traffd 82 G5
Crofts of Dipple Moray 157 Q6
Crofts of Savoch Abers 159 P5
Crofty Swans 28 F6
Crogen Gwynd 68 D7
Croggan Ag & B 130 E2
Croglin Cumb 111 L11
Croick Highld 162 B8
Cromarty Highld 156 D4
Crombie Fife 134 D11
Cromdale Highld 149 K2
Cromer Herts 50 G5
Cromer Norfk 77 J3
Cromford Derbys 84 C9
Cromhall S Glos 32 C6
Cromhall Common S Glos 32 C7
Cromor W Isls 168 j5
Crompton Fold Oldham 89 Q9
Cromwell Notts 85 N8
Cronberry E Ayrs 115 M3
Crondall Hants 23 L5
Cronkbourne IoM 80 e6
Cronk-y-Voddy IoM 80 d4
Cronton Knows 81 P7
Crook Cumb 101 N11
Crook Dur 103 N3
Crookdake Cumb 100 G2
Crooke Wigan 88 H9
Crooked End Gloucs 46 B11
Crookedholm E Ayrs 125 M10
Crooked Soley Wilts 34 B10
Crookes Sheff 84 D3
Crookhall Dur 112 H10
Crookham Nthumb 118 H3
Crookham W Berk 22 F2
Crookham Village Hants 23 L4
Crook Inn Border 116 G5
Crooklands Cumb 95 L4
Crook of Devon P & K 134 C7
Cropper Derbys 71 N7
Cropredy Oxon 48 E5
Cropston Leics 72 F8
Cropthorne Worcs 47 J5
Cropton N York 98 F3
Cropwell Bishop Notts 72 H3
Cropwell Butler Notts 72 H3
Cros W Isls 168 k1
Crosbost W Isls 168 i5
Crosby Cumb 100 E3
Crosby IoM 80 d6
Crosby N Linc 92 E8
Crosby Sefton 81 L5
Crosby Garret Cumb 102 D9
Crosby Ravensworth Cumb 102 B8
Crosby Villa Cumb 100 E3
Croscombe Somset 19 Q6
Crosemere Shrops 69 M9
Crosland Edge Kirk 90 E8
Crosland Hill Kirk 90 E8
Cross Somset 19 M4
Crossaig Ag & B 123 P9
Crossapoll Ag & B 136 B7
Cross Ash Mons 45 N11
Cross-at-Hand Kent 26 C2
Crossbush W Susx 24 B9
Crosscanonby Cumb 100 E3
Cross Coombe Cnwll 3 J3
Crossdale Street Norfk 77 J4
Cross End Bed 61 N9
Cross End Essex 52 E5
Crossens Sefton 88 D6
Cross Flatts C Brad 90 E2
Crossford Fife 134 D10
Crossford S Lans 126 E8
Crossgate Cnwll 5 N4
Crossgate Lincs 74 D5
Crossgate Staffs 70 G7
Crossgatehall E Loth 128 B6
Crossgates E Ayrs 125 K9
Crossgates Fife 134 E10
Cross Gates Leeds 91 K4
Crossgates N York 99 L4
Crossgates Powys 44 F2
Crossgill Lancs 95 M8
Cross Green Devon 5 P4
Cross Green Leeds 91 J4
Cross Green Staffs 58 D3
Cross Green Suffk 64 A11
Cross Green Suffk 64 B10
Cross Green Suffk 64 D11
Cross Hands Carmth 28 G2
Crosshands Carmth 41 N6
Crosshands E Ayrs 125 M11
Cross Hands Pembks 41 L8
Cross Hill Derbys 84 F11
Crosshill Fife 134 F8
Crosshill S Ayrs 114 F6
Cross Hills N York 96 F11
Crosshouse E Ayrs 125 K10
Cross Houses Shrops 57 J3
Cross Houses Shrops 57 M6
Cross in Hand E Susx 25 N6
Cross Inn Cerdgn 42 G3
Cross Inn Cerdgn 43 K2
Cross Inn Pembks 41 M9
Cross Inn Rhondd 30 E8
Cross Keys Ag & B 132 C10
Crosskeys Caerph 30 H6
Cross Keys Wilts 32 G10
Crosskirk Highld 166 H3
Crosslands Cumb 94 G3
Cross Lane IoW 14 F9
Cross Lane Head Shrops 57 N5
Cross Lanes Cnwll 2 H9
Cross Lanes Cnwll 3 K5
Cross Lanes N York 98 A8
Crosslanes Shrops 69 K11
Cross Lanes Wrexhm 69 L5
Crosslee Rens 125 L4
Crossley Kirk 90 G6
Crossmichael D & G 108 F7
Cross Oak Powys 44 G10
Cross of Jackston Abers 158 H11
Cross o' th' hands Derbys 71 P5
Crosspost W Susx 24 G6
Crossroads Abers 150 F6
Crossroads Abers 151 K9
Cross Street Suffk 64 H6
Crosston Angus 143 J6
Cross Town Ches E 82 G9
Crossway Mons 45 N11
Crossway Powys 44 F3
Crossway Green Mons 31 P6
Crossway Green Worcs 58 B11
Crossways Dorset 12 C7
Crosswell Pembks 41 M3
Crosthwaite Cumb 95 J2
Croston Lancs 88 F7
Crostwick Norfk 77 K8
Crostwight Norfk 77 L6
Crouch Kent 37 P9
Crouch Kent 39 J10
Crouch End Gt Lon 36 H3
Croucheston Wilts 21 L9
Crouch Hill Dorset 11 Q2
Crough House Green Kent 37 K11
Croughton Nhants 48 F8
Crovie Abers 159 K4
Crow Hants 13 L4
Crowan Cnwll 2 G7
Crowborough E Susx 25 M4
Crowborough Town E Susx 25 M4
Crowcombe Somset 18 F7
Crowdecote Derbys 83 P11
Crowden Derbys 83 N5
Crowden Devon 8 C5
Crowdhill Hants 22 E10
Crowdleham Kent 37 N9
Crow Edge Barns 83 Q4
Crowell Oxon 35 K5
Crow End Cambs 62 D9
Crowfield Nhants 48 H6
Crowfield Suffk 64 G10
Crowfield Green Suffk 64 G10
Crowgate Street Norfk 77 L7
Crow Green Essex 51 N11
Crowhill E Loth 129 J5
Crow Hill Herefs 46 B9
Crowhole Derbys 84 D5
Crowhurst E Susx 26 C9
Crowhurst Surrey 37 J11
Crowhurst Lane End Surrey 37 J11
Crowland Lincs 74 D8
Crowland Suffk 64 E7
Crowlas Cnwll 2 E7
Crowle N Linc 92 C8
Crowle Worcs 46 H3
Crowle Green Worcs 46 H3
Crowmarsh Gifford Oxon 34 H7
Crown Corner Suffk 65 K7
Crownhill C Plym 6 D7
Crownhill Crematorium M Keyn 49 M7
Crownpits Surrey 23 Q6
Crownthorpe Norfk 76 F11
Crowntown Cnwll 2 G7
Crows-an-Wra Cnwll 2 B8
Crow's Green Essex 51 Q5
Crowshill Norfk 76 D10
Crow's Nest Cnwll 5 M8
Crowsnest Shrops 56 F4
Crowthorne Wokham 23 M2
Crowton Ches W 82 C10
Croxall Staffs 59 J2
Croxby Lincs 93 L11
Croxdale Dur 103 Q3
Croxden Staffs 71 K7
Croxley Green Herts 50 C11
Croxteth Lpool 81 N5
Croxton Cambs 62 B8
Croxton N Linc 93 J8
Croxton Norfk 64 B4
Croxton Norfk 76 D5
Croxton Staffs 70 D8
Croxtonbank Staffs 70 D8
Croxton Green Ches E 69 Q4
Croxton Kerrial Leics 73 L5
Croy Highld 156 D8
Croy N Lans 126 C2
Croyde Devon 16 G4
Croyde Bay Devon 16 G4
Croydon Cambs 62 D11
Croydon Gt Lon 36 H7
Croydon Crematorium Gt Lon 36 H7
Crubenmore Highld 148 B9
Cruckmeole Shrops 56 G3
Cruckton Shrops 56 G2
Cruden Bay Abers 159 Q10
Crudgington Wrekin 70 A11
Crudwell Wilts 33 J6
Cruft Devon 8 D5
Crug Powys 56 B10
Crugmeer Cnwll 4 E6
Crugybar Carmth 43 N7
Crug-y-byddar Powys 56 B8
Crumlin Caerph 30 H5
Crumplehorn Cnwll 5 L11
Crumpsall Manch 82 H4
Crundale Kent 27 J2
Crundale Pembks 41 J7
Crunwear Pembks 41 N8
Cruwys Morchard Devon 9 L2
Crux Easton Hants 22 D3
Cruxton Dorset 11 N5
Crwbin Carmth 28 E2
Cryers Hill Bucks 35 N5
Crymych Pembks 41 N4
Crynant Neath 29 L4
Crystal Palace Gt Lon 36 H6
Cuaig Highld 153 N6
Cuan Ag & B 130 F5
Cubbington Warwks 59 M11
Cubert Cnwll 4 B10
Cubley Barns 90 G10
Cublington Bucks 49 M10
Cublington Herefs 45 N7
Cuckfield W Susx 24 H5
Cucklington Somset 20 E9
Cuckney Notts 85 J6
Cuckoo Bridge Lincs 74 D6
Cuckoo's Corner Hants 23 K6
Cuckoo's Nest Ches W 69 L2
Cuddesdon Oxon 34 G4
Cuddington Bucks 35 K2
Cuddington Ches W 82 C10
Cuddington Heath Ches W 69 N5
Cuddy Hill Lancs 88 F3
Cudham Gt Lon 37 K9
Cudliptown Devon 8 D9
Cudnell Bmouth 13 J5
Cudworth Barns 91 K9
Cudworth Somset 10 H2
Cuerdley Cross Warrtn 82 B7
Cufaude Hants 23 J3
Cuffley Herts 50 H10
Cuil Highld 138 H6
Culbokie Highld 155 R6
Culbone Somset 17 Q2
Culburnie Highld 155 N9
Culcabock Highld 156 B9
Culcharry Highld 156 F7
Culcheth Warrtn 82 E6
Culdrain Abers 158 D11
Culduie Highld 153 N9
Culford Suffk 64 A7
Culgaith Cumb 102 B5
Culham Oxon 34 F5
Culkein Highld 164 B10
Culkein Drumbeg Highld 164 D10
Culkerton Gloucs 32 H5
Cullen Moray 158 D4
Cullercoats N Tyne 113 N6
Cullerlie Abers 151 K7
Cullicudden Highld 156 A5
Cullingworth C Brad 90 D3
Cuillin Hills Highld 144 G3
Cullipool Ag & B 130 E5
Cullivoe Shet 169 s3
Culloden Highld 156 C8
Cullompton Devon 9 P3
Cullompton Services Devon 9 P3
Culm Davy Devon 18 F11
Culmington Shrops 56 H8
Culmstock Devon 10 C2
Culnacraig Highld 160 H6
Culnaightrie D & G 108 G10
Culnaknock Highld 153 J5
Culpho Suffk 53 M2
Culrain Highld 162 D8
Culross Fife 134 B10
Culroy S Ayrs 114 F5
Culsalmond Abers 158 G11
Culscadden D & G 107 N8
Culshabbin D & G 107 K7
Culswick Shet 169 p9
Cultercullen Abers 151 N3
Cults C Aber 151 M7
Culverstone Green Kent 37 P8
Culverthorpe Lincs 73 Q2
Culworth Nhants 48 F5
Culzean Castle & Country Park S Ayrs 114 D5
Cumbernauld N Lans 126 D3
Cumbernauld Village N Lans 126 D2
Cumberworth Lincs 87 P6
Cumdivock Cumb 110 F11
Cuminestown Abers 159 K7
Cumledge Border 129 K8
Cummersdale Cumb 110 G10
Cummertrees D & G 109 P7
Cummingston Moray 157 L4
Cumnock E Ayrs 115 L3
Cumnor Oxon 34 E4
Cumrew Cumb 111 L10
Cumrue D & G 109 N3
Cumwhinton Cumb 111 J10
Cumwhitton Cumb 111 K10
Cundall N York 97 P6
Cunninghamhead N Ayrs 125 K9
Cunningsburgh Shet 169 r10
Cupar Fife 135 K5
Cupar Muir Fife 135 K5
Curbar Derbys 84 C6
Curbridge Hants 14 F4
Curbridge Oxon 34 B3
Curdridge Hants 14 F4
Curdworth Warwks 59 J6
Curland Somset 19 J11
Curridge W Berk 34 E10
Currie C Edin 127 M4
Curry Mallet Somset 19 K10
Curry Rivel Somset 19 L9
Curteis Corner Kent 26 E4
Curtisden Green Kent 26 B3
Curtisknowle Devon 7 J8
Cury Cnwll 2 H9
Cushnie Abers 150 E5
Cushuish Somset 18 G8
Cusop Herefs 45 J6
Cutcloy D & G 107 N11
Cutcombe Somset 18 B7
Cutgate Rochdl 89 P8
Cuthill Highld 162 H9
Cutiau Gwynd 67 L11
Cutler's Green Essex 51 N4
Cutmadoc Cnwll 4 H9
Cutmere Cnwll 5 N9
Cutnall Green Worcs 58 C11
Cutsdean Gloucs 47 L8
Cutsyke Wakefd 91 L6
Cutthorpe Derbys 84 D6
Cuttivett Cnwll 5 P9
Cuxham Oxon 35 J5
Cuxton Medway 38 B8
Cuxwold Lincs 93 L10
Cwm Blae G 30 G3
Cwm Denbgs 80 F9
Cwmafan Neath 29 L6
Cwmaman Rhondd 30 D5
Cwmann Carmth 43 L5
Cwmavon Torfn 31 J3
Cwm-bach Carmth 28 E4
Cwmbach Carmth 41 Q5
Cwmbach Powys 44 H7
Cwmbach Rhondd 30 D4
Cwmbach Llechrhyd Powys 44 E4
Cwmbelan Powys 55 L8
Cwmbran Torfn 31 J6
Cwmbrwyno Cerdgn 54 G8
Cwm Capel Carmth 28 E4
Cwmcarn Caerph 30 H6
Cwmcarvan Mons 31 N3
Cwm-celyn Blae G 30 H3
Cwm-Cewydd Gwynd 55 K2
Cwm-cou Cerdgn 41 Q2
Cwm Crawnon Powys 44 G11
Cwmdare Rhondd 30 C4
Cwmdu Carmth 43 M8
Cwmdu Powys 44 H10
Cwmdu Swans 28 H6
Cwmduad Carmth 42 G8
Cwm Dulais Swans 28 H4
Cwmdwr Carmth 43 P8
Cwmfelin Brdgnd 29 N7
Cwmfelin Myr Td 30 E4
Cwmfelin Boeth Carmth 41 N7
Cwmfelinfach Caerph 30 G6
Cwmfelin Mynach Carmth 41 P6
Cwmffrwd Carmth 42 H11
Cwmgiedd Powys 29 L2
Cwmgorse Carmth 29 K2
Cwmgwili Carmth 28 G2
Cwmgwrach Neath 29 N4
Cwmhiraeth Carmth 42 F7
Cwm-Ifor Carmth 43 N9
Cwm Irfon Powys 44 B5
Cwmisfael Carmth 43 J11
Cwm Llinau Powys 55 J3
Cwmllynfell Neath 29 K2
Cwmmawr Carmth 28 F2
Cwm Morgan Carmth 41 Q4
Cwmparc Rhondd 29 P5
Cwmpengraig Carmth 42 G7
Cwm Penmachno Conwy 67 P5
Cwmpennar Rhondd 30 D4
Cwmrhos Powys 44 H10
Cwmrhydyceirw Swans 29 J5
Cwmsychbant Cerdgn 43 J5
Cwmtillery Blae G 30 H3
Cwm-twrch Isaf Powys 29 L2
Cwm-twrch Uchaf Powys 29 L2
Cwm-y-glo Carmth 28 G2
Cwm-y-glo Gwynd 67 K2
Cwmyoy Mons 45 K10
Cwmystwyth Cerdgn 54 H10
Cwrt Gwynd 54 F5
Cwrt-newydd Cerdgn 43 J5
Cwrt-y-gollen Powys 45 J11
Cyfarthfa Castle Museum Myr Td 30 D3
Cyfronydd Powys 55 Q3
Cylibebyll Neath 29 K4
Cymau Flints 69 J3
Cymer Neath 29 N5
Cymmer Rhondd 30 D6
Cynghordy Carmth 43 R6
Cynheidre Carmth 28 E3
Cynonville Neath 29 M5
Cynwyd Denbgs 68 E6
Cynwyl Elfed Carmth 42 G9

D

Daccombe Devon 7 N5
Dacre Cumb 101 N5
Dacre N York 97 J8
Dacre Banks N York 97 J8
Daddry Shield Dur 102 G3
Dadford Bucks 49 J7
Dadlington Leics 72 C11
Dafen Carmth 28 F4
Daffy Green Norfk 76 D10
Dagenham Gt Lon 37 M4
Daglingworth Gloucs 33 J3
Dagnall Bucks 49 Q11
Dagworth Suffk 64 E9
Dailly S Ayrs 114 E7
Dainton Devon 7 M5
Dairsie Fife 135 L4
Daisy Hill Bolton 82 E4
Daisy Hill Leeds 90 H5
Dalabrog W Isls 168 c15
Dalavich Ag & B 131 K5
Dalbeattie D & G 108 H8
Dalbury Derbys 71 P8
Dalby IoM 80 b6
Dalby Lincs 87 M7
Dalby N York 98 C6
Dalcapon P & K 141 N7
Dalchalm Highld 163 L5
Dalchreichart Highld 146 H5
Dalchruin P & K 133 L4
Dalcrue P & K 134 C2
Dalderby Lincs 87 J7
Dalditch Devon 9 P8
Daldowie Crematorium C Glas 126 B5
Dale Cumb 101 P2
Dale Derbys 72 C3
Dale Pembks 40 F9
Dale Bottom Cumb 101 J6
Dale End Derbys 84 B8
Dale End N York 96 E11
Dale Hill E Susx 26 B5
Dalehouse N York 105 L7
Dalelia Highld 138 C4
Dalgarven N Ayrs 124 H8
Dalgety Bay Fife 134 F11
Dalgig E Ayrs 115 L5
Dalginross P & K 133 M3
Dalguise P & K 141 N8
Dalhalvaig Highld 166 E6
Dalham Suffk 63 M8
Daliburgh W Isls 168 c15
Dalkeith Mdloth 127 Q4
Dallas Moray 157 L7
Dallinghoo Suffk 65 K10
Dallington E Susx 25 Q7
Dallington Nhants 60 F8
Dallow N York 97 J6
Dalmally Ag & B 131 P2
Dalmary Stirlg 132 G8
Dalmellington E Ayrs 115 J6
Dalmeny C Edin 127 L2
Dalmore Highld 156 B4
Dalmuir W Duns 125 M3
Dalnabreck Highld 138 C4
Dalnacardoch P & K 140 H3
Dalnahaitnach Highld 148 F4
Dalnaspidal P & K 140 F3
Dalnawillan Lodge Highld 166 H8
Daloist P & K 141 J6
Dalqueich P & K 134 D7
Dalquhairn S Ayrs 114 F8
Dalreavoch Lodge Highld 162 H5
Dalry N Ayrs 124 H8
Dalrymple E Ayrs 114 G5
Dalserf S Lans 126 D7
Dalsmeran Ag & B 120 B9
Dalston Cumb 110 G10
Dalston Gt Lon 36 H4
Dalswinton D & G 109 K3
Dalton Cumb 95 L5
Dalton D & G 109 P6
Dalton Lancs 88 F9
Dalton N York 97 P5
Dalton N York 103 M9
Dalton Nthumb 112 H6
Dalton Rothm 84 G2
Dalton-in-Furness Cumb 94 E6
Dalton-le-Dale Dur 113 P11
Dalton Magna Rothm 84 G2
Dalton-on-Tees N York 103 Q9
Dalton Parva Rothm 84 G2
Dalton Piercy Hartpl 104 E4
Dalveich Stirlg 133 J3
Dalwhinnie Highld 147 Q11
Dalwood Devon 10 E4
Damask Green Herts 50 G5
Damerham Hants 21 M11
Damgate Norfk 77 N10
Dam Green Norfk 64 E4
Damnaglaur D & G 106 F10
Danaway Kent 38 E9
Danbury Essex 52 C10
Danby N York 105 K9
Danby Bottom N York 105 J10
Danby Wiske N York 104 B11
Dandaleith Moray 157 P8
Danderhall Mdloth 127 Q4
Danebridge Ches E 83 L11
Dane End Herts 50 H6
Danegate E Susx 25 N4
Danehill E Susx 25 K5
Dane Hills C Leic 72 F10
Danemoor Green Norfk 76 F10
Danesford Shrops 57 N6
Danesmoor Derbys 84 F8
Dane Street Kent 39 J11
Daniel's Water Kent 26 G3
Danshillock Abers 158 H6
Danskine E Loth 128 F6
Danthorpe E R Yk 93 N4
Danzey Green Warwks 58 H11
Dapple Heath Staffs 71 J9
Darby Green Hants 23 M2
Darcy Lever Bolton 89 L9
Dardy Powys 45 J11
Daren-felen Mons 30 H2
Darenth Kent 37 N6
Daresbury Halton 82 C8
Darfield Barns 91 L10
Darfoulds Notts 85 J5
Dargate Kent 39 J9
Darite Cnwll 5 M8
Darland Medway 38 C8
Darland Wrexhm 69 L3
Darlaston Wsall 58 E5
Darlaston Green Wsall 58 E5
Darley N York 97 K9
Darley Abbey C Derb 72 B3
Darley Bridge Derbys 84 C8
Darley Dale Derbys 84 C8
Darley Green Solhll 59 J10
Darleyhall Herts 50 D6
Darley Head N York 97 J9
Darlingscott Warwks 47 P6
Darlington Darltn 103 Q8
Darlington Crematorium Darltn 103 Q8
Darliston Shrops 69 Q8
Darlton Notts 85 N6
Darnford Staffs 58 H3
Darnick Border 117 Q4
Darowen Powys 55 J4
Darra Abers 158 H8
Darracott Devon 16 C8
Darracott Devon 16 H4
Darras Hall Nthumb 113 J6
Darrington Wakefd 91 M7
Darsham Suffk 65 N8
Darshill Somset 20 B6
Dartford Kent 37 M6
Dartington Devon 7 K6
Dartmeet Devon 6 H4
Dartmoor National Park Devon 8 G9
Dartmouth Devon 7 M8
Darton Barns 91 J8
Darvel E Ayrs 125 P10
Darwell Hole E Susx 25 Q7
Darwen Bl w D 89 K6
Datchet W & M 35 Q9
Datchworth Herts 50 G7
Datchworth Green Herts 50 G7
Daubhill Bolton 89 L9
Daugh of Kinermony Moray 157 N9
Dauntsey Wilts 33 J8
Dava Highld 157 J10
Davenham Ches W 82 E10
Davenport Stockp 83 K7
Davenport Green Ches E 82 H9
Davenport Green Traffd 82 H7
Daventry Nhants 60 C8
Davidson's Mains C Edin 127 N2
Davidstow Cnwll 5 K4
David Street Kent 37 P8
Davington D & G 117 J10
Davington Hill Kent 38 H9
Daviot Abers 151 J2
Daviot Highld 156 C10
Daviot House Highld 156 C9
Davis's Town E Susx 25 M7
Davoch of Grange Moray 158 C7
Davyhulme Traffd 82 G5
Daw End Wsall 58 F4
Dawesgreen Surrey 36 F11
Dawley Wrekin 57 M3
Dawlish Devon 9 N9
Dawlish Warren Devon 9 N9
Dawn Conwy 80 B10

Eccleston - Farnham 275

Eccleston St Hel 81 P5
Eccleston Green Lancs 88 G7
Echt Abers 151 J6
Eckford Border 118 D5
Eckington Derbys 84 F5
Eckington Worcs 46 H6
Ecton Nhants 60 H8
Ecton Staffs 71 K3
Edale Derbys 83 P7
Eday Ork 169 e3
Eday Airport Ork 169 e3
Edburton W Susx 24 F8
Edderside Cumb 109 P11
Edderton Highld 162 G10
Eddington Kent 39 L8
Eddleston Border 127 N8
Eddlewood S Lans 126 C7
Edenbridge Kent 37 K11
Edenfield Lancs 89 N7
Edenhall Cumb 101 Q4
Edenham Lincs 73 R6
Eden Mount Cumb 95 J5
Eden Park Gt Lon 37 J7
Eden Project Cnwll 3 Q3
Edensor Derbys 84 B7
Edentaggart Ag & B 132 C9
Edenthorpe Donc 91 Q9
Edern Gwynd 66 D7
Edgarley Somset 19 P7
Edgbaston Birm 58 G8
Edgcombe Cnwll 3 J7
Edgcott Bucks 49 J10
Edgcott Somset 17 Q4
Edge Gloucs 32 F3
Edge Shrops 56 F3
Edgebolton Shrops 69 Q10
Edge End Gloucs 31 Q2
Edgefield Norfk 76 F5
Edgefield Green Norfk 76 F5
Edgefold Bolton 89 L9
Edge Green Ches W 69 N4
Edgehill Warwks 48 C5
Edgerley Shrops 69 L11
Edgerton Kirk 90 E7
Edgeside Lancs 89 N6
Edgeworth Gloucs 32 H3
Edgeworthy Devon 9 K2
Edginswell Torbay 7 M5
Edgiock Worcs 47 K2
Edgmond Wrekin 70 C11
Edgmond Marsh Wrekin 70 C10
Edgton Shrops 56 F7
Edgware Gt Lon 36 E2
Edgworth Bl w D 89 L7
Edinbane Highld 152 E7
Edinburgh C Edin 127 P3
Edinburgh Airport C Edin 127 L3
Edinburgh Castle C Edin 127 P3
Edinburgh Old & New Town C Edin 127 P3
Edinburgh Royal Botanic Gardens C Edin 127 N2
Edinburgh Zoo C Edin 127 N3
Edingale Staffs 59 K2
Edingham D & G 108 H8
Edingley Notts 85 L9
Edingthorpe Norfk 77 L5
Edingthorpe Green Norfk 77 L5
Edington Border 129 M9
Edington Nthumb 113 J4
Edington Somset 19 L7
Edington Wilts 20 H4
Edington Burtle Somset 19 L6
Edingworth Somset 19 L4
Edistone Devon 16 D7
Edithmead Somset 19 K5
Edith Weston Rutlnd 73 N9
Edlesborough Bucks 49 Q11
Edlingham Nthumb 119 M9
Edlington Lincs 86 H6
Edmond Castle Cumb 111 J9
Edmondsham Dorset 13 J2
Edmondsley Dur 113 K11
Edmondthorpe Leics 73 M7
Edmonton Cnwll 4 F7
Edmonton Gt Lon 36 H2
Edmundbyers Dur 112 F10
Ednam Border 118 D3
Ednaston Derbys 71 N6
Edradynate P & K 141 L7
Edrom Border 129 L8
Edstaston Shrops 69 P8
Edstone Warwks 47 N2
Edvin Loach Herefs 46 C3
Edwalton Notts 72 F3
Edwardstone Suffk 52 F3
Edwardsville Myr Td 30 E5
Edwinsford Carmth 43 M8
Edwinstowe Notts 85 K7
Edworth C Beds 50 F2
Edwyn Ralph Herefs 46 B3
Edzell Angus 143 L4
Edzell Woods Abers 143 L4
Efail-fach Neath 29 L5
Efail Isaf Rhondd 30 E8
Efailnewydd Gwynd 66 F7
Efail-Rhyd Powys 68 G9
Efailwen Carmth 41 M5
Efenechtyd Denbgs 68 F3
Effgill D & G 110 F2
Effingham Surrey 36 D10
Efflinch Staffs 71 M11
Efford Devon 9 L4
Efford Crematorium C Plym 6 E7
Egbury Hants 22 D4
Egdean W Susx 23 Q10
Egerton Bolton 89 L8
Egerton Kent 26 F2
Egerton Forstal Kent 26 E2
Eggborough N York 91 P6
Eggbuckland C Plym 6 E7
Eggesford Devon 17 M9
Eggington C Beds 49 Q9
Egginton Derbys 71 P9
Egglescliffe S on T 104 D8
Eggleston Dur 103 J6
Egham Surrey 36 B6
Egham Wick Surrey 35 Q10
Egleton Rutlnd 73 M9
Eglingham Nthumb 119 M7
Egloshayle Cnwll 4 G7
Egloskerry Cnwll 5 M4
Eglwysbach Conwy 79 Q10
Eglwys-Brewis V Glam 30 D11
Eglwys Cross Wrexhm 69 N6
Eglwys Fach Cerdgn 54 F5
Eglwyswrw Pembks 41 M3
Egmanton Notts 85 M7
Egremont Cumb 100 D8
Egremont Wirral 81 L6
Egton N York 105 M9
Egton Bridge N York 105 M10
Egypt Bucks 35 Q7
Egypt Hants 22 E6
Eigg Highld 144 G10
Eight Ash Green Essex 52 F6
Eilanreach Highld 145 P4
Eilean Donan Castle Highld 145 Q2
Eisteddfa Gurig Cerdgn 54 H8
Elan Valley Powys 44 B2
Elan Village Powys 44 C2
Elberton S Glos 32 B7
Elbridge W Susx 15 P6
Elburton C Plym 6 E8
Elcombe Swindn 33 M8
Elcot W Berk 34 C11
Eldernell Cambs 74 F11
Eldersfield Worcs 46 E8
Elderslie Rens 125 L5
Elder Street Essex 51 N4
Eldon Dur 103 P5
Eldwick C Brad 90 E2
Elfhill Abers 151 L10
Elford Nthumb 119 N4
Elford Staffs 59 J2
Elgin Moray 157 N5
Elgol Highld 144 H5
Elham Kent 27 L3
Elie Fife 135 M7
Elilaw Nthumb 119 J9
Elim IoA 78 F8
Eling Hants 14 C4
Elkesley Notts 85 L5
Elkstone Gloucs 33 J2
Ella Abers 158 F6
Ellacombe Torbay 7 N6
Elland Calder 90 E6
Elland Lower Edge Calder 90 E6
Ellary Ag & B 123 M4
Ellastone Staffs 71 L6
Ellel Lancs 95 K9
Ellemford Border 129 J7
Ellenabeich Ag & B 130 E4
Ellenborough Cumb 100 D3
Ellenbrook Salfd 82 F4
Ellenhall Staffs 70 E9
Ellen's Green Surrey 24 C3
Ellerbeck N York 104 D11
Ellerby N York 105 L8
Ellerdine Heath Wrekin 69 R10
Ellerhayes Devon 9 N4
Elleric Ag & B 139 J8
Ellerker E R Yk 92 F5
Ellers N York 90 C2
Ellerton E R Yk 92 B3
Ellerton N York 103 Q11
Ellerton Shrops 70 C9
Ellesborough Bucks 35 M3
Ellesmere Shrops 69 L8
Ellesmere Port Ches W 81 N9
Ellingham Hants 13 K3
Ellingham Norfk 65 M3
Ellingham Nthumb 119 N5
Ellingstring N York 97 J4
Ellington Cambs 61 Q6
Ellington Nthumb 113 L2
Ellington Thorpe Cambs 61 Q6
Elliots Green Somset 20 E5
Ellisfield Hants 22 H5
Ellishader Highld 153 J4
Ellistown Leics 72 C8
Ellon Abers 159 N11
Ellonby Cumb 101 M3
Ellough Suffk 65 N4
Elloughton E R Yk 92 F5
Ellwood Gloucs 31 Q3
Elm Cambs 75 J9
Elmbridge Worcs 58 D11
Elmdon Essex 51 L3
Elmdon Solhll 59 J8
Elmdon Heath Solhll 59 J8
Elmer W Susx 15 Q6
Elmers End Gt Lon 37 J7
Elmer's Green Lancs 88 G9
Elmesthorpe Leics 72 D11
Elm Green Essex 52 C10
Elmhurst Staffs 58 H2
Elmley Castle Worcs 47 J6
Elmley Lovett Worcs 58 C11
Elmore Gloucs 46 E11
Elmore Back Gloucs 46 E11
Elm Park Gt Lon 37 M3
Elmscott Devon 16 C7
Elmsett Suffk 53 J2
Elms Green Worcs 57 N11
Elmstead Heath Essex 53 J7
Elmstead Market Essex 53 J7
Elmstead Row Essex 53 J7
Elmsted Kent 27 K3
Elmstone Kent 39 N9
Elmstone Hardwicke Gloucs 46 H9
Elmswell E R Yk 99 K9
Elmswell Suffk 64 D9
Elmton Derbys 84 H6
Elphin Highld 161 L4
Elphinstone E Loth 128 B6
Elrick Abers 151 L6
Elrig D & G 107 K8
Elrington Nthumb 112 C8
Elsdon Nthumb 112 D2
Elsecar Barns 91 K11
Elsenham Essex 51 M5
Elsfield Oxon 34 F2
Elsham N Linc 92 H8
Elsing Norfk 76 F8
Elslack N York 96 D11
Elson Hants 14 H6
Elson Shrops 69 L7
Elsrickle S Lans 116 F2
Elstead Surrey 23 P6
Elsted W Susx 23 M11
Elsthorpe Lincs 73 R6
Elstob Dur 104 B6
Elston Lancs 88 H4
Elston Notts 85 N11
Elston Wilts 21 L6
Elstone Devon 17 M8
Elstow Bed 61 N11
Elstree Herts 50 E11
Elstronwick E R Yk 93 M4
Elswick Lancs 88 E3
Elswick N u Ty 113 K8
Elsworth Cambs 62 D8
Elterwater Cumb 101 K10
Eltham Gt Lon 37 K6
Eltham Crematorium Gt Lon 37 K6
Eltisley Cambs 62 C9
Elton Bury 89 M8
Elton Cambs 61 N2
Elton Ches W 81 P9
Elton Derbys 84 B8
Elton Gloucs 32 D2
Elton Herefs 56 H10
Elton Notts 73 K3
Elton S on T 104 D7
Elton Green Ches W 81 P10
Eltringham Nthumb 112 G8
Elvanfoot S Lans 116 D7
Elvaston Derbys 72 C4
Elveden Suffk 63 P4
Elvetham Heath Hants 23 M3
Elvingston E Loth 128 D5
Elvington C York 98 E11
Elvington Kent 39 N11
Elwell Devon 17 M5
Elwick Hartpl 104 E4
Elwick Nthumb 119 M3
Elworth Ches E 70 C2
Elworthy Somset 18 E8
Ely Cambs 62 H4
Ely Cardif 30 F9
Emberton M Keyn 49 N5
Embleton Cumb 100 G4
Embleton Dur 104 D5
Embleton Nthumb 119 P6
Embo Highld 163 J8
Emborough Somset 20 B4
Embo Street Highld 163 J8
Embsay N York 96 F10
Emery Down Hants 13 N3
Emley Kirk 90 G8
Emley Moor Kirk 90 G8
Emmbrook Wokham 35 M11
Emmer Green Readg 35 K9
Emmett Carr Derbys 84 G5
Emmington Oxon 35 K4
Emneth Norfk 75 J9
Emneth Hungate Norfk 75 K9
Empingham Rutlnd 73 N9
Empshott Hants 23 L8
Empshott Green Hants 23 K8
Emstrey Crematorium Shrops 57 J2
Emsworth Hants 15 K5
Enborne W Berk 34 D11
Enborne Row W Berk 22 D2
Enchmarsh Shrops 57 J5
Enderby Leics 72 E11
Endmoor Cumb 95 L4
Endon Staffs 70 G4
Endon Bank Staffs 70 G4
Enfield Gt Lon 51 J11
Enfield Crematorium Gt Lon 50 H11
Enfield Lock Gt Lon 51 J11
Enfield Wash Gt Lon 51 J11
Enford Wilts 21 M4
Engine Common S Glos 32 C8
England's Gate Herefs 45 Q4
Englefield W Berk 34 H10
Englefield Green Surrey 35 Q10
Engleseabrook Ches E 70 D4
English Bicknor Gloucs 46 A11
Englishcombe BaNES 20 D2
English Frankton Shrops 69 N9
Engollan Cnwll 4 D7
Enham-Alamein Hants 22 C5
Enmore Somset 18 H7
Enmore Green Dorset 20 G10
Ennerdale Bridge Cumb 100 E7
Enniscaven Cnwll 4 F10
Enochdhu P & K 141 Q5
Ensay Ag & B 137 K6
Ensbury Bmouth 13 J5
Ensdon Shrops 69 M11
Ensis Devon 17 K6
Enson Staffs 70 G9
Enstone Oxon 48 C10
Enterkinfoot D & G 116 B10
Enterpen N York 104 E9
Enville Staffs 58 B7
Eolaigearraidh W Isls 168 c17
Epney Gloucs 32 E2
Epperstone Notts 85 L11
Epping Essex 51 L10
Epping Green Essex 51 K9
Epping Green Herts 50 G9
Epping Upland Essex 51 K10
Eppleby N York 103 N8
Eppleworth E R Yk 92 H4
Epsom Surrey 36 F8
Epwell Oxon 48 C6
Epworth N Linc 92 C10
Epworth Turbary N Linc 92 C10
Erbistock Wrexhm 69 L6
Erdington Birm 58 H6
Eridge Green E Susx 25 N3
Eridge Station E Susx 25 M4
Erines Ag & B 123 Q4
Eriska Ag & B 138 G9
Eriskay W Isls 168 c17
Eriswell Suffk 63 M5
Erith Gt Lon 37 M5
Erlestoke Wilts 21 J4
Ermington Devon 6 G8
Erpingham Norfk 76 H5
Erriottwood Kent 38 F10
Errogie Highld 147 P3
Errol P & K 134 G3
Erskine Rens 125 M3
Ervie D & G 106 D4
Erwarton Suffk 53 M5
Erwood Powys 44 F6
Eryholme N York 104 B9
Eryrys Denbgs 68 H3
Escalls Cnwll 2 B8
Escomb Dur 103 N4
Escott Somset 18 E7
Escrick N York 91 Q2
Esgair Carmth 42 G9
Esgair Cerdgn 54 D11
Esgairgeiliog Powys 54 H3
Esgerdawe Carmth 43 M6
Esgyryn Conwy 79 Q9
Esh Dur 103 N2
Esher Surrey 36 D8
Esholt C Brad 90 F2
Eshott Nthumb 119 P11
Eshton N York 96 D9
Esh Winning Dur 103 N2
Eskadale Highld 155 N9
Eskbank Mdloth 127 Q4
Eskdale Green Cumb 100 F10
Eskdalemuir D & G 117 K11
Eskham Lincs 93 Q11
Eskholme Donc 91 Q7
Esperley Lane Ends Dur 103 M6
Esprick Lancs 88 E3
Essendine Rutlnd 73 Q8
Essendon Herts 50 G9
Essich Highld 156 A10
Essington Staffs 58 E4
Esslemont Abers 151 N2
Eston R & Cl 104 F7
Etal Nthumb 118 H3
Etchilhampton Wilts 21 K2
Etchingham E Susx 26 B6
Etchinghill Kent 27 L4
Etchinghill Staffs 71 J11
Etchingwood E Susx 25 M6
Etling Green Norfk 76 E9
Etloe Gloucs 32 C3
Eton W & M 35 Q9
Eton Wick W & M 35 P9
Etruria C Stke 70 F5
Etteridge Highld 148 B9
Ettersgill Dur 102 G5
Ettiley Heath Ches E 70 C2
Ettingshall Wolves 58 D5
Ettington Warwks 47 Q5
Etton C Pete 74 B9
Etton E R Yk 92 G2
Ettrick Border 117 K8
Ettrickbridge Border 117 M6
Ettrickhill Border 117 K8
Etwall Derbys 71 P8
Eudon George Shrops 57 M7
Euston Suffk 64 B6
Euximoor Drove Cambs 75 J11
Euxton Lancs 88 H7
Evancoyd Powys 45 K2
Evanton Highld 155 R4
Evedon Lincs 86 E11
Evelith Shrops 57 N3
Evelix Highld 162 H8
Evenjobb Powys 45 K2
Evenley Nhants 48 G8
Evenlode Gloucs 47 P9
Evenwood Dur 103 N6
Evenwood Gate Dur 103 N6
Evercreech Somset 20 B7
Everingham E R Yk 92 D2
Everleigh Wilts 21 P4
Everley N York 99 K3
Eversholt C Beds 49 Q8
Evershot Dorset 11 M4
Eversley Hants 23 L2
Eversley Cross Hants 23 L2
Everthorpe E R Yk 92 F4
Everton C Beds 62 B10
Everton Hants 13 N6
Everton Lpool 81 L6
Everton Notts 85 L2
Evertown D & G 110 G5
Evesbatch Herefs 46 C5
Evesham Worcs 47 K6
Evington C Leic 72 G10
Ewden Village Sheff 90 H11
Ewell Surrey 36 F8
Ewell Minnis Kent 27 N3
Ewelme Oxon 34 H6
Ewen Gloucs 33 K5
Ewenny V Glam 29 P9
Ewerby Lincs 86 F11
Ewerby Thorpe Lincs 86 F11
Ewhurst Surrey 24 C2
Ewhurst Green E Susx 26 C7
Ewhurst Green Surrey 24 C3
Ewloe Flints 81 L11
Ewloe Green Flints 81 K11
Ewood Bl w D 89 K5
Ewood Bridge Lancs 89 M6
Eworthy Devon 8 B5
Ewshot Hants 23 M5
Ewyas Harold Herefs 45 M9
Exbourne Devon 8 F4
Exbury Hants 14 D6
Exceat E Susx 25 M11
Exebridge Somset 18 B10
Exelby N York 97 L3
Exeter Devon 9 M6
Exeter Airport Devon 9 N6
Exeter & Devon Crematorium Devon 9 M6
Exeter Services Devon 9 N6
Exford Somset 17 R4
Exfordsgreen Shrops 56 H3
Exhall Warwks 47 M3
Exhall Warwks 59 N7
Exlade Street Oxon 35 J8
Exley Head C Brad 90 C2
Exminster Devon 9 M7
Exmoor National Park 17 R4
Exmouth Devon 9 P8
Exning Suffk 63 K7
Exted Kent 27 L3
Exton Devon 9 N7
Exton Hants 22 H10
Exton Rutlnd 73 N8
Exton Somset 18 B8
Exwick Devon 9 M6
Eyam Derbys 84 B5
Eydon Nhants 48 F5
Eye C Pete 74 D10
Eye Herefs 45 P2
Eye Suffk 64 G7
Eye Green C Pete 74 D10
Eye Kettleby Leics 73 J7
Eyemouth Border 129 N7
Eyeworth C Beds 62 C11
Eyhorne Street Kent 38 D11
Eyke Suffk 65 L11
Eynesbury Cambs 61 Q9
Eynsford Kent 37 M7
Eynsham Oxon 34 D3
Eype Dorset 11 J6
Eyre Highld 152 G7
Eythorne Kent 27 N2
Eyton Herefs 45 P2
Eyton Shrops 56 F2
Eyton Shrops 56 F7
Eyton Shrops 69 M10
Eyton Wrexhm 69 L6
Eyton on Severn Shrops 57 K3
Eyton upon the Weald Moors Wrekin 57 M2

F

Faccombe Hants 22 C3
Faceby N York 104 E10
Fachwen Powys 68 D11
Facit Lancs 89 P7
Fackley Notts 84 G8
Faddiley Ches E 69 Q4
Fadmoor N York 98 D3
Faerdre Swans 29 J4
Fagwyr Swans 29 J4
Faifley W Duns 125 M3
Failand N Som 31 P10
Failford S Ayrs 115 J2
Failsworth Oldham 83 J4
Fairbourne Gwynd 54 E2
Fairburn N York 91 M5
Fairfield Derbys 83 N10
Fairfield Kent 26 G6
Fairfield Worcs 58 D9
Fairford Gloucs 33 N4
Fairford Park Gloucs 33 N4
Fairgirth D & G 109 J9
Fair Green Norfk 75 N7
Fairhaven Lancs 88 C5
Fair Isle Shet 169 t12
Fairlands Surrey 23 Q4
Fairlie N Ayrs 124 G7
Fairlight E Susx 26 E9
Fairmile Devon 10 B5
Fairmile Surrey 36 D8
Fairnilee Border 117 P4
Fair Oak Hants 22 E11
Fairoak Staffs 70 D8
Fair Oak Green Hants 23 J2
Fairseat Kent 37 P8
Fairstead Essex 52 C8
Fairstead Norfk 75 M6
Fairstead Norfk 77 K7
Fairwarp E Susx 25 L5
Fairwater Cardif 30 F9
Fairy Cross Devon 16 G7
Fakenham Norfk 76 C6
Fakenham Magna Suffk 64 C6
Fala Mdloth 128 C7
Fala Dam Mdloth 128 C7
Falcut Nhants 48 G6
Faldingworth Lincs 86 E4
Faldouet Jersey 11 c2
Falfield S Glos 32 C6
Falkenham Suffk 53 N4
Falkirk Falk 133 P11
Falkirk Crematorium Falk 133 P11
Falkirk Wheel Falk 133 P11
Falkland Fife 134 H6
Fallburn S Lans 116 D3
Fallgate Derbys 84 E8
Fallin Stirlg 133 N9
Fallodon Nthumb 119 N6
Fallowfield Manch 83 J6
Fallowfield Nthumb 112 D7
Falls of Blarghour Ag & B 131 K5
Falmer E Susx 25 J9
Falmouth Cnwll 3 L7
Falnash Border 117 M9
Falsgrave N York 99 L3
Falstone Nthumb 111 P3
Fanagmore Highld 164 E7
Fancott C Beds 50 B5
Fanellan Highld 155 N9
Fangdale Beck N York 98 B2
Fangfoss E R Yk 98 F10
Fanmore Ag & B 137 L7
Fannich Lodge Highld 154 H4
Fans Border 118 B2
Far Bletchley M Keyn 49 N8
Farcet Cambs 62 B2
Far Cotton Nhants 60 G9
Farden Shrops 57 K9
Fareham Hants 14 G5
Far End Cumb 101 K11
Farewell Staffs 58 G2
Far Forest Worcs 57 N9
Farforth Lincs 87 K5
Far Green Gloucs 32 E4
Faringdon Oxon 33 Q5
Farington Lancs 88 G5
Farlam Cumb 111 L9
Farleigh N Som 31 P11
Farleigh Surrey 37 J8
Farleigh Hungerford Somset 20 F3
Farleigh Wallop Hants 22 H5
Farlesthorpe Lincs 87 N6
Farleton Cumb 95 L4
Farleton Lancs 95 M7
Farley Derbys 84 C8
Farley Staffs 71 K6
Farley Wilts 21 P9
Farley Green Suffk 63 M10
Farley Green Surrey 36 C11
Farley Hill Wokham 23 K2
Farleys End Gloucs 32 E2
Farlington C Port 15 J5
Farlington N York 98 C7
Farlow Shrops 57 L8
Farmborough BaNES 20 C2
Farmbridge End Essex 51 P8
Farmcote Gloucs 47 L9
Farmcote Shrops 57 P6
Farmers Carmth 43 M6
Farmington Gloucs 47 M11
Farmoor Oxon 34 E3
Far Moor Wigan 82 B4
Farms Common Cnwll 2 H7
Farm Town Leics 72 B7
Farmtown Moray 158 D7
Farnah Green Derbys 84 D11
Farnborough Gt Lon 37 K8
Farnborough Hants 23 N4
Farnborough W Berk 34 D8
Farnborough Warwks 48 D5
Farnborough Park Hants 23 N3
Farnborough Street Hants 23 N3
Farncombe Surrey 23 Q6
Farndish Bed 61 K8
Farndon Ches W 69 M4
Farndon Notts 85 N10
Farne Islands Nthumb 119 P3
Farnell Angus 143 L6
Farnham Dorset 21 J11
Farnham Essex 51 L6
Farnham N York 97 M8
Farnham Suffk 65 M9
Farnham Surrey 23 M5

278 Goatham Green - Grimston

Goatham Green E Susx 26 D7
Goathill Dorset 20 C11
Goathland N York 105 M10
Goathurst Somset 19 J8
Goathurst Common Kent 37 L10
Goat Lees Kent 26 H2
Gobowen Shrops 69 K8
Godalming Surrey 23 Q6
Goddard's Corner Suffk 65 K8
Goddard's Green Kent 26 D5
Goddards Green W Susx 24 G6
Godford Cross Devon 10 C4
Godington Oxon 48 H9
Godley Tamesd 83 L5
Godmanchester Cambs 62 B6
Godmanstone Dorset 11 P5
Godmersham Kent 39 J11
Godney Somset 19 N6
Godolphin Cross Cnwll 2 G7
Godre'r-graig Neath 29 L3
Godshill Hants 21 N11
Godshill IoW 14 F10
Godstone Staffs 71 J8
Godstone Surrey 37 J10
Godsworthy Devon 8 D9
Godwinscroft Hants 13 L5
Goetre Mons 31 K3
Goff's Oak Herts 50 H10
Gofilon Mons 31 J2
Gogar C Edin 127 M3
Goginan Cerdgn 54 F8
Golan Gwynd 67 J6
Golant Cnwll 5 J11
Golberdon Cnwll 5 N7
Golborne Wigan 82 D5
Golcar Kirk 90 D7
Goldcliff Newpt 31 L8
Golden Cross E Susx 25 M8
Golden Green Kent 37 P11
Golden Grove Carmth 43 L11
Goldenhill C Stke 70 F4
Golden Hill Pembks 41 J10
Golden Pot Hants 23 K6
Golden Valley Derbys 84 F10
Golders Green Gt Lon 36 F3
Golders Green Crematorium Gt Lon 36 G3
Goldfinch Bottom W Berk 22 F2
Goldhanger Essex 52 F10
Gold Hill Cambs 62 H2
Gold Hill Dorset 12 D2
Golding Shrops 57 J4
Goldington Bed 61 N10
Goldsborough N York 97 N9
Goldsborough N York 105 M8
Golds Green Sandw 58 E6
Goldsithney Cnwll 2 E7
Goldstone Kent 39 N9
Goldstone Shrops 70 C9
Goldsworth Park Surrey 23 Q3
Goldthorpe Barns 91 M10
Goldworthy Devon 16 F7
Golford Kent 26 C4
Golford Green Kent 26 C4
Gollanfield Highld 156 E7
Gollinglith Foot N York 96 H4
Golly Wrexhm 69 K3
Golsoncott Somset 18 D7
Golspie Highld 163 J6
Gomeldon Wilts 21 N7
Gomersal Kirk 90 G5
Gomshall Surrey 36 C11
Gonalston Notts 85 L11
Gonerby Hill Foot Lincs 73 N3
Gonfirth Shet 169 q7
Goodameavy Devon 6 E6
Good Easter Essex 51 P8
Gooderstone Norfk 75 Q10
Goodleigh Devon 17 L5
Goodmanham E R Yk 92 E2
Goodmayes Gt Lon 37 L3
Goodnestone Kent 38 H9
Goodnestone Kent 39 N11
Goodrich Herefs 45 R11
Goodrington Torbay 7 M7
Goodshaw Lancs 89 N5
Goodshaw Fold Lancs 89 N5
Goodstone Devon 7 K4
Goodwick Pembks 40 H3
Goodworth Clatford Hants 22 C6
Goodyers End Warwks 59 M7
Goole E R Yk 92 B6
Goole Fields E R Yk 92 C6
Goom's Hill Worcs 47 K4
Goonbell Cnwll 3 J4
Goonhavern Cnwll 3 K3
Goonvrea Cnwll 3 J4
Goosecruives Abers 151 K11
Gooseford Devon 8 G6
Goose Green Essex 53 K6
Goose Green Kent 26 D4
Goose Green Kent 37 P10
Goose Green S Glos 32 C10
Goose Green W Susx 24 D7
Goose Green Wigan 82 C4
Gooseham Cnwll 16 C8
Gooseham Mill Cnwll 16 C8
Goosehill Green Worcs 46 H2
Goose Pool Herefs 45 P7
Goosey Oxon 34 C6
Goosnargh Lancs 88 H3
Goostrey Ches E 82 G10
Gordano Services N Som 31 P9
Gorddinog Conwy 79 M10
Gordon Border 118 B2
Gordon Arms Hotel Border 117 L5
Gordonstown Abers 158 E6
Gordonstown Abers 158 H10
Gore Powys 45 K3
Gorebridge Mdloth 127 Q5
Gorefield Cambs 74 H8
Gore Pit Essex 52 E8
Gores Wilts 21 M3
Gore Street Kent 39 N8
Gorey Jersey 11 c2
Goring Oxon 34 H8
Goring-by-Sea W Susx 24 D10
Goring Heath Oxon 35 J9
Gorleston on Sea Norfk 77 Q11
Gornal Wood Crematorium Dudley 58 D6
Gorrachie Abers 158 H6
Gorran Churchtown Cnwll 3 P5
Gorran Haven Cnwll 3 Q5
Gorran High Lanes Cnwll 3 P5
Gorrig Cerdgn 42 H6
Gors Cerdgn 54 E9
Gorsedd Flints 80 H9
Gorse Hill Swindn 33 N7
Gorseinon Swans 28 G5
Gorseybank Derbys 71 P4
Gorsgoch Cerdgn 43 J4
Gorslas Carmth 28 G2
Gorsley Gloucs 46 C9
Gorsley Common Herefs 46 C9
Gorstage Ches W 82 D10
Gorstan Highld 155 L5
Gorstella Ches W 69 L2
Gorst Hill Worcs 57 N10
Gorsty Hill Staffs 71 L9
Gorten Ag & B 138 C11
Gorthleck Highld 147 N3
Gorton Manch 83 J5
Gosbeck Suffk 64 H10
Gosberton Lincs 74 D4
Gosberton Clough Lincs 74 C5
Gosfield Essex 52 C6
Gosford Devon 10 C5
Gosforth Cumb 100 E10
Gosforth N u Ty 113 K7
Gosling Street Somset 19 P8
Gosmore Herts 50 E5
Gospel End Staffs 58 C6
Gospel Green W Susx 23 P8
Gosport Hants 14 H7
Gossard's Green C Beds 49 Q6
Gossington Gloucs 32 D4
Goswick Nthumb 119 L2
Gotham Notts 72 E4
Gotherington Gloucs 47 J9
Gotton Somset 18 H9
Goudhurst Kent 26 B4
Goulceby Lincs 87 J5
Gourdas Abers 159 J9
Gourdie C Dund 142 F11
Gourdon Abers 143 Q3
Gourock Inver 124 G2
Govan C Glas 125 N4
Goveton Devon 7 K9
Gowdall E R Yk 91 Q6
Gower Highld 155 P6
Gower Swans 28 F6
Gowerton Swans 28 G5
Gowkhall Fife 134 D10
Gowthorpe E R Yk 98 F10
Goxhill E R Yk 93 L2
Goxhill N Linc 93 K6
Grabhair W Isls 168 i6
Graby Lincs 74 A5
Grade Cnwll 3 J11
Gradeley Green Ches E 69 Q4
Graffham W Susx 23 P11
Grafham Cambs 61 Q7
Grafham Surrey 24 B2
Grafton Herefs 45 P7
Grafton N York 97 P8
Grafton Oxon 33 Q4
Grafton Shrops 69 M11
Grafton Worcs 46 A2
Grafton Worcs 47 J7
Grafton Flyford Worcs 47 J3
Grafton Regis Nhants 49 L5
Grafton Underwood Nhants 61 K4
Grafty Green Kent 26 E2
Graianrhyd Denbgs 68 H3
Graig Conwy 79 Q10
Graig Denbgs 80 F10
Graig-fechan Denbgs 68 F4
Grain Medway 38 E6
Grains Bar Oldham 90 B9
Grainsby Lincs 93 N11
Grainthorpe Lincs 93 Q11
Grampound Cnwll 3 N4
Grampound Road Cnwll 3 N3
Gramsdal W Isls 168 d12
Gramsdale W Isls 168 d12
Granborough Bucks 49 L9
Granby Notts 73 K3
Grandborough Warwks 59 Q11
Grand Chemins Jersey 11 c2
Grandes Rocques Guern 10 b1
Grandtully P & K 141 M7
Grange Cumb 101 J7
Grange Medway 38 C8
Grange P & K 134 H2
Grange Wirral 81 J7
Grange Crossroads Moray 158 C7
Grange Hall Moray 157 K5
Grangehall S Lans 116 D2
Grange Hill Essex 37 K2
Grangemill Derbys 84 B9
Grange Moor Kirk 90 G7
Grangemouth Falk 133 Q11
Grange of Lindores Fife 134 H4
Grange-over-Sands Cumb 95 J5
Grangepans Falk 134 C11
Grangetown R & Cl 104 F6
Grangetown Sundld 113 P10
Grange Villa Dur 113 K10
Gransmoor E R Yk 99 N9
Gransmore Green Essex 51 Q6
Granston Pembks 40 G4
Grantchester Cambs 62 F9
Grantham Lincs 73 N3
Grantham Crematorium Lincs 73 N3
Granton C Edin 127 N2
Grantown-on-Spey Highld 149 J2
Grantsfield Herefs 45 Q2
Grantshouse Border 129 L6
Grappenhall Warrtn 82 D7
Grasby Lincs 93 J10
Grasmere Cumb 101 K9
Grasscroft Oldham 83 L4
Grassendale Lpool 81 M7
Grassgarth Cumb 101 K2
Grass Green Essex 52 B4
Grassington N York 96 F8
Grassmoor Derbys 84 F7
Grassthorpe Notts 85 N7
Grateley Hants 21 Q6
Gratwich Staffs 71 J8
Graveley Cambs 62 C8
Graveley Herts 50 F5
Gravelly Hill Birm 58 H6
Gravelsbank Shrops 56 E4
Graveney Kent 39 J9
Gravesend Kent 37 Q6
Gravir W Isls 168 i6
Grayingham Lincs 92 F11
Grayrigg Cumb 101 Q11
Grays Thurr 37 P5
Grayshott Hants 23 N7
Grayson Green Cumb 100 C5
Grayswood Surrey 23 P8
Graythorpe Hartpl 104 F5
Grazeley Wokham 35 J11
Greasbrough Rothm 91 L11
Greasby Wirral 81 K7
Greasley Notts 84 G11
Great Abington Cambs 62 H11
Great Addington Nhants 61 L5
Great Alne Warwks 47 M3
Great Altcar Lancs 88 C9
Great Amwell Herts 51 J8
Great Asby Cumb 102 C8
Great Ashfield Suffk 64 D8
Great Ayton N York 104 G8
Great Baddow Essex 52 B11
Great Badminton S Glos 32 F8
Great Bardfield Essex 51 Q4
Great Barford Bed 61 P10
Great Barr Sandw 58 F5
Great Barrington Gloucs 33 P2
Great Barrow Ches W 81 P11
Great Barton Suffk 64 B8
Great Barugh N York 98 E5
Great Bavington Nthumb 112 E4
Great Bealings Suffk 53 M2
Great Bedwyn Wilts 21 Q2
Great Bentley Essex 53 K7
Great Billing Nhants 60 H8
Great Bircham Norfk 75 Q4
Great Blakenham Suffk 64 G11
Great Blencow Cumb 101 N4
Great Bolas Wrekin 70 A10
Great Bookham Surrey 36 D10
Great Bosullow Cnwll 2 C7
Great Bourton Oxon 48 E5
Great Bowden Leics 60 F3
Great Bradley Suffk 63 L10
Great Braxted Essex 52 E9
Great Bricett Suffk 64 E11
Great Brickhill Bucks 49 P8
Great Bridgeford Staffs 70 F9
Great Brington Nhants 60 E7
Great Bromley Essex 53 J6
Great Broughton Cumb 100 E4
Great Broughton N York 104 F9
Great Budworth Ches W 82 E9
Great Burdon Darltn 104 B7
Great Burstead Essex 37 Q2
Great Busby N York 104 F9
Great Canfield Essex 51 N7
Great Carlton Lincs 87 M3
Great Casterton Rutlnd 73 Q9
Great Chalfield Wilts 20 G2
Great Chart Kent 26 G3
Great Chatwell Staffs 57 P2
Great Chell C Stke 70 F4
Great Chesterford Essex 51 M2
Great Cheverell Wilts 21 J4
Great Chishill Cambs 51 K3
Great Clacton Essex 53 L8
Great Cliffe Wakefd 91 J7
Great Clifton Cumb 100 D5
Great Coates NE Lin 93 M9
Great Comberton Worcs 47 J6
Great Comp Kent 37 P9
Great Corby Cumb 111 J10
Great Cornard Suffk 52 E3
Great Cowden E R Yk 93 M2
Great Coxwell Oxon 33 Q6
Great Cransley Nhants 60 H5
Great Cressingham Norfk 76 B11
Great Crosthwaite Cumb 101 J6
Great Cubley Derbys 71 M7
Great Cumbrae Island N Ayrs 124 F6
Great Dalby Leics 73 J8
Great Doddington Nhants 61 J8
Great Doward Herefs 45 Q11
Great Dunham Norfk 76 B9
Great Dunmow Essex 51 P6
Great Durnford Wilts 21 M7
Great Easton Essex 51 P5
Great Easton Leics 60 H2
Great Eccleston Lancs 88 E2
Great Edstone N York 98 E4
Great Ellingham Norfk 64 E2
Great Elm Somset 20 D5
Great Everdon Nhants 60 C9
Great Eversden Cambs 62 E10
Great Fencote N York 97 L2
Greatfield Wilts 33 L7
Great Finborough Suffk 64 E10
Greatford Lincs 74 A8
Great Fransham Norfk 76 B9
Great Gaddesden Herts 50 B8
Greatgate Staffs 71 K7
Great Gidding Cambs 61 P4
Great Givendale E R Yk 98 G10
Great Glemham Suffk 65 L9
Great Glen Leics 72 H11
Great Gonerby Lincs 73 M3
Great Gransden Cambs 62 C9
Great Green Cambs 50 G2
Great Green Norfk 65 K4
Great Green Suffk 64 C10
Great Green Suffk 64 C8
Great Habton N York 98 F5
Great Hale Lincs 74 B2
Great Hallingbury Essex 51 M7
Greatham Hants 23 L8
Greatham Hartpl 104 E5
Greatham W Susx 24 B7
Great Hampden Bucks 35 M4
Great Harrowden Nhants 61 J6
Great Harwood Lancs 89 L4
Great Haseley Oxon 34 H4
Great Hatfield E R Yk 93 L2
Great Haywood Staffs 70 H10
Great Heck N York 91 P6
Great Henny Essex 52 E4
Great Hinton Wilts 20 H3
Great Hockham Norfk 64 D3
Great Holland Essex 53 M8
Great Hollands Br For 35 N11
Great Horkesley Essex 52 G5
Great Hormead Herts 51 K5
Great Horton C Brad 90 E4
Great Horwood Bucks 49 L8
Great Houghton Barns 91 L9
Great Houghton Nhants 60 G9
Great Hucklow Derbys 83 Q9
Great Kelk E R Yk 99 N9
Great Kimble Bucks 35 M3
Great Kingshill Bucks 35 N5
Great Langdale Cumb 101 J9
Great Langton N York 103 Q11
Great Leighs Essex 52 B8
Great Limber Lincs 93 K9
Great Linford M Keyn 49 N6
Great Livermere Suffk 64 B7
Great Longstone Derbys 84 B6
Great Lumley Dur 113 L11
Great Lyth Shrops 56 H3
Great Malvern Worcs 46 E5
Great Maplestead Essex 52 D5
Great Marton Bpool 88 C3
Great Massingham Norfk 75 Q6
Great Melton Norfk 76 G10
Great Meols Wirral 81 J6
Great Milton Oxon 34 H4
Great Missenden Bucks 35 N4
Great Mitton Lancs 89 L3
Great Mongeham Kent 39 Q11
Great Moulton Norfk 64 H3
Great Munden Herts 51 J6
Great Musgrave Cumb 102 E8
Great Ness Shrops 69 L11
Great Notley Essex 52 B7
Great Oak Mons 31 L2
Great Oakley Essex 53 L6
Great Oakley Nhants 61 J3
Great Offley Herts 50 D5
Great Ormside Cumb 102 D7
Great Orton Cumb 110 F10
Great Ouseburn N York 97 P8
Great Oxendon Nhants 60 F4
Great Oxney Green Essex 51 Q9
Great Palgrave Norfk 76 A9
Great Pattenden Kent 26 B3
Great Paxton Cambs 62 B8
Great Plumpton Lancs 88 D4
Great Plumstead Norfk 77 L9
Great Ponton Lincs 73 N4
Great Potheridge Devon 17 J9
Great Preston Leeds 91 L5
Great Purston Nhants 48 F7
Great Raveley Cambs 62 C4
Great Rissington Gloucs 47 N11
Great Rollright Oxon 48 B8
Great Rudbaxton Pembks 41 J6
Great Ryburgh Norfk 76 D6
Great Ryle Nthumb 119 K8
Great Ryton Shrops 56 H4
Great Saling Essex 51 Q5
Great Salkeld Cumb 101 Q3
Great Sampford Essex 51 P3
Great Saredon Staffs 58 E3
Great Saughall Ches W 81 M11
Great Saxham Suffk 63 N8
Great Shefford W Berk 34 C9
Great Shelford Cambs 62 G10
Great Smeaton N York 104 B10
Great Snoring Norfk 76 C5
Great Somerford Wilts 33 J8
Great Soudley Shrops 70 C9
Great Stainton Darltn 104 B6
Great Stambridge Essex 38 E3
Great Staughton Cambs 61 P8
Great Steeping Lincs 87 M8
Great Stoke S Glos 32 B8
Great Stonar Kent 39 P10
Greatstone-on-Sea Kent 27 J7
Great Strickland Cumb 101 Q6
Great Stukeley Cambs 62 B6
Great Sturton Lincs 86 H5
Great Sutton Ches W 81 M9
Great Sutton Shrops 57 J8
Great Swinburne Nthumb 112 D5
Great Tew Oxon 48 D9
Great Tey Essex 52 E6
Great Thurlow Suffk 63 L10
Great Torrington Devon 16 H8
Great Tosson Nthumb 119 K10
Great Totham Essex 52 E9
Great Totham Essex 52 E9
Great Tows Lincs 86 H2
Great Urswick Cumb 94 F6
Great Wakering Essex 38 F4
Great Waldingfield Suffk 52 F3
Great Walsingham Norfk 76 C4
Great Waltham Essex 51 Q8
Great Warford Ches E 82 H9
Great Warley Essex 37 N2
Great Washbourne Gloucs 47 J8
Great Weeke Devon 8 H7
Great Weldon Nhants 61 K3
Great Weinetham Suffk 64 B10
Great Wenham Suffk 53 J4
Great Whittington Nthumb 112 F6
Great Wigborough Essex 52 G8
Great Wilbraham Cambs 63 J9
Great Wishford Wilts 21 L7
Great Witchingham Norfk 76 G7
Great Witcombe Gloucs 32 H2
Great Witley Worcs 57 P11
Great Wolford Warwks 47 Q8
Greatworth Nhants 48 G6
Great Wratting Suffk 63 L11
Great Wymondley Herts 50 F5
Great Wyrley Staffs 58 E3
Great Wytheford Shrops 69 Q11
Great Yarmouth Norfk 77 Q10
Great Yarmouth Crematorium Norfk 77 Q11
Great Yeldham Essex 52 C4
Grebby Lincs 87 M7
Greeba IoM 80 d5
Green Denbgs 80 F11
Green Bank Cumb 94 H4
Greenburn W Loth 126 G5
Greencroft Hall Dur 113 J11
Green Cross Surrey 23 N7
Green Down Somset 19 Q4
Green End Bed 61 M11
Green End Bed 61 N8
Green End Bed 61 P10
Green End Bed 61 P8
Green End Cambs 61 Q4
Green End Cambs 62 B6
Green End Cambs 62 E9
Green End Cambs 62 G7
Green End Cambs 62 G8
Green End Herts 50 G4
Green End Herts 50 H4
Green End Herts 50 H6
Greenend Oxon 48 B10
Green End Warwks 59 L7
Greenfield Ag & B 131 Q9
Greenfield C Beds 50 C4
Greenfield Flints 80 H9
Greenfield Highld 146 G7
Greenfield Oldham 83 L4
Greenfield Oxon 35 K6
Greenford Gt Lon 36 D4
Greengairs N Lans 126 D3
Greengates C Brad 90 F3
Greengill Cumb 100 F3
Greenhalgh Lancs 88 E3
Greenham Somset 18 E10
Greenham W Berk 34 E11
Green Hammerton N York 97 Q9
Greenhaugh Nthumb 111 Q3
Green Head Cumb 110 G11
Greenhead Nthumb 111 N7
Green Heath Staffs 58 E2
Greenheys Salfd 82 F4
Greenhill D & G 109 P5
Greenhill Falk 126 E2
Greenhill Herefs 46 D5
Greenhill Kent 39 L8
Greenhill S Lans 116 C4
Green Hill Wilts 33 L7
Greenhillocks Derbys 84 F11
Greenhithe Kent 37 N5
Greenholm E Ayrs 125 N10
Greenholme Cumb 101 Q9
Greenhouse Border 117 R6
Greenhow Hill N York 96 H8
Greenland Highld 167 M3
Greenland Sheff 84 E3
Greenlands Bucks 35 L7
Green Lane Devon 9 J9
Green Lane Worcs 47 L2
Greenlaw Border 129 J10
Greenlea D & G 109 M5
Greenloaning P & K 133 N6
Green Moor Barns 90 H11
Greenmount Bury 89 M8
Green Oak E R Yk 92 D5
Greenock Inver 124 H2
Greenock Crematorium Inver 124 H2
Greenodd Cumb 94 G4
Green Ore Somset 19 Q4
Green Quarter Cumb 101 N10
Greensgate Norfk 76 G8
Greenshields S Lans 116 E2
Greenside Gatesd 112 H8
Greenside Kirk 90 F7
Greens Norton Nhants 49 J5
Greenstead Green Essex 52 D6
Greensted Essex 51 M10
Green Street E Susx 26 C9
Green Street Gloucs 46 G11
Green Street Herts 50 E11
Green Street Herts 51 L6
Green Street Worcs 46 G5
Green Street Green Gt Lon 37 L8
Green Street Green Kent 37 N6
Greenstreet Green Suffk 52 H2
Green Tye Herts 51 K7
Greenway Gloucs 46 D8
Greenway Somset 19 K10
Greenway V Glam 30 E10
Greenway Worcs 57 N10
Greenwich Gt Lon 37 J5
Greenwich Maritime Gt Lon 37 J5
Greet Gloucs 47 K8
Greete Shrops 57 K10
Greetham Lincs 87 K6
Greetham Rutlnd 73 N8
Greetland Calder 90 D6
Gregson Lane Lancs 88 H5
Greinton Somset 19 M7
Grenaby IoM 80 c7
Grendon Nhants 61 J8
Grendon Warwks 59 L5
Grendon Green Herefs 46 A3
Grendon Underwood Bucks 49 J10
Grenofen Devon 6 D4
Grenoside Sheff 84 D2
Grenoside Crematorium Sheff 84 D2
Greosabhagh W Isls 168 g8
Gresford Wrexhm 69 K4
Gresham Norfk 76 H4
Greshornish House Hotel Highld 152 E7
Gressenhall Norfk 76 D8
Gressenhall Green Norfk 76 D8
Gressingham Lancs 95 M7
Gresty Green Ches E 70 C4
Greta Bridge Dur 103 L8
Gretna D & G 110 F7
Gretna Green D & G 110 F7
Gretna Services D & G 110 F7
Gretton Gloucs 47 K8
Gretton Nhants 61 J2
Gretton Shrops 57 J5
Grewelthorpe N York 97 K5
Grey Friars Suffk 65 P7
Greygarth N York 97 J6
Grey Green N Linc 92 C9
Greylake Somset 19 L8
Greyrigg D & G 109 N3
Greys Green Oxon 35 K8
Greysouthen Cumb 100 E5
Greystoke Cumb 101 M4
Greystone Angus 143 J9
Greywell Hants 23 K4
Gribb Dorset 10 H4
Gribthorpe E R Yk 92 C3
Griff Warwks 59 N7
Griffithstown Torfn 31 J5
Griffydam Leics 72 C7
Griggs Green Hants 23 M8
Grimeford Village Lancs 89 J8
Grimesthorpe Sheff 84 E3
Grimethorpe Barns 91 L9
Grimley Worcs 46 F2
Grimmet S Ayrs 114 F5
Grimoldby Lincs 87 L3
Grimpo Shrops 69 L9
Grimsargh Lancs 88 H4
Grimsby NE Lin 93 N8
Grimsby Crematorium NE Lin 93 N9
Grimscote Nhants 49 J4
Grimscott Cnwll 16 D10
Grimshader W Isls 168 j5
Grimshaw Bl w D 89 L6
Grimshaw Green Lancs 88 F8
Grimsthorpe Lincs 73 Q6
Grimston E R Yk 93 N3

Hickleton - Hook Street 281

Hickleton Donc 91 M9
Hickling Norfk 77 N7
Hickling Notts 72 H5
Hickling Green Norfk 77 N7
Hickling Heath Norfk 77 N7
Hickmans Green Kent 39 J10
Hicks Forstal Kent 39 L9
Hickstead W Susx 24 G6
Hidcote Bartrim Gloucs 47 N6
Hidcote Boyce Gloucs 47 N6
High Ackworth Wakefd 91 L7
Higham Barns 91 J9
Higham Derbys 84 E9
Higham Kent 37 P11
Higham Kent 38 B7
Higham Lancs 89 N3
Higham Suffk 52 H4
Higham Suffk 63 M7
Higham Dykes Nthumb 112 H5
Higham Ferrers Nhants 61 L7
Higham Gobion C Beds 50 D4
Higham Hill Gt Lon 37 J2
Higham on the Hill Leics 72 B11
Highampton Devon 8 C4
Highams Park Gt Lon 37 J2
High Angerton Nthumb 112 G3
High Ardwell D & G 106 E8
High Auldgirth D & G 109 K3
High Bankhill Cumb 101 Q2
High Beach Essex 51 K11
High Bentham N York 95 P7
High Bewaldeth Cumb 100 H4
High Bickington Devon 17 L7
High Biggins Cumb 95 N5
High Birkwith N York 96 B5
High Blantyre S Lans 126 B6
High Bonnybridge Falk 126 E2
High Borrans Cumb 101 M10
High Bradley N York 96 F11
High Bray Devon 17 M5
Highbridge Hants 22 E10
Highbridge Somset 19 K5
Highbrook W Susx 25 J4
High Brooms Kent 25 N2
High Bullen Devon 17 J7
Highburton Kirk 90 F8
Highbury Gt Lon 36 H3
Highbury Somset 20 C5
High Buston Nthumb 119 P9
High Callerton Nthumb 113 J6
High Casterton Cumb 95 N5
High Catton E R Yk 98 E10
Highclere Hants 22 D3
Highcliffe Dorset 13 M6
High Close Dur 103 N7
High Cogges Oxon 34 C3
High Common Norfk 76 D10
High Coniscliffe Darltn 103 P7
High Crosby Cumb 111 J9
High Cross Cnwll 3 J8
High Cross E Ayrs 125 L8
High Cross Hants 23 K9
High Cross Herts 51 J7
Highcross Lancs 88 C3
High Cross W Susx 24 F7
High Cross Warwks 59 K11
High Drummore D & G 106 F10
High Dubmire Sundld 113 M11
High Easter Essex 51 P8
High Eggborough N York 91 P6
High Ellington N York 97 J4
Higher Alham Somset 20 C6
Higher Ansty Dorset 12 C4
Higher Ballam Lancs 88 D4
Higher Bartle Lancs 88 G4
Higher Berry End C Beds 49 Q8
Higher Bockhampton Dorset 12 B6
Higher Brixham Torbay 7 N8
Higher Burrowton Devon 9 P5
Higher Burwardsley Ches W 69 P3
High Ercall Wrekin 69 Q11
Higher Chillington Somset 10 H2
Higher Clovelly Devon 16 E7
Highercombe Somset 18 B8
Higher Coombe Dorset 11 L6
Higher Disley Ches E 83 L8
Higher Folds Wigan 82 E4
Higherford Lancs 89 P2
Higher Gabwell Devon 7 N5
Higher Halstock Leigh Dorset 11 L3
Higher Harpers Lancs 89 N3
Higher Heysham Lancs 95 J8
Higher Hurdsfield Ches E 83 K10
Higher Irlam Salfd 82 F5
Higher Kingcombe Dorset 11 L5
Higher Kinnerton Flints 69 K2
Higher Marston Ches W 82 E9
Higher Muddiford Devon 17 K4
Higher Nyland Dorset 20 D10
Higher Ogden Rochdl 90 B8
Higher Pentire Cnwll 2 H8
Higher Penwortham Lancs 88 G5
Higher Prestacott Devon 5 P2
Higher Studfold N York 96 B6
Higher Town Cnwll 3 L5
Higher Town Cnwll 4 G9
Higher Town IoS 2 c1
Higher Tregantle Cnwll 5 Q11
Higher Walton Lancs 88 H5
Higher Walton Warrtn 82 C7
Higher Wambrook Somset 10 F3
Higher Waterston Dorset 11 Q5
Higher Whatcombe Dorset 12 D4
Higher Wheelton Lancs 89 J6
Higher Whitley Ches W 82 D8
Higher Wincham Ches W 82 E9
Higher Wraxhall Dorset 11 M4
Higher Wych Ches W 69 N6
High Etherley Dur 103 N5
High Ferry Lincs 87 L11
Highfield E R Yk 92 B3
Highfield Gatesd 112 H9
Highfield N Ayrs 125 J7
Highfields Donc 91 N9
High Flats Kirk 90 G9
High Garrett Essex 52 C6
Highgate E Susx 25 K4
Highgate Gt Lon 36 G3
Highgate Kent 26 C5
High Grange Dur 103 N4
High Grantley N York 97 K7
High Green Cumb 101 M10
High Green Kirk 90 G8
High Green Norfk 64 H4
High Green Norfk 76 G10
High Green Sheff 91 J11
High Green Shrops 57 N8
High Green Suffk 64 B9
High Green Worcs 46 G5
Highgreen Manor Nthumb 112 B2
High Halden Kent 26 E4
High Halstow Medway 38 C6
High Ham Somset 19 M8
High Harrington Cumb 100 D5
High Harrogate N York 97 M9
High Haswell Dur 104 C2
High Hatton Shrops 69 R10
High Hauxley Nthumb 119 Q10
High Hawsker N York 105 P9
High Hesket Cumb 101 N2
High Hoyland Barns 90 H9
High Hunsley E R Yk 92 G3
High Hurstwood E Susx 25 L5
High Hutton N York 98 F7
High Ireby Cumb 100 H3
High Kelling Norfk 76 G3
High Kilburn N York 97 R5
High Killerby N York 99 M4
High Knipe Cumb 101 P7
High Lands Dur 103 M5
Highlane Ches E 83 J11
Highlane Derbys 84 F4
High Lane Stockp 83 L7
High Lanes Cnwll 2 F6
High Laver Essex 51 M9
Highlaws Cumb 109 P11
Highleadon Gloucs 46 E10
High Legh Ches E 82 F8
Highleigh W Susx 15 M7
High Leven S on T 104 E8
Highley Shrops 57 N8
High Littleton BaNES 20 B3
High Lorton Cumb 100 G5
High Marishes N York 98 G5
High Marnham Notts 85 P6
High Melton Donc 91 N10
High Mickley Nthumb 112 G8
Highmoor Cumb 110 E11
Highmoor Oxon 35 K8
Highmoor Cross Oxon 35 K8
Highmoor Hill Mons 31 N7
High Moorsley Sundld 113 M11
Highnam Gloucs 46 E11
Highnam Green Gloucs 46 E10
High Newport Sundld 113 N10
High Newton Cumb 95 J4
High Nibthwaite Cumb 94 F3
High Offley Staffs 70 D9
High Ongar Essex 51 N10
High Onn Staffs 70 E11
High Park Corner Essex 52 H7
High Pennyvenie E Ayrs 115 J6
High Post Wilts 21 N7
Highridge N Som 31 Q11
High Roding Essex 51 P7
High Row Cumb 101 L3
High Row Cumb 101 L6
High Salter Lancs 95 N8
High Salvington W Susx 24 D9
High Scales Cumb 110 C11
High Seaton Cumb 100 D4
High Shaw N York 96 C2
High Side Cumb 100 H4
High Spen Gatesd 112 H9
Highstead Kent 39 M8
Highsted Kent 38 F9
High Stoop Dur 103 M2
High Street Cnwll 3 P3
High Street Kent 26 B5
Highstreet Kent 39 J9
High Street Suffk 65 N10
High Street Suffk 65 N7
Highstreet Green Essex 52 C5
Highstreet Green Surrey 23 Q7
Hightae D & G 109 N5
Highter's Heath Birm 58 G9
High Throston Hartpl 104 E4
Hightown Ches E 70 F2
Hightown Hants 13 L4
Hightown Sefton 81 L4
High Town Staffs 58 E2
Hightown Green Suffk 64 D10
High Toynton Lincs 87 J7
High Trewhitt Nthumb 119 K9
High Urpeth Dur 113 K10
High Valleyfield Fife 134 C10
High Warden Nthumb 112 D7
Highway Herefs 45 P5
Highway Wilts 33 K10
Highweek Devon 7 L4
High Westwood Dur 112 H9
Highwood Staffs 71 K8
Highwood Hill Gt Lon 36 F2
High Woolaston Gloucs 31 Q5
High Worsall N York 104 C9
Highworth Swindn 33 P6
High Wray Cumb 101 L11
High Wych Herts 51 L8
High Wycombe Bucks 35 N6
Hilborough Norfk 75 R10
Hilcote Derbys 84 G9
Hilcott Wilts 21 M3
Hildenborough Kent 37 N11
Hilden Park Kent 37 N11
Hildersham Cambs 62 H11
Hilderstone Staffs 70 H8
Hilderthorpe E R Yk 99 P7
Hilfield Dorset 11 N3
Hilgay Norfk 75 M11
Hill S Glos 32 B5
Hill Warwks 59 Q11
Hillam N York 91 N5
Hillbeck Cumb 102 E7
Hillborough Kent 39 M8
Hill Brow Hants 23 L9
Hillbutts Dorset 12 G4
Hill Chorlton Staffs 70 D7
Hillcliffiane Derbys 71 P5
Hill Common Norfk 77 N7
Hill Common Somset 18 F9
Hill Deverill Wilts 20 G6
Hilldyke Lincs 87 K11
Hill End Dur 103 K3
Hill End Fife 134 C8
Hillend Fife 134 E11
Hill End Gloucs 46 H7
Hillend Mdloth 127 P4
Hillend N Lans 126 E4
Hillend Swans 28 D6
Hillersland Gloucs 31 Q2
Hillerton Devon 8 H5
Hillesden Bucks 49 J9
Hillesley Gloucs 32 E7
Hillfarrance Somset 18 G10
Hill Green Kent 38 D9
Hillgrove W Susx 23 P9
Hillhampton Herefs 46 A5
Hillhead Abers 158 E10
Hillhead Devon 7 N8
Hill Head Hants 14 F6
Hillhead S Lans 116 D2
Hillhead of Cocklaw Abers 159 Q9
Hilliard's Cross Staffs 59 J2
Hilliclay Highld 167 L4
Hillingdon Gt Lon 36 C4
Hillington C Glas 125 N5
Hillington Norfk 75 P5
Hillis Corner IoW 14 E8
Hillmorton Warwks 60 B6
Hillock Vale Lancs 89 M5
Hill of Beath Fife 134 F9
Hill of Fearn Highld 163 J11
Hillowton D & G 108 G8
Hillpool Worcs 58 C9
Hillpound Hants 22 G11
Hill Ridware Staffs 71 K11
Hillside Abers 151 N8
Hillside Angus 143 N5
Hillside Devon 7 J6
Hill Side Kirk 90 F7
Hill Side Worcs 46 E2
Hills Town Derbys 84 G7
Hillstreet Hants 22 B11
Hillswick Shet 169 p6
Hill Top Dur 103 J6
Hill Top Hants 14 D6
Hill Top Kirk 90 D8
Hill Top Rothm 84 E2
Hill Top Sandw 58 E6
Hill Top Wakefd 91 J7
Hillwell Shet 169 q12
Hilmarton Wilts 33 K9
Hilperton Wilts 20 G3
Hilperton Marsh Wilts 20 G3
Hilsea C Port 15 J6
Hilston E R Yk 93 N4
Hiltingbury Hants 22 D10
Hilton Border 129 M9
Hilton Cambs 62 C7
Hilton Cumb 102 D6
Hilton Derbys 71 N8
Hilton Dorset 12 C4
Hilton Dur 103 N6
Hilton Highld 156 F2
Hilton S on T 104 E8
Hilton Shrops 57 P5
Hilton Park Services Staffs 58 E4
Himbleton Worcs 46 H3
Himley Staffs 58 C6
Hincaster Cumb 95 L4
Hinchley Wood Surrey 36 E7
Hinckley Leics 59 P6
Hinderclay Suffk 64 E6
Hinderwell N York 105 L7
Hindford Shrops 69 K8
Hindhead Surrey 23 N7
Hindle Fold Lancs 89 L4
Hindley Nthumb 112 F9
Hindley Wigan 82 D4
Hindley Green Wigan 82 D4
Hindlip Worcs 46 G3
Hindolveston Norfk 76 E6
Hindon Wilts 20 H8
Hindringham Norfk 76 D4
Hingham Norfk 76 E11
Hinksford Staffs 58 C7
Hinstock Shrops 70 B9
Hintlesham Suffk 53 J3
Hinton Gloucs 32 C4
Hinton Hants 13 M5
Hinton Herefs 45 L7
Hinton S Glos 32 D9
Hinton Shrops 56 G3
Hinton Shrops 57 M8
Hinton Admiral Hants 13 M5
Hinton Ampner Hants 22 H9
Hinton Blewett BaNES 19 Q3
Hinton Charterhouse BaNES 20 E3
Hinton Green Worcs 47 K6
Hinton-in-the-Hedges Nhants 48 G7
Hinton Marsh Hants 22 G9
Hinton Martell Dorset 12 H3
Hinton on the Green Worcs 47 K6
Hinton Parva Swindn 33 P8
Hinton St George Somset 11 J2
Hinton St Mary Dorset 20 E11
Hinton Waldrist Oxon 34 C5
Hints Shrops 57 L10
Hints Staffs 59 J4
Hinwick Bed 61 K8
Hinxhill Kent 26 H3
Hinxton Cambs 62 G11
Hinxworth Herts 50 F2
Hipperholme Calder 90 E5
Hipsburn Nthumb 119 P8
Hipswell N York 103 N11
Hirn Abers 151 J7
Hirnant Powys 68 D10
Hirst Nthumb 113 L3
Hirst Courtney N York 91 Q6
Hirwaen Denbgs 68 F2
Hirwaun Rhondd 30 C3
Hiscott Devon 17 J6
Histon Cambs 62 F8
Hitcham Suffk 64 D11
Hitcham Causeway Suffk 64 D11
Hitcham Street Suffk 64 D11
Hitchin Herts 50 E5
Hither Green Gt Lon 37 J6
Hittisleigh Devon 8 H5
Hive E R Yk 92 D4
Hixon Staffs 71 J9
Hoaden Kent 39 N10
Hoar Cross Staffs 71 L10
Hoarwithy Herefs 45 Q9
Hoath Kent 39 M9
Hoathly Kent 25 Q3
Hobarris Shrops 56 E9
Hobbles Green Suffk 63 M10
Hobbs Cross Essex 51 L11
Hobbs Cross Essex 51 L8
Hobkirk Border 118 A8
Hobland Hall Norfk 77 Q11
Hobsick Notts 84 G11
Hobson Dur 113 J9
Hoby Leics 72 H7
Hoccombe Somset 18 F9
Hockering Norfk 76 F9
Hockerton Notts 85 M9
Hockley Ches E 83 K8
Hockley Covtry 59 L9
Hockley Essex 38 D3
Hockley Staffs 59 K4
Hockley Heath Solhll 59 J10
Hockliffe C Beds 49 Q9
Hockwold cum Wilton Norfk 63 M3
Hockworthy Devon 18 D11
Hoddesdon Herts 51 J9
Hoddlesden Bl w D 89 L6
Hoddom Cross D & G 110 C6
Hoddom Mains D & G 110 C6
Hodgehill Ches E 82 H11
Hodgeston Pembks 41 K11
Hodnet Shrops 69 R9
Hodsock Notts 85 K3
Hodsoll Street Kent 37 P8
Hodson Swindn 33 N8
Hodthorpe Derbys 84 H5
Hoe Hants 22 G11
Hoe Norfk 76 D8
Hoe Gate Hants 14 H4
Hoff Cumb 102 C7
Hogben's Hill Kent 38 H10
Hoggards Green Suffk 64 B10
Hoggeston Bucks 49 M10
Hoggrill's End Warwks 59 K6
Hog Hill E Susx 26 E8
Hoghton Lancs 89 J5
Hoghton Bottoms Lancs 89 J5
Hognaston Derbys 71 N4
Hogsthorpe Lincs 87 P6
Holbeach Lincs 74 G6
Holbeach Bank Lincs 74 G5
Holbeach Clough Lincs 74 G5
Holbeach Drove Lincs 74 F8
Holbeach Hurn Lincs 74 G5
Holbeach St Johns Lincs 74 G7
Holbeach St Mark's Lincs 74 G4
Holbeach St Matthew Lincs 74 H4
Holbeck Notts 84 H6
Holbeck Woodhouse Notts 84 H6
Holberrow Green Worcs 47 K3
Holbeton Devon 6 G8
Holborn Gt Lon 36 H4
Holborough Kent 38 B9
Holbrook Derbys 72 B2
Holbrook Sheff 84 F4
Holbrook Suffk 53 L4
Holbrook Moor Derbys 84 E11
Holbrooks Covtry 59 M8
Holburn Nthumb 119 K3
Holbury Hants 14 D6
Holcombe Devon 7 P4
Holcombe Somset 20 C5
Holcombe Rogus Devon 18 E11
Holcot Nhants 60 G7
Holden Lancs 96 A11
Holdenby Nhants 60 E7
Holden Gate Calder 89 P6
Holder's Green Essex 51 P5
Holdgate Shrops 57 K7
Holdingham Lincs 86 E11
Holditch Dorset 10 G4
Holdsworth Calder 90 D5
Holehouse Derbys 83 M6
Hole-in-the-Wall Herefs 46 B9
Holemoor Devon 16 G10
Hole Street W Susx 24 D8
Holford Somset 18 G6
Holgate C York 98 B10
Holker Cumb 94 H5
Holkham Norfk 76 B3
Hollacombe Devon 16 F11
Holland Fen Lincs 86 H11
Holland Lees Lancs 88 G9
Holland-on-Sea Essex 53 L8
Hollandstoun Ork 169 g1
Hollee D & G 110 E7
Hollesley Suffk 53 Q3
Hollicombe Torbay 7 M6
Hollingbourne Kent 38 D10
Hollingbury Br & H 24 H9
Hollingdon Bucks 49 N9
Hollingthorpe Leeds 91 K4
Hollington Derbys 71 N7
Hollington Staffs 71 K7
Hollingworth Tamesd 83 M5
Hollinlane Ches E 82 H8
Hollins Bury 89 N9
Hollins Derbys 84 D6
Hollins Staffs 70 H5
Hollinsclough Staffs 83 N11
Hollins End Sheff 84 E4
Hollins Green Warrtn 82 E6
Hollins Lane Lancs 95 K10
Hollinswood Wrekin 57 N3
Hollinwood Shrops 69 P7
Hollinwood Crematorium Oldham 83 K4
Hollingrove E Susx 25 Q6
Hollocombe Devon 17 L9
Holloway Derbys 84 D9
Holloway Gt Lon 36 H3
Holloway Wilts 20 G8
Hollowell Nhants 60 E6
Hollowmoor Heath Ches W 81 P11
Hollows D & G 110 G5
Hollybush Caerph 30 G4
Hollybush E Ayrs 114 G4
Hollybush Herefs 46 E7
Holly End Norfk 75 J9
Holly Green Worcs 46 G6
Hollyhurst Ches E 69 Q6
Hollym E R Yk 93 P5
Hollywood Worcs 58 G9
Holmbridge Kirk 90 E9
Holmbury St Mary Surrey 24 D2
Holmbush Cnwll 3 Q3
Holmcroft Staffs 70 G10
Holme Cambs 61 Q3
Holme Cumb 95 L5
Holme Kirk 90 E9
Holme N Linc 92 F9
Holme N York 97 N4
Holme Notts 85 P9
Holme Chapel Lancs 89 P5
Holme Green N York 91 P2
Holme Hale Norfk 76 B10
Holme Lacy Herefs 45 R7
Holme Marsh Herefs 45 L4
Holme next the Sea Norfk 75 P2
Holme on the Wolds E R Yk 99 K11
Holme Pierrepont Notts 72 G3
Holmer Herefs 45 Q6
Holmer Green Bucks 35 P5
Holme St Cuthbert Cumb 109 P11
Holmes Chapel Ches E 82 G11
Holmesfield Derbys 84 D5
Holmes Hill E Susx 25 M8
Holmeswood Lancs 88 E7
Holmethorpe Surrey 36 G10
Holme upon Spalding Moor E R Yk 92 D3
Holmewood Derbys 84 F7
Holmfield Calder 90 D5
Holmfirth Kirk 90 E9
Holmhead E Ayrs 115 L3
Holmpton E R Yk 93 Q6
Holmrook Cumb 100 E11
Holmsford Bridge Crematorium N Ayrs 125 K10
Holmshurst E Susx 25 P5
Holmside Dur 113 K11
Holmwrangle Cumb 111 K11
Holne Devon 7 J5
Holnest Dorset 11 P3
Holnicote Somset 18 B5
Holsworthy Devon 16 E11
Holsworthy Beacon Devon 16 F10
Holt Dorset 12 H4
Holt Norfk 76 F4
Holt Wilts 20 G2
Holt Worcs 46 F2
Holt Wrexhm 69 M4
Holtby C York 98 D10
Holt End Worcs 58 G11
Holt Fleet Worcs 46 F2
Holt Green Lancs 88 D9
Holt Heath Dorset 13 J4
Holt Heath Worcs 46 F2
Holton Oxon 34 H3
Holton Somset 20 C9
Holton Suffk 65 N6
Holton cum Beckering Lincs 86 F4
Holton Heath Dorset 12 F6
Holton Hill E Susx 25 Q5
Holton le Clay Lincs 93 N10
Holton le Moor Lincs 93 J11
Holton St Mary Suffk 53 J4
Holt Street Kent 39 N11
Holtye E Susx 25 L3
Holway Flints 80 H9
Holwell Dorset 11 P2
Holwell Herts 50 E4
Holwell Leics 73 J6
Holwell Oxon 33 P3
Holwick Dur 102 H5
Holworth Dorset 12 C8
Holybourne Hants 23 K6
Holy Cross Worcs 58 D9
Holyfield Essex 51 J10
Holyhead IoA 78 C8
Holy Island IoA 78 D8
Holy Island Nthumb 119 M2
Holy Island Nthumb 119 M2
Holymoorside Derbys 84 D7
Holyport W & M 35 N9
Holystone Nthumb 119 J10
Holytown N Lans 126 D5
Holytown Crematorium N Lans 126 D5
Holywell C Beds 50 B7
Holywell Cambs 62 D6
Holywell Cnwll 4 B10
Holywell Dorset 11 M4
Holywell Flints 80 H9
Holywell Nthumb 113 M6
Holywell Warwks 59 K11
Holywell Green Calder 90 D7
Holywell Lake Somset 18 F10
Holywell Row Suffk 63 M5
Holywood D & G 109 K4
Holywood Village D & G 109 L5
Homer Shrops 57 L4
Homer Green Sefton 81 L4
Homersfield Suffk 65 K4
Homescales Cumb 95 M3
Hom Green Herefs 46 A10
Homington Wilts 21 M9
Honeyborough Pembks 40 H9
Honeybourne Worcs 47 M6
Honeychurch Devon 8 F4
Honey Hill Kent 39 K9
Honeystreet Wilts 21 M2
Honey Tye Suffk 52 G4
Honiley Warwks 59 K10
Honing Norfk 77 L6
Honingham Norfk 76 G9
Honington Lincs 73 N2
Honington Suffk 64 C7
Honington Warwks 47 Q6
Honiton Devon 10 D4
Honley Kirk 90 E8
Honnington Wrekin 70 C11
Honor Oak Crematorium Gt Lon 37 J6
Hoo Kent 39 N9
Hoobrook Worcs 58 B10
Hood Green Barns 91 J10
Hood Hill Rothm 91 K11
Hooe C Plym 6 E8
Hooe E Susx 25 Q8
Hoo End Herts 50 E6
Hoo Green Ches E 82 F8
Hoohill Bpool 88 C3
Hook Cambs 62 F2
Hook Devon 10 G3
Hook E R Yk 92 C5
Hook Gt Lon 36 E8
Hook Hants 14 F5
Hook Hants 23 K4
Hook Pembks 41 J8
Hook Wilts 33 L8
Hookagate Shrops 56 H3
Hook Bank Worcs 46 F6
Hooke Dorset 11 L4
Hook End Essex 51 N10
Hookgate Staffs 70 C7
Hook Green Kent 25 Q3
Hook Green Kent 37 P6
Hook Norton Oxon 48 C8
Hook Street Gloucs 32 C5
Hook Street Wilts 33 L8

284 Kingsley - Langley

Kingsley Ches W 82 C10
Kingsley Hants 23 L7
Kingsley Staffs 71 J5
Kingsley Green W Susx 23 N8
Kingsley Park Nhants 60 G8
Kingslow Shrops 57 P5
King's Lynn Norfk 75 M6
Kings Meaburn Cumb 102 B6
Kingsmead Hants 14 G4
King's Mills Guern 10 b2
King's Moss St Hel 81 Q4
Kingsmuir Angus 142 H8
Kings Muir Border 117 K3
Kingsmuir Fife 135 N6
Kings Newnham Warwks 59 Q9
King's Newton Derbys 72 B5
Kingsnorth Kent 26 H4
King's Norton Birm 58 G9
King's Norton Leics 72 H10
Kings Nympton Devon 17 M8
King's Pyon Herefs 45 N4
Kings Ripton Cambs 62 C5
King's Somborne Hants 22 C8
King's Stag Dorset 11 Q2
King's Stanley Gloucs 32 F4
King's Sutton Nhants 48 E7
Kingstanding Birm 58 G6
Kingsteignton Devon 7 M4
King Sterndale Derbys 83 N10
Kingsthorne Herefs 45 P8
Kingsthorpe Nhants 60 G8
Kingston Cambs 62 D9
Kingston Cnwll 5 P6
Kingston Devon 6 G9
Kingston Devon 9 Q7
Kingston Dorset 12 C3
Kingston Dorset 12 G9
Kingston E Loth 128 E3
Kingston Hants 13 K4
Kingston IoW 14 E10
Kingston Kent 39 L11
Kingston W Susx 24 C10
Kingston Bagpuize Oxon 34 D5
Kingston Blount Oxon 35 K5
Kingston Deverill Wilts 20 F7
Kingstone Herefs 45 N7
Kingstone Somset 10 H2
Kingstone Staffs 71 K9
Kingstone Winslow Oxon 33 Q7
Kingston Lacy House & Gardens Dorset 12 G4
Kingston Lisle Oxon 34 B7
Kingston near Lewes E Susx 25 J9
Kingston on Soar Notts 72 E5
Kingston on Spey Moray 157 Q4
Kingston Russell Dorset 11 M6
Kingston St Mary Somset 18 H9
Kingston Seymour N Som 31 M11
Kingston Stert Oxon 35 K4
Kingston upon Hull C KuH 93 J5
Kingston upon Thames Gt Lon 36 E7
Kingston upon Thames Crematorium Gt Lon 36 E7
Kingstown Cumb 110 G9
King's Walden Herts 50 E6
Kingswear Devon 7 M8
Kingswells C Aber 151 M6
Kings Weston Bristl 31 P9
Kingswinford Dudley 58 C7
Kingswood Bucks 49 J11
Kingswood Gloucs 32 D6
Kingswood Kent 38 D11
Kingswood Powys 56 C4
Kingswood S Glos 32 B10
Kingswood Somset 18 F7
Kingswood Surrey 36 F9
Kingswood Warwks 59 J10
Kingswood Brook Warwks 59 J10
Kingswood Common Herefs 45 K4
Kingswood Common Staffs 58 B4
Kings Worthy Hants 22 E8
Kingthorpe Lincs 86 F5
Kington Herefs 45 K3
Kington S Glos 32 B6
Kington Worcs 47 J3
Kington Langley Wilts 32 H9
Kington Magna Dorset 20 E10
Kington St Michael Wilts 32 H9
Kingussie Highld 148 D7
Kingweston Somset 19 P8
Kinharrachie Abers 159 M11
Kinharvie D & G 109 K7
Kinkell Bridge P & K 133 Q4
Kinknockie Abers 159 P9
Kinleith C Edin 127 M4
Kinlet Shrops 57 N8
Kinloch Highld 144 F8
Kinloch Highld 164 H10
Kinloch Highld 165 N6
Kinloch P & K 142 A9
Kinlochard Stirlg 132 F7
Kinlochbervie Highld 164 F5
Kinlocheil Highld 138 H2
Kinlochewe Highld 154 D5
Kinloch Hourn Highld 146 B6
Kinlochlaggan Highld 147 N10
Kinlochleven Highld 139 M5
Kinlochmoidart Highld 138 C3
Kinlochnanuagh Highld 145 M11
Kinloch Rannoch P & K 140 G6
Kinloss Moray 157 K5
Kinmel Bay Conwy 80 D8
Kinmuck Abers 151 L4
Kinmundy Abers 151 M4
Kinnabus Ag & B 122 C11
Kinnadie Abers 159 N9
Kinnaird P & K 141 N6
Kinneff Abers 143 Q2
Kinnelhead D & G 116 E10
Kinnell Angus 143 L7
Kinnerley Shrops 69 K10
Kinnersley Herefs 45 L5
Kinnersley Worcs 46 G6
Kinnerton Powys 45 J2
Kinnerton Shrops 56 F5
Kinnerton Green Flints 69 K2
Kinnesswood P & K 134 F7
Kinninvie Dur 103 L6
Kinnordy Angus 142 F6
Kinoulton Notts 72 H4
Kinross P & K 134 E7
Kinrossie P & K 142 B11
Kinross Services P & K 134 E7
Kinsbourne Green Herts 50 D7
Kinsey Heath Ches E 70 B6
Kinsham Herefs 56 F11
Kinsham Worcs 46 H7
Kinsley Wakefd 91 L8
Kinson Bmouth 13 J5
Kintail Highld 146 B4
Kintbury W Berk 34 C11
Kintessack Moray 157 J5
Kintillo P & K 134 E4
Kinton Herefs 56 G10
Kinton Shrops 69 L11
Kintore Abers 151 K4
Kintour Ag & B 122 G9
Kintra Ag & B 122 D10
Kintra Ag & B 137 J10
Kintraw Ag & B 130 G7
Kintyre Ag & B 120 D4
Kinveachy Highld 148 G4
Kinver Staffs 58 B8
Kiplin N York 103 Q11
Kippax Leeds 91 L4
Kippen Stirlg 133 J9
Kippford or Scaur D & G 108 H10
Kipping's Cross Kent 25 P2
Kirbister Ork 169 c6
Kirby Bedon Norfk 77 K10
Kirby Bellars Leics 73 J7
Kirby Cane Norfk 65 M3
Kirby Corner Covtry 59 L9
Kirby Cross Essex 53 M7
Kirby Fields Leics 72 E10
Kirby Grindalythe N York 99 J7
Kirby Hill N York 97 N7
Kirby Hill N York 103 M9
Kirby Knowle N York 97 Q3
Kirby le Soken Essex 53 M7
Kirby Misperton N York 98 F5
Kirby Muxloe Leics 72 E10
Kirby Sigston N York 97 P2
Kirby Underdale E R Yk 98 G9
Kirby Wiske N York 97 N4
Kirdford W Susx 24 B5
Kirk Highld 167 N5
Kirkabister Shet 169 r10
Kirkandrews D & G 108 D11
Kirkandrews upon Eden Cumb 110 G9
Kirkbampton Cumb 110 F9
Kirkbean D & G 109 L9
Kirk Bramwith Donc 91 Q8
Kirkbride Cumb 110 D9
Kirkbridge N York 97 L2
Kirkbuddo Angus 143 J9
Kirkburn Border 117 K3
Kirkburn E R Yk 99 K9
Kirkburton Kirk 90 F8
Kirkby Knows 81 N5
Kirkby Lincs 86 E2
Kirkby N York 104 F9
Kirkby Fleetham N York 97 L2
Kirkby Green Lincs 86 E9
Kirkby in Ashfield Notts 84 G9
Kirkby-in-Furness Cumb 94 E4
Kirkby la Thorpe Lincs 86 E11
Kirkby Lonsdale Cumb 95 N5
Kirkby Malham N York 96 C8
Kirkby Mallory Leics 72 D10
Kirkby Malzeard N York 97 K6
Kirkby Mills N York 98 E3
Kirkbymoorside N York 98 D3
Kirkby on Bain Lincs 86 H8
Kirkby Overblow N York 97 M11
Kirkby Stephen Cumb 102 E9
Kirkby Thore Cumb 102 B5
Kirkby Underwood Lincs 73 R5
Kirkby Wharf N York 91 N2
Kirkby Woodhouse Notts 84 G10
Kirkcaldy Fife 134 H9
Kirkcaldy Crematorium Fife 134 H9
Kirkcambeck Cumb 111 K7
Kirkchrist D & G 108 E10
Kirkcolm D & G 106 D4
Kirkconnel D & G 115 P5
Kirkconnell D & G 109 L7
Kirkcowan D & G 107 K5
Kirkcudbright D & G 108 E10
Kirkdale Lpool 81 L6
Kirk Deighton N York 97 N10
Kirk Ella E R Yk 92 H5
Kirkfieldbank S Lans 116 B2
Kirkgunzeon D & G 109 J7
Kirk Hallam Derbys 72 D2
Kirkham Lancs 88 E4
Kirkham N York 98 E7
Kirkhamgate Wakefd 90 H6
Kirk Hammerton N York 97 Q9
Kirkharle Nthumb 112 F4
Kirkhaugh Nthumb 111 N11
Kirkheaton Kirk 90 F7
Kirkheaton Nthumb 112 F5
Kirkhill Highld 155 Q8
Kirkhope S Lans 116 D9
Kirkhouse Cumb 111 L9
Kirkhouse Green Donc 91 Q8
Kirkibost Highld 145 J4
Kirkinch P & K 142 E9
Kirkinner D & G 107 M7
Kirkintilloch E Duns 126 B3
Kirk Ireton Derbys 71 P4
Kirkland Cumb 100 E7
Kirkland Cumb 102 B4
Kirkland D & G 109 M3
Kirkland D & G 115 P5
Kirkland D & G 115 R9
Kirkland Guards Cumb 100 G2
Kirk Langley Derbys 71 P7
Kirkleatham R & Cl 104 G6
Kirklevington S on T 104 D9
Kirkley Suffk 65 Q3
Kirklington N York 97 M4
Kirklington Notts 85 L9
Kirklinton Cumb 110 H7
Kirkliston C Edin 127 L3
Kirkmabreck D & G 107 N6
Kirkmaiden D & G 106 F10
Kirk Merrington Dur 103 Q4
Kirk Michael IoM 80 d3
Kirkmichael P & K 141 Q6
Kirkmichael S Ayrs 114 F6
Kirkmuirhill S Lans 126 D9
Kirknewton Nthumb 118 H4
Kirknewton W Loth 127 L4
Kirkney Abers 158 D11
Kirk of Shotts N Lans 126 E5
Kirkoswald Cumb 101 Q2
Kirkoswald S Ayrs 114 D6
Kirkpatrick D & G 109 K2
Kirkpatrick Durham D & G 108 G6
Kirkpatrick-Fleming D & G 110 E6
Kirk Sandall Donc 91 Q9
Kirksanton Cumb 94 C4
Kirk Smeaton N York 91 N7
Kirkstall Leeds 90 H3
Kirkstead Lincs 86 G8
Kirkstile Abers 158 D10
Kirkstile D & G 110 G2
Kirkstone Pass Inn Cumb 101 M9
Kirkstyle Highld 167 P2
Kirkthorpe Wakefd 91 K6
Kirkton Abers 150 G2
Kirkton D & G 109 L4
Kirkton Fife 135 K2
Kirkton Highld 145 P2
Kirkton Highld 154 B9
Kirkton P & K 134 B4
Kirkton Manor Border 117 J3
Kirkton of Airlie Angus 142 E7
Kirkton of Auchterhouse Angus 142 E10
Kirkton of Barevan Highld 156 E8
Kirkton of Collace P & K 142 B11
Kirkton of Glenbuchat Abers 150 B4
Kirkton of Logie Buchan Abers 151 P2
Kirkton of Menmuir Angus 143 J5
Kirkton of Monikie Angus 143 J10
Kirkton of Rayne Abers 158 G11
Kirkton of Skene Abers 151 L6
Kirkton of Strathmartine Angus 142 F10
Kirkton of Tealing Angus 142 G10
Kirkton of Tough Abers 150 G5
Kirktown Abers 159 N4
Kirktown Abers 159 Q7
Kirktown of Alvah Abers 158 G5
Kirktown of Bourtie Abers 151 L2
Kirktown of Fetteresso Abers 151 M10
Kirktown of Mortlach Moray 157 Q10
Kirktown of Slains Abers 151 Q2
Kirkurd Border 116 G2
Kirkwall Ork 169 d5
Kirkwall Airport Ork 169 d6
Kirkwhelpington Nthumb 112 E4
Kirk Yetholm Border 118 F5
Kirmington N Linc 93 K8
Kirmond le Mire Lincs 86 G2
Kirn Ag & B 124 F2
Kirriemuir Angus 142 F7
Kirstead Green Norfk 65 K2
Kirtlebridge D & G 110 D6
Kirtling Cambs 63 L9
Kirtling Green Cambs 63 L9
Kirtlington Oxon 48 E11
Kirtomy Highld 166 B4
Kirton Lincs 74 F3
Kirton Notts 85 L7
Kirton Suffk 53 N3
Kirton End Lincs 74 E2
Kirtonhill W Duns 125 K2
Kirton Holme Lincs 74 E2
Kirton in Lindsey N Linc 92 F11
Kirwaugh D & G 107 M7
Kishorn Highld 153 Q10
Kislingbury Nhants 60 E9
Kitebrook Warwks 47 P8
Kite Green Warwks 59 J11
Kites Hardwick Warwks 59 Q11
Kitleigh Cnwll 5 L2
Kitt Green Wigan 88 G9
Kittisford Somset 18 E10
Kittle Swans 28 G7
Kitt's Green Birm 59 J7
Kittybrewster C Aber 151 N6
Kitwood Hants 23 J8
Kivernoll Herefs 45 P8
Kiveton Park Rothm 84 G4
Knaith Lincs 85 P4
Knaith Park Lincs 85 P3
Knap Corner Dorset 20 F10
Knaphill Surrey 23 Q3
Knapp Somset 19 K9
Knapp Hill Hants 22 D10
Knapthorpe Notts 85 M9
Knapton C York 98 B10
Knapton N York 98 H5
Knapton Norfk 77 L5
Knapton Green Herefs 45 N4
Knapwell Cambs 62 D8
Knaresborough N York 97 N9
Knarsdale Nthumb 111 N10
Knaven Abers 159 L9
Knayton N York 97 P3
Knebworth Herts 50 G6
Knedlington E R Yk 92 B5
Kneesall Notts 85 M8
Kneesworth Cambs 50 H2
Kneeton Notts 85 M11
Knelston Swans 28 E7
Knenhall Staffs 70 G7
Knettishall Suffk 64 D5
Knightacott Devon 17 M4
Knightcote Warwks 48 D4
Knightley Staffs 70 E9
Knightley Dale Staffs 70 E10
Knighton C Leic 72 G10
Knighton Devon 6 E9
Knighton Dorset 11 N2
Knighton Poole 12 H5
Knighton Powys 56 D10
Knighton Somset 18 G6
Knighton Staffs 70 C6
Knighton Staffs 70 D9
Knighton Wilts 33 Q10
Knighton on Teme Worcs 57 L11
Knightsbridge Gloucs 46 G9
Knightsmill Cnwll 4 H5
Knightwick Worcs 46 D3
Knill Herefs 45 K2
Knipton Leics 73 L4
Knitsley Dur 112 H11
Kniveton Derbys 71 N4
Knock Cumb 102 C5
Knock Highld 145 L6
Knock Moray 158 D7
Knock W Isls 168 j4
Knockally Highld 167 K11
Knockan Highld 161 L4
Knockando Moray 157 M9
Knockbain Highld 155 Q9
Knockbain Highld 156 A6
Knock Castle N Ayrs 124 F5
Knockdee Highld 167 L4
Knockdow Ag & B 124 E3
Knockdown Wilts 32 F7
Knockeen S Ayrs 114 F8
Knockenkelly N Ayrs 121 K6
Knockentiber E Ayrs 125 L10
Knockhall Kent 37 N6
Knockholt Kent 37 L9
Knockholt Pound Kent 37 L9
Knockin Shrops 69 K10
Knockinlaw E Ayrs 125 L10
Knockmill Kent 37 N8
Knocknain D & G 106 C5
Knockrome Ag & B 123 J5
Knocksharry IoM 80 c4
Knocksheen D & G 108 C4
Knockvennie Smithy D & G 108 G6
Knodishall Suffk 65 N9
Knodishall Common Suffk 65 N9
Knole Somset 19 N9
Knole Park S Glos 31 Q8
Knolls Green Ches E 82 H9
Knolton Wrexhm 69 L7
Knook Wilts 20 H6
Knossington Leics 73 L9
Knott End-on-Sea Lancs 94 H11
Knotting Bed 61 M8
Knotting Green Bed 61 M8
Knottingley Wakefd 91 N6
Knotty Ash Lpool 81 N6
Knotty Green Bucks 35 P6
Knowbury Shrops 57 K9
Knowe D & G 107 K3
Knowehead D & G 115 M9
Knoweside S Ayrs 114 E5
Knowle Bristl 32 B10
Knowle Devon 9 J4
Knowle Devon 9 P3
Knowle Devon 9 Q8
Knowle Devon 16 H4
Knowle Shrops 57 K10
Knowle Solhll 59 J9
Knowle Somset 18 C6
Knowle Cross Devon 9 P5
Knowlefield Cumb 110 H9
Knowle Green Lancs 89 J3
Knowle Hill Surrey 35 Q11
Knowle St Giles Somset 10 G2
Knowle Village Hants 14 G5
Knowle Wood Calder 89 Q6
Knowl Green Essex 52 C3
Knowl Hill W & M 35 M9
Knowlton Dorset 12 H3
Knowlton Kent 39 N11
Knowsley Knows 81 N5
Knowsley Safari Park Knows 81 P6
Knowstone Devon 17 Q7
Knox N York 97 L9
Knox Bridge Kent 26 C3
Knucklas Powys 56 D10
Knuston Nhants 61 K7
Knutsford Ches E 82 G9
Knutsford Services Ches E 82 F9
Knutton Staffs 70 E5
Krumlin Calder 90 D7
Kuggar Cnwll 3 J10
Kyleakin Highld 145 N2
Kyle of Lochalsh Highld 145 N2
Kylerhea Highld 145 N3
Kylesku Highld 164 F10
Kylesmorar Highld 145 P9
Kyles Scalpay W Isls 168 h8
Kylestrome Highld 164 F10
Kynaston Herefs 46 B7
Kynaston Shrops 69 L10
Kynnersley Wrekin 70 B11
Kyre Green Worcs 46 B2
Kyre Park Worcs 46 B2
Kyrewood Worcs 57 K11
Kyrle Somset 18 E10

L

La Bellieuse Guern 10 b2
Lacasaigh W Isls 168 i5
Lacasdal W Isls 168 j4
Laceby NE Lin 93 M9
Lacey Green Bucks 35 M4
Lach Dennis Ches W 82 F10
Lackenby R & Cl 104 G7
Lackford Suffk 63 N6
Lackford Green Suffk 63 N6
Lacock Wilts 32 H11
Ladbroke Warwks 48 D3
Ladderedge Staffs 70 H4
Laddingford Kent 37 Q11
Lade Bank Lincs 87 L10
Ladock Cnwll 3 M3
Lady Ork 169 f2
Ladybank Fife 135 J6
Ladycross Cnwll 5 N4
Ladygill S Lans 116 C5
Lady Hall Cumb 94 D3
Ladykirk Border 129 M10
Ladyridge Herefs 46 A8
Lady's Green Suffk 63 N9
Ladywood Birm 58 G7
Ladywood Worcs 46 G2
La Fontenelle Guern 10 c1
La Fosse Guern 10 b2
Lag D & G 109 J3
Laga Highld 138 A5
Lagavulin Ag & B 122 F10
Lagg N Ayrs 121 J7
Laggan Highld 146 H8
Laggan Highld 147 Q9
Lagganlia Highld 148 F7
La Greve Guern 10 c1
La Greve de Lecq Jersey 11 a1
La Hougue Bie Jersey 11 c2
La Houguette Guern 10 b2
Laid Highld 165 K5
Laide Highld 160 E8
Laig Highld 144 G10
Laigh Clunch E Ayrs 125 M8
Laigh Fenwick E Ayrs 125 M9
Laigh Glenmuir E Ayrs 115 M3
Laighstonehall S Lans 126 C7
Laindon Essex 37 Q3
Lairg Highld 162 D5
Laisterdyke C Brad 90 F4
Laithes Cumb 101 N4
Lake Devon 8 D7
Lake Devon 17 K5
Lake IoW 14 G10
Lake Wilts 21 M7
Lake District National Park Cumb 100 H9
Lakenheath Suffk 63 M4
Laker's Green Surrey 24 B3
Lakesend Norfk 75 K11
Lakeside Cumb 94 H3
Laleham Surrey 36 C7
Laleston Brdgnd 29 N9
Lamanva Cnwll 3 K7
Lamarsh Essex 52 E4
Lamas Norfk 77 J7
Lambden Border 118 D2
Lamberhurst Kent 25 Q3
Lamberhurst Down Kent 25 Q3
Lamberton Border 129 P8
Lambeth Gt Lon 36 H5
Lambeth Crematorium Gt Lon 36 G6
Lambfair Green Suffk 63 M10
Lambley Notts 85 K11
Lambley Nthumb 111 N9
Lambourn W Berk 34 B9
Lambourne End Essex 37 L2
Lambourn Woodlands W Berk 34 B9
Lamb Roe Lancs 89 L3
Lambs Green W Susx 24 F3
Lambston Pembks 40 H7
Lamellion Cnwll 5 L9
Lamerton Devon 8 C9
Lamesley Gatesd 113 L9
Lamington S Lans 116 D4
Lamlash N Ayrs 121 K5
Lamonby Cumb 101 M3
Lamorick Cnwll 4 G9
Lamorna Cnwll 2 C9
Lamorran Cnwll 3 M5
Lampen Cnwll 5 K8
Lampeter Cerdgn 43 L5
Lampeter Velfrey Pembks 41 N8
Lamphey Pembks 41 K10
Lamplugh Cumb 100 E6
Lamport Nhants 60 G6
Lamyatt Somset 20 C7
Lana Devon 5 N2
Lana Devon 16 E10
Lanark S Lans 116 B2
Lancaster Lancs 95 K8
Lancaster & Morecambe Crematorium Lancs 95 K8
Lancaster Services Lancs 95 L10
Lancaut Gloucs 31 P5
Lanchester Dur 113 J11
Lancing W Susx 24 E10
L'Ancresse Guern 10 c1
Landbeach Cambs 62 G7
Landcross Devon 16 H7
Landerberry Abers 151 J7
Landford Wilts 21 Q11
Land-hallow Highld 167 L10
Landican Crematorium Wirral 81 K7
Landimore Swans 28 E6
Landkey Devon 17 K5
Landore Swans 29 J5
Landrake Cnwll 5 P9
Landscove Devon 7 K5
Land's End Cnwll 2 A8
Land's End Airport Cnwll 2 B8
Landshipping Pembks 41 K8
Landue Cnwll 5 P6
Landulph Cnwll 6 C6
Landwade Suffk 63 K7
Lane Cnwll 4 C9
Laneast Cnwll 5 L5
Lane Bottom Lancs 89 P3
Lane End Bucks 35 M6
Lane End Cnwll 4 G8
Lane End Hants 22 G9
Lane End Kent 37 N6
Lane End Lancs 96 C11
Lane End Warrtn 82 E6
Lane End Wilts 20 F5
Lane Ends Derbys 71 N8
Lane Ends Lancs 89 M4
Lane Ends N York 90 B2
Lane Green Staffs 58 C4
Laneham Notts 85 P5
Lanehead Dur 102 F2
Lane Head Dur 103 M8
Lanehead Nthumb 111 Q3
Lane Head Wigan 82 D5
Lane Head Wsall 58 E4
Lane Heads Lancs 88 E3
Laneshaw Bridge Lancs 89 Q2
Lane Side Lancs 89 M6
Langaford Devon 5 Q2
Langaller Somset 19 J9
Langar Notts 73 J4
Langbank Rens 125 K3
Langbar N York 96 G10
Langbaurgh N York 104 G8
Langcliffe N York 96 B8
Langdale End N York 99 J2
Langdon Cnwll 5 N4
Langdon Beck Dur 102 G4
Langdown Hants 14 D5
Langdyke Fife 135 J7
Langenhoe Essex 52 H8
Langford C Beds 50 E2
Langford Devon 9 P4
Langford Essex 52 D10
Langford N Som 19 N2
Langford Notts 85 P9
Langford Oxon 33 P4
Langford Budville Somset 18 F10
Langham Dorset 20 E9
Langham Essex 52 H5
Langham Norfk 76 E3
Langham Rutlnd 73 L8
Langham Suffk 64 D8
Langho Lancs 89 L4
Langholm D & G 110 G4
Langland Swans 28 H7
Langlee Border 117 Q3
Langley Ches E 83 K10

Langley - Little Budworth 285

Langley Derbys 84 F11
Langley Gloucs 47 K9
Langley Hants 14 D6
Langley Herts 50 F6
Langley Kent 38 D11
Langley Nthumb 112 B8
Langley Oxon 47 Q11
Langley Rochdl 89 P9
Langley Slough 36 B5
Langley Somset 18 E9
Langley W Susx 23 M9
Langley Warwks 47 N2
Langley Burrell Wilts 32 H9
Langley Castle Nthumb 112 B8
Langley Common Derbys 71 P7
Langley Green Derbys 71 P7
Langley Green Essex 52 E7
Langley Green Warwks 47 N2
Langley Lower Green Essex 51 K4
Langley Marsh Somset 18 E9
Langley Mill Derbys 84 F11
Langley Moor Dur 103 Q2
Langley Park Dur 113 K11
Langley Street Norfk 77 M11
Langley Upper Green Essex 51 K4
Langney E Susx 25 P10
Langold Notts 85 J3
Langore Cnwll 5 M4
Langport Somset 19 M9
Langrick Lincs 87 J11
Langridge BaNES 32 D11
Langridgeford Devon 17 K7
Langrigg Cumb 110 C11
Langrish Hants 23 K10
Langsett Barns 90 G10
Langside P & K 133 M5
Langstone Hants 15 K6
Langstone Newpt 31 L7
Langthorne N York 97 K2
Langthorpe N York 97 N7
Langthwaite N York 103 K10
Langtoft E R Yk 99 L7
Langtoft Lincs 74 B8
Langton Dur 103 N7
Langton Lincs 86 H7
Langton Lincs 87 L6
Langton N York 98 F7
Langton by Wragby Lincs 86 F5
Langton Green Kent 25 M3
Langton Green Suffk 64 G7
Langton Herring Dorset 11 N8
Langton Long Blandford Dorset 12 F3
Langton Matravers Dorset 12 H9
Langtree Devon 16 H8
Langtree Week Devon 16 H8
Langwathby Cumb 101 Q4
Langwell House Highld 163 Q2
Langwith Derbys 84 H7
Langwith Junction Derbys 84 H7
Langworth Lincs 86 E5
Lanhydrock House & Gardens Cnwll 4 H9
Lanivet Cnwll 4 G9
Lanjeth Cnwll 3 P3
Lank Cnwll 4 H6
Lanlivery Cnwll 4 H10
Lanner Cnwll 3 J6
Lanoy Cnwll 5 M6
Lanreath Cnwll 5 K10
Lansallos Cnwll 5 K11
Lanteglos Cnwll 4 H5
Lanteglos Highway Cnwll 5 J11
Lanton Border 118 B6
Lanton Nthumb 118 H4
La Passee Guern 10 b1
Lapford Devon 8 H3
Laphroaig Ag & B 122 E10
Lapley Staffs 58 C2
La Pulente Jersey 11 a2
Lapworth Warwks 59 J10
Larachbeg Highld 138 B8
Larbert Falk 133 P11
Larbreck Lancs 88 E2
Largie Abers 158 F11
Largiemore Ag & B 131 J10
Largoward Fife 135 M6
Largs N Ayrs 124 G6
Largybeg N Ayrs 121 K7
Largymore N Ayrs 121 K7
Larkbeare Devon 9 Q5
Larkfield Inver 124 G2
Larkfield Kent 38 B10
Larkhall S Lans 126 D7
Larkhill Wilts 21 M6
Larling Norfk 64 D4
La Rocque Jersey 11 c2
La Rousaillerie Guern 10 b1
Lartington Dur 103 K7
Lasborough Gloucs 32 F6
Lasham Hants 23 J6
Lashbrook Devon 8 B3
Lashbrook Devon 16 G10
Lashenden Kent 26 D3
Lask Edge Staffs 70 G3
Lasswade Mdloth 127 Q4
Lastingham N York 98 E2
Latcham Somset 19 M5
Latchford Herts 51 J6
Latchford Oxon 35 J4
Latchingdon Essex 52 E11
Latchley Cnwll 5 Q7
Lately Common Warrtn 82 E5
Lathbury M Keyn 49 N6
Latheron Highld 167 M10
Latheronwheel Highld 167 L10
Lathones Fife 135 M6
Latimer Bucks 50 B11
Latteridge S Glos 32 C8
Lattiford Somset 20 C9
Latton Wilts 33 L5
Lauder Border 128 E10
Laugharne Carmth 28 B2
Laughterton Lincs 85 P5
Laughton E Susx 25 L8
Laughton Leics 60 E3
Laughton Lincs 74 A4
Laughton Lincs 92 D11
Laughton-en-le-Morthen Rothm 84 H3
Launcells Cnwll 16 C10
Launcells Cross Cnwll 16 D10
Launceston Cnwll 5 N5
Launton Oxon 48 H10
Laurencekirk Abers 143 N3
Laurieston D & G 108 E8
Laurieston Falk 126 G2
Lavendon M Keyn 49 P4
Lavenham Suffk 52 F2
Lavernock V Glam 30 G11
Laversdale Cumb 111 J8
Laverstock Wilts 21 N8
Laverstoke Hants 22 E5
Laverton Gloucs 47 L7
Laverton N York 97 K6
Laverton Somset 20 E4
La Villette Guern 10 b2
Lavister Wrexhm 69 L3
Law S Lans 126 E7
Lawers P & K 140 G10
Lawford Essex 53 J5
Lawford Somset 18 F7
Law Hill S Lans 126 E7
Lawhitton Cnwll 5 P5
Lawkland N York 95 R7
Lawkland Green N York 96 A7
Lawley Wrekin 57 M3
Lawnhead Staffs 70 E9
Lawns Wood Crematorium Leeds 90 H3
Lawrenny Pembks 41 K9
Lawshall Suffk 64 B11
Lawshall Green Suffk 64 B11
Lawton Herefs 45 N3
Laxay W Isls 168 i5
Laxdale W Isls 168 j4
Laxey IoM 80 f5
Laxfield Suffk 65 K7
Laxford Bridge Highld 164 F7
Laxo Shet 169 r7
Laxton E R Yk 92 C5
Laxton Nhants 73 P11
Laxton Notts 85 M7
Laycock C Brad 90 C2
Layer Breton Essex 52 F8
Layer-de-la-Haye Essex 52 G7
Layer Marney Essex 52 F8
Layham Suffk 52 H3
Layland's Green W Berk 34 C11
Laymore Dorset 10 H4
Layter's Green Bucks 35 Q6
Laytham E R Yk 92 B3
Laythes Cumb 110 D9
Lazenby R & Cl 104 G7
Lazonby Cumb 101 P3
Lea Derbys 84 D9
Lea Herefs 46 C10
Lea Lincs 85 P3
Lea Shrops 56 F7
Lea Shrops 56 G3
Lea Wilts 33 J7
Leachkin Highld 156 A9
Leadburn Border 127 N6
Leadenham Lincs 86 B10
Leaden Roding Essex 51 N8
Leadgate Dur 112 H10
Leadgate Nthumb 112 H9
Leadhills S Lans 116 B7
Leadingcross Green Kent 38 E11
Leadmill Derbys 84 B4
Leafield Oxon 48 B11
Leagrave Luton 50 C6
Leahead Ches W 70 B2
Lea Heath Staffs 71 J9
Leake N York 97 P2
Leake Common Side Lincs 87 L10
Lealholm N York 105 L9
Lealholm Side N York 105 L9
Lealt Highld 153 J5
Leam Derbys 84 B5
Lea Marston Warwks 59 K6
Leamington Hastings Warwks 59 P11
Leamington Spa Warwks 59 M11
Leamside Dur 113 M11
Leap Cross E Susx 25 N8
Leasgill Cumb 95 K4
Leasingham Lincs 86 E11
Leasingthorne Dur 103 Q4
Leatherhead Surrey 36 E9
Leathley N York 97 K11
Leaton Shrops 69 N11
Leaton Wrekin 57 L2
Lea Town Lancs 88 F4
Leaveland Kent 38 H11
Leavenheath Suffk 52 G4
Leavening N York 98 F8
Leaves Green Gt Lon 37 K8
Lea Yeat Cumb 95 R3
Lebberston N York 99 M4
Le Bigard Guern 10 b2
Le Bourg Guern 10 b2
Le Bourg Jersey 11 c2
Lechlade on Thames Gloucs 33 P5
Lecht Gruinart Ag & B 122 C6
Leck Lancs 95 N5
Leckbuie P & K 140 H9
Leckford Hants 22 C7
Leckhampstead Bucks 49 K7
Leckhampstead W Berk 34 D9
Leckhampstead Thicket W Berk 34 D9
Leckhampton Gloucs 46 H11
Leckmelm Highld 161 K9
Leckwith V Glam 30 G10
Leconfield E R Yk 92 H2
Ledaig Ag & B 138 G10
Ledburn Bucks 49 P10
Ledbury Herefs 46 D7
Leddington Gloucs 46 C8
Ledgemoor Herefs 45 N4
Ledicot Herefs 45 N2
Ledmore Junction Highld 161 L4
Ledsham Ches W 81 M10
Ledsham Leeds 91 M5
Ledston Leeds 91 L5
Ledstone Devon 7 J9
Ledston Luck Leeds 91 L4
Ledwell Oxon 48 D9
Lee Devon 16 H2
Lee Gt Lon 37 J5
Lee Hants 22 C11
Lee Shrops 69 M8
Leebotwood Shrops 56 H5
Lee Brockhurst Shrops 69 P9
Leece Cumb 94 E7
Lee Chapel Essex 37 Q3
Lee Clump Bucks 35 P4
Lee Common Bucks 35 P4
Leeds Kent 38 D11
Leeds Leeds 90 H4
Leeds Bradford Airport Leeds 90 G2
Leeds Castle Kent 38 D11
Leedstown Cnwll 2 G7
Lee Green Ches E 70 B2
Leek Staffs 70 H3
Leek Wootton Warwks 59 L11
Lee Mill Devon 6 F7
Leeming C Brad 90 C4
Leeming N York 97 L3
Leeming Bar N York 97 L3
Lee Moor Devon 6 F6
Lee-on-the-Solent Hants 14 G6
Lees C Brad 90 C3
Lees Derbys 71 P7
Lees Oldham 83 L4
Lees Green Derbys 71 P7
Leesthorpe Leics 73 K8
Lee Street Surrey 24 G2
Leeswood Flints 69 J2
Leetown P & K 134 G3
Leftwich Ches W 82 E10
Legar Powys 45 J11
Legbourne Lincs 87 L4
Legburthwaite Cumb 101 K7
Legerwood Border 118 A2
Legoland W & M 35 P10
Le Gron Guern 10 b2
Legsby Lincs 86 F3
Le Haguais Jersey 11 c2
Le Hocq Jersey 11 c2
Leicester C Leic 72 F10
Leicester Forest East Leics 72 E10
Leicester Forest East Services Leics 72 E10
Leigh Devon 17 N9
Leigh Dorset 11 N3
Leigh Gloucs 46 G9
Leigh Kent 37 M11
Leigh Shrops 56 E4
Leigh Surrey 36 F11
Leigh Wigan 82 E5
Leigh Wilts 33 L6
Leigh Worcs 46 E4
Leigh Beck Essex 38 D5
Leigh Delamere Wilts 32 G9
Leigh Delamere Services Wilts 32 G9
Leigh Green Kent 26 F5
Leigh Knoweglass S Lans 125 Q7
Leighland Chapel Somset 18 D7
Leigh-on-Sea Sthend 38 D4
Leigh Park Dorset 12 H5
Leigh Sinton Worcs 46 E4
Leighswood Wsall 58 G4
Leighterton Gloucs 32 F6
Leighton N York 97 J5
Leighton Powys 56 C3
Leighton Shrops 57 L3
Leighton Somset 20 D6
Leighton Bromswold Cambs 61 P5
Leighton Buzzard C Beds 49 P9
Leigh upon Mendip Somset 20 C5
Leigh Woods N Som 31 Q10
Leinthall Earls Herefs 56 G11
Leinthall Starkes Herefs 56 G11
Leintwardine Herefs 56 G10
Leire Leics 60 B3
Leiston Suffk 65 N9
Leith C Edin 127 P2
Leitholm Border 118 E2
Lelant Cnwll 2 E6
Lelley E R Yk 93 M4
Lem Hill Worcs 57 N9
Lempitlaw Border 118 E4
Lemreway W Isls 168 i6
Lemsford Herts 50 F8
Lenchwick Worcs 47 K5
Lendalfoot S Ayrs 114 B9
Lendrick Stirlg 132 H6
Lendrum Terrace Abers 159 R9
Lenham Kent 38 E11
Lenham Heath Kent 26 F2
Lenie Highld 147 N2
Lennel Border 118 G2
Lennox Plunton D & G 108 D10
Lennoxtown E Duns 125 Q2
Lent Bucks 35 P8
Lenton C Nott 72 F3
Lenton Lincs 73 Q4
Lenwade Norfk 76 F8
Lenzie E Duns 126 B3
Leochel-Cushnie Abers 150 E5
Leomansley Staffs 58 H3
Leominster Herefs 45 P3
Leonard Stanley Gloucs 32 F4
Leoville Jersey 11 a1
Lepe Hants 14 D7
Lephin Highld 152 B8
Leppington N York 98 F8
Lepton Kirk 90 G7
Lerags Ag & B 130 H2
L'Erée Guern 10 a2
Lerryn Cnwll 5 J10
Lerwick Shet 169 r9
Les Arquets Guern 10 b2
Lesbury Nthumb 119 P8
Les Hubits Guern 10 c2
Leslie Abers 150 F3
Leslie Fife 134 H7
Les Lohiers Guern 10 b2
Lesmahagow S Lans 126 E10
Les Murchez Guern 10 b2
Lesnewth Cnwll 5 J3
Les Nicolles Guern 10 b2
Les Quartiers Guern 10 c1
Les Quennevais Jersey 11 a2
Les Sages Guern 10 b2
Lessingham Norfk 77 M6
Lessonhall Cumb 110 D10
Lestowder Cnwll 3 K9
Les Villets Guern 10 b2
Leswalt D & G 106 D5
L'Etacq Jersey 11 a1
Letchmore Heath Herts 50 E11
Letchworth Garden City Herts 50 F4
Letcombe Bassett Oxon 34 C8
Letcombe Regis Oxon 34 C7
Letham Angus 143 J8
Letham Border 118 C9
Letham Falk 133 P10
Letham Fife 135 J5
Letham Grange Angus 143 L8
Lethendy P & K 142 A9
Lethenty Abers 150 F3
Lethenty Abers 159 K9
Letheringham Suffk 65 K10
Letheringsett Norfk 76 F4
Lettaford Devon 8 H8
Letterewe Highld 154 C3
Letterfearn Highld 145 Q3
Letterfinlay Lodge Hotel Highld 146 H9
Lettermorar Highld 145 M10
Letters Highld 161 K9
Lettershaw S Lans 116 B6
Letterston Pembks 40 H5
Lettoch Highld 149 J4
Lettoch Highld 157 L11
Letton Herefs 45 L5
Letton Herefs 56 F10
Lett's Green Kent 37 L9
Letty Green Herts 50 G8
Letwell Rothm 85 J3
Leuchars Fife 135 M3
Leumrabhagh W Isls 168 i6
Leurbost W Isls 168 i5
Levalsa Meor Cnwll 3 Q4
Levedale Staffs 70 F11
Level's Green Essex 51 L6
Leven E R Yk 99 N11
Leven Fife 135 K7
Levens Cumb 95 K3
Levens Green Herts 51 J6
Levenshulme Manch 83 J6
Levenwick Shet 169 r11
Leverburgh W Isls 168 f9
Leverington Cambs 74 H8
Leverstock Green Herts 50 C9
Leverton Lincs 87 M11
Le Villocq Guern 10 b1
Levington Suffk 53 M4
Levisham N York 98 G2
Lew Oxon 34 B3
Lewannick Cnwll 5 M5
Lewdown Devon 8 C7
Lewes E Susx 25 K8
Leweston Pembks 40 H6
Lewisham Gt Lon 37 J6
Lewisham Crematorium Gt Lon 37 J6
Lewiston Highld 147 N2
Lewistown Brdgnd 29 P7
Lewis Wych Herefs 45 L3
Lewknor Oxon 35 K5
Leworthy Devon 16 E11
Leworthy Devon 17 M4
Lewson Street Kent 38 G9
Lewth Lancs 88 F3
Lewtrenchard Devon 8 C7
Lexden Essex 52 G6
Lexworthy Somset 19 J7
Ley Cnwll 5 K8
Leybourne Kent 37 Q9
Leyburn N York 96 H2
Leycett Staffs 70 D5
Leygreen Herts 50 E6
Ley Hill Bucks 35 Q4
Leyland Lancs 88 G6
Leyland Green St Hel 82 C4
Leylodge Abers 151 K5
Leys Abers 159 P7
Leys P & K 142 D10
Leysdown-on-Sea Kent 38 H7
Leysmill Angus 143 L8
Leys of Cossans Angus 142 F8
Leysters Herefs 45 R2
Leyton Gt Lon 37 J3
Leytonstone Gt Lon 37 J3
Lezant Cnwll 5 N6
Lezerea Cnwll 2 H7
Lhanbryde Moray 157 P5
Libanus Powys 44 D9
Libberton S Lans 116 D2
Liberton C Edin 127 P4
Lichfield Staffs 58 H3
Lickey Worcs 58 E9
Lickey End Worcs 58 E10
Lickey Rock Worcs 58 E10
Lickfold W Susx 23 P9
Liddaton Green Devon 8 C8
Liddesdale Highld 138 D6
Liddington Swindn 33 P8
Lidgate Derbys 84 D5
Lidgate Suffk 63 M9
Lidget Donc 91 R10
Lidgett Notts 85 K7
Lidham Hill E Susx 26 D8
Lidlington C Beds 49 Q7
Lidsing Kent 38 C9
Liff Angus 142 E11
Lifford Birm 58 G8
Lifton Devon 5 P4
Liftondown Devon 5 P4
Lighthorne Warwks 48 B3
Lighthorne Heath Warwks 48 C3
Lightwater Surrey 23 P2
Lightwater Valley Theme Park N York 97 L5
Lightwood C Stke 70 G6
Lightwood Green Ches E 70 A6
Lightwood Green Wrexhm 69 L6
Lilbourne Nhants 60 C5
Lilburn Tower Nthumb 119 K6
Lilleshall Wrekin 70 C11
Lilley Herts 50 D5
Lilley W Berk 34 D9
Lilliesleaf Border 117 Q5
Lillingstone Dayrell Bucks 49 K7
Lillingstone Lovell Bucks 49 K6
Lillington Dorset 11 N2
Lilliput Poole 12 H7
Lilstock Somset 18 G5
Lilyhurst Shrops 57 N2
Limbrick Lancs 89 J7
Limbury Luton 50 C6
Limebrook Herefs 56 F11
Limefield Bury 89 N8
Limekilnburn S Lans 126 C7
Limekilns Fife 134 D11
Limerigg Falk 126 F3
Limerstone IoW 14 D10
Limestone Brae Nthumb 111 Q11
Lime Street Worcs 46 F8
Limington Somset 19 P10
Limmerhaugh E Ayrs 115 M2
Limpenhoe Norfk 77 M11
Limpley Stoke Wilts 20 E2
Limpsfield Surrey 37 K10
Limpsfield Chart Surrey 37 K10
Linby Notts 84 H10
Linchmere W Susx 23 N8
Lincluden D & G 109 L5
Lincoln Lincs 86 C6
Lincoln Crematorium Lincs 86 C6
Lincomb Worcs 57 Q11
Lincombe Devon 7 J10
Lincombe Devon 16 H2
Lindale Cumb 95 J4
Lindal in Furness Cumb 94 E5
Lindfield W Susx 24 H5
Lindford Hants 23 M7
Lindley Kirk 90 E7
Lindley N York 97 K11
Lindores Fife 134 H4
Lindow End Ches E 82 H9
Lindridge Worcs 57 M11
Lindsell Essex 51 P5
Lindsey Suffk 52 G2
Lindsey Tye Suffk 52 G2
Liney Somset 19 L7
Linford Hants 13 L3
Linford Thurr 37 Q5
Lingbob C Brad 90 D3
Lingdale R & Cl 105 J7
Lingen Herefs 56 F11
Lingfield Surrey 25 J2
Lingwood Norfk 77 M10
Linicro Highld 152 F4
Linkend Worcs 46 F8
Linkenholt Hants 22 C3
Linkhill Kent 26 D6
Linkinhorne Cnwll 5 N7
Linktown Fife 134 H9
Linkwood Moray 157 N5
Linley Shrops 56 F6
Linley Green Herefs 46 C4
Linleygreen Shrops 57 M5
Linlithgow W Loth 126 H2
Linshiels Nthumb 118 G9
Linsidemore Highld 162 C7
Linslade C Beds 49 P9
Linstead Parva Suffk 65 L6
Linstock Cumb 110 H9
Linthurst Worcs 58 E10
Linthwaite Kirk 90 E8
Lintlaw Border 129 L8
Lintmill Moray 158 D4
Linton Border 118 E5
Linton Cambs 63 J11
Linton Derbys 71 P11
Linton Herefs 46 C9
Linton Kent 38 C11
Linton Leeds 97 N11
Linton N York 96 E8
Linton Nthumb 113 L2
Linton Heath Derbys 71 P11
Linton Hill Herefs 46 C10
Linton-on-Ouse N York 97 Q8
Linwood Hants 13 L3
Linwood Lincs 86 F3
Linwood Rens 125 L5
Lionacleit W Isls 168 c13
Lional W Isls 168 k1
Lions Green E Susx 25 N7
Liphook Hants 23 M8
Lipley Shrops 70 C8
Liscard Wirral 81 K6
Liscombe Somset 18 A8
Liskeard Cnwll 5 M9
Lismore Ag & B 138 E9
Liss Hants 23 L9
Lissett E R Yk 99 N9
Liss Forest Hants 23 L9
Lissington Lincs 86 F4
Liston Essex 52 E3
Lisvane Cardif 30 G8
Liswerry Newpt 31 K7
Litcham Norfk 76 B8
Litchard Brdgnd 29 P8
Litchborough Nhants 48 H4
Litchfield Hants 22 E4
Litherland Sefton 81 L5
Litlington Cambs 50 H2
Litlington E Susx 25 M10
Little Abington Cambs 62 H11
Little Addington Nhants 61 L6
Little Airies D & G 107 M8
Little Almshoe Herts 50 F5
Little Alne Warwks 47 M2
Little Altcar Sefton 88 C9
Little Amwell Herts 51 J8
Little Asby Cumb 102 C9
Little Aston Staffs 58 G5
Little Atherfield IoW 14 E11
Little Ayton N York 104 G8
Little Baddow Essex 52 C10
Little Badminton S Glos 32 F8
Little Bampton Cumb 110 E9
Little Bardfield Essex 51 Q4
Little Barford Bed 61 Q9
Little Barningham Norfk 76 G5
Little Barrington Gloucs 33 P2
Little Barrow Ches W 81 P11
Little Barugh N York 98 F5
Little Bavington Nthumb 112 E5
Little Bealings Suffk 53 M2
Littlebeck N York 105 N10
Little Bedwyn Wilts 33 Q11
Little Bentley Essex 53 K6
Little Berkhamsted Herts 50 G9
Little Billing Nhants 60 H8
Little Billington C Beds 49 P10
Little Birch Herefs 45 Q8
Little Bispham Bpool 88 C2
Little Blakenham Suffk 53 K2
Little Blencow Cumb 101 N4
Little Bloxwich Wsall 58 F4
Little Bognor W Susx 24 B6
Little Bolehill Derbys 71 P4
Little Bollington Ches E 82 F7
Little Bookham Surrey 36 D10
Littleborough Devon 9 K2
Littleborough Notts 85 P4
Littleborough Rochdl 89 Q7
Littlebourne Kent 39 M10
Little Bourton Oxon 48 E6
Little Bowden Leics 60 F3
Little Bradley Suffk 63 L10
Little Brampton Herefs 45 L2
Little Brampton Shrops 56 F8
Little Braxted Essex 52 D9
Little Brechin Angus 143 K5
Littlebredy Dorset 11 M7
Little Brickhill M Keyn 49 P8
Little Bridgeford Staffs 70 F9
Little Brington Nhants 60 E8
Little Bromley Essex 53 J6
Little Broughton Cumb 100 E4
Little Budworth Ches W 82 C11

Llantysilio - Low Toynton 287

Llantysilio Denbgs 68 G6
Llanuwchllyn Gwynd 68 A8
Llanvaches Newpt 31 M6
Llanvair Discoed Mons 31 M6
Llanvapley Mons 31 L2
Llanvetherine Mons 45 M11
Llanveynoe Herefs 45 L8
Llanvihangel Crucorney Mons 45 L10
Llanvihangel Gobion Mons 31 K3
Llanvihangel-Ystern-Llewern Mons 31 M2
Llanwarne Herefs 45 Q9
Llanwddyn Powys 68 D11
Llanwenarth Mons 31 J2
Llanwenog Cerdgn 43 J5
Llanwern Newpt 31 L7
Llanwinio Carmth 41 Q5
Llanwnda Gwynd 66 H3
Llanwnda Pembks 40 H3
Llanwnnen Cerdgn 43 K5
Llanwnog Powys 55 N6
Llanwonno Rhondd 30 D5
Llanwrda Carmth 43 P8
Llanwrin Powys 54 H4
Llanwrthwl Powys 44 D2
Llanwrtyd Powys 44 B5
Llanwrtyd Wells Powys 44 B5
Llanwyddelan Powys 55 P4
Llanyblodwel Shrops 68 H10
Llanybri Carmth 28 B2
Llanybydder Carmth 43 K6
Llanycefn Pembks 41 L6
Llanychaer Bridge Pembks 41 J3
Llanycrwys Carmth 43 M5
Llanymawddwy Gwynd 68 B11
Llanymynech Powys 69 J10
Llanynghenedl IoA 78 E8
Llanynys Denbgs 68 F2
Llan-y-pwll Wrexhm 69 L4
Llanyre Powys 44 E2
Llanystumdwy Gwynd 66 H7
Llanywern Powys 44 G9
Llawhaden Pembks 41 L7
Llawnt Shrops 68 H8
Llawryglyn Powys 55 L6
Llay Wrexhm 69 K3
Llechcynfarwy IoA 78 F8
Llechfaen Powys 44 F9
Llechrhyd Caerph 30 F3
Llechryd Cerdgn 41 P2
Llechylched IoA 78 E9
Lledrod Cerdgn 54 E10
Lleyn Peninsula Gwynd 66 E7
Llidiardau Gwynd 68 A7
Llidiartnenog Carmth 43 K7
Llidiart-y-parc Denbgs 68 F6
Llithfaen Gwynd 66 F6
Lloc Flints 80 G9
Llowes Powys 44 H6
Llwydcoed Rhondd 30 C4
Llwydcoed Crematorium Rhondd 30 C3
Llwydiarth Powys 68 D11
Llwyn Denbgs 68 E2
Llwyncelyn Cerdgn 42 H3
Llwyndafydd Cerdgn 42 G3
Llwynderw Powys 56 C4
Llwyn-drain Pembks 41 Q4
Llwyn-du Mons 45 K11
Llwyndyrys Gwynd 66 F6
Llwyngwril Gwynd 54 D3
Llwynhendy Carmth 28 F5
Llwynmawr Wrexhm 68 H7
Llwyn-on Myr Td 30 D2
Llwyn-y-brain Carmth 41 N8
Llwyn-y-groes Cerdgn 43 L3
Llwynypia Rhondd 30 C6
Llynclys Shrops 69 J10
Llynfaes IoA 78 G9
Llyn-y-pandy Flints 81 J11
Llysfaen Conwy 80 B9
Llyswen Cerdgn 43 J2
Llyswen Powys 44 G7
Llysworney V Glam 30 C10
Llys-y-frân Pembks 41 K6
Llywel Powys 44 B8
Load Brook Sheff 84 C3
Loan Falk 126 H2
Loanend Nthumb 129 N9
Loanhead Mdloth 127 P4
Loaningfoot D & G 109 L9
Loans S Ayrs 125 J11
Lobb Devon 16 H4
Lobhillcross Devon 8 C7
Lochailort Highld 145 N11
Lochaline Highld 138 B9
Lochans D & G 106 E6
Locharbriggs D & G 109 L4
Lochavich Ag & B 131 J4
Lochawe Ag & B 131 N2
Loch Baghasdail W Isls 168 c16
Lochboisdale W Isls 168 c16
Lochbuie Ag & B 137 Q10
Lochcarron Highld 154 A10
Lochdon Ag & B 138 C11
Lochdonhead Ag & B 138 C11
Lochead Ag & B 123 N4
Lochearnhead Stirlg 132 H3
Lochee C Dund 142 F11
Locheilside Station Highld 138 H2
Lochend Highld 155 Q10
Locheport W Isls 168 d11
Loch Euphort W Isls 168 d11
Lochfoot D & G 109 J6
Lochgair Ag & B 131 J9
Lochgelly Fife 134 F9
Lochgilphead Ag & B 130 H10
Lochgoilhead Ag & B 131 Q7
Lochieheads Fife 134 H5
Lochill Moray 157 P5
Lochindorb Lodge Highld 156 H10
Lochinver Highld 160 H2
Loch Lomond and The Trossachs National Park 132 E5
Lochluichart Highld 155 K5
Lochmaben D & G 109 N4
Lochmaddy W Isls 168 e11
Loch Maree Hotel Highld 154 B3
Loch nam Madadh W Isls 168 e11
Loch Ness Highld 147 N2
Lochore Fife 134 F8
Lochranza N Ayrs 124 A7
Lochside Abers 143 N5
Lochside D & G 109 L5
Lochside Highld 156 E7
Lochslin Highld 163 J10
Lochton S Ayrs 107 J2
Lochty Angus 143 J5
Lochty Fife 135 N6
Lochuisge Highld 138 D6
Lochwinnoch Rens 125 K6
Lochwood D & G 116 F11
Lockengate Cnwll 4 G9
Lockerbie D & G 109 P4
Lockeridge Wilts 33 M11
Lockerley Hants 22 B9
Locking N Som 19 L3
Locking Stumps Warrtn 82 D6
Lockington E R Yk 99 K11
Lockington Leics 72 D5
Lockleywood Shrops 70 B9
Locksbottom Gt Lon 37 K7
Locksgreen IoW 14 D8
Locks Heath Hants 14 F5
Lockton N York 98 G3
Loddington Leics 73 K10
Loddington Nhants 60 H5
Loddiswell Devon 7 J9
Loddon Norfk 65 M2
Lode Cambs 62 H8
Lode Heath Solhll 59 J8
Loders Dorset 11 K6
Lodge Hill Crematorium Birm 58 F8
Lodsworth W Susx 23 P10
Lofthouse Leeds 91 J5
Lofthouse N York 96 H6
Lofthouse Gate Wakefd 91 J6
Loftus R & Cl 105 K7
Logan E Ayrs 115 L3
Loganbeck Cumb 94 D2
Loganlea W Loth 126 H5
Loggerheads Staffs 70 C7
Logie Angus 143 M5
Logie Fife 135 L3
Logie Moray 157 J7
Logie Coldstone Abers 150 C7
Logie Newton Abers 158 G10
Logie Pert Angus 143 M5
Logierait P & K 141 N7
Logierieve Abers 151 N2
Login Carmth 41 N6
Lolworth Cambs 62 E8
Lonbain Highld 153 M7
Londesborough E R Yk 98 H11
London Gt Lon 36 G5
London Apprentice Cnwll 3 Q4
London Beach Kent 26 E4
London Colney Herts 50 E10
Londonderry N York 97 M3
London End Nhants 61 K7
London Gateway Services Gt Lon 36 E2
Londonthorpe Lincs 73 P3
London Zoo ZSL Gt Lon 36 G4
Londubh Highld 160 D10
Lonemore Highld 153 P2
Long Ashton N Som 31 P10
Long Bank Worcs 57 P10
Long Bennington Lincs 73 L2
Longbenton N Tyne 113 L7
Longborough Gloucs 47 N9
Long Bredy Dorset 11 M6
Longbridge Birm 58 F9
Longbridge Warwks 47 Q2
Longbridge Deverill Wilts 20 G6
Long Buckby Nhants 60 D7
Longburgh Cumb 110 F9
Longburton Dorset 11 N2
Long Cause Devon 7 K6
Long Clawson Leics 73 J5
Longcliffe Derbys 84 B9
Longcombe Devon 7 L7
Long Common Hants 14 F4
Long Compton Staffs 70 F10
Long Compton Warwks 47 Q8
Longcot Oxon 33 Q6
Long Crendon Bucks 35 J3
Long Crichel Dorset 12 G2
Longcroft Cumb 110 D9
Longcross Surrey 35 Q11
Longden Shrops 56 G3
Longden Common Shrops 56 G3
Long Ditton Surrey 36 E7
Longdon Staffs 58 G2
Longdon Worcs 46 F7
Longdon Green Staffs 58 G2
Longdon Heath Worcs 46 F7
Longdon upon Tern Wrekin 69 R11
Longdown Devon 9 L6
Longdowns Cnwll 3 J7
Long Drax N York 92 A5
Long Duckmanton Derbys 84 F6
Long Eaton Derbys 72 D4
Longfield Kent 37 P7
Longford Covtry 59 N8
Longford Derbys 71 N7
Longford Gloucs 46 F10
Longford Gt Lon 36 C5
Longford Kent 37 M9
Longford Shrops 70 A8
Longford Wrekin 70 C11
Longforgan P & K 134 H2
Longformacus Border 128 H8
Longframlington Nthumb 119 M10
Long Green Ches W 81 P10
Long Green Worcs 46 F8
Longham Dorset 13 J5
Longham Norfk 76 C8
Long Hanborough Oxon 34 D2
Longhaven Abers 159 R10
Long Hedges Lincs 87 L11
Longhirst Nthumb 113 K3
Longhope Gloucs 46 C11
Longhope Ork 169 c7
Longhorsley Nthumb 112 H2
Longhoughton Nthumb 119 P7
Long Itchington Warwks 59 P11
Longlands Cumb 101 J3
Longlane Derbys 71 N7
Long Lawford Warwks 59 Q9
Longleat Safari & Adventure Park Wilts 20 F6
Longlevens Gloucs 46 G11
Longley Calder 90 D6
Longley Kirk 90 E9
Longley Green Worcs 46 D4
Longleys P & K 142 D9
Long Load Somset 19 N10
Longmanhill Abers 158 H5
Long Marston Herts 49 N11
Long Marston N York 97 R10
Long Marston Warwks 47 N5
Long Marton Cumb 102 C6
Long Meadowend Shrops 56 G8
Long Melford Suffk 52 E2
Longmoor Camp Hants 23 L8
Longmorn Moray 157 N6
Longmoss Ches E 83 J10
Long Newnton Gloucs 32 H6
Longnewton Border 118 A5
Long Newton E Loth 128 E7
Longnewton S on T 104 C7
Longney Gloucs 32 E2
Longniddry E Loth 128 C4
Longnor Shrops 56 H4
Longnor Staffs 71 K2
Longparish Hants 22 D5
Longpark Cumb 110 H8
Long Preston N York 96 B9
Longridge Lancs 89 J3
Longridge Staffs 70 G11
Longridge W Loth 126 G5
Longriggend N Lans 126 E3
Long Riston E R Yk 93 K2
Longrock Cnwll 2 E7
Longsdon Staffs 70 H4
Longshaw Wigan 82 B4
Longside Abers 159 P8
Long Sight Oldham 89 Q9
Longslow Shrops 70 B7
Longstanton Cambs 62 E7
Longstock Hants 22 C7
Longstone Pembks 41 M9
Longstowe Cambs 62 D10
Long Stratton Norfk 64 H3
Long Street M Keyn 49 L5
Longstreet Wilts 21 M4
Long Sutton Hants 23 K5
Long Sutton Lincs 74 H6
Long Sutton Somset 19 N9
Longthorpe C Pete 74 C11
Long Thurlow Suffk 64 E8
Longthwaite Cumb 101 M6
Longton C Stke 70 G6
Longton Lancs 88 F5
Longtown Cumb 110 G7
Longtown Herefs 45 L9
Longueville Jersey 11 c2
Longville in the Dale Shrops 57 J6
Long Waste Wrekin 69 R11
Long Whatton Leics 72 D6
Longwick Bucks 35 L3
Long Wittenham Oxon 34 F6
Longwitton Nthumb 112 G3
Longwood D & G 108 F8
Longwood Shrops 57 L3
Longworth Oxon 34 C5
Longyester E Loth 128 E7
Lon-las Swans 29 K5
Lonmay Abers 159 P6
Lonmore Highld 152 D8
Looe Cnwll 5 M11
Loose Kent 38 C11
Loosebeare Devon 8 H3
Loosegate Lincs 74 F5
Loosley Row Bucks 35 M4
Lootcherbrae Abers 158 F7
Lopcombe Corner Wilts 21 Q7
Lopen Somset 11 J2
Loppington Shrops 69 N9
Lorbottle Nthumb 119 K9
Lordington W Susx 15 L5
Lordsbridge Norfk 75 L8
Lords Wood Medway 38 C9
Lornty P & K 142 B8
Loscoe Derbys 84 F11
Loscombe Dorset 11 K5
Lossiemouth Moray 157 N3
Lostford Shrops 69 R8
Lostock Gralam Ches W 82 E10
Lostock Green Ches W 82 E10
Lostock Hall Lancs 88 G5
Lostock Hall Fold Bolton 89 K9
Lostock Junction Bolton 89 K9
Lostwithiel Cnwll 5 J10
Lothbeg Highld 163 L4
Lothersdale N York 96 E11
Lothmore Highld 163 M4
Loudwater Bucks 35 P6
Loughborough Leics 72 E7
Loughborough Crematorium Leics 72 E7
Loughor Swans 28 G5
Loughton Essex 51 K11
Loughton M Keyn 49 M7
Loughton Shrops 57 L8
Lound Lincs 73 R7
Lound Notts 85 L3
Lound Suffk 65 Q2
Lounston Devon 9 J9
Lount Leics 72 B7
Louth Lincs 87 K3
Love Clough Lancs 89 N5
Lovedean Hants 15 J4
Lover Wilts 21 P10
Loversall Donc 91 P11
Loves Green Essex 51 P10
Lovesome Hill N York 104 C11
Loveston Pembks 41 L9
Lovington Somset 19 Q8
Low Ackworth Wakefd 91 M7
Low Angerton Nthumb 112 G4
Lowbands Gloucs 46 E8
Low Barbeth D & G 106 D4
Low Barlings Lincs 86 E6
Low Bell End N York 105 K11
Low Bentham N York 95 N7
Low Biggins Cumb 95 N5
Low Borrowbridge Cumb 102 B10
Low Bradfield Sheff 84 C2
Low Bradley N York 96 F11
Low Braithwaite Cumb 101 M2
Low Burnham N Linc 92 C10
Low Buston Nthumb 119 P9
Lowca Cumb 100 C6
Low Catton E R Yk 98 E10
Low Coniscliffe Darltn 103 Q8
Low Crosby Cumb 110 H9
Lowdham Notts 85 L11
Low Dinsdale Darltn 104 B8
Lowe Shrops 69 N8
Lowe Hill Staffs 70 H3
Low Ellington N York 97 K4
Lower Aisholt Somset 18 H7
Lower Ansty Dorset 12 C4
Lower Apperley Gloucs 46 G9
Lower Arncott Oxon 48 H11
Lower Ashton Devon 9 K8
Lower Assendon Oxon 35 K8
Lower Ballam Lancs 88 D4
Lower Bartle Lancs 88 F4
Lower Basildon W Berk 34 H9
Lower Bearwood Herefs 45 M3
Lower Beeding W Susx 24 F5
Lower Benefield Nhants 61 L3
Lower Bentley Worcs 58 E11
Lower Beobridge Shrops 57 P6
Lower Birchwood Derbys 84 F10
Lower Boddington Nhants 48 E4
Lower Boscaswell Cnwll 2 B7
Lower Bourne Surrey 23 M6
Lower Brailes Warwks 48 B7
Lower Breakish Highld 145 L3
Lower Bredbury Stockp 83 K6
Lower Broadheath Worcs 46 F3
Lower Broxwood Herefs 45 M4
Lower Buckenhill Herefs 46 B8
Lower Bullingham Herefs 45 Q7
Lower Burgate Hants 21 N11
Lower Burrowton Devon 9 P5
Lower Burton Herefs 45 N3
Lower Caldecote C Beds 61 Q11
Lower Cam Gloucs 32 D4
Lower Canada N Som 19 L3
Lower Catesby Nhants 60 B9
Lower Chapel Powys 44 E7
Lower Chicksgrove Wilts 21 J9
Lower Chute Wilts 22 B4
Lower Clapton Gt Lon 36 H3
Lower Clent Worcs 58 D9
Lower Creedy Devon 9 K4
Lower Crossings Derbys 83 M8
Lower Cumberworth Kirk 90 G9
Lower Darwen Bl w D 89 K5
Lower Dean Bed 61 N7
Lower Denby Kirk 90 G9
Lower Diabaig Highld 153 P5
Lower Dicker E Susx 25 N8
Lower Dinchope Shrops 56 H8
Lower Down Shrops 56 E8
Lower Dunsforth N York 97 P8
Lower Egleton Herefs 46 B5
Lower Elkstone Staffs 71 K3
Lower Ellastone Staffs 71 L6
Lower End Bucks 35 J3
Lower End M Keyn 49 P7
Lower End Nhants 60 H9
Lower End Nhants 61 J8
Lower Everleigh Wilts 21 N4
Lower Exbury Hants 14 D7
Lower Eythorne Kent 27 N2
Lower Failand N Som 31 P10
Lower Farringdon Hants 23 K7
Lower Feltham Gt Lon 36 C6
Lower Fittleworth W Susx 24 B7
Lower Foxdale IoM 80 c6
Lower Frankton Shrops 69 L8
Lower Freystrop Pembks 41 J8
Lower Froyle Hants 23 L6
Lower Gabwell Devon 7 N5
Lower Gledfield Highld 162 D8
Lower Godney Somset 19 N6
Lower Gornal Dudley 58 D6
Lower Gravenhurst C Beds 50 D3
Lower Green Herts 50 E4
Lower Green Herts 51 K4
Lower Green Kent 25 N2
Lower Green Kent 25 P2
Lower Green Norfk 76 D4
Lower Green Staffs 58 D3
Lower Green Suffk 63 M7
Lower Hacheston Suffk 65 L10
Lower Halliford Surrey 36 C7
Lower Halstock Leigh Dorset 11 L3
Lower Halstow Kent 38 E8
Lower Hamworthy Poole 12 G6
Lower Hardres Kent 39 L11
Lower Harpton Herefs 45 K2
Lower Hartlip Kent 38 D9
Lower Hartshay Derbys 84 E10
Lower Hartwell Bucks 35 L2
Lower Hatton Staffs 70 E7
Lower Hawthwaite Cumb 94 E3
Lower Hergest Herefs 45 K3
Lower Heyford Oxon 48 E10
Lower Heysham Lancs 95 J8
Lower Higham Kent 38 B7
Lower Holbrook Suffk 53 L4
Lower Hordley Shrops 69 L9
Lower Horncroft W Susx 24 B7
Lowerhouse Lancs 89 N4
Lower Houses Kirk 90 F7
Lower Howsell Worcs 46 E5
Lower Irlam Salfd 82 F6
Lower Kilburn Derbys 72 B2
Lower Kilcott Gloucs 32 E7
Lower Killeyan Ag & B 122 C11
Lower Kingcombe Dorset 11 M5
Lower Kingswood Surrey 36 F10
Lower Kinnerton Ches W 69 K2
Lower Langford N Som 19 N2
Lower Largo Fife 135 L7
Lower Leigh Staffs 71 J7
Lower Lemington Gloucs 47 P8
Lower Llanfadog Powys 55 M11
Lower Lovacott Devon 17 J6
Lower Loxhore Devon 17 L4
Lower Lydbrook Gloucs 46 A11
Lower Lye Herefs 56 G11
Lower Machen Newpt 30 H7
Lower Maes-coed Herefs 45 L8
Lower Mannington Dorset 13 J4
Lower Marston Somset 20 E6
Lower Meend Gloucs 31 Q4
Lower Merridge Somset 18 H8
Lower Middleton Cheney Nhants 48 F6
Lower Milton Somset 19 P5
Lower Moor Worcs 47 J5
Lower Morton S Glos 32 B6
Lower Nazeing Essex 51 J9
Lower Norton Warwks 47 P2
Lower Nyland Dorset 20 E10
Lower Penarth V Glam 30 G11
Lower Penn Staffs 58 C5
Lower Pennington Hants 13 P6
Lower Penwortham Lancs 88 G5
Lower Peover Ches E 82 F10
Lower Place Rochdl 89 Q8
Lower Pollicott Bucks 35 K2
Lower Quinton Warwks 47 N5
Lower Rainham Medway 38 D8
Lower Raydon Suffk 52 H4
Lower Roadwater Somset 18 D7
Lower Salter Lancs 95 N8
Lower Seagry Wilts 33 J8
Lower Sheering Essex 51 L8
Lower Shelton C Beds 49 Q6
Lower Shiplake Oxon 35 L9
Lower Shuckburgh Warwks 48 E2
Lower Slaughter Gloucs 47 N10
Lower Soothill Kirk 90 H6
Lower Soudley Gloucs 32 C3
Lower Standen Kent 27 M3
Lower Stanton St Quintin Wilts 32 H8
Lower Stoke Medway 38 D6
Lower Stone Gloucs 32 C6
Lower Stonnall Staffs 58 G4
Lower Stow Bedon Norfk 64 D3
Lower Street Dorset 12 D5
Lower Street E Susx 26 B9
Lower Street Norfk 77 K4
Lower Street Suffk 63 N10
Lower Street Suffk 64 G11
Lower Stretton Warrtn 82 D8
Lower Stroud Dorset 11 K5
Lower Sundon C Beds 50 C5
Lower Swanwick Hants 14 E5
Lower Swell Gloucs 47 N9
Lower Tadmarton Oxon 48 D7
Lower Tale Devon 9 Q4
Lower Tean Staffs 71 J7
Lower Thurlton Norfk 65 N2
Lower Town Cnwll 2 H8
Lower Town Devon 7 J4
Lower Town Herefs 46 B6
Lower Town Pembks 41 J3
Lower Trebullett Cnwll 5 N6
Lower Treluswell Cnwll 3 K6
Lower Tysoe Warwks 48 B5
Lower Ufford Suffk 65 K11
Lower Upcott Devon 9 L8
Lower Upham Hants 22 F11
Lower Upnor Medway 38 C7
Lower Vexford Somset 18 F7
Lower Walton Warrtn 82 D7
Lower Waterston Dorset 12 B5
Lower Weare Somset 19 M4
Lower Weedon Nhants 60 D9
Lower Welson Herefs 45 K4
Lower Westmancote Worcs 46 H7
Lower Whatcombe Dorset 12 D4
Lower Whatley Somset 20 D5
Lower Whitley Ches W 82 D9
Lower Wick Gloucs 32 D5
Lower Wick Worcs 46 F4
Lower Wield Hants 22 H6
Lower Willingdon E Susx 25 N10
Lower Withington Ches E 82 H11
Lower Woodend Bucks 35 M7
Lower Woodford Wilts 21 M7
Lower Wraxhall Dorset 11 M4
Lower Wyche Worcs 46 E6
Lower Wyke C Brad 90 F5
Lowesby Leics 73 J9
Lowestoft Suffk 65 Q3
Loweswater Cumb 100 F6
Low Fell Gatesd 113 L9
Lowfield Heath W Susx 24 G3
Low Gartachorrans Stirlg 132 F10
Low Gate Nthumb 112 D8
Low Gettbridge Cumb 111 K9
Lowgill Cumb 102 B11
Lowgill Lancs 95 P8
Low Grantley N York 97 K6
Low Green N York 97 K9
Low Habberley Worcs 57 Q9
Low Ham Somset 19 M9
Low Harrogate N York 97 L9
Low Hawsker N York 105 P9
Low Hesket Cumb 111 J11
Low Hutton N York 98 F7
Lowick Cumb 94 F3
Lowick Nhants 61 L4
Lowick Nthumb 119 K3
Lowick Bridge Cumb 94 F3
Lowick Green Cumb 94 F3
Low Knipe Cumb 101 P7
Low Laithe N York 97 J8
Lowlands Dur 103 M5
Lowlands Torfn 31 J5
Low Langton Lincs 86 G5
Low Leighton Derbys 83 M7
Low Lorton Cumb 100 G5
Low Marishes N York 98 G5
Low Marnham Notts 85 P7
Low Middleton Nthumb 119 M3
Low Mill N York 105 J11
Low Moor C Brad 90 F5
Low Moorsley Sundld 113 M11
Low Moresby Cumb 100 C6
Low Newton Cumb 95 J4
Low Row Cumb 100 G2
Low Row Cumb 101 L3
Low Row Cumb 111 L8
Low Row N York 103 J11
Low Salchrie D & G 106 D4
Low Santon N Linc 92 F8
Lowsonford Warwks 59 J11
Low Street Norfk 77 L7
Low Street Thurr 37 Q5
Low Tharston Norfk 64 H2
Lowther Cumb 101 P6
Lowther Castle Cumb 101 P6
Lowthorpe E R Yk 99 M8
Lowton Devon 8 G4
Lowton Somset 18 G11
Lowton Wigan 82 D5
Lowton Common Wigan 82 D5
Lowton St Mary's Wigan 82 D5
Low Torry Fife 134 C10
Low Toynton Lincs 87 J6

Mayals - Monk Bretton 289

Mayals Swans 28 H7
May Bank Staffs 70 F5
Maybole S Ayrs 114 E6
Maybury Surrey 36 B9
Mayes Green Surrey 24 D3
Mayfield E Susx 25 N5
Mayfield Mdloth 128 B7
Mayfield Staffs 71 M5
Mayford Surrey 23 Q3
May Hill Gloucs 46 D10
Mayland Essex 52 F11
Maylandsea Essex 52 F11
Maynard's Green E Susx 25 N7
Maypole Birm 58 G9
Maypole Kent 39 M9
Maypole Mons 45 P11
Maypole Green Norfk 65 N2
Maypole Green Suffk 64 C10
Maypole Green Suffk 65 K8
May's Green Oxon 35 K8
May's Green Surrey 36 C9
Mead Devon 16 C8
Meadgate BaNES 20 C3
Meadle Bucks 35 M3
Meadowfield Dur 103 P3
Meadowtown Shrops 56 E4
Meadwell Devon 5 Q5
Meaford Staffs 70 F7
Meal Bank Cumb 101 P11
Mealrigg Cumb 109 P11
Mealsgate Cumb 100 H2
Meanwood Leeds 90 H3
Mearbeck N York 96 B8
Meare Somset 19 N6
Meare Green Somset 19 J10
Meare Green Somset 19 K9
Mearns E Rens 125 N6
Mears Ashby Nhants 60 H7
Measham Leics 72 A8
Meathop Cumb 95 J4
Meaux E R Yk 93 J3
Meavy Devon 6 E5
Medbourne Leics 60 H2
Meddon Devon 16 D8
Meden Vale Notts 85 J7
Medlam Lincs 87 K9
Medlar Lancs 88 E3
Medmenham Bucks 35 M8
Medomsley Dur 112 H10
Medstead Hants 23 J7
Medway Crematorium Kent 38 B9
Medway Services Medway 38 D9
Meerbrook Staffs 70 H2
Meer Common Herefs 45 M4
Meesden Herts 51 K4
Meeson Wrekin 70 A10
Meeth Devon 17 J10
Meeting Green Suffk 63 M9
Meeting House Hill Norfk 77 L6
Meidrim Carmth 41 Q6
Meifod Powys 56 B2
Meigle P & K 142 D9
Meikle Carco D & G 115 Q5
Meikle Earnock S Lans 126 C7
Meikle Kilmory Ag & B 124 D5
Meikle Obney P & K 141 P10
Meikleour P & K 142 B10
Meikle Wartle Abers 158 H11
Meinciau Carmth 28 E2
Meir C Stke 70 G6
Meir Heath Staffs 70 G6
Melbourn Cambs 51 J2
Melbourne Derbys 72 B5
Melbourne E R Yk 92 C2
Melbur Cnwll 3 N3
Melbury Devon 16 F8
Melbury Abbas Dorset 20 G10
Melbury Bubb Dorset 11 M3
Melbury Osmond Dorset 11 M3
Melbury Sampford Dorset 11 M3
Melchbourne Bed 61 M7
Melcombe Bingham Dorset 12 C4
Meldon Devon 8 E6
Meldon Nthumb 112 H4
Meldon Park Nthumb 112 H3
Meldreth Cambs 62 E11
Meldrum Stirlg 133 L8
Melfort Ag & B 130 G5
Meliden Denbgs 80 F8
Melinau Pembks 41 N8
Melin-byrhedyn Powys 55 J5
Melincourt Neath 29 M4
Melin-y-coed Conwy 67 Q2
Melin-y-ddol Powys 55 P3
Melin-y-wig Denbgs 68 D5
Melkinthorpe Cumb 101 Q5
Melkridge Nthumb 111 P8
Melksham Wilts 20 H2
Mellangoose Cnwll 2 H8
Mell Green W Berk 34 E9
Mellguards Cumb 110 H11
Melling Lancs 95 M6
Melling Sefton 81 M4
Melling Mount Sefton 81 N4
Mellis Suffk 64 F7
Mellon Charles Highld 160 C8
Mellon Udrigle Highld 160 D7
Mellor Lancs 89 K4
Mellor Stockp 83 L7
Mellor Brook Lancs 89 J4
Mells Somset 20 D5
Mells Suffk 65 N6
Melmerby Cumb 102 B3
Melmerby N York 96 G3
Melmerby N York 97 M5
Melness Highld 165 N4
Melon Green Suffk 64 A10
Melplash Dorset 11 K5
Melrose Border 117 Q4
Melsetter Ork 169 b8
Melsonby N York 103 N9
Meltham Kirk 90 E8
Meltham Mills Kirk 90 E8
Melton E R Yk 92 G5
Melton Suffk 65 K11
Meltonby E R Yk 98 F10
Melton Constable Norfk 76 E5
Melton Mowbray Leics 73 K7
Melton Ross N Linc 93 J8
Melvaig Highld 160 A9
Melverley Shrops 69 K11
Melverley Green Shrops 69 K11
Melvich Highld 166 E4
Membury Devon 10 F4
Membury Services W Berk 34 B9
Memsie Abers 159 N5
Memus Angus 142 G6
Menabilly Cnwll 4 H11
Menagissey Cnwll 3 J4
Menai Bridge IoA 79 K10
Mendham Suffk 65 K5
Mendip Crematorium Somset 19 Q6
Mendip Hills 19 P4
Mendlesham Suffk 64 G8
Mendlesham Green Suffk 64 F9
Menheniot Cnwll 5 M9
Menithwood Worcs 57 N11
Mennock D & G 115 R6
Menston C Brad 90 F2
Menstrie Clacks 133 P8
Menthorpe N York 92 B4
Mentmore Bucks 49 P11
Meoble Highld 145 N10
Meole Brace Shrops 56 H2
Meonstoke Hants 22 H11
Meopham Kent 37 P7
Meopham Green Kent 37 P7
Meopham Station Kent 37 P7
Mepal Cambs 62 F4
Meppershall C Beds 50 D3
Merbach Herefs 45 L5
Mere Ches E 82 F8
Mere Wilts 20 F8
Mere Brow Lancs 88 E7
Mereclough Lancs 89 P4
Mere Green Birm 58 H5
Mere Green Worcs 47 J2
Mere Heath Ches W 82 E10
Meresborough Medway 38 D9
Mereworth Kent 37 Q10
Meriden Solhll 59 K8
Merkadale Highld 152 F11
Merley Poole 12 H5
Merlin's Bridge Pembks 40 H8
Merrington Shrops 69 N10
Merrion Pembks 40 H11
Merriott Somset 11 J2
Merrivale Devon 8 D9
Merrow Surrey 36 B10
Merry Field Hill Dorset 12 H4
Merry Hill Herts 36 D2
Merryhill Wolves 58 C5
Merry Lees Leics 72 D9
Merrymeet Cnwll 5 M8
Mersea Island Essex 52 H8
Mersham Kent 27 J3
Merstham Surrey 36 G10
Merston W Susx 15 N6
Merstone IoW 14 F9
Merther Cnwll 3 M5
Merthyr Carmth 42 G10
Merthyr Cynog Powys 44 D7
Merthyr Dyfan V Glam 30 F11
Merthyr Mawr Brdgnd 29 N9
Merthyr Tydfil Myr Td 30 D3
Merthyr Vale Myr Td 30 E5
Merton Devon 17 J9
Merton Gt Lon 36 G6
Merton Norfk 64 C2
Merton Oxon 48 G11
Meshaw Devon 17 P8
Messing Essex 52 E8
Messingham N Linc 92 E10
Metfield Suffk 65 K5
Metherell Cnwll 5 Q8
Metheringham Lincs 86 E8
Methil Fife 135 K8
Methilhill Fife 135 K7
Methley Leeds 91 K5
Methley Junction Leeds 91 K5
Methlick Abers 159 L10
Methven P & K 134 C2
Methwold Norfk 63 M2
Methwold Hythe Norfk 63 M2
Mettingham Suffk 65 M4
Metton Norfk 76 J4
Mevagissey Cnwll 3 Q5
Mexborough Donc 91 M10
Mey Highld 167 N2
Meyllteyrn Gwynd 66 C8
Meysey Hampton Gloucs 33 M4
Miabhig W Isls 168 f4
Miavaig W Isls 168 f4
Michaelchurch Herefs 45 Q9
Michaelchurch Escley Herefs 45 L8
Michaelchurch-on-Arrow Powys 45 J4
Michaelstone-y-Fedw Newpt 30 H8
Michaelston-le-Pit V Glam 30 G10
Michaelstow Cnwll 4 H6
Michaelwood Services Gloucs 32 D5
Michelcombe Devon 6 H5
Micheldever Hants 22 F7
Micheldever Station Hants 22 F6
Michelmersh Hants 22 B9
Mickfield Suffk 64 G9
Micklebring Donc 84 H2
Mickleby N York 105 M8
Micklefield Leeds 91 L4
Micklefield Green Herts 50 B11
Mickleham Surrey 36 E10
Mickleover C Derb 71 Q8
Micklethwaite C Brad 90 E2
Micklethwaite Cumb 110 E10
Mickleton Dur 103 J6
Mickleton Gloucs 47 N6
Mickletown Leeds 91 L5
Mickle Trafford Ches W 81 N11
Mickley Derbys 84 D5
Mickley N York 97 L5
Mickley Green Suffk 64 A10
Mickley Square Nthumb 112 G8
Mid Ardlaw Abers 159 M5
Midbea Ork 169 d2
Mid Beltie Abers 150 G7
Mid Bockhampton Dorset 13 L5
Mid Calder W Loth 127 K4
Mid Clyth Highld 167 N9
Mid Culbeuchly Abers 158 G5
Middle Assendon Oxon 35 K7
Middle Aston Oxon 48 E9
Middle Barton Oxon 48 D9
Middlebie D & G 110 D5
Middlebridge P & K 141 L4
Middle Chinnock Somset 11 K2
Middle Claydon Bucks 49 K9
Middlecliffe Barns 91 L9
Middlecott Devon 8 H7
Middle Duntisbourne Gloucs 33 J3
Middleham N York 96 H3
Middle Handley Derbys 84 F5
Middle Harling Norfk 64 D4
Middlehill Cnwll 5 M8
Middlehill Wilts 32 F11
Middlehope Shrops 56 H7
Middle Kames Ag & B 131 J10
Middle Littleton Worcs 47 L5
Middle Madeley Staffs 70 D5
Middle Maes-coed Herefs 45 L8
Middlemarsh Dorset 11 P3
Middle Mayfield Staffs 71 L6
Middle Mill Pembks 40 F5
Middlemore Devon 6 D4
Middle Quarter Kent 26 E4
Middle Rasen Lincs 86 E3
Middle Rocombe Devon 7 N5
Middle Salter Lancs 95 N8
Middlesbrough Middsb 104 E7
Middlesceugh Cumb 101 M2
Middleshaw Cumb 95 M3
Middlesmoor N York 96 G6
Middle Stoford Somset 18 G10
Middle Stoke Medway 38 D6
Middlestone Dur 103 Q4
Middlestone Moor Dur 103 P4
Middle Stoughton Somset 19 M5
Middlestown Wakefd 90 H7
Middle Street Gloucs 32 E4
Middle Taphouse Cnwll 5 K9
Middlethird Border 118 C2
Middleton Ag & B 136 A7
Middleton Cumb 95 N3
Middleton Derbys 71 M2
Middleton Derbys 84 C9
Middleton Essex 52 E4
Middleton Hants 22 D6
Middleton Herefs 57 J11
Middleton Lancs 95 J9
Middleton Leeds 91 J5
Middleton N York 96 H11
Middleton N York 98 F3
Middleton Nhants 60 H3
Middleton Norfk 75 N7
Middleton Nthumb 112 G4
Middleton Nthumb 119 M3
Middleton P & K 134 E6
Middleton Rochdl 89 P9
Middleton Shrops 57 J9
Middleton Shrops 69 K9
Middleton Suffk 65 N8
Middleton Swans 28 D7
Middleton Warwks 59 J5
Middleton Cheney Nhants 48 E6
Middleton Crematorium Rochdl 89 P9
Middleton Green Staffs 70 H7
Middleton Hall Nthumb 119 J5
Middleton-in-Teesdale Dur 102 H5
Middleton Moor Suffk 65 N8
Middleton One Row Darltn 104 C8
Middleton-on-Leven N York 104 E9
Middleton-on-Sea W Susx 15 Q6
Middleton on the Hill Herefs 45 Q2
Middleton on the Wolds E R Yk 99 J11
Middleton Park C Aber 151 N5
Middleton Priors Shrops 57 L6
Middleton Quernhow N York 97 M5
Middleton St George Darltn 104 B8
Middleton Scriven Shrops 57 M7
Middleton Stoney Oxon 48 F10
Middleton Tyas N York 103 P9
Middletown Cumb 100 C9
Middle Town IoS 2 b3
Middletown N Som 31 N10
Middletown Powys 56 E2
Middle Tysoe Warwks 48 B6
Middle Wallop Hants 21 Q7
Middlewich Ches E 82 F11
Middle Winterslow Wilts 21 P8
Middlewood Cnwll 5 M6
Middlewood Herefs 45 K6
Middle Woodford Wilts 21 M7
Middlewood Green Suffk 64 F9
Middleyard E Ayrs 125 N11
Middle Yard Gloucs 32 F4
Middlezoy Somset 19 L8
Middridge Dur 103 P5
Midford BaNES 20 E2
Midge Hall Lancs 88 G6
Midgeholme Cumb 111 M9
Midgham W Berk 34 G11
Midgley Calder 90 C5
Midgley Wakefd 90 H8
Mid Holmwood Surrey 36 E11
Midhopestones Sheff 90 G11
Midhurst W Susx 23 N10
Mid Lavant W Susx 15 N5
Midlem Border 117 Q5
Mid Mains Highld 155 M10
Midney Somset 19 N9
Midpark Ag & B 124 C6
Midsomer Norton BaNES 20 C4
Midtown Highld 165 N4
Midville Lincs 87 L9
Mid Warwickshire Crematorium Warwks 48 B3
Midway Ches E 83 K8
Mid Yell Shet 169 s4
Migvie Abers 150 C6
Milborne Port Somset 20 C11
Milborne St Andrew Dorset 12 D5
Milborne Wick Somset 20 C10
Milbourne Nthumb 112 H5
Milbourne Wilts 33 J7
Milburn Cumb 102 C5
Milbury Heath S Glos 32 C6
Milby N York 97 P7
Milcombe Oxon 48 D8
Milden Suffk 52 G2
Mildenhall Suffk 63 M6
Mildenhall Wilts 33 P11
Milebrook Powys 56 E10
Milebush Kent 26 C2
Mile Elm Wilts 33 J11
Mile End Essex 52 G6
Mile End Gloucs 31 Q2
Mile End Suffk 65 L4
Mileham Norfk 76 C8
Mile Oak Br & H 24 F9
Mile Oak Kent 25 Q2
Mile Oak Staffs 59 J4
Miles Hope Herefs 45 R2
Milesmark Fife 134 D10
Miles Platting Manch 83 J5
Mile Town Kent 38 F7
Milfield Nthumb 118 H4
Milford Derbys 84 E11
Milford Devon 16 C7
Milford Powys 55 P6
Milford Staffs 70 H10
Milford Surrey 23 P6
Milford Haven Pembks 40 H9
Milford on Sea Hants 13 N6
Milkwall Gloucs 31 Q3
Millais Jersey 11 a1
Milland W Susx 23 M9
Milland Marsh W Susx 23 M9
Mill Bank Calder 90 C6
Millbeck Cumb 101 J5
Millbreck Abers 159 P9
Millbridge Surrey 23 M6
Millbrook C Beds 50 B3
Millbrook C Sotn 14 C4
Millbrook Cnwll 6 C8
Millbrook Jersey 11 b2
Millbrook Tamesd 83 L5
Mill Brow Stockp 83 L7
Millbuie Abers 151 K6
Millbuie Highld 155 Q7
Millcombe Devon 7 L9
Mill Common Norfk 77 L11
Mill Common Suffk 65 N5
Millcorner E Susx 26 D7
Millcraig Highld 156 B3
Mill Cross Devon 7 J6
Milldale Staffs 71 L4
Mill End Bucks 35 L7
Mill End Cambs 62 D4
Millend Gloucs 32 D5
Mill End Herts 50 H4
Millerhill Mdloth 127 Q4
Miller's Dale Derbys 83 P10
Millers Green Derbys 71 P4
Miller's Green Essex 51 N9
Millerston C Glas 125 Q4
Millgate Lancs 89 P7
Mill Green Cambs 63 K11
Mill Green Essex 51 P10
Mill Green Herts 50 F8
Mill Green Lincs 74 D6
Mill Green Norfk 64 G5
Millgreen Shrops 70 B9
Mill Green Staffs 58 G4
Mill Green Staffs 71 K10
Mill Green Suffk 52 G3
Mill Green Suffk 64 D10
Mill Green Suffk 64 G9
Mill Green Suffk 65 L9
Millhalf Herefs 45 K5
Millhayes Devon 10 E4
Millhead Lancs 95 K6
Millheugh S Lans 126 C7
Mill Hill E Susx 25 P9
Mill Hill Gt Lon 36 F2
Millhouse Ag & B 124 B3
Millhouse Cumb 101 L3
Millhousebridge D & G 109 P3
Millhouse Green Barns 90 G10
Millhouses Barns 91 L10
Millhouses Sheff 84 D4
Milliken Park Rens 125 L5
Millin Cross Pembks 41 J8
Millington E R Yk 98 G10
Millmeece Staffs 70 E8
Millness Cumb 95 L4
Mill of Drummond P & K 133 N4
Mill of Haldane W Duns 132 D11
Millom Cumb 94 D4
Millook Cnwll 5 K2
Millpool Cnwll 2 F7
Millpool Cnwll 5 J7
Millport N Ayrs 124 F7
Mill Side Cumb 95 J4
Mill Street Kent 37 Q9
Mill Street Norfk 76 F8
Mill Street Suffk 64 F7
Millthorpe Derbys 84 D5
Millthrop Cumb 95 P2
Milltimber C Aber 151 M7
Milltown Abers 149 P6
Milltown Abers 150 D4
Milltown Cnwll 5 J10
Milltown D & G 110 F5
Milltown Derbys 84 E8
Milltown Devon 17 K4
Milltown of Campfield Abers 150 H7
Milltown of Edinvillie Moray 157 P9
Milltown of Learney Abers 150 G7
Milnathort P & K 134 E7
Milngavie E Duns 125 P3
Milnrow Rochdl 89 Q8
Milnthorpe Cumb 95 K4
Milnthorpe Wakefd 91 J7
Milovaig Highld 152 B8
Milson Shrops 57 L10
Milstead Kent 38 F10
Milston Wilts 21 N5
Milthorpe Lincs 74 B4
Milthorpe Nhants 48 G5
Milton C Stke 70 G4
Milton Cambs 62 G8
Milton Cumb 111 L8
Milton D & G 106 H7
Milton D & G 108 H6
Milton D & G 109 K5
Milton Derbys 71 Q9
Milton Highld 153 N9
Milton Highld 155 N11
Milton Highld 155 Q8
Milton Highld 156 D3
Milton Highld 167 P6
Milton Inver 125 K4
Milton Kent 37 Q6
Milton Moray 149 M4
Milton Moray 158 D5
Milton N Som 19 K2
Milton Newpt 31 L7
Milton Notts 85 M6
Milton Oxon 34 E6
Milton Oxon 48 E7
Milton P & K 141 Q5
Milton Pembks 41 K10
Milton Somset 19 N10
Milton Stirlg 132 G7
Milton W Duns 125 L3
Milton Abbas Dorset 12 D4
Milton Abbot Devon 5 Q6
Milton Bridge Mdloth 127 P5
Milton Bryan C Beds 49 Q8
Milton Clevedon Somset 20 C7
Milton Combe Devon 6 D5
Milton Common Oxon 35 J4
Milton Damerel Devon 16 F9
Milton End Gloucs 32 D2
Milton End Gloucs 33 M4
Milton Ernest Bed 61 M9
Milton Green Ches W 69 N3
Milton Hill Oxon 34 E6
Milton Keynes M Keyn 49 N7
Milton Lilbourne Wilts 21 N2
Milton Malsor Nhants 60 F9
Milton Morenish P & K 140 F10
Milton of Auchinhove Abers 150 F7
Milton of Balgonie Fife 135 J7
Milton of Buchanan Stirlg 132 E9
Milton of Campsie E Duns 126 B2
Milton of Leys Highld 156 B9
Milton of Murtle C Aber 151 M7
Milton of Tullich Abers 150 B8
Milton on Stour Dorset 20 E9
Milton Regis Kent 38 F9
Milton Street E Susx 25 M10
Milton-under-Wychwood Oxon 47 Q11
Milverton Somset 18 F9
Milverton Warwks 59 M11
Milwich Staffs 70 H8
Milwr Flints 80 H10
Minard Ag & B 131 K8
Minchington Dorset 12 G2
Minchinhampton Gloucs 32 G4
Mindrum Nthumb 118 F4
Minehead Somset 18 C5
Minera Wrexhm 69 J4
Minety Wilts 33 K6
Minffordd Gwynd 67 K7
Mingarrypark Highld 138 B4
Miningsby Lincs 87 K8
Minions Cnwll 5 M7
Minishant S Ayrs 114 F5
Minllyn Gwynd 55 K2
Minnigaff D & G 107 M4
Minnis Bay Kent 39 N8
Minnonie Abers 159 J5
Minshull Vernon Ches E 70 B2
Minskip N York 97 N8
Minstead Hants 13 N2
Minsted W Susx 23 N10
Minster Kent 38 G7
Minster Kent 39 P9
Minsterley Shrops 56 F3
Minster Lovell Oxon 34 B2
Minsterworth Gloucs 46 E11
Minterne Magna Dorset 11 P4
Minterne Parva Dorset 11 P4
Minting Lincs 86 G6
Mintlaw Abers 159 N8
Mintlyn Crematorium Norfk 75 N7
Minto Border 117 R6
Minton Shrops 56 G6
Minwear Pembks 41 K8
Minworth Birm 59 J6
Mirehouse Cumb 100 C7
Mireland Highld 167 P4
Mirfield Kirk 90 G7
Miserden Gloucs 32 H3
Miskin Rhondd 30 D5
Miskin Rhondd 30 D8
Misson Notts 85 L2
Misterton Leics 60 C4
Misterton Notts 85 N2
Misterton Somset 11 K3
Mistley Essex 53 K5
Mistley Heath Essex 53 K5
Mitcham Gt Lon 36 G7
Mitcheldean Gloucs 46 C11
Mitchell Cnwll 3 M3
Mitchellslacks D & G 116 D11
Mitchel Troy Mons 31 N2
Mitford Nthumb 113 J3
Mithian Cnwll 3 J3
Mitton Staffs 70 F11
Mixbury Oxon 48 H8
Mixenden Calder 90 D5
Moats Tye Suffk 64 E10
Mobberley Ches E 82 G9
Mobberley Staffs 71 J6
Moccas Herefs 45 M6
Mochdre Conwy 79 Q9
Mochdre Powys 55 P7
Mochrum D & G 107 K8
Mockbeggar Hants 13 L3
Mockbeggar Kent 26 B2
Mockerkin Cumb 100 E6
Modbury Devon 6 H8
Moddershall Staffs 70 G7
Moelfre IoA 79 J7
Moelfre Powys 68 G9
Moel Tryfan Gwynd 67 J3
Moffat D & G 116 F9
Mogador Surrey 36 F10
Moggerhanger C Beds 61 P11
Moira Leics 71 Q11
Molash Kent 38 H11
Mol-chlach Highld 144 G5
Mold Flints 68 H2
Moldgreen Kirk 90 F7
Molehill Green Essex 51 N6
Molehill Green Essex 52 B7
Molescroft E R Yk 92 H2
Molesden Nthumb 112 H4
Molesworth Cambs 61 N5
Molland Devon 17 Q6
Mollington Ches W 81 M10
Mollington Oxon 48 D5
Mollinsburn N Lans 126 C3
Monachty Cerdgn 43 K2
Mondynes Abers 143 P2
Monewden Suffk 65 J10
Moneydie P & K 134 D2
Moneyrow Green W & M 35 N9
Moniaive D & G 115 Q9
Monifieth Angus 142 H11
Monikie Angus 142 H10
Monimail Fife 134 H5
Monington Pembks 41 M2
Monk Bretton Barns 91 K9

290 Monken Hadley - Nettlestone

Monken Hadley Gt Lon 50 F11
Monk Fryston N York 91 N5
Monkhide Herefs 46 B6
Monkhill Cumb 110 F9
Monkhopton Shrops 57 L6
Monkland Herefs 45 P3
Monkleigh Devon 16 H7
Monknash V Glam 29 P10
Monkokehampton Devon 8 E3
Monkseaton N Tyne 113 M6
Monks Eleigh Suffk 52 G2
Monk's Gate W Susx 24 F5
Monks Heath Ches E 82 H10
Monk Sherborne Hants 22 H3
Monks Horton Kent 27 K3
Monksilver Somset 18 E7
Monks Kirby Warwks 59 Q8
Monk Soham Suffk 65 J8
Monkspath Solhll 58 H9
Monks Risborough Bucks 35 M4
Monksthorpe Lincs 87 M7
Monk Street Essex 51 P5
Monkswood Mons 31 K4
Monkton Devon 10 D4
Monkton Kent 39 N9
Monkton S Ayrs 114 G2
Monkton S Tyne 113 M8
Monkton V Glam 29 P10
Monkton Combe BaNES 20 E2
Monkton Deverill Wilts 20 G7
Monkton Farleigh Wilts 32 F11
Monkton Heathfield Somset 19 J9
Monkton Up Wimborne Dorset 12 H2
Monkton Wyld Dorset 10 G5
Monkwearmouth Sundld 113 N9
Monkwood Hants 23 J8
Monmore Green Wolves 58 D5
Monmouth Mons 31 P2
Monnington on Wye Herefs 45 M6
Monreith D & G 107 L9
Montacute Somset 19 N11
Montcliffe Bolton 89 K8
Montford Shrops 56 G2
Montford Bridge Shrops 69 M11
Montgarrie Abers 150 F4
Montgomery Powys 56 C5
Monton Salfd 82 G5
Montrose Angus 143 N6
Mont Saint Guern 10 b2
Monxton Hants 22 B6
Monyash Derbys 83 Q11
Monymusk Abers 150 H4
Monzie P & K 133 P2
Moodiesburn N Lans 126 B3
Moonzie Fife 135 J4
Moor Allerton Leeds 91 J3
Moorbath Dorset 11 J5
Moorby Lincs 87 J8
Moorcot Herefs 45 M3
Moor Crichel Dorset 12 G3
Moordown Bmouth 13 J6
Moore Halton 82 C8
Moor End C Beds 49 Q10
Moor End Calder 90 D5
Moor End Devon 17 M10
Moorend Gloucs 32 D4
Moor End Lancs 88 D2
Moor End N York 91 Q3
Moorends Donc 92 A7
Moorgreen Hants 22 E11
Moor Green Herts 50 H5
Moorgreen Notts 84 G11
Moorhall Derbys 84 D6
Moorhampton Herefs 45 M5
Moorhead C Brad 90 E3
Moor Head Leeds 90 G5
Moorhouse Cumb 110 E10
Moorhouse Cumb 110 F9
Moorhouse Donc 91 M8
Moorhouse Notts 85 N7
Moorhouse Bank Surrey 37 K10
Moorland Somset 19 K8
Moorlinch Somset 19 L7
Moor Monkton N York 97 R9
Moor Row Cumb 100 D8
Moor Row Cumb 110 D11
Moorsholm R & Cl 105 J8
Moorside Dorset 20 E11
Moor Side Lancs 88 E4
Moor Side Lancs 88 F3
Moorside Leeds 90 G3
Moor Side Lincs 87 J9
Moorside Oldham 89 Q9
Moorstock Kent 27 K4
Moor Street Birm 58 E8
Moor Street Medway 38 D8
Moorswater Cnwll 5 L9
Moorthorpe Wakefd 91 M8
Moortown Devon 6 E4
Moortown Hants 13 L4
Moortown IoW 14 D10
Moortown Leeds 90 H3
Moortown Lincs 93 J11
Moortown Wrekin 69 R11
Morangie Highld 162 H10
Morar Highld 145 L9
Moray Crematorium Moray 158 A5
Morborne Cambs 61 P2
Morchard Bishop Devon 9 J3
Morcombelake Dorset 11 J6
Morcott Rutlnd 73 N10
Morda Shrops 69 J9
Morden Dorset 12 F5
Morden Gt Lon 36 G7
Mordiford Herefs 45 R7
Mordon Dur 104 B5
More Shrops 56 E6
Morebath Devon 18 C9
Morebattle Border 118 E6
Morecambe Lancs 95 J8
Moredon Swindn 33 M7
Morefield Highld 161 J7
Morehall Kent 27 M4
Moreleigh Devon 7 K8
Morenish P & K 140 F10
Moresby Parks Cumb 100 C7
Morestead Hants 22 F9
Moreton Dorset 12 D7
Moreton Essex 51 M9
Moreton Herefs 45 Q2
Moreton Oxon 35 J4
Moreton Staffs 70 D11
Moreton Staffs 71 L9
Moreton Wirral 81 K7
Moreton Corbet Shrops 69 Q10
Moretonhampstead Devon 9 J7
Moreton-in-Marsh Gloucs 47 P8
Moreton Jeffries Herefs 46 B5
Moretonmill Shrops 69 Q10
Moreton Morrell Warwks 48 B3
Moreton on Lugg Herefs 45 Q5
Moreton Paddox Warwks 48 B4
Moreton Pinkney Nhants 48 G5
Moreton Say Shrops 70 A8
Moreton Valence Gloucs 32 E3
Morfa Cerdgn 42 F4
Morfa Bychan Gwynd 67 J7
Morfa Dinlle Gwynd 66 G3
Morfa Glas Neath 29 N3
Morfa Nefyn Gwynd 66 D6
Morganstown Cardif 30 F8
Morgan's Vale Wilts 21 N10
Morham E Loth 128 F5
Moriah Cerdgn 54 E9
Morland Cumb 102 B6
Morley Ches E 82 H8
Morley Derbys 72 B2
Morley Dur 103 M5
Morley Leeds 90 H5
Morley Green Ches E 82 H8
Morley St Botolph Norfk 64 F2
Mornick Cnwll 5 N7
Morningside C Edin 127 N3
Morningside N Lans 126 E6
Morningthorpe Norfk 65 J3
Morpeth Nthumb 113 J3
Morphie Abers 143 N5
Morrey Staffs 71 L11
Morridge Side Staffs 71 J4
Morriston Swans 29 J5
Morston Norfk 76 E3
Mortehoe Devon 16 H2
Morthen Rothm 84 G3
Mortimer W Berk 23 J2
Mortimer Common W Berk 35 J11
Mortimer's Cross Herefs 45 N2
Mortimer West End Hants 22 H2
Mortlake Gt Lon 36 F5
Mortlake Crematorium Gt Lon 36 E5
Morton Cumb 101 N3
Morton Cumb 110 G10
Morton Derbys 84 F8
Morton IoW 14 H9
Morton Lincs 74 A6
Morton Lincs 85 P2
Morton Notts 85 M10
Morton Shrops 69 J10
Morton Hall Lincs 85 Q8
Mortonhall Crematorium C Edin 127 P4
Morton-on-Swale N York 97 M2
Morton on the Hill Norfk 76 G8
Morton Tinmouth Dur 103 N6
Morvah Cnwll 2 C6
Morval Cnwll 5 M10
Morvich Highld 146 B3
Morville Shrops 57 M6
Morville Heath Shrops 57 M6
Morwenstow Cnwll 16 C8
Mosborough Sheff 84 F4
Moscow E Ayrs 125 M9
Mose Shrops 57 P6
Mosedale Cumb 101 L4
Moseley Birm 58 G8
Moseley Wolves 58 D5
Moseley Worcs 46 F3
Moses Gate Bolton 89 L9
Moss Ag & B 136 B7
Moss Donc 91 P8
Moss Wrexhm 69 K4
Mossat Abers 150 D4
Mossbank Shet 169 r6
Moss Bank St Hel 81 Q5
Mossbay Cumb 100 C5
Mossblown S Ayrs 114 H3
Mossbrow Traffd 82 F7
Mossburnford Border 118 C7
Mossdale D & G 108 E6
Mossdale E Ayrs 115 J7
Moss Edge Lancs 88 E2
Moss End Ches E 82 E9
Mossend N Lans 126 C5
Mosser Mains Cumb 100 F5
Mossley Ches E 70 F2
Mossley Tamesd 83 L4
Mosspaul Hotel Border 117 M11
Moss Side Cumb 110 C10
Moss-side Highld 156 F6
Moss Side Lancs 88 D4
Moss Side Sefton 81 M4
Mosstodloch Moray 157 Q6
Mossyard D & G 107 P7
Mossy Lea Lancs 88 G8
Mosterton Dorset 11 K3
Moston Manch 83 J4
Moston Shrops 69 Q9
Moston Green Ches E 70 C2
Mostyn Flints 80 H8
Motcombe Dorset 20 G9
Mothecombe Devon 6 G9
Motherby Cumb 101 M5
Motherwell N Lans 126 C6
Motspur Park Gt Lon 36 F7
Mottingham Gt Lon 37 K6
Mottisfont Hants 22 B9
Mottistone IoW 14 D10
Mottram in Longdendale Tamesd 83 L5
Mottram St Andrew Ches E 83 J9
Mouilpied Guern 10 b2
Mouldsworth Ches W 81 Q10
Moulin P & K 141 M6
Moulsecoomb Br & H 24 H9
Moulsford Oxon 34 G8
Moulsoe M Keyn 49 P6
Moultavie Highld 156 A3
Moulton Ches W 82 E11
Moulton Lincs 74 F6
Moulton N York 103 P10
Moulton Nhants 60 G7
Moulton Suffk 63 L8
Moulton V Glam 30 E11
Moulton Chapel Lincs 74 E7
Moulton St Mary Norfk 77 M10
Moulton Seas End Lincs 74 F5
Mount Cnwll 4 B10
Mount Cnwll 5 J8
Mount Kirk 90 D7
Mountain C Brad 90 D4
Mountain Ash Rhondd 30 D5
Mountain Cross Border 127 M8
Mountain Street Kent 39 J11
Mount Ambrose Cnwll 3 J5
Mount Bures Essex 52 F5
Mountfield E Susx 26 B7
Mountgerald House Highld 155 Q5
Mount Hawke Cnwll 3 J4
Mount Hermon Cnwll 2 H10
Mountjoy Cnwll 4 D9
Mount Lothian Mdloth 127 P6
Mountnessing Essex 51 P11
Mounton Mons 31 P6
Mount Pleasant Ches E 70 E3
Mount Pleasant Derbys 71 P11
Mount Pleasant Derbys 84 D11
Mount Pleasant Dur 103 Q4
Mount Pleasant E R Yk 93 N3
Mount Pleasant E Susx 25 K7
Mount Pleasant Norfk 64 D3
Mount Pleasant Suffk 63 M11
Mount Pleasant Worcs 47 K2
Mountsett Crematorium Dur 113 J10
Mountsorrel Leics 72 F8
Mount Sorrel Wilts 21 K10
Mount Tabor Calder 90 D5
Mousehill Surrey 23 P6
Mousehole Cnwll 2 D8
Mouswald D & G 109 N6
Mow Cop Ches E 70 F3
Mowhaugh Border 118 F6
Mowmacre Hill C Leic 72 F9
Mowsley Leics 60 D3
Moy Highld 147 L11
Moy Highld 156 D11
Moyle Highld 145 Q4
Moylegrove Pembks 41 M2
Muasdale Ag & B 120 C3
Muchalls Abers 151 N9
Much Birch Herefs 45 Q8
Much Cowarne Herefs 46 B5
Much Dewchurch Herefs 45 P8
Muchelney Somset 19 M10
Muchelney Ham Somset 19 M10
Much Hadham Herts 51 K7
Much Hoole Lancs 88 F6
Much Hoole Town Lancs 88 F6
Muchlarnick Cnwll 5 L10
Much Marcle Herefs 46 C8
Much Wenlock Shrops 57 L5
Muck Highld 144 F12
Mucking Thurr 37 Q4
Muckingford Thurr 37 Q5
Muckleburgh Collection Norfk 76 G3
Muckleford Dorset 11 N6
Mucklestone Staffs 70 C7
Muckley Shrops 57 L5
Muckton Lincs 87 L4
Muddiford Devon 17 K4
Muddles Green E Susx 25 M8
Mudeford Dorset 13 L6
Mudford Somset 19 Q11
Mudford Sock Somset 19 Q11
Mudgley Somset 19 N5
Mud Row Kent 38 H7
Mugdock Stirlg 125 P2
Mugeary Highld 152 G10
Mugginton Derbys 71 P6
Muggintonlane End Derbys 71 P6
Muggleswick Dur 112 F11
Muirden Abers 158 H7
Muirdrum Angus 143 K10
Muiresk Abers 158 G8
Muirhead Angus 142 E11
Muirhead Fife 134 H6
Muirhead N Lans 126 B4
Muirkirk E Ayrs 115 N2
Muirmill Stirlg 133 L11
Muir of Fowlis Abers 150 F5
Muir of Miltonduff Moray 157 M6
Muir of Ord Highld 155 P7
Muirshearlich Highld 146 E11
Muirtack Abers 159 N10
Muirton P & K 133 Q5
Muirton Mains Highld 155 N7
Muirton of Ardblair P & K 142 B9
Muker N York 102 H11
Mulbarton Norfk 76 H11
Mulben Moray 157 R7
Mulfra Cnwll 2 D7
Mull Ag & B 137 Q9
Mullacott Cross Devon 17 J3
Mullion Cnwll 2 H10
Mullion Cove Cnwll 2 H10
Mumby Lincs 87 P6
Munderfield Row Herefs 46 B4
Munderfield Stocks Herefs 46 C4
Mundesley Norfk 77 L4
Mundford Norfk 63 P2
Mundham Norfk 65 L2
Mundon Hill Essex 52 E11
Mundy Bois Kent 26 F2
Mungrisdale Cumb 101 L4
Munlochy Highld 156 A7
Munnoch N Ayrs 124 H8
Munsley Herefs 46 C6
Munslow Shrops 57 J7
Murchington Devon 8 G7
Murcot Worcs 47 L6
Murcott Oxon 48 G11
Murcott Wilts 33 J6
Murkle Highld 167 L3
Murlaggan Highld 146 C9
Murrell Green Hants 23 K3
Murroes Angus 142 H10
Murrow Cambs 74 G9
Mursley Bucks 49 M9
Murston Kent 38 F9
Murthill Angus 142 H6
Murthly P & K 141 R10
Murton C York 98 C10
Murton Cumb 102 D6
Murton Dur 113 N11
Murton N Tyne 113 M6
Murton Nthumb 129 P10
Musbury Devon 10 F6
Muscoates N York 98 D5
Musselburgh E Loth 127 Q3
Muston Leics 73 L3
Muston N York 99 M5
Mustow Green Worcs 58 C10
Muswell Hill Gt Lon 36 G3
Mutehill D & G 108 E11
Mutford Suffk 65 P4
Muthill P & K 133 P4
Mutterton Devon 9 P3
Muxton Wrekin 57 N2
Mybster Highld 167 L6
Myddfai Carmth 43 Q8
Myddle Shrops 69 N10
Mydroilyn Cerdgn 43 J3
Myerscough Lancs 88 F3
Mylor Cnwll 3 L6
Mylor Bridge Cnwll 3 L6
Mynachlog ddu Pembks 41 M4
Myndd-llan Flints 80 H10
Myndtown Shrops 56 F7
Mynydd-bach Mons 31 N6
Mynydd-Bach Swans 29 J5
Mynydd Buch Cerdgn 54 G9
Mynyddgarreg Carmth 28 D3
Mynydd Isa Flints 69 J2
Mynydd Llandygai Gwynd 79 L11
Mynytho Gwynd 66 E8
Myrebird Abers 151 J8
Myredykes Border 118 A11
Mytchett Surrey 23 N3
Mytholm Calder 90 B5
Mytholmroyd Calder 90 C5
Mythop Lancs 88 D4
Myton-on-Swale N York 97 P7

N

Naast Highld 160 C10
Nab's Head Lancs 89 J5
Na Buirgh W Isls 168 f8
Naburn C York 98 B11
Nab Wood Crematorium C Brad 90 E3
Naccolt Kent 27 J3
Nackington Kent 39 L11
Nacton Suffk 53 M3
Nafferton E R Yk 99 M9
Nag's Head Gloucs 32 G5
Nailbridge Gloucs 46 B11
Nailsbourne Somset 18 H9
Nailsea N Som 31 N10
Nailstone Leics 72 C9
Nailsworth Gloucs 32 F5
Nairn Highld 156 F6
Nalderswood Surrey 36 F11
Nancegollan Cnwll 2 G7
Nancledra Cnwll 2 D6
Nanhoron Gwynd 66 D8
Nannerch Flints 80 H11
Nanpantan Leics 72 E7
Nanpean Cnwll 4 F10
Nanquidno Cnwll 2 B8
Nanstallon Cnwll 4 G8
Nant-ddu Powys 30 D2
Nanternis Cerdgn 42 G3
Nantgaredig Carmth 43 J10
Nantgarw Rhondd 30 F7
Nant-glas Powys 55 M11
Nantglyn Denbgs 68 D2
Nantgwyn Powys 55 M9
Nant Gwynant Gwynd 67 L4
Nantlle Gwynd 67 J4
Nantmawr Shrops 69 J10
Nantmel Powys 55 N11
Nantmor Gwynd 67 L5
Nant Peris Gwynd 67 L3
Nantwich Ches E 70 B4
Nant-y-Bwch Blae G 30 F2
Nant-y-caws Carmth 43 J11
Nant-y-derry Mons 31 K3
Nantyffyllon Brdgnd 29 M6
Nantyglo Blae G 30 G2
Nant-y-gollen Shrops 68 H9
Nant-y-moel Brdgnd 29 P6
Nant-y-pandy Conwy 79 M10
Naphill Bucks 35 M5
Napleton Worcs 46 G5
Nappa N York 96 C10
Napton on the Hill Warwks 48 E2
Narberth Pembks 41 M8
Narborough Leics 72 E11
Narborough Norfk 75 P8
Narkurs Cnwll 5 N10
Nasareth Gwynd 66 H5
Naseby Nhants 60 E5
Nash Bucks 49 L8
Nash Gt Lon 37 K8
Nash Herefs 45 L2
Nash Newpt 31 K8
Nash Shrops 57 L10
Nash End Worcs 57 P8
Nash Lee Bucks 35 M3
Nash's Green Hants 23 J5
Nash Street Kent 37 P7
Nassington Nhants 73 R11
Nastend Gloucs 32 E3
Nasty Herts 51 J6
Nateby Cumb 102 E9
Nateby Lancs 88 F2
National Memorial Arboretum Staffs 59 J2
National Motor Museum (Beaulieu) Hants 14 C6
National Space Science Centre C Leic 72 F9
Natland Cumb 95 L3
Naughton Suffk 52 H2
Naunton Gloucs 47 M10
Naunton Worcs 46 G7
Naunton Beauchamp Worcs 47 J4
Navenby Lincs 86 C9
Navestock Essex 51 M11
Navestock Side Essex 51 N11
Navidale House Hotel Highld 163 N3
Navity Highld 156 D5
Nawton N York 98 D4
Nayland Suffk 52 G5
Nazeing Essex 51 K9
Nazeing Gate Essex 51 K9
Neacroft Hants 13 L5
Neal's Green Warwks 59 M8
Neap Shet 169 s8
Near Cotton Staffs 71 K5
Near Sawrey Cumb 101 L11
Neasden Gt Lon 36 F3
Neasham Darltn 104 B8
Neath Neath 29 L5
Neatham Hants 23 K6
Neatishead Norfk 77 L7
Nebo Cerdgn 54 C11
Nebo Conwy 67 Q3
Nebo Gwynd 66 H4
Nebo IoA 78 H6
Necton Norfk 76 B10
Nedd Highld 164 D10
Nedderton Nthumb 113 K4
Nedging Suffk 52 G2
Nedging Tye Suffk 52 H2
Needham Norfk 65 J5
Needham Lake & Nature Reserve Suffk 64 F10
Needham Market Suffk 64 F10
Needham Street Suffk 63 M7
Needingworth Cambs 62 D6
Neen Savage Shrops 57 M9
Neen Sollars Shrops 57 M10
Neenton Shrops 57 L7
Nefyn Gwynd 66 E6
Neilston E Rens 125 M6
Nelson Caerph 30 F5
Nelson Lancs 89 P3
Nemphlar S Lans 116 B2
Nempnett Thrubwell BaNES 19 P2
Nenthall Cumb 111 Q11
Nenthead Cumb 102 E2
Nenthorn Border 118 C3
Neopardy Devon 9 J5
Nep Town W Susx 24 F7
Nercwys Flints 68 H2
Nereabolls Ag & B 122 B8
Nerston S Lans 125 Q6
Nesbit Nthumb 119 J4
Nesfield N York 96 G11
Ness Ches W 81 L9
Nesscliffe Shrops 69 L11
Neston Ches W 81 K9
Neston Wilts 32 G11
Netchwood Shrops 57 L6
Nether Alderley Ches E 82 H9
Netheravon Wilts 21 M5
Nether Blainslie Border 117 Q2
Netherbrae Abers 159 J6
Nether Broughton Leics 72 H5
Netherburn S Lans 126 D8
Netherbury Dorset 11 K5
Netherby Cumb 110 G6
Netherby N York 97 M11
Nether Cerne Dorset 11 P5
Nethercleuch D & G 109 P3
Nether Compton Dorset 19 Q11
Nethercote Warwks 60 B8
Nethercott Devon 5 P2
Nethercott Devon 16 H4
Nether Crimond Abers 151 L3
Nether Dallachy Moray 157 R5
Netherend Gloucs 31 Q4
Nether Exe Devon 9 M4
Netherfield E Susx 26 B8
Netherfield Leics 72 F7
Netherfield Notts 72 G2
Nether Fingland S Lans 116 C8
Nethergate N Linc 92 C11
Nethergate Norfk 76 F6
Netherhampton Wilts 21 M9
Nether Handley Derbys 84 F5
Nether Handwick Angus 142 F9
Nether Haugh Rothm 91 L11
Netherhay Dorset 11 J3
Nether Headon Notts 85 M5
Nether Heage Derbys 84 E10
Nether Heyford Nhants 60 E9
Nether Howcleugh S Lans 116 E8
Nether Kellet Lancs 95 L7
Nether Kinmundy Abers 159 Q9
Netherland Green Staffs 71 L8
Nether Langwith Notts 84 H6
Netherlaw D & G 108 F12
Netherley Abers 151 M9
Nethermill D & G 109 M3
Nethermuir Abers 159 M9
Netherne-on-the-Hill Surrey 36 G9
Netheroyd Hill Kirk 90 E7
Nether Padley Derbys 84 B5
Netherplace E Rens 125 N6
Nether Poppleton C York 98 B10
Nether Row Cumb 101 K3
Netherseal Derbys 59 L2
Nether Silton N York 97 Q2
Nether Skyborry Shrops 56 D10
Nether Stowey Somset 18 G7
Nether Street Essex 51 N8
Netherstreet Wilts 21 J2
Netherthong Kirk 90 E9
Netherthorpe Derbys 84 F6
Netherton Angus 143 J6
Netherton Devon 7 M4
Netherton Dudley 58 D7
Netherton Hants 22 C3
Netherton Herefs 45 Q9
Netherton Kirk 90 E8
Netherton N Lans 126 D7
Netherton Nthumb 119 J9
Netherton Oxon 34 D5
Netherton P & K 142 A7
Netherton Shrops 57 N8
Netherton Stirlg 125 P2
Netherton Wakefd 90 H7
Netherton Worcs 47 J6
Nethertown Cumb 100 C9
Nethertown Highld 167 Q1
Nethertown Lancs 89 L3
Nethertown Staffs 71 L11
Netherurd Border 116 G2
Nether Wallop Hants 22 B7
Nether Wasdale Cumb 100 F10
Nether Welton Cumb 110 G11
Nether Westcote Gloucs 47 P10
Nether Whitacre Warwks 59 K6
Nether Whitecleuch S Lans 116 A7
Nether Winchendon Bucks 35 K2
Netherwitton Nthumb 112 G2
Nethy Bridge Highld 149 J3
Netley Hants 14 E5
Netley Marsh Hants 13 P2
Nettlebed Oxon 35 J7
Nettlebridge Somset 20 B5
Nettlecombe Dorset 11 L5
Nettlecombe IoW 14 F11
Nettleden Herts 50 B8
Nettleham Lincs 86 D5
Nettlestead Kent 37 Q10
Nettlestead Green Kent 37 Q10
Nettlestone IoW 14 H8

292 North Curry - Osbaldeston

North Curry Somset 19 K9
North Dalton E R Yk 99 J10
North Deighton N York 97 N10
North Devon Crematorium Devon 17 J5
Northdown Kent 39 Q7
North Downs 38 F10
North Duffield N York 92 A3
North Duntulm Highld 152 G3
North East Surrey Crematorium Gt Lon 36 F7
Northedge Derbys 84 E7
North Elham Kent 27 L3
North Elkington Lincs 87 J2
North Elmham Norfk 76 D7
North Elmsall Wakefd 91 M8
Northend Bucks 35 K6
North End C Port 15 J6
North End Cumb 110 F9
North End Dorset 20 F9
North End E R Yk 93 L2
North End E R Yk 93 N4
North End Essex 51 Q7
North End Hants 21 M11
North End Hants 22 G9
North End Leics 72 F7
North End Lincs 74 D2
North End Lincs 87 M3
North End Lincs 92 H11
North End Lincs 93 P10
North End N Linc 93 K6
North End N Som 31 M11
North End Nhants 61 L7
North End Norfk 64 D3
North End Nthumb 119 M10
North End Sefton 81 L4
North End W Susx 15 Q6
North End W Susx 24 D9
Northend Warwks 48 C4
Northenden Manch 82 H7
Northend Woods Bucks 35 P7
North Erradale Highld 160 A10
North Evington C Leic 72 G10
North Fambridge Essex 38 E2
North Ferriby E R Yk 92 G5
Northfield Birm 58 F9
Northfield C Aber 151 N6
Northfield E R Yk 92 H5
Northfields Lincs 73 Q9
Northfleet Kent 37 P6
North Frodingham E R Yk 99 N10
North Gorley Hants 13 L2
North Green Norfk 65 J4
North Green Suffk 65 L9
North Green Suffk 65 M8
North Greetwell Lincs 86 D6
North Grimston N York 98 G7
North Halling Medway 38 B8
North Haven Shet 169 t12
North Hayling Hants 15 K6
North Hazelrigg Nthumb 119 L4
North Heasley Devon 17 N5
North Heath W Susx 24 C6
North Hele Devon 18 D10
North Hill Cnwll 5 M6
North Hillingdon Gt Lon 36 C4
North Hinksey Village Oxon 34 E3
North Holmwood Surrey 36 E11
North Huish Devon 7 J7
North Hykeham Lincs 86 B7
Northiam E Susx 26 D7
Northill C Beds 61 P11
Northington Gloucs 32 D3
Northington Hants 22 G7
North Kelsey Lincs 92 H10
North Kessock Highld 156 B8
North Killingholme N Linc 93 K7
North Kilvington N York 97 P3
North Kilworth Leics 60 D4
North Kingston Hants 13 L4
North Kyme Lincs 86 G10
North Landing E R Yk 99 Q6
Northlands Lincs 87 K10
Northleach Gloucs 33 M2
North Lee Bucks 35 M3
North Lees N York 97 L6
Northleigh Devon 10 D5
Northleigh Devon 17 L5
North Leigh Kent 27 K2
North Leigh Oxon 34 C2
North Leverton with Habblesthorpe Notts 85 N4
Northlew Devon 8 D5
North Littleton Worcs 47 L5
Northload Bridge Somset 19 N7
North Lopham Norfk 64 E5
North Luffenham RutInd 73 N10
North Marden W Susx 23 M11
North Marston Bucks 49 L10
North Middleton Mdloth 128 B8
North Middleton Nthumb 119 J6
North Millbrex Abers 159 K9
North Milmain D & G 106 E7
North Molton Devon 17 N6
Northmoor Oxon 34 D4
North Moreton Oxon 34 G7
Northmuir Angus 142 F7
North Mundham W Susx 15 N6
North Muskham Notts 85 N9
North Newbald E R Yk 92 F3
North Newington Oxon 48 D6
North Newnton Wilts 21 M3
North Newton Somset 19 K8
Northney Hants 15 K6
North Nibley Gloucs 32 D5
North Oakley Hants 22 F4
North Ockendon Gt Lon 37 N3
Northolt Gt Lon 36 D4
Northop Flints 81 J11
Northop Hall Flints 81 K11
North Ormesby Middsb 104 F7
North Ormsby Lincs 87 J2
Northorpe Kirk 90 G6
Northorpe Lincs 74 A7
Northorpe Lincs 74 D3
Northorpe Lincs 86 E11
North Otterington N York 97 N3
Northover Somset 19 N7
Northover Somset 19 P10
North Owersby Lincs 86 E2
Northowram Calder 90 E5
North Perrott Somset 11 K3
North Petherton Somset 19 J8
North Petherwin Cnwll 5 M4
North Pickenham Norfk 76 B10
North Piddle Worcs 47 J4
North Poorton Dorset 11 L5
Northport Dorset 12 F7
North Poulner Hants 13 L3
North Queensferry Fife 134 E11
North Radworthy Devon 17 P5
North Rauceby Lincs 86 D11
Northrepps Norfk 77 J4
North Reston Lincs 87 L4
North Rigton N York 97 L11
North Ripley Hants 13 L5
North Rode Ches E 83 J11
North Ronaldsay Ork 169 g1
North Ronaldsay Airport Ork 169 g1
North Row Cumb 100 H4
North Runcton Norfk 75 M7
North Scale Cumb 94 D7
North Scarle Lincs 85 P7
North Seaton Nthumb 113 L3
North Seaton Colliery Nthumb 113 L3
North Shian Ag & B 138 G9
North Shields N Tyne 113 N7
North Shoebury Sthend 38 F4
North Shore Bpool 88 C3
North Side C Pete 74 E11
North Side Cumb 100 C5
North Skelton R & Cl 105 J7
North Somercotes Lincs 93 R11
North Stainley N York 97 L5
North Stainmore Cumb 102 F8
North Stifford Thurr 37 P4
North Stoke BaNES 32 D11
North Stoke Oxon 34 H7
North Stoke W Susx 24 B8
North Street Cambs 63 J7
North Street Hants 21 N11
North Street Hants 22 H8
North Street Kent 38 H10
North Street Medway 38 D7
North Street W Berk 34 H10
North Sunderland Nthumb 119 P4
North Tamerton Cnwll 5 N2
North Tawton Devon 8 G4
North Third Stirlg 133 M10
North Thoresby Lincs 93 N11
North Togston Nthumb 119 P10
Northton W Isls 168 e9
North Town Devon 17 J10
North Town Somset 19 Q6
North Town W & M 35 N8
North Tuddenham Norfk 76 E9
North Uist W Isls 168 c10
Northumberland National Park Nthumb 118 G10
North Walbottle N u Ty 113 J7
North Walsham Norfk 77 K5
North Waltham Hants 22 G5
North Warnborough Hants 23 K4
Northway Somset 18 F9
Northway Swans 28 G7
North Weald Bassett Essex 51 L10
North Wheatley Notts 85 N3
North Whilborough Devon 7 M5
Northwich Ches W 82 E10
North Wick BaNES 31 Q11
Northwick S Glos 31 Q7
Northwick Somset 19 L5
Northwick Worcs 46 F3
North Widcombe BaNES 19 Q3
North Willingham Lincs 86 G3
North Wingfield Derbys 84 F7
North Witham Lincs 73 N6
Northwold Norfk 75 Q11
Northwood C Stke 70 F5
Northwood Derbys 84 C8
Northwood Gt Lon 36 C2
Northwood IoW 14 E8
Northwood Shrops 69 N8
Northwood Green Gloucs 46 D11
North Wootton Dorset 11 P2
North Wootton Norfk 75 M6
North Wootton Somset 19 Q6
North Wraxall Wilts 32 F9
North Wroughton Swindn 33 M8
North York Moors National Park 105 K10
Norton Donc 91 N7
Norton E Susx 25 L10
Norton Gloucs 46 G10
Norton Halton 82 C8
Norton Herts 50 F4
Norton IoW 13 P7
Norton Mons 45 N10
Norton N Som 19 K2
Norton Nhants 60 C8
Norton Notts 85 J6
Norton Powys 56 E11
Norton S on T 104 D6
Norton Sheff 84 E4
Norton Shrops 56 H8
Norton Shrops 57 K3
Norton Shrops 57 L8
Norton Shrops 57 N4
Norton Suffk 64 D8
Norton Swans 28 H7
Norton W Susx 15 P5
Norton Wilts 32 G8
Norton Worcs 46 G4
Norton Worcs 47 K5
Norton Bavant Wilts 20 H6
Norton Bridge Staffs 70 F8
Norton Canes Staffs 58 F3
Norton Canes Services Staffs 58 F3
Norton Canon Herefs 45 M5
Norton Corner Norfk 76 F6
Norton Disney Lincs 85 Q9
Norton Ferris Wilts 20 E7
Norton Fitzwarren Somset 18 G9
Norton Green IoW 13 P7
Norton Hawkfield BaNES 19 Q2
Norton Heath Essex 51 P10
Norton in Hales Shrops 70 C7
Norton in the Moors C Stke 70 F4
Norton-Juxta-Twycross Leics 59 M3
Norton-le-Clay N York 97 P6
Norton Lindsey Warwks 47 P2
Norton Little Green Suffk 64 D8
Norton Malreward BaNES 20 B2
Norton Mandeville Essex 51 N10
Norton-on-Derwent N York 98 F6
Norton St Philip Somset 20 E3
Norton Subcourse Norfk 65 N2
Norton sub Hamdon Somset 19 N11
Norton Wood Herefs 45 M5
Norwell Notts 85 N8
Norwell Woodhouse Notts 85 M8
Norwich Norfk 77 J10
Norwich Airport Norfk 77 J9
Norwich (St Faith) Crematorium Norfk 77 J8
Norwick Shet 169 t2
Norwood Clacks 133 P9
Norwood Derbys 84 G4
Norwood Kent 27 J5
Norwood End Essex 51 N9
Norwood Green Calder 90 E5
Norwood Green Gt Lon 36 D5
Norwood Hill Surrey 24 F2
Norwoodside Cambs 74 H11
Noseley Leics 73 J11
Noss Mayo Devon 6 F9
Nosterfield N York 97 L4
Nosterfield End Cambs 51 P2
Nostie Highld 145 Q2
Notgrove Gloucs 47 M10
Nottage Brdgnd 29 M9
Notter Cnwll 5 P9
Nottingham C Nott 72 F3
Nottington Dorset 11 P8
Notton Wakefd 91 J8
Notton Wilts 32 H11
Nounsley Essex 52 C9
Noutard's Green Worcs 57 Q11
Nowton Suffk 64 B9
Nox Shrops 56 G2
Nuffield Oxon 35 J7
Nunburnholme E R Yk 98 G11
Nuncargate Notts 84 H10
Nunclose Cumb 111 J11
Nuneaton Warwks 59 N6
Nuneham Courtenay Oxon 34 G5
Nunhead Gt Lon 36 H5
Nunkeeling E R Yk 99 N11
Nun Monkton N York 97 R9
Nunney Somset 20 D6
Nunney Catch Somset 20 D6
Nunnington Herefs 45 R6
Nunnington N York 98 D5
Nunsthorpe NE Lin 93 N9
Nunthorpe C York 98 C10
Nunthorpe Middsb 104 F8
Nunthorpe Village Middsb 104 F8
Nunton Wilts 21 N9
Nunwick N York 97 M6
Nunwick Nthumb 112 C6
Nupdown S Glos 32 B5
Nup End Bucks 49 N11
Nupend Gloucs 32 E3
Nuptown Br For 35 N10
Nursling Hants 22 C11
Nursted Hants 23 L10
Nursteed Wilts 21 K2
Nurton Staffs 58 B5
Nutbourne W Susx 15 L5
Nutbourne W Susx 24 C7
Nutfield Surrey 36 H10
Nuthall Notts 72 E2
Nuthampstead Herts 51 K4
Nuthurst W Susx 24 E5
Nutley E Susx 25 K5
Nutley Hants 22 H6
Nuttall Bury 89 M7
Nutwell Donc 91 Q10
Nybster Highld 167 Q4
Nyetimber W Susx 15 N7
Nyewood W Susx 23 M10
Nymans W Susx 24 G5
Nymet Rowland Devon 17 N10
Nymet Tracey Devon 8 H4
Nympsfield Gloucs 32 F4
Nynehead Somset 18 F10
Nythe Somset 19 M8
Nyton W Susx 15 P5

O

Oadby Leics 72 G10
Oad Street Kent 38 E9
Oakall Green Worcs 46 F2
Oakamoor Staffs 71 J6
Oakbank W Loth 127 K4
Oak Cross Devon 8 D5
Oakdale Caerph 30 G5
Oake Somset 18 G9
Oaken Staffs 58 C4
Oakenclough Lancs 95 L11
Oakengates Wrekin 57 N2
Oakenholt Flints 81 K10
Oakenshaw Dur 103 N3
Oakenshaw Kirk 90 F5
Oakerthorpe Derbys 84 E10
Oakford Cerdgn 43 J3
Oakford Devon 18 B10
Oakfordbridge Devon 18 B10
Oakgrove Ches E 83 K11
Oakham RutInd 73 M9
Oakhanger Ches E 70 D4
Oakhanger Hants 23 L7
Oakhill Somset 20 B5
Oakhurst Kent 37 N10
Oakington Cambs 62 F8
Oaklands Powys 44 E4
Oakle Street Gloucs 46 E11
Oakley Bed 61 M10
Oakley Bucks 34 H2
Oakley Fife 134 C10
Oakley Hants 22 G4
Oakley Oxon 35 L4
Oakley Poole 12 H5
Oakley Suffk 64 H6
Oakley Green W & M 35 P9
Oakley Park Powys 55 M7
Oakridge Lynch Gloucs 32 H4
Oaks Lancs 89 K4
Oaks Shrops 56 G4
Oaksey Wilts 33 J6
Oaks Green Derbys 71 M8
Oakshaw Ford Cumb 111 K5
Oakshott Hants 23 K9
Oakthorpe Leics 59 M2
Oak Tree Darltn 104 C8
Oakwood C Derb 72 B3
Oakwood Nthumb 112 D7
Oakworth C Brad 90 C3
Oare Kent 38 H9
Oare Somset 17 P2
Oare Wilts 21 N2
Oasby Lincs 73 Q3
Oath Somset 19 L9
Oathlaw Angus 142 H6
Oatlands Park Surrey 36 C7
Oban Ag & B 130 H2
Oban Airport Ag & B 138 G10
Obley Shrops 56 E9
Obney P & K 141 P10
Oborne Dorset 20 C11
Obthorpe Lincs 74 A8
Occold Suffk 64 H7
Occumster Highld 167 N9
Ochiltree E Ayrs 115 K3
Ockbrook Derbys 72 C3
Ocker Hill Sandw 58 E6
Ockeridge Worcs 46 E2
Ockham Surrey 36 C9
Ockle Highld 137 P1
Ockley Surrey 24 D2
Ocle Pychard Herefs 46 A5
Octon E R Yk 99 L7
Odcombe Somset 19 P11
Odd Down BaNES 20 D2
Oddingley Worcs 46 H3
Oddington Gloucs 47 P9
Oddington Oxon 48 G11
Odell Bed 61 L9
Odham Devon 8 C4
Odiham Hants 23 K4
Odsal C Brad 90 F5
Odsey Cambs 50 G3
Odstock Wilts 21 M9
Odstone Leics 72 B9
Offchurch Warwks 59 N11
Offenham Worcs 47 L5
Offerton Stockp 83 K7
Offerton Sundld 113 M9
Offham E Susx 25 K8
Offham Kent 37 Q9
Offham W Susx 24 B9
Offleymarsh Staffs 70 D9
Offord Cluny Cambs 62 B7
Offord D'Arcy Cambs 62 B7
Offton Suffk 53 J2
Offwell Devon 10 D5
Ogbourne Maizey Wilts 33 N10
Ogbourne St Andrew Wilts 33 N10
Ogbourne St George Wilts 33 P10
Ogden Calder 90 D4
Ogle Nthumb 112 H5
Oglet Lpool 81 N8
Ogmore V Glam 29 N9
Ogmore-by-Sea V Glam 29 N9
Ogmore Vale Brdgnd 29 P6
Ogwen Bank Gwynd 79 L11
Okeford Fitzpaine Dorset 12 D2
Okehampton Devon 8 E5
Oker Side Derbys 84 C8
Okewood Hill Surrey 24 D3
Olchard Devon 9 L9
Old Nhants 60 G6
Old Aberdeen C Aber 151 N6
Old Alresford Hants 22 G8
Oldany Highld 164 C10
Old Auchenbrack D & G 115 Q8
Old Basford C Nott 72 F2
Old Basing Hants 23 J4
Old Beetley Norfk 76 D8
Oldberrow Warwks 58 H11
Old Bewick Nthumb 119 L6
Old Bolingbroke Lincs 87 L7
Old Bramhope Leeds 90 G2
Old Brampton Derbys 84 D6
Old Bridge of Urr D & G 108 G7
Old Buckenham Norfk 64 F3
Old Burghclere Hants 22 E3
Oldbury Kent 37 N9
Oldbury Sandw 58 E7
Oldbury Shrops 57 N6
Oldbury Warwks 59 M6
Oldbury Naite S Glos 32 B6
Oldbury-on-Severn S Glos 32 B6
Oldbury on the Hill Gloucs 32 F7
Old Byland N York 98 B3
Old Cantley Donc 91 Q10
Old Cassop Dur 104 B3
Old Castle Brdgnd 29 P9
Oldcastle Mons 45 L10
Oldcastle Heath Ches W 69 N5
Old Catton Norfk 77 J9
Old Churchstoke Powys 56 D6
Old Clee NE Lin 93 N9
Old Cleeve Somset 18 D6
Old Clipstone Notts 85 K8
Old Colwyn Conwy 80 B9
Oldcotes Notts 85 J3
Old Dailly S Ayrs 114 D8
Old Dalby Leics 72 H6
Old Dam Derbys 83 P9
Old Deer Abers 159 N8
Old Ditch Somset 19 P5
Old Edlington Donc 91 N11
Old Eldon Dur 103 P5
Old Ellerby E R Yk 93 L3
Old Felixstowe Suffk 53 P4
Oldfield C Brad 90 C3
Oldfield Worcs 46 F2
Old Fletton C Pete 74 C11
Oldford Somset 20 E4
Old Forge Herefs 45 R11
Old Furnace Herefs 45 P10
Old Glossop Derbys 83 M6
Old Goole E R Yk 92 B6
Old Grimsby IoS 2 b1
Old Hall Green Herts 51 J6
Oldhall Green Suffk 64 B10
Old Hall Street Norfk 77 L5
Oldham Oldham 83 K4
Oldhamstocks E Loth 129 J5
Old Harlow Essex 51 L8
Old Heath Essex 52 H7
Old Hunstanton Norfk 75 N2
Old Hurst Cambs 62 D5
Old Hutton Cumb 95 M3
Old Inns Services N Lans 126 D2
Old Kea Cnwll 3 L5
Old Kilpatrick W Duns 125 M3
Old Knebworth Herts 50 F6
Old Lakenham Norfk 77 J10
Oldland S Glos 32 C10
Old Langho Lancs 89 L3
Old Laxey IoM 80 f5
Old Leake Lincs 87 M10
Old Malton N York 98 F6
Oldmeldrum Abers 151 L2
Oldmill Cnwll 5 P7
Old Milverton Warwks 59 L11
Oldmixon N Som 19 K3
Old Newton Suffk 64 F9
Old Quarrington Dur 104 B3
Old Radford C Nott 72 F2
Old Radnor Powys 45 K3
Old Rayne Abers 150 H2
Old Romney Kent 26 H7
Old Shoreham W Susx 24 F9
Oldshoremore Highld 164 F5
Old Soar Kent 37 P10
Old Sodbury S Glos 32 E8
Old Somerby Lincs 73 P4
Oldstead N York 98 A5
Old Stratford Nhants 49 L6
Old Struan P & K 141 K4
Old Swarland Nthumb 119 N10
Old Swinford Dudley 58 D8
Old Tebay Cumb 102 B9
Old Thirsk N York 97 P4
Old Town Calder 90 C5
Old Town Cumb 95 M4
Old Town Cumb 101 N2
Old Town E Susx 25 N11
Old Town IoS 2 c2
Old Trafford Traffd 82 H5
Old Tupton Derbys 84 E7
Oldwall Cumb 111 J8
Oldwalls Swans 28 E6
Old Warden C Beds 50 D2
Oldways End Somset 17 R7
Old Weston Cambs 61 N5
Old Wick Highld 167 Q7
Old Windsor W & M 35 Q10
Old Wives Lees Kent 39 J11
Old Woking Surrey 36 B9
Old Wolverton M Keyn 49 M6
Old Woodhall Lincs 86 H7
Old Woods Shrops 69 N10
Olgrinmore Highld 167 J6
Olive Green Staffs 71 L11
Oliver's Battery Hants 22 E9
Ollaberry Shet 169 q5
Ollach Highld 153 J10
Ollerton Ches E 82 G9
Ollerton Notts 85 L7
Ollerton Shrops 70 A9
Olmarch Cerdgn 43 M3
Olmstead Green Cambs 51 P2
Olney M Keyn 49 N4
Olrig House Highld 167 L3
Olton Solhll 58 H8
Olveston S Glos 32 B7
Ombersley Worcs 46 F2
Ompton Notts 85 L7
Once Brewed Nthumb 111 P7
Onchan IoM 80 e6
Onecote Staffs 71 J3
Onehouse Suffk 64 E10
Onen Mons 31 M2
Ongar Street Herefs 56 F11
Onibury Shrops 56 H9
Onich Highld 139 J5
Onllwyn Neath 29 M2
Onneley Staffs 70 D6
Onslow Green Essex 51 Q7
Onslow Village Surrey 23 Q5
Onston Ches W 82 C10
Openwoodgate Derbys 84 E11
Opinan Highld 153 N3
Orbliston Moray 157 Q6
Orbost Highld 152 D9
Orby Lincs 87 N7
Orchard Portman Somset 18 H10
Orcheston Wilts 21 L5
Orcop Herefs 45 P9
Orcop Hill Herefs 45 P9
Ord Abers 158 F6
Ordhead Abers 150 H5
Ordie Abers 150 D7
Ordiequish Moray 157 Q6
Ordley Nthumb 112 D9
Ordsall Notts 85 M5
Ore E Susx 26 D9
Oreleton Common Herefs 56 H11
Oreton Shrops 57 M8
Orford Suffk 65 N11
Orford Warrtn 82 D6
Organford Dorset 12 F6
Orgreave Staffs 71 L11
Orkney Islands Ork 169 d6
Orkney Neolithic Ork 169 b5
Orlestone Kent 26 H5
Orleton Herefs 56 H11
Orleton Worcs 57 N11
Orlingbury Nhants 61 J6
Ormathwaite Cumb 101 J5
Ormesby R & Cl 104 F7
Ormesby St Margaret Norfk 77 P9
Ormesby St Michael Norfk 77 P9
Ormiscaig Highld 160 D8
Ormiston E Loth 128 C6
Ormsaigmore Highld 137 M3
Ormsary Ag & B 123 M5
Ormskirk Lancs 88 E9
Ornsby Hill Dur 113 J11
Oronsay Ag & B 136 b4
Orphir Ork 169 c6
Orpington Gt Lon 37 L7
Orrell Sefton 81 L5
Orrell Wigan 82 B4
Orrell Post Wigan 88 G9
Orrisdale IoM 80 d3
Orroland D & G 108 G11
Orsett Thurr 37 P4
Orslow Staffs 70 E11
Orston Notts 73 K2
Orthwaite Cumb 101 J4
Ortner Lancs 95 L10
Orton Cumb 102 B9
Orton Nhants 60 H5
Orton Staffs 58 C5
Orton Longueville C Pete 74 C11
Orton-on-the-Hill Leics 59 M4
Orton Rigg Cumb 110 F10
Orton Waterville C Pete 74 C11
Orwell Cambs 62 E10
Osbaldeston Lancs 89 J4

Osbaldeston Green - Pentonbridge 293

Osbaldeston Green Lancs 89 J4
Osbaldwick C York 98 C10
Osbaston Leics 72 C10
Osbaston Shrops 69 K10
Osborne IoW 14 F8
Osborne House IoW 14 F8
Osbournby Lincs 73 R3
Oscroft Ches W 81 Q11
Ose Highld 152 E9
Osgathorpe Leics 72 C7
Osgodby Lincs 86 E2
Osgodby N York 91 Q4
Osgodby N York 99 M4
Oskaig Highld 153 J10
Oskamull Ag & B 137 M7
Osmaston Derbys 71 M6
Osmington Dorset 11 Q8
Osmington Mills Dorset 12 B8
Osmondthorpe Leeds 91 J4
Osmotherley N York 104 E11
Osney Oxon 34 E3
Ospringe Kent 38 H9
Ossett Wakefd 90 H6
Ossington Notts 85 N8
Ostend Essex 38 F2
Osterley Gt Lon 36 E5
Oswaldkirk N York 98 C5
Oswaldtwistle Lancs 89 L5
Oswestry Shrops 69 J9
Otford Kent 37 M9
Otham Kent 38 C11
Otham Hole Kent 38 D11
Othery Somset 19 L8
Otley Leeds 97 K11
Otley Suffk 65 J10
Otley Green Suffk 65 J10
Otterbourne Hants 22 E10
Otterburn N York 96 C9
Otterburn Nthumb 112 C2
Otter Ferry Ag & B 131 J11
Otterham Cnwll 5 K3
Otterhampton Somset 18 H6
Otterham Quay Kent 38 D8
Otterham Station Cnwll 5 K4
Otternish W Isls 168 e10
Ottershaw Surrey 36 B8
Otterswick Shet 169 s5
Otterton Devon 10 B7
Otterwood Hants 14 D6
Ottery St Mary Devon 10 C5
Ottinge Kent 27 L3
Ottringham E R Yk 93 N6
Oughterby Cumb 110 E9
Oughtershaw N York 96 C4
Oughterside Cumb 100 F2
Oughtibridge Sheff 84 D2
Oughtrington Warrtn 82 E7
Oulston N York 98 A6
Oulton Cumb 110 D10
Oulton Leeds 91 K5
Oulton Norfk 76 G6
Oulton Staffs 70 D10
Oulton Staffs 70 G7
Oulton Suffk 65 Q3
Oulton Broad Suffk 65 Q3
Oulton Street Norfk 76 H6
Oundle Nhants 61 M3
Ounsdale Staffs 58 C6
Our Dynamic Earth C Edin 127 P3
Ousby Cumb 102 B4
Ousden Suffk 63 M9
Ousefleet E R Yk 92 D6
Ouston Dur 113 L10
Outchester Nthumb 119 M4
Out Elmstead Kent 39 M11
Outgate Cumb 101 L11
Outhgill Cumb 102 E10
Outhill Warwks 58 H11
Outlands Staffs 70 D8
Outlane Kirk 90 D7
Out Newton E R Yk 93 Q6
Out Rawcliffe Lancs 88 E2
Outwell Norfk 75 K10
Outwick Hants 21 M11
Outwood Surrey 36 H11
Outwood Wakefd 91 J6
Outwood Gate Bury 89 M9
Outwoods Leics 72 C7
Outwoods Staffs 70 D11
Ouzlewell Green Leeds 91 J5
Ovenden Calder 90 D5
Over Cambs 62 E6
Over Ches W 82 D11
Over Gloucs 46 F11
Over S Glos 31 Q8
Over Burrows Derbys 71 P7
Overbury Worcs 47 J7
Overcombe Dorset 11 P8
Over Compton Dorset 19 Q11
Overdale Crematorium Bolton 89 K9
Over End Cambs 61 N2
Overgreen Derbys 84 D6
Over Green Warwks 59 J6
Over Haddon Derbys 84 B7
Over Kellet Lancs 95 L7
Over Kiddington Oxon 48 D10
Overleigh Somset 19 N7
Overley Staffs 71 M11
Over Monnow Mons 31 P2
Over Norton Oxon 48 B9
Over Peover Ches E 82 G10
Overpool Ches W 81 M9
Overscaig Hotel Highld 161 Q2
Overseal Derbys 71 P11
Over Silton N York 97 P2
Oversland Kent 39 J10
Oversley Green Warwks 47 L3
Overstone Nhants 60 G7
Over Stowey Somset 18 G7
Overstrand Norfk 77 J3
Over Stratton Somset 19 M11
Overstreet Wilts 21 L7
Over Tabley Ches E 82 F9
Overthorpe Nhants 48 E6
Overton C Aber 151 M5
Overton Ches W 81 Q9
Overton Hants 22 F5
Overton Lancs 95 J9
Overton N York 98 B9
Overton Shrops 57 J10
Overton Swans 28 E7
Overton Wakefd 90 H7
Overton Wrexhm 69 L6
Overton Bridge Wrexhm 69 L6
Overton Green Ches E 70 E2
Overtown Lancs 95 N5
Overtown N Lans 126 E7
Overtown Swindn 33 N9
Overtown Wakefd 91 K7
Over Wallop Hants 21 Q7
Over Whitacre Warwks 59 L6
Over Woodhouse Derbys 84 G6
Over Worton Oxon 48 D9
Overy Oxon 34 G6
Oving Bucks 49 L10
Oving W Susx 15 P6
Ovingdean Br & H 25 J10
Ovingham Nthumb 112 G8
Ovington Dur 103 M8
Ovington Essex 52 C3
Ovington Hants 22 G8
Ovington Norfk 76 C11
Ovington Nthumb 112 G8
Ower Hants 14 E6
Ower Hants 22 B11
Owermoigne Dorset 12 C7
Owlbury Shrops 56 E6
Owlerton Sheff 84 D3
Owlpen Gloucs 32 E5
Owl's Green Suffk 65 K8
Owlsmoor Br For 23 M2
Owlswick Bucks 35 L3
Owmby Lincs 86 D3
Owmby Lincs 93 J10
Owslebury Hants 22 F10
Owston Donc 91 P8
Owston Leics 73 K9
Owston Ferry N Linc 92 D10
Owstwick E R Yk 93 N4
Owthorne E R Yk 93 P5
Owthorpe Notts 72 H4
Owton Manor Hartpl 104 E5
Oxborough Norfk 75 P10
Oxbridge Dorset 11 K5
Oxcombe Lincs 87 K5
Oxcroft Derbys 84 G6
Oxen End Essex 51 Q5
Oxenholme Cumb 95 L3
Oxenhope C Brad 90 C4
Oxen Park Cumb 94 G3
Oxenpill Somset 19 M6
Oxenton Gloucs 47 J8
Oxenwood Wilts 22 B3
Oxford Oxon 34 F3
Oxford Airport Oxon 48 E11
Oxford Crematorium Oxon 34 G3
Oxford Services Oxon 34 H4
Oxhey Herts 50 D11
Oxhill Dur 113 J10
Oxhill Warwks 48 B5
Oxley Wolves 58 D4
Oxley Green Essex 52 F9
Oxley's Green E Susx 25 Q6
Oxlode Cambs 62 G3
Oxnam Border 118 C7
Oxnead Norfk 77 J7
Oxshott Surrey 36 D8
Oxshott Heath Surrey 36 D8
Oxspring Barns 90 H10
Oxted Surrey 37 J10
Oxton Border 128 D9
Oxton N York 91 N2
Oxton Notts 85 K10
Oxwich Swans 28 E7
Oxwich Green Swans 28 E7
Oxwick Norfk 76 C6
Oykel Bridge Hotel Highld 161 P6
Oyne Abers 150 H2
Oystermouth Swans 28 H7
Ozleworth Gloucs 32 E6

P

Pabail W Isls 168 k4
Packers Hill Dorset 11 Q2
Packington Leics 72 B8
Packmoor C Stke 70 F4
Packmores Warwks 59 L11
Padanaram Angus 142 G7
Padbury Bucks 49 K8
Paddington Gt Lon 36 G4
Paddington Warrtn 82 D7
Paddlesworth Kent 27 L4
Paddlesworth Kent 37 Q8
Paddock Wood Kent 25 Q2
Paddolgreen Shrops 69 P8
Padfield Derbys 83 M5
Padgate Warrtn 82 D7
Padhams Green Essex 51 P11
Padiham Lancs 89 M4
Padside N York 97 J9
Padstow Cnwll 4 E6
Padworth W Berk 34 H11
Page Bank Dur 103 P3
Pagham W Susx 15 N7
Paglesham Essex 38 F3
Paignton Torbay 7 M6
Pailton Warwks 59 Q8
Paine's Cross E Susx 25 P6
Painleyhill Staffs 71 J8
Painscastle Powys 44 H5
Painshawfield Nthumb 112 G8
Painsthorpe E R Yk 98 G9
Painswick Gloucs 32 G3
Painter's Forstal Kent 38 G10
Paisley Rens 125 M5
Paisley Woodside Crematorium Rens 125 M5
Pakefield Suffk 65 Q3
Pakenham Suffk 64 C8
Pale Gwynd 68 C7
Pale Green Essex 51 Q2
Palestine Hants 21 Q6
Paley Street W & M 35 N9
Palfrey Wsall 58 F5
Palgrave Suffk 64 G6
Pallington Dorset 12 C6
Palmersbridge Cnwll 5 K6
Palmers Green Gt Lon 36 H2
Palmerston E Ayrs 115 K4
Palmerstown V Glam 30 F11
Palnackie D & G 108 H9
Palnure D & G 107 N5
Palterton Derbys 84 G7
Pamber End Hants 22 H3
Pamber Green Hants 22 H3
Pamber Heath Hants 22 H2
Pamington Gloucs 46 H8
Pamphill Dorset 12 G4
Pampisford Cambs 62 G11
Panborough Somset 19 N5
Panbride Angus 143 K10
Pancrasweek Devon 16 D10
Pancross V Glam 30 D11
Pandy Caerph 30 G7
Pandy Gwynd 54 E4
Pandy Gwynd 68 A9
Pandy Mons 45 L10
Pandy Powys 55 L4
Pandy Wrexhm 68 G7
Pandy'r Capel Denbgs 68 E4
Pandy Tudur Conwy 67 R2
Panfield Essex 52 B6
Pangbourne W Berk 34 H9
Pangdean W Susx 24 G8
Panks Bridge Herefs 46 B5
Pannal N York 97 M10
Pannal Ash N York 97 L10
Pannanich Wells Hotel Abers 150 C8
Pant Shrops 69 J10
Pantasaph Flints 80 H9
Panteg Pembks 40 H4
Pantersbridge Cnwll 5 K8
Pant-ffrwyth Brdgnd 29 P8
Pant Glas Gwynd 66 H5
Pantglas Powys 54 H5
Pant-Gwyn Carmth 43 L9
Pant-lasau Swans 29 J4
Pant Mawr Powys 55 J8
Panton Lincs 86 G5
Pant-pastynog Denbgs 68 D2
Pantperthog Gwynd 54 G4
Pant-y-dwr Powys 55 M10
Pant-y-ffridd Powys 56 B4
Pantyffynnon Carmth 28 H2
Pantygaseg Torfn 31 J5
Pant-y-gog Brdgnd 29 P6
Pantymenyn Carmth 41 M5
Pant-y-mwyn Flints 68 G2
Panxworth Norfk 77 M9
Papa Westray Airport Ork 169 d1
Papcastle Cumb 100 F4
Papigoe Highld 167 Q6
Papple E Loth 128 F5
Papplewick Notts 84 H10
Papworth Everard Cambs 62 C8
Papworth St Agnes Cambs 62 C8
Par Cnwll 3 R3
Paramour Street Kent 39 N9
Parbold Lancs 88 F8
Parbrook Somset 19 Q7
Parbrook W Susx 24 C5
Parc Gwynd 68 A8
Parc Gwyn Crematorium Pembks 41 M8
Parcllyn Cerdgn 42 D4
Parc Seymour Newpt 31 M6
Pardshaw Cumb 100 E6
Parham Suffk 65 L9
Park D & G 109 K2
Park Nthumb 111 N8
Park Bottom Cnwll 2 H5
Park Bridge Tamesd 83 K4
Park Corner E Susx 25 M3
Park Corner Oxon 35 J7
Park Corner W & M 35 N8
Park Crematorium Lancs 88 D5
Park End Bed 49 Q4
Parkend Gloucs 32 B3
Park End Nthumb 112 C5
Parkers Green Kent 37 P11
Parkeston Essex 53 M5
Parkeston Quay Essex 53 M5
Park Farm Kent 26 H4
Parkgate Ches W 81 K9
Parkgate Cumb 110 D11
Parkgate D & G 109 M3
Parkgate E Susx 26 B9
Parkgate Essex 51 Q5
Park Gate Hants 14 F5
Parkgate Kent 26 E5
Parkgate Kent 37 M8
Park Gate Leeds 90 F2
Parkgate Surrey 24 F2
Park Gate Worcs 58 D10
Park Green Essex 51 L5
Park Green Suffk 64 G9
Parkgrove Crematorium Angus 143 L8
Parkhall W Duns 125 M3
Parkham Devon 16 F7
Parkham Ash Devon 16 F7
Park Head Derbys 84 E10
Park Hill Gloucs 31 Q5
Parkhouse Mons 31 P4
Parkmill Swans 28 F7
Park Royal Gt Lon 36 E4
Parkside Dur 113 P11
Parkside N Lans 126 E6
Parkside Wrexhm 69 L3
Parkstone Poole 12 H6
Park Street Herts 50 D10
Park Street W Susx 24 D4
Park Wood Crematorium Calder 90 E6
Parley Green Dorset 13 K5
Parmoor Bucks 35 L7
Parndon Essex 51 K9
Parndon Wood Crematorium Essex 51 K9
Parracombe Devon 17 M2
Parrog Pembks 41 L3
Parsonby Cumb 100 F3
Parson Cross Sheff 84 D2
Parson Drove Cambs 74 G9
Parson's Heath Essex 52 H6
Parson's Hill Derbys 71 P9
Partick C Glas 125 N4
Partington Traffd 82 F6
Partney Lincs 87 M7
Parton Cumb 100 C6
Partridge Green W Susx 24 E7
Partrishow Powys 45 K10
Parwich Derbys 71 M4
Paslow Wood Common Essex 51 N10
Passenham Nhants 49 L7
Passfield Hants 23 M8
Passingford Bridge Essex 51 M11
Paston C Pete 74 C10
Paston Norfk 77 L5
Pasturefields Staffs 70 H10
Patchacott Devon 8 C5
Patcham Br & H 24 H9
Patchetts Green Herts 50 D11
Patching W Susx 24 C9
Patchole Devon 17 L3
Patchway S Glos 32 B8
Pateley Bridge N York 97 J7
Paternoster Heath Essex 52 F8
Pathe Somset 19 L8
Pathhead Fife 134 H9
Pathhead Mdloth 128 B7
Pathlow Warwks 47 N3
Path of Condie P & K 134 D5
Patmore Heath Herts 51 K5
Patna E Ayrs 114 H5
Patney Wilts 21 L3
Patrick IoM 80 b5
Patrick Brompton N York 97 K2
Patricroft Salfd 82 G5
Patrington E R Yk 93 P6
Patrington Haven E R Yk 93 P6
Patrixbourne Kent 39 L10
Patterdale Cumb 101 L7
Pattingham Staffs 57 Q5
Pattishall Nhants 49 J4
Pattiswick Green Essex 52 D7
Patton Shrops 57 K5
Paul Cnwll 2 D8
Paulerspury Nhants 49 K5
Paull E R Yk 93 L5
Paul's Dene Wilts 21 M8
Paulton BaNES 20 C3
Paunton Herefs 46 C4
Pauperhaugh Nthumb 119 M11
Pave Lane Wrekin 70 D11
Pavenham Bed 61 L9
Pawlett Somset 19 J6
Pawston Nthumb 118 G4
Paxford Gloucs 47 N7
Paxton Border 129 N9
Payden Street Kent 38 F11
Payhembury Devon 10 B4
Paynter's Lane End Cnwll 2 H5
Paythorne Lancs 96 B10
Paytoe Herefs 56 G10
Peacehaven E Susx 25 K10
Peak Dale Derbys 83 N9
Peak District National Park 83 Q6
Peak Forest Derbys 83 P9
Peak Hill Lincs 74 E7
Peakirk C Pete 74 C9
Pearson's Green Kent 25 Q2
Peartree Green Herefs 46 A8
Peasedown St John BaNES 20 D3
Peasehill Derbys 84 F11
Peaseland Green Norfk 76 F8
Peasemore W Berk 34 E9
Peasenhall Suffk 65 M8
Pease Pottage W Susx 24 G4
Peaslake Surrey 24 C2
Peasley Cross St Hel 81 Q6
Peasmarsh E Susx 26 E7
Peasmarsh Somset 10 G2
Peasmarsh Surrey 23 Q5
Peathill Abers 159 M4
Peat Inn Fife 135 M6
Peatling Magna Leics 60 C2
Peatling Parva Leics 60 C3
Peaton Shrops 57 J7
Pebmarsh Essex 52 E5
Pebworth Worcs 47 M5
Pecket Well Calder 90 B5
Peckforton Ches E 69 P3
Peckham Gt Lon 36 H5
Peckleton Leics 72 D10
Pedairffordd Powys 68 F10
Pedlinge Kent 27 K4
Pedmore Dudley 58 D8
Pedwell Somset 19 M7
Peebles Border 117 K2
Peel IoM 80 b5
Peel Lancs 88 D4
Peel Common Hants 14 G6
Peene Kent 27 L4
Peening Quarter Kent 26 E6
Peggs Green Leics 72 C7
Pegsdon C Beds 50 D4
Pegswood Nthumb 113 K3
Pegwell Kent 39 Q9
Peinchorran Highld 153 J11
Peinlich Highld 152 G6
Pelcomb Pembks 40 H7
Pelcomb Bridge Pembks 40 H7
Pelcomb Cross Pembks 40 H7
Peldon Essex 52 G8
Pell Green E Susx 25 P4
Pelsall Wsall 58 F4
Pelsall Wood Wsall 58 F4
Pelton Dur 113 L10
Pelton Fell Dur 113 L10
Pelutho Cumb 109 P11
Pelynt Cnwll 5 L10
Pemberton Carmth 28 F4
Pemberton Wigan 82 C4
Pembles Cross Kent 26 E2
Pembrey Carmth 28 D4
Pembridge Herefs 45 M3
Pembroke Pembks 41 J10
Pembroke Dock Pembks 41 J10
Pembrokeshire Coast National Park Pembks 40 F6
Pembury Kent 25 P2
Pen-allt Herefs 45 R9
Penallt Mons 31 P2
Penally Pembks 41 M11
Penare Cnwll 3 P5
Penarth V Glam 30 G10
Penblewin Pembks 41 M7
Pen-bont Rhydybeddau Cerdgn 54 F8
Penbryn Cerdgn 42 E4
Pencader Carmth 42 H7
Pencaenewydd Gwynd 66 G6
Pencaitland E Loth 128 C6
Pencarnisiog IoA 78 F10
Pencarreg Carmth 43 K5
Pencarrow Cnwll 5 J5
Pencelli Powys 44 F9
Penclawdd Swans 28 F5
Pencoed Brdgnd 30 C8
Pencombe Herefs 46 A4
Pencoyd Herefs 45 Q9
Pencraig Herefs 45 R10
Pencraig Powys 68 D9
Pendeen Cnwll 2 B7
Penderyn Rhondd 29 P3
Pendine Carmth 41 P9
Pendlebury Salfd 82 G4
Pendleton Lancs 89 M3
Pendock Worcs 46 E8
Pendoggett Cnwll 4 G6
Pendomer Somset 11 L2
Pendoylan V Glam 30 E9
Pendre Brdgnd 29 P8
Penegoes Powys 54 H4
Penelewey Cnwll 3 L5
Pen-ffordd Pembks 41 L6
Pengam Caerph 30 G5
Pengam Cardif 30 H9
Penge Gt Lon 37 J6
Pengelly Cnwll 4 H5
Pengorffwysfa IoA 78 H6
Pengover Green Cnwll 5 M8
Pen-groes-oped Mons 31 K3
Pengwern Denbgs 80 E9
Penhale Cnwll 2 H10
Penhale Cnwll 4 E10
Penhale Cnwll 4 H9
Penhale Cnwll 5 Q11
Penhallow Cnwll 3 K3
Penhalurick Cnwll 3 J6
Penhalvean Cnwll 3 J6
Penhill Swindn 33 N7
Penhow Newpt 31 M6
Penhurst E Susx 25 Q7
Peniarth Gwynd 54 E3
Penicuik Mdloth 127 N6
Peniel Carmth 42 H10
Peniel Denbgs 68 D2
Penifiler Highld 152 H9
Peninver Ag & B 120 E7
Penisarwaun Gwynd 67 K2
Penistone Barns 90 G10
Penjerrick Cnwll 3 K7
Penketh Warrtn 82 C7
Penkill S Ayrs 114 D8
Penkridge Staffs 58 D2
Penlean Cnwll 5 L2
Penleigh Wilts 20 G4
Penley Wrexhm 69 M6
Penllergaer Swans 28 H5
Pen-llyn IoA 78 F8
Penllyn V Glam 30 C9
Pen-lon IoA 78 G11
Penmachno Conwy 67 P4
Penmaen Caerph 30 G5
Penmaen Swans 28 F7
Penmaenan Conwy 79 N9
Penmaenmawr Conwy 79 N9
Penmaenpool Gwynd 67 M11
Penmark V Glam 30 E11
Penmon IoA 79 L8
Penmorfa Gwynd 67 J6
Penmount Crematorium Cnwll 3 L4
Penmynydd IoA 79 J10
Penn Bucks 35 P6
Penn Wolves 58 C5
Pennal Gwynd 54 F4
Pennan Abers 159 K4
Pennant Cerdgn 43 K2
Pennant Denbgs 68 D8
Pennant Powys 55 K5
Pennant-Melangell Powys 68 D9
Pennard Swans 28 G7
Pennerley Shrops 56 F5
Pennicott Devon 9 L4
Pennines 90 B3
Pennington Cumb 94 F5
Pennington Hants 13 P5
Pennington Green Wigan 89 J9
Pennorth Powys 44 G9
Penn Street Bucks 35 P5
Pennsylvania S Glos 32 D10
Penny Bridge Cumb 94 G4
Pennycross Ag & B 137 N10
Pennygate Norfk 77 L7
Pennyghael Ag & B 137 N10
Pennyglen S Ayrs 114 E5
Penny Green Derbys 84 H5
Penny Hill Lincs 74 G5
Pennymoor Devon 9 L2
Pennywell Sundld 113 N9
Penparc Cerdgn 42 D5
Penparcau Cerdgn 54 D8
Penpedairheol Caerph 30 F5
Penpedairheol Mons 31 K4
Penperlleni Mons 31 K4
Penpethy Cnwll 4 H4
Penpillick Cnwll 4 H10
Penpol Cnwll 3 L6
Penpoll Cnwll 5 J11
Penponds Cnwll 2 G6
Penpont Cnwll 4 H7
Penpont D & G 108 H2
Penpont Powys 44 D9
Penquit Devon 6 G8
Penrest Cnwll 5 N6
Penrherber Carmth 41 Q3
Pen-rhiw Pembks 41 P2
Penrhiwceiber Rhondd 30 E5
Pen Rhiwfawr Neath 29 K2
Penrhiw-llan Cerdgn 42 G6
Penrhiw-pal Cerdgn 42 F5
Penrhos Gwynd 66 E8
Penrhos IoA 78 D8
Penrhos Mons 31 M2
Penrhos Powys 29 M2
Penrhos garnedd Gwynd 79 K10
Penrhyn Bay Conwy 79 Q8
Penrhyncoch Cerdgn 54 E8
Penrhyndeudraeth Gwynd 67 L7
Penrhyn-side Conwy 79 Q8
Penrice Swans 28 E7
Penrioch N Ayrs 120 G3
Penrith Cumb 101 P4
Penrose Cnwll 4 D7
Penruddock Cumb 101 M5
Penryn Cnwll 3 K7
Pensarn Conwy 80 D9
Pensax Worcs 57 N11
Pensby Wirral 81 K8
Penselwood Somset 20 E8
Pensford BaNES 20 B2
Pensham Worcs 46 H6
Penshaw Sundld 113 M10
Penshurst Kent 25 M2
Penshurst Station Kent 37 M11
Pensilva Cnwll 5 M7
Pensnett Dudley 58 D7
Penstone Devon 9 J4
Penstrowed Powys 55 P6
Pentewan Cnwll 3 Q4
Pentir Gwynd 79 K11
Pentire Cnwll 4 B9
Pentlepoir Pembks 41 M9
Pentlow Essex 63 P11
Pentlow Street Essex 63 P11
Pentney Norfk 75 P8
Pentonbridge Cumb 110 H5

296 Reepham - Rumford

Reepham Norfk 76 G7
Reeth N York 103 K11
Reeves Green Solhll 59 L9
Regaby IoM 80 f2
Regil N Som 19 P2
Reiff Highld 160 F4
Reigate Surrey 36 G10
Reighton N York 99 N5
Reisque Abers 151 M4
Reiss Highld 167 P6
Rejerrah Cnwll 4 B10
Releath Cnwll 2 H7
Relubbus Cnwll 2 F7
Relugas Moray 156 H8
Remenham Wokham 35 L8
Remenham Hill Wokham 35 L8
Rempstone Notts 72 F6
Rendcomb Gloucs 33 K3
Rendham Suffk 65 L9
Rendlesham Suffk 65 L11
Renfrew Rens 125 N4
Renhold Bed 61 N10
Renishaw Derbys 84 G5
Rennington Nthumb 119 P7
Renton W Duns 125 K2
Renwick Cumb 101 Q2
Repps Norfk 77 N8
Repton Derbys 71 Q9
Resaurie Highld 156 C8
Rescassa Cnwll 3 P5
Rescorla Cnwll 3 P4
Resipole Highld 138 C5
Reskadinnick Cnwll 2 G5
Resolis Highld 156 B4
Resolven Neath 29 M4
Rest and be thankful
Ag & B 131 Q6
Reston Border 129 M7
Restronguet Cnwll 3 L6
Reswallie Angus 143 J7
Reterth Cnwll 4 E9
Retford Notts 85 M4
Retire Cnwll 4 G9
Rettendon Essex 38 C2
Retyn Cnwll 4 D10
Revesby Lincs 87 J8
Rew Devon 7 J11
Rew Devon 7 K4
Rewe Devon 9 M5
Rew Street IoW 14 E8
Rexon Devon 5 Q4
Reydon Suffk 65 P6
Reymerston Norfk 76 E10
Reynalton Pembks 41 L9
Reynoldston Swans 28 E7
Rezare Cnwll 5 P6
Rhadyr Mons 31 L4
Rhandirmwyn Carmth 43 Q6
Rhayader Powys 55 M11
Rheindown Highld 155 P8
Rhes-y-cae Flints 80 H10
Rhewl Denbgs 68 F2
Rhewl Denbgs 68 G6
Rhewl-fawr Flints 80 G8
Rhewl Mostyn Flints 80 H8
Rhicarn Highld 164 C11
Rhiconich Highld 164 G6
Rhicullen Highld 156 B3
Rhigos Rhondd 29 P3
Rhireavach Highld 160 G7
Rhives Highld 163 J6
Rhiwbina Cardif 30 G8
Rhiwbryfdir Gwynd 67 M5
Rhiwderyn Newpt 31 J7
Rhiwen Gwynd 67 K2
Rhiwinder Rhondd 30 D7
Rhiwlas Gwynd 68 B7
Rhiwlas Gwynd 79 K11
Rhiwlas Powys 68 G8
Rhiwsaeson Rhondd 30 E8
Rhode Somset 19 J8
Rhoden Green Kent 37 Q11
Rhodesia Notts 85 J5
Rhodes Minnis Kent 27 L3
Rhodiad-y-brenin
Pembks 40 E5
Rhonehouse D & G 108 F9
Rhoose V Glam 30 E11
Rhos Carmth 42 G7
Rhos Denbgs 68 F2
Rhos Neath 29 K4
Rhosbeirio IoA 78 F6
Rhoscefnhir IoA 79 J9
Rhoscolyn IoA 78 D9
Rhoscrowther Pembks 40 H10
Rhosesmor Flints 81 J11
Rhos-fawr Gwynd 66 F7
Rhosgadfan Gwynd 67 J3
Rhosgoch IoA 78 G7
Rhosgoch Powys 44 H5
Rhos Haminiog Cerdgn 43 K2
Rhoshill Pembks 41 N2
Rhoshirwaun Gwynd 66 C9
Rhoslan Gwynd 66 H6
Rhoslefain Gwynd 54 D3
Rhosllanerchrugog
Wrexhm 69 J5
Rhôs Lligwy IoA 78 H7
Rhosmaen Carmth 43 M10
Rhosmeirch IoA 78 H9
Rhosneigr IoA 78 E10
Rhosnesni Wrexhm 69 L4
Rhôs-on-Sea Conwy 79 Q8
Rhosrobin Wrexhm 69 K4
Rhossili Swans 28 D7
Rhostryfan Gwynd 66 H3
Rhostyllen Wrexhm 69 K5
Rhosybol IoA 78 G7
Rhos y-brithdir Powys 68 F10
Rhosygadfa Shrops 69 K8
Rhos-y-garth Cerdgn 54 E10
Rhos-y-gwaliau Gwynd 68 B8
Rhos-y-llan Gwynd 66 C7
Rhosymedre Wrexhm 69 J6
Rhos-y-meirch Powys 56 D11
Rhu Ag & B 132 B11
Rhuallt Denbgs 80 F9
Rhubodach Ag & B 124 C3
Rhuddall Heath Ches W 69 Q2
Rhuddlan Cerdgn 43 J6
Rhuddlan Denbgs 80 E9
Rhulen Powys 44 G5
Rhunahaorine Ag & B 123 M10
Rhyd Gwynd 67 L6
Rhydargaeau Carmth 42 H9
Rhydcymerau Carmth 43 L7
Rhydd Worcs 46 F5
Rhyd-Ddu Gwynd 67 K4
Rhydding Neath 29 K5
Rhydgaled Conwy 68 C2
Rhydlanfair Conwy 67 Q4
Rhydlewis Cerdgn 42 F5
Rhydlios Gwynd 66 B9
Rhyd-lydan Conwy 68 A4
Rhydowen Cerdgn 42 H5
Rhydrosser Cerdgn 54 D11
Rhydspence Herefs 45 J5
Rhydtalog Flints 68 H4
Rhyd-uchaf Gwynd 68 B7
Rhyd-y-clafdy Gwynd 66 E8
Rhydycroesau Shrops 68 H8
Rhydyfelin Cerdgn 54 D9
Rhydyfelin Rhondd 30 E7
Rhyd-y-foel Conwy 80 C9
Rhydyfro Neath 29 K3
Rhyd-y-groes Gwynd 79 K11
Rhydymain Gwynd 67 Q10
Rhyd-y-meirch Mons 31 K3
Rhydymwyn Flints 81 J11
Rhyd-y pennau Cerdgn 54 E7
Rhyd-yr-onnen Gwynd 54 E4
Rhyd-y-sarn Gwynd 67 M6
Rhyl Denbgs 80 E8
Rhymney Caerph 30 F3
Rhynd P & K 134 F3
Rhynie Abers 150 D2
Rhynie Highld 163 J11
Ribbesford Worcs 57 P10
Ribbleton Lancs 88 H4
Ribby Lancs 88 E4
Ribchester Lancs 89 K3
Riber Derbys 84 D9
Riby Lincs 93 L9
Riccall N York 91 Q3
Riccarton Border 111 K2
Riccarton E Ayrs 125 L10
Richards Castle Herefs 56 H11
Richings Park Bucks 36 B5
Richmond Gt Lon 36 E6
Richmond N York 103 N10
Richmond Sheff 84 F3
Richmond Fort Guern 10 b2
Rich's Holford Somset 18 F8
Rickerscote Staffs 70 G10
Rickford N Som 19 N3
Rickham Devon 7 K11
Rickinghall Suffk 64 E6
Rickling Essex 51 L4
Rickling Green Essex 51 M5
Rickmansworth Herts 36 C2
Riddell Border 117 Q6
Riddings Derbys 84 F10
Riddlecombe Devon 17 L9
Riddlesden C Brad 90 D2
Ridge BaNES 19 Q3
Ridge Dorset 12 F7
Ridge Herts 50 F10
Ridge Wilts 21 J8
Ridgebourne Powys 44 F2
Ridge Green Surrey 36 H11
Ridge Lane Warwks 59 L6
Ridge Row Kent 27 M3
Ridgeway Derbys 84 F4
Ridgeway Worcs 47 K2
Ridgeway Cross Herefs 46 D5
Ridgewell Essex 52 B3
Ridgewood E Susx 25 L7
Ridgmont C Beds 49 Q7
Riding Mill Nthumb 112 F8
Ridley Kent 37 P8
Ridley Nthumb 111 Q8
Ridley Green Ches E 69 Q4
Ridlington Norfk 77 L5
Ridlington Rutlnd 73 L10
Ridlington Street Norfk 77 L5
Ridsdale Nthumb 112 D4
Rievaulx N York 98 B3
Rigg D & G 110 E7
Riggend N Lans 126 D3
Righoul Highld 156 F7
Rigmadon Park Cumb 95 N4
Rigsby Lincs 87 M5
Rigside S Lans 116 B3
Riley Green Lancs 89 J5
Rileyhill Staffs 58 H2
Rilla Mill Cnwll 5 M7
Rillaton Cnwll 5 M7
Rillington N York 98 H6
Rimington Lancs 96 B11
Rimpton Somset 20 B10
Rimswell E R Yk 93 P5
Rinaston Pembks 41 J5
Rindleford Shrops 57 N5
Ringford D & G 108 E9
Ringinglow Sheff 84 C4
Ringland Norfk 76 G9
Ringles Cross E Susx 25 L6
Ringlestone Kent 38 E10
Ringley Bolton 89 M9
Ringmer E Susx 25 K8
Ringmore Devon 6 H9
Ringmore Devon 7 N4
Ring o'Bells Lancs 88 F8
Ringorm Moray 157 P9
Ring's End Cambs 74 G10
Ringsfield Suffk 65 N4
Ringsfield Corner Suffk 65 N4
Ringshall Herts 35 Q2
Ringshall Suffk 64 E11
Ringshall Stocks Suffk 64 F11
Ringstead Nhants 61 L5
Ringstead Norfk 75 P2
Ringwood Hants 13 L3
Ringwould Kent 27 Q2
Rinsey Cnwll 2 F8
Rinsey Croft Cnwll 2 G8
Ripe E Susx 25 M8
Ripley Derbys 84 E10
Ripley Hants 13 L5
Ripley N York 97 L8
Ripley Surrey 36 C9
Riplingham E R Yk 92 G4
Riplington Hants 23 J10
Ripon N York 97 M6
Rippingale Lincs 74 A5
Ripple Kent 39 Q11
Ripple Worcs 46 G7
Ripponden Calder 90 C7
Risabus Ag & B 122 D11
Risbury Herefs 45 Q4
Risby N Linc 92 F8
Risby Suffk 63 P7
Risca Caerph 30 H6
Rise E R Yk 93 L2
Riseden E Susx 25 P4
Riseden Kent 26 B4
Risegate Lincs 74 D5
Riseholme Lincs 86 C5
Risehow Cumb 100 D4
Riseley Bed 61 M8
Riseley Wokham 23 K2
Rishangles Suffk 64 H8
Rishton Lancs 89 L4
Rishworth Calder 90 C7
Rising Bridge Lancs 89 M5
Risley Derbys 72 D3
Risley Warrtn 82 E6
Risplith N York 97 K7
Rivar Wilts 22 B2
Rivenhall End Essex 52 D8
River Kent 27 N3
River W Susx 23 P10
River Bank Cambs 62 H7
Riverford Highld 155 P7
Riverhead Kent 37 M9
Rivers Corner Dorset 12 C2
Rivington Lancs 89 J8
Rivington Services Lancs 89 J8
Roachill Devon 17 R7
Roade Nhants 49 L4
Road Green Norfk 65 K3
Roadhead Cumb 111 K6
Roadmeetings S Lans 126 F8
Roadside E Ayrs 115 L4
Roadside Highld 167 L4
Roadwater Somset 18 D7
Roag Highld 152 D9
Roa Island Cumb 94 E7
Roan of Craigoch S Ayrs 114 E7
Roast Green Essex 51 L4
Roath Cardif 30 G9
Roberton Border 117 N8
Roberton S Lans 116 C5
Robertsbridge E Susx 26 B7
Roberttown Kirk 90 F6
Robeston Wathen
Pembks 41 L7
Robgill Tower D & G 110 D6
Robin Hill Staffs 70 G3
Robin Hood Lancs 88 G8
Robin Hood Leeds 91 J5
Robin Hood
Crematorium Solhll 58 H8
Robin Hood Doncaster
Sheffield Airport
Donc 91 R11
Robinhood End Essex 52 B4
Robin Hood's Bay N York 105 Q9
Roborough Devon 6 E6
Roborough Devon 17 K8
Roby Knows 81 N6
Roby Mill Lancs 88 G9
Rocester Staffs 71 L7
Roch Pembks 40 G6
Rochdale Rochdl 89 P8
Rochdale
Crematorium Rochdl 89 P8
Roche Cnwll 4 F9
Rochester Medway 38 B8
Rochester Nthumb 118 F11
Rochford Essex 38 E3
Rochford Worcs 57 L11
Roch Gate Pembks 40 G6
Rock Cnwll 4 E6
Rock Neath 29 L6
Rock Nthumb 119 P6
Rock W Susx 24 D8
Rock Worcs 57 N10
Rockbeare Devon 9 P6
Rockbourne Hants 21 M11
Rockcliffe Cumb 110 G8
Rockcliffe D & G 108 H10
Rockcliffe Cross Cumb 110 F8
Rock End Staffs 70 F3
Rockend Torbay 7 N6
Rock Ferry Wirral 81 L7
Rockfield Highld 163 L10
Rockfield Mons 31 N2
Rockford Devon 17 P2
Rockford Hants 13 L3
Rockgreen Shrops 57 J9
Rockhampton S Glos 32 C6
Rockhead Cnwll 4 H5
Rockhill Shrops 56 D9
Rock Hill Worcs 58 E11
Rockingham Nhants 61 J2
Rockland All Saints
Norfk 64 D2
Rockland St Mary Norfk 77 L11
Rockland St Peter Norfk 64 D2
Rockley Notts 85 M6
Rockley Wilts 33 N10
Rockliffe Lancs 89 P6
Rockville Ag & B 131 Q9
Rockwell End Bucks 35 L7
Rockwell Green Somset 18 F10
Rodborough Gloucs 32 F4
Rodbourne Swindn 33 M7
Rodbourne Wilts 32 H8
Rodd Herefs 45 L2
Roddam Nthumb 119 K6
Rodden Dorset 11 N8
Roddymoor Dur 103 N3
Rode Somset 20 F4
Rode Heath Ches E 70 E3
Rode Heath Ches E 83 J11
Rodel W Isls 168 f9
Roden Wrekin 69 Q11
Rodhuish Somset 18 D7
Rodington Wrekin 57 K2
Rodington Heath Wrekin 57 K2
Rodley Gloucs 32 D2
Rodley Leeds 90 G3
Rodmarton Gloucs 32 H5
Rodmell E Susx 25 K9
Rodmersham Kent 38 F9
Rodmersham Green
Kent 38 F9
Rodney Stoke Somset 19 N5
Rodsley Derbys 71 N6
Rodway Somset 19 J6
Roecliffe N York 97 N7
Roe Cross Tamesd 83 L5
Roe Green Herts 50 F9
Roe Green Herts 50 H4
Roe Green Salfd 82 G4
Roehampton Gt Lon 36 F6
Roffey W Susx 24 E4
Rogart Highld 162 G6
Rogate W Susx 23 M10
Roger Ground Cumb 101 L11
Rogerstone Newpt 31 J7
Roghadal W Isls 168 f9
Rogiet Mons 31 N7
Roke Oxon 34 H6
Roker Sundld 113 P9
Rollesby Norfk 77 N8
Rolleston Leics 73 J10
Rolleston Notts 85 M10
Rolleston on Dove Staffs 71 N9
Rolston E R Yk 93 M2
Rolstone N Som 19 L2
Rolvenden Kent 26 D5
Rolvenden Layne Kent 26 E5
Romaldkirk Dur 103 J6
Romanby N York 97 N2
Romanno Bridge Border 127 M8
Romansleigh Devon 17 N7
Romden Castle Kent 26 E3
Romesdal Highld 152 G7
Romford Dorset 13 J3
Romford Gt Lon 37 M3
Romiley Stockp 83 K6
Romney Street Kent 37 N8
Romsey Hants 22 C10
Romsley Shrops 57 P8
Romsley Worcs 58 E8
Rona Highld 153 L6
Ronachan Ag & B 123 M9
Rood Ashton Wilts 20 G3
Rookhope Dur 102 H2
Rookley IoW 14 F10
Rookley Green IoW 14 F10
Rooks Bridge Somset 19 L4
Rooks Nest Somset 18 E8
Rookwith N York 97 K3
Roos E R Yk 93 N4
Roose Cumb 94 E7
Roosebeck Cumb 94 F7
Roothams Green Bed 61 N9
Ropley Hants 22 H8
Ropley Dean Hants 22 H8
Ropley Soke Hants 23 J8
Ropsley Lincs 73 P4
Rora Abers 159 Q7
Rorrington Shrops 56 E4
Rosarie Moray 158 A7
Rose Cnwll 3 K3
Roseacre Lancs 88 E3
Rose Ash Devon 17 P7
Rosebank S Lans 126 E8
Rosebush Pembks 41 L5
Rosecare Cnwll 5 K2
Rosecliston Cnwll 4 C10
Rosedale Abbey N York 105 K11
Rose Green Essex 52 F6
Rose Green Suffk 52 F4
Rose Green Suffk 52 G3
Rose Green W Susx 15 P7
Rosehall Highld 162 B6
Rosehearty Abers 159 M4
Rose Hill E Susx 25 L7
Rose Hill Lancs 89 N4
Rosehill Shrops 69 N11
Roseisle Moray 157 L4
Roselands E Susx 25 P10
Rosemarket Pembks 41 J9
Rosemarkie Highld 156 C6
Rosemary Lane Devon 10 D2
Rosemount P & K 142 B9
Rosenannon Cnwll 4 F8
Rosenithon Cnwll 3 L9
Roser's Cross E Susx 25 M6
Rosevean Cnwll 4 G10
Rosevine Cnwll 3 M6
Rosewarne Cnwll 2 G6
Rosewell Mdloth 127 P5
Roseworth S on T 104 D6
Roseworthy Cnwll 2 G6
Rosgill Cumb 101 P7
Roskestal Cnwll 2 B9
Roskhill Highld 152 D9
Roskorwell Cnwll 3 K9
Rosley Cumb 110 F11
Roslin Mdloth 127 P5
Rosliston Derbys 71 N11
Rosneath Ag & B 132 B11
Ross D & G 108 D12
Ross Nthumb 119 M3
Rossett Wrexhm 69 L3
Rossett Green N York 97 L10
Rossington Donc 91 Q11
Rossland Rens 125 L3
Ross-on-Wye Herefs 46 A10
Roster Highld 167 N9
Rostherne Ches E 82 F8
Rosthwaite Cumb 101 J8
Roston Derbys 71 L6
Rosudgeon Cnwll 2 F8
Rosyth Fife 134 E11
Rothbury Nthumb 119 L10
Rotherby Leics 72 H7
Rotherfield E Susx 25 N5
Rotherfield Greys Oxon 35 K8
Rotherfield Peppard
Oxon 35 K8
Rotherham Rothm 84 F2
Rotherham
Crematorium Rothm 84 G2
Rothersthorpe Nhants 60 F9
Rotherwick Hants 23 K3
Rothes Moray 157 P8
Rothesay Ag & B 124 D5
Rothiebrisbane Abers 158 H10
Rothiemay Moray 158 E8
Rothiemurchus Lodge
Highld 148 H6
Rothiemurchus Visitor
Centre Highld 148 G5
Rothienorman Abers 158 H10
Rothley Leics 72 F8
Rothley Nthumb 112 F3
Rothmaise Abers 158 G11
Rothwell Leeds 91 J5
Rothwell Lincs 93 K11
Rothwell Nhants 60 H4
Rotsea E R Yk 99 M10
Rottal Lodge Angus 142 F4
Rottingdean Br & H 25 J10
Rottington Cumb 100 C8
Roucan D & G 109 M5
Roucan Loch
Crematorium D & G 109 M5
Roud IoW 14 F10
Rougham Norfk 76 A7
Rougham Suffk 64 C9
Rough Close Staffs 70 G7
Rough Common Kent 39 K10
Roughlee Lancs 89 N2
Roughpark Abers 149 Q5
Roughton Lincs 86 H8
Roughton Norfk 77 J4
Roughton Shrops 57 P6
Roughway Kent 37 P10
Roundbush Essex 52 E11
Round Bush Herts 50 D11
Roundbush Green Essex 51 N8
Round Green Luton 50 D6
Roundham Somset 11 J3
Roundhay Leeds 91 J3
Rounds Green Sandw 58 E7
Round Street Kent 37 Q7
Roundstreet Common
W Susx 24 C5
Roundway Wilts 21 K2
Roundyhill Angus 142 F7
Rousay Ork 169 c3
Rousdon Devon 10 F6
Rousham Oxon 48 E10
Rous Lench Worcs 47 K4
Routenburn N Ayrs 124 F5
Routh E R Yk 93 J2
Rout's Green Bucks 35 L5
Row Cnwll 4 H6
Row Cumb 95 K3
Row Cumb 102 B4
Rowanburn D & G 110 H5
Rowardennan Stirlg 132 D8
Rowarth Derbys 83 M7
Row Ash Hants 14 F4
Rowberrow Somset 19 N3
Rowborough IoW 14 E10
Rowde Wilts 21 J2
Rowden Devon 8 F5
Rowen Conwy 79 P10
Rowfield Derbys 71 M5
Rowfoot Nthumb 111 N8
Rowford Somset 18 H9
Row Green Essex 52 B7
Rowhedge Essex 52 H7
Rowhook W Susx 24 D4
Rowington Warwks 59 K11
Rowland Derbys 84 B6
Rowland's Castle Hants 15 K4
Rowland's Gill Gatesd 113 J9
Rowledge Surrey 23 M6
Rowley Dur 112 G11
Rowley E R Yk 92 G4
Rowley Shrops 56 E3
Rowley Hill Kirk 90 F8
Rowley Regis Sandw 58 E7
Rowley Regis
Crematorium Sandw 58 E7
Rowlstone Herefs 45 M9
Rowly Surrey 24 B2
Rowner Hants 14 G6
Rowney Green Worcs 58 F10
Rownhams Hants 22 C11
Rownhams Services
Hants 22 C11
Rowrah Cumb 100 E7
Rowsham Bucks 49 M11
Rowsley Derbys 84 C7
Rows of Trees Ches E 82 H9
Rowstock Oxon 34 E7
Rowston Lincs 86 E9
Rowthorne Derbys 84 G8
Rowton Ches W 69 M2
Rowton Shrops 56 F2
Rowton Shrops 56 G8
Rowton Wrekin 69 R11
Row Town Surrey 36 B8
Roxburgh Border 118 C4
Roxby N Linc 92 F7
Roxby N York 105 L7
Roxton Bed 61 Q10
Roxwell Essex 51 P9
Royal Leamington Spa
Warwks 59 M11
Royal Oak Darltn 103 P6
Royal Oak Lancs 81 N4
Royal's Green Ches E 69 R6
Royal Sutton Coldfield
Birm 58 H5
Royal Tunbridge Wells
Kent 25 N3
Royal Wootton
Bassett Wilts 33 L8
Royal Yacht Britannia
C Edin 127 P2
Roy Bridge Highld 146 H11
Roydhouse Kirk 90 G8
Roydon Essex 51 K8
Roydon Norfk 64 G5
Roydon Norfk 75 P6
Roydon Hamlet Essex 51 K9
Royston Barns 91 K8
Royston Herts 51 J2
Royton Oldham 89 Q9
Rozel Jersey 11 c1
Ruabon Wrexhm 69 K6
Ruaig Ag & B 136 D6
Ruan High Lanes Cnwll 3 N6
Ruan Lanihorne Cnwll 3 M5
Ruan Major Cnwll 3 J10
Ruan Minor Cnwll 3 J10
Ruardean Gloucs 46 B11
Ruardean Hill Gloucs 46 B11
Ruardean Woodside
Gloucs 46 B11
Rubery Birm 58 E9
Rubha Ban W Isls 168 c16
Ruckcroft Cumb 101 P2
Ruckhall Herefs 45 P7
Ruckinge Kent 26 H5
Ruckland Lincs 87 K5
Ruckley Shrops 57 J4
Rudby N York 104 E9
Rudchester Nthumb 112 H7
Ruddington Notts 72 F4
Ruddle Gloucs 32 C2
Ruddlemoor Cnwll 3 Q3
Rudford Gloucs 46 E10
Rudge Somset 20 F4
Rudgeway S Glos 32 B7
Rudgwick W Susx 24 C4
Rudhall Herefs 46 B9
Rudheath Ches W 82 E10
Rudheath Woods Ches E 82 F10
Rudley Green Essex 52 D11
Rudloe Wilts 32 F10
Rudry Caerph 30 H7
Rudston E R Yk 99 M7
Rudyard Staffs 70 H3
Ruecastle Border 118 B6
Rufford Lancs 88 F7
Rufford Abbey Notts 85 K8
Rufforth C York 98 A10
Rug Denbgs 68 E6
Rugby Warwks 60 B5
Rugeley Staffs 71 J11
Ruishton Somset 19 J9
Ruislip Gt Lon 36 C3
Rùm Highld 144 E8
Rumbach Moray 158 A7
Rumbling Bridge P & K 134 C8
Rumburgh Suffk 65 L5
Rumby Hill Dur 103 N4
Rumford Cnwll 4 D7
Rumford Falk 126 G2

298 Scarba - Sicklesmere

Scarba Ag & B 130 D7
Scarborough N York 99 L3
Scarcewater Cnwll 3 N3
Scarcliffe Derbys 84 G7
Scarcroft Leeds 91 K2
Scarfskerry Highld 167 N2
Scargill Dur 103 L8
Scarinish Ag & B 136 C7
Scarisbrick Lancs 88 D8
Scarness Cumb 100 H4
Scarning Norfk 76 D9
Scarrington Notts 73 J2
Scarth Hill Lancs 88 E9
Scarthingwell N York 91 M3
Scartho NE Lin 93 N9
Scatsta Airport Shet 169 q6
Scawby N Linc 92 G9
Scawsby Donc 91 N10
Scawthorpe Donc 91 P9
Scawton N York 98 A4
Scayne's Hill W Susx 25 J6
Scethrog Powys 44 G9
Scholar Green Ches E 70 E3
Scholemoor Crematorium C Brad 90 E4
Scholes Kirk 90 F5
Scholes Kirk 90 F9
Scholes Leeds 91 K3
Scholes Rothm 91 K11
Scholes Wigan 88 H9
School Aycliffe Dur 103 Q6
School Green C Brad 90 E4
School Green Ches W 70 A2
Schoolgreen Wokham 35 K11
School House Dorset 10 H4
Scissett Kirk 90 G8
Scleddau Pembks 40 H4
Scofton Notts 85 K4
Scole Norfk 64 H6
Scone P & K 134 E2
Sconser Highld 153 J11
Scoonie Fife 135 K7
Scopwick Lincs 86 E9
Scoraig Highld 160 G7
Scorborough E R Yk 99 L11
Scorrier Cnwll 3 J5
Scorriton Devon 7 J5
Scorton Lancs 95 L11
Scorton N York 103 Q10
Sco Ruston Norfk 77 K7
Scotby Cumb 110 H9
Scotch Corner N York 103 P9
Scotforth Lancs 95 K9
Scot Hay Staffs 70 D5
Scothern Lincs 86 D5
Scotland Lincs 73 Q4
Scotland Gate Nthumb 113 L4
Scotlandwell P & K 134 F7
Scot Lane End Bolton 89 J9
Scotscalder Station Highld 167 J5
Scotsdike Cumb 110 G6
Scot's Gap Nthumb 112 F3
Scotsmill Abers 150 F4
Scotstoun C Glas 125 N4
Scotswood N u Ty 113 K8
Scotter Lincs 92 E10
Scotterthorpe Lincs 92 E10
Scottish Seabird Centre E Loth 128 F2
Scottish Wool Centre Stirlg 132 G7
Scottlethorpe Lincs 73 R6
Scotton Lincs 92 E11
Scotton N York 97 M9
Scotton N York 103 N11
Scottow Norfk 77 K7
Scott Willoughby Lincs 73 R3
Scoulton Norfk 76 D11
Scounslow Green Staffs 71 K9
Scourie Highld 164 E8
Scourie More Highld 164 D8
Scousburgh Shet 169 q12
Scouthead Oldham 90 B9
Scrabster Highld 167 K2
Scraesburgh Border 118 C7
Scrafield Lincs 87 K7
Scrainwood Nthumb 119 J9
Scrane End Lincs 74 G2
Scraptoft Leics 72 G9
Scratby Norfk 77 Q8
Scrayingham N York 98 E9
Scrays E Susx 26 C8
Scredington Lincs 74 A2
Scremby Lincs 87 M7
Scremerston Nthumb 129 Q10
Screveton Notts 73 J2
Scrivelsby Lincs 87 J7
Scriven N York 97 M9
Scrooby Notts 85 L2
Scropton Derbys 71 M8
Scrub Hill Lincs 86 H9
Scruton N York 97 L2
Scuggate Cumb 110 H6
Scullomie Highld 165 P4
Sculthorpe Norfk 76 B5
Scunthorpe N Linc 92 E8
Scurlage Swans 28 E7
Sea Somset 10 G2
Seaborough Dorset 11 J3
Seabridge Staffs 70 E6
Seabrook Kent 27 L4
Seaburn Sundld 113 P9
Seacombe Wirral 81 L6
Seacroft Leeds 91 K3
Seacroft Lincs 87 Q8
Seadyke Lincs 74 F3
Seafield Highld 152 H9
Seafield W Loth 127 J4
Seafield Crematorium C Edin 127 P2
Seaford E Susx 25 L11
Seaforth Sefton 81 L5
Seagrave Leics 72 G7
Seagry Heath Wilts 33 J8
Seaham Dur 113 P11
Seahouses Nthumb 119 P4
Seal Kent 37 N9
Sealand Flints 81 M11
Seale Surrey 23 N5
Seamer N York 99 L4
Seamer N York 104 E8
Seamill N Ayrs 124 G8
Sea Palling Norfk 77 N6
Searby Lincs 93 J9
Seasalter Kent 39 J9
Seascale Cumb 100 D10
Seathwaite Cumb 100 H11
Seathwaite Cumb 100 H8
Seatle Cumb 94 H4
Seatoller Cumb 100 H8
Seaton Cnwll 5 N11
Seaton Cumb 100 D4
Seaton Devon 10 E6
Seaton Dur 113 N11
Seaton E R Yk 99 P11
Seaton Kent 39 M10
Seaton Nthumb 113 M5
Seaton Rutlnd 73 N11
Seaton Burn N Tyne 113 K6
Seaton Carew Hartpl 104 F5
Seaton Delaval Nthumb 113 M5
Seaton Ross E R Yk 92 C2
Seaton Sluice Nthumb 113 M5
Seatown Dorset 11 J6
Seave Green N York 104 G10
Seaview IoW 14 H8
Seaville Cumb 110 C10
Seavington St Mary Somset 11 J2
Seavington St Michael Somset 19 M11
Sebastopol Torfn 31 J5
Sebergham Cumb 101 L2
Seckington Warwks 59 L3
Sedbergh Cumb 95 P2
Sedbury Gloucs 31 P6
Sedbusk N York 96 C2
Sedgeberrow Worcs 47 K7
Sedgebrook Lincs 73 M3
Sedge Fen Suffk 63 L4
Sedgefield Dur 104 C5
Sedgeford Norfk 75 P3
Sedgehill Wilts 20 G9
Sedgemoor Services Somset 19 L4
Sedgley Dudley 58 D6
Sedgley Park Bury 82 H4
Sedgwick Cumb 95 L3
Sedlescombe E Susx 26 C8
Sedrup Bucks 35 M2
Seed Kent 38 F10
Seend Wilts 20 H2
Seend Cleeve Wilts 20 H2
Seer Green Bucks 35 Q6
Seething Norfk 65 L2
Sefton Sefton 81 M4
Sefton Town Sefton 81 L4
Seghill Nthumb 113 L6
Seighford Staffs 70 F9
Seion Gwynd 79 J11
Seisdon Staffs 58 B5
Selattyn Shrops 69 J8
Selborne Hants 23 K8
Selby N York 91 Q4
Selham W Susx 23 P10
Selhurst Gt Lon 36 H7
Selkirk Border 117 P5
Sellack Herefs 45 R9
Sellafirth Shet 169 s4
Sellan Cnwll 2 C7
Sellick's Green Somset 18 H11
Sellindge Kent 27 J4
Selling Kent 38 H10
Sells Green Wilts 20 H2
Selly Oak Birm 58 F8
Selmeston E Susx 25 M9
Selsdon Gt Lon 37 J8
Selsey Gloucs 32 F4
Selsey W Susx 15 N8
Selsfield Common W Susx 24 H4
Selside Cumb 101 P11
Selside N York 96 A5
Selsted Kent 27 M3
Selston Notts 84 G10
Selworthy Somset 18 B5
Semer Suffk 52 G2
Semington Wilts 20 G2
Semley Wilts 20 G9
Sempringham Lincs 74 B4
Send Surrey 36 B9
Send Marsh Surrey 36 B9
Senghenydd Caerph 30 F6
Sennen Cnwll 2 B8
Sennen Cove Cnwll 2 B8
Sennybridge Powys 44 C9
Serlby Notts 85 K3
Sessay N York 97 Q5
Setchey Norfk 75 M8
Setley Hants 13 P4
Seton Mains E Loth 128 C4
Settle N York 96 B8
Settrington N York 98 G6
Seven Ash Somset 18 G8
Sevenhampton Gloucs 47 K10
Sevenhampton Swindn 33 P6
Seven Hills Crematorium Suffk 53 M3
Seven Kings Gt Lon 37 L3
Sevenoaks Kent 37 M9
Sevenoaks Weald Kent 37 M10
Seven Sisters Neath 29 M3
Seven Springs Gloucs 47 J11
Seven Star Green Essex 52 F6
Severn Beach S Glos 31 P8
Severn Stoke Worcs 46 G6
Severn View Services S Glos 31 Q7
Sevick End Bed 61 N10
Sevington Kent 26 H3
Sewards End Essex 51 N3
Sewardstonebury Essex 51 J11
Sewell C Beds 49 Q10
Sewerby E R Yk 99 P7
Seworgan Cnwll 3 J7
Sewstern Leics 73 M6
Sexhow N York 104 E9
Sezincote Gloucs 47 N8
Sgiogarstaigh W Isls 168 k1
Shabbington Bucks 35 J3
Shackerley Shrops 57 Q3
Shackerstone Leics 72 B9
Shacklecross Derbys 72 C4
Shackleford Surrey 23 P5
Shade Calder 89 Q6
Shader W Isls 168 i2
Shadforth Dur 104 B2
Shadingfield Suffk 65 N5
Shadoxhurst Kent 26 G4
Shadwell Leeds 91 J3
Shadwell Norfk 64 C5
Shaftenhoe End Herts 51 K3
Shaftesbury Dorset 20 G10
Shaftholme Donc 91 P9
Shafton Barns 91 K8
Shafton Two Gates Barns 91 K8
Shakerley Wigan 82 E4
Shalbourne Wilts 22 B2
Shalcombe IoW 14 C9
Shalden Hants 23 J6
Shalden Green Hants 23 K6
Shaldon Devon 7 N4
Shalfleet IoW 14 D9
Shalford Essex 52 B6
Shalford Surrey 36 B11
Shalford Green Essex 52 B6
Shallowford Staffs 70 F9
Shalmsford Street Kent 39 J11
Shalstone Bucks 48 H7
Shamley Green Surrey 24 B2
Shandford Angus 142 H5
Shandon Ag & B 132 B10
Shandwick Highld 156 F2
Shangton Leics 73 J11
Shankhouse Nthumb 113 L5
Shanklin IoW 14 G10
Shap Cumb 101 Q7
Shapinsay Ork 169 e5
Shapwick Dorset 12 F4
Shapwick Somset 19 M7
Shard End Birm 59 J7
Shardlow Derbys 72 C4
Shareshill Staffs 58 D3
Sharlston Wakefd 91 K7
Sharlston Common Wakefd 91 K7
Sharman's Cross Solhll 58 H9
Sharnal Street Medway 38 C7
Sharnbrook Bed 61 L9
Sharneyford Lancs 89 P6
Sharnford Leics 59 Q6
Sharnhill Green Dorset 11 Q3
Sharoe Green Lancs 88 G4
Sharow N York 97 M6
Sharpenhoe C Beds 50 C4
Sharperton Nthumb 119 J10
Sharp Green Norfk 77 M7
Sharpness Gloucs 32 C4
Sharpthorne W Susx 25 J4
Sharptor Cnwll 5 M7
Sharpway Gate Worcs 58 E11
Sharrington Norfk 76 E4
Shatterford Worcs 57 P8
Shatterling Kent 39 N10
Shatton Derbys 84 B4
Shaugh Prior Devon 6 E6
Shave Cross Dorset 11 J5
Shavington Ches E 70 B4
Shaw C Brad 90 C3
Shaw Oldham 89 Q9
Shaw Swindn 33 M7
Shaw W Berk 34 E11
Shaw Wilts 32 G11
Shawbirch Wrekin 57 L2
Shawbost W Isls 168 h3
Shawbury Shrops 69 Q10
Shawclough Rochdl 89 P8
Shaw Common Gloucs 46 C9
Shawdon Hill Nthumb 119 L8
Shawell Leics 60 B4
Shawford Hants 22 E9
Shawforth Lancs 89 P6
Shaw Green Herts 50 H4
Shaw Green Lancs 88 G7
Shaw Green N York 97 L10
Shawhead D & G 109 J5
Shaw Mills N York 97 L8
Shawsburn S Lans 126 D7
Shear Cross Wilts 20 G6
Shearington D & G 109 M7
Shearsby Leics 60 D2
Shearston Somset 19 J8
Shebbear Devon 16 G10
Shebdon Staffs 70 D9
Shebster Highld 166 H4
Sheddens E Rens 125 P6
Shedfield Hants 14 G4
Sheen Staffs 71 L2
Sheepbridge Derbys 84 E6
Sheep Hill Dur 113 J9
Sheepridge Kirk 90 F7
Sheepscar Leeds 91 J4
Sheepscombe Gloucs 32 G2
Sheepstor Devon 6 F5
Sheepwash Devon 8 C3
Sheepwash Nthumb 113 L3
Sheepway N Som 31 N9
Sheepy Magna Leics 72 A10
Sheepy Parva Leics 72 A10
Sheering Essex 51 M8
Sheerness Kent 38 F7
Sheerwater Surrey 36 B8
Sheet Hants 23 L10
Sheffield Cnwll 2 D8
Sheffield Sheff 84 E3
Sheffield Bottom W Berk 34 H11
Sheffield City Road Crematorium Sheff 84 E3
Sheffield Green E Susx 25 K5
Sheffield Park E Susx 25 K6
Shefford C Beds 50 D3
Sheigra Highld 164 E4
Sheinton Shrops 57 L4
Shelderton Shrops 56 G9
Sheldon Birm 58 J8
Sheldon Derbys 83 Q11
Sheldon Devon 10 C3
Sheldwich Kent 38 H10
Sheldwich Lees Kent 38 H10
Shelf Calder 90 E5
Shelfanger Norfk 64 G5
Shelfield Warwks 47 M2
Shelfield Wsall 58 F4
Shelfield Green Warwks 47 M2
Shelford Notts 72 H2
Shelford Warwks 59 P7
Shellacres Nthumb 118 G2
Shelley Essex 51 N9
Shelley Kirk 90 G8
Shelley Suffk 52 H4
Shelley Far Bank Kirk 90 G8
Shellingford Oxon 34 B6
Shellow Bowells Essex 51 P9
Shelsley Beauchamp Worcs 46 D2
Shelsley Walsh Worcs 46 D2
Shelton Bed 61 M7
Shelton Norfk 65 J3
Shelton Notts 73 K2
Shelton Shrops 56 H2
Shelton Green Norfk 65 J3
Shelton Lock C Derb 72 B4
Shelton Under Harley Staffs 70 E7
Shelve Shrops 56 E5
Shelwick Herefs 45 Q6
Shenfield Essex 51 P11
Shenington Oxon 48 C6
Shenley Herts 50 E10
Shenley Brook End M Keyn 49 M7
Shenleybury Herts 50 E10
Shenley Church End M Keyn 49 M7
Shenmore Herefs 45 M7
Shennanton D & G 107 K5
Shenstone Staffs 58 H4
Shenstone Worcs 58 C10
Shenstone Woodend Staffs 58 H4
Shenton Leics 72 B11
Shenval Moray 149 N2
Shepeau Stow Lincs 74 F8
Shephall Herts 50 G6
Shepherd's Bush Gt Lon 36 F4
Shepherd's Green Oxon 35 K8
Shepherds Patch Gloucs 32 D4
Shepherdswell Kent 27 N2
Shepley Kirk 90 F9
Shepperdine S Glos 32 B5
Shepperton Surrey 36 C7
Shepperton Green Surrey 36 C7
Shepreth Cambs 62 E11
Shepshed Leics 72 D7
Shepton Beauchamp Somset 19 M11
Shepton Mallet Somset 20 B6
Shepton Montague Somset 20 C8
Shepway Kent 38 C11
Sheraton Dur 104 D3
Sherborne Dorset 20 B11
Sherborne Gloucs 33 N2
Sherborne Somset 19 Q3
Sherborne St John Hants 22 H3
Sherbourne Warwks 47 Q2
Sherburn Dur 104 B2
Sherburn N York 99 K5
Sherburn Hill Dur 104 B2
Sherburn in Elmet N York 91 M4
Shere Surrey 36 C11
Shereford Norfk 76 B6
Sherfield English Hants 21 Q10
Sherfield on Loddon Hants 23 J3
Sherfin Lancs 89 M5
Sherford Devon 7 K10
Sherford Dorset 12 F6
Sheriffhales Shrops 57 P2
Sheriff Hutton N York 98 D7
Sheringham Norfk 76 H3
Sherington M Keyn 49 N5
Shermanbury W Susx 24 F7
Shernborne Norfk 75 P4
Sherrington Wilts 21 J7
Sherston Wilts 32 G7
Sherwood C Nott 72 F2
Sherwood Forest Notts 85 K8
Sherwood Forest Crematorium Notts 85 L7
Shetland Islands Shet 169 r8
Shettleston C Glas 125 Q5
Shevington Wigan 88 G9
Shevington Moor Wigan 88 G8
Shevington Vale Wigan 88 G9
Sheviock Cnwll 5 P10
Shibden Head C Brad 90 D5
Shide IoW 14 F9
Shidlaw Nthumb 118 F3
Shiel Bridge Highld 146 A4
Shieldaig Highld 153 Q7
Shieldhill D & G 109 M3
Shieldhill Falk 126 F2
Shieldhill House Hotel S Lans 116 E2
Shields N Lans 126 D6
Shielfoot Highld 138 B3
Shielhill Angus 142 G6
Shielhill Inver 124 G3
Shifford Oxon 34 C4
Shifnal Shrops 57 N3
Shilbottle Nthumb 119 N9
Shildon Dur 103 P5
Shillford E Rens 125 M6
Shillingford Devon 18 C10
Shillingford Oxon 34 G6
Shillingford Abbot Devon 9 M7
Shillingford St George Devon 9 M7
Shillingstone Dorset 12 D2
Shillington C Beds 50 D4
Shillmoor Nthumb 118 G9
Shilton Oxon 33 Q3
Shilton Warwks 59 P8
Shimpling Norfk 64 H5
Shimpling Suffk 64 B11
Shimpling Street Suffk 64 B11
Shincliffe Dur 103 Q2
Shiney Row Sundld 113 M10
Shinfield Wokham 35 K11
Shingay Cambs 62 D11
Shingle Street Suffk 53 Q3
Shinnersbridge Devon 7 K6
Shinness Highld 162 C4
Shipbourne Kent 37 N10
Shipdham Norfk 76 D10
Shipham Somset 19 M3
Shiphay Torbay 7 M5
Shiplake Oxon 35 L9
Shiplake Row Oxon 35 K9
Shiplate N Som 19 L3
Shipley C Brad 90 F3
Shipley Derbys 72 C2
Shipley Shrops 57 Q5
Shipley W Susx 24 D6
Shipley Bridge Surrey 24 H2
Shipley Hatch Kent 26 H4
Shipmeadow Suffk 65 M3
Shippea Hill Station Cambs 63 K4
Shippon Oxon 34 E5
Shipston-on-Stour Warwks 47 Q6
Shipton Bucks 49 L9
Shipton Gloucs 47 K11
Shipton N York 98 B9
Shipton Shrops 57 K6
Shipton Bellinger Hants 21 P5
Shipton Gorge Dorset 11 K6
Shipton Green W Susx 15 M7
Shipton Moyne Gloucs 32 G7
Shipton-on-Cherwell Oxon 48 E11
Shiptonthorpe E R Yk 92 E2
Shipton-under-Wychwood Oxon 47 Q11
Shirburn Oxon 35 J5
Shirdley Hill Lancs 88 D8
Shire Cumb 102 B3
Shirebrook Derbys 84 H7
Shiregreen Sheff 84 E2
Shirehampton Bristl 31 P9
Shiremoor N Tyne 113 M6
Shirenewton Mons 31 N6
Shire Oak Wsall 58 G4
Shireoaks Notts 85 J4
Shirkoak Kent 26 F4
Shirland Derbys 84 F9
Shirlett Shrops 57 L5
Shirley C Sotn 14 D4
Shirley Derbys 71 N6
Shirley Gt Lon 37 J7
Shirley Solhll 58 H9
Shirl Heath Herefs 45 N3
Shirrell Heath Hants 14 G4
Shirvan Ag & B 123 Q3
Shirwell Devon 17 L4
Shiskine N Ayrs 120 H6
Shittlehope Dur 103 K3
Shobdon Herefs 45 N2
Shobley Hants 13 L3
Shobrooke Devon 9 L4
Shoby Leics 72 H6
Shocklach Ches W 69 M5
Shocklach Green Ches W 69 M5
Shoeburyness Sthend 38 F4
Sholden Kent 39 Q11
Sholing C Sotn 14 E4
Shoot Hill Shrops 56 G2
Shop Cnwll 4 D7
Shop Cnwll 16 C9
Shopwyke W Susx 15 N5
Shore Rochdl 89 Q7
Shoreditch Gt Lon 36 H4
Shoreditch Somset 18 H10
Shoreham Kent 37 M8
Shoreham Airport W Susx 24 F9
Shoreham-by-Sea W Susx 24 F9
Shoreswood Nthumb 129 N10
Shorley Hants 22 G9
Shorncote Gloucs 33 K5
Shorne Kent 37 Q6
Shorta Cross Cnwll 5 M10
Shortbridge E Susx 25 L6
Shortfield Common Surrey 23 M6
Shortgate E Susx 25 L7
Short Heath Birm 58 G6
Shortheath Hants 23 L7
Short Heath Wsall 58 E4
Shortlanesend Cnwll 3 L4
Shortlees E Ayrs 125 L10
Shortstown Bed 61 N11
Shorwell IoW 14 E10
Shoscombe BaNES 20 D3
Shotesham Norfk 65 J2
Shotgate Essex 38 C3
Shotley Suffk 53 M4
Shotley Bridge Dur 112 G10
Shotleyfield Nthumb 112 G10
Shotley Gate Suffk 53 M5
Shotley Street Suffk 53 M4
Shottenden Kent 38 H11
Shottermill Surrey 23 N8
Shottery Warwks 47 N4
Shotteswell Warwks 48 D5
Shottisham Suffk 53 P3
Shottle Derbys 71 Q5
Shottlegate Derbys 71 Q5
Shotton Dur 104 C5
Shotton Dur 104 D3
Shotton Flints 81 L11
Shotton Nthumb 113 K5
Shotton Nthumb 118 F4
Shotton Colliery Dur 104 C2
Shotts N Lans 126 F6
Shotwick Ches W 81 L10
Shougle Moray 157 N6
Shouldham Norfk 75 N9
Shouldham Thorpe Norfk 75 N9
Shoulton Worcs 46 F3
Shover's Green E Susx 25 Q4
Shraleybrook Staffs 70 D5
Shrawardine Shrops 69 L11
Shrawley Worcs 57 Q11
Shreding Green Bucks 36 B4
Shrewley Warwks 59 K11
Shrewsbury Shrops 56 H2
Shrewton Wilts 21 L6
Shripney W Susx 15 P6
Shrivenham Oxon 33 P7
Shropham Norfk 64 D3
Shrub End Essex 52 G7
Shucknall Herefs 46 A6
Shudy Camps Cambs 51 P2
Shuna Ag & B 130 F6
Shurdington Gloucs 46 H11
Shurlock Row W & M 35 M10
Shurnock Worcs 47 K2
Shurrery Highld 166 H5
Shurrery Lodge Highld 166 H5
Shurton Somset 18 H6
Shustoke Warwks 59 K6
Shute Devon 9 L4
Shute Devon 10 F5
Shutford Oxon 48 C6
Shut Heath Staffs 70 F10
Shuthonger Gloucs 46 G7
Shutlanger Nhants 49 K5
Shutterton Devon 9 N9
Shutt Green Staffs 58 C3
Shuttington Warwks 59 L3
Shuttlewood Derbys 84 G6
Shuttleworth Bury 89 N7
Siabost W Isls 168 h3
Siadar W Isls 168 i2
Sibbertoft Nhants 60 E4
Sibdon Carwood Shrops 56 G8
Sibford Ferris Oxon 48 C7
Sibford Gower Oxon 48 C7
Sible Hedingham Essex 52 C5
Sibley's Green Essex 51 P5
Siblyback Cnwll 5 L7
Sibsey Lincs 87 L10
Sibsey Fenside Lincs 87 K10
Sibson Cambs 74 A11
Sibson Leics 72 B10
Sibster Highld 167 P6
Sibthorpe Notts 85 M6
Sibthorpe Notts 85 N11
Sibton Suffk 65 M8
Sicklesmere Suffk 64 B9

Sicklinghall - South Wingate 299

Sicklinghall N York 97 N11
Sidbrook Somset 19 J9
Sidbury Devon 10 C6
Sidbury Shrops 57 M7
Sid Cop Barns 91 K9
Sidcot N Som 19 M3
Sidcup Gt Lon 37 L6
Siddick Cumb 100 D4
Siddington Ches E 82 H10
Siddington Gloucs 33 K5
Sidemoor Worcs 58 E10
Sidestrand Norfk 77 K4
Sidford Devon 10 C6
Sidlesham W Susx 15 N7
Sidlesham Common W Susx 15 N7
Sidley E Susx 26 B10
Sidmouth Devon 10 C7
Siefton Shrops 56 H8
Sigford Devon 7 K4
Sigglesthorne E R Yk 99 P11
Sigingstone V Glam 30 C10
Signet Oxon 33 P2
Silchester Hants 22 H2
Sileby Leics 72 G7
Silecroft Cumb 94 C4
Silfield Norfk 64 G2
Silian Cerdgn 43 L4
Silkstead Hants 22 D10
Silkstone Barns 90 H9
Silkstone Common Barns 90 H10
Silk Willoughby Lincs 73 R2
Silloth Cumb 109 P10
Silpho N York 99 K2
Silsden C Brad 96 F11
Silsoe C Beds 50 C3
Silton Dorset 20 E9
Silverburn Mdloth 127 N5
Silverdale Lancs 95 K6
Silverdale Staffs 70 E5
Silver End Essex 52 D8
Silverford Abers 159 J5
Silvergate Norfk 76 H6
Silverlace Green Suffk 65 L9
Silverley's Green Suffk 65 K6
Silverstone Nhants 49 J6
Silver Street Kent 38 E9
Silver Street Somset 19 P8
Silverton Devon 9 N4
Silverwell Cnwll 3 J4
Silvington Shrops 57 L9
Simister Bury 89 N9
Simmondley Derbys 83 M6
Simonburn Nthumb 112 C6
Simonsbath Somset 17 P4
Simonsburrow Devon 18 F11
Simonstone Lancs 89 M4
Simonstone N York 96 C2
Simprim Border 129 L11
Simpson M Keyn 49 N7
Simpson Cross Pembks 40 G7
Sinclair's Hill Border 129 L9
Sinclairston E Ayrs 115 J4
Sinderby N York 97 M4
Sinderhope Nthumb 112 B10
Sinderland Green Traffd 82 F7
Sindlesham Wokham 35 L11
Sinfin C Derb 72 A4
Singleborough Bucks 49 L8
Single Street Gt Lon 37 K9
Singleton Kent 26 H3
Singleton Lancs 88 D3
Singleton W Susx 15 N4
Singlewell Kent 37 Q6
Sinkhurst Green Kent 26 D3
Sinnarhard Abers 150 D5
Sinnington N York 98 E3
Sinton Worcs 46 F2
Sinton Worcs 46 F2
Sinton Green Worcs 46 F2
Sipson Gt Lon 36 C5
Sirhowy Blae G 30 F2
Sissinghurst Kent 26 C4
Siston S Glos 32 C9
Sitcott Devon 5 P3
Sithney Cnwll 2 G8
Sithney Common Cnwll 2 G8
Sithney Green Cnwll 2 G8
Sittingbourne Kent 38 F9
Six Ashes Shrops 57 P7
Six Bells Blae G 30 H4
Sixhills Lincs 86 G3
Six Mile Bottom Cambs 63 J9
Sixmile Cottages Kent 27 K3
Sixpenny Handley Dorset 21 J11
Six Rues Jersey 11 b1
Sizewell Suffk 65 P9
Skaill Ork 169 e6
Skara Brae Ork 169 b5
Skares E Ayrs 115 K4
Skateraw Abers 151 N9
Skateraw E Loth 129 J5
Skeabost Highld 152 G8
Skeeby N York 103 N10
Skeffington Leics 73 J10
Skeffling E R Yk 93 Q7
Skegby Notts 84 G8
Skegby Notts 85 N7
Skegness Lincs 87 Q8
Skelbo Highld 162 H7
Skelbo Street Highld 162 H8
Skelbrooke Donc 91 N8
Skeldyke Lincs 74 F3
Skellingthorpe Lincs 86 B6
Skellorn Green Ches E 83 K8
Skellow Donc 91 N8
Skelmanthorpe Kirk 90 G8
Skelmersdale Lancs 88 F9
Skelmorlie N Ayrs 124 F4
Skelpick Highld 166 B5
Skelston D & G 108 H3
Skelton C York 98 B9
Skelton Cumb 101 M3
Skelton E R Yk 92 C5
Skelton N York 97 N7
Skelton N York 103 L10
Skelton R & Cl 105 J7
Skelwith Bridge Cumb 101 K10
Skendleby Lincs 87 M7
Skene House Abers 151 K5
Skenfrith Mons 45 P10
Skerne E R Yk 99 L9
Skerray Highld 165 Q4
Skerricha Highld 164 F6
Skerton Lancs 95 K8
Sketchley Leics 59 P6
Sketty Swans 28 H6
Skewen Neath 29 K5
Skewsby N York 98 C6
Skeyton Norfk 77 J6
Skeyton Corner Norfk 77 K6
Skiall Highld 166 H3
Skidbrooke Lincs 87 M2
Skidbrooke North End Lincs 93 R11
Skidby E R Yk 92 H4
Skigersta W Isls 168 k1
Skilgate Somset 18 C9
Skillington Lincs 73 M5
Skinburness Cumb 109 P9
Skinflats Falk 133 Q11
Skinidin Highld 152 C8
Skinners Green W Berk 34 D11
Skinningrove R & Cl 105 K7
Skipness Ag & B 123 R8
Skipper's Bridge D & G 110 G4
Skiprigg Cumb 110 G11
Skipsea E R Yk 99 P10
Skipsea Brough E R Yk 99 P10
Skipton N York 96 E10
Skipton-on-Swale N York 97 N5
Skipwith N York 91 R3
Skirlaugh E R Yk 93 K3
Skirling Border 116 F3
Skirmett Bucks 35 L6
Skirpenbeck E R Yk 98 E9
Skirwith Cumb 102 B4
Skirwith N York 95 Q6
Skirza Highld 167 Q3
Skitby Cumb 110 H7
Skittle Green Bucks 35 L4
Skokholm Island Pembks 40 D10
Skomer Island Pembks 40 D9
Skulamus Highld 145 L3
Skyborry Green Shrops 56 D10
Skye Green Essex 52 E7
Skye of Curr Highld 148 H3
Skyreholme N York 96 G8
Slack Calder 90 B5
Slackcote Oldham 90 B9
Slack Head Cumb 95 K5
Slackholme End Lincs 87 P6
Slacks of Cairnbanno Abers 159 K8
Slad Gloucs 32 G3
Slade Devon 10 C3
Slade Devon 17 J2
Slade Devon 17 Q6
Slade End Oxon 34 G6
Slade Green Gt Lon 37 M5
Slade Heath Staffs 58 D3
Slade Hooton Rothm 84 H3
Sladesbridge Cnwll 4 G7
Slades Green Worcs 46 F8
Slaggyford Nthumb 111 N10
Slaidburn Lancs 95 Q10
Slaithwaite Kirk 90 D8
Slaley Derbys 84 C9
Slaley Nthumb 112 E9
Slamannan Falk 126 F3
Slapton Bucks 49 P10
Slapton Devon 7 L9
Slapton Nhants 48 H5
Slattocks Rochdl 89 P9
Slaugham W Susx 24 G5
Slaughterford Wilts 32 F10
Slawston Leics 60 G2
Sleaford Hants 23 M7
Sleaford Lincs 86 E11
Sleagill Cumb 101 Q7
Sleap Shrops 69 N9
Sleapford Wrekin 70 A11
Sleapshyde Herts 50 E9
Sleasdairidh Highld 162 E7
Slebech Pembks 41 K7
Sledge Green Worcs 46 F8
Sledmere E R Yk 99 J8
Sleetbeck Cumb 111 K5
Sleight Dorset 12 G5
Sleightholme Dur 103 J8
Sleights N York 105 N9
Slepe Dorset 12 F6
Slickly Highld 167 N3
Sliddery N Ayrs 120 H7
Sligachan Highld 144 G2
Sligrachan Ag & B 131 P9
Slimbridge Gloucs 32 D4
Slimbridge Wetland Centre Gloucs 32 D3
Slindon Staffs 70 E8
Slindon W Susx 15 Q5
Slinfold W Susx 24 D4
Sling Gwynd 79 L11
Slingsby N York 98 D6
Slip End C Beds 50 C7
Slip End Herts 50 G3
Slipton Nhants 61 L5
Slitting Mill Staffs 71 J11
Slockavullin Ag & B 130 G8
Sloley Norfk 77 K7
Sloncombe Devon 8 H7
Sloothby Lincs 87 N6
Slough Slough 35 Q9
Slough Crematorium Bucks 35 Q8
Slough Green Somset 19 J11
Slough Green W Susx 24 G5
Slumbay Highld 154 A10
Slyfield Green Surrey 23 Q4
Slyne Lancs 95 K7
Smailholm Border 118 B3
Smallbridge Rochdl 89 Q7
Smallbrook Devon 9 L5
Smallbrook Gloucs 31 Q4
Smallburgh Norfk 77 L7
Smalldale Derbys 83 N9
Smalldale Derbys 83 Q8
Small Dole W Susx 24 F8
Smalley Derbys 72 C2
Smalley Common Derbys 72 C2
Smalley Green Derbys 72 C2
Smallfield Surrey 24 H2
Small Heath Birm 58 H7
Small Hythe Kent 26 E5
Smallridge Devon 10 G4
Smallthorne C Stke 70 F4
Smallways N York 103 M8
Smallwood Ches E 70 E2
Small Wood Hey Lancs 94 H11
Smallworth Norfk 64 E5
Smannell Hants 22 C5
Smardale Cumb 102 D9
Smarden Kent 26 E3
Smarden Bell Kent 26 E3
Smart's Hill Kent 25 M2
Smeafield Nthumb 119 L3
Smearisary Highld 138 A2
Smeatharpe Devon 10 D2
Smeeth Kent 27 J4
Smeeton Westerby Leics 60 E2
Smelthouses N York 97 J8
Smerral Highld 167 L10
Smestow Staffs 58 C6
Smethwick Sandw 58 F7
Smethwick Green Ches E 70 E2
Smisby Derbys 72 A7
Smitheclose IoW 14 F8
Smith End Green Worcs 46 E4
Smithfield Cumb 110 H7
Smith Green Lancs 95 K9
Smithies Barns 91 K9
Smithincott Devon 9 Q2
Smith's End Herts 51 K3
Smith's Green Essex 51 N6
Smith's Green Essex 51 Q2
Smithstown Highld 160 B11
Smithton Highld 156 C8
Smithy Bridge Rochdl 89 Q7
Smithy Green Ches E 82 F10
Smithy Green Stockp 83 J7
Smithy Houses Derbys 84 E11
Smockington Leics 59 Q7
Smoo Highld 165 K3
Smythe's Green Essex 52 F8
Snade D & G 108 H3
Snailbeach Shrops 56 F4
Snailwell Cambs 63 K7
Snainton N York 99 J4
Snaith E R Yk 91 Q6
Snake Pass Inn Derbys 83 P6
Snape N York 97 L4
Snape Suffk 65 M10
Snape Green Lancs 88 D8
Snape Street Suffk 65 M10
Snaresbrook Gt Lon 37 K3
Snarestone Leics 72 A9
Snarford Lincs 86 D4
Snargate Kent 26 G6
Snave Kent 26 H6
Sneachill Worcs 46 H4
Snead Powys 56 E6
Sneath Common Norfk 64 H4
Sneaton N York 105 N9
Sneatonthorpe N York 105 P9
Snelland Lincs 86 E4
Snelson Ches E 82 H10
Snelston Derbys 71 M6
Snetterton Norfk 64 D3
Snettisham Norfk 75 N4
Snibston Leics 72 C8
Snig's End Gloucs 46 E9
Snitter Nthumb 119 K10
Snitterby Lincs 86 C2
Snitterfield Warwks 47 P3
Snitterton Derbys 84 C8
Snitton Shrops 57 K9
Snoadhill Kent 26 F3
Snodhill Herefs 45 L6
Snodland Kent 38 B9
Snoll Hatch Kent 37 Q11
Snowden Hill Barns 90 H10
Snowdon Gwynd 67 L4
Snowdon Kent 39 M11
Snowdonia National Park 67 Q9
Snow End Herts 51 K4
Snowshill Gloucs 47 L8
Snow Street Norfk 64 F5
Soake Hants 15 J4
Soar Cardif 30 E8
Soar Devon 7 J11
Soar Powys 44 D8
Soay Highld 144 F5
Soberton Hants 22 H11
Soberton Heath Hants 14 H4
Sockbridge Cumb 101 N5
Sockburn Darltn 104 B9
Sodom Denbgs 80 F10
Sodylt Bank Shrops 69 K7
Soham Cambs 63 J6
Soham Cotes Cambs 63 J5
Solas W Isls 168 d10
Solbury Pembks 40 G8
Soldon Devon 16 E9
Soldon Cross Devon 16 E9
Soldridge Hants 23 J7
Sole Street Kent 27 J2
Sole Street Kent 37 Q7
Solihull Solhll 59 J9
Sollers Dilwyn Herefs 45 N3
Sollers Hope Herefs 46 B8
Sollom Lancs 88 F7
Solva Pembks 40 F6
Solwaybank D & G 110 F5
Somerby Leics 73 K8
Somerby Lincs 93 J9
Somercotes Derbys 84 F10
Somerford Dorset 13 L6
Somerford Keynes Gloucs 33 K5
Somerley W Susx 15 M7
Somerleyton Suffk 65 P2
Somersal Herbert Derbys 71 L7
Somersby Lincs 87 K6
Somersham Cambs 62 E5
Somersham Suffk 53 J2
Somerton Oxon 48 E9
Somerton Somset 19 N9
Somerton Suffk 63 P10
Somerwood Shrops 57 K2
Sompting W Susx 24 E9
Sonning Wokham 35 L9
Sonning Common Oxon 35 K8
Sonning Eye Oxon 35 K9
Sontley Wrexhm 69 K5
Sopley Hants 13 L5
Sopworth Wilts 32 F7
Sorbie D & G 107 M8
Sordale Highld 167 K4
Sorisdale Ag & B 136 H3
Sorn E Ayrs 115 L2
Sortat Highld 167 N4
Sotby Lincs 86 H5
Sots Hole Lincs 86 F8
Sotterley Suffk 65 N5
Soughton Flints 81 J11
Soulbury Bucks 49 N9
Soulby Cumb 101 N5
Soulby Cumb 102 D8
Souldern Oxon 48 F8
Souldrop Bed 61 L8
Sound Ches E 70 A5
Sound Muir Moray 157 R7
Soundwell S Glos 32 C9
Sourton Devon 8 D6
Soutergate Cumb 94 E4
South Acre Norfk 75 R8
South Alkham Kent 27 M3
Southall Gt Lon 36 D5
South Allington Devon 7 K11
South Alloa Falk 133 P9
Southam Gloucs 47 J9
Southam Warwks 48 D2
South Ambersham W Susx 23 P10
Southampton C Sotn 14 D4
Southampton Airport Hants 22 E11
Southampton Crematorium Hants 22 D11
South Anston Rothm 84 H4
South Ascot W & M 35 P11
South Ashford Kent 26 H3
South Baddesley Hants 14 C7
South Ballachulish Highld 139 K6
South Bank C York 98 B10
South Bank R & Cl 104 F6
South Barrow Somset 20 B9
South Beddington Gt Lon 36 G8
South Beer Cnwll 5 N3
South Benfleet Essex 38 C4
South Bersted W Susx 15 P6
South Bockhampton Dorset 13 L5
Southborough Gt Lon 37 K7
Southborough Kent 25 N2
Southbourne Bmouth 13 K6
Southbourne W Susx 15 L5
South Bowood Dorset 11 J5
South Bramwith Donc 91 Q8
South Brent Devon 6 H6
South Brewham Somset 20 D7
South Bristol Crematorium Bristl 31 Q11
South Broomhill Nthumb 119 P11
Southburgh Norfk 76 E10
South Burlingham Norfk 77 M10
Southburn E R Yk 99 K10
South Cadbury Somset 20 B9
South Carlton Lincs 86 B5
South Carlton Notts 85 J4
South Cave E R Yk 92 F4
South Cerney Gloucs 33 K5
South Chailey E Susx 25 J7
South Chard Somset 10 G3
South Charlton Nthumb 119 N6
South Cheriton Somset 20 C10
South Church Dur 103 P5
Southchurch Sthend 38 F4
South Cleatlam Dur 103 M7
South Cliffe E R Yk 92 E3
South Clifton Notts 85 P6
South Cockerington Lincs 87 L3
South Cornelly Brdgnd 29 M8
Southcott Cnwll 5 K2
Southcott Devon 8 D5
Southcott Devon 9 J8
Southcott Devon 16 G8
Southcott Wilts 21 N3
Southcourt Bucks 35 M2
South Cove Suffk 65 P5
South Creake Norfk 76 B4
South Crosland Kirk 90 E8
South Croxton Leics 72 H8
South Dalton E R Yk 99 K11
South Darenth Kent 37 N7
South Downs National Park 25 J9
South Duffield N York 92 A4
Southease E Susx 25 K9
South Elkington Lincs 87 J3
South Elmsall Wakefd 91 M8
Southend Ag & B 120 C10
South End E R Yk 93 Q7
South End Hants 21 M11
South End Herefs 46 D6
South End N Linc 93 K6
South End Norfk 64 D3
Southend Wilts 33 N10
Southend Airport Essex 38 E4
Southend Crematorium Sthend 38 E4
Southend-on-Sea Sthend 38 E4
Southernby Cumb 101 L3
Southernden Kent 26 E2
Southerndown V Glam 29 N10
Southerness D & G 109 L10
South Erradale Highld 153 N3
Southerton Devon 10 B6
Southery Norfk 63 K2
South Essex Crematorium Gt Lon 37 N3
South Fambridge Essex 38 E3
South Fawley W Berk 34 C8
South Ferriby N Linc 92 G6
South Field E R Yk 92 H5
Southfield Falk 126 E3
Southfleet Kent 37 P6
Southford IoW 14 F11
Southgate Gt Lon 36 G2
Southgate Norfk 75 N4
Southgate Norfk 76 B4
Southgate Norfk 76 G7
Southgate Swans 28 G7
South Godstone Surrey 37 J11
South Gorley Hants 13 L2
South Gosforth N u Ty 113 K7
South Green Essex 37 Q2
South Green Essex 52 H8
South Green Kent 38 E9
South Green Norfk 76 F9
South Green Suffk 64 H6
South Gyle C Edin 127 M3
South Hanningfield Essex 38 B2
South Harting W Susx 23 L11
South Hayling Hants 15 K7
South Hazelrigg Nthumb 119 L4
South Heath Bucks 35 P4
South Heighton E Susx 25 K10
South Hetton Dur 113 N11
South Hiendley Wakefd 91 K8
South Hill Cnwll 5 N7
South Hill Somset 19 N9
South Hinksey Oxon 34 F4
South Hole Devon 16 C7
South Holmwood Surrey 24 E2
South Hornchurch Gt Lon 37 M4
South Horrington Somset 19 Q5
South Huish Devon 6 H10
South Hykeham Lincs 86 B8
South Hylton Sundld 113 N9
Southill C Beds 50 E2
Southington Hants 22 F5
South Kelsey Lincs 92 H11
South Kessock Highld 156 B8
South Killingholme N Linc 93 K7
South Kilvington N York 97 P4
South Kilworth Leics 60 D4
South Kirkby Wakefd 91 L8
South Knighton Devon 7 L4
South Kyme Lincs 86 G11
South Lanarkshire Crematorium S Lans 126 B6
Southleigh Devon 10 E6
South Leigh Oxon 34 C3
South Leverton Notts 85 N4
South Littleton Worcs 47 L5
South London Crematorium Gt Lon 36 G7
South Lopham Norfk 64 E5
South Luffenham Rutlnd 73 N10
South Malling E Susx 25 K8
South Marston Swindn 33 N7
South Merstham Surrey 36 G10
South Middleton Nthumb 119 J6
South Milford N York 91 M4
South Milton Devon 6 J10
South Mimms Herts 50 F10
South Mimms Services Herts 50 F10
Southminster Essex 38 G2
South Molton Devon 17 N6
South Moor Dur 113 J10
Southmoor Oxon 34 C5
South Moreton Oxon 34 G7
Southmuir Angus 142 F7
South Mundham W Susx 15 N6
South Muskham Notts 85 N9
South Newbald E R Yk 92 F3
South Newington Oxon 48 D8
South Newton Wilts 21 L8
South Normanton Derbys 84 F9
South Norwood Gt Lon 36 H7
South Nutfield Surrey 36 H11
South Ockendon Thurr 37 N4
Southoe Cambs 61 Q8
Southolt Suffk 64 H8
South Ormsby Lincs 87 L5
Southorpe C Pete 74 A10
South Ossett Wakefd 90 H7
South Otterington N York 97 N3
Southover Dorset 11 N6
Southover E Susx 25 Q5
South Owersby Lincs 86 E2
Southowram Calder 90 E6
South Park Surrey 36 F11
South Perrott Dorset 11 K3
South Petherton Somset 19 M11
South Petherwin Cnwll 5 N5
South Pickenham Norfk 76 B11
South Pill Cnwll 5 Q10
South Pool Devon 7 K10
South Poorton Dorset 11 L5
Southport Sefton 88 C7
Southport Crematorium Lancs 88 D8
South Queensferry C Edin 127 L2
South Radworthy Devon 17 N5
South Rauceby Lincs 86 D11
South Raynham Norfk 76 B7
South Reddish Stockp 83 J6
Southrepps Norfk 77 K4
South Reston Lincs 87 M4
Southrey Lincs 86 F7
South Ronaldsay Ork 169 d8
Southrop Gloucs 33 N4
Southrope Hants 23 J6
South Runcton Norfk 75 M9
South Scarle Notts 85 P8
Southsea C Port 15 J7
Southsea Wrexhm 69 K4
South Shian Ag & B 138 G9
South Shields S Tyne 113 N7
South Shields Crematorium S Tyne 113 M8
South Shore Bpool 88 C4
Southside Dur 103 M5
South Somercotes Lincs 87 M2
South Stainley N York 97 M8
South Stifford Thurr 37 N5
South Stoke BaNES 20 D2
South Stoke Oxon 34 G8
South Stoke W Susx 24 B9
South Stour Kent 26 H4
South Street Kent 37 P8
South Street Kent 39 J10
South Street Kent 39 K8
South Tarbrax S Lans 127 J7
South Tawton Devon 8 G6
South Tehidy Cnwll 2 H5
South Thoresby Lincs 87 M5
South Thorpe Dur 103 M8
South Town Hants 23 J7
Southtown Norfk 77 Q10
Southtown Somset 19 K11
South Uist W Isls 168 d14
Southwaite Cumb 110 H11
Southwaite Services Cumb 110 H11
South Walsham Norfk 77 M9
Southwark Gt Lon 36 H5
South Warnborough Hants 23 K5
Southwater W Susx 24 E5
Southwater Street W Susx 24 D5
Southway Somset 19 P6
South Weald Essex 37 N2
Southwell Dorset 11 P10
Southwell Notts 85 L10
South West Middlesex Crematorium Gt Lon 36 D6
South Weston Oxon 35 K5
South Wheatley Cnwll 5 L3
Southwick Hants 14 H5
Southwick Nhants 61 M2
Southwick Somset 19 L5
Southwick Sundld 113 N9
Southwick W Susx 24 F9
Southwick Wilts 20 F3
South Widcombe BaNES 19 Q3
South Wigston Leics 72 F11
South Willesborough Kent 26 H3
South Willingham Lincs 86 G4
South Wingate Dur 104 D4

300 South Wingfield - Stonegate

South Wingfield Derbys 84 E9
South Witham Lincs 73 N7
Southwold Suffk 65 Q6
South Wonston Hants 22 E7
Southwood Norfk 77 M10
Southwood Somset 19 Q8
South Woodham Ferrers Essex 38 D2
South Wootton Norfk 75 M6
South Wraxall Wilts 20 F2
South Zeal Devon 8 G6
Sowerby Calder 90 C6
Sowerby N York 97 P4
Sowerby Bridge Calder 90 D6
Sowerby Row Cumb 101 L2
Sower Carr Lancs 88 D2
Sowerhill Somset 18 A10
Sowhill Torfn 31 J4
Sowley Green Suffk 63 M10
Sowood Calder 90 D7
Sowton Devon 6 E5
Sowton Devon 9 N6
Soyland Town Calder 90 C6
Spa Common Norfk 77 K5
Spain's End Essex 51 Q3
Spalding Lincs 74 D6
Spaldington E R Yk 92 C4
Spaldwick Cambs 61 P6
Spalford Notts 85 P7
Spanby Lincs 74 A3
Spanish Green Hants 23 J3
Sparham Norfk 76 F8
Sparhamill Norfk 76 F8
Spark Bridge Cumb 94 G4
Sparket Cumb 101 M5
Sparkford Somset 20 B9
Sparkhill Birm 58 H8
Sparkwell Devon 6 F7
Sparrow Green Norfk 76 C9
Sparrowpit Derbys 83 N8
Sparrows Green E Susx 25 P4
Sparsholt Hants 22 D8
Sparsholt Oxon 34 B7
Spartylea Nthumb 112 C11
Spath Staffs 71 K7
Spaunton N York 98 E3
Spaxton Somset 18 H7
Spean Bridge Highld 146 G11
Spear Hill W Susx 24 D7
Spearywell Hants 22 B9
Speen Bucks 35 M5
Speen W Berk 34 E11
Speeton N York 99 P6
Speke Lpool 81 N8
Speldhurst Kent 25 N2
Spellbrook Herts 51 L7
Spelmonden Kent 26 B4
Spelsbury Oxon 48 B10
Spen Kirk 90 F5
Spencers Wood Wokham 35 K11
Spen Green Ches E 70 E2
Spennithorne N York 96 H3
Spennymoor Dur 103 Q4
Spernall Warwks 47 L2
Spetchley Worcs 46 G4
Spetisbury Dorset 12 F4
Spexhall Suffk 65 M5
Spey Bay Moray 157 R4
Speybridge Highld 149 J2
Speyview Moray 157 P9
Spilsby Lincs 87 M7
Spindlestone Nthumb 119 N4
Spinkhill Derbys 84 G5
Spinningdale Highld 162 F9
Spion Kop Notts 85 J7
Spirthill Wilts 33 J9
Spital Wirral 81 L8
Spital Hill Donc 85 K2
Spital in the Street Lincs 86 C2
Spithurst E Susx 25 K7
Spittal E Loth 128 D4
Spittal E R Yk 98 F10
Spittal Highld 167 L6
Spittal Nthumb 129 Q9
Spittal Pembks 41 J6
Spittalfield P & K 141 R9
Spittal of Glenmuick Abers 149 Q10
Spittal of Glenshee P & K 141 R4
Spittal-on-Rule Border 118 A7
Spixworth Norfk 77 J8
Splatt Cnwll 4 E6
Splatt Cnwll 5 L4
Splatt Devon 8 F3
Splayne's Green E Susx 25 K6
Splottlands Cardif 30 H9
Spofforth N York 97 N10
Spondon C Derb 72 C3
Spon Green Flints 69 J2
Spooner Row Norfk 64 F2
Sporle Norfk 76 A9
Spott E Loth 128 H4
Spottiswoode Border 128 G10
Spratton Nhants 60 F7
Spreakley Surrey 23 M6
Spreyton Devon 8 G5
Spriddlestone Devon 6 E8
Spridlington Lincs 86 D4
Springburn C Glas 125 Q4
Springfield D & G 110 F7
Springfield Essex 52 B10
Springfield Fife 135 J5
Springhill Staffs 58 E4
Springhill Staffs 58 G3
Springholm D & G 108 H6
Springside N Ayrs 125 K10
Springthorpe Lincs 85 Q3
Spring Vale Barns 90 H10
Springwell Sundld 113 L9
Springwood Crematorium Lpool 81 N7
Sproatley E R Yk 93 L4
Sproston Green Ches W 82 F11
Sprotbrough Donc 91 N10
Sproughton Suffk 53 K3
Sprouston Border 118 E3
Sprowston Norfk 77 K9
Sproxton Leics 73 M6
Sproxton N York 98 C4
Spunhill Shrops 69 M8
Spurstow Ches E 69 Q3
Spyway Dorset 11 L6
Square & Compass Pembks 40 F4
Stableford Shrops 57 P5
Stableford Staffs 70 E7
Stacey Bank Sheff 84 C2
Stackhouse N York 96 B7
Stackpole Pembks 41 J11
Stacksford Norfk 64 F3
Stacksteads Lancs 89 P6
Staddiscombe C Plym 6 E8
Staddlethorpe E R Yk 92 D5
Staden Derbys 83 N10
Stadhampton Oxon 34 H5
Stadhlaigearraidh W Isls 168 c14
Staffield Cumb 101 P2
Staffin Highld 152 H4
Stafford Staffs 70 G10
Stafford Crematorium Staffs 70 H10
Stafford Services (Northbound) Staffs 70 F8
Stafford Services (Southbound) Staffs 70 F8
Stagsden Bed 49 Q5
Stainborough Barns 91 J10
Stainburn Cumb 100 D5
Stainburn N York 97 L11
Stainby Lincs 73 N6
Staincross Barns 91 J8
Staindrop Dur 103 M6
Staines-upon-Thames Surrey 36 B6
Stainfield Lincs 74 A6
Stainfield Lincs 86 F6
Stainforth Donc 91 Q8
Stainforth N York 96 B7
Staining Lancs 88 C3
Stainland Calder 90 D7
Stainsacre N York 105 P9
Stainsby Derbys 84 G7
Stainton Cumb 95 L3
Stainton Cumb 101 N5
Stainton Cumb 110 G9
Stainton Donc 85 J2
Stainton Dur 103 L7
Stainton Middsb 104 E8
Stainton N York 103 M11
Stainton by Langworth Lincs 86 E5
Staintondale N York 105 Q11
Stainton le Vale Lincs 86 G2
Stainton with Adgarley Cumb 94 E6
Stair Cumb 100 H6
Stair E Ayrs 114 H3
Stairfoot Barns 91 K9
Stairhaven D & G 106 H7
Staithes N York 105 L7
Stakeford Nthumb 113 L3
Stake Pool Lancs 95 J11
Stakes Hants 15 J5
Stalbridge Dorset 20 D11
Stalbridge Weston Dorset 20 D11
Stalham Norfk 77 M6
Stalham Green Norfk 77 M7
Stalisfield Green Kent 38 G11
Stalland Common Norfk 64 E2
Stallen Dorset 20 B11
Stallingborough NE Lin 93 L8
Stalling Busk N York 96 D3
Stallington Staffs 70 G7
Stalmine Lancs 94 H11
Stalmine Moss Side Lancs 94 H11
Stalybridge Tamesd 83 L5
Stambourne Essex 52 B4
Stambourne Green Essex 51 Q3
Stamford Lincs 73 Q9
Stamford Nthumb 119 P7
Stamford Bridge Ches W 81 P11
Stamford Bridge E R Yk 98 E9
Stamfordham Nthumb 112 G6
Stamford Hill Gt Lon 36 H3
Stanah Lancs 88 D2
Stanborough Herts 50 F8
Stanbridge C Beds 49 Q10
Stanbridge Dorset 12 H4
Stanbury C Brad 90 C3
Stand Bury 89 M9
Stand N Lans 126 D4
Standburn Falk 126 G3
Standeford Staffs 58 D3
Standen Kent 26 E3
Standen Street Kent 26 D5
Standerwick Somset 20 F4
Standford Hants 23 M8
Standingstone Cumb 100 E4
Standish Gloucs 32 E3
Standish Wigan 88 H8
Standish Lower Ground Wigan 88 H9
Standlake Oxon 34 C4
Standon Hants 22 D9
Standon Herts 51 J6
Standon Staffs 70 E7
Standon Green End Herts 51 J7
Standwell Green Suffk 64 G8
Stane N Lans 126 F6
Stanfield Norfk 76 C7
Stanford C Beds 50 E2
Stanford Kent 27 K4
Stanford Shrops 56 E2
Stanford Bishop Herefs 46 C4
Stanford Bridge Worcs 57 N11
Stanford Bridge Wrekin 70 C10
Stanford Dingley W Berk 34 G10
Stanford in the Vale Oxon 34 B6
Stanford le Hope Thurr 37 Q4
Stanford on Avon Nhants 60 C5
Stanford on Soar Notts 72 E6
Stanford on Teme Worcs 57 N11
Stanford Rivers Essex 51 M10
Stanfree Derbys 84 G6
Stanghow R & Cl 105 J7
Stanground C Pete 74 D11
Stanhill Lancs 89 L5
Stanhoe Norfk 75 R3
Stanhope Border 116 G5
Stanhope Dur 103 J3
Stanhope Kent 26 H3
Stanhope Bretby Derbys 71 P10
Stanion Nhants 61 K3
Stanklin Worcs 58 C10
Stanley Derbys 72 C2
Stanley Dur 113 J10
Stanley Notts 84 G8
Stanley P & K 141 R11
Stanley Shrops 57 N8
Stanley Staffs 70 G4
Stanley Wakefd 91 J6
Stanley Common Derbys 72 C2
Stanley Crook Dur 103 N3
Stanley Ferry Wakefd 91 K6
Stanley Gate Lancs 88 E9
Stanley Moor Staffs 70 G4
Stanley Pontlarge Gloucs 47 K8
Stanmer Br & H 24 H9
Stanmore Gt Lon 36 E2
Stanmore Hants 22 E9
Stanmore W Berk 34 E9
Stannersburn Nthumb 111 P3
Stanningfield Suffk 64 B10
Stanningley Leeds 90 G4
Stannington Nthumb 113 K5
Stannington Sheff 84 C3
Stannington Station Nthumb 113 K4
Stansbatch Herefs 45 L2
Stansfield Suffk 63 N10
Stanshope Staffs 71 L4
Stanstead Suffk 52 D2
Stanstead Abbotts Herts 51 J8
Stansted Kent 37 P8
Stansted Airport Essex 51 M6
Stansted Mountfitchet Essex 51 M5
Stanton Derbys 71 P11
Stanton Gloucs 47 L8
Stanton Mons 45 L10
Stanton Nthumb 112 H2
Stanton Staffs 71 L5
Stanton Suffk 64 D7
Stanton by Bridge Derbys 72 B5
Stanton by Dale Derbys 72 D3
Stanton Drew BaNES 19 Q2
Stanton Fitzwarren Swindn 33 N6
Stanton Harcourt Oxon 34 D3
Stanton Hill Notts 84 G8
Stanton in Peak Derbys 84 B8
Stanton Lacy Shrops 56 H9
Stanton Lees Derbys 84 C8
Stanton Long Shrops 57 K6
Stanton on the Wolds Notts 72 G4
Stanton Prior BaNES 20 C2
Stanton St Bernard Wilts 21 L2
Stanton St John Oxon 34 G3
Stanton St Quintin Wilts 32 H9
Stanton Street Suffk 64 D8
Stanton under Bardon Leics 72 D8
Stanton upon Hine Heath Shrops 69 Q10
Stanton Wick BaNES 20 B2
Stantway Gloucs 32 D2
Stanwardine in the Field Shrops 69 M10
Stanwardine in the Wood Shrops 69 M9
Stanway Essex 52 F7
Stanway Gloucs 47 L8
Stanway Green Essex 52 G7
Stanway Green Suffk 65 J7
Stanwell Surrey 36 C6
Stanwell Moor Surrey 36 B6
Stanwick Nhants 61 L6
Stanwix Cumb 110 H9
Staoinebrig W Isls 168 c14
Stape N York 98 F2
Stapehill Dorset 13 J4
Stapeley Ches E 70 B5
Stapenhill Staffs 71 P10
Staple Kent 39 N10
Staple Cross Devon 18 D10
Staplecross E Susx 26 C7
Staplefield W Susx 24 G5
Staple Fitzpaine Somset 19 J11
Stapleford Cambs 62 G10
Stapleford Herts 50 H7
Stapleford Leics 73 L7
Stapleford Lincs 85 Q9
Stapleford Notts 72 D3
Stapleford Wilts 21 L7
Stapleford Abbotts Essex 37 M2
Stapleford Tawney Essex 51 M11
Staplegrove Somset 18 H9
Staplehay Somset 18 H10
Staple Hill Worcs 58 E10
Staplehurst Kent 26 C3
Staplers IoW 14 F9
Staplestreet Kent 39 J9
Stapleton Cumb 111 K6
Stapleton Herefs 56 E11
Stapleton Leics 72 C11
Stapleton N York 103 Q8
Stapleton Shrops 56 H4
Stapleton Somset 19 N10
Stapley Somset 10 D2
Staploe Bed 61 Q8
Staplow Herefs 46 C6
Star Fife 135 J7
Star Pembks 41 P4
Star Somset 19 M3
Starbeck N York 97 M9
Starbotton N York 96 E6
Starcross Devon 9 N8
Stareton Warwks 59 M10
Starkholmes Derbys 84 D9
Starlings Green Essex 51 L4
Starr's Green E Susx 26 C8
Starston Norfk 65 J5
Start Devon 7 L10
Startforth Dur 103 K7
Startley Wilts 32 H8
Statenborough Kent 39 P10
Statham Warrtn 82 E7
Stathe Somset 19 L9
Stathern Leics 73 K4
Station Town Dur 104 D3
Staughton Green Cambs 61 P7
Staughton Highway Cambs 61 P8
Staunton Gloucs 31 Q2
Staunton Gloucs 46 E9
Staunton in the Vale Notts 73 L2
Staunton on Arrow Herefs 45 M2
Staunton on Wye Herefs 45 M6
Staveley Cumb 94 H3
Staveley Cumb 101 N11
Staveley Derbys 84 F6
Staveley N York 97 N8
Staverton Devon 7 K6
Staverton Gloucs 46 G10
Staverton Nhants 60 B8
Staverton Wilts 20 G2
Staverton Bridge Gloucs 46 G10
Stawell Somset 19 L7
Stawley Somset 18 E10
Staxigoe Highld 167 Q6
Staxton N York 99 L5
Staylittle Cerdgn 54 E7
Staylittle Powys 55 K6
Staynall Lancs 88 D2
Staythorpe Notts 85 N10
Stead C Brad 96 H11
Stean N York 96 G6
Stearsby N York 98 C6
Steart Somset 19 J5
Stebbing Essex 51 Q6
Stebbing Green Essex 51 Q6
Stechford Birm 58 H7
Stede Quarter Kent 26 E4
Stedham W Susx 23 N10
Steel Nthumb 112 D9
Steel Cross E Susx 25 M4
Steelend Fife 134 C9
Steele Road Border 111 K2
Steel Green Cumb 94 D5
Steel Heath Shrops 69 P7
Steen's Bridge Herefs 45 Q3
Steep Hants 23 K9
Steephill IoW 14 F11
Steep Lane Calder 90 C6
Steeple Dorset 12 F8
Steeple Essex 52 F11
Steeple Ashton Wilts 20 H3
Steeple Aston Oxon 48 E9
Steeple Barton Oxon 48 D10
Steeple Bumpstead Essex 51 Q2
Steeple Claydon Bucks 49 K9
Steeple Gidding Cambs 61 P4
Steeple Langford Wilts 21 K7
Steeple Morden Cambs 50 G2
Steeton C Brad 90 C2
Stein Highld 152 D6
Stella Gatesd 113 J8
Stelling Minnis Kent 27 K2
Stembridge Somset 19 M10
Stenalees Cnwll 4 G10
Stenhouse D & G 115 R9
Stenhousemuir Falk 133 P11
Stenigot Lincs 86 H4
Stenscholl Highld 152 H4
Stenson Fields Derbys 72 A4
Stenton E Loth 128 G5
Steornabhagh W Isls 168 j4
Stepaside Pembks 41 M9
Stepford D & G 109 J4
Stepney Gt Lon 37 J4
Stepping Hill Stockp 83 K7
Steppingley C Beds 50 B3
Stepps N Lans 126 B4
Sternfield Suffk 65 M9
Stert Wilts 21 K3
Stetchworth Cambs 63 K9
Stevenage Herts 50 F5
Steven's Crouch E Susx 26 B8
Stevenston N Ayrs 124 H9
Steventon Hants 22 F5
Steventon Oxon 34 E6
Steventon End Essex 51 N2
Stevington Bed 49 Q4
Stewartby Bed 50 B2
Stewartfield S Lans 125 Q6
Stewarton E Ayrs 125 L8
Stewkley Bucks 49 N9
Stewley Somset 19 K11
Stewton Lincs 87 L3
Steyne Cross IoW 14 H9
Steyning W Susx 24 E8
Steynton Pembks 40 H9
Stibb Cnwll 16 C9
Stibbard Norfk 76 D6
Stibb Cross Devon 16 G9
Stibb Green Wilts 21 P2
Stibbington Cambs 74 A11
Stichill Border 118 D3
Sticker Cnwll 3 P3
Stickford Lincs 87 L8
Sticklepath Devon 8 F6
Sticklepath Somset 18 D7
Stickling Green Essex 51 L4
Stickney Lincs 87 K9
Stiffkey Norfk 76 D3
Stifford's Bridge Herefs 46 D5
Stiff Street Kent 38 E9
Stile Bridge Kent 26 C2
Stileway Somset 19 N6
Stilligarry W Isls 168 c14
Stillingfleet N York 91 P2
Stillington N York 98 B7
Stillington S on T 104 C6
Stilton Cambs 61 Q3
Stinchcombe Gloucs 32 D5
Stinsford Dorset 11 Q6
Stiperstones Shrops 56 F4
Stirchley Birm 58 G8
Stirchley Wrekin 57 M3
Stirling Abers 159 R9
Stirling Stirlg 133 M9
Stirling Castle Stirlg 133 M9
Stirling Services Stirlg 133 N10
Stirtloe Cambs 61 Q7
Stirton N York 96 E10
Stisted Essex 52 D7
Stitchcombe Wilts 33 P11
Stithians Cnwll 3 J6
Stivichall Covtry 59 M9
Stixwould Lincs 86 G7
Stoak Ches W 81 N10
Stobo Border 116 H3
Stoborough Dorset 12 F7
Stoborough Green Dorset 12 F7
Stobs Castle Border 117 Q9
Stobswood Nthumb 119 P11
Stock Essex 51 Q11
Stock N Som 19 N2
Stockbridge Hants 22 C7
Stockbriggs S Lans 126 D10
Stockbury Kent 38 D9
Stockcross W Berk 34 D11
Stockdalewath Cumb 110 G11
Stocker's Hill Kent 38 G11
Stockerston Leics 73 L11
Stock Green Worcs 47 J3
Stocking Herefs 46 B8
Stockingford Warwks 59 M6
Stocking Pelham Herts 51 L5
Stockland Devon 10 E4
Stockland Bristol Somset 18 H6
Stockland Green Kent 25 N2
Stockleigh English Devon 9 L3
Stockleigh Pomeroy Devon 9 L4
Stockley Wilts 33 J11
Stockley Hill Herefs 45 M7
Stocklinch Somset 19 L11
Stockmoor Herefs 45 M4
Stockport Stockp 83 J6
Stockport Crematorium Stockp 83 K7
Stocksbridge Sheff 90 H11
Stocksfield Nthumb 112 G8
Stockton Herefs 45 Q2
Stockton Norfk 65 M3
Stockton Shrops 56 D4
Stockton Shrops 57 N5
Stockton Warwks 48 D2
Stockton Wilts 21 J7
Stockton Wrekin 70 D11
Stockton Brook Staffs 70 G4
Stockton Heath Warrtn 82 D7
Stockton-on-Tees S on T 104 D7
Stockton on Teme Worcs 57 N11
Stockton on the Forest C York 98 D9
Stockwell Gloucs 32 H2
Stockwell End Wolves 58 C4
Stockwell Heath Staffs 71 K10
Stockwood Bristl 32 B11
Stockwood Dorset 11 M3
Stock Wood Worcs 47 K3
Stodday Lancs 95 K9
Stodmarsh Kent 39 M9
Stody Norfk 76 F4
Stoer Highld 164 B11
Stoford Somset 11 M2
Stoford Wilts 21 L7
Stogumber Somset 18 E7
Stogursey Somset 18 H6
Stoke Covtry 59 N9
Stoke Devon 16 C7
Stoke Hants 15 K6
Stoke Hants 22 D4
Stoke Medway 38 D7
Stoke Abbott Dorset 11 K4
Stoke Albany Nhants 60 H3
Stoke Ash Suffk 64 G7
Stoke Bardolph Notts 72 G2
Stoke Bliss Worcs 46 C2
Stoke Bruerne Nhants 49 K5
Stoke by Clare Suffk 52 B3
Stoke-by-Nayland Suffk 52 G4
Stoke Canon Devon 9 M5
Stoke Charity Hants 22 E7
Stoke Climsland Cnwll 5 P7
Stoke Cross Herefs 46 B4
Stoke D'Abernon Surrey 36 D9
Stoke Doyle Nhants 61 M3
Stoke Dry RutInd 73 M11
Stoke Edith Herefs 46 B6
Stoke End Warwks 59 J5
Stoke Farthing Wilts 21 L9
Stoke Ferry Norfk 75 P10
Stoke Fleming Devon 7 M9
Stokeford Dorset 12 E7
Stoke Gabriel Devon 7 M7
Stoke Gifford S Glos 32 B9
Stoke Golding Leics 72 B11
Stoke Goldington M Keyn 49 M5
Stoke Green Bucks 35 Q8
Stokeham Notts 85 N5
Stoke Hammond Bucks 49 N9
Stoke Heath Shrops 70 B9
Stoke Heath Worcs 58 D11
Stoke Holy Cross Norfk 77 J11
Stokeinteignhead Devon 7 N4
Stoke Lacy Herefs 46 B5
Stoke Lyne Oxon 48 G9
Stoke Mandeville Bucks 35 M2
Stokenchurch Bucks 35 L5
Stoke Newington Gt Lon 36 H3
Stokenham Devon 7 L10
Stoke-on-Trent C Stke 70 F5
Stoke Orchard Gloucs 46 H9
Stoke Poges Bucks 35 Q8
Stoke Pound Worcs 58 E11
Stoke Prior Herefs 45 Q3
Stoke Prior Worcs 58 D11
Stoke Rivers Devon 17 L4
Stoke Rochford Lincs 73 N5
Stoke Row Oxon 35 J8
Stoke St Gregory Somset 19 K9
Stoke St Mary Somset 19 J10
Stoke St Michael Somset 20 C5
Stoke St Milborough Shrops 57 K8
Stokesay Shrops 56 G8
Stokesby Norfk 77 N9
Stokesley N York 104 F9
Stoke sub Hamdon Somset 19 N11
Stoke Talmage Oxon 35 J5
Stoke Trister Somset 20 D9
Stoke upon Tern Shrops 70 A9
Stoke-upon-Trent C Stke 70 F5
Stoke Wake Dorset 12 C3
Stoke Wharf Worcs 58 E11
Stolford Somset 18 H5
Stondon Massey Essex 51 N10
Stone Bucks 35 L2
Stone Gloucs 32 C5
Stone Kent 37 N6
Stone Rothm 85 J3
Stone Somset 19 Q8
Stone Staffs 70 G8
Stone Worcs 58 C9
Stonea Cambs 62 G2
Stone Allerton Somset 19 L4
Ston Easton Somset 20 B4
Stonebridge N Som 19 L3
Stonebridge Norfk 64 C3
Stonebridge Warwks 59 K8
Stone Bridge Corner C Pete 74 E10
Stonebroom Derbys 84 F9
Stone Chair Calder 90 E5
Stone Cross E Susx 25 M5
Stone Cross E Susx 25 P10
Stone Cross E Susx 25 P4
Stone Cross Kent 25 M3
Stone Cross Kent 26 H4
Stone Cross Kent 39 P10
Stonecross Green Suffk 63 P9
Stonecrouch Kent 26 B5
Stone-edge-Batch N Som 31 N10
Stoneferry C KuH 93 K4
Stonefield Castle Hotel Ag & B 123 Q5
Stonegate E Susx 25 Q5

Stonegate - Tallington 301

Stonegate N York 105 L9
Stonegrave N York 98 D5
Stonehall Worcs 46 G5
Stonehaugh Nthumb 111 Q5
Stonehaven Abers 151 M10
Stonehenge Wilts 21 M6
Stone Hill Donc 92 A9
Stonehouse C Plym 6 D8
Stone House Cumb 95 R3
Stonehouse Gloucs 32 F3
Stonehouse Nthumb 111 N9
Stonehouse S Lans 126 D8
Stone in Oxney Kent 26 F6
Stoneleigh Warwks 59 M10
Stoneley Green Ches E 69 R4
Stonely Cambs 61 P7
Stoner Hill Hants 23 K9
Stonesby Leics 73 L6
Stonesfield Oxon 48 C11
Stones Green Essex 53 L6
Stone Street Kent 37 N10
Stone Street Suffk 52 G4
Stone Street Suffk 52 H3
Stone Street Suffk 65 M5
Stonestreet Green Kent 27 J4
Stonethwaite Cumb 101 J8
Stonewells Moray 157 P4
Stonewood Kent 37 N6
Stoneybridge W Isls 168 c14
Stoneybridge Worcs 58 D9
Stoneyburn W Loth 126 H5
Stoney Cross Hants 13 N2
Stoneygate C Leic 72 G10
Stoneyhills Essex 38 G2
Stoneykirk D & G 106 E7
Stoney Middleton Derbys 84 B5
Stoney Stanton Leics 59 Q6
Stoney Stoke Somset 20 D8
Stoney Stratton Somset 20 C7
Stoney Stretton Shrops 56 F3
Stoneywood C Aber 151 M5
Stoneywood Falk 133 M11
Stonham Aspal Suffk 64 G10
Stonnall Staffs 58 G4
Stonor Oxon 35 K7
Stonton Wyville Leics 73 J11
Stony Cross Herefs 46 D5
Stony Cross Herefs 57 J11
Stonyford Hants 22 B11
Stony Houghton Derbys 84 G7
Stony Stratford M Keyn 49 L6
Stonywell Staffs 58 G2
Stoodleigh Devon 17 M5
Stoodleigh Devon 18 B11
Stop 24 Services Kent 27 K4
Stopham W Susx 24 B7
Stopsley Luton 50 D6
Stoptide Cnwll 4 E6
Storeton Wirral 81 L8
Storeyard Green Herefs 46 D6
Stornoway W Isls 168 j4
Stornoway Airport W Isls 168 j4
Storridge Herefs 46 E5
Storrington W Susx 24 C8
Storth Cumb 95 K5
Storwood E R Yk 92 B2
Stotfield Moray 157 N3
Stotfold C Beds 50 F3
Stottesdon Shrops 57 M8
Stoughton Leics 72 G10
Stoughton Surrey 23 Q4
Stoughton W Susx 15 M4
Stoulton Worcs 46 H5
Stourbridge Dudley 58 C8
Stourbridge Crematorium Dudley 58 C8
Stourhead Wilts 20 E8
Stourpaine Dorset 12 E3
Stourport-on-Severn Worcs 57 Q10
Stour Provost Dorset 20 E10
Stour Row Dorset 20 F10
Stourton Leeds 91 J4
Stourton Staffs 58 C8
Stourton Warwks 47 Q7
Stourton Wilts 20 E8
Stourton Caundle Dorset 20 D11
Stout Somset 19 M8
Stove Shet 169 r11
Stoven Suffk 65 N5
Stow Border 117 P2
Stow Lincs 85 Q4
Stow Bardolph Norfk 75 M9
Stow Bedon Norfk 64 D2
Stowbridge Norfk 75 M9
Stow-cum-Quy Cambs 62 H8
Stowe Gloucs 31 Q3
Stowe Shrops 56 E10
Stowe by Chartley Staffs 71 J9
Stowehill Nhants 60 D9
Stowell Somset 20 C10
Stowey BaNES 19 Q3
Stowford Devon 8 B5
Stowford Devon 8 B7
Stowford Devon 10 C7
Stowford Devon 17 M3
Stowlangtoft Suffk 64 D8
Stow Longa Cambs 61 P6
Stow Maries Essex 38 D2
Stowmarket Suffk 64 E10
Stow-on-the-Wold Gloucs 47 N9
Stowting Kent 27 K3
Stowting Common Kent 27 K3
Stowupland Suffk 64 F9
Straanruie Highld 148 H4
Strachan Abers 150 H9
Strachur Ag & B 131 M7
Stradbroke Suffk 65 J7
Stradbrook Wilts 20 H4
Stradishall Suffk 63 N10
Stradsett Norfk 75 N9
Stragglethorpe Lincs 86 B10
Stragglethorpe Notts 72 H3
Straight Soley Wilts 34 B10
Straiton Mdloth 127 P4
Straiton S Ayrs 114 G7
Straloch Abers 151 M3
Straloch P & K 141 P5
Stramshall Staffs 71 K7
Strang IoM 80 e6
Strangeways Salfd 82 H5
Strangford Herefs 46 A9
Stranraer D & G 106 E5
Strata Florida Cerdgn 54 G11
Stratfield Mortimer W Berk 23 J2
Stratfield Saye Hants 23 J2
Stratfield Turgis Hants 23 J3
Stratford C Beds 61 Q11
Stratford Gt Lon 37 J4
Stratford St Andrew Suffk 65 M9
Stratford St Mary Suffk 52 H5
Stratford sub Castle Wilts 21 M8
Stratford Tony Wilts 21 L9
Stratford-upon-Avon Warwks 47 P3
Strath Highld 160 B11
Strathan Highld 160 H2
Strathan Highld 165 N4
Strathaven S Lans 126 C9
Strathblane Stirlg 125 P2
Strathcanaird Highld 161 K6
Strathcarron Highld 154 B9
Strathcoil Ag & B 138 B11
Strathdon Abers 150 B5
Strathkinness Fife 135 M4
Strathloanhead W Loth 126 G3
Strathmashie House Highld 147 P9
Strathmiglo Fife 134 G6
Strathpeffer Highld 155 N6
Strathtay P & K 141 M7
Strathwhillan N Ayrs 121 K4
Strathy Highld 166 D4
Strathy Inn Highld 166 D3
Strathyre Stirlg 132 H4
Stratton Cnwll 16 C10
Stratton Dorset 11 P6
Stratton Gloucs 33 K4
Stratton Audley Oxon 48 H9
Stratton-on-the-Fosse Somset 20 C4
Stratton St Margaret Swindn 33 N7
Stratton St Michael Norfk 65 J3
Stratton Strawless Norfk 77 J7
Stream Somset 18 E7
Streat E Susx 25 J7
Streatham Gt Lon 36 H6
Streatley C Beds 50 C5
Streatley W Berk 34 G8
Street Devon 10 D7
Street Lancs 95 L10
Street N York 105 K10
Street Somset 19 N7
Street Ashton Warwks 59 Q8
Street Dinas Shrops 69 K7
Street End E Susx 25 P6
Street End Kent 39 K11
Street End W Susx 15 N7
Street Gate Gatesd 113 K9
Streethay Staffs 58 H2
Street Houses N York 98 A11
Streetlam N York 104 B11
Street Lane Derbys 84 E11
Streetly Wsall 58 G5
Streetly Crematorium Wsall 58 G5
Streetly End Cambs 63 K11
Street on the Fosse Somset 20 B7
Strefford Shrops 56 G7
Strelitz P & K 142 B10
Strelley Notts 72 E2
Strensall C York 98 C8
Strensham Services (northbound) Worcs 46 G6
Strensham Services (southbound) Worcs 46 H6
Stretcholt Somset 19 J6
Strete Devon 7 L9
Stretford Herefs 45 N3
Stretford Herefs 45 Q3
Stretford Traffd 82 G6
Strethall Essex 51 L3
Stretham Cambs 62 H6
Strettington W Susx 15 N5
Stretton Ches W 69 M4
Stretton Derbys 84 E8
Stretton Rutlnd 73 N7
Stretton Staffs 58 C2
Stretton Staffs 71 P9
Stretton Warrtn 82 D8
Stretton en le Field Leics 59 M2
Stretton Grandison Herefs 46 B6
Stretton-on-Dunsmore Warwks 59 P10
Stretton on Fosse Warwks 47 P7
Stretton Sugwas Herefs 45 P6
Stretton under Fosse Warwks 59 Q8
Stretton Westwood Shrops 57 K5
Strichen Abers 159 M6
Strines Stockp 83 L7
Stringston Somset 18 G6
Strixton Nhants 61 K8
Stroat Gloucs 31 Q5
Stroma Highld 167 Q1
Stromeferry Highld 153 R11
Stromness Ork 169 b6
Stronachlachar Stirlg 132 E5
Stronafian Ag & B 131 L11
Stronchrubie Highld 161 L3
Strone Ag & B 131 P11
Strone Highld 146 E11
Strone Highld 147 N2
Stronenaba Highld 146 G11
Stronmilchan Ag & B 131 P2
Stronsay Ork 169 f4
Stronsay Airport Ork 169 f4
Strontian Highld 138 E5
Strood Kent 26 E5
Strood Medway 38 B8
Strood Green Surrey 36 F11
Strood Green W Susx 24 B6
Stroud Gloucs 32 G3
Stroud Hants 23 K10
Stroude Surrey 36 B7
Stroud Green Essex 38 E3
Stroud Green Gloucs 32 F3
Stroxton Lincs 73 N4
Struan Highld 152 E10
Struan P & K 141 K4
Strubby Lincs 87 N4
Strumpshaw Norfk 77 L10
Strutherhill S Lans 126 D8
Struthers Fife 135 K6
Struy Highld 155 M9
Stryd-y-Facsen IoA 78 E8
Stryt-issa Wrexhm 69 J5
Stuartfield Abers 159 N8
Stubbers Green Wsall 58 F4
Stubbington Hants 14 G6
Stubbins Lancs 89 M7
Stubbs Green Norfk 65 K2
Stubhampton Dorset 12 F2
Stubley Derbys 84 D5
Stubshaw Cross Wigan 82 C5
Stubton Lincs 85 Q11
Stuckton Hants 13 L2
Studfold N York 96 B7
Stud Green W & M 35 N9
Studham C Beds 50 B7
Studholme Cumb 110 E9
Studland Dorset 12 H8
Studley Warwks 47 L2
Studley Wilts 33 J10
Studley Common Warwks 47 L2
Studley Roger N York 97 L7
Studley Royal N York 97 L6
Studley Royal Park & Fountains Abbey N York 97 L7
Stuntney Cambs 63 J5
Stunts Green E Susx 25 P8
Sturbridge Staffs 70 E8
Sturgate Lincs 85 Q3
Sturmer Essex 51 Q2
Sturminster Common Dorset 12 C2
Sturminster Marshall Dorset 12 G4
Sturminster Newton Dorset 12 C2
Sturry Kent 39 L9
Sturton N Linc 92 G10
Sturton by Stow Lincs 85 Q4
Sturton le Steeple Notts 85 N4
Stuston Suffk 64 G6
Stutton N York 91 M2
Stutton Suffk 53 L5
Styal Ches E 82 H8
Stydd Lancs 89 K3
Stynie Moray 157 Q5
Styrrup Notts 85 K2
Succoth Ag & B 132 B6
Suckley Worcs 46 D4
Suckley Green Worcs 46 D4
Sudborough Nhants 61 L4
Sudbourne Suffk 65 N11
Sudbrook Lincs 73 P2
Sudbrook Mons 31 P7
Sudbrooke Lincs 86 D5
Sudbury Derbys 71 M8
Sudbury Gt Lon 36 E3
Sudbury Suffk 52 E3
Sudden Rochdl 89 P8
Sudgrove Gloucs 32 H3
Suffield N York 99 K2
Suffield Norfk 77 J5
Sugdon Wrekin 69 R11
Sugnall Staffs 70 D8
Sugwas Pool Herefs 45 P6
Suisnish Highld 145 J4
Sulby IoM 80 e3
Sulgrave Nhants 48 G6
Sulham W Berk 34 H10
Sulhamstead W Berk 34 H11
Sulhamstead Abbots W Berk 34 H11
Sulhamstead Bannister W Berk 34 H11
Sullington W Susx 24 C8
Sullom Shet 169 q6
Sullom Voe Shet 169 r6
Sully V Glam 30 G11
Sumburgh Airport Shet 169 q12
Summerbridge N York 97 K8
Summercourt Cnwll 4 D10
Summerfield Norfk 75 Q3
Summerfield Worcs 58 B10
Summer Heath Bucks 35 K6
Summerhill Pembks 41 N9
Summerhill Staffs 58 G3
Summer Hill Wrexhm 69 K4
Summerhouse Darltn 103 P7
Summerlands Cumb 95 L3
Summerley Derbys 84 E5
Summersdale W Susx 15 N5
Summerseat Bury 89 M8
Summertown Oxon 34 F3
Summit Oldham 89 Q9
Summit Rochdl 89 Q7
Sunbiggin Cumb 102 C9
Sunbury-on-Thames Surrey 36 D7
Sundaywell D & G 108 H4
Sunderland Ag & B 122 B7
Sunderland Cumb 100 G3
Sunderland Lancs 95 J9
Sunderland Sundld 113 N9
Sunderland Bridge Dur 103 Q3
Sunderland Crematorium Sundld 113 N9
Sundhope Border 117 L5
Sundon Park Luton 50 C5
Sundridge Kent 37 L9
Sunk Island E R Yk 93 N7
Sunningdale W & M 35 Q11
Sunninghill W & M 35 P11
Sunningwell Oxon 34 E4
Sunniside Dur 103 M3
Sunniside Gatesd 113 K9
Sunny Brow Dur 103 N4
Sunnyhill C Derb 72 A4
Sunnyhurst Bl w D 89 K6
Sunnylaw Stirlg 133 M8
Sunnymead Oxon 34 F3
Sunton Wilts 21 P4
Surbiton Gt Lon 36 E7
Surfleet Lincs 74 E5
Surfleet Seas End Lincs 74 E5
Surlingham Norfk 77 L10
Surrex Essex 52 E7
Surrey & Sussex Crematorium W Susx 24 G3
Sustead Norfk 76 H4
Susworth Lincs 92 D10
Sutcombe Devon 16 E9
Sutcombemill Devon 16 E9
Suton Norfk 64 F2
Sutterby Lincs 87 L6
Sutterton Lincs 74 E3
Sutton C Beds 62 B11
Sutton C Pete 74 A11
Sutton Cambs 62 F5
Sutton Devon 7 J10
Sutton Devon 8 H4
Sutton Donc 91 P8
Sutton E Susx 25 L11
Sutton Gt Lon 36 G8
Sutton Kent 27 P2
Sutton N York 91 M5
Sutton Norfk 77 M7
Sutton Notts 73 K3
Sutton Oxon 34 D3
Sutton Pembks 40 H7
Sutton Shrops 57 J2
Sutton Shrops 57 N7
Sutton Shrops 69 L9
Sutton Shrops 70 B8
Sutton St Hel 82 B6
Sutton Staffs 70 D10
Sutton Suffk 53 P2
Sutton W Susx 23 Q11
Sutton Abinger Surrey 36 D11
Sutton at Hone Kent 37 N7
Sutton Bassett Nhants 60 G2
Sutton Benger Wilts 32 H9
Sutton Bingham Somset 11 L2
Sutton Bonington Notts 72 E6
Sutton Bridge Lincs 75 J6
Sutton Cheney Leics 72 C10
Sutton Coldfield Birm 58 H5
Sutton Coldfield Crematorium Birm 58 H5
Sutton Courtenay Oxon 34 F6
Sutton Crosses Lincs 74 H6
Sutton cum Lound Notts 85 L4
Sutton Fields Notts 72 D5
Sutton Green Surrey 36 B10
Sutton Green Wrexhm 69 M5
Sutton Howgrave N York 97 M5
Sutton in Ashfield Notts 84 G9
Sutton-in-Craven N York 90 C2
Sutton in the Elms Leics 60 B2
Sutton Lane Ends Ches E 83 K10
Sutton Maddock Shrops 57 N4
Sutton Mallet Somset 19 L7
Sutton Mandeville Wilts 21 J9
Sutton Manor St Hel 81 Q6
Sutton Marsh Herefs 45 R6
Sutton Montis Somset 20 B10
Sutton-on-Hull C KuH 93 K4
Sutton on Sea Lincs 87 P4
Sutton-on-the-Forest N York 98 B8
Sutton on the Hill Derbys 71 N8
Sutton on Trent Notts 85 N7
Sutton Poyntz Dorset 11 Q8
Sutton St Edmund Lincs 74 G8
Sutton St James Lincs 74 G7
Sutton St Nicholas Herefs 45 Q5
Sutton Scotney Hants 22 E7
Sutton Street Kent 38 D10
Sutton-under-Brailes Warwks 48 B7
Sutton-under-Whitestonecliffe N York 97 Q4
Sutton upon Derwent E R Yk 98 E11
Sutton Valence Kent 26 D2
Sutton Veny Wilts 20 H6
Sutton Waldron Dorset 20 G11
Sutton Weaver Ches W 82 B9
Sutton Wick BaNES 19 Q3
Sutton Wick Oxon 34 E6
Swaby Lincs 87 L5
Swadlincote Derbys 71 P11
Swaffham Norfk 75 R9
Swaffham Bulbeck Cambs 63 J8
Swaffham Prior Cambs 63 J8
Swafield Norfk 77 K5
Swainby N York 104 E10
Swainshill Herefs 45 P6
Swainsthorpe Norfk 77 J11
Swainswick BaNES 32 E11
Swalcliffe Oxon 48 C7
Swalecliffe Kent 39 K8
Swallow Lincs 93 L10
Swallow Beck Lincs 86 B7
Swallowcliffe Wilts 21 J9
Swallowfield Wokham 23 K2
Swallow Nest Rothm 84 G3
Swallows Cross Essex 51 P11
Swampton Hants 22 D4
Swanage Dorset 12 H9
Swanbourne Bucks 49 M9
Swanbridge V Glam 30 G11
Swancote Shrops 57 N6
Swan Green Ches W 82 F10
Swanland E R Yk 92 G5
Swanley Kent 37 M7
Swanley Village Kent 37 M7
Swanmore Hants 22 G11
Swannington Leics 72 C7
Swannington Norfk 76 G8
Swanpool Garden Suburb Lincs 86 C7
Swanscombe Kent 37 P6
Swansea Swans 29 J6
Swansea Airport Swans 28 G6
Swansea Crematorium Swans 29 J5
Swansea West Services Swans 28 H5
Swan Street Essex 52 E6
Swanton Abbot Norfk 77 K6
Swanton Morley Norfk 76 E8
Swanton Novers Norfk 76 E5
Swanton Street Kent 38 E10
Swan Village Sandw 58 E6
Swanwick Derbys 84 F10
Swanwick Hants 14 F5
Swanwick Crematorium Derbys 84 F10
Swarby Lincs 73 Q2
Swardeston Norfk 77 J11
Swarkestone Derbys 72 B5
Swarland Nthumb 119 N10
Swarraton Hants 22 G7
Swartha C Brad 96 G11
Swarthmoor Cumb 94 F5
Swaton Lincs 74 B3
Swavesey Cambs 62 E7
Sway Hants 13 N5
Swayfield Lincs 73 P6
Swaythling C Soth 22 D11
Sweet Green Worcs 46 B2
Sweetham Devon 9 L5
Sweethaws E Susx 25 M5
Sweetlands Corner Kent 26 C2
Sweets Cnwll 5 K2
Sweetshouse Cnwll 4 H9
Swefling Suffk 65 L9
Swepstone Leics 72 B8
Swerford Oxon 48 C8
Swettenham Ches E 82 H11
Swffryd Blae G 30 H5
Swift's Green Kent 26 E3
Swilland Suffk 64 H11
Swillbrook Lancs 88 F4
Swillington Leeds 91 K4
Swimbridge Devon 17 L5
Swimbridge Newland Devon 17 L5
Swinbrook Oxon 33 Q2
Swincliffe Kirk 90 G5
Swincliffe N York 97 K9
Swincombe Devon 17 M3
Swinden N York 96 C10
Swinderby Lincs 85 Q8
Swindon Gloucs 46 H9
Swindon Nthumb 119 J11
Swindon Staffs 58 C6
Swindon Swindn 33 M8
Swine E R Yk 93 K3
Swinefleet E R Yk 92 C6
Swineford S Glos 32 C11
Swineshead Bed 61 N7
Swineshead Lincs 74 D2
Swineshead Bridge Lincs 74 D2
Swiney Highld 167 M9
Swinford Leics 60 C5
Swinford Oxon 34 D3
Swingfield Minnis Kent 27 M3
Swingfield Street Kent 27 M3
Swingleton Green Suffk 52 G2
Swinhoe Nthumb 119 P5
Swinhope Lincs 93 M11
Swinithwaite N York 96 F3
Swinmore Common Herefs 46 C6
Swinscoe Staffs 71 L5
Swinside Cumb 100 H6
Swinstead Lincs 73 Q6
Swinthorpe Lincs 86 E4
Swinton Border 129 L10
Swinton N York 97 K5
Swinton N York 98 F6
Swinton Rothm 91 M11
Swinton Salfd 82 G4
Swithland Leics 72 F8
Swordale Highld 155 Q4
Swordland Highld 145 N9
Swordly Highld 166 B4
Sworton Heath Ches E 82 E8
Swyddffynnon Cerdgn 54 F11
Swyncombe Oxon 35 J6
Swynnerton Staffs 70 F7
Swyre Dorset 11 L7
Sycharth Powys 68 H9
Sychnant Powys 55 M9
Sychtyn Powys 55 M3
Sydallt Wrexhm 69 K3
Syde Gloucs 33 J2
Sydenham Gt Lon 37 J6
Sydenham Oxon 35 K4
Sydenham Damerel Devon 5 Q6
Sydenhurst Surrey 23 Q8
Syderstone Norfk 76 A5
Sydling St Nicholas Dorset 11 N5
Sydmonton Hants 22 E3
Sydnal Lane Shrops 57 Q3
Syerston Notts 85 M11
Syke Rochdl 89 P7
Sykehouse Donc 91 Q7
Syleham Suffk 65 J6
Sylen Carmth 28 F3
Symbister Shet 169 s7
Symington S Ayrs 125 K11
Symington S Lans 116 D3
Symondsbury Dorset 11 J6
Symonds Yat Herefs 45 R11
Sympson Green C Brad 90 F3
Synderford Dorset 10 H4
Synod Inn Cerdgn 42 H4
Syre Highld 165 Q8
Syreford Gloucs 47 K10
Syresham Nhants 48 H6
Syston Leics 72 G8
Syston Lincs 73 N2
Sytchampton Worcs 58 B11
Sywell Nhants 60 H7

T

Tabley Hill Ches E 82 F9
Tackley Oxon 48 E11
Tacolneston Norfk 64 G2
Tadcaster N York 91 M2
Taddington Derbys 83 P10
Taddington Gloucs 47 L8
Taddiport Devon 16 H8
Tadley Hants 22 H2
Tadlow Cambs 62 C11
Tadmarton Oxon 48 C7
Tadwick BaNES 32 D10
Tadworth Surrey 36 F9
Tafarnaubach Blae G 30 F2
Tafarn-y-bwlch Pembks 41 L4
Tafarn-y-Gelyn Denbgs 68 G2
Taff's Well Rhondd 30 F8
Tafolwern Powys 55 K4
Taibach Neath 29 L7
Tain Highld 162 H10
Tain Highld 167 M3
Tai'n Lôn Gwynd 66 G4
Tairbeart W Isls 168 g7
Tai'r Bull Powys 44 D9
Takeley Essex 51 N6
Takeley Street Essex 51 M6
Talachddu Powys 44 F8
Talacre Flints 80 G8
Talaton Devon 9 Q5
Talbenny Pembks 40 F8
Talbot Green Rhondd 30 D8
Talbot Village Bmouth 13 J6
Taleford Devon 10 B5
Talerddig Powys 55 L4
Talgarreg Cerdgn 42 H4
Talgarth Powys 44 H8
Talisker Highld 152 E11
Talke Staffs 70 E4
Talke Pits Staffs 70 E4
Talkin Cumb 111 L9
Talladale Highld 154 B3
Talla Linnfoots Border 116 G6
Tallaminnock S Ayrs 114 H8
Tallarn Green Wrexhm 69 M6
Tallentire Cumb 100 F3
Talley Carmth 43 M8
Tallington Lincs 74 A9

302 Tallwrn - Tidbury Green

Tallwrn Wrexhm 69 J5
Talmine Highld 165 N4
Talog Carmth 42 F9
Talsarn Cerdgn 43 K3
Talsarnau Gwynd 67 L7
Talskiddy Cnwll 4 E8
Talwrn IoA 78 H9
Talwrn Wrexhm 69 L5
Tal-y-bont Cerdgn 54 F7
Tal-y-Bont Conwy 79 P11
Tal-y-bont Gwynd 67 K10
Tal-y-bont Gwynd 79 L10
Talybont-on-Usk Powys 44 G10
Tal-y-Cafn Conwy 79 P10
Tal-y-coed Mons 45 N11
Tal-y-garn Rhondd 30 D9
Tal-y-llyn Gwynd 54 G3
Talysarn Gwynd 66 H4
Tal-y-Waun Torfn 31 J4
Talywern Powys 55 J4
Tamar Valley Mining District Devon 6 C5
Tamer Lane End Wigan 82 D4
Tamerton Foliot C Plym 6 D6
Tamworth Staffs 59 K4
Tamworth Green Lincs 74 G2
Tamworth Services Warwks 59 K4
Tancred N York 97 Q9
Tancredston Pembks 40 G5
Tandridge Surrey 37 J10
Tanfield Dur 113 J9
Tanfield Lea Dur 113 J10
Tangiers Pembks 41 J7
Tangley Hants 22 B4
Tangmere W Susx 15 P5
Tangusdale W Isls 168 b17
Tan Hill N York 102 G9
Tankerness Ork 169 e6
Tankersley Barns 91 J11
Tankerton Kent 39 K8
Tannach Highld 167 P7
Tannachie Abers 151 K11
Tannadice Angus 142 H6
Tanner's Green Worcs 58 G10
Tannington Suffk 65 J8
Tannochside N Lans 126 C5
Tansley Derbys 84 D9
Tansor Nhants 61 N2
Tantobie Dur 113 J10
Tanton N York 104 F8
Tanwood Worcs 58 D10
Tanworth in Arden Warwks 58 H10
Tan-y-Bwlch Gwynd 67 M6
Tan-y-fron Conwy 68 C2
Tan-y-fron Wrexhm 69 J4
Tan-y-grisiau Gwynd 67 M5
Tan-y-groes Cerdgn 42 E5
Taobh Tuath W Isls 168 e9
Taplow Bucks 35 P8
Tarbert Ag & B 123 L9
Tarbert Ag & B 123 Q6
Tarbert W Isls 168 g7
Tarbet Ag & B 132 C7
Tarbet Highld 145 N9
Tarbet Highld 164 E7
Tarbock Green Knows 81 P7
Tarbolton S Ayrs 114 H2
Tarbrax S Lans 127 J6
Tardebigge Worcs 58 E11
Tarfside Angus 142 H2
Tarland Abers 150 D7
Tarleton Lancs 88 F6
Tarlscough Lancs 88 E8
Tarlton Gloucs 33 J5
Tarnock Somset 19 L4
Tarns Cumb 109 P11
Tarnside Cumb 95 J2
Tarporley Ches W 69 Q2
Tarr Somset 17 R5
Tarrant Crawford Dorset 12 F4
Tarrant Gunville Dorset 12 F2
Tarrant Hinton Dorset 12 F2
Tarrant Keyneston Dorset 12 F4
Tarrant Launceston Dorset 12 F3
Tarrant Monkton Dorset 12 F3
Tarrant Rawston Dorset 12 F3
Tarrant Rushton Dorset 12 F3
Tarring Neville E Susx 25 K10
Tarrington Herefs 46 B6
Tarskavaig Highld 145 J5
Tarves Abers 159 L11
Tarvin Ches W 81 P11
Tarvin Sands Ches W 81 P11
Tasburgh Norfk 64 H2
Tasley Shrops 57 M6
Taston Oxon 48 C10
Tatenhill Staffs 71 N10
Tathall End M Keyn 49 M5
Tatham Lancs 95 N7
Tathwell Lincs 87 K4
Tatsfield Surrey 37 K9
Tattenhall Ches W 69 N3
Tatterford Norfk 76 B6
Tattersett Norfk 76 A6
Tattershall Lincs 86 H9
Tattershall Bridge Lincs 86 G9
Tattershall Thorpe Lincs 86 H9
Tattingstone Suffk 53 K4
Tattingstone White Horse Suffk 53 K4
Tatton Park Ches E 82 F8
Tatworth Somset 10 G3
Tauchers Moray 157 R8
Taunton Somset 18 H10
Taunton Deane Crematorium Somset 18 H10
Taunton Deane Services Somset 18 G10
Taverham Norfk 76 H9
Taverners Green Essex 51 N7
Tavernspite Pembks 41 N8
Tavistock Devon 6 D4
Tavistock Devon 6 D4
Taw Green Devon 8 G5
Tawstock Devon 17 K6
Taxal Derbys 83 M9
Taychreggan Hotel Ag & B 131 L3
Tay Forest Park P & K 141 J5
Tayinloan Ag & B 123 L10
Taynton Gloucs 46 D10
Taynton Oxon 33 P2
Taynuilt Ag & B 139 J11
Tayport Fife 135 M2
Tayvallich Ag & B 130 E10
Tealby Lincs 86 G2
Tealing Angus 142 G10
Team Valley Gatesd 113 K9
Teangue Highld 145 L6
Teanord Highld 155 Q5
Tebay Cumb 102 B10
Tebay Services Cumb 102 B9
Tebworth C Beds 49 Q9
Tedburn St Mary Devon 9 K6
Teddington Gloucs 47 J8
Teddington Gt Lon 36 E6
Tedstone Delamere Herefs 46 C3
Tedstone Wafer Herefs 46 C3
Teesport R & Cl 104 F6
Teesside Crematorium Middsb 104 E7
Teesside Park S on T 104 E7
Teeton Nhants 60 E6
Teffont Evias Wilts 21 J8
Teffont Magna Wilts 21 J8
Tegryn Pembks 41 P4
Teigh Rutlnd 73 M7
Teigncombe Devon 8 G7
Teigngrace Devon 7 M4
Teignmouth Devon 7 N4
Teindside Border 117 N9
Telford Wrekin 57 M3
Telford Crematorium Wrekin 57 N2
Telford Services Shrops 57 N3
Tellisford Somset 20 F3
Telscombe E Susx 25 K10
Telscombe Cliffs E Susx 25 K10
Tempar P & K 140 G6
Templand D & G 109 N3
Temple Cnwll 5 J7
Temple Mdloth 127 Q6
Temple Balsall Solhll 59 K9
Temple Bar Cerdgn 43 K4
Temple Cloud BaNES 20 B3
Templecombe Somset 20 D10
Temple End Suffk 63 L10
Temple Ewell Kent 27 N3
Temple Grafton Warwks 47 M3
Temple Guiting Gloucs 47 L9
Temple Herdewyke Warwks 48 C4
Temple Hirst N York 91 Q6
Temple Normanton Derbys 84 F7
Temple of Fiddes Abers 151 L11
Temple Sowerby Cumb 102 B5
Templeton Devon 9 L2
Templeton Pembks 41 M8
Templetown Dur 112 H10
Tempsford C Beds 61 Q10
Tenbury Wells Worcs 57 K11
Tenby Pembks 41 M10
Tendring Essex 53 K7
Tendring Green Essex 53 K6
Tendring Heath Essex 53 K6
Ten Mile Bank Norfk 75 L11
Tenpenny Heath Essex 53 J7
Tenterden Kent 26 E5
Terling Essex 52 C8
Tern Wrekin 69 R11
Ternhill Shrops 70 A8
Terregles D & G 109 K5
Terrington N York 98 D6
Terrington St Clement Norfk 75 L6
Terrington St John Norfk 75 K8
Terry's Green Warwks 58 H10
Teston Kent 38 B11
Testwood Hants 14 C4
Tetbury Gloucs 32 G6
Tetbury Upton Gloucs 32 G5
Tetchill Shrops 69 L8
Tetcott Devon 5 N2
Tetford Lincs 87 K6
Tetney Lincs 93 P10
Tetney Lock Lincs 93 P10
Tetsworth Oxon 35 J4
Tettenhall Wolves 58 C4
Tettenhall Wood Wolves 58 C5
Teversal Notts 84 G8
Teversham Cambs 62 G9
Teviothead Border 117 N9
Tewin Herts 50 G8
Tewin Wood Herts 50 G7
Tewkesbury Gloucs 46 G8
Teynham Kent 38 G9
Thackley C Brad 90 F3
Thackthwaite Cumb 100 F6
Thackthwaite Cumb 101 M5
Thainstone Abers 151 K4
Thakeham W Susx 24 D7
Thame Oxon 35 K3
Thames Ditton Surrey 36 E7
Thamesmead Gt Lon 37 L4
Thamesport Medway 38 E7
Thanet Crematorium Kent 39 Q8
Thanington Kent 39 K10
Thankerton S Lans 116 D3
Tharston Norfk 64 H3
Thatcham W Berk 34 F11
Thatto Heath St Hel 81 Q6
Thaxted Essex 51 P4
Theakston N York 97 M3
Thealby N Linc 92 E7
Theale Somset 19 N5
Theale W Berk 34 H10
Thearne E R Yk 93 J3
The Bank Ches E 70 E3
The Bank Shrops 57 L5
The Beeches Gloucs 33 K4
Theberton Suffk 65 N8
The Blythe Staffs 71 J9
The Bog Shrops 56 F5
The Bourne Worcs 47 J3
The Braes Highld 153 J11
The Bratch Staffs 58 C6
The Broad Herefs 45 P2
The Brunt E Loth 128 H5
The Bungalow IoM 80 e4
The Burf Worcs 57 Q11
The Butts Gloucs 46 G11
The Camp Gloucs 32 H3
The Chequer Wrexhm 69 N6
The City Bed 61 P9
The City Bucks 35 L5
The Common Oxon 47 Q9
The Common Wilts 21 P8
The Common Wilts 33 K7
The Corner Kent 26 B3
The Counties Crematorium Nhants 60 F9
The Cronk IoM 80 d2
Theddingworth Leics 60 E3
Theddlethorpe All Saints Lincs 87 N3
Theddlethorpe St Helen Lincs 87 N3
The Den N Ayrs 125 J7
The Forest of Dean Crematorium Gloucs 32 B2
The Forge Herefs 45 L3
The Forstal Kent 26 H4
The Fouralls Shrops 70 B8
The Garden of England Crematorium Kent 38 E8
The Green Cumb 94 D4
The Green Essex 52 C8
The Green N York 105 L9
The Green Wilts 20 G8
The Grove Worcs 46 G6
The Haven W Susx 24 C4
The Haw Gloucs 46 F9
The Headland Hartpl 104 F4
The Hill Cumb 94 D4
The Holt Wokham 35 M9
The Hundred Herefs 45 Q2
Thelbridge Cross Devon 9 J2
The Leacon Kent 26 G5
The Lee Bucks 35 P4
The Lhen IoM 80 e1
The Linn Crematorium E Rens 125 P6
Thelnetham Suffk 64 E6
The Lochs Moray 157 Q5
Thelveton Norfk 64 H5
Thelwall Warrtn 82 E7
The Manchester Crematorium Manch 82 H6
The Marsh Powys 56 E5
Themelthorpe Norfk 76 F7
The Middles Dur 113 K10
The Moor Kent 26 C6
The Mumbles Swans 28 H7
The Murray S Lans 125 Q7
The Mythe Gloucs 46 G8
The Narth Mons 31 P3
The Neuk Abers 151 J8
Thenford Nhants 48 F6
Theobald's Green Wilts 33 K11
The Park Crematorium Hants 23 N5
The Quarry Gloucs 32 D5
The Quarter Kent 26 E3
The Reddings Gloucs 46 H10
Therfield Herts 50 H3
The Rhôs Powys 44 H8
The Rose Hill Crematorium Donc 91 Q10
The Ross P & K 133 M3
The Sands Surrey 23 N5
The Shoe Wilts 32 F10
The Smithies Shrops 57 M5
The Spring Warwks 59 L10
The Square Torfn 31 J5
The Stair Kent 37 P11
The Stocks Kent 26 F6
The Straits Hants 23 L7
The Strand Wilts 20 H3
Thetford Norfk 64 B5
Thetford Forest Park 63 P3
Thethwaite Cumb 101 L2
The Towans Cnwll 2 F6
The Vale Crematorium Luton 50 D6
The Vauld Herefs 45 Q5
The Wyke Shrops 57 N3
Theydon Bois Essex 51 K11
Thicket Priory N York 92 A2
Thickwood Wilts 32 F10
Thimbleby Lincs 86 H6
Thimbleby N York 104 D11
Thingwall Wirral 81 K8
Thirkleby N York 97 Q5
Thirlby N York 97 Q4
Thirlestane Border 128 F10
Thirn N York 97 K3
Thirsk N York 97 P4
Thirtleby E R Yk 93 L4
Thistleton Lancs 88 E3
Thistleton Rutlnd 73 N7
Thistley Green Suffk 63 L5
Thixendale N York 98 G8
Thockrington Nthumb 112 E5
Tholomas Drove Cambs 74 H9
Tholthorpe N York 97 Q7
Thomas Chapel Pembks 41 M9
Thomas Close Cumb 101 M2
Thomastown Abers 158 E10
Thomas Town Warwks 47 L2
Thompson Norfk 64 C2
Thong Kent 37 Q6
Thoralby N York 96 F3
Thoresby Notts 85 K6
Thoresthorpe Lincs 87 N5
Thoresway Lincs 93 L11
Thorganby Lincs 93 M11
Thorganby N York 92 A2
Thorgill N York 105 K11
Thorington Suffk 65 N7
Thorington Street Suffk 52 H4
Thorlby N York 96 E10
Thorley Herts 51 L7
Thorley IoW 14 C9
Thorley Houses Herts 51 L6
Thorley Street IoW 14 C9
Thormanby N York 97 Q6
Thornaby-on-Tees S on T 104 E7
Thornage Norfk 76 F4
Thornborough Bucks 49 K8
Thornborough N York 97 L5
Thornbury C Brad 90 F4
Thornbury Devon 16 G10
Thornbury Herefs 46 B3
Thornbury S Glos 32 B6
Thornby Cumb 110 E10
Thornby Nhants 60 E5
Thorncliff Staffs 71 J3
Thorncliffe Crematorium Cumb 94 D6
Thorncombe Dorset 10 H4
Thorncombe Street Surrey 23 Q6
Thorncott Green C Beds 61 Q11
Thorncross IoW 14 D10
Thorndon Suffk 64 G8
Thorndon Cross Devon 8 D6
Thorne Donc 92 A8
Thorne Coffin Somset 19 P11
Thornecroft Devon 7 K5
Thornehillhead Devon 16 G8
Thorner Leeds 91 K2
Thornes Staffs 58 G4
Thornes Wakefd 91 J7
Thorne St Margaret Somset 18 F10
Thorney Bucks 36 B5
Thorney C Pete 74 E10
Thorney Notts 85 Q6
Thorney Somset 19 M10
Thorney Hill Hants 13 M5
Thorney Island W Susx 15 L6
Thorney Toll Cambs 74 F10
Thornfalcon Somset 19 J10
Thornford Dorset 11 N2
Thorngrafton Nthumb 111 Q7
Thorngrove Somset 19 L8
Thorngumbald E R Yk 93 M5
Thornham Norfk 75 P2
Thornham Magna Suffk 64 G7
Thornham Parva Suffk 64 G7
Thornhaugh C Pete 73 R10
Thornhill C Sotn 14 E4
Thornhill Caerph 30 G8
Thornhill Cumb 100 D9
Thornhill D & G 116 B11
Thornhill Derbys 83 Q8
Thornhill Kirk 90 H7
Thornhill Stirlg 133 K7
Thornhill Crematorium Cardif 30 G8
Thornhill Lees Kirk 90 G7
Thornhills Calder 90 F6
Thornholme E R Yk 99 N8
Thornicombe Dorset 12 E4
Thornington Nthumb 118 G4
Thornley Dur 103 M3
Thornley Dur 104 C3
Thornley Gate Nthumb 112 B9
Thornliebank E Rens 125 P6
Thorns Suffk 63 M9
Thornsett Derbys 83 M7
Thorns Green Ches E 82 G8
Thornthwaite Cumb 100 H5
Thornthwaite N York 97 J9
Thornton Angus 142 F8
Thornton Bucks 49 K7
Thornton C Brad 90 D4
Thornton E R Yk 98 F11
Thornton Fife 134 H8
Thornton Lancs 88 C2
Thornton Leics 72 D9
Thornton Lincs 86 H7
Thornton Middsb 104 E8
Thornton Nthumb 129 P10
Thornton Pembks 40 H9
Thornton Sefton 81 L4
Thornton Curtis N Linc 93 J7
Thornton Garden of Rest Crematorium Sefton 81 L4
Thorntonhall S Lans 125 P6
Thornton Heath Gt Lon 36 H7
Thornton Hough Wirral 81 L8
Thornton-in-Craven N York 96 D11
Thornton in Lonsdale N York 95 P6
Thornton-le-Beans N York 97 N2
Thornton-le-Clay N York 98 D7
Thornton-le-Dale N York 98 G4
Thornton le Moor Lincs 92 H11
Thornton-le-Moor N York 97 N3
Thornton-le-Moors Ches W 81 N10
Thornton-le-Street N York 97 P3
Thorntonloch E Loth 129 K5
Thornton Rust N York 96 E3
Thornton Steward N York 97 J3
Thornton Watlass N York 97 K3
Thornwood Common Essex 51 L10
Thornydykes Border 128 G10
Thornythwaite Cumb 101 L6
Thoroton Notts 73 K2
Thorp Arch Leeds 97 P11
Thorpe Derbys 71 M4
Thorpe E R Yk 99 K11
Thorpe Lincs 87 N4
Thorpe N York 96 F8
Thorpe Norfk 65 N2
Thorpe Notts 85 N11
Thorpe Surrey 36 B7
Thorpe Abbotts Norfk 64 H6
Thorpe Acre Leics 72 E7
Thorpe Arnold Leics 73 K6
Thorpe Audlin Wakefd 91 M7
Thorpe Bassett N York 98 H6
Thorpe Bay Sthend 38 F4
Thorpe by Water Rutlnd 73 M11
Thorpe Common Rothm 91 K11
Thorpe Constantine Staffs 59 L3
Thorpe End Norfk 77 K9
Thorpe Green Essex 53 L7
Thorpe Green Lancs 88 H6
Thorpe Green Suffk 64 C11
Thorpe Hesley Rothm 91 K11
Thorpe in Balne Donc 91 P8
Thorpe Langton Leics 60 F2
Thorpe Larches Dur 104 C5
Thorpe Lea Surrey 36 B6
Thorpe le Fallows Lincs 86 B4
Thorpe-le-Soken Essex 53 L7
Thorpe le Street E R Yk 92 D2
Thorpe Malsor Nhants 60 H5
Thorpe Mandeville Nhants 48 F6
Thorpe Market Norfk 77 J4
Thorpe Marriot Norfk 76 H8
Thorpe Morieux Suffk 64 C11
Thorpeness Suffk 65 P10
Thorpe on the Hill Leeds 91 J5
Thorpe on the Hill Lincs 86 B7
Thorpe Park Surrey 36 B7
Thorpe St Andrew Norfk 77 K10
Thorpe St Peter Lincs 87 N8
Thorpe Salvin Rothm 84 H4
Thorpe Satchville Leics 73 J8
Thorpe Thewles S on T 104 C6
Thorpe Tilney Lincs 86 F9
Thorpe Underwood N York 97 Q9
Thorpe Underwood Nhants 60 G4
Thorpe Waterville Nhants 61 M4
Thorpe Willoughby N York 91 P4
Thorpland Norfk 75 M9
Thorrington Essex 53 J8
Thorverton Devon 9 M4
Thrales End C Beds 50 D7
Thrandeston Suffk 64 G6
Thrapston Nhants 61 L5
Threapland Cumb 100 G3
Threapland N York 96 E8
Threapwood Ches W 69 M6
Threapwood Staffs 71 J6
Threapwood Head Staffs 71 J6
Threave S Ayrs 114 F6
Three Ashes Herefs 45 Q10
Three Bridges W Susx 24 G3
Three Burrows Cnwll 3 J4
Three Chimneys Kent 26 D4
Three Cocks Powys 44 H7
Three Counties Crematorium Essex 52 C6
Three Crosses Swans 28 G6
Three Cups Corner E Susx 25 P6
Three Gates Worcs 46 C2
Threehammer Common Norfk 77 L8
Three Hammers Cnwll 5 L4
Three Holes Norfk 75 K10
Threekingham Lincs 74 A3
Three Leg Cross E Susx 25 Q4
Three Legged Cross Dorset 13 J3
Three Mile Cross Wokham 35 K11
Threemilestone Cnwll 3 K4
Three Miletown W Loth 127 K2
Three Oaks E Susx 26 D9
Threlkeld Cumb 101 K5
Threshers Bush Essex 51 L9
Threshfield N York 96 E8
Thrigby Norfk 77 P9
Thringarth Dur 102 H6
Thringstone Leics 72 C7
Thrintoft N York 97 M2
Thriplow Cambs 62 F11
Throapham Rothm 84 H3
Throckenhalt Lincs 74 G9
Throcking Herts 50 H4
Throckley N u Ty 113 J7
Throckmorton Worcs 47 J4
Throop Bmouth 13 K5
Throop Dorset 12 D6
Throphill Nthumb 112 H3
Thropton Nthumb 119 K10
Throsk Stirlg 133 P9
Througham Gloucs 32 H3
Throughgate D & G 109 J4
Throwleigh Devon 8 G6
Throwley Kent 38 G10
Throwley Forstal Kent 38 G11
Thrumpton Notts 72 E4
Thrumpton Notts 85 M4
Thrumster Highld 167 P7
Thrunscoe NE Lin 93 P9
Thrunton Nthumb 119 L8
Thrup Oxon 33 Q5
Thrupp Gloucs 32 G4
Thrupp Oxon 48 E11
Thrushelton Devon 8 B7
Thrussington Leics 72 H7
Thruxton Hants 21 Q5
Thruxton Herefs 45 N8
Thrybergh Rothm 91 M11
Thulston Derbys 72 C4
Thundersley Essex 38 C4
Thurcaston Leics 72 F8
Thurcroft Rothm 84 G3
Thurdon Cnwll 16 D9
Thurgarton Norfk 76 H5
Thurgarton Notts 85 L11
Thurgoland Barns 90 H10
Thurlaston Leics 72 E11
Thurlaston Warwks 59 Q10
Thurlbear Somset 19 J10
Thurlby Lincs 74 A7
Thurlby Lincs 86 B8
Thurlby Lincs 87 N5
Thurleigh Bed 61 N9
Thurlestone Devon 6 H10
Thurloxton Somset 19 J8
Thurlstone Barns 90 G10
Thurlton Norfk 65 N2
Thurlwood Ches E 70 E3
Thurmaston Leics 72 G9
Thurnby Leics 72 G10
Thurne Norfk 77 N8
Thurnham Kent 38 D10
Thurning Nhants 61 N4
Thurning Norfk 76 F6
Thurnscoe Barns 91 M9
Thurrock Services Thurr 37 N5
Thursby Cumb 110 F10
Thursden Lancs 89 Q4
Thursford Norfk 76 D5
Thursley Surrey 23 P7
Thurso Highld 167 K3
Thurstaston Wirral 81 J8
Thurston Suffk 64 C8
Thurston Clough Oldham 90 B9
Thurstonfield Cumb 110 F9
Thurstonland Kirk 90 F8
Thurston Planch Suffk 64 C9
Thurton Norfk 77 L11
Thurvaston Derbys 71 N7
Thuxton Norfk 76 E10
Thwaite N York 102 G11
Thwaite Suffk 64 G8
Thwaite Head Cumb 94 G2
Thwaites C Brad 90 D2
Thwaite St Mary Norfk 65 L2
Thwaites Brow C Brad 90 D2
Thwing E R Yk 99 L6
Tibbermore P & K 134 C3
Tibbers D & G 116 B11
Tibberton Gloucs 46 E10
Tibberton Worcs 46 H3
Tibberton Wrekin 70 B10
Tibbie Shiels Inn Border 117 J6
Tibenham Norfk 64 G4
Tibshelf Derbys 84 F8
Tibshelf Services Derbys 84 F8
Tibthorpe E R Yk 99 K9
Ticehurst E Susx 25 Q4
Tichborne Hants 22 G8
Tickencote Rutlnd 73 P9
Tickenham N Som 31 N10
Tickford End M Keyn 49 N6
Tickhill Donc 85 J2
Ticklerton Shrops 56 H6
Ticknall Derbys 72 B6
Tickton E R Yk 93 J2
Tidbury Green Solhll 58 H9

Tidcombe - Tring 303

Tidcombe Wilts 21 Q3
Tiddington Oxon 34 H4
Tiddington Warwks 47 P3
Tiddleywink Wilts 32 G9
Tidebrook E Susx 25 P4
Tideford Cnwll 5 P10
Tideford Cross Cnwll 5 N9
Tidenham Gloucs 31 Q5
Tideswell Derbys 83 Q9
Tidmarsh W Berk 34 H10
Tidmington Warwks 47 Q7
Tidpit Hants 21 L11
Tidworth Wilts 21 P5
Tiers Cross Pembks 40 H8
Tiffield Nhants 49 K4
Tigerton Angus 143 J5
Tigh a Ghearraidh W Isls 168 c10
Tigharry W Isls 168 c10
Tighnabruaich Ag & B 124 B3
Tigley Devon 7 K6
Tilbrook Cambs 61 N7
Tilbury Thurr 37 P5
Tilbury Dock Thurr 37 P5
Tilbury Green Essex 52 B3
Tilbury Juxta Clare Essex 52 C3
Tile Cross Birm 59 J7
Tile Hill Covtry 59 L9
Tilehouse Green Solhll 59 J9
Tilehurst Readg 35 J10
Tilford Surrey 23 N6
Tilgate W Susx 24 G4
Tilgate Forest Row W Susx 24 G4
Tilham Street Somset 19 Q7
Tillers Green Gloucs 46 C8
Tillicoultry Clacks 133 Q8
Tillietudlem S Lans 126 E8
Tillingham Essex 52 G11
Tillington Herefs 45 P6
Tillington W Susx 23 Q10
Tillington Common Herefs 45 P5
Tillybirloch Abers 150 H6
Tillyfourie Abers 150 G5
Tillygreig Abers 151 M3
Tillyrie P & K 134 E6
Tilmanstone Kent 39 P11
Tilney All Saints Norfk 75 L7
Tilney High End Norfk 75 L7
Tilney St Lawrence Norfk 75 K8
Tilshead Wilts 21 K5
Tilstock Shrops 69 P7
Tilston Ches W 69 N4
Tilstone Bank Ches W 69 Q3
Tilstone Fearnall Ches W 69 Q2
Tilsworth C Beds 49 Q10
Tilton on the Hill Leics 73 J9
Tiltups End Gloucs 32 F5
Tilty Essex 51 N5
Timberland Lincs 86 F9
Timbersbrook Ches E 70 F2
Timberscombe Somset 18 C6
Timble N York 97 J10
Timewell Devon 18 C9
Timpanheck D & G 110 F6
Timperley Traffd 82 G7
Timsbury BaNES 20 C3
Timsbury Hants 22 B10
Timsgarry W Isls 168 f4
Timsgearraidh W Isls 168 f4
Timworth Suffk 64 B8
Timworth Green Suffk 64 B8
Tincleton Dorset 12 C6
Tindale Cumb 111 M9
Tindale Crescent Dur 103 N5
Tingewick Bucks 49 J8
Tingley Leeds 90 H5
Tingrith C Beds 50 B4
Tingwall Airport Shet 169 r9
Tingwell Ork 169 d4
Tinhay Devon 5 P4
Tinker's Hill Hants 22 D5
Tinkersley Derbys 84 C8
Tinsley Sheff 84 F2
Tinsley Green W Susx 24 G3
Tintagel Cnwll 4 H4
Tintern Parva Mons 31 P4
Tintinhull Somset 19 N11
Tintwistle Derbys 83 M5
Tinwald D & G 109 M4
Tinwell Rutlnd 73 Q9
Tippacott Devon 17 P2
Tipp's End Norfk 75 K11
Tiptoe Hants 13 N5
Tipton Sandw 58 E6
Tipton Green Sandw 58 E6
Tipton St John Devon 10 B6
Tiptree Essex 52 E8
Tiptree Heath Essex 52 E8
Tirabad Powys 44 B6
Tiree Ag & B 136 C7
Tiree Airport Ag & B 136 C7
Tiretigan Ag & B 123 M7
Tirley Gloucs 46 F9
Tiroran Ag & B 137 M10
Tirphil Caerph 30 F4
Tirril Cumb 101 P5
Tir-y-fron Flints 69 J3
Tisbury Wilts 20 H9
Tisman's Common W Susx 24 C4
Tissington Derbys 71 M4
Titchberry Devon 16 C6
Titchfield Hants 14 F5
Titchfield Common Hants 14 F5
Titchmarsh Nhants 61 M5
Titchwell Norfk 75 Q2
Tithby Notts 72 H3
Titley Herefs 45 L2
Titmore Green Herts 50 F5
Titsey Surrey 37 K10
Titson Cnwll 16 C11
Tittensor Staffs 70 F7
Tittleshall Norfk 76 B7
Titton Worcs 58 B11
Tiverton Ches W 69 Q2
Tiverton Devon 9 N2
Tivetshall St Margaret Norfk 64 H4
Tivetshall St Mary Norfk 64 H4
Tivington Somset 18 B5
Tivy Dale Barns 90 H9
Tixall Staffs 70 H10
Tixover Rutlnd 73 P10
Toab Shet 169 q12
Toadhole Derbys 84 E9
Toadmoor Derbys 84 D10
Tobermory Ag & B 137 N4
Toberonochy Ag & B 130 E6
Tobha Mor W Isls 168 c14
Tocher Abers 158 G11
Tochieneal Moray 158 D4
Tockenham Wilts 33 K9
Tockenham Wick Wilts 33 K8
Tocketts R & Cl 104 H7
Tockholes Bl w D 89 K6
Tockington S Glos 32 B7
Tockwith N York 97 Q10
Todber Dorset 20 E11
Todburn Nthumb 119 M11
Toddington C Beds 50 B5
Toddington Gloucs 47 K8
Toddington Services C Beds 50 B5
Todds Green Herts 50 F5
Todenham Gloucs 47 P7
Todhills Angus 142 G10
Todhills Cumb 110 G8
Todhills Dur 103 P4
Todhills Services Cumb 110 G8
Todmorden Calder 89 Q6
Todwick Rothm 84 G4
Toft Cambs 62 E9
Toft Ches E 82 G9
Toft Lincs 73 R7
Toft Shet 169 r6
Toft Warwks 59 Q10
Toft Hill Dur 103 N5
Toft Hill Lincs 86 H8
Toft Monks Norfk 65 N3
Toft next Newton Lincs 86 D3
Toftrees Norfk 76 B6
Toftwood Norfk 76 D9
Togston Nthumb 119 P10
Tokavaig Highld 145 K5
Tokers Green Oxon 35 K9
Tolastadh W Isls 168 k3
Toldish Cnwll 4 E10
Tolland Somset 18 F8
Tollard Farnham Dorset 21 J11
Tollard Royal Wilts 20 H11
Toll Bar Donc 91 P9
Tollbar End Covtry 59 N9
Toller Fratrum Dorset 11 M5
Toller Porcorum Dorset 11 M5
Tollerton N York 97 R8
Tollerton Notts 72 G4
Toller Whelme Dorset 11 L4
Tollesbury Essex 52 G9
Tolleshunt D'Arcy Essex 52 F9
Tolleshunt Knights Essex 52 F9
Tolleshunt Major Essex 52 F9
Tollingham E R Yk 92 D3
Tolpuddle Dorset 12 C6
Tolsta W Isls 168 k3
Tolworth Gt Lon 36 E7
Tomatin Highld 148 E2
Tomchrasky Highld 146 H5
Tomdoun Highld 146 F7
Tomich Highld 147 J2
Tomich Highld 155 P8
Tomich Highld 156 B3
Tomich Highld 162 E5
Tomintoul Moray 149 M4
Tomlow Warwks 48 E2
Tomnacross Highld 155 P9
Tomnavoulin Moray 149 N2
Tompkin Staffs 70 G4
Ton Mons 31 K4
Ton Mons 31 L5
Tonbridge Kent 37 N11
Tondu Brdgnd 29 N8
Tonedale Somset 18 F10
Ton fanau Gwynd 54 D4
Tong C Brad 90 G4
Tong Kent 38 G10
Tong Shrops 57 P3
Tonge Leics 72 C6
Tong Green Kent 38 G11
Tongham Surrey 23 N5
Tongland D & G 108 E10
Tong Norton Shrops 57 P3
Tongue Highld 165 N5
Tongue End Lincs 74 C7
Tongwynlais Cardif 30 F8
Tonmawr Neath 29 M5
Tonna Neath 29 L5
Ton-teg Rhondd 30 E7
Tonwell Herts 50 H7
Tonypandy Rhondd 30 C6
Tonyrefail Rhondd 30 D7
Toot Baldon Oxon 34 G4
Toot Hill Essex 51 M10
Toothill Hants 22 C11
Toothill Swindn 33 M8
Tooting Gt Lon 36 G6
Tooting Bec Gt Lon 36 G6
Topcliffe N York 97 N5
Topcroft Norfk 65 K3
Topcroft Street Norfk 65 K3
Top End Bed 61 M8
Topham Donc 91 Q7
Top of Hebers Rochdl 89 P9
Toppesfield Essex 52 B4
Toprow Norfk 64 H2
Topsham Devon 9 N7
Top-y-rhos Flints 69 J3
Torbeg N Ayrs 120 G6
Torboll Highld 162 H7
Torbreck Highld 156 A9
Torbryan Devon 7 L5
Torcastle Highld 139 L2
Torcross Devon 7 L10
Tore Highld 155 R7
Torfrey Cnwll 5 J11
Torinturk Ag & B 123 P7
Torksey Lincs 85 P5
Tormarton S Glos 32 E9
Tormore N Ayrs 120 G5
Tornagrain Highld 156 D7
Tornaveen Abers 150 G6
Torness Highld 147 P2
Toronto Dur 103 N4
Torpenhow Cumb 100 H3
Torphichen W Loth 126 H3
Torphins Abers 150 G7
Torpoint Cnwll 6 C7
Torquay Torbay 7 N6
Torquay Crematorium Torbay 7 N5
Torquhan Border 128 C10
Torr Devon 6 F8
Torran Highld 153 K8
Torrance E Duns 125 Q3
Torranyard N Ayrs 125 K9
Torre Somset 18 D7
Torridon Highld 154 B6
Torridon House Highld 153 R6
Torrin Highld 145 J3
Torrisdale Ag & B 120 E4
Torrisdale Highld 165 Q4
Torrish Highld 163 M3
Torrisholme Lancs 95 K8
Torrobull Highld 162 D6
Torry C Aber 151 N6
Torryburn Fife 134 C10
Torteval Guern 10 a2
Torthorwald D & G 109 M5
Tortington W Susx 24 B10
Torton Worcs 58 B10
Tortworth S Glos 32 D6
Torvaig Highld 152 H9
Torver Cumb 94 F2
Torwood Falk 133 N10
Torwoodlee Border 117 P3
Torworth Notts 85 L3
Tosberry Devon 16 D7
Toscaig Highld 153 N10
Toseland Cambs 62 B8
Tosside Lancs 95 R9
Tostock Suffk 64 D9
Totaig Highld 152 C7
Tote Highld 152 G8
Tote Highld 153 J5
Tote Hill W Susx 23 N10
Totford Hants 22 G7
Tothill Lincs 87 M4
Totland IoW 13 P7
Totley Sheff 84 D5
Totley Brook Sheff 84 D4
Totnes Devon 7 L6
Toton Notts 72 E4
Totronald Ag & B 136 F4
Totscore Highld 152 F4
Tottenham Gt Lon 36 H2
Tottenhill Norfk 75 M8
Totteridge Gt Lon 36 F2
Totternhoe C Beds 49 Q10
Tottington Bury 89 M8
Tottleworth Lancs 89 L4
Totton Hants 14 C4
Touchen End W & M 35 N9
Toulston N York 91 M2
Toulton Somset 18 G8
Toulvaddie Highld 163 K10
Tovil Kent 38 C11
Towan Cnwll 3 Q4
Towan Cnwll 4 D7
Toward Ag & B 124 E4
Toward Quay Ag & B 124 E4
Towcester Nhants 49 J5
Towednack Cnwll 2 D6
Tower of London Gt Lon 36 H4
Towersey Oxon 35 K3
Towie Abers 150 C5
Tow Law Dur 103 M3
Town End Cambs 74 H11
Town End Cumb 95 J4
Town End Cumb 101 K9
Town End Cumb 102 B5
Townend W Duns 125 K2
Towngate Cumb 111 K11
Towngate Lincs 74 B8
Town Green Lancs 88 E9
Town Green Norfk 77 M9
Townhead Barns 83 Q4
Townhead Cumb 100 E3
Town Head Cumb 101 M10
Townhead Cumb 102 B4
Townhead D & G 109 M3
Town Head N York 96 B9
Townhead of Greenlaw D & G 108 F8
Townhill Fife 134 E10
Town Kelloe Dur 104 C3
Townlake Devon 5 Q7
Town Lane Wigan 82 E5
Town Littleworth E Susx 25 K7
Town of Lowton Wigan 82 D5
Town Row E Susx 25 N4
Towns End Hants 22 G3
Townsend Somset 10 H2
Townshend Cnwll 2 F7
Town Street Suffk 63 N3
Townwell S Glos 32 D6
Town Yetholm Border 118 F5
Towthorpe C York 98 C9
Towthorpe E R Yk 98 H8
Towton N York 91 M3
Towyn Conwy 80 D9
Toxteth Lpool 81 M7
Toynton All Saints Lincs 87 L8
Toynton Fen Side Lincs 87 L8
Toynton St Peter Lincs 87 M8
Toy's Hill Kent 37 L10
Trabboch E Ayrs 114 H3
Trabbochburn E Ayrs 115 J3
Traboe Cnwll 3 J9
Tracebridge Somset 18 E10
Tradespark Highld 156 F6
Trallong Powys 44 D9
Tranent E Loth 128 C5
Tranmere Wirral 81 L7
Trantelbeg Highld 166 E6
Trantlemore Highld 166 E6
Tranwell Nthumb 113 J4
Trap Carmth 43 N11
Traprain E Loth 128 F4
Trap's Green Warwks 58 H11
Trapshill W Berk 22 C2
Traquair Border 117 L4
Trash Green W Berk 35 J11
Trawden Lancs 89 Q3
Trawscoed Cerdgn 54 F10
Trawsfynydd Gwynd 67 N7
Trealaw Rhondd 30 D6
Treales Lancs 88 E4
Trearddur Bay IoA 78 D9
Treaslane Highld 152 F7
Treator Cnwll 4 E6
Tre Aubrey V Glam 30 D10
Trebanog Rhondd 30 D6
Trebanos Neath 29 K4
Trebartha Cnwll 5 M6
Trebarwith Cnwll 4 H4
Trebeath Cnwll 5 M4
Trebetherick Cnwll 4 E6
Treborough Somset 18 D7
Trebudannon Cnwll 4 D9
Trebullett Cnwll 5 N6
Treburgett Cnwll 4 H6
Treburley Cnwll 5 P6
Treburrick Cnwll 4 D7
Trebyan Cnwll 4 H9
Trecastle Powys 44 B9
Trecogo Cnwll 5 N5
Trecott Devon 8 F4
Trecwn Pembks 41 J4
Trecynon Rhondd 30 C4
Tredaule Cnwll 5 L5
Tredavoe Cnwll 2 D8
Tredegar Blae G 30 F3
Tredethy Cnwll 4 H7
Tredington Gloucs 46 H9
Tredington Warwks 47 Q6
Tredinnick Cnwll 4 E7
Tredinnick Cnwll 4 G10
Tredinnick Cnwll 5 K8
Tredinnick Cnwll 5 L10
Tredinnick Cnwll 5 M10
Tredomen Powys 44 G8
Tredrissi Pembks 41 L2
Tredrizzick Cnwll 4 F6
Tredunnock Mons 31 L6
Tredustan Powys 44 G8
Treen Cnwll 2 B9
Treen Cnwll 2 C6
Treesmill Cnwll 4 H10
Treeton Rothm 84 F3
Trefasser Pembks 40 G3
Trefdraeth IoA 78 G10
Trefecca Powys 44 G8
Trefeglwys Powys 55 M6
Trefenter Cerdgn 54 E11
Treffgarne Pembks 41 J6
Treffgarne Owen Pembks 40 G5
Trefforest Rhondd 30 E7
Treffynnon Pembks 40 G5
Trefil Blae G 30 F2
Trefilan Cerdgn 43 K3
Trefin Pembks 40 F4
Treflach Wood Shrops 69 J9
Trefnannau Powys 68 H11
Trefnant Denbgs 80 F10
Trefonen Shrops 69 J9
Trefor Gwynd 66 F5
Trefor IoA 78 F8
Trefrew Cnwll 5 J5
Trefriw Conwy 67 P2
Tregadillett Cnwll 5 M5
Tre-gagle Mons 31 P3
Tregaian IoA 78 H8
Tregare Mons 31 M2
Tregarne Cnwll 3 K9
Tregaron Cerdgn 43 N3
Tregarth Gwynd 79 L11
Tregaswith Cnwll 4 D9
Tregatta Cnwll 4 H4
Tregawne Cnwll 4 G8
Tregeare Cnwll 5 L4
Tregeiriog Wrexhm 68 G8
Tregele IoA 78 F6
Tregellist Cnwll 4 G6
Tregenna Cnwll 3 M5
Tregeseal Cnwll 2 B7
Tregew Cnwll 3 L7
Tre-Gibbon Rhondd 30 C3
Tregidden Cnwll 3 K9
Tregiskey Cnwll 3 Q4
Treglemais Pembks 40 F5
Tregole Cnwll 5 K2
Tregolls Cnwll 3 J6
Tregonce Cnwll 4 E7
Tregonetha Cnwll 4 F9
Tregonning & Gwinear Mining District Cnwll 2 F7
Tregony Cnwll 3 N5
Tregoodwell Cnwll 5 J5
Tregorrick Cnwll 3 Q3
Tregoss Cnwll 4 F9
Tregoyd Powys 44 H7
Tregrehan Mills Cnwll 3 Q3
Tre-groes Cerdgn 42 H6
Tregullon Cnwll 4 H9
Tregunna Cnwll 4 F7
Tregunnon Cnwll 5 L5
Tregurrian Cnwll 4 D8
Tregynon Powys 55 P5
Tre-gynwr Carmth 42 H11
Trehafod Rhondd 30 D6
Trehan Cnwll 5 Q10
Treharris Myr Td 30 E5
Treharrock Cnwll 4 G6
Trehemborne Cnwll 4 D7
Treherbert Carmth 43 L5
Treherbert Rhondd 29 P5
Trehunist Cnwll 5 N9
Trekenner Cnwll 5 N6
Treknow Cnwll 4 H4
Trelan Cnwll 3 J10
Trelash Cnwll 5 K3
Trelassick Cnwll 3 M3
Trelawne Cnwll 5 L11
Trelawnyd Flints 80 F9
Treleague Cnwll 3 K9
Treleaver Cnwll 3 K10
Trelech Carmth 41 Q4
Trelech a'r Betws Carmth 42 F9
Treleddyd-fawr Pembks 40 E5
Trelew Cnwll 3 L6
Trelewis Myr Td 30 F5
Treligga Cnwll 4 G5
Trelights Cnwll 4 F6
Trelill Cnwll 4 G6
Trelinnoe Cnwll 5 N5
Trelion Cnwll 3 N3
Trelissick Cnwll 3 L6
Trellech Mons 31 P3
Trelleck Grange Mons 31 N4
Trelogan Flints 80 G8
Trelow Cnwll 4 E8
Trelowarren Cnwll 3 J9
Trelowia Cnwll 5 M10
Treluggan Cnwll 3 M6
Trelystan Powys 56 D4
Tremadog Gwynd 67 K7
Tremail Cnwll 5 K4
Tremain Cerdgn 42 D5
Tremaine Cnwll 5 L4
Tremar Cnwll 5 M8
Trematon Cnwll 5 P10
Trembraze Cnwll 5 M8
Tremeirchion Denbgs 80 F10
Tremethick Cross Cnwll 2 C7
Tremore Cnwll 4 G9
Tre-Mostyn Flints 80 G9
Trenance Cnwll 3 L9
Trenance Cnwll 4 D8
Trenance Cnwll 4 E7
Trenarren Cnwll 3 Q4
Trench Wrekin 57 M2
Trench Green Oxon 35 J9
Trendeal Cnwll 3 M3
Trendrine Cnwll 2 D6
Treneague Cnwll 4 F7
Trenear Cnwll 2 H7
Treneglos Cnwll 5 L4
Trenerth Cnwll 2 G6
Trenewan Cnwll 5 K11
Trenewth Cnwll 4 H6
Trengune Cnwll 5 K3
Treninnick Cnwll 4 C9
Trenowah Cnwll 4 B10
Trenoweth Cnwll 3 K7
Trent Dorset 19 Q11
Trentham C Stke 70 F6
Trentishoe Devon 17 L2
Trentlock Derbys 72 D4
Trent Port Lincs 85 P4
Trent Vale C Stke 70 F6
Trenwheal Cnwll 2 G7
Treoes V Glam 29 P9
Treorchy Rhondd 30 C5
Trequite Cnwll 4 G6
Tre'r-ddol Cerdgn 54 F6
Trerhyngyll V Glam 30 D9
Trerulefoot Cnwll 5 N10
Tresaith Cerdgn 42 E4
Tresawle Cnwll 3 M4
Tresco IoS 2 b2
Trescott Staffs 58 C5
Trescowe Cnwll 2 F7
Tresean Cnwll 4 B10
Tresham Gloucs 32 E6
Treshnish Isles Ag & B 136 G7
Tresillian Cnwll 3 M4
Tresinney Cnwll 5 J5
Treskinnick Cross Cnwll 5 L2
Tresmeer Cnwll 5 L4
Tresparrett Cnwll 5 J3
Tressait P & K 141 K5
Tresta Shet 169 q8
Tresta Shet 169 t4
Treswell Notts 85 N5
Treswithian Cnwll 2 G5
Treswithian Downs Crematorium Cnwll 2 G5
Tre Taliesin Cerdgn 54 F6
Trethevey Cnwll 4 H4
Trethewey Cnwll 2 B9
Trethomas Caerph 30 G7
Trethosa Cnwll 3 N3
Trethurgy Cnwll 4 G10
Tretio Pembks 40 E5
Tretire Herefs 45 Q10
Tretower Powys 44 H10
Treuddyn Flints 69 J3
Trevadlock Cnwll 5 M6
Trevalga Cnwll 4 H3
Trevalyn Wrexhm 69 L3
Trevanger Cnwll 4 F6
Trevanson Cnwll 4 F7
Trevarrack Cnwll 2 D7
Trevarren Cnwll 4 E9
Trevarrian Cnwll 4 D8
Trevarrick Cnwll 3 P5
Trevarth Cnwll 3 J5
Trevaughan Carmth 41 P7
Tre-Vaughan Carmth 42 G10
Treveal Cnwll 2 D5
Treveal Cnwll 4 B10
Treveighan Cnwll 4 H6
Trevellas Downs Cnwll 3 J3
Trevelmond Cnwll 5 L9
Trevemper Cnwll 4 C10
Treveor Cnwll 3 P5
Treverbyn Cnwll 3 M4
Treverbyn Cnwll 4 G10
Treverva Cnwll 3 K7
Trevescan Cnwll 2 B9
Trevethin Torfn 31 J4
Trevia Cnwll 4 H5
Trevigro Cnwll 5 N8
Trevilla Cnwll 3 L6
Trevilson Cnwll 4 C10
Treviscoe Cnwll 4 E10
Treviskey Cnwll 3 N5
Trevithick Cnwll 3 P4
Trevithick Cnwll 4 D9
Trevoll Cnwll 4 C10
Trevone Cnwll 4 D6
Trevor Wrexhm 69 J6
Trevorgans Cnwll 2 C8
Trevorrick Cnwll 4 E7
Trevose Cnwll 4 D6
Trew Cnwll 2 G8
Trewalder Cnwll 4 H5
Trewalkin Powys 44 H8
Trewarmett Cnwll 4 H4
Trewassa Cnwll 5 J4
Trewavas Cnwll 2 F8
Trewavas Mining District Cnwll 2 F8
Treween Cnwll 5 L5
Trewellard Cnwll 2 B7
Trewen Cnwll 5 M5
Trewennack Cnwll 2 H8
Trewent Pembks 41 K11
Trewern Powys 56 D2
Trewetha Cnwll 4 G5
Trewethern Cnwll 4 G6
Trewidland Cnwll 5 M10
Trewillis Cnwll 3 K10
Trewint Cnwll 5 L5
Trewint Cnwll 5 M9
Trewithian Cnwll 3 M6
Trewoodloe Cnwll 5 N7
Trewoon Cnwll 2 H10
Trewoon Cnwll 3 P3
Treworga Cnwll 3 M5
Treworgan Cnwll 3 L4
Treworlas Cnwll 3 M6
Treworld Cnwll 5 J3
Treworthal Cnwll 3 M6
Tre-wyn Mons 45 L10
Treyarnon Cnwll 4 D7
Treyford W Susx 23 M11
Trickett's Cross Dorset 13 J4
Triermain Cumb 111 L7
Triffleton Pembks 41 J6
Trillacott Cnwll 5 M4
Trimdon Dur 104 C4
Trimdon Colliery Dur 104 C3
Trimdon Grange Dur 104 C3
Trimingham Norfk 77 K4
Trimley Lower Street Suffk 53 N4
Trimley St Martin Suffk 53 N4
Trimley St Mary Suffk 53 N4
Trimpley Worcs 57 P9
Trimsaran Carmth 28 E4
Trims Green Herts 51 L7
Trimstone Devon 17 J3
Trinafour P & K 140 H5
Trinant Caerph 30 H5
Tring Herts 35 P2

Distances and journey times

The mileage chart shows distances in miles between two towns along AA-recommended routes. Using motorways and other main roads this is normally the fastest route, though not necessarily the shortest.

The journey times, shown in hours and minutes, are average off-peak driving times along AA-recommended routes. These times should be used as a guide only and do not allow for unforeseen traffic delays, rest breaks or fuel stops.

For example, the 378 miles (608 km) journey between Glasgow and Norwich should take approximately 7 hours 28 minutes.

Journey times

The diagonal labels (top-left to bottom-right) list the towns in order:

Aberdeen, Aberystwyth, Barnstaple, Birmingham, Brighton, Bristol, Cambridge, Cardiff, Carlisle, Carmarthen, Dorchester, Dover, Edinburgh, Exeter, Fort William, Glasgow, Gloucester, Guildford, Hereford, Holyhead, Hull, Inverness, Kendal, Leeds, Lincoln, Liverpool, Maidstone, Manchester, Middlesbrough, Newcastle, Northampton, Norwich, Nottingham, Oxford, Penzance, Perth, Peterborough, Plymouth, Portsmouth, Preston, Salisbury, Sheffield, Shrewsbury, Southampton, Stoke-on-Trent, Stranraer, Taunton, Wick, York, LONDON

Distances in miles (one mile equals 1.6093 km)